10000 JAPANESE IDIOMS

William de Lange

Edited by

Hiromi Miyagi-Lusthaus

For more on books by William de Lange visit:
www.williamdelange.com

First edition, 2005
Second, expanded and revised edition, 2018

Published by TOYO PRess
Visit us at: www.toyopress.com

Copyright © 2018 by William de Lange

The moral right of the author has been asserted.

All rights reserved. No part of this publication may be reproduced, stored or introduced into a retrieval system, or transmitted, in any form or by any means (electronic, mechanical, photo-copying, recording or otherwise), without the prior written permission of both the copyright owner and the above publisher of this book

ISBN: 978-94-92722-102

Preface

Idioms are perhaps the most difficult aspect of a foreign language for a student to master. Indeed, even the most advanced speakers of a foreign language may occasionally get the idiom wrong. Thus, politicians, artists, and even writers entertaining foreign audiences, may resort to a figure of speech that seems appropriate in the context of their own language, but will only be the cause of puzzlement, hilarity, or even embarrassment when rendered into the language of their hosts. This is because idioms are so firmly rooted in the culture, tradition, beliefs, and habits of a people.

This applies as well if not more so when rendering Japanese into English. There are profound differences between the cultures of the Far East and the West, and such differences are often directly reflected in the makeup of an idiom. To those familiar with Japan's long feudal history, it will come as no surprise that many of its idiomatic expressions derive from a martial context. Two examples that draw directly on the Japanese art of fencing are the expressions 鍔を割る (to smash a hand guard) and 鐺が詰まる (to have the tip of one's sheath obstructed—and thus be unable to draw one's sword). Though both have gone out of fashion, the former may still be used to describe a desperate fight or, more figuratively, a fierce competition, and the latter to describe someone who is in financial trouble or in dire straits. Another idiom that has its roots in Japan's feudal history is the expression 鉾を向ける (to direct one's halberd at someone), which now means to attack someone verbally, as in an argument. Other idioms have their roots in more peaceful pastimes, such as the drinking of tea. Though shared by other nations, in Japan, where it has become a ritual in its own right, the drinking of tea has spawned such expressions as 茶を言う (to talk tea), which means to talk nonsense. Another Japanese idiom related to tea is お茶を濁す (to make the tea turbid), which can be used either to indicate that something is done in a halfhearted way or, to use the English equivalent, when someone is "beating about the bush." Even the absence of certain idioms in a language can reveal a lot about those who speak it. Unlike, for instance, the English, Dutch, and Hispanic languages, which are spoken by peoples who have a longstanding seafaring tradition, for an island people, the Japanese have remarkably few idioms that derive from a nautical context.

A large number of Japanese idioms involve parts of the human body, perhaps more so than in any other language. The head, the ears, the eyes, the nose, the mouth, the chin, the jaw, the neck, the arms, the elbows, the hands, the fingers, the nails, the chest, the heart, the liver, the stomach, the veins, the navel, the

Preface

groin, the legs, the knees, the heels, indeed the body itself, whether in the form of 体, 体 or 身, are at the center of the large majority of Japanese idioms.

Entries

In compiling the main entries for this dictionary a few basic principles have been observed. Care has been taken to avoid the unnecessary inclusion of synonymous entries. There are in Japanese, as in Chinese, a large number of single and compound nouns that are exceedingly close in meaning. Words such as 恩 and 恩義 (a favor) or 刑 and 刑罰 (punishment), essentially have the same meaning. Although they may differ in nuance or in the specific context or sentence structure in which they are used, such synonyms tend to combine with the same verbs to create identical idiomatic expressions. Consequently, it is pointless to include different versions of such synonyms here. As a rule, preference has been given to nouns that consist of just one Chinese character, simply because they feature in a larger number of idiomatic expressions. Needless to say that in those cases where the various synonyms of a noun *do* combine with one or more completely different verbs to create new or different idiomatic expressions, such nouns have been included among the main entries.

At first glance, the reader will notice that a considerable number of sub-entries in this dictionary are not purely idiomatic, that is, their meaning follows logically from the sum of their constituent parts, and in many cases their constituent parts can simply be replaced by another word similar in meaning. Most of the sub-entries, however, are sufficiently unpredictable to pose a stumbling block to the foreign student. Thus obvious and straightforward noun-verb combinations such as 歌を歌う (sing a song) or 金で買う (buy with money) have been left out, but an expression such as 金を掛ける (invest money), has been included, simply to bring it to the attention of the foreign student and to distinguish it from the homonymous expression 金を賭ける (bet money). Indeed, the choice for many of the verbs that occur in strictly non-idiomatic expressions are far from obvious and at times even bewildering. One only has to think of instances such as 果実を結ぶ (bear fruit), 富が落ちる (win a prize in a lottery), 記事を差し止める (ban a newspaper article), or 異を差し挟む (hold uncommon views), to realize that, especially for the beginning student, the inclusion of such expressions is essential.

Particles

Another major stumbling block for foreign students lies in the difficulty of choos-

Preface

ing the right postpositional particle: が, で, と, に, は, へ, or を (助詞). Often a student will be quite sure as to which verb combines with which noun, but to choose the right particle to join them together is often frustratingly difficult. Perhaps the easiest aspect in the context of the idioms presented in this book is the distinction between the particles が and を; the former being used in combination with intransitive verbs (自動詞), as in 気が抜ける, the latter in combination with transitive verbs (他動詞), such as 気を抜く.

Nothing, however, prepares the student fully for other combinations, which seem quite arbitrary and offer no clue as to which particle they require. Which particle, for instance, joins the noun 山 (mountain) with the verb 登る (climb) to express in Japanese the phrase "climb a mountain," を or に? (the latter). And which particle combines 人 (person) with 成る (become) to express the phrase "to grow up," or "come to oneself," に or と? (the latter). To complicate matters, the use of a different particle may even radically change the meaning of an expression, such as in 顔に出す (show one's emotions) and 顔を出す (show up), or as in 鍵に掛ける (deceive someone) and 鍵を掛ける (lock something up). Given the important role of the particle in the meaning of an idiom, all the idioms listed in this dictionary are arranged under the particle by which the noun and verb are combined: ガ, デ, ト, ニ, ハ, or ヲ.

Senses

Another difficulty with Japanese idiomatic expressions is the many senses that a single expression may cover. In many cases the two given senses derive simply from the difference between the literal and figurative meaning of an expression, as in 垢を抜く which in its literal sense means to "wash off the dirt" and in its figurative sense means to "clear one's name." In other cases senses may even seem to contradict each other, such as in (人を)自由にする, which may either mean to "set someone free," or to "have someone at one's mercy." Another example is 幕を切る, which can either mean to "start on something" or to "bring something to an end." In these cases, only the context in which the expression occurs will solve the paradox. Then there are a number of expressions that have a bewilderingly large number of senses. Expressions such as 手を入れる, for example, which, depending on the context, may either mean to "touch something up," to "sound someone out," to "find a means," or to "make a raid." Here, too, the sense that applies is usually suggested by the context, although only a full grasp of all the nuances will lead to a correct interpretation.

5

Preface

In most cases, there is no profound distinction between the basic senses of the intransitive and transitive form of an idiom. Usually, there is a slight difference in intentionality, the intransitive form having a more passive tone, while the transitive form has a more active tone. However, idioms being what they are, here too, there may be considerable differences in meaning from case to case, while certain senses may only derive from either the intransitive or the transitive form. A case in point is the earlier mentioned idioms 気が抜ける and 気を抜く which have not one sense in common while the former has the additional meaning of to "lose flavor," "go flat," or "go stale."

Patterns

Luckily, there is some consistency in the way in which some verbs combine with certain nouns. Think, for instance, of the verbs 上がる (rise) or 貸す (lend) and the nouns 腕 (arm) and 手 (hand). One of the aims of this dictionary is to help the foreign reader to develop a feeling for such patterns of usage. Thus, as one grows familiar with the makeup of Japanese idioms, one will find that verbs such as 陥る frequently combine with nouns denoting trouble, difficulty or any kind of situation one can get into or fall into. Thus, the verb 抱く often combines with nouns denoting doubt, suspicion, and other emotions that can be entertained, harbored, or cherished. And thus the verb 背く tends to combine well with nouns denoting rule, custom, morality, and other things that can be violated or contravened. There is, however, no hard and fast rule, as the same verbs will combine with far less obvious nouns, as in 羽目に陥る (be in a quandary), 膝を抱く (implore someone), or 名に背く (belie one's name).

When these many and often difficult hurdles have finally been overcome, the student can turn his or her full attention to the thousands of truly idiomatic expressions that have a meaning completely removed from the literal meanings of their constituent parts. Idioms such as 鯖を読む (cheat in counting) or 鰹節に使う (make a cat's paw of someone), the application of which seems to bear no relation to the individual meanings of their constituent parts. These are the most difficult to master, as the key to their meaning and usage lies deeply buried in old and, to the student, alien customs and traditions. They are quintessentially Japanese and, as such, they are a source of joy to those who have mastered them, as they will have brought them yet a step closer to the essence of the people and culture that have spawned them.

Preface

Symbols

Where relevant, different senses of meaning for each entry are indicated by the symbols ❶, ❷, ❸, etc. The senses are generally listed with the sense used most frequently appearing first.

Other symbols used throughout this dictionary are listed with their meanings below. Please note that the usage of the symbols differs slightly for the main entries, the sub-entries, and the sample phrases.

Main entries:
- Ⓐ archaic
- Ⓗ historic
- Ⓓ dialect
- Ⓔ elegant
- Ⓒ colloquial
- Ⓥ vulgar
- Ⓢ slang

Sub-entries
- ⓐ archaic
- ⓞ obsolete
- ⓓ dialect
- ⓔ elegant
- ⓒ colloquial
- ⓥ vulgar
- ⓢ slang

Sample phrases
- ⓘ idiomatic equivalent
- Ⓐ abstract equivalent
- Ⓛ literal equivalent
- Ⓔ elegant equivalent
- Ⓒ colloquial equivalent
- Ⓥ vulgar equivalent
- Ⓢ slang equivalent

ア

愛 love

N ⓐ ～に愛持つ be blinded by love. ～に溢れる overflow with love. ～に溺れる dote on *sb*; ⓒ be mad about *sb*. ～に答える requite *sb's* love; love *sb* in return. ～に背く betray *one's/sb's* love. ～に絆される be a slave of love; be tied to *sb* by love. ～に報いる return *sb's* love; requite *sb's* love.

を ～を受ける be the object of *sb's* love. ～を受け入れる accept *sb's* love. ～を失う lose *sb's* love. ～を打ち明ける ⓔ confess (one's) love. ～を奪う ⓔ steal (one's) love away. ～を得る win *sb's* love; gain *sb's* love. ～を勝ち取る gain *sb's* affections; conquer *sb's* affection. ～を感じる feel love. ～を割く suppress one's feelings of love; abandon one's feelings of love; ⓔ forsake *sb's* love. ～を囁き合う whisper words of love. ～を示す express (one's) love; demonstrate one's love. ～を誓い合う promise to love each other; ⓔ exchange tender vows. ～を告げる declare (one's) love; ⓔ testify to one's feelings. ～を報いる return *sb's* love; requite *sb's* love; love *sb* back. ～を持つ be charming; be attractive.

愛嬌 charms; winsomeness

A ～が有る be attractive; be charming; be endearing; be cute. ～が付く become lovable; gain in charm; ⓒ grow winsome. ～が零れる be overflowing with smiles.

を ～を売る sell one's favors; ⓔ traffic in one's charms; ⓘ curry favor with *sb*. ～を呉れる [*kabuki*] delight the crowds. ～を零す ❶ be alluring; be seductive. ❷ alienate *sb*. ～を振り巻く please everyone; spread one's charms around; be all smiles; ⓒ ⓘ turn on the charm.

愛顧 patronage; favor

を ～を受ける receive *sb's* favors; be patronized. ～を失う lose favor with *sb*; ⓘ fall from grace. ～を乞う solicit *sb's* patronage; ask for *sb's* favor.

愛情 affection; love

N ～に飢える be starved for love; be deprived of affection. ～に溺れる be infatuated with *sb*. ～に報いる requite *sb's* love.

を ～を抱く hold *sb* in affection. ～を得る gain *sb's* affection; win *sb's* love. ～を捧げる give one's love to *sb*; be devoted to *sb*. ～を注ぐ shower *sb* with affection; ⓔ pour one's affection on *sb*. ～を持つ feel affection toward *sb*. 〜を求める seek *sb's* affection; crave *sb's* affection.

あいそう
愛想 friendliness; amiability

A 〜が尽きる despair of *sb*; be disgusted with *sb*; be through with *sb*; © be fed up with *sb*.

を 〜を言う pay *sb* a compliment. 〜を尽かす despair of *sb*; be disgusted with *sb*; be exasperated with *sb*; © be fed up with *sb*. 〜をする give *sb* a cordial reception; be hospitable; receive *sb* warmly.

あいだ
間 an interval; a space ▶ 間

N 〜に立つ mediate between. 〜に入る mediate between.

する 〜へ入る mediate between.

を 〜を置く leave an interval. 〜を裂く estrange *sb* from *sb* else. 〜を塞ぐ drive two people apart. 〜を詰める leave no space.

あいづち
相槌 Ⅲ alternate hammering

を 〜を打つ © ❶ hammer (a sword) alternately. © ❷ make verbal responses (to smoothen the conversation); echo *sb's* words; repeat *sb's* sentiments; ① chime in with *sb*.

あいて
相手 a partner; an opponent

N 〜にする ❶ deal with *sb*; engage with *sb*. ❷ take notice of *sb*; take *sb* seriously. ❸ make a companion of *sb*; treat *sb* as a partner. ❹ take *sb* on; take *sb* up on a challenge; play against *sb*.

を 〜をする ❶ keep *sb* company; be a companion to *sb*. ❷ entertain *sb*; bear *sb* company. ❸ take *sb* on; take *sb* up on a challenge; play against *sb*.

あいま
合間 an interval

を 〜を縫う use the spare moments.

あおいき
青息 distress

を 〜を吹く sigh with worry; be in distress; © be at one's last gasp.

あおすじ
青筋 a blue vein

を 〜を立てる turn purple with rage. 〜を張る turn purple with rage.

あお
煽ち a gust of wind

N ⓐ 〜に乗る be taken in by *sb*; be led astray.

あおり
障泥 a saddle flap

を ⓑ 〜を打つ spur *sb* on; egg *sb* on; encourage *sb*.

あおり
煽り a blast; a gust; influnece

を ⓒ 〜を食う ❶ be influenced by *sb*; be swayed by *sb*. ❷ suffer from the repercussions of *sth*; be hit by *sth*.

垢 dirt; filth; grime

[A] 〜が付く become dirty; become soiled. 〜が出る exude dirt. 〜が抜ける ❶ become sophisticated. ❷ clear one's name; be cleared of suspicion.

[を] 〜を落とす wash off the dirt; rinse *sth* out; clean *sth*. 〜を抜く ❶ wash off the dirt. ❷ clear one's name; be cleared of suspicion; be vindicated.

証 proof; evidence

[A] 〜を立つ be vindicated; be proven innocent; ⓔ be exonerated.

[を] 〜を立てる prove *sth*; give evidence; testify to *sth*.

赤字 a deficit; red figures

[N] 〜に陥る ⓘ fall into the red; ⓘ go in the red. 〜になる suffer a loss; ⓘ go in the red.

[を] 〜を埋める make up a loss; cover a deficit. 〜を出す run up a deficit; ⓘ go in the red.

赤腹 a brown thrush; a dace

[を] ⓐ 〜を垂れる tell a lie.

明かり a light; a lamp; light

[A] ⓐ 〜が立つ be vindicated; prove *sth* to be groundless; be cleared of suspicion.

[を] ⓐ 〜を走る be evident; be obvious; be clear to all.

秋 autumn; (the) fall

[を] ⓘ 〜を吹かす love starts to cool.

秋風 the autumn wind

[A] 〜が立つ love starts to cool.

[を] ⓘ 〜を吹かす love starts to cool; fall out of love.

諦め resignation; acceptance

[A] 〜が付く be reconciled; come to terms with; resign oneself to *sth*.

空家 a vacant house

[を] 〜を叩く ❶ be ignored in spite of one's efforts; make futile efforts; exert oneself to no purpose. ⓐ ❷ call in vain.

悪 evil; wickedness

[N] 〜に与する be a party to vice. 〜に誘う entice *sb* to vice; tempt *sb*. 〜に染まる sink into vice; ⓔ be steeped in vice. 〜に陥る fall into evil ways. 〜に走る take to crime. 〜に耽る ⓔ abandon oneself to evil; ⓔ be given to evil ways. 〜に負ける yield to evil; be conquered by evil.

[を] 〜を一掃する root out evil. 〜を重ねる repeat malpractices. 〜を滅ぼす overthrow evil.

灰汁 lye; ash; harshness

[A] ～が強い be assertive; be tenacious. ～が抜ける become polished; become refined; be free from vulgarity.

[を] ～を去る ❶ become polished; become refined; ⓔ be free from vulgarity. ⓓ ❷ draw out the harshness; ⓒ skim off the scum. ～を抜く draw out the harshness; ⓒ skim off the scum.

悪意 malice; evil intent; ill will

[N] ～に取る take sth amiss; take sth the wrong way; ⓔ put a bad construction on sth.

[を] ～を抱く harbor ill will (against sb); bear a grudge against sb.

悪事 an evil deed; vice; a crime

[N] ～に耽る indulge in vice; give oneself over to evil.

[を] ～を行う do evil; practice evil. ～を重ねる commit one crime after another. ～を薦める put a bad idea into sb's head; give sb bad ideas; incite sb to do wrong. ～を企む plot evil; plan a crime. ～を働く do evil; work evil; commit a crime.

悪態 abuse; foul language

[を] ～を吐く insult sb; abuse sb; call sb names; ⓘ fling dirt at sb.

悪天候 bad weather

[を] ⓣ ～を売る make a profit on the prospect of a poor harvest. ⓣ ～を買う make a loss on the prospect of a poor harvest.

欠伸 a yawn; yawning

[を] ～を隠す hide a yawn (behind one's hand). ～を噛み殺す stifle a yawn; choke down a yawn. ～を移す infect sb with one's yawning. ～をさせる be boring; make sb yawn.

悪名 a bad name; notoriety

[A] ⓢ ～が高い have a bad name; be notorious.

[を] ～を轟かせる gain a bad name; become notorious; gain notoriety. ～を馳せる gain a bad name; become notorious; gain notoriety.

胡座 cross-legged

[を] ～を掻く ❶ sit cross-legged. ❷ ⓘ rest on one's laurels.

朱 red; cinnabar; blood ▶朱

[N] ～に染まる be smeared with blood; ⓔ welter in blood. ～に成る ❶ dye sth red. ❷ be smeared with blood; be covered in blood.

揚げ足 a raised leg

[A] ～を打つ sit cross-legged. ～を取

る ❶ catch *sb* tripping; trip *sb* up. ❷ find fault with *sb*; carp at *sb's* faults.

揚げ壺 a gambling trick

[を] ⓢ ～を食う be deceived; ⓒ be taken in; ⓒ be conned; ⓒ be duped.

顎 the chin; the jaw

[A] ～が奪われる be stranded; be tied up. ⓒ ～が多い be talkative; ⓒ be loquacious; ⓒ be a chatterbox; ⓒ talk people's head off. ～が落ちる ❶ be delicious. ❷ have fits of laughter; ⓒⓘ fall over laughing; ⓒⓘ kill oneself laughing. ～が食い違う be frustrated; be disappointed. ～が草臥れる get tired of talking. Ⓐ ～が怖い be argumentative; be glib-tongued. ～が出る be exhausted; become tired out; ⓢ be knackered. ～が外れる ❶ have one's jaw dislocated. ❷ have fits of laughter; ⓒⓘ fall over laughing; ⓒⓘ kill oneself laughing. ～が干上がる suffer loss of income; lose one's means of livelihood.

[Av] ～で扱き使う boss *sb* around; ⓘ have *sb* at one's beck and call; ⓘ wrap *sb* round one's little finger. ～で射る point to *sth* with one's chin. ～で示す point *sth* out with one's chin. ～で使う ❶ deceive *sb*; ⓘ take *sb* in; ⓒⓘ lead *sb* by the nose. ❷ boss *sb* around; ⓘ have *sb* at one's beck and call; ⓘ wrap *sb* round one's little finger.

[を] ～を捌る ⓘ turn up one's nose. ～を出す be exhausted; become tired out; ⓢ be knackered. ～を突き出す ❶ stick one's chin out; thrust one's chin out. ❷ show resolve; be resolute. ～を撫でる ❶ rub one's chin; stroke one's chin. ❷ pride oneself on *sth*; be elated. ～を外す have fits of laughter; ⓒⓘ fall over laughing; ⓒⓘ kill oneself laughing. ～を引く put on a brave face. ⓢ ～を養う make a living; get by; support oneself; ⓒ earn one's daily bread.

足 a foot; a leg

[A] ⓐ ～が上がる lose one's job. ～が重い have leaden feet; be disinclined (to visit *sb*). ～が有る have a means of transport. ～が軽い have light feet; be light-footed. ⓐ ～が近い visit each other frequently; see much of each other. ～が付く ❶ be traced; be tracked down. ❷ put donw one's foot; find a footing. ❸ be found out; be exposed. ❹ keep bad company; have a ne'er-do-well as a lover; have a good-for-nothing boyfriend. ～が強い ❶ [nautical] be a fast sailor. ❷ keep well; last a long time. ～が出る ❶ exceed the budg-

5

et; ① break the bank. ❷ have one's faults exposed; ① show the cloven hoof; ⓒ ① show oneself up. 〜が遠い visit each other infrequently; see little of each other. 〜が鈍る be less eager to; lose enthusiasm for *sth*. 〜が早い ❶ be quick on one's feet. ❷ go bad quickly; be perishable. 〜が向く head for (a place); go somewhere; ⓒ turn one's steps toward (a place). 〜が弱い ❶ have a poor leg; be a bad walker. ❷ [nautical] be a slow sailer. ❸ have thin tires. ❹ go bad quickly; be perishable.

A 〜を洗う ❶ give up (one's bad habits); make a new start. ❷ be through with *sb*; ① wash one's hands of (a matter). 〜を痛める injure one's leg. 〜を入れる set foot in (a place). 〜を奪う strand *sb*; deprive *sb* of transportation. 〜を屈める bend one's legs. 〜を固める secure a foothold. 〜を組む cross one's legs; sit with crossed legs. 〜を掬う trip *sb* up; sweep *sb's* legs from under him/her. 〜を揃える keep pace with *sb*; walk in step. 〜を出す ❶ be short of money; ① go in the red. ❷ betray oneself; reveal one's true character; ① show one's true colors; ① show the cloven hoof. ❸ have a breech delivery. ❹ have an unexpected result. 〜を解く unwind one's legs. 〜を止め る stop in one's tracks; force *sb* to stay. 〜を取られる ❶ lose one's footing. ❷ be short of money; be in dire straits. 〜を抜く extricate oneself (from an awkward situation). 〜を延ばす ❶ stretch one's legs; make oneself at home. ❷ extend one's journey; go farther. 〜を運ぶ call on *sb*; pay *sb* a visit; visit a place. 〜を早める quicken one's pace. 〜を払う trip *sb* up; sweep *sb's* legs from under him/her. 〜を引っ張る stand in *sb's* way; drag *sb* down. 〜を踏み入れる give *sth* a try; get involved in *sth*; ① have a shot at *sth*. 〜を踏み換える change foot. 〜を踏み外す make a false step; take a wrong step. 〜を踏む ① step on *sb's* foot. 〜を向ける ❶ head for (a place); go somewhere; ⓒ turn one's steps toward (a place). ❷ contemplate *sth*; consider *sth*. 〜を緩める slacken one's pace.

味 taste; flavor; savor

A 〜が有る have flavor; have depth; have body. 〜が薄い have a weak taste; have little flavor. 〜が旨い taste delicious; taste great. 〜が変わる the taste changes; turn sour; go stale. 〜が濃い have a strong taste; have a rich taste; be rich. (何かの)〜がする taste of *sth*. 〜が強い have a strong taste; have

～が抜ける lose flavor. ～が分かる ❶ be able to taste *sth*; have a sense taste. ❷ be a gourmet. ❸ have experience of *sth*; know *sth* by experience.
を ～を覚える ❶ remember the taste. ❷ have experience of *sth*. (何かの)～を感じる sense a (certain) taste; (be able to) taste *sth*. ～を聞く try *sth*; taste *sth*. ～を占める take a liking to *sth*; ⓒ get a taste for *sth*. ～を知る ❶ know the taste of *sth*; ❷ have experience of *sth*; know *sth* by experience. ⓥ ⓢ (女の) ❸ know a woman; have slept with a woman; ⓔ have carnal knowledge of a woman. ～を付ける flavor (food); season (food). ～を見る try the taste of *sth*; taste *sth*; sample (food).

足掛かり a footing; a foothold

N ～になる give one a foothold.
を ～を得る gain a foothold. ～を捜す seek a foothold. ～を作る establish a foothold.

足手 arms and legs

を ～を引く exert oneself (on behalf of *sb*/sth); be busily engaged in *sth*.

足並 a pace; a step

A ～が揃う fall into step; fall into line; ⓔ act in concert. ～が乱れる fall out of step; fall apart.
を ～を揃える fall into step; ⓒ act in concert. ～を乱す be out of tune; be in disarray.

足下 the soles of one's feet

A ～が危ない have an unsteady gait; be unsteady on one's feet. ～がふらつく have an unsteady gait; be unsteady on one's feet.
を ～を上げる dismiss *sb*; discharge *sb*; ⓒ fire *sb*; ⓢ ⓘ give *sb* the sack; ⓒ ⓘ send *sb* packing. ～を見る take advantage of *sb*'s weakness.

梓 A a catalpa tree

N ⓑ ～に刻む ❶ print books; make a book. ❷ issue a book; publish a book. ⓑ ～に鏤める ❶ print books; make a book. ❷ issue a book; publish a book.

汗 sweat; perspiration

A ～が滴る drip with sweat. ～が出る sweat; perspire. ～が噴き出す break out in sweat.
N ～に塗れる be soaked in sweat. ～になる ❶ sweat profusely. ❷ be anxious; be nervous.
を ～を入れる take a rest; ⓒ have a breather. ～をかく sweat; perspire. ～を流す ❶ take a sweat (in a bath).

❷ labor hard; work hard; do one's utmost; exert oneself; give one's all. ～を握(にぎ)る be nervous; be on edge; ⓒ be kept on tenterhooks. ～を拭(ぬぐ)う wipe away perspiration; mop (one's brow). ～を絞(しぼ)る wring out the sweat. ～を揉(も)む labor hard; work hard; exert oneself.

仇(あだ) a foe; an enemy

Ⓝ ～になる become enemies; turn into an enemy.

Ⓦ ～を討(う)つ avenge *sb*; take revenge for *sb*; ⓘ settle old scores (with *sb*); ⓘ square accounts with *sb*. ～を返(かえ)す revenge oneself on *sb*. ～をする do *sb* harm; do *sb* a disservice. ～を為(な)す ❶ make enemies; harm *sb*; ⓘ breed bad blood. ❷ hold a grudge against *sb*; ⓔ harbor a private malice; ⓘ have a chip on one's shoulder. ⓒ ～を結(むす)ぶ ❶ revenge oneself on *sb*; get one's revenge. ❷ harm *sb*; do *sb* harm. ❸ harbor ill will (against *sb*); bear a grudge against *sb*; ⓘ have a chip on one's shoulder.

頭(あたま) the head; the brain ▶ 頭(かしら) ▶ 頭(ず)

Ⓐ ⓞ ～が荒(あら)い be short of breath; breathe hard. ～が良(い)い be clear-headed; be clever; be bright. ～が痛(いた)む ❶ have a headache. ❷ worry about *sb*/*sth*; fret over *sb*/*sth*. ～が要(い)る require brains. ～が可笑(おか)しい be mad; be crazy; ⓒ be mental. ～が重(おも)い have a headache. ～が固(かた)い have fixed ideas; be inflexible; be set in one's ways; ⓘ be dyed in the wool. ～が固(かた)まる become fixed in one's ideas. ～が切(き)れる have a sharp mind; be a quick thinker; be quick on one's feet; ⓢ ⓘ be on the ball. ～が臭(くさ)い have smelly hair. ⓞ ～が苦(くる)しい be suffocating; ⓒ be stuffy. ～が下(さ)がる ❶ bow one's head (in greeting); bow to one; ⓘ take off one's hat to *sb* ❷ admire *sb*; be impressed by *sb*; ⓘ take off one's hat to *sb*. ～が鋭(するど)い be sharp-witted. ～が高(たか)い be arrogant; be haughty; be proud; have an overbearing attitude. ～が違(ちが)う have a different mind. ⓞ ～が長(なが)い have a long breath; keep well. ～が鈍(にぶ)い be dull-witted. ～が働(はたら)く have the presence of mind (to); have the sense (to). ～が低(ひく)い be courteous; be humble; ⓘ keep a low profile. ～が古(ふる)い have outdated ideas; ⓘ be of the old school. ～が弱(よわ)い be weak-heade; be feeble-minded. ～が悪(わる)い be slow-witted; be muddle-headed; ⓒ be brainless.

Ⓝ ～に入(い)れる learn *sth* by heart. ～に浮(う)かぶ come to mind; occur to

one. 〜に描（えが）く picture (a situation); envisage (a scene). 〜に置（お）く take *sth* into consideration; bear *sth* in mind; ⓘ take *sth* on board. 〜に来（く）る ⓒ ❶ get mad; lose one's temper; be vexed by *sth*; ⓢ ⓘ blow a fuse. ❷ ⓘ go to one's head; ⓘ lose one's head; ⓢ ⓘ lose one's marbles; ⓢ freak out. ❸ become nervous; get flustered; fret over *sth*. 〜に閃（ひらめ）く flash across one's mind.
［する］〜へ来（く）る ❶ ⓘ lose one's head ⓢ ⓘ lose one's marbles; ⓢ freak out. ❷ become nervous; worry over *sth*; fret over *sth*.
［を］〜を上（あ）げる show oneself. 〜を痛（いた）める worry about *sth*; fret over *sth*. 〜を動（うご）かせる think about *sth*; ponder over *sth*. 〜を抑（おさ）える keep *sb* under control; ⓘ keep *sb* under one's thumb; hold *sb* down. 〜を抱（かか）える ❶ think hard about *sth*; ⓒ ⓘ rack one's brains. ❷ be at a loss (about what to do); ⓘ be at one's wits' end; ⓘ be all at sea. 〜を掻（か）く scratch one's head. 〜を下（さ）げる ❶ bow one's head (in greeting); bow to one. ❷ show one's respect. ❸ give up; give in. 〜を搾（しぼ）る think hard about *sth*; ⓒ ⓘ rack one's brains. 〜を垂（た）れる ❶ drop one's head. ❷ be discouraged; lose heart. 〜を使（つか）う use one's brains; ⓢ ⓘ use one's loaf. 〜を突（つ）っ

込（こ）む ❶ thrust one's head (into). ❷ take part in *sth*; ⓒ dabble in *sth*. 〜を撫（な）でる pat *sb* on the head. 〜を悩（なや）ませる be worried about *sth*. 〜を撥（は）ねる ❶ cut off *sb's* head. ❷ extort money from *sb*; take a percentage. 〜を捻（ひね）る think hard about *sth*; ⓒ ⓘ rack one's brains. 〜を冷（ひ）やす settle down; calm down; ⓐ cool down. 〜を解（ほぐ）す ⓘ clear one's head. 〜を丸（まる）める become a Buddhist priest; take the tonsure. 〜を擡（もた）げる ❶ gain power; ⓘ be in the ascendant. ❷ come to mind; gain hold; come to the fore. 〜を割（わ）る ❶ fracture one's skull. ❷ fret over *sth*; ⓒ ⓘ rack one's brains.

当（あ）たり a hit; a success

［A］〜が有（あ）る [fishing] have a bite. 〜が良（い）い hit well. 〜が付（つ）く ❶ have a mind to do *sth*; be inclined to do *sth*. ❷ be possible to guess; have a general idea. ❸ be a success; ⓒ win aclaim; ⓒ be a hit. 〜が無（な）い [fishing] have no bite. 〜が悪（わる）い hit badly.
［を］〜を付（つ）ける ❶ fall in love with *sb*; ⓘ fall for *sb*; ⓒ be enamored by *sb*. ❷ make an estimation; have a guess. 〜を取（と）る ❶ be a success; ⓒ win aclaim; ⓒ be a hit. ❷ make an estimation; have a guess.

辺り the vicinity; surroundings

[を] 〜を構う have regard for those around one. 〜を輝かす have charisma; be charismatic; ① catch the eye. 〜を見回す look around. 〜を払う ❶ keep people at bay; drive the crowd away. ⑩ ❷ be overbearing; overshadow others.

呆気 surprise; amazement

[N] 〜に取られる be surprised; be startled; be shocked; be baffled; be flabbergasted; ① be taken aback.

悪口 abuse; slander

[を] 〜を切る say bad things about *sb*; speak ill of *sb*; foul *sb*'s name.

圧迫 pressure; oppression

[を] 〜を受ける be under pressure; be pressed. 〜を加える put pressure on *sb*; bring pressure to bear on *sb*; ① turn the screws on. 〜を続ける keep up the pressure. 〜を強める intensify the pressure; raise the stakes. 〜を除く take off the pressure.

当て an object; an aim; an end

[A] 〜が違う fall short of one's expectations; ① belie one's expectations. 〜が付く be possible to guess; have a general idea. 〜が外れる be disappointed (in one's hopes); be frustrated; prove a disappointment. [N] 〜になる rely on *sb*/*sth*; put one's trust in *sb*/*sth*. 〜になる be reliable; be trustworthy. [を] 〜を付ける ❶ take aim at *sth*; aim at *sth*. ❷ make an estimation; have a guess. ❸ make an innuendo; insinuate *sth*; ① voice indirect criticism of *sb*..

当てずっぽう [S] a random guess

[N] 〜に答える give a random answer; guess at *sth*; ① try a shot in the dark.

[を] ⑤ 〜を言う have a guess; guess at *sth*; ① try a shot in the dark.

後 the back; the future

[N] (事の) 〜に続く follow *sth*. 〜になる fall behind. 〜に残る stay behind; remain behind; be left; (人の) survive *sb*. 〜に引けない refuse to yield; ① hold the line.
[A] 〜で引く turn back.
[を] 〜へ回す postpone *sth*; put *sth* of; lay *sth* aside; ① put *sth* on ice.
[を] 〜を黒む [military] protect the rear flank; guard the rear. 〜を立てる re-establish an extinct family. 〜を継ぐ succeed *sb*; step into *sb*'s shoes. 〜を詰める ❶ come to a setlement; reach an understanding;

アト　　　　　　　　　　　　　　アトシマツ

settle a matter. ⓥ ⓢ ❷ have a prostitute for the night.
　〜を弔(とむら)う perform religious rites for the repose of sb's soul. 〜を濁(にご)す leave a bad impression. 〜を引(ひ)く be unable to stop; find it hard to quit; grow on one.

跡(あと) a mark; a stain; a trace

Ⓐ 〜が絶(た)える disappear without a trace; leave no trace; become extinct; go out of existence; die out. 〜が付(つ)く leave traces.
Ⓝ 〜に習(なら)う follow a precedent.
Ⓐ ⓢ 〜で座(すわ)る succeed sb; ⓘ step into sb's shoes.
Ⓚ 〜を追(お)う ❶ trail sb; stalk sb; run after sb; ⓘ follow up the scent. ❷ follow sb in death. 〜を隠(かく)す conceal one's whereabouts. 〜を晦(くら)ます conceal one's whereabouts; ⓘ erase one's steps; ⓘ cover up one's tracks. 〜を絶(た)つ be exterminated; be wiped out; put an end to sth; wipe out; disappear without a trace. 〜を辿(たど)る trace sb; follow up a lead. ⓢ 〜を垂(た)る set an example. 〜を付(つ)ける trace sb; trail sb; track sb down. 〜を取(と)る succeed sb; step into sb's shoes. 〜を残(のこ)す leave traces. 〜を踏(ふ)む step in sb's footsteps. 〜を守(まも)る continue a (family) tradition; take charge of the house. 〜を譲(ゆず)る make place for sb else; transfer control; ⓘ pass the reins to sb else.

迎合(あど) Ⓑ a supporting actor

Ⓚ ⓒ 〜を打(う)つ make verbal responses (to smoothen the conversation); echo sb's words; repeat sb's sentiments; ⓘ chime in with sb.

後釜(あとがま) Ⓑ a successor

Ⓝ ⓢ 〜に座(すわ)る succeed sb; replace sb; ⓘ step into sb's shoes. ⓢ 〜に据(す)える install sb in another's place.

後口(あとぐち) an aftertaste

Ⓝ 〜に回(まわ)す leave sth till later; put sth off; ⓒ procrastinate on an issue.
Ⓚ 〜を清(きよ)める wash away the taste of sth (with a glass of beer).

後先(あとさき) the front and rear

Ⓚ 〜を考(かんが)える be prudent; look ahead; be circumspicious; reflect on the effect of one's actions.

後知恵(あとぢえ) Ⓑ wisdom after the event

Ⓚ ⓢ 〜を動(うご)かす use the wisdom of hindsight; second-guess.

後始末(あとしまつ) settlement; clearance

Ⓚ 〜を付(つ)ける round (a matter) off; settle (an affair); put an end to sth; bring sth to a close.

11

あとばら
後腹 afterpains; after-trouble

[A] 〜が痛む suffer the consequences of one's actions.

あとぼう
後棒 a palanquin's hind bearer

[を] 〜を担ぐ ❶ bear a palanquin. ❷ be involved in an intrigue; ⓒ be party to a conspiracy; ⓓ have a hand in a plot; ⓔⓓ be in cahoots.

あとまわし
後回し postponement

[N] 〜にする postpone *sth*; put *sth* off; sidetrack a matter. 〜になる be postponed; be put off; be sidetracked.

あとめ
跡目 [田] the family headship

[N] 〜に継ぐ succeed *sb* as head of the family; become the new family heir.

[を] 〜を譲る ❶ pass on the family leadership. ❷ go into seclusion; become a hermit; renounce the world; ⓒ retire from the world.

あな
穴 a hole; a burrow; a gap ▶ 穴

[A] 〜が開く ❶ suffer a loss; ⓔ incur losses. ❷ lose time; be behind (on schedule). 〜が埋まる ❶ recoup a loss; make good a loss. ❷ make up for lost time; ⓓ catch up.

[を] 〜を開ける ❶ make a hole; drill a hole. ❷ cause a deficit; ⓓ go in the red. ❸ lose time; get behind (on schedule). 〜を言う criticize *sb*; point out *sb's* shortcomings. 〜を穿つ expose *sb*; penetrate a situation; ⓓ blow *sb's* cover. 〜を埋める ❶ fill up a hole. ❷ make up a loss. ❸ be supplied with *sth*. 〜を捜す find fault with *sb*; carp at *sb's* faults. 〜を探る find fault with *sb*; point out *sb's* shortcomings; carp at *sb's* faults. 〜を塞ぐ fill a hole; close a gap. 〜を掘る dig a hole.

あぶら
油 oil

[A] 〜が切れる ❶ run out of oil. ❷ lose energy; ⓒⓓ run out of steam.

[を] 〜を言う incite *sb* to action; wheedle *sb* into doing *sth*; egg *sb* on. 〜を売る ❶ sell oil. ❷ idle one's time away; ⓒ dawdle away one's time; ⓔ loaf around. ⓐ 〜を掛ける incite *sb* to action; wheedle *sb* into doing *sth*. 〜を濾す filter oil. 〜を差す encourage *sb*; egg *sb* on. 〜を絞る ❶ extract oil from *sth*. ❷ take *sb* to task; ⓒ tell *sb* off; ⓓ haul *sb* over the coals. ❸ work hard; do one's best; ⓓ work one's fingers to the bone; ⓓ scrape to earn a living. ❹ cause *sb* to suffer great hardships; give *sb* a hard time. (火に)〜を注ぐ ⓓ pour oil (on the flames); ⓓ add fuel to the fire; fuel *sb's* anger. 〜を

アブラ

付ける put oil on *sth*; anoint *sb*; grease sth. 〜を採る ❶ extract oil. ❷ reprimand *sb*; ⓒ haul *sb* over the coals. ❸ cross-examine *sb*; [leave rest of entry] ❹ flatter *sb*; ⓒ pay lipservice; ⓒ flannel *sb*. ❺ skimp one's work; ⓢⓒ skate on the job. 〜を載せる ❶ flatter *sb*; fawn on *sb*; ⓒ curry favor with *sb*. ❷ exaggerate *sth*; ⓒ indulge in hyperbole; ⓒ stretch the facts; ⓢⓒ pile it on; ⓢⓒ lay it on thick.

脂 fat

Ⓐ 〜が乗る ❶ put on fat. ❷ be at its best; ⓒ be in one's prime. ❸ ⓒ get into one's stride; ⓒ get into the swing of things. ❹ be at the height of one's skill; ⓔ be at the zenith of power. ❺ be interested in *sth*.

阿呆 a fool; a simpleton; an ass

ⓦ ⓢ 〜を尽くす play the fool.

甘茶 hydrangea tea

ⓦ 〜を飲ます humor *sb*; ⓒ curry favor with *sb*; ⓔ ingratiate oneself with *sb*.

網 a net; a dragnet; a net trap

Ⓐ ⓢ 〜が上がる resolve a situation; reveal (*sth* hidden). 〜が下りる be brought to justice; be sentenced.

アヤマチ

Ⓝ 〜に掛かる ❶ be caught in a net; be netted. (法の) ❷ be caught in the meshes (of the law); fall into the clutches (of the law). 〜に絡まる be entangled in a net. 〜に漏れる ❶ slip through the meshes of a net. (法の) ❷ escape the clutches of the law; evade the law.

ⓦ 〜を打つ throw a net; cast a net. 〜を潜る ❶ slip through the meshes of a net. (法の) ❷ escape the clutches of the law; evade the law. 〜を張る ❶ pitch a net; lay a net. ❷ set a trap. 〜を広げる spread a net.

飴 candy; a sweet; barley sugar

ⓦ ⓢ 〜を食わす ❶ let *sb* win on purpose; give in to *sb* on purpose. ❷ let *sb* off lightly; let *sb* have his/her way. ❸ cajole *sb*; ⓒ talk *sb* into *sth*. 〜をしゃぶる eat candy; suck on a sweet. 〜を嘗めさせる ❶ let *sb* win on purpose; give in to *sb* on purpose. ❷ let *sb* off lightly; let *sb* have his/her way. ❸ cajole *sb*; ⓒ talk *sb* into *sth*.

過ち a mistake; an error

Ⓝ 〜に陥る fall into bad ways.
ⓦ 〜を犯す ❶ make a mistake; commit an error; ⓒ ⓒ drop the ball. ⓔ ❷ have an extramarital affair; ⓔ commit adultery. ⓢ 〜を文ざる

粗 fish bones; a fault

⎣を⎦ ～を捜す find fault with *sb*; carp at *sb's* faults. ～を拾う find fault with *sb*; carp at *sb's* faults. ～を穿つ be critical of *sb's* faults; pick at *sb's* faults; ① split hairs.

新 ⒈ brand-new; fresh

⎣A⎦ ① ～で買う buy *sth* brand-new.

荒胆 bewilderment; shock

⎣を⎦ ～を抜く strike terror into *sb's* heart; ① scare the living daylights out of *sb*; ① scare *sb* out of his/her wits. ～を拉ぐ strike terror into *sb's* heart; ① scare the living daylights out of *sb*; ① scare *sb* out of his/her wits.

泡 bubbles; foam; scum

⎣に⎦ ～となる come to nothing; end in failure; ① go up in smoke. ⎣を⎦ ～を噛む ❶ be in agony; be tormented. ❷ be vexed; be frustrated;

keep up appearances; gloss over a mistake. ～を悟る be convinced of one's error; see one's mistake. ～を正す correct one's mistake; put right an error. ～を認める acknowledge one's error; recognize one's mistake. ～を詫びる apologize for one's mistake.

be chagrined. ❸ ～を食う be confused; be flurried; be taken aback. ～を立てる make foam; create bubbles. ～を吹かす upset *sb*; cause *sb* distress. ～を吹く froth at the mouth; blow bubbles.

哀れ sorrow; grief; pathos

⎣と⎦ ～と思う be moved to pity; be touched with compassion. ⎣を⎦ ～を訴える plead for mercy; appeal for *sb's* mercy. ～を交す exchange tender feelings; be moved by each other. ～を誘う add pathos; move one to pity. ～をそそる excite one's pity. ～を留める ❶ be a pitiable sight; be pathetic. ❷ leave a pathetic impression. ～を増す deepen one's sorrow; add to one's loneliness. ～を催す be moved to pity; be touched with compassion.

哀れみ compassion; pity

⎣を⎦ ～を掛ける treat *sb* with compassion; take pity on *sb*. ～を請う ❶ beg for mercy; appeal for *sb's* pity. ❷ beg for alms. ～を蒙る engage *sb's* compassion. ～を垂れる treat *sb* with compassion; take pity on *sb*.

案 an idea; a plan; a scheme

⎣N⎦ ～に落つ go according to plan;

アン / イ

prove a success; work out well. ～に違う fall short of one's expectations; ⓔ belie one's expectations.
[を] ～を立てる work out a plan. ～を出す present a plan; launch an idea. ～を作る make a plan; hatch an idea; draw up a plan. ～を練る elaborate on a plan; scrutinize a scheme. ～を述べる present one's plan; explain an idea; give one's opinion. ～を廻らす work out a plan; ⓔ tax one's ingenuity.

安 peace; tranquility; calm
[を] ～を偸む live a quiet life; live free from care.

暗礁 a hidden reef
[N] ～に乗り上げる ❶ strike a hidden rock; be stranded on a hidden reef; run aground. ❷ be deadlocked; ⓒ ⓘ hit a snag.

安否 safety; one's welfare
[を] ～を尋ねる inquire after sb's health; find out how sb is doing. ～を問う inquire after sb's health; find out how sb is doing.

按摩 a massage; a masseur
[を] ～をする give sb a massage. ～を取る have a massage; call in a masseur.

イ

意 a mind; a will; heart; sense
[A] ⓒ ～が有る have a mind to do sth; be inclined to do sth.
[と] ⓒ ～と為す mind about sth; give heed to sth; ⓘ take sth to heart.
[N] ⓐ ～に中たる meet one's/sb's expectations. ～に介する worry about; care about; give heed to sth. ～に適う be agreeable; be pleasing. ～に従う do as sb says; ⓒ yield to sb's wishes. ～に染む be willing; be inclined to. ～に任す leave sth to sb's discretion. ～に満たす satisfy one; be satisfactory.
[を] ～を表わす show one's approval; ⓒ voice one's satisfaction. ⓒ ～を安じる feel at ease; be at ease. ⓐ ～を致す express one's thoughts. ～を受ける do as sb says; ⓒ comply with sb's wishes. ～を得る be satisfactory; meet one's approval; have one's way. ～を酌む take sb's thoughts into consideration; bear sth in mind; ⓘ take sth on board. ～を決する make up one's mind; set one's mind on sth. ～を探る sound sb's mind. ～を示す hint at sth. ～を注ぐ make an effort; pay attention to. ～を体する ⓒ be in compliance with sb's wishes. ～を通じる ❶ make oneself understood; make one's intentions

15

known. ❷ contact *sb* secretly; make secret overtures. 〜を尽くす express oneself carefully. 〜を唱える voice one's disapproval; raise an objection; ⓔ take exception to *sth*. 〜を曲げる force oneself (to do *sth*). ⓐ 〜を迎える humor *sb*; ⓔ ingratiate oneself with *sb*; ⓘ curry favor with *sb*. 〜を用いる take care with *sth*; pay attention to *sth*.

威 dignity; authority; influence

Ⓐ 〜を借りる shelter under *sb's* influence; ⓘ ride on *sb's* coat-tails. 〜を示す display one's power. 〜を振るう wield power; exercise influence.

異 uncommonness; strangeness

Ⓐ 〜を差し挟む hold uncommon views; ⓔ assert a heterodox opinion. 〜を立てる do *sth* uncommon; ⓔ depart from convention. 〜を唱える voice one's disapproval; raise an objection; ⓔ take exception to *sth*.

帷 Ⓝ a curtain; hangings

Ⓐ ⓐⓔ 〜を下す open a private school.

言い掛かり a false charge

Ⓐ 〜を付ける accuse *sb* falsely; trump up charges.

言い分 one's say; a complaint

Ⓐ 〜を聞く listen to both sides of the argument. 〜を通す have one's say; get one's point across. 〜を述べる state one's case; make one's point.

言い訳 an apology; an excuse

Ⓐ 〜が立たない be inexcusable; be unpardonable; be unjustifiable.

家 a house; a household; home

Ⓝ 〜に杖突く be fifty years old. Ⓐ ⓐ 〜を明ける vacate a house; stay away from home. 〜を出ず ❶ leave home; go out into the world; enter the real world. ❷ become a Buddhist priest; take the tonsure; enter a Buddhist monastery. 〜を失う become homeless. 〜を興す ❶ make one's fortune. ⓑ ❷ found a clan. ⓒ 〜を傾ける exhaust one's family fortune; be bankrupt. 〜を構える ⓒ take up one's abode. 〜を知る become the head of a household. 〜を建てる build a house. 〜を飛び出す run away from home. 〜を持つ own a house.

家路 Ⓝ one's way home

Ⓝ 〜につく make one's way home. Ⓐ ⓒ 〜を辿る return home; ⓒ wend one's way home.

意外 unexpected; unforeseen

N ～に驚く be astonished; be surprised at sth. ～に思う think sth strange; think sth odd; be surprised; be taken aback.

鋳型 a mold

N ～に注ぎ込む pour (metal) into a mold; cast iron. ～に嵌める mold sb/sth to the same example.
を ～を取る cast a mold. ～を放す strip a mold.

怒り anger; a rage; wrath

A ～が解ける relent toward sb; calm down; ⓐ cool down.
N ～に触れる arouse sb's anger; offend sb; ⓔ incur sb's anger. ～に任せる lose one's temper; give way to anger; ⓔ be borne away with anger. ～に燃える be irate; burn with anger; ⓔ be consumed with rage.
を ～を遷す vent one's anger on sb; lash out against sb; ⓒ ⓘ take it out on sb. ～を抑える restrain one's anger; ⓔ suppress one's wrath. ～を買う arouse sb's anger; make sb angry. ～を静める calm oneself down; ⓔ quell one's anger; ⓔ appease one's anger. ～を宥める calm sb's anger; calm sb down; ⓔ appease sb's anger. ～をぶちまける fly into a rage; ⓔ open the floodgates of wrath; ⓒ ⓘ fly off the handle. ～を招く invite sb's anger; trigger sb's anger; ⓔ incur sb's wrath. ～を漏らす betray one's anger; vent one's anger; ⓒ ⓘ let off steam.

錨 an anchor

A ～がずれる the anchor drags.
を ～を上げる raise anchor; weigh anchor. ～を打つ ❶ the anchor finds bottom. ⓒ ❷ establish oneself; find one's footing. ～を下ろす ❶ drop anchor; let go the anchor; cast anchor; lie at anchor. ❷ sit down; squat on one's haunches. ～を切る ❶ cut loose the anchor. ⓒ ❷ become independent; ⓘ cut the cord. ～を引きずる drag one's anchor. ～を巻く weigh anchor.

息 one's breath; breathing

A ～が合う be in harmony; be in tune. ～が上がる have difficulty in breathing. ～が掛かる be under sb's patronage; be backed up by sb; enjoy sb's interest. ～が通う touch sb's heart; ⓔ call forth a response in sb's heart; ⓘ strike a sympathetic cord. ～が切れる be out of breath; run out of steam; ebb away. ～が臭い have a foul breath; have bad breath. ～が絶える pass away; ⓔ ⓘ breathe one's last. ～が続く

ⓒ have a long wind. ～が詰(つ)まる ❶ be suffocated; be stifled. ❷ be very nervous; ⓘ be on tenterhooks. ～が長(なが)い have endurance, endure, hold long. ～が弾(はず)む be out of breath. ⓒ ～が短(みじか)い have a short temper; be hot-tempered; be touchy.

[を] ～を入(い)れる take a breath. ～を切(き)らす be out of breath; lose one's breath. ～を凝(こ)らす hold one's breath; ⓒ do *sth* with bated breath. ～を殺(ころ)す hold one's breath: ⓒ anticipate *sth* with bated breath. ～を吸(す)う take a deep breath. ～をする breathe (in); take in air. ～を吐(つ)く ❶ draw breath; take breath; breathe a sigh of relief. ❷ make a living; support oneself (on a pittance). ～を継(つ)ぐ ❶ gather breath. ❷ take a short rest. ～を詰(つ)める hold one's breath. ～を閉(と)じる hold one's breath. ～を止(と)める ❶ catch one's breath; hold one's breath. ❷ strangle *sb*; choke *sb*. ～を抜(ぬ)く ❶ take a breath. ❷ give a sigh of relief; be able to breathe again. ❸ feel relieved; be reassured; be put at ease. Ⓐ ～を延(の)ぶ ❶ give a sigh of relief; be able to breathe again. ❷ feel relieved; be reassured; be put at ease. ～を呑(の)む ❶ swallow one's breath. ❷ be astonished; gasp in amazement. ～を吐(は)く breathe out. ～を弾(はず)ませる ❶ gasp for breath; pant

for breath. ❷ be excited; be flustered. ⓒ ～を張(は)る take a deep breath. 潜(ひそ)める gather breath; catch one's breath. ～を引(ひ)き取(と)る pass away; ⓒ ⓘ breathe one's last. ～を引(ひ)く ❶ draw breath; breathe in; inhale. ⓒ ❷ suffer from asthma. ～を吹(ふ)き返(かえ)す revive (the economy); come back to life. ～を吹(ふ)き込(こ)む breathe new life into (a project).

意気(いき) spirit; heart; morale

[A] ～が揚(あ)がる be in high spirits; be elated; ⓘ be gung ho.
[N] ～に燃(も)える be full with *sth*; burn with exitement.
[を] ～を立(た)てる keep up morale; maintain one's spirit; keep courage; ⓘ hold oneself high.

異議(いぎ) objection; a protest

[A] ～が有(あ)る take exception to *sth*; have an objection.
[N] ～に及(およ)ぶ dodge an issue; ⓒ equivocate on an issue; ⓒ ⓘ pussyfoot an issue; ⓘ beat about the bush.
[を] ～を差(さ)し挟(はさ)む make a protest; lodge a complaint. ～を唱(とな)える voice one's disapproval; raise an objection; ⓒ take exception to *sth*. ～を申(もう)し立(た)てる lodge a complaint; voice an objection.

イギ

威儀(いぎ) dignity
[を] 〜を正(ただ)す maintain one's dignity; keep up one's state.

勢(いきお)い vigor; drive; momentum
[A] 〜が付(つ)く be enlivened; live up; gain vigor; gain momentum.
[N] ⓔ 〜に乗(じょう)じる use the momentum; seize a good opportunity; go with the current.
[を] 〜を殺(そ)がれる be discouraged; lose momentum; lose vigor. 〜が付ける encourage sb; brace sb up; add momentum. 〜を振(ふ)るう wield influence; exersize authority. 〜を増(ま)す gather strength; gain momentum.

生(い)き血(ち) blood of a living being
[を] 〜を搾(しぼ)る sacrifice others for one's own ends. 〜を吸(す)う suck the lifeblood out of sb/sth. 〜を啜(すす)る sacrifice others for one's own ends.

息杖(いきづえ) Ⓝ a palanquin's carrying pole
[を] ⓒ 〜を立(た)てる coax a tip out of sb.

生(い)き恥(はじ) 'the shame of living (on)'
[N] 〜を曝(さら)す live in disgrace; live in shame; ⓒ live ignominiously.

委曲(いきょく) details; specifics
[を] ⓒ 〜を尽(つ)くす explain sth in detail; ⓔ elaborate on sth.

イケン

意気地(いくじ) spirit; willpower; pride
[A] 〜が無(な)い be weak-willed; be infirm; be spineless; ⓒ have no guts; ⓒ be a milksop.

意見(いけん) an opinion; a view
[A] 〜が合(あ)う be like-minded; get along well; ⓔ be congenial to one; ⓘ see eye to eye; ⓒ ⓘ hit it off. 〜が食(く)い違(ちが)う have conflicting views (on a matter).
[N] 〜に従(したが)う yield to sb's opinion. 〜に付(つ)く yield to sb's opinion; follow sb's advice.
[を] 〜を改(あらた)める modify one's opinion. 〜を言(い)う give one's opinion; speak one's piece. 〜を抱(いだ)く cherish an idea, entertain an opinion. 〜を入(い)れる accept sb's opinion. 〜を受け入れる accept sb's opinion. 〜を聞(き)く ask sb's opinion. 〜を決(き)める form an opinion. ⓒ 〜を懲(ちょう)する consult sb; ask for sb's advice; seek sb's opinion; ⓔ take counsel with sb. 〜を探(さぐ)る sound sb out; feel sb out. 〜を確(たし)かめる ascertain sb's opinion; make sure of sb's view. 〜を尋(たず)ねる ask sb's opinion. 〜を戦(たたか)わす debate each other's opinions. 〜を叩(たた)く sound sb out; feel sb out; ⓘ feel sb's pulse. 〜を立(た)てる form an opinion; come to hold a viewpoint. 〜を通(とお)す gain one's point; carry one's point. 〜を唱(とな)

える advocate an opinion. ～を述べる state one's opinion; express one's views. ～を持つ have an opinion. ～を求める seek sb's opinion.

威厳 dignity; gravity; august

N ～に関わる reflect on one's dignity; be below one's dignity.
を ～を冒す insult sb's dignity; ⓔ affront sb's dignity. ～を落とす damage one's/sb's dignity. ～を示す show dignity; display dignity; be august. ～を保つ maintain one's dignity; keep up one's state; Ⓢ keep one's cool. ～を作る be on one's dignity; get on one's dignity.

意向 intention; inclination

を ～を探る sound sb out; feel sb out. ～を確かめる ascertain sb's intentions; make sure of sb's intentions. ～を質す inquire after sb's intentions; ask sb's intention. ～を漏らす reveal one's intentions; ⓔ disclose one's intentions.

遺恨 a grudge; spite; enmity

A ～が有る bear a grudge (against sb); ⓔ nurse a rancor (against sb); ⓘ have a chip on one's shoulders.
N ～を抱く bear a grudge (against sb); ⓔ nurse a rancor (against sb); ⓘ have a chip on one's shoulders. ～を達す avenge sb; take revenge for sb; ⓘ settle old scores (with sb); ⓘ square accounts (with sb). ～を晴らす avenge sb; take revenge for sb; ⓘ settle old scores (with sb); ⓘ square accounts (with sb).

委細 particulars; details

を ～を調べる conduct a thorough inquiry; investigate the details. ～を述べる go into the details; give a detailed account; tell all.

異彩 a conspicuous color

を ～を放つ stand out; be conspicuous; ⓘ cut a brilliant figure.

勲 ⓔ distinguished service

を ⓔ ～を立てる do (the state) a great service; ⓔ render distinguished service.

潔し gallantry; bravery; grace

と ～としない be too proud to do sth; be ashamed to do sth; scorn to do sth; disdain to doing sth.

勇み valor; bravery; pluck

を ～を付ける encourage sb; cheer sb on.

勇み足 overstep the sumo ring

を ～を遣る overstep the mark;

overreach oneself; commit a blunder.

諫め いさめ remonstrance; admonition
[を] ～を聞く heed sb's advice; yield to remonstrance; ⓒ ⓘ lend sb an ear.

意志 いし will; volition
[A] ～が通じる be well understood; make oneself understood.
[N] ～に屈する yield to sb; give in to sb's wishes; ⓒ bend to sb's will. ～に従う obey sb's will. ～に反する be against one's will.
[を] ～を働かせる exercise one's will. ～を曲げる yield to sb; give in to sb's wishes; ⓒ bend to sb's will.

意思 いし an intention; a mind
[N] ～に沿う go along with sb's wishes; comply with sb's wishes. ～に背く go against sb's wishes; be contrary to sb's intentions.
[を] ～を変える change one's mind. ～を通じる make oneself understood; get one's across one's intentions. ～を洩らす reveal one's intentions; express one's intentions.

意地 いじ temper; disposition
[A] ～が有る have a strong will; have pride. ～が汚い be greedy; be

mean; ⓒ be avaricious. ～が悪い be malicious; be ill-natured.
[N] ～に掛かる refuse to give in; be obstinate; be stubborn. ～になる refuse to give in; be obstinate; be stubborn.
[を] ～を通す have one's own way; do as one wants. ～を張る refuse to give in; persevere in one's ideas; hold on; ⓒ ⓘ dig in one's heels.

意識 いしき consciousness; awareness
[N] ～に上せる become conscious of; grow aware of.
[を] ～を失う lose consciousness; pass out; ⓒ black out.

礎 いしずえ 🄔 a foundation stone
[を] ～を得る gain a foothold. ～を築く ❶ lay a foundation (for a house). ❷ lay the basis for sth; pave the way for sth. ～を据える ❶ lay a foundation (for a house). ❷ lay the basis for sth; pave the way for sth.

意匠 いしょう a design
[を] ～を凝らす be elaborate; be intricate. ～を作る make a design.

威信 いしん 🄔 prestige; dignity
[N] ⓒ ～に係わる affect one's prestige. ⓒ ～を保つ maintain one's dignity; keep up one's state; ⓢ keep

one's cool. ⓔ ～を傷(きず)つける injure *sb's* prestige; mar *sb's* reputation.

圀 ⓓ ～を保(たも)つ maintain one's dignity; ⓔ keep one's cool.

異心(いしん) treacherous intentions

圀 ～を抱(いだ)く harbour treacherous intentions; ⓔ have evil designs. ～を挟(はさ)む harbour treacherous intentions; ⓔ have evil designs.

椅子(いす) a chair; a post; a position

圀 ～を失(うしな)う lose one's post; ⓒ ① be thrown out of the saddle. ～を占(し)める occupy a post; hold a post. ～を勤(つと)める offer *sb* a chair. ～を保(たも)つ occupy a post; ⓒ ① be in the saddle. ～を並(なら)べる set chairs. ～を狙(ねら)う have one's eye on a post; covet a post. ～を張(は)る upholster a chair.

居住(いず)まい one's way of sitting

圀 ～を正(ただ)す straighten oneself; sit up straight. ～を直(なお)す straighten oneself; sit up straight.

異性(いせい) the other sex

圓 ⓔ ～に接(せっ)する know a (wo)man; have sexual experience; ⓔ have carnal knowledge of a (wo)man.

圀 ～を知(し)る know a (wo)man; have sexual experience; ⓔ have carnal knowledge of a (wo)man.

板(いた) a board; a plank; a plate

圄 ～で囲(かこ)う board (a place) up. ～で塞(ふさ)ぐ board (a window) up.

圓 ～に付(つ)く be at home in (a subject); get used to *sth*; ⓔ be well versed in (a subject). ⓒ ～に載(の)せる put a play on the stage. ⓒ ～に上(のぼ)す publish (a book); issue a book.

悪戯(いたずら) mischief; a prank; a joke

圓 ～になる come to nothing; be wasted; ① go up in smoke.

圀 ～をする ❶ do mischief; play a trick on *sb*; be mischievious. ❷ molest (a woman). ～を始(はじ)める get into trouble; be in mischief.

市(いち) a market; a fair

圄 ～が栄(さか)える all's well that ends well. ～が立(た)つ a fair is held.

圓 ～に出(で)る appear in the market; ⓒ hit the market.

圂 ～へ出(だ)す take one's products to market; put *sth* on the market.

圀 ～を立(た)てる open a market; hold a fair. ～を為(な)す ❶ open a market; hold a fair. ❷ flock together; form a crowd. ～を開(ひら)く open a market; hold a fair.

一議(いちぎ) 圓 a complaint; criticizm

圓 ⓔ ～に及(およ)ばず without complaint; ⓔ without further consideration.

イチギ / イッサン

一隅 a corner; a nook
[を] 〜を照らす brighten one's corner of the world; ⓒ do one's bit [to improve society].

一道 ⓔ one road; an art
[N] ⓒ 〜に秀でる excel in an art.

一二 one or two; a few
[を] 〜を争う contend for the first place; ⓒ vie for first position.

一命 a life; a single order
[A] 〜が危ない be in grave danger; ⓒ be in peril of one's life.
[N] 〜に関わる be a matter of life and death; be lethal; be deadly. 〜に賭けて…する do sth at the risk of one's life; stake one's life on sth.
[を] 〜を失う lose one's life. 〜を賭ける risk one's life; hazard one's life; ⓒ put one's life at stake. 〜を下す give a single order. 〜を捧げる devote one's life (to a cause). 〜を救う rescue sb; save sb's life. 〜を捨てる throw away one's life; give up one's life. 〜を助ける rescue sb; save sb's life. 〜を繋ぐ stay alive; keep on living; eke out a living. 〜を賭する risk one's life; ⓒ hazard one's life. 〜を取り留める escape with one's life; be saved from death; ⓒ have a close call. 〜を投げ打つ lay down one's life (for a cause); pay for sth with one's life.

意中 (be) on one's mind
[を] 〜を明かす open (up) one's mind to sb; bare one's heart to sb. 〜を察する read sb's mind. 〜を漏らす say what is on one's mind; reveal one's thoughts.

一翼 one wing
[を] 〜を担う play a part in sth; contribute to sth; have a share in sth; have a stake in sth.

一家 a house(hold); a family
[を] 〜を治める manage a household; run a household. 〜を構える make a home of one's own; keep house. 〜を立てる set up house; start housekeeping. 〜を成す develop one's own style; establish oneself.

一驚 ⓔ surprise; astonishment
[A] ⓒ 〜を喫する be surprised; be startled; be shocked; be baffled; be flabbergasted; ⓒ be taken aback.

一粲 ⓔ a laugh; a diversion
[N] ⓒ 〜に供する offer sb a gift; send sb a one of one's own poems.
[を] ⓒ 〜を博す read out one's own poem (by way of diversion).

いっさん
一盞 a sake cup
- 図 〜を傾ける have a drink.

いっし
一矢 回 an arrow
- 図 ⓒ 〜を報いる ❶ shoot back; return fire. ❷ fight back; retaliate. ❸ talk back; ⓒ rebut (a charge).

いっし
一指 回 a finger; one('s) finger
- 図 〜を染める try one's hand at sth; take sth up; have a try at sth; get a taste of sth.

いっしょ
一緒 together; united
- N 〜に行く go with sb; go together; join sb. 〜に住む live together; live with sb. 〜にする unite two people; marry two people; mate sb with sb else. 〜になる ❶ get together; join sb; keep sb company; join in. ❷ be united; be married; ⓘ become man and wife.

いっしょう
一生 a lifetime; one's life
- 図 〜を誤る make a failure of one's life; ruin one's life; ⓔ wreck one's chances in life. 〜を得る be saved. 〜を終える pass away; reach the end of one's life. 〜を送る spend one's life; go through life. 〜を賭ける risk one's life; stake one's life. 〜を捧げる devote one's life to (a cause); give one's life to (a cause).

いっしょう
一笑 a laugh; a smile
- N ⓔ 〜に付し去る laugh sb down; dismiss sth with a laugh. 〜に付す laugh sb down.
- 図 〜を買う be laughed at; be scorned; ⓔ invite ridicule.

いっしん
一身 a body; one('s) body
- 図 〜を誤る go astray; go to the bad; ⓔ stray from virtue. 〜を捧げる devote one's life to (a cause); dedicate oneself to (a cause). 〜に賭して…する do sth at the risk of one's life; stake one's life on sth.

いっしん
一新 renewal; reform
- 図 〜を画する make a complete change; revolutionize sth; make a fresh start.

いっせい
一世 a generation; an age
- 図 〜を驚かす startle the world; create a sensation; ⓘ make a stir. 〜を風靡する dominate one's age; ⓔ take the world by storm.

いっせいめん
一生面 a new field (of activity)
- 図 〜を開く open up a new field; depart from convention; create a new style.

いっせき
一石 one stone
- 図 〜を投じる cause excitement; be

much talked about; ⓐ make a stir; ⓒ give rise to a controversy.

一戦 a battle; an engagement
を ～を交える exchange fire; fight a battle; ⓒ engage an enemy.

一線 one line
を ～を画する draw a clear line; make a sharp distinction (between).

一着 the first arrival
N ～になる be the first to come in; finish first.
を ～を輸する lose a match; come second; lag behind.

一籌 Ⓘ a tally (to keep a score)
を ～を輸す be slightly inferior; fall short of a standard.

一丁字 one single character
を ～を識らず be unable to read a single character; be completely illiterate.

一途 Ⓘ a road; a course; a way
を ～を辿る follow a route; continue on a (certain) course; sustain a (certain) trend.

一頭地 the height of one head
を ～を抜く rise above the crowd; tower above one's peers; cut a prominent figure.

一臂 Ⓘ an elbow; one's elbow
を ⓒ ～を貸す give sb assistance; lend sb a helping ha; ⓒ do one's bit.

一歩 one step
を ～を退く take a step backward; retrace one step; take a step backward. ～を進む advance a step; take a step forward. ～を誤る take a wrong step; make a wrong move. ～を進める go one step farther; carry sth a step forwards. ～を譲る recede one step; yield a step; ⓒ concede a point.

一本 one; a piece; a roll
N ～にする line up; unify sth; standardize sth. ⓒ ～になる become a fully fledged geisha.
を ～を取られる be beaten. ⓒ ～を補う buy a book. ～を参る give sb a blow; upset sb; baffle sb; ⓒ ⓐ put sb out of countenance.

井手 a dam; a sluice
A ～が上がる increase profits; run a good business; do well out of sth.

糸 thread; yarn; filament
を ～を繰る reel thread. ～を手繰る

[fishing] haul in the line; draw up the line. 〜を垂れる cast a line; fish; angle. 〜を紡ぐ spin thread; spin yarn. 〜を通す thread a needle. 〜を解く unravel thread. 〜を抜く take out the stitches. 〜を伸ばす [fishing] let out a line. 〜を引く ❶ pull a rope. ❷ manipulate (a situation); ⓒ work the wires. 〜を巻く quill. 〜を縒る twist thread.

絃 a guitar string; a chord; gut

図 〜を締める tighten a string. 〜を付ける string a guitar. 〜を張る tighten a string.

意図 an intent; a design; an aim

図 〜を隠す hide one's intentions; ⓒ cover one's tracks. 〜を挫く frustrate sb's plans; thwart sb's aims. 〜を見抜く see through sb's plot; penetrate sb's mind.

糸口 a beginning; a start; a clue

図 〜となる lead to (a success); become the first step (to success). 図 〜を失う lose the clue. 〜を得る find a clue; have a key to (a problem). 〜を捜す look for a clue; search for a key (to a problem). 〜を掴む find a clue; have a key to (a problem). 〜を開く pave the way (for sb/sth); make a beginning.

暇 leisure; spare time ▶ 暇

A 〜が出る ❶ be dismissed; ⓒ be relieved of one's post; ⓒ be fired; ⓢ ⓘ get the sack. ❷ get time off; have time off. ❸ be divorced.

N 〜になる be dismissed; ⓒ be relieved of one's post; ⓒ be fired; ⓢ ⓘ get the sack.

図 〜を乞う ❶ ask for a vacation; ask for time off. ❷ ask to be relieved of one's post. ❸ take one's leave; ⓒ bid sb farewell. 〜を出す ❶ dismiss sb; discharge sb; ⓒ fire sb; ⓢ ⓘ give sb the sack; ⓒ ⓘ send sb packing. ❷ give sb time off. ❸ get divorced (from one's wife); get separated. 〜を告げる say goodbye; take one's leave; ⓒ bid sb farewell. 〜を取る ❶ resign from one's post; tender one's resignation. ❷ take time off; have a vacation. ❸ get divorced (from one's husband); get separated. 〜を願う ❶ ask for a vacation; ask for time off. ❷ take one's leave; ⓒ bid sb farewell. 〜を遣る ❶ dismiss sb; discharge sb; ⓒ fire sb; ⓢ ⓘ give sb the sack. ❷ get divorced (from one's wife).

糸目 a fine line; the strings

図 〜を付ける set a limit; ⓘ draw a line.

犬 a dog

|を| ～を飼う keep a dog. ～を悦ばす throw up; vomit *sth* out; spew *sth* up; fetch up; be sick; puke; ⓒ ① shoot the cat.

命 life ▶ 命

|A| ～が危ない be in grave danger; ⓒ be in peril of one's life. ～が助かる be saved; escape death; survive. ～が無い be lifeless; be dead; be without life; show no signs of life. ～が長い have a long life; be long-lived. ～が延びる take on a new life; ⓒ ① get a new lease of life. ～が短い have a short life; be short-lived.

|と| ～と頼む rely on *sth* with one's life; ⓒ regard *sth* as the wellspring of one's life.

|N| ～に換える value *sth* as much as one's own life; do *sth* in the face of death. ～に関わる be a matter of life and death. ～に賭けて…する do *sth* at the risk of one's life; stake one's life on *sth*. ～に向かう be life-staking; be perilous.

|を| ～を預ける put one's life in *sb's* hands; entrust one life to *sb*. ～を失う lose one's life. ～を打ち込む put one's heart and soul into *sth*. ～を奪う take *sb's* life; kill *sb*. ～を得る gain life; have life. ～を惜しむ value life (above *sth* else). ⓒ hold one's life dear. ～を落とす pass away. ～を賭ける risk one's life; hazard one's life; ⓒ put one's life at stake. ～を削る shorten one's life; ① drive a nail into one's coffin. ～を支える support life. ～を捧げる devote one's life (to a cause). ～を救う save *sb's* life; reque *sb's* life. ～を捨てる throw away one's life; give up one's life. ～を託する put one's life in *sb's* hands; entrust one life to *sb*. ～を保つ stay alive; keep on living; maintain life; ⓒ preserve life. ～を縮める shorten one's life. ① drive a nail into one's coffin. ～を継ぐ eke out a living; stay alive; keep on living. ～を付け狙う seek *sb's* life. ～を繋ぐ eke out a living; stay alive; keep on living. ～を尊ぶ value life; hold life dear. ～を取られる pay with one's life. ～を取る take *sb's* life; kill *sb*. ～を投げ打つ throw away one's life; give up one's life. ～を投げ出す risk one's life; hazard one's life; ⓒ put one's life at stake. ～を狙う seek after *sb's* life; ⓒ have a design on *sb's* life. ～を拾う escape with one's life; get out alive; get away unscathed. ～を貪る outlive one's span of life; live to no purpose; live a useless life. ～を譲る sacrifice one's life.

いの
祈り prayers; a supplication
[A] ～が叶う have one's prayers answered.
[を] ～を捧げる offer up a prayer; say a prayer. ～をする say a prayer.

いはい
位牌 a Buddhist mortuary tablet
[を] ～を汚す soil the family name; mar the reputation of a clan. ～を守る uphold family honor; keep up the name of one's clan.

いばら
茨 brambles; thorny shrubs
[を] ⓒ～を負う do penance; take the responsibility for the crimes of others. ～を開く ❶ make one's way through brambles. ❷ reclaim waste land; cultivate land; open up land.

いびき
鼾 a snore
[を] ～をかく snore; sleep audibly.

いひょう
意表 Ⓔ the unexpected
[N] ～に出る take sb by surprise; surprise sb; baffle sb.
[を] ～を突く take sb by surprise; surprise sb; baffle sb.

いま
今 now; the present
[を] ～を時めく be at the height of one's powers; enjoy great fame and influence.

いみ
意味 meaning; significance
[を] ～を失う lose its meaning. ～を掴む grasp the meaning. ～を伝える convey the meaning. ～を取る understand sth; comprehend sth. ～を為す make sense of sth; stand to reason.

いも
芋 a potato
[を] ～を洗う be thrown together; be shoulder to shoulder.

いやけ
嫌気 aversion; dislike; disgust
[A] ～が差す feel a repugnance for; be tired of; ⓒ get sick (and tired) of sb/sth.
[を] ～を起こす cause sb to dislike sb/sth; make sb sick of sth; ⓒ put sb out of conceit with sb/sth.

いらか
甍 Ⓔ a roof tile; a tiled roof
[を] ⓒ～を争う (buildings) stand close together. ⓒ～を並べる (buildings) stand side by side; stand in a row.

いろ
色 a color; a hue; love; lust
[A] ～が褪せる ❶ a color fades; lose color; turn pale. ❷ lose attractiveness. ～が薄い have a light color. ～が濃い have a deep color.
[N] ～に溺れる be addicted to sensual pleasures; be a slave to lust. ～に

出る show one's emotions; betray one's feelings.
｢を｣ ～を漁る dangle after women; go in for sensual pleasures. ～を失う ❶ lose color; turn pale. ❷ get worked up; ⓒ lose one's composure. ⓐ ❸ lose the ball. ～を売る prostitute oneself; ⓒ sell one's favors; ⓘ go on the streets. ～を変える change the color of sth. ～を好む be amorous; be sensual; be lustful; be lascivious. ～を添える give sth color; ⓒ jazz sth up. ～を損ず be upset; be mad; get angry. ～を正す look stern; ⓒ put on a grave face. ～を作る make oneself up; put on make-up. ～を付ける ❶ color sth; paint sth. ❷ lay on the colors; embellish sth. ❸ make a concession; ⓒ throw in sth extra. ⓒ ～を作る turn red with anger; ⓒ flare up; ⓢ lose it. ～を抜く decolorize sth; remove the color from sth; bleach sth. ～を塗る ❶ color sth; paint sth. ❷ lay on the colors; embellish sth. ⓒ ～を粥ぐ prostitute oneself; ⓒ sell one's favors. ～を持つ have a lover; have a sweetheart.

色目 ⑤ an amorous glance
｢を｣ ⓢ ～を使う leer at sb; ⓒ cast an amorous glance at sb; ⓘ give sb the eye; ⓘ make eyes at sb.

岩 a rock; a crag
｢A｣ ～が物言う a rumor spreads.

韻 a rhyme
｢を｣ ～を合わせる rhyme the lines. ～を押す rhyme with sth. ～を探る make sth shyme; find the right words to rhyme. ～を踏む rhyme with sth.

陰 ⑤ shade; the hidden, yin ♦ 陰
｢N｣ ⓒ ～に閉ず ❶ remain inside; stay indoors. ❷ become silent; be quiet. ⓒ ～に籠る ❶ be pent up; hide one's resentment. ❷ be gloomy; feel dejected; be cast down; be in low spirits; ⓒ ⓘ have the blues.

印 a seal; a stamp
｢を｣ ～を押す seal sth; stamp sth; put one's seal to sth. ～を結ぶ make symbolic signs with the fingers.

員 a (committee) member
｢と｣ ～に備わる join a group; be part of a group; be ranked among a group's members.

淫 ⑤ license; indulgence
｢を｣ ⓒ ～を好む be licentious. ⓒ ～を提ぐ prostitute oneself; ⓘ go on the streets.

陰影 (いんえい) shadow; gloom
- N ⓔ 〜に富む be full of nuances; be profound; ⓒ be deep.
- を ⓔ 〜を付ける shade (a picture). ⓒ 〜を投じる cast shadows; cast a gloom over *sth*.

因果 (いんが) cause and effect; karma
- と 〜と諦める accept one's karma; ⓒ resign oneself to one's fate.
- を 〜を含める tell *sb* to accept their karma; ⓒ persuade *sb* to reconcile themselves to their fate.

咽喉 (いんこう) the throat
- を ⓔ 〜を扼する ⓘ have the upper hand over *sb*; ⓘ hold all the cards; ⓒ ⓘ have the drop on *sb*.

韻字 (いんじ) rhyming words
- を 〜を探る make *sth* rhyme; find the right words to rhyme.

印綬 (いんじゅ) an official seal
- を 〜を帯びる be appointed to a post; hold a position. 〜を解く release *sb* from office.

印象 (いんしょう) an impression
- を 〜を与える make an impression; impress *sb*. 〜を残す leave an impression; leave one's mark. 〜を述べる voice one's impression; express one's views. 〜を深める deepen an impression.

引導 (いんどう) the last words
- を ⓔ 〜を渡す address the last words to a deceased person; give *sb* his/her notice; put *sb* to death; ⓒ send *sb* to glory.

因縁 (いんねん) cause; occasion; karma
- を 〜を付ける find a pretext to pick a fight; accuse *sb* falsely.

陰謀 (いんぼう) a plot; a conspiracy
- N 〜に加わる join in a conspiracy; be implicated in a plot. 〜に巻き込まれる be entangled in a plot.
- を 〜を暴く expose a plot; reveal a plot; ⓘ blow the gaff on *sb*. 〜を嗅ぎ付ける scent a plot. 〜を企てる conspire against *sb*; lay a plot. 〜を企む conspire against *sb*; lay a plot. 〜を幇助する abet a plot. 〜を回らす weave a plot. 〜を巡らす devise a plot; plot against *sb*.

ウ

飢え (うえ) hunger; starvation
- N 〜に泣く suffer from starvation.
- を 〜を凌ぐ stave off hunger; ⓘ keep the wolf from the door. 〜を忍ぶ endure starvation.

ウカガイ　　　　　　　　　　　　　　　　ウサ

伺い a call; a visit; an inquiry

[を] 〜を立てる inquire of *sb*; ask *sb* for instructions; invoke an oracle.

浮き足 imballance

[N] 〜になる ❶ be unsteady on one's feet; lose one's footing. ❷ begin to waver; start to falter.

浮き名 回 a romance; a scandal

[を] ⓒ 〜を立てる cause a scandal; ⓒ ⓘ become the talk of the town; be talked about. ⓒ 〜を流す cause a scandal; ⓒ ⓘ become the talk of the town; be talked about.

憂き日 回 a wretched life

[を] ⓒ 〜を送る lead a miserable existence; have a wretched life.

浮き彫り a relief; a carving

[N] 〜にする ❶ carve *sth* in relief. ❷ throw *sth* into (sharp) relief.

憂き身 回 hardships

[を] ⓒ 〜を窶す devote oneself to *sth*; be absorbed in *sth*; pine for (*sb's*) love).

憂き目 hardships; hard times

[を] 〜を見る have a hard time; suffer great hardships; ⓒ have trials and tribulations; ⓘ come to grief.

浮き世 the (fleeting) world; life

[を] 〜を捨てる renounce the world; turn one's back on life. ⓒ 〜を立つ earn one's living; make one's way through the world.

受け a support; popularity

[A] [*shōgi*] 〜が旨い have a good defence. [*shōgi*] 〜が不味い have a poor defence. 〜が良い be popular; be well recieved; be in favor; have a good reputation. 〜が悪い be unpopular; be ill recieved; be out of favor; have a bad reputation.

[N] 〜に立つ vouch for *sb*; stand guarantee for *sb*; go security for *sb*.

[を] [*shōgi*] 〜を誤る make the wrong move in one's defense.

有卦 回 a period of good luck

[N] ⓒ 〜に入る ❶ come into good luck; enjoy a period of good luck; ⓒ have one's star in the ascendancy. ❷ be fortunate; be lucky.

動き movement; motion

[A] 〜がとれない be constrained; ⓘ be bogged down; ⓘ be in a fix; ⓘ be stuck in the mud.

憂さ sorrow; gloom; melancholy

[を] 〜を晴らす divert one's mind; drive way the gloom. 〜を紛らす

divert one's mind; drive way the gloom.

牛 cattle; a cow; a bull; a steer

[N] ⓒ ～に喰らわる be deceived; ① be taken in; ⓒ be duped. ～を飼う keep cows; raise cattle.

後ろ the back; the rear

[N] ～に隠れる hide behind sb/sth. ～に忍び寄る sneak up on sb from behind. ～に回る move behind sb/sth.
[を] ⓐ ～を切る vanish; disappear; ① erase one's steps; ① cover up one's tracks. ～を見せる run away; reveal one's weakness; ① show one's heels. ～を見る look over one's shoulders; look behind one. ～を向く ① turn on one's heels.

後ろ髪 "rear hair"

[を] ～を引かれる be loath to leave; tear oneself away.

後ろ楯 backing; support

[A] ～が有る have (sb's) support; have sb's backing.
[N] ～になる give sb support; be supportive; support sb. ～に持つ have (sb's) support; have sb's backing.
[を] ～を得る gain support; find support; be backed; get support.

後ろ手 "rear hands"

[N] ～に縛る tie sb's hands behind their back; tie sb's hands behind their back.

後向き face backwwards

[N] ～になる ❶ face towards the rear; face backwards. ❶ turn one's back upon sb; ① give sb the cold shoulder.

後ろ指 a hind toe

[を] ～を指す ❶ point at sb (behind their back. ❷ talk about sb behind their back; gossip about sb.

渦 a whirlpool; a vortex

[を] ～を巻く ❶ make a whirl; whirl around. ❷ arouse exitement; ① create a stirr. ⓒ ❸ be shy; be coy.

薄氷 thin ice

[を] ～を踏む take great risks; ① be skating on thin ice.

嘘 a lie; an untruth; a falsehood

[A] ～で固める back (one's story) up with lies; ⓒ be a pack of lies.
[を] ～を言いふらす circulate a lie. ～

を教える misinform sb; tell sb a lie ～をつく tell a lie. ～を面責する reprove sb for telling a lie; ⓒ give sb the lie.

疑い doubt; suspicion

を ～を抱く have doubts; entertain suspicions. ～を入れる be open to doubt; offer room for doubt. ～を受ける be under suspicion; ⓔ incur suspicion. ～を起こす begin to doubt. ～を掛ける cast suspicion on sb/sth; attach suspicion to sb/sth. ～を挟む raise questions about sb/sth; throw doubt on sb/sth; cast doubt upon sb/sth. ～を解く dissipate doubts; allay suspicion; clear oneself of suspicion ～を晴らす dispel doubts; allay suspicion; clear oneself of suspicion. ～を招く invite suspicion; ⓔ incur suspicion. ～を持つ have doubts; ⓔ entertain suspicions.

内 the inside; the interior; home

N ～にいる be at home; be in. ～に帰る return home. ～に閉じ籠る stay at home; shut oneself up. ～に入る ❶ enter a house. ❷ be a number of a family; belong to a family. を ～を空ける stay out; stay away from home. ～を治める rule over a people; ⓔ conduct the affairs of state. ～を出る leave home; go out.

団扇 a (round) fan

を ～を使う use a fan; fan oneself; cool oneself. ～を上げる decide in favor of sb; declare sb the winner.

現 alive; awake; conscious

を ～を抜かす be engrossed in sth; abandon oneself to sb; be besotted by sb; ⓒ be mad about sb/sth.

討手 Ⓝ a punitive force

を ～を差し向ける send a punitive force against sb.

鬱憤 resentment; rancor; wrath

を ～を押える control one's anger; hide one's resentment. ～を晴らす vent one's anger; ⓒ satisfy one's resentment. ～を漏らす betray one's anger; vent one's anger; ⓒⓘ let off steam.

腕 the arm; the wrist; skill

A ～が上がる ❶ get better at sth; acquire more skill. ❷ (be able to) drink more. ～が有る have skill; ⓘ be a good hand. ～が良い have skill; ⓘ be a good hand. ～が旨い have skill; ⓘ be a good hand. ～が利く be skilled; be capable; ⓒⓘ be a dab hand at sth. ～が冴える get better at sth; acquire more skill. ～が立つ be able; be skillful. ～が鳴る

33

be eager to do *sth*; itch for action; be rearing to go. ～が鈍る lose one's touch.
[N] ～に縋る lean on *sb*'s arm.
[を] ～を上げる ⓐ improve one's skill. ⓑ (be able to) drink more. ～を買う esteem *sb*'s ability; value *sb*'s skills. ～を貸す give one's arm to *sb* (in friendship). ～を醤る fall into a trap; ⓒ step into a snare; ⓓ be taken in; ⓔ be duped; ⓕ be conned. ～を挫く sprain one's arm. ～を組む fold one's arms; lock arms with *sb*. ～を拱く stand by idly; remain an onlooker; ⓖ sit on the fence. ～を摩る be eager to show one's skill. ～を示す show skill; display talent. ～を試す try one's hand; put one's skill to the test. ～を鳴らす gain recognition; win reputation. ～を伸ばす ⓐ stretch out one's arm; reach out. ⓑ develop one's skill to the full. ⓒ ～を引く make a solemn vow; make a blood-oath. ⓓ ～を撫す be eager to show one's skill. ～を揮う display one's skill. ～を捲る ⓔ roll up one's sleeves. ～を磨く polish one's skills; brush up one's skills. ～を見せる display one's skill; show one's ability.

項 thin nape of the neck

[を] ～を反らす be haughty; be proud; be precocious.

産声 the cry of a newborn

[を] ～を上げる ⓐ be born; ⓑ utter one's first cry. ⓒ come into being; ⓓ see the light of day.

馬 a horse; a pony

[A] ～が合う be like-minded; get along well; ⓔ be congenial to one; ⓕ see eye to eye; ⓖ ⓗ hit it off.
[N] ～に乗る mount a horse; ride a horse. ～に跨る sit astride a horse.
[を] ～を急がす spur on a horse. ～を飼う keep a horse; rear a horse. ～を換える change horses. ～を繋ぐ ⓐ hitch a horse. ⓑ fawn on *sb*; ⓒ curry favor with *sb*; ⓓ butter *sb* up; ⓔ soft-soap *sb*. ～を止める check one's horse. ～を慣らす train a horse; break in a horse. ～を乗り潰す ride a horse down. ～を走らす gallop one's horse; course one's horse. ～を放す unhitch a horse. ～を引く ⓐ lead a horse. ⓑ be followed by a bill collector. ～を雇う hire a horse.

海 the sea; the ocean

[N] ～に落ちる fall into the sea; fall overboard. ～に出す put (a ship) to sea. ⓐ ～に涌く (fish) come to the surface.
[へ] ～へ行く go to the seaside.
[を] ～を渡る ⓐ go abroad; go over-

seas. ❷ come from abroad; come from overseas.

有耶無耶(うやむや) obscurity
[N] 〜に終(おわ)る come to nothing; ⓘ go up in smoke. 〜にする obscure (an issue); leave *sth* undecided; ⓒ ⓘ hush *sth* up. 〜になる come to nothing; ⓘ go up in smoke.

烏有(うゆう) 回 an imaginary person
[N] ⓒ 〜に帰(き)す ❶ be completely destroyed by fire; be burned down; be reduced to ashes. ❷ come to nothing; ⓘ go up in smoke. ⓒ 〜に属(ぞく)す ❶ be completely destroyed by fire; be burned down; be reduced to ashes. ❷ come to nothing; ⓘ go up in smoke.

裏(うら) the reverse; the other side ▸ 裏(り)
[A] 〜が有(あ)る have another side; have a doubloe meaning.
[亙] 〜へ回(まわ)る ❶ go to the rear (of a building); go round to the back. ❷ do *sth* in secret; do *sth* by stealth; ⓢ do *sth* on the sly.
[を] ⓒ 〜を言(い)う be ironical; be sardonic. 〜を行(い)く baffle *sb*; outwit *sb*; outsmart *sb*. 〜を返(かえ)す ❶ turn *sth* over; turn *sth* inside out; turn *sth* upside down. ❷ do *sth* a second time; repeat an action. ❸ flatten the tip of a protruding nail. ❹ give (a wall) a coating. ⓒ ❺ visit the same prostitute twice. 〜をかく ❶ baffle *sb*; outwit *sb*; outsmart *sb*. ⓒ ❷ drive a spear through *sb*; run *sb* through; impale *sb* on one's sword. 〜を掛(か)ける turn (a record) over; play the reverse side of a record. (法律(ほうりつ)の)〜を潜(くぐ)る slip through the meshes of the law. 〜を付ける line a coat. 〜を取(と)る verify (a story); ⓔ ascertain the truth. 〜を封(ふう)す seal a letter. 〜を見透(みす)かす see through *sb*'s schemes. 〜を行(ゆ)く baffle *sb*; outwit *sb*; outsmart *sb*.

恨(うら)み a grudge; resentment
[A] 〜が有(あ)る hold a grudge against *sb*; ⓔ harbor a private malice; ⓘ have a chip on one's shoulder. 〜が解(と)ける satisfy one's grudge; get back at *sb*.
[N] 〜に思(おも)う feel bitter toward *sb*; ⓘ keep a score on wrongs; ⓘ have a chip on one's shoulder.
[を] 〜を言(い)う reproach *sb*. 〜を抱(いだ)く hold a grudge against *sb*; ⓔ harbor a private malice; ⓒ have it in for *sb*; ⓘ have a chip on one's shoulder. 〜を買(か)う cause *sb* to hold a grudge against one; make an enemy of *sb*; ⓘ breed bad blood; ⓔ incur *sb's* enmity. 〜を飲(の)む repress one's anger; swallow one's words; pocket

an insult. ～を晴らす vent one's spite; take revenge upon sb; ⓒ settle old scores with sb; ⓓ square accounts with sb. ～を招く earn sb's enmity; ⓒ breed bad blood. ～を持つ hold a grudge against sb; ⓔ harbor a private malice; ⓒ have it in for sb; ⓒ have a chip on one's shoulder. ～を忘れる forget one's grudges; let bygones be bygones.

裏目 the reverse side
N ～に出る produce the opposite result; go against one; backfire.

譫言 gibberish; rigmarole
を ～を言う talk in a delerium; talk deleriously; rave.

噂 a rumor; a report; gossip
A ～が立つ a rumor spreads. N ～に聞く hear sth by rumor; ⓒ get wind of sth; ⓒ hear sth on the grapevine. ～に上る be talked about; ⓒⓒ become the talk of the town; ⓒⓒ go the rounds. を ～をする gossip about sb/sth; ⓒ spread tales about sb/sth. ～を立てる start a rumor; spread a rumor. ～を流す start a rumor; spread a rumor. ～を広める spread a rumor; circulate a story. ～を揉み消す kill a rumor; stifle a rumor.

上手 the upper part; upstream
N ～に出る outdo sb; gain the lead; ⓒ gain the upper hand.
を ～を行く be superior to sb. ～を持つ [shōgi] occupy the superior side of the board.

上荷 the top/upper load
N ～を撥ねる ❶ steal part of a cargo. ❷ have a secret affair with sb's wife; carry on with sb's wife.

上辺 the exterior; the outside
を ～を飾る gloss over a mistakes; ⓒ keep up appearances. ～を繕う save appearances; ⓒ save one's face.

上米 ⓜ a commission, a kickback
を ～を取る take a percentage; take a commission; take a rake-off. ～を履く take a percentage; take a commission. ～を跳ねる take a percentage; ⓒ take a rake-off.

上前 ⓜ the outer skirt
を ～を合わせる arrange the outer skirt. ～を取る take a percentage; take a commission; take a rake-off. ～を履く take a percentage; take a commission; take a rake-off. ～を跳ねる take a percentage; ⓒ take a rake-off.

ウワムキ　　　　　　　　　　　　　　　ウンメイ

うわむき
上向き facing upward; an upturn

[N] 〜にする face *sth* upward; turn *sth* upward. 〜になる ⓐ look upward; face upward. ⓑ look up; have an upward tendency.

うわめ
上目 an upward glance/look

[を] 〜を使う look upwards; cast one's eyes upwards.

うん
運 destiny; fate; fortune

[A] 〜が尽きる meet one's doom; run out of luck; be at the end of one's luck. 〜が蹲う meet one's doom; run out of luck. 〜が強い have luck on one's side; be fortunate. 〜が無い be out of luck; ⓒⓓ have a bad break. 〜が開く be in luck's way; be favored by fortune. 〜が向く be in luck's way; ⓒ be favored by fortune. 〜が良い be fortunate; be lucky; be auspicious. 〜が悪い be unfortunate; be unlucky; be inauspicious.
[N] 〜に任せる trust to chance; ⓒ trust to Providence. 〜に恵まれる be fortunate; be lucky; ⓒ be favored by fortune.
[を] 〜を試す take chances; try one's luck. 〜を開く create one's own luck; ⓓ sieze the day.

うんき
運気 fate

[を] 〜を刎ねる ⓐ decapitate *sb*; cut off *sb's* head. ⓑ put *sb* to death; sentence *sb* to death.

うんじょう
運上 旧 business tax

[を] 〜を取る ⓐ be out of *sb's* league; ⓒ be a cut above the rest.

うんせい
運勢 one's star; one's fortune

[A] 〜が衰える fortunes are waning.
[を] 〜を見る tell *sb's* fortune.

うんちく
蘊蓄 旧 one's stock of knowledge

[を] ⓒ 〜を傾ける pour all one's learning into (one's work); freely draw on one's profound learning.

うんのう
蘊奥 旧 principles; doctrine

[を] ⓒ 〜を窮める master the secrets of (an ancient craft); be initiated in the mysteries of (an art).

うんぴょう
雲表 旧 "above the clouds"

[N] ⓒ 〜に聳える soar above the clouds; tower above the clouds.

うんめい
運命 destiny; fate; fortune

[と] 〜と諦める resign oneself to one's fate. 〜と戦う fight one's fate; ⓒ strive against fate.
[N] 〜に甘んじる resign oneself to one's fate; submit to fate. 〜に逆らう go against fate. 〜に任せる leave *sb* to his/her fate; abandon oneself

to fate. 〜に弄(もてあそ)ばれる be the sport of fortune; ⓘ drop in the lap of fate. 【を】〜を託(かこ)つ howl at one's fate; ⓔ bewail one's predicament. 〜を決(けっ)する seal one's/*sb's* fate. 〜を作(つく)る mold one's destiny; carve out one's fate. 〜を共(とも)にする join fortunes with *sb*; ⓘ throw in one's lot.

エ

絵(え) a picture; a painting; a sketch
【A】〜が腐(くさ)る ❶ be left with an ace in one's hand. ❷ miss the occasion; miss a golden opportunity. 〜が付(つ)く ❶ be dealt a good set of cards. ❷ have a stroke of luck; be lucky. 〜が分(わか)る have an eye for paintings.
【を】〜を描(か)く paint a picture.

栄(えい) 【E】 glory; honor
【を】〜を得(え)る receive honors. 〜を蒙(こうむ)る receive honors. 〜を担(にな)う be bestowed the honor.

鋭(えい) 【E】 sharpness
【を】ⓔ (...の)〜を鈍(にぶ)らす blunt the edges of (a sword). ⓔ (...の)〜を避(よ)ける avoid the brunt of (an atack).

穎(えい) an awn; a glume; an arista
【を】〜を脱(だっ)す gain recognition; ⓔ rise above one's peers.

酔(え)い 【E】 intoxication
【N】〜に乗(の)る do *sth* with Dutch courage.

鋭意(えいい) eagerness; diligence
【N】〜に当(あ)たる apply oneself to (one's work); devote oneself (to a cause). 〜に従(したが)う apply oneself to (one's work); devote oneself (to a cause).

影響(えいきょう) influence; effect
【N】〜に働(はたら)かされる be susceptible to an influence.
【を】〜を与(あた)える exert an influence over. 〜を受(う)ける be influenced by; be affected by. 〜を及(およ)ぼす exert influence; have an effect.

英風(えいふう) 【E】 lofty virtues
【を】ⓔ 〜を慕(した)う admire *sb*; look up to *sb*; have a high regard for *sb*.

永別(えいべつ) 【E】 the last parting
【を】ⓔ 〜を告(つ)げる say one's last good-bye; take leave of *sb*; ⓔ bid one's last farewell.

易(えき) fortune-telling; divination
【を】〜を立(た)てる tell *sb's* fortune; cast a horoscope. 〜を見(み)る tell *sb's* fortune; ⓔ cast a horoscope.

エダ　　　　　　　　　　　　　　　　　　　　　エン

枝 a branch; a bough; a limb
N ～に分かれる ❶ⓑ branch out. ❷ⓐ branch out; branch off. を ～を折る break off a branch. ～を下ろす prune a tree; lop off branches. ⓐ ～を交える have an intimate relationship with sb. ～を切る prune a tree; lop off branches. ～を出す shoot out branches. ～を垂らす weep. ～を挿げる be argumentative; ⓓ split hairs. ⓐ ～を鳴らさず be at peace. ～を払う prune a tree; lop off branches. ～を広げる ❶ⓑ branch out. ❷ⓐ branch out; spread into branches; branch off.

悦 joy; content
N ～に入る ❶ be in a good mood; be in raptures. ❷ be pleased with oneself; chuckle over sth.

笑壺 a smiling face
N ～に入る smile to oneself; chuckle to oneself; amuse oneself.

餌 a bait; a lure
N ～に飼う lure sb into a trap; ensnarl s; ⓓ set sb up.

烏帽子 ⓕ a nobleman's headgear
を ⓒ ～を着せる make an outrageous claim; ⓒ ⓓ speak through the back of one's neck.

衣紋 dress; clothes; a coat
を ～を繕う straighten one's clothes; adjust one's dress.

鰓 the gills of a fish
A ～が過ぎる boast about sth; brag about sth; ⓒ ⓓ blow one's own horn (trumpet); ⓓ talk big.

襟 the neck; a collar; a neckband
N ～に付く flatter sb; ⓓ curry favor with sb. を ～を正す ❶ adjust one's dress; straighten oneself. ❷ be awed; ⓒ stand in awe. ～を立てる turn up one's collar. ～を掴む seize sb by the collar; collar sb. ～を開く open oneself up to sb; take sb into one's confidence; ⓓ pour out one's heart to sb; ⓒ unbosom oneself.

縁 a relation; a connection ▶ 縁
A ～が切れる be cut off; get separated; be disowned.
N ⓐ ～に付く marry a man; get married. ⓐ ～に付ける give one's daughter in marriage; marry one's daughter off. ～に繋がる be related to; be connected with. ～に引かされる be drawn together.
を ～を切る ❶ break off relations; ⓒ sever one's connections with sb. ❷ disown sb; disinherit sb; ⓓ cut sb

39

off without a penny. ❸ divorce *sb*; get separated; ⓔ secure a divorce; ⓒ split up. 〜を断つ ❶ break off relations; ⓒ sever one's connections with *sb*. ❷ disown *sb*; disinherit *sb*; ⓘ cut *sb* off without a penny. ❸ divorce *sb*; get divorced; get separated; ⓔ secure a divorce; ⓒ split up. 〜を辿る hunt up one's connections. Ⓐ 〜を離る live an ascetic life. 〜を結ぶ form a connection with *sb*; marry *sb*; ⓒⓘ tie the knot.

宴 ⒺⒶ banquet; a feast; a party
Ⓝ ⓔ 〜に列する attend a banquet; be present at a dinner.
を ⓔ 〜を張る hold a banquet; give a dinner; ⓒ throw a party. ⓔ 〜を催す hold a banquet; give a dinner; ⓒ throw a party

円 yen; circle; ring; round
Ⓝ 〜に替える convert into yen.
を 〜を描く draw a circle.

縁起 the history; the origin
Ⓐ 〜が良い be a good omen; bode well. 〜が悪い be a bad omen; do not bode well.
を 〜を祝う wish *sb* good luck; welcome a sign of good luck. 〜を担ぐ be superstitious; believe in omens. 〜を直す change one's fortune.

怨言 Ⓔ bitter remarks
を ⓔ 〜を放つ mutter words of discontent; voice one's misgivings.

冤罪 Ⓔ a false charge
Ⓝ ⓔ 〜に泣く be falsely charged; be accused wrongly.
を ⓔ 〜を雪ぐ exonerate oneself; clear oneself of a false charge; ⓔ vindicate oneself. ⓔ 〜を被る be falsely charged; be accused wrongly.

援助 assistance; aid
を 〜を仰ぐ look for help. 〜を与える give aid; ⓔ render assistance. 〜を得る receive aid; get assistance. 〜を約する promise help; ⓒ pledge one's assistance.

宴席 Ⓔ a seat in a dining hall
Ⓝ ⓔ 〜に侍る wait at a banquet. ⓔ 〜に列する attend a banquet; be present at a dinner.
を ⓔ 〜を設ける hold a banquet.

遠島 Ⓐ a distant island
を 〜を申し付ける banish *sb* to a distant island; send *sb* into exile.

猿臂 Ⓔ "a monkey's elbow"
を ⓔ 〜を伸ばす stretch out one's arms; extend one's arms.

えんまく
煙幕 a smoke screen

を ～を張る ❶ ⓛ lay down a smoke screen. ❷ hide one's true intentions; ⓛ lay down a smoke screen.

えんりょ
遠慮 reserve; forethought

A ～が有る have forethought; be farsighted.
を ～を欠く lack forethought; lack restraint. ～を捨てる throw off restraint. ～を忘れる forget one's reserve; break through reserve.

お
尾 a tail; a brush; a train

A ～が出る be exposed; come to light. ⓐ ～が掛かる be in hot pursuit; chase sb. ⓐ ～が見える be exposed; come to light.
N ～に付く echo sb's words; parrot sb; ⓒ copycat sb.
を ～を現わす expose oneself; betray oneself; ⓛ give oneself away. ⓐ ～を滑る be dispirited. ～を出す expose oneself; betray oneself. ～を引く leave traces; have a lasting effect; linger on. ～を振る ❶ wag its tail; whisk its tail. ❷ try to please (a superior); ingratiate oneself with sb. ～を巻く ❶ loop its tail. ❷ sneak away; ⓛ beat a retreat. ～を見せる expose oneself; betray oneself.

お
老い old age; the aged

を ～を労る tend to the old; look after the elderly. ～を送る live out the rest of one's days. ～を養う live out the last days of one's life.

おめ
負い目 debts; indebtedness

N ～に成る be indebted to sb; be obliged to sb; owe sb a favor.
を ～を感じる feel indebted toward sb; ⓒ be beholden to sb; be grateful to sb.

おう
王 a king; a monarch

を ～を立てる put a king on the throne; enthrone a king. ～を詰める [shōgi] checkmate the king. ～を廃する depose a king; dethrone a king.

おうい
王位 the throne; the crown

N ～に在る be on the throne; hold the throne. ～に就く take the throne; ⓒ accede to the throne. ～に登る mount the throne; ⓒ ascend the throne; ⓒ accede to the throne.
を ～を争う contend for the throne. ～を失う ⓒ forfeit one's crown. ～を奪う usurp the throne. ～を捨てる abdicate; resign the kingship. ～を継ぐ succeed to the throne. ～を譲る abdicate in sb's favor; make over the throne to sb.

おうぎ
扇 a (folding) fan

[を] ⓑ ～を請（う）く master the secrets of (an ancient craft); be initiated in the mysteries of (an art). ～を翳（かざ）す shade one's eyes with a fan. ～を使（つか）う fan oneself. ～を鳴（な）らす beckon *sb*.

おうし
横死 an untimely death

[を] ～を遂（と）げる die a violent death.

おうへい
横柄 arrogance; haughtiness

[N] ～に扱（あつか）う treat *sb* with disdain. ～に構（かま）える assume an attitude of superiority. ～に振（ふ）る舞（ま）う behave arrogantly; act haughtily.

[を] ⓐ ～を捌（さば）く behave haughtily; ⓒ lord it over *sb*.

おおぐち
大口 a big mouth

[を] ～を叩（たた）く boast about *sth*; brag about *sth*; ⓒ ⓘ blow one's own horn (trumpet); ⓘ talk big.

おおげさ
大袈裟 exaggeration; hyperbole

[N] ～に言（い）う stretch the facts; indulge in hyperbole; ⓢ ⓘ pile it on; ⓢ ⓘ lay it on thick. ～にする take *sth* too far; make too much out of *sth*; ⓘ make a mountain out of a molehill.

おおなた
大鉈 a large hatchet; a big axe

[を] ～を振（ふ）るう ❶ wield a large hatchet; swing a big axe. ❷ take drastic measures; introduce sweeping reforms; make a huge cut in the budget; axe (extra expenditures).

おおぶね
大船 a large boat

[N] ～に乗（の）る feel relieved; be reassured; be put at ease.

おおぶろしき
大風呂敷 bragging; boasting

[を] ～を拡（ひろ）げる boast about *sth*; brag about *sth*; ⓒ ⓘ blow one's own horn (trumpet); ⓘ talk big.

おおぼね
大骨 big bones; large bones

[を] ～を折（お）る ❶ take great pains to do *sth*; make strenuous efforts. ❷ suffer extreme hardships.

おおみえ
大見得 a grand appearance

[を] ～を切（き）る assume a grand posture; make a grand gesture.

おおめ
大目 extra; surplus; ample

[N] ～に見（み）る condone *sth*; pass over *sth*; overlook *sth*; let *sth* pass; let *sb* off (lightly); ⓢ ⓘ give *sb* a break.

おおめだま
大目玉 a large eyeball

[を] ⓢ ～を食（く）う be severely scolded; be told off in no uncertain terms; be given a thorough dressing-down.

お株 one's forte; a favorite trick

[を] ⓐ 〜を言う repeat oneself; ⓘ harp on the same string. 〜を奪われる be outdone in one's own forte; ⓘ be beaten at one's own game.

お釜 a pot; a kettle

[A] ⓒ 〜が割れる ❶ be divorced; a family breaks up. ❷ go to ruin; be a failure; ⓒ make a mess of *sth*.
[N] ⓒ 〜に掛ける deride one's superior(s); scoff at one's superior(s).
[を] ⓒ 〜を興す increase the family fortune; cause one's house to flourish. ⓒ ⓥ 〜を掘る practice sodomy.

沖 the offing; the open sea

[N] 〜にいる ⓒ be out at sea; ⓒ be in the offing. 〜に出る gain an offing; stand out to sea.
[を] ⓒ 〜を泳ぐ indulge in lewd pleasures. 〜を漕ぐ ❶ excel in *sth*. ❷ indulge in lewd pleasures. ⓐ 〜を越える ❶ excel in *sth*. ❷ go too far; carry things too far. 〜を眺める gaze out across the sea.

燠 embers; live coals

[N] 〜に成る ❶ be reduced to embers. ❷ come to nothing; be wasted; ⓘ go up in smoke.
[を] 〜を掻き立てる stoke embers; stir the coals.

置網 [E] standing nets

[を] ⓐ ⓒ 〜を言う talk prematurely; talk rashly; tempt providence.

掟 a rule; a law; a regulation

[N] 〜に従う comply with the rules; obey the law. 〜に背く violate a law. 〜による be according to law.
[を] 〜を定める lay down the law; establish a rule. 〜を守る observe the law; ⓒ stick to the rules. 〜を破る break the law; violate the rules.

奥義 [E] the innermost secrets

[を] ⓒ 〜を窮める master the secrets of (an ancient craft). ⓒ 〜を授ける initiate *sb* into the inner-most secrets of (an ancient art).

奥の手 a last resort; one's trump

[A] 〜が有る have a last resort; ⓘ have a card up one's sleeve.
[を] 〜を出す use one's last resort; ⓘ play one's trump card.

臆病風 "a cowardly cold"

[N] 〜に吹かれる be overcome by fear; ⓘ get cold feet.

お蔵 a warehouse; a storehouse

[を] 〜にする put *sth* on hold; shelve (a plan); cancel (a performance).

遅れ a delay; a time lag
[を] 〜を取る be beaten; be routed. 〜を取り戻す catch up with sb; work off arrears. 〜を見せる be intimidated by sb; shrink from sth; recoil from sth; wince at sth.

杠 a (merchant's) carrying pole
[を] ⓐ 〜を折る suffer a devastating financial loss; be bankrupted.

抑え weight; pressure; control
[A] 〜が利く have sth under control; be in control; be under control; ⓢ ⓘ call the shots.

お先棒 a front palanquin bearer
[N] 〜に使う use sb; involve sb in (one's excuses); ⓘ make a cat's paw of sb; ⓘ make a scapegoat of sb. 〜になる act as a person's tool; ⓘ be used as a cat's paw.
[を] 〜を担ぐ use sb; involve sb in (one's excuses); ⓘ make a cat's paw of sb; ⓘ make a scapegoat of sb.

お里 [回] one's home (town)
[A] ⓒ 〜が知れる reveal one's upbringing; show one's true nature; ⓘ give oneself away.

納まり a conclusion; settlement
[A] 〜が付く be brought to a conclusion; be settled; be over and done with.
[を] 〜を付ける bring sth to a conclusion; settle sth; put an end to sth.

押し a push; a weight; audacity
[A] 〜が利く have influence; be influential; ⓘ carry weight. 〜が強い be pushing; be aggressive; ⓒ be pushy.
[を] 〜をする put pressure on sb/sth; put sb/sth under pressure.

教え teachings; a lesson
[を] 〜を仰ぐ ask for instruction; ⓔ seek instruction. 〜を受ける be taught; study under sb.

怖気 fear; fright ▶ 怖気
[N] 〜がつく be overcome with fear; lose one's nerve; lose courage; get cold feet.

お釈迦 [回] a failure; a waster
[N] ⓢ 〜になる be a failure; end in failure; be unusable; be botched.

お上手 flattery; feighning
[を] 〜を言う flatter sb; humor sb; ⓘ curry favor with sb; ⓘ find sb's soft side. 〜を遣う flatter sb; humor sb; ⓘ curry favor with sb; ⓘ find sb's soft side.

汚職 corruption; graft; bribery
[を] 〜を一掃する root out corruption; wipe out corruption. 〜を生む breed corruption.

汚辱 disgrace; ignominy
[を] 〜を加える cast a slur on *sb*; ⓒ ⓘ sling mud at *sb*. 〜を被る be subjected to slander. 〜を忍ぶ endure ignominy; ⓘ eat humble pie.

白粉 toilet powder; face paint
[を] 〜を遣う use powder. 〜を付ける powder one's face; paint one's face. 〜を塗り立てる powder one's face thickly; make a heavy toilet; paint one's face thickly.

お世辞 a compliment; flattery
[を] 〜を言う ❶ say nice things to *sb*; pay *sb* a compliment. ❷ flatter *sb*; ⓒ ⓘ soft-soap *sb*; ⓒ ⓘ butter *sb* up; ⓢ ⓘ lay it on thick.

怖気 fear; fright ▶ 怖気
[A] 〜が立つ ❶ be overcome with fear; lose one's nerve; lose courage; get cold feet. ❷ be horrified; be disgusted; be appalled.
[を] 〜を振るう be overcome with fear; lose one's nerve; lose courage; get cold feet.

恐れ fear; dread; terror; horror
[A] 〜が有る be in danger of; run the risk of.
[を] 〜を抱く be filled with fear; be afraid of. 〜を為す be scared; be frightened.

おだ (小田原評定) empty palaver
[を] 〜を上げる indulge in idle talk; engage in gossip; argue for the sake of argument; ⓒ tittle-tattle.

煽て flattery; cajoling
[N] 〜に乗る ❶ be taken in by *sb*; be cajoled into *sth*; ⓒ be duped. ❷ give in to *sb's* flattery.

落ち a slip; the point (of a joke)
[A] 〜が有る contain an omission. 〜が来る win esteem; be cheered; be lauded; be applauded. 〜が分かる understand the gist (of a joke); ⓒ ⓘ get the point; ⓢ ⓘ get it.
[を] 〜を取る win esteem; be lauded; be lauded; be applauded. (人の)〜を拾う pick up *sb's* mistake; make good *sb's* omission.

落ち着き composure; serenity
[を] 〜を失う get worked up; ⓔ lose one's composure. 〜を取り戻す regain one's presence of mind; ⓔ recover one's composure.

おつ
乙 ⑬ strange; odd; queer

[N] ⓢ ～に絡む make witty remarks about *sb*; make fun of *sb*.
[を] ⓢ ～を澄ます strike an affectedly serene pose; ⓘ put on airs.

おと
音 a sound; a noise; a report

[A] ～がする hear a noise.
[N] ～に聞く ❶ be famous; be well known; be notorious. ❷ hear *sth* by rumor; ⓒ get wind of *sth*; ⓘ hear *sth* through the grapevine.
[を] ～を消す stifle the noise; absorb the sound. ～を出す produce a sound. ～を立てる make a noise.

おとがい
頤 ⑬ the chin; the mentum

[A] ⓒ ～が落ちる ❶ be delicious. ❷ shiver with cold. ❸ be talkative; ⓒ be loquacious; ⓒ be a chatterbox; ⓘ talk people's head off.
[A] ～を使う have *sb* at one's beck and call; boss *sb* around; ⓘ turn *sb* round one's little finger.
[を] ⓒ ～を利く wag one's tongue; babble. ⓒ ～を叩く wag one's tongue; babble. ⓒ ～を解く make *sb* laugh; ⓘ set the table roaring. ⓒ ～を鳴らす wag one's tongue; babble. ⓒ ～を吐く say bad things about *sb*; abuse *sb*; speak ill of *sb*; bad-mouth *sb*; ⓢ slur *sb*. ～を放つ roar with laughter. ⓒ ～を開く be talkative;

ⓒ be loquacious; ⓒ be a chatterbox; ⓘ talk people's head off. ⓒ ～を養う make a living; support oneself; ⓒ earn one's daily bread.

おとこ
男 a man; a male; menfolk

[A] ～が廃る lose one's honor; be ashamed of oneself. ～が立つ have one's honor satisgied; have one's own way; ⓘ save one's face.
[N] ～にする make a man out of *sb*. ～に成す celebrate a child's coming of age. ～に成る ❶ become a man; reach adulthood. ❷ reach the crtitical age; go through the menopause. ❸ return to secular life; renounce the cloth.
[を] ～を上げる build up one's image; rise in public estimation. ～を売る widen one's reputation; win fame. ～を拵える find a lover; desert one's husband; ⓒ carry on with a man. ～を下げる fall in public estimation; be disgraced; ⓘ lose face. ～を知る know a man; have slept with a man; ⓒ have carnal knowledge of a man. ～を立てる satisfy one's honor; ⓘ save one's face. ～を作る ❶ build up one's character. ❷ find oneself a man; find a lover. ～を振り捨てる desert a man for *sb* else; jilt one's lover. ～を磨く ❶ build up one's character. ❷ attempt to preserve

one's honor. ～を見せる show one's manliness. ～を持つ have a husband; have a lover; be married.

音骨 a voice; a sound
[を] ～を立てる raise one's voice.

囮 a decoy; a lure; a bait
[N] ～に使う use *sth* as a decoy.

お中 the stomach; one's inside
[A] ～が痛い have a stomach ache. ～が大きい be pregnant; ⓒ be heavy with child. ～がくちい have a full stomach; have no appetite. ～が空く have an empty stomach; be hungry; feel hungry. ～が出来る have a pot-belly; fatten around the waist. ⓒ ～が減る have an empty stomach; be hungry; feel hungry.
[を] ⓒ ～を拵える have a meal to fortify oneself; satisfy one's appetite; eat one's fill.

鬼 a devil; an ogre; a goblin
[N] (心を)～にする harden one's heart (against pity); steel oneself. ～に責められる be visited by a bebt collector; ⓒ be importuned for payment of debts.
[を] ～を欺く ❶ be terribly ugly; be monstrous-like; look like a savage. ❷ be fiersome; be a firebrand.

斧 an axe; a hatchet
[を] ～を入れる reclaim wasteland; open up wasteland; cut down woods; ⓒ put (virgin land) to the plow. ～を加える take an axe to (a tree). ⓒ ～を投ぐ resolve to take up learning.

己 oneself; myself
[N] ～に克つ conquer oneself.
[を] ～を知る know oneself. ～を捨てる rise above oneself. ～を枉ぐ act against oneself; ⓒ compromise one's principles.

お歯黒 tooth dye
[を] ～を付ける dye one's teeth.

お箱 ⓒ one's pet topic/hobby
[を] ⓒ ～を出す ride one's hobby; mount one's hobby horse.

お鉢 ⓒ a rice tub; one's turn
[A] ⓒ ～が回る one's turn comes; be picked out; be next in line.

お払い箱 a paybox; dismissal
[N] ～にする dismiss *sb*; ⓘ sack *sb*; ⓘ give *sb* the bucket. ～になる be dismissed; be sacked; get fired; get the can/gate/boot.

帯 a belt; a sash; a girdle
[を] ～を締める tie a girdle; put on a

sash. 〜を解く ❶ ungirdle oneself; undo a sash. ❷ take a rest. 〜を結ぶ tie a sash. 〜を緩める feel relieved; feel relaxed.

お百度 ⑤ a hundred times prayer

[を] ⓪ 〜を踏む ❶ circle a shrine a hundred times (in prair). ❷ visit sb repeatedly; make repeaded calls on sb. ❸ request sb repeatedly; make repeated requests to sb.

尾鰭 tail and fin

[A] 〜が有る have dignity; have presence.
[を] 〜を付ける resort to hyperbole; embellish a story; ⓪ stretch the facts; ⓪ embroider the truth; ⓪ paint sth in high colors; ⑤ ⓪ lay it on thick.

お布施 a monetary offering

[を] 〜を上げる make a monetary offering. 〜を包む make a monetary offering.

おべっか ⑤ flattery; sycophancy

[A] ⑤ 〜が旨い be a flatterer; be a toady; ⓪ have a well-oiled tongue; ⓪ have a smoothe tongue.
[N] ⑤ 〜に乗る give in to sb's flattery; be taken in by sb; be cajoled into sth.

[を] ⑤ 〜を言う flatter sb; humor sb; ⓪ curry favor with sb; ⓪ find sb's soft side. ⑤ 〜を使う flatter sb; humor sb; ⓪ curry favor with sb; ⓪ find sb's soft side.

お祭り ⑤ a festival; a fair; a fete

[A] ⓪ ⓥ ⑤ 〜が渡る have sexual intercourse; sleep with each other.

お神籤 a written oracle

[を] 〜を引く draw a written oracle.

汚名 a stigma; a slur; a taint

[を] 〜を被る have one's good name stained; be stigmatized. 〜を濯ぐ clear one's name; live down one's reputation.

お眼鏡 ⑤ a pair of glasses

[N] ⓪ 〜に適う ❶ pass muster; be recognized; be acknowledged. ❷ find favor (with one's master); be liked; take sb's fancy.

思い a thought; feelings

[A] 〜が届く get one's ideas across. 〜が積もる have mixed feelings. 〜が残る have a lingering regret.
[N] 〜に掛ける be troubled by sth; ⓪ weigh on one's mind.
[を] ⓪ 〜を致す take sth into consideration; give thought to; ⓪ take sth

on board. ～を掛ける give one's heart to; take a fancy to. ～を砕く ❶ worry about *sth*; fret over *sth*; ⓒ ① rack one's brains. ❷ have a hard time; suffer great hardships. ～を焦がす pine for *sb*; languish for. ～を凝らす think hard about *sth*; ⓒ apply one's mind to *sth*; ⓒ ① rack one's brains. ～を遂げる achieve one's aims; satisfy one's desire. ～を残す pass away with regrets. ～を馳せる think about (home); long for; pine for. ～を晴らす ❶ relieve one's mind. ❷ accomplish one's aim; see one's dream through. ❸ settle old scores; revenge oneself on *sb*; ⓒ wreak one's wrath; ① get one's own back. ～を潜める ponder on *sth*; think deeply. ～を巡らす turn *sth* over in one's mind. ～を寄せる lose one's heart to *sb*; fall in love with *sb*; give one's heart to *sb*; take a fancy to *sb*; set one's heart on *sb*.

重き weight; dignity

Ⓚ ～を置く lay stress on *sth*; emphasize *sth*; attach importance to *sth*. ～を加える gain in significance. ～を為す ❶ be held in high esteem; be thought of highly. ❷ have authority; ① carry weight.

玩具 a toy; a plaything

Ⓝ ～にする ❶ play with *sth*; triffle with *sth*. ❷ make fun of *sb*; triffle with *sb*; ① turn *sb* around one's little finger; ① make a fool of *sb*.

表 the surface; the exterior

Ⓐ ～へ出る go out of doors. Ⓐⱽ ～で遊ぶ play outdoors. Ⓚ ～を飾る save appearances; ① keep up appearances. ～を出す face upwards; face outward. ～を張る ① keep up appearances.

面 the (sur)face ▶面 ▶面

Ⓐ ～が立つ save one's honor; maintain one's dignity; ① save one's face; ① stand proud. Ⓝ ～に負く be intimidated by *sb*; become afraid of *sb*. Ⓚ ～を合わす meet face to face. ～を冒す defy *sb*; ⓒ reprove *sb* to his/her face; ⓒ tell *sb* off. ～を起こす ❶ look up; raise one's head. ❷ gain honor; get credit for *sth*. ～を変える change color; turn pale; lose color. ～を汚す injure *sb's* dignity; cause *sb* to lose face; ⓒ blight *sb's* honor. ～を曝す ❶ show oneself; appear in public; step into the public eye. ❷ disgrace oneself in public; bring shame on oneself. ～を伏す ❶ drop one's head in one's hands;

hang one's head. ❷ be embarrassed; ① lose face. 〜を向ける ❶ turn to face *sb*; face *sb*. ❷ offer resistance; stand against *sb*; oppose *sb*. 〜を和らげる soften one's expression; look benign. 〜を汚す disgrace *sb*; humiliate *sb*; ① take *sb* down a peg.

重荷 a heavy burden

⦗を⦘ 〜を下ろす unburden oneself. 〜を負わせる burden *sb*. 〜を担う shoulder a burden. (心の)〜を除く take a load off one's mind.

折 a time; an occasion; a chance

⦗A⦘ 〜が悪い be inopportune; be badly timed; be inauspicious.
⦗N⦘ 〜に触れる ❶ meet the occasion; ① sieze the day. ❷ on an occasion; at a time.
⦗を⦘ 〜を得る have an opportunity; get a chance. 〜を待つ wait until the time is ripe; wait for an opportunity; ⓔ bide one's time. 〜を見る look for an opportunity; ⓔ bide one's time.

折紙 folded paper; a certificate

⦗A⦘ 〜を付ける certify *sth*; warrant *sth*; vouch for *sb*; stand guarantee for *sb*; go security for *sb*.

終わり an end; a close; a finish

⦗を⦘ 〜を告げる come to an end; mark the end of *sth*; ⓒ ① wind *sth* up. ⓐ 〜を取る die; pass away; ⓔ ① breathe one's last. 〜を全うする end well; come to a good end; make a happy ending of *sth*.

恩 a favor; an obligation

⦗N⦘ 〜に受ける be indebted to *sb*; be obliged to *sb*; owe *sb* a favor. 〜に掛ける make *sb* feel obliged; expect a favor in return. 〜に着せる make *sb* feel obliged; expect a favor in return. 〜に着る feel deeply indebted toward *sb*; be deeply grateful to *sb*. 〜に報いる return a favor.
⦗を⦘ 〜を知る have a sense of gratitude; be sensible to kindness. 〜を売る try to win *sb's* favors. 〜を返す repay *sb* a favor; return a favor. 〜を感じる feel indebted; have a sense of obligation. 〜を着せる make *sb* feel obliged; expect a favor in return. ⓒ 〜を着る feel deeply indebted toward *sb*. 〜を蒙る receive favors; enjoy *sb's* patronage. 〜を知る be grateful (to *sb*). 〜を報ずる repay kindness; return a favor. 〜を施す do *sb* a favor; oblige *sb*. 〜を忘れる be ungrateful; forget one's obligations.

恩寵 grace; favor

⦗を⦘ ① 〜を受ける receive *sb's* favor;

win sb's favor. ⓔ ～を失う lose sb's favor; fall from grace. ⓕ ～を蒙る be in sb's favor; be favored.

音頭 leading in singing

[を] ～を取る ❶ lead in singing; lead a chorus. ❷ take the lead; ⓘ play first violin; ⓒ ⓘ call the shots.

女 a woman; womenfolk

[N] ～になる become a woman. ～に逆上せる be mad about a woman; be infatuated with a woman; ⓒ ⓘ run after a woman.
[を] ～を囲う keep a woman. ～を知る know a woman; have slept with a woman; ⓔ have carnal knowledge of a woman. ～を拵える find a lover; desert one's wife; ⓒ carry on with a woman. ～を弄ぶ make a plaything of a woman.

力

我 oneself; the self; I ▶ 我

[A] ～が折れる give in to sb's demand; drop one's stubborn attitude. ～が張る refuse to give in; be obstinate; be stubborn.
[N] ⓐ ～に成る ❶ act willfully; have one's way. ❷ give oneself airs; be pompous; ⓔ be ostentatious; ⓘ put on airs; ⓒ be stuck-up.

[を] ～を折る yield to sb's will; give in. ～を殺す suppress one's ego; efface oneself. ～を出す reveal one's true self. ～を立てる be self-willed; assert oneself; ⓒ ⓘ stick to one's colors. ～を通す have one's own way. ～を張る cling to; persist in.

会 a meeting; a party

[N] ～に加える attend a meeting; participate in a meeting. ～に付する submit (an issue) to conference; bring (a matter) before the council. ⓔ ～に召す summon sb to council. ～に列する take part in a conference; attend a meeting.
[を] ～を操る manipulate a meeting. ～を閉じる close a meeting. ～を始める be in conference. ～を開く hold a meeting; sit in council. ～を催す convene a meeting; hold a meeting; give a party.

貝 a shellfish

[N] ～になる ❶ remain silent; ⓘ bite one's lip; ⓒ ⓘ button one's lips. ❷ remain indoors; shut oneself up.
[を] ⓐ ～を作る be close to tears; be ready to cry; be almost in tears. ～を拾う gather shellfish. ～を吹き鳴らす blow on a shell. ～を伏す pile sth up; herd sth together; hoard sth. ～を掘る dig up shellfish.

戒 a (Buddhist) commandment

[を] ～を受ける become a Buddhist priest; take the tonsure. ～を授ける give sb the Buddhist commandments; ordain sb to the priesthood. ～を守る observe the Buddhist commandments.

櫂 an oar; a paddle

[A] ⓐ ～が回る live a life of leisure; ⓒ be well off.
[を] ～を納める lay in the oars; boat an oar; ⓒ ship the oars. ～を漕ぐ pull an oar. ～を揃える keep stroke (in rowing). ～を立てる up the paddles (in salute). ～を外す take out the oars; ⓒ unship the oars. ～を嵌める lay in the oars; boat an oar; ⓒ ship the oars.

骸 a skeleton

[を] ⓐ ～を乞う tender one's resignation; ⓒ beg to be relieved of one's post.

甲斐 an effect; a result

[A] ～が有る be worthwhile; be rewarding; be worth doing.

害 injury; hurt; harm; damage

[を] ～を与える damage sth; do injury to sb/sth; work evil on sb. ～を受ける ❶ suffer damage; be injured; be damaged; suffer a loss. ❷ be injured; be hurt. ～を及ぼす cause injury to sb/sth. ～を加える inflict injury on sb; injure sb. ～を被る suffer damage; be damaged; be affected (negatively). ～を避ける avoid being injured; keep out of harm's way.

我意 self-will

[を] ～を通す have one's own way. ～を張る assert oneself; be self-willed; ⓒ stick to one's own opinion.

凱歌 a triumphal song

[を] ⓒ ～を揚げる be victorious; win a victory; ⓒ ～を奏する sing in triumph; crow over the enemy.

骸骨 a skeleton

[を] ⓐ ～を乞う beg to be relieved of one's post; ⓒ tender one's resignation.

解釈 an interpretation

[を] ～を誤る have a false idea of sth; ⓒ ① hold the wrong end of the stick; ⓒ ① get the boot on the wrong leg. ～を下す put an interpretation on sth.

灰燼 ashes

[N] ⓒ ～に帰す be completely

destroyed by fire; be burned down; be reduced to ashes.

外聞(がいぶん) reputation; honor

[A] 〜が立(た)つ preserve one's honor; be saved from disgrace. 〜が良(よ)く無(な)い be bad for one's reputation; do not sound respectable. 〜が悪(わる)い be disreputable; be shameful.
[N] 〜に関(かか)わる affect one's reputation; ⓒ compromise one's (good) name; reflect (badly) on one's reputation.
[を] 〜を失(うしな)う be disgraced; ⓔ bring disgrace upon oneself; ⓘ lose face. 〜を重(おも)んじる be keen on one's reputation; ⓔ be jealous of one's good name. 〜を欠(か)く be embarrassed; ⓔ ⓘ be put out of countenance. 〜を繕(つくろ)う save appearances; ⓘ keep up appearances. 〜を憚(はばか)る ❶ be wary of public opinion. ❷ be a liability; be a threat to one's good name.

顔(かお) a face; looks; features

[A] 〜が合(あ)う ❶ meet face to face. ❷ run into *sb*; come across *sb*. ❸ [sports] compete with *sb*; play a match. 〜が厚(あつ)い be impudent; be cheeky. 〜が売(う)れる ❶ be popular; be widely known. ❷ have influence; have authority. 〜が利(き)く be influential; have authority. 〜が揃(そろ)う have full attendance; come together. 〜が立(た)つ save one's honor; maintain one's dignity; keep up one's state; ⓢ keep one's cool. 〜が潰(つぶ)れる be disgraced; ⓘ lose face. 〜が通(とお)る be famous; be widely known; be popular. 〜が広(ひろ)い be widely known; have wide connections; ⓒ get around. 〜が汚(よご)れる be disgraced; ⓔ bring disgrace upon oneself; ⓘ lose face. 〜が悪(わる)い ❶ be untrustworthy; be unreliable. ❷ be ugly; be bad-looking.
[N] 〜に出(だ)す show one's emotions; betray one's feelings. 〜に免(めん)ずる let *sb* off (so as to preserve face); (do *sth*) for *sb's* sake.
[を] 〜を赤(あか)らめる go red in the face; blush; be ashamed. 〜を上(あ)げる look up; raise one's head. 〜を合(あ)わせる ❶ meet face to face. ❷ make a simultaneous appearance; appear on stage together; act together. ❸ meet in duel; ⓘ cross swords. ❹ be able to look *sb* in the face. 〜を洗(あら)う wash one's face. 〜を打(う)つ strike *sb* in the face. 〜を売(う)る make oneself known; gain influence. 〜を犯(おか)す defy *sb*; ⓔ reprove *sb* to his/her face. 〜を覚(おぼ)える remember *sb's* face; recognize *sb's* face. 〜を貸(か)す assist *sb* (to help them gain standing); lend oneself for *sth*; meet *sb's* wishes. 〜を利(き)かす use one's

influence; ⓘ pull the strings. 〜を曇らす make a dark face; ⓔ cloud one's face. 〜を顰める make grimaces; make a wry face; ⓒ wrinkle one's face. 〜をする ❶ ⓘ pull a face. ❷ do one's makeup; powder one's face. 〜を背ける turn aside; look away. 〜を染める ❶ paint one's face; apply makeup. ❷ blush; be ashamed. 〜を出す ❶ stick one's head out (of the window). ❷ protrude; break through; stick out; appear (from behind sth). ❸ make one's appearance; attend (a meeting); show up. ❹ pay sb a visit; ⓘ pay one's respects; visit sb. 〜を立てる ⓘ save sb's face; back sb up; ⓔ ⓘ keep sb in countenance. 〜を作る ❶ ⓘ make a face (forcefully). ❷ put on one's makeup; powder one's face. 〜を繋ぐ ❶ introduce sb to sb else. ❷ maintain contacts; keep up one's contacts. 〜を潰す injure sb's dignity; cause sb to lose face; ⓔ blight sb's honor. 〜を直す ❶ regain one's presence of mind; ⓔ recover one's composure; ⓘ pull oneself together. ❷ redo one's makeup. 〜を拭う ❶ wipe one's face; ❷ bear the shame; endure ignominy. 〜を伏せる hang one's head; drop one's head in one's hands. ⓐ 〜を踏む injure sb's dignity; cause sb to lose face; ⓔ blight sb's honor. 〜を振る ❶ shake one's head (in denial). ❷ turn one's face away. ❸ refuse an offer; turn down a request. 〜を綻ばす break into a smile; have a beaming face. 〜を見せる make one's appearance; show up; visit sb; attend (a meeting). 〜を向ける turn to face sb. 〜を和らげる soften one's expression; look benign. 〜を歪める ❶ make faces; ⓒ ⓘ pull faces. 〜を汚す disgrace sb; humiliate sb; ⓘ take sb down a peg.

かおいろ
顔色 complexion; countenance

Ⓐ 〜が良い have good color; look fine. 〜が変わる go pale; lose color. 〜が黒い have a dark complexion. 〜が白い have a fair complexion. 〜が勝れない look unwell; look poorly; ⓔ have a unhealthy complexion. 〜が悪い have no color; look pale; look unwell.

Ⓐᵥ 〜で察する read sb's thoughts; tell sth by sb's expression.

Ⓝ 〜に出す betray one's emotions; show one's feelings.

Ⓥ 〜を窺う gauge sb's feelings; sound sb out; ⓒ check sb's mood; ⓔ consult sb's pleasure. 〜を失う lose color; go pale; ⓔ turn livid. 〜を犯す defy sb; ⓔ reprove sb to his/her face. 〜を変える change color; turn pale; lose color. ～を正す compose oneself; make a straight face. ～を和らげる relax one's expression. ～を読む read sb's expression.

踵 the heel ♦ 踵 ♦ 踵

[を] ⓐ ～を狙う take advantage of sb's condition; ⓘ aim below the belt. ～を踏む follow sb closely; ⓘ be hot on sb's heels; ⓘ breathe down sb's neck.

垣 a fence; a railing; a hedge

[N] ⓐ ～に鬩ぐ have a private dispute; quarrel among each other.
[を] ～を作る put up a fence: fence (a place) off. ～を廻らす enclose (a garden) with a fence. ～を結う put up a fence; fence (a place) off.

鍵 a key; a hook; a clue

[N] ⓒ ～に掛かる be deceived; ⓘ be taken in; ⓒⓘ be led by the nose. ⓒ ～に掛ける deceive sb; ⓘ take sb in; ⓒⓘ lead sb by the nose. ⓒ ～になる become partners in crime.
[を] ～を開ける unlock (a door); open a lock with a key. ～を掛ける lock sth up; turn a key on sth. ～を握る have a solution; ⓐ hold the key to (a secret/problem). ～を回す turn the key.

陰 the back; the dark ♦ 陰

[A] ～で笑う laugh behind sb's back; ⓒ poke fun at sb.
[N] ～に置けない be shrewd; be insiduous; not to be triffled with; not to be taken lightly. ～に隠す take sb in protection; place sb/sth under one's protection. ～に隠れる hide in the shade; hide behind sth. ～に潜む be concealed; lay hidden; lurk in the dark. ～に回る do sth behind sb's back.
[を] ～へ回る do sth behind sb's back.
[を] ～をする hide oneself; go into hiding; ⓘ lie low. ⓐ ～を頼む ask for sb's help; rely on sb. ～を付ける shade (a picture).

影 light; a reflection; a sign

[A] ～が薄い ❶ be in eclipse; be insignificant; ⓘ be on the way out. ❷ be on the verge of death; ⓘ be at death's door. ～が映る throw a shadow; cast a reflection; be silhouetted. ～が射す ❶ catch a glimpse of sb; appear suddenly. ❷ cast a shadow. ❸ be illuminated. ❹ show symptoms (of a disease).
[と] ～と添う follow sth closely; stick to sth like a shadow.
[を] ～を致す hide oneself; go into hiding; ⓘ lie low; ⓘ go to ground. ⓐ ～を搗つ find no response; beat the

air; ⓘ draw a blank. 〜を映す reflect an image; mirror a reflection. 〜を追う chase a phantom. 〜を落とす ❶ cast a shadow on *sth*. ❷ be a blight on (one's honor). ❸ throw light upon *sth*; illuminate *sth*. 〜を隠す hide oneself; go into hiding; ⓘ lie low; ⓘ go to ground. 〜を投げる cast a shadow on *sth*; throw a shadow on *sth*. 〜を潜める conceal oneself; disappear from sight; lay hidden; ⓘ lie low. 〜を踏む cast a shadow; throw a shadow.

かげぐち
陰口 backbiting

Ⓝ 〜を利く talk behind *sb's* back; backbite *sb*; ⓔ disparage *sb*. 〜を叩く talk behind *sb's* back; backbite *sb*; ⓔ disparage *sb*.

かこ
過去 the past; bygone days

Ⓝ 〜に生きる live in the past. 〜に遡る be retroactive; go back in time. 〜に葬る put *sth* behind one; bury *sth* in the past; let bygones be bygones; ⓘ bury the axe.

Ⓦ 〜を思う think of the past. 〜を顧みる reflect on the past. 〜を振り返る look back upon the past.

かさ
傘 an umbrella

Ⓝ ⓘ 〜に乗る ❶ hide under *sb's* umbrella; shelter under an umrella. ❷ become (too) excited; ⓘ get carried away. 〜に入る hide under *sb's* umbrella; shelter under an umrella.

Ⓦ 〜をさす open an umbrella; raise an umbrella; put up an umbrella. 〜を窄める close an umbrella; furl an umbrella; fold an umbrella. 〜を閉じる close an umbrella; furl an umbrella; fold an umbrella. 〜を拡げる open an umbrella; spread an umbrella.

かさ
笠 a bamboo hat; a lamp shade

Ⓝ (人を)〜に着る hide behind (*sb's* authority); do *sth* under *sb's* aegis; ⓘ ride on *sb's* coattails.

Ⓦ ⓐ 〜を揚ぐ raise one's hat in surrender; ⓘ throw in the towel.

かさ
嵩 bulk; quantity; volume; size

Ⓐ 〜が張る be voluminous; be unwieldy; be bulky.

Ⓝ 〜に懸かる ❶ (ab)use one's superior position; follow up one's advantage over *sb*; take advantage of the circumstances. ❷ be high-handed; be overbearing; ⓔ lord it over *sb*. 〜に懸ける spur oneself on; brace oneself up. 〜に回す attain superiority (over *sb*); ⓘ gain the upper hand over *sb*.

Ⓦ 〜を懸く ❶ abuse one's superior position; follow up one's advantage over *sb*; take advantage of the circumstances. ❷ exaggerate; ⓒ indulge in hyperbole; ⓘ stretch the facts; ⓢ ⓘ pile it on; ⓢ ⓘ lay it on thick. ◎ ～を着す exaggerate; ⓒ indulge in hyperbole; ⓘ stretch the facts; ⓢ ⓘ pile it on; ⓢ ⓘ lay it on thick.

風穴 an air hole; a windhole
N ～を開ける sun *sb* through (with a spear); fill *sb* with lead.

風上 the windward
N ～に出る get to the windward of (another boat). ～に向かう face to windward. ～に向ける beat to windward.

風下 the leeward
N ～にあう lie leeward. ～に当たる face leeward. (人の)～に居る ❶ be under *sb*'s influence; be under *sb*'s spell. ❷ imitate *sb*'s style; follow *sb* slavishly. ❸ be defeated by *sb*; be routed by *sb*.

風向き the wind-direction
A ～が良い the prospects are good; the situation is favorable; ⓒ things look good. ～が悪い the prospects are gloomy; the situation is unfavorable; ⓒ things look bad.

飾り an ornament; headdress
を ～を下ろす ❶ shave one's head. ❷ become a Buddhist priest; ⓘ take the tonsure. ～を付ける face (a coat); trim (a hat).

舵 a rudder; a helm
を ～を取る ❶ steer (a ship); ⓒ be at the helm. ❷ be in control; ⓢ ⓘ call the shots. ❸ humor *sb*; ingratiate oneself with *sb*; ⓘ curry favor with *sb*. ～を誤る steer (a ship) in the wrong direction.

火事 a fire; a conflagration
Av ～で焼ける be burnt in a fire. N ～に遭う be in a fire. を ～を消す put out a fire. ～を出す start a fire.

過失 an error; a blunder; a fault
を ～を改める correct a mistake. ～を犯す commit an error; make a mistake; ⓒ ⓘ drop the ball. ～を認める acknowledge one's mistake.

果実 fruit
を ～を結ぶ bear fruit.

頭 the head; a leader ▶ 頭 ▶ 頭
A ⓒ ～が打つ have a severe headache; ⓒ have a splitting headache.

[N] ～に立つ take the lead; stand at the head.
[を] ～を下ろす ❶ shave one's head. ❷ become a Buddhist priest; take the tonsure. ～を傾ける ❶ find. ❷ ponder *sth* deeply; think hard about *sth*.

柏 an oak
[N] ～に寝る sleep between a folded futon; roll oneself up in a futon.

拍手 open hands
[N] ～を打つ clap one's hands in worship at a Shinto shrine.

数 a number
[A] ～が少ない be few in number. ～が増える grow in number. ～が減る fall in number.
[A] ～でこなす make profit by selling *sth* in large quantities.
[N] ～に入れる include in the number; take into account.
[を] ～を覚える keep count of. ～を数える take count of. ～を揃える complete the number. ～を尽す be in abundance. ～を増す increase the number.

霞 a haze; a mist
[A] ～がかかる the mist is setting; be hazy; be misty.

[N] ～に隠れる be hidden in the mist. ～に消える disappear in the mist; vanish in the mist. ～に包まれる be covered in mist; be shrouded/veiled in mist.
[N] ～を食う live on air.

掠り a rake-off; a kickback
[を] Ⓐ Ⓢ ～を食う be forced to pay a percentage; Ⓒ pay *sb* a rake-off. Ⓢ ～を取る take a percentage; Ⓒ take a rake-off.

風 a wind; a breeze ▶風
[A] ～が変わる ❶ the wind changes. ❷ have a change of mood. ～が吹く the wind blows; the wind is up. ～が悪い ❶ [nautical] have a poor wind. ❷ have the tide against one; face an uphill struggle.
[N] ～に当たる expose oneself to the wind; have a walk in the wind; Ⓒ go for a blow. ～に戦ぐ rustle in the wind; Ⓔ be stirred by the wind. ～に付く come before the wind. ～になびく bend before the wind; yield to the wind. ～に乗る come before the wind. ～に運ばれる be carried forward by the wind; Ⓒ be windborne. ～に翻る wave in the wind; flutter in the wind. ～に向かう face the wind.
[を] ～を入れる ventilate; let air into. ～を追う make haste. ～を切る ❶ go

against the wind. ❷ work vigorously; ⓒ be full of go. 〜を食(く)らう suspect *sth*; sense *sth*; get wind of *sth*. 〜を掴(つか)む say impossible things; ⓒ ① talk rubbish. 〜を繋(つな)ぐ say impossible things; ⓒ ① talk rubbish. 〜を通(とお)す admit fresh air into (a room); draw a draft. 〜を捕(とら)える clutch air. (帆(ほ)が)〜を孕(はら)む fill with wind; swell with the wind. 〜を吹(ふ)かす give oneself airs; ① put on airs; ⓒ be stuck-up. ⓒ 〜を結(むす)ぶ say impossible things; ⓒ ① talk rubbish.

風邪(かぜ) a cold; the common cold

[を] 〜を移(うつ)す pass on a cold. 〜を引(ひ)く catch a cold.

稼(かせ)ぎ labor; work

[N] 〜にありつく make one's way in the world; make a living. 〜に出(で)る go to work; go for work. 〜になる pay well; carry good pay.

方(かた) a manner; a side; a person

[Aj] 〜が付(つ)く be settled; be brought to a conclusion; come to a close. [を] 〜を付(つ)ける settle *sth*; reach an agreement; bring *sth* to a close.

肩(かた) the shoulder

[Aj] 〜が良(い)い [sports] have a good throw. 〜が怒(いか)る ❶ become worked up. ❷ have square shoulders. ❸ have a stiff neck. ❸ stand tall; feel proud; be confident. 〜が薄(うす)い look down and out; look disheveled; look seedy. 〜が利(き)く have strong shoulders; be powerful. 〜が凝(こ)る ❶ have stiff shoulders; have a stiff neck. ❷ be tiresome; be (a) difficult (read). ❸ be ill at ease; feel uncomfortable. ⓒ 〜が窄(すぼ)る feel inferior; feel small. 〜が狭(せま)い be ashamed; ⓒ ① lose countenance. Ⓐ 〜が閊(つか)える have stiff shoulders; have a stiff neck. 〜が抜(ぬ)ける feel relieved; fulfill one's duty. 〜が張(は)る ❶ have stiff shoulders. ❷ feel constrained; be tense. ❸ have square shoulders. ❹ stand tall; feel proud; be confident. Ⓐ 〜が良(よ)い ❶ be fortunate; be lucky. ❷ be good at throwing *sth*; be a good throw. Ⓐ 〜が悪(わる)い ❶ be unfortunate be unlucky. ❷ be bad at throwing *sth*; be a poor throw.
[Av] 〜で押(お)し退(の)ける push *sb* away with one's shoulder; shoulder *sb* aside. 〜で笑(わら)う shake with laughter; ridicule *sb*; make fun of *sb*.
[N] 〜に掛(か)かる be charged with (a responsibility). 〜に担(かつ)ぐ bear a burden; carry *sth* on one's shoulders; shoulder *sth*. 〜にする bear a burden; carry *sth* on one's shoulders; shoulder *sth*. 〜に乗(の)せる lift *sth* on

one's shoulders. ～に凭れ掛かる lean against sb's shoulder; rest (one's head) on sb's shoulder. 图 ～を怒らせる ❶ square one's shoulders; throw back one's shoulders. ❷ get worked up. ❸ grow confident; swell with pride. ～を入れる ❶ put one's shoulders under sth. ❷ back sb/sth up; patronize sb. ～を落とす ❶ drop one's shoulders. ❷ feel dejected; lose courage. ～を変える ❶ shift (a burden) from one shoulder to the other. ❷ take turns. ～を貸す ① give sb a shoulder; assist sb. ～を越す ❶ surpass sb; outstrip sb. ❷ exceed a limit; overstep the bounds. ❸ pass over one's shoulder; miss the mark. ❹ be nonplussed; be taken aback; be flabbergasted. ～を凝らす swell with pride. ～を竦める shrug one's shoulders. ～を窄める shrug one's shoulders. ～を聳やかす ❶ swell with pride. ❷ grow confident; swell with pride. ～を叩く ❶ massage one's shoulders. ❷ tap sb on the shoulder. ❸ urge sb to resign. ～を並べる ❶ stand in line; walk in file; be shoulder to shoulder. ❷ be on a par with sb; rank with sb; equal to sb. Ⓐ (事から)～を抜く escape one's responsibility; unburden oneself. ～を脱ぐ ❶ bare one's shoulder(s). ❷ give sb a shoulder;

assist sb. ～を張る open one's shoulders. ～を解す ❶ relax one's shoulders. ❷ feel relieved; feel relaxed. ～を持つ support sb; side with sb; stand by sb; take sb's side. ～を焼く see into the future; divine the future; prophesy the future.

型 a model; a mold; a pattern
Ⓝ ～に嵌まる be set in a model; be unconventional; run to a pattern; fall into a rut. ～に嵌める Ⓐ force sb into a pattern; make sb conform. 图 ～を破る break with tradition; go against convention.

形 shape; a pledge ♦ 形
Ⓐ ～が崩れる go out of shape; lose shape.
Ⓝ ～に取る keep sth as security; receive sth as security.

片 settlement; disposal
Ⓐ ～が付く be settled; come to a close; be disposed of.
图 ～を付ける ❶ settle a matter; set things in order. ❷ finish one's work; bring (a project) to a close. ❸ pay off (one's debts).

片意地 stubbornness; obstinacy
图 ～を張る refuse to give in; be obstinate; be stubborn.

敵 labor; work ▶ 敵

[N] ～を討つ avenge *sb*; take revenge for *sb*; ⓒ settle old scores (with *sb*); ⓒ square accounts with *sb*; ⓒ get even with *sb*. ～を取る avenge *sb*; take revenge for *sb*; ⓒ settle old scores (with *sb*); ⓒ square accounts with *sb*; ⓒ get even with *sb*.

固唾 [E] saliva

[を] ～を呑む hold one's breath; catch one's breath; be intensely anxious.

形 a form; a shape; a figure ▶ 形

[A] ～が崩れる go out of shape; lose shape. ～が出来る ❶ take shape; acquire a form. ❷ become an adult; ⓒ come of age.
[を] ～を与える give shape to. ～を改める sit up straight; straighten oneself. ～を変える take another form; disguise oneself. ～を正す sit up straight; straighten oneself. ～を繕う save appearances; ⓒ keep up appearances. ～を取る take (a certain) form.

刀 a sword

[N] ～に懸けて...する do *sth* on one's honor; do *sth* at the risk of one's life; stake one's life on *sth*.
[を] ～を納める sheathe a sword. ～を構える raise a sword; hold a sword;

aim a sword. ～を試す try a (new) sword. ～を抜く draw a sword. ～を振り上げる raise a sword. ～を振り回す brandish a sword.

片肌 one bare shoulder

[A] ～を脱ぐ ❶ bare one of one's shoulders. ❷ give *sb* a hand; help *sb* out; join in.

片棒 a palanquin bearer

[を] ～を担ぐ be involved in an intrigue; ⓒ be a party to a conspiracy; ⓘ have a hand in a plot; ⓢ ⓘ be in cahoots.

肩身 public honor

[A] ⓐ ～が窄る feel inferior; feel small. ～が狭い feel inferior; be shy; ⓒ ⓘ be a shrinking daisy. ～が広い stand tall; feel at ease.
[を] ～を窄める fear the public gaze; ⓒ shrink from the public eye.

片目 one eye

[A] ～が明く ❶ learn to read a bit. ❷ [sumō] have one's firsth win; have a victory at last.
[A] ～で見る look with one eye.
[を] ～を潰す lose one eye; lose the sight in one eye; become blind in one eye.

勝ち a victory; a conquest

- N ～に乗る follow up a victory.
- を ～を得る gain a victory; carry/win the day. ～を占める gain a victory; win the day. ～を拾う gain an unexpected victory. ～を譲る give sb a game; ⓪ yield one's palm.

価値 value; worth; merit

- A ～がある be of value; be worthwhile.
- を ～を失う lose value. ～を落とす drop the value (of); depreciate the value (of sth). ～を損じる impair the value (of sth). ～を高める heighten the value (of sth). ～を認める recognize the value (of sth).

活 live; living; resuscitation

- を ～を入れる ❶ resuscitate sb; bring sb round. ❷ encourage sb; rally sb's strength; ❸ buck sb up.

渇 回 thirst

- を ⓒ ～を癒す quench one's thirst. ⓒ ～を訴える complain of thirst. ⓒ ～を覚える feel thirsty.

鰹節 dried bonito

- N ⓐ ～にする use sth as a pretext. ⓐ ～に使う involve sb in (one's excuses); ⓪ make a cat's paw of sb; ⓪ make a scapegoat of sb.

活眼 回 a quick eye; insight

- を ⓒ ～を開く penetrate a situation; have insight; have a keen eye.

活気 vigor; spirit; zest

- A ～がある be lively. ～が付く become animated; liven up.
- N ～に富む be full of life. ～に満ちる brim with life.
- を ～を失う lose vigor. ～を帯びる pick up vigor. ～を添える put life into sth; give life to sth. ⓒ ～を呈する display vigor.

客気 回 youthful ardor; rashness

- N ⓒ ～に駆られる be carried away by youthful ardor; act on impulse.

格好 shape; form; appearances

- A ～が崩れる get out of shape; look worse. ～が良い look good; be attractive; be stylish; look smart; be well-cut; ⓢ be cool. ～が悪い look bad; be unattractive; ⓒ be unseemly; look clumsy; ⓢ be uncool.
- を ～を付ける give shape to sth; add style to one's appearance; try to look good.

喝采 applause; an ovation

- を ～を受ける receive an ovation. ～を博する win applause; receive an ovation.

勝手 one's own way; willfulness

[A] ～が違う be out of one's element; ⓘ be not in one's line. ～が分かる be familiar with; know how to do; ⓘ know the ropes.
[N] ～に合う suit one's fancy. ～に変える take (great) liberties with. ～にする do as one pleases; have one's own way. ～に使う appropriate sb's things for one's own use; make free use of sb's things. ⓘ ～に付く do as one pleases; have one's own way. ～に振る舞う act in a willful manner; behave selfishly.
[を] ～を知る be familiar with sth; know how to do sth; ⓘ know the ropes; ⓒ get the knack of sth. ～を飲み込む grasp the situation; ⓒ get the hang of sth. ～を計る be self-seeking. ～を許す ⓘ give sb a free hand; ⓘ give sb plenty of rope.

家庭 a household; a home

[を] ～を作る settle down; set up house; start a home. ～を持つ settle down; set up house; start a home.

合点 understanding; grasp

[A] ～が行く ❶ make sense of sth; grasp the meaning; ⓘ catch the idea. ❷ be convinced; be won over; be persuaded; ⓘ come round to sb's point of view. ～が遅い be slow to understand sth; be slow-witted. ～が早い be quick to understand sth; be quick-witted.

角 a corner; an edge ▶ 角

[A] ～が立つ arouse bitterness; cause offense; aggravate sb; have a rough going. ～が取れる ❶ round off one's rough edges; become sociable; become affable. ❷ be sophisticated; be refined; be polished.
[を] ⓘ ～を入る look angry. ～を落とす round off the corners. ～を立てる speak harshly; make matters worse; ⓔ aggravate a situation. ～を取る mellow out; round off the rough corners. ⓒ soften up. ～を曲がる turn a corner.

門 a door; a gate ▶ 門

[A] (お)～が違う ❶ go to the wrong place; visit the wrong person. ❷ accuse the wrong person; ⓒ ⓘ bark up the wrong tree.
[を] ⓐ ～を出ず ❶ leave home; go out into the world; enter the real world. ❷ become a Buddhist priest; take the tonsure; enter a Buddhist monastery. ～を売る sell sth from door to door; set up shop. ⓐ ～を広ぐ increase the number of one's family. ⓐ ～を塞ぐ feel awkward to visit sb; have leaden feet.

廉 (かど) a charge; a suspicion

- N ~を倒さぬ be well mannered (in spite of one's shabby appearance); keep up appearances (in spite of one's poverty); keep on a brave face; hold one's head high. ~を質す investigate a charge; look into a matter; follow a lead.

鼎 (かなえ) a tripod kettle

- を ~を扛ぐ be very strong; have great strenth. ~を定む designate the place of the capital; fix the capita. ~を問われる have one's ability questioned.

金轡 (かなぐつ) a bit

- を ~を嵌める offer a bribe; bribe sb; ① grease sb's palm; ① shut sb up.

悲しみ (かな) sorrow; sadness; grief

- N ~に暮れる give way to grief. ~に沈む be overwhelmed with sorrow; be lost in sorrow. ~に堪える bear the sorrow.
- を ~を和らげる lessen the sorrow; alleviate one's sorrow; ① blunt the edge of sorrow.

金棒 (かなぼう) an iron rod

- を ~を引く spread scandal; stir up rumors; go about gossiping.

金 (かね) money; wealth; riches

- A ~が唸る be rolling in money; wallow in money. ~が掛かる require (a lot of) money. ~が切れる run out of money. ~が溜まる have some money saved. ~が出来る grow rich; make money. ~が入る come into money.
- A ~で釣る bait sb with money.
- と ~と転ぶ be swayed by money.
- N ~に飽かす use one's money freely; lavish money on sth. ~に困る be out of money; ⊙ ① be hard up. ~に転ぶ be swayed by money. ~に付く ingratiate oneself with the rich; ① curry favor with the rich; flirt with wealth. ~になる be profitable; make money.
- を ~を遊ばせる let money lie idle; ① sit on one's money. ~を扱う handle money. ~を得る earn money; obtain money; gain (access to) money. ~を送る send money; remit money. ~をおろす draw money (from a bank). ~を掛ける spend money; invest money. ~を賭ける bet money (on sth); stake money on (a race). ~を返す repay money; give back money. ~を貸す lend money. ~を稼ぐ earn money; make money. ~を借りる borrow money. ⊙ ~を切る break (into small) money; change money. ⓊU ~を食う

be expensive; eat money. 〜を崩す break (into small) money; change money. 〜を工面する raise money. 〜を拵える raise money. 〜を死蔵する lock money away. ⓒ 〜を摩る lose one's money (in speculation). 〜をせびる pester sb for money; extort money from sb. 〜を出す give money; hand out money; furnish the money. 〜を溜める save money; hoard money. 〜を使う use money; spend money. 〜を投じる throw money at (a project); sink money into (a project). 〜を取る charge money; take money. 〜を握らせる bribe sb with money; ⓒ ⓞ grease sb's palm. 〜を寝かす let money lie idle; ⓞ sit on one's money. 〜を残す have surplus money; leave money to sb. (有り)〜を叩く use all one's money; ⓒ ⓞ go for broke. 〜を払う pay money. 〜を散蒔く be a spendthrift; ⓒ fling money about. 〜を纏める save some money; collect some money. 〜を回す circulate capital; invest money; finance (a project). 〜を儲ける make a profit; earn money; make good money.

鐘 a bell; a gong

[A] 〜が打つ the bell strikes; the bell tolls. 〜が鳴る the bell rings; the bell chimes.

[を] ⓐ 〜を打つ ❶ make a promise; make a vow. ❷ give something up; quit halfway. 〜をつく strike a bell; toll a bell. 〜を鳴らす ring a bell.

過半数 more than half

[を] 〜を得る obtain a majority; win a majority. 〜を占める hold a majority.

黴 mold; mildew; must

[A] 〜が生える ❶ go moldy; go stale. ❷ go out of fashion, become outdated; become old-fashioned.
[を] 〜を取り除く remove the mold; get the mold off sth. 〜を防ぐ keep sth from getting moldy.

華美 [N] splendor; gorgeousness

[N] ⓒ 〜に流れる be carried away by an urge for ostentation. ⓒ 〜に耽る indulge in luxury.
[を] ⓒ 〜を競う vie with each other in splendor. ⓒ 〜を戒める admonish against luxurious living. ⓒ 〜を極める make sth exquisite; ⓒ explore the boundaries of ostentation.

株 stocks; shares; a stump

[A] 〜が上がる ❶ one's stock rises. ❷ rise in public esteem; gain status; ⓒ be in the ascendant.
[を] (お)〜を奪う beat sb at his/her

own game; outdo *sb* in his/her own forte. 〜を売る sell one's assets. 〜を買う buy shares; invest in stocks. 〜を買い占める buy up shares; ⓘ corner the market. 〜を取る beat *sb* at his/her own game; outdo *sb* in his/her own forte. 〜を持つ hold shares (in a company). 〜を譲る transfer the goodwill (of an enterprise).

下風 ㊐ the leeward

Ⓝ ⓔ 〜に至る serve *sb*; be in a subordinate position; ⓘ play second fiddle to *sb*. ⓔ 〜に立つ serve *sb*; be in a subordinate position; ⓘ play second fiddle to *sb*. ⓔ 〜に着く serve *sb*; be in a subordinate position; ⓘ play second fiddle to *sb*.

兜 a (military) helmet

㊄ 〜を脱ぐ ❶ take off one's helmet; remove one's helmet. ❷ admit defeat; give *sb* best; give up; ⓘ take off one's hat to *sb*.

壁 a wall; a barrier

Ⓐ 〜で囲む wall (a place) off. ㊁ ⓒ 〜と見る ridicule *sb*; ⓔ hold *sb* in contempt; despise *sb*; look down on *sb*. Ⓝ ⓒ 〜にする ridicule *sb*; despise *sb*; look down on *sb*. ⓔ hold *sb* in contempt. 〜に突き当たる face unsurmountable difficulties; ⓘ run into a stone wall; ⓒ ⓘ hit a snag. 〜にぶつかる be bogged down; have difficulties; ⓘ run into a stone wall. ㊄ 〜を穿つ study on water and bread; study amidst great poverty. ⓒ 〜を背負う squat against a wall; sit against a wall. 〜を塗る plaster a wall. 〜を破る tear down a wall; break through a wall.

画餅 ㊐ a painted rice cake

Ⓝ ⓒ 〜に帰す come to nothing; end in failure; fall through; ⓘ go up in smoke. ⓒ 〜に属す come to nothing; end in failure; fall through; ⓘ go up in smoke.

釜 a pot; a kettle; a cauldron

㊄ ⓐ ⓥ 〜を抜く practice sodomy. ⓥ 〜を掘る practice sodomy.

鎌 a sickle; a scythe; a hook

Ⓐ ⓒ 〜が切れる go well; yield results. ㊄ 〜を掛ける ❶ put an enticing question; ask a leading question. ❷ entice *sb* to speak; draw *sb* out; pump out a secret.

竈 a kitchen range; a furnace

Ⓐ 〜が賑わう live the good life.

N Ⓐ ～に媚ぶ ❶ flatter the cook; ① curry favor with the cook. ❷ ingratiate oneself with the men behind the scene. Ⓐ ～に跨がる surpass one's parents.

を Ⓞ ～を起す increase the family fortune; cause one's house to flourish. Ⓞ ～を覆す lose one's fortune; go bankrupt; ⑤ go bust. Ⓞ ～を占める run a household; manage a household. Ⓞ ～を立てる set up a house; start housekeeping. Ⓞ ～を持つ possess a fortune. Ⓞ ～を破る be ruined; go bankrupt; waste a fortune. Ⓞ ～を分つ set up a branch family; keep a separate house.

神 a god; a goddess; a deity ♦ 神

N ～に祈る pray to God/the gods. ～に捧げる dedicate to God/the gods; make offerings to God/the gods. ～になる be elevated to godhood. ～に祭る deify sb; enshrine sb; apotheosize sb.

を ～を敬う be pious; revere God/the gods. ～を畏れる fear God/the gods. ～を信じる believe in God/the gods. ～を祭る worship God/the gods.

紙 paper

N ～に書く write on paper. ～に包む wrap sth in paper. ～に捻る ❶ wrap sth up in paper. ❷ give sb a tip; give sth as a gratuity. ❸ make a votive offering.

を ～を畳む unfold a sheet of paper. ～を伸ばす flatten crumpled paper. ～を張る paper a wall; paste paper on sth. ～を広げる unfold a sheet of paper.

髪 hair; hairdo; locks

Ⓐ ～が抜ける lose one's hair.

を ～を編む braid one's hair. ～を下ろす ❶ shave one's head. ❷ become a Buddhist priest; take the tonsure. ～を刈る have one's hair cut. Ⓞ ～を梳る comb one's hair. ～を梳く comb one's hair. ～を束ねる bind one's hair. ～を縮らす curl one's hair. ～を解く let down one's hair; take down one's hair. ～を直す tidy one's hair. ～を撫でる caress sb's hair; stroke sb's hair. ～を伸ばす let one's hair grow long. ～を乱す rumple one's hair; tousle one's hair. ～を毟る tear one's hair; rend one's hair. ～を結う dress one's hair. ～を分ける split one's hair.

裃 Ⓝ a *kamishimo* [garment]

を ～を着る be ceremonious; be formal. ～を脱ぐ be relaxed; be unceremonious.

かみなり
雷 thunder; a thunderbolt

[A] ～が落ちる ❶ be struck by lightning. ❷ be scolded; ⓒ be told off; ⓒ ⓓ be given a dressing-down. [を] ～を落とす scold sb; ⓒ tell sb off; ⓒ haul sb over the coals.

かめん
仮面 a mask

[を] ～を被る ❶ put on a mask. ❷ hide one's feelings; play the hypocrite; ⓒ keep a straight face. ～を脱ぐ ❶ pull off one's mask. ❷ reveal oneself; owe up to sth; ⓒ show one's true colors. ～を剥ぐ expose sb; ⓒ blow sb's cover; ⓒ unmask sb.

かも
鴨 a (wild) duck; a drake

[N] ⓒ ～にする target sb; victimize sb.

から
空 emptiness; vacancy ◆ 空 ◆ 空

[N] ～にする empty (a box). ～になる become empty; be emptied. [を] ⓒ ～を踏む be disappointed (in one's hopes); be frustrated; prove a disappointment.

から
殻 a husk; a hull; a shell

[を] ⓐ ～を言う exaggerate; stretch the facts; ⓒ indulge in hyperbole; ⓒ ⓓ pile it on; ⓒ ⓓ lay it on thick. ～を抜かす stretch the facts; indulge in hyperbole; ⓒ ⓓ pile it on; ⓒ ⓓ lay it on thick. ～を破る ⓐ break out of one's shell; shake off one's inhibitions.

がら
柄 a build; a pattern; a design

[A] ～が大きい be of large build; be burly; be big. ～が小さい be of small build; be slender; be small. [N] ～に無く be out of character; be unlike one.

からあし
空足 a misstep

[を] ～を踏む ⓒ make a misstep; lose one's balance; ⓒ totter.

からだ
体 the body; physique ◆ 体

[A] ～が空く have time to oneself; be free; be vacant; have time on one's hands. ～が続く keep going strong; be in good health; ⓔ be in good fettle. ～が強い have a strong constitution. ～が太る gain weight; put on weight. ～が弱る become weak; be run down. ～が痩せる lose weight; lose flesh. ～が弱い have a weak constitution. ～が弱る become weak; be run down. [A] ～で覚える know sth through experience; learn from experience; (learn to) do sth by instinct. [N] ～に合う ❶ fit (one's body) well. ❷ agree with one. ～に障る be harmful to one's health; injure one's health. 〜に良い be good for the body; be healthy. 〜に悪い be bad for the body; be unhealthy. 囲 〜を惜しむ spare oneself (the trouble); be idle; be lazy. 〜を固める be settled down. 〜を壊す impair one's health; ruin one's health; lose one's health; make oneself ill. 〜を沈める go down in the world; ⓒ fall into reduced circumstances; ⓢⓞ go to the dogs. 〜を調べる go through sb's pockets; search sb. 〜を作る build up one's body. 〜を張る ❶ do sth at the risk of one's life; devote oneself to (a cause); throw oneself into sth heart and soul. ❷ prostitute oneself; sell one's body. 〜を拭く dry one's body; dry oneself. 〜を休める rest one's body; have a rest; give oneself a rest. (男に)〜を許す give oneself to a man; sleep with a man; ⓒⓞ go all the way. 〜を悪くする injure one's health.

からたち
枳殻 a trifoliate orange

N 〜に成る have a change of heart; mend one's ways; ⓞ turn over a new leaf.

からつば
空唾 saliva without mucus

囲 〜を呑む hold one's breath; be intensely anxious; ⓞ catch one's breath.

がりょうてんせい
画竜点睛 ⒺⓃ the finishing touch

N ⓒ 〜を欠く lack the finishing touch; ⓒ be devoid of life; have no essence; carry no meaning. ⓒ 〜を施す give a finishing touch to sth; bring (a piece of art) to life.

かわ
川 a river; a stream; a rivulet

A ⓐ 〜が明く a river is cleared. ⓐ 〜が止まる a river too high to wade across. 囲 〜へ流す put sth behind one; bury sth in the past; let bygones be bygones; ⓘ bury the axe. 囲 〜を下る go down a river. 〜を遡る go up a river. 〜を渡る cross a river; wade across a stream.

かわ
皮 the skin; a hide; a pelt; a fur

囲 〜を被る play the hypocrite; feign innocence. 〜を殺ぐ pare leather. 〜を鞣す tan hide. 〜を剥ぐ skin (an animal, a tree). 〜を剥く peel off the skin.

かん
勘 an intuition; a hunch

A 〜が有る have a sixth sense; have a knack for (a trade). 〜が良い have a good intuition; be sharp; be perceptive; ⓘ have a good nose. 〜が付く have a general idea. 〜が悪い have a poor intuition; be dull; ⓘ have a bad nose.

勘 ～で分かる know sth by intuition; ⓒ have a hunch; ⓘ feel sth in one's bones. 🈂 ～を覆す reconsider the facts. ～を付ける be perceptive; be sharp; be quick-witted. ～を働かす use one's intuition; ⓒⓘ play one's hunch. ～を持つ have a sixth sense; have a good intuition; be perceptive; be sharp; ⓘ have a good nose.

癇 a quick temper; mettle

🅰 ～が高ぶる lose one's temper; become irate; ⓢⓘ blow a fuse. ～が立つ lose one's temper; ⓒⓘ fly off the handle; ⓢⓘ blow a fuse.

🄽 ～に障る irritate one; ⓘ cut one to the quick; ⓘ rub one the wrong way; ⓒ get on one's nerves. ～に触れる irritate one; ⓘ strike a raw nerve; ⓘ rub one the wrong way; ⓒ get on one's nerves.

🈂 ～を起こす lose one's temper; become irate; ⓒⓘ fly off the handle; ⓢⓘ blow a fuse.

観 🅴 a look; an appearance

🅰 ～が有る have (a certain look); have (a certain) appearance; look (like).

🈂 ～を起こす penetrate the deeper meanings of life; gain profound insight; see through things.

燗 heated *sake*

🅰 ～が通る *sake* with exactly the right temperature.

🈂 ～をする warm up *sake* in a bottle. ～を付ける warm up sake in a bottle.

棺 a coffin; a casket

🄽 ～に蓋う leave this world (behind); pass away; draw one's last breath; ⓒ breathe one's last. ～に納める lay *sb* in a coffin.

閑 🅴 leisure; time off

🈂 ⓒ ～を得る have time to oneself; be free; be vacant; ⓘ have time on one's hands. ⓒ ～を盗む steal time (to do *sth*).

巻 a volume; a reel; a tome

🈂 ～を追う read a book volume by volume. ⓒ ～を掩う close a book; finish reading a book.

款 🅴 an article; goodwill

🈂 ⓒ ～を通じる make friends with *sb*; ⓒ enter into friendly relations with *sb*; make secret overtures (to the enemy).

官 🅴 government; high office

🄽 ⓒ ～に就く enter government service; take office.

カン

を ⓔ ～を辞する leave office; step down from public service. ⓔ ～をす enter public service; take office.

感 Ⓔ a feeling ; a sensation
Ⓝ ⓔ ～に堪える show deep signs of emotion; be deeply impressed.
を ⓔ ～を与える strike *sb* (as); leave an impression.

冠 Ⓔ a crown; a coronet ▶ 冠むり
を ⓐⓔ ～を掛く resign from one's post; ⓔ tender one's resignation.

甲 a high pitch; a high key ▶ 甲こう
を ～を取る [music] play at a high pitch; sing in a high key.

寛 Ⓔ leniency; generosity
Ⓝ ⓔ ～に過ぎる be too lenient; be too generous.

歓 Ⓔ delight; pleasure; joy
を ⓔ ～を尽す make merry; have a good time.

願 a prayer; a wish; a vow
Ⓐ ～が叶う have one's prayer answered.
Ⓝ ⓐ ～に懸ける ❶ worry over *sth*; fret about *sth*. ❷ be haunted by; prey on one's mind. ❸ offer a prayer; make a vow.

を ⓞ ～を起こす offer a prayer; make a vow. ～を懸ける offer a prayer; make a vow. ～を立てる offer a prayer; make a vow. ～を解く revoke a vow.

眼 Ⓔ the eye; eyesight
を ⓢ ～を付ける glare at *sb* (with envy); stare at *sb* (suspiciously); ⓔ fasten one's eyes on *sb*.

干戈 Ⓔ arms; weapons
Ⓝ ⓞⓔ ～に訴える resort to arms.
を ⓐⓔ ～を動かす open hostilities; take up arms against *sb*. ⓐⓔ ～を納める lay down arms. ⓐⓔ ～を交える open hostilities; go to war; cross swords with *sb*; fight each other.

眼下 under one's eyes
Ⓝ ～に見る ❶ look down upon (a place); command a view of (a place). ❷ look down upon *sb*; ⓔ hold *sb* in low esteem; think little of *sb*.

カンガエ

考え thought; ideas; a notion
Ⓐ ～が有る have an idea. ～が浮かぶ come to mind; occur to one. ～が固まる an idea takes shape. ～が変わる change one's mind. ～がつく form an opinion.
Ⓝ ～に入れる take *sth* into consideration; ⓞ take *sth* on board. ～に沈

む be lost in thought. 〜に耽る be deep in thought.
[を] 〜を改める revise one's thinking. 〜を抱く entertain a thought. 〜を起こす get an idea. 〜を決める make up one's mind; ⓐ take sth into one's head. 〜を捨てる relinquish a thought; drop an idea. 〜を伝える convey one's thoughts. 〜を盗む steal sb's idea. 〜を述べる express one's views; speak one's mind. 〜を纏める collect one's thoughts. 〜を持つ entertain a thought.

感覚 sensation; sense; feeling
[N] 〜に訴える appeal to the senses.
[を] 〜を失う lose feeling (in one's limbs); become past feeling.

寒気 cold weather; the cold
[A] 〜が増す grow cold.
[N] 〜に堪える bear the cold; stand the cold. 〜に負ける yield to the cold.
[を] 〜を凌ぐ ward off the cold. 〜を冒す brave the cold.

感興 interest; inspiration; fun
[A] 〜が湧く become interested in sth; warm up to (an idea).
[を] 〜を誘う arouse sb's interest. 〜を殺ぐ spoil the fun; dampen sb's enthusiasm. 〜をそそる excite sb's interest. 〜を求める seek new sensations; seek pleasure.

雁首 the bowl of a pipe
[を] 〜を揃える hold a meeting of slavish followers; attend a meeting out of mere obligation.

関係 a relation; a relationship
[A] 〜がある ❶ be related; ⓒ have something to do with sb/sth. ⓒ ❷ have a sexual relation with sb.
[を] 〜を促進する promote relations. 〜を改善する improve relations. 〜を断つ cut one's ties with sb; break off relations; ⓒ sever one's connections with sb. 〜を続ける sustain a relation. 〜を結ぶ establish a connection with. 〜を持つ entertain relations with.

奸計 [E] evil designs; a trick
[N] ⓒ 〜に掛かる fall prey to a plot; be the victim of an evil scheme.
[を] ⓒ 〜を廻らす work out a vicous plan; plot against sb.

間隙 a gap; an aperture
[N] 〜に乗じる take advantage of an unguarded moment; catch sb off guard.
[を] 〜を埋める stop a gap; bridge a divide. 〜を生じる fall out with sb.

カンゲキ

~を縫ぬう slip through a gap; pass between two obstacles.

寒暄かんけん cold and warmth
- ㊅ ~を叙じょす exchange the compliments of the season; exchange seasonal greetings. ~を延のぶ extend seasonal greetings.

勧告かんこく advice; counsel
- Ⓝ ~に従したがう take *sb's* advice.
- ㊅ ~を受うけるtake *sb's* advice.

感かんじ feelings; sense
- Ⓐ ~がする have a feeling.
- ㊅ ~を与あたえる produce a feeling.

感謝かんしゃ gratitude; appreciation
- Ⓝ ~に値あたいする be worthy of one's appreciation; deserve one's thanks.
- ㊅ ~を受うける receive thanks. ~を捧ささげる offer thanks; give thanks.

慣習かんしゅう tradition; custom; habit
- ㊅ ~を捨すてる do away with tradition. ~を守まもる uphold a tradition; keep a tradition alive. ~を破やぶる break with tradition.

干渉かんしょう interference; meddling
- ㊅ ~を受うける be interfered with. ~をする meddle in *sb's* affairs. ~を招まねく invite interference.

カンジョウ

感情かんじょう feelings; emotions
- Ⓐ ~が薄うすらぐ calm down; ⓐ cool down. ~が篭こもる be impassioned; be full of emotion. ~が高たかまる get excited; let one's feelings run high. ~が燃もえ上あがる get passionate over *sth*; let emotions flare up.
- Ⓝ ~に訴うったえる appeal to *sb's* sentiments. ~に駆かられる do *sth* on the impulse of the moment; be driven by emotions. ~に走はしる give way to one's emotions. ~に任まかせる give vent to one's emotions. ~に負まける let one's emotions get the better of one; be swayed by emotions.
- ㊅ ~を表あらわす express one's feelings. ~を偽いつわる feign one's feelings. ~を動うごかす work up one's/*sb's* feelings. ~を押おさえる contain one's passions; suppress one's feelings. ⓒ ~を害がいする hurt one's/*sb's* feelings. ~を隠かくす hide one's feelings; ⓘ keep a straight face. ~を込こめる do *sth* with feeling; ⓘ put one's heart into *sth*. ~を刺激しげきする excite one's/*sb's* emotions; stir one's/*sb's* feelings. ~を和やわらげる appease *sb*; ⓒ pacify one's/*sb's* sentiments.

勘定かんじょう counting; reckoning
- Ⓐ ~が合あう the accounts tally. ~が嵩かさむ run up bills.
- Ⓝ ~に入いれる count *sth* in; take *sth*

73

into account. ～に組み入れる place to sb's account. ～に付ける charge sb's account.
［を］ ～を締め切る close accounts. ～を締める add up accounts. ～をする settle one's accounts; foot the bill. ～を溜める run up bills. ～を付ける pay money; foot the bill. ～を取る collect a bill. ～を延ばす postpone one's payment. ～を払う pay money; foot the bill. ～を引き合わせる check account.

関心 concern; interest
［A］ ～が薄らぐ interest wanes; lose interest.
［を］ ～を抱く have an interest in sth. ～を示す show concern; display interest. ～を引く draw one's/sb's interest; arouse concern; capture sb's interest. ～を持つ be interested; be concerned; take notice. ～を寄せる give thought to; take an interest in.

歓心 favor; goodwill; approval
［を］ ～を買う ingratiate oneself with sb; ⓘ curry favor with sb.

肝胆 E the liver and gallbladder
［を］ ⓐⓒ ～を出す show one's good faith toward sb; do sth with devotion. ⓐⓒ ～を傾ける unbosom one-self; ⓘ pour out one's heart to sb. ⓐⓒ ～を砕く devote oneself to sth. ⓐⓒ ～を吐く reveal one's real intentions; ⓘ put one's cards on the table. ⓐⓒ ～を披く unbosom oneself; ⓘ pour out one's heart to sb.

眼中 consideration; account
［N］ ～に入れる take sb/sth into consideration; take sb/sth into account. ～に置く take sth/sb into consideration; take sth/sb into account. ～に無い take no notice of sb/sth; have no eye for sb/sth; think nothing of sb/sth; ignore sb/sth; ⓔ set sth at naught.

官途 E government service
［N］ ⓒ ～に就く enter government service; take up a government post.

勘所 a vital spot; the crux
［を］ ～を押える grasp the crux (of a matter); get it right; ⓘ be on the mark; ⓒⓘ get the point; ⓢⓘ get it.

肝脳 E the liver and brains
［を］ ～を絞る apply one's mind to sth; think hard about sth; ⓒⓘ rack one's brains.

看板 a signboard; a sign
［A］ ～が泣く be not true to one's

name; be not worthy of one's reputation.
图 ～を下(お)ろす close down (a shop). ～を出(だ)す put up a sign. ～を塗(ぬ)り替(か)える ❶ repaint a signboard. ❷ change one's policy; change occupation; Ⓐ change one's colors.

冠(かんむり) a crown; a coronet ▶ 冠(かん)
图 Ⓐ ～を掛(か)く step down from office; Ⓔ retire from public office. ～を被(かぶ)せる crown sb. ～を加(くわ)える ❶ crown sb. ❷ celebrate one's coming of age. ～を着(き)ける put a crown on one's head; wear a crown. Ⓐ ～を弾(はじ)く prepare for public office. ～を曲(ま)げる be offended; take offense at sth; Ⓒ Ⓐ get sour.

歓楽(かんらく) pleasure; merriment; mirth
Ⓝ ～に耽(ふけ)る indulge in pleasure; live wild; Ⓒ Ⓘ live it up. ～に酔(よ)う indulge in pleasure.
图 ～を追(お)う pursue (a life of) pleasure. ～を尽(つ)くす give oneself up to pleasure. ～を求(もと)める seek pleasure.

感涙(かんるい) Ⓔ tears of gratitude
Ⓝ Ⓔ ～に噎(むせ)ぶ be choked with tears of gratitude.

慣例(かんれい) custom; normal practice
Ⓝ ～に従(したが)う conform to the custom; follow normal practice; Ⓘ fall into line. ～に背(そむ)く go against normal practice. ～による be according to custom.
图 ～を残(のこ)す set a precedent. ～を廃(はい)する abandon normal practice; do away with custom. ～を破(やぶ)る violate custom; break with custom.

貫禄(かんろく) dignity; presence
Ⓐ ～が有(あ)る command respect; be influential; have influence; Ⓘ carry weight. ～が付(つ)く gather prestige; gain in reputation; increase one's stature; Ⓘ gather weight.

キ

気(き) spirit; a mind; a heart
Ⓐ ～が合(あ)う be like-minded; get along well; Ⓔ be congenial to one; Ⓘ see eye to eye; Ⓒ Ⓘ hit it off. ～が焦(あせ)る be impatient. ～が荒(あら)い be quarrelsome; be ill-tempered. ～が改(あらた)まる be braced up; feel renewed; feel refreshed. ～がある have a mind to; be interested in; be ready to (take sth up). ～が良(い)い be good-natured; be generous. ～が行(い)く be attentive. Ⓒ ～が痛(いた)む ❶ fret over sth; worry about sth. ❷ feel inferior; feel small. ～が入(い)る ❶ fret over sth; worry about sth. ❷ be impassioned;

be full of emotion. ⓒ ～が煎(い)れる be anxious; be nervous; be upset; be nettled. ～が飢(う)える ❶ be dejected; feel depressed; ⓒ feel blue. ❷ feel frustrated; be discouraged; become fed up with *sth*; grow weary of *sth*. ～が多(おお)い ❶ be fickle; be flighty. ❷ be inconstant; be unfaithful. ～が大(おお)きい be broad-minded; be large-hearted; be generous. ～が後(おく)れる lose one's nerve; be daunted by; become diffident. ～が置(お)ける feel ill at ease. ⓒ ～が落(お)つ be disappointed; feel discouraged; be dejected; lose heart; lose courage. ～が重(おも)い be downcast; be in low spirits. ～が折(お)れる be discouraged; lose heart. ～が勝(か)つ be strong-willed; be opinionated; ⓢ be hard-nosed. ～が軽(かる)い be cheerful; be sociable; be easy to get on with. ～が変(か)わる change one's mind; have a change of heart. ～が利(き)く ❶ be clever; be sensible. ❷ be tactful; be thoughtful; be smart; ⓢ ⓒ be on the ball. ❸ be chic; be fashionable; ⓒ be hip; ⓢ be cool. ～が腐(くさ)る ❶ be dejected; feel depressed; ⓒ feel blue. ❷ feel frustrated; be discouraged; become fed up with *sth*; grow weary of *sth*. ～が挫(くじ)ける be discouraged; lose heart. ～が狂(くる)う lose one's mind; go mad; ⓢ go crazy; ⓢ ⓒ lose one's marbles.

～が冴(さ)える be cheerful; have a sunny disposition. ～が差(さ)す feel guilty; ⓒ feel the pricks of conscience. ～が静(しず)まる calm down; settle down; ⓒ regain one's composure. ～が沈(しず)む be depressed; be in low spirits; feel gloomy. ～が進(すす)む feel like doing *sth*; be in the mood (to do *sth*); ⓒ be in the right frame of mind. ～が済(す)む be satisfied; be appeased; feel content. ～がする get a certain notion; feel as if; believe that. ～が座(すわ)る feel relieved; be at ease. ～が急(せ)く be impatient; be anxious; be in a hurry; be eager; ⓒ chafe at the bit. ～が殺(そ)がれる lose enthusiasm; be dampened in spirit. ～が外(そ)れる be distracted; fail to pay attention. ～が高(たか)い be high-handed; be haughty. ～が立(た)つ be upset; be agitated; be on edge; be wrought up. ～が小(ちい)さい be timid; be faint-hearted; be cautious. ～が違(ちが)う be out of one's mind; be mad; ⓢ be crazy. ～が散(ち)る be distracted; lose one's concentration; ⓒ lose it. ～が支(つか)える be distraught; be dejected; feel depressed. ～が尽(つ)きる ❶ lose spirit; run out of energy; ⓒ become enervated; ⓒ lose one's zest for life. ❷ be bored; feel weary. ❸ feel wretched; be out of sorts. ～が付(つ)く ❶ notice *sth*; be aware of *sth*; dawn on one. ❷ be attentive; thoughtful; be considerate. ❸ regain consciousness; Ⓒ come to; Ⓘ come round. 〜が詰(つ)まる feel oppressed; feel uncomfortable; be ill at ease. 〜が強(つよ)い be bold; be daring; be strong-willed. 〜が出(で)る feel like doing *sth*; be in the mood (to do *sth*); Ⓔ be in the right frame of mind. 〜が通(とお)る be worldly-wise; know the world; be street-wise. 〜が咎(とが)める have a guilty conscience; feel guilty; be sorry. 〜が閉(と)じる be depressed; be gloomy; feel dejected; be cast down; be in low spirits; Ⓒ Ⓘ have the blues. 〜が直(なお)る recover one's spirit. 〜が長(なが)い be patient; be self-composed; Ⓒ be laid-back. 〜が抜(ぬ)ける ❶ lose consciousness; pass out; Ⓒ black out. ❷ be let down; be frustrated. ❸ lose flavor; go flat; go stale. 〜が練(ね)れる have a good temper; be gentle; be patient. 〜が上(のぼ)る ❶ have a rush of blood to the head; feel dizzy. ❷ go mad; lose one's senses; Ⓢ Ⓘ lose one's marbles. 〜が乗(の)る take interest in *sth*; be excited by *sth*; Ⓢ Ⓘ be on a roll. 〜が入(はい)る get into *sth*; put one's mind to *sth*. 〜が弾(はず)む be in high spirits; get excited; have a light heart; be merry. 〜が早(はや)い ❶ be hasty; be rash. ❷ have a quick temper; be short-tem-

pered. 〜が逸(はや)る be hasty; be impatient; be rash. 〜が張(は)り詰(つ)める be on the alert; Ⓘ be on tenterhooks. 〜が張(は)る strain one's nerves; be tense; be under stress; be anxious. 〜が晴(は)れる feel relieved; be cheered up. 〜が引(ひ)き締(し)める feel bolstered (by *sth*). 〜が引(ひ)ける feel timorous; feel inferior; feel small; be ashamed. Ⓒ 〜が開(ひら)く feel relieved; become merry; become cheerful. 〜が広(ひろ)い be calm; be laid-back. 〜が鬱(ふさ)ぐ feel depressed; be low-spirited; be low. 〜が触(ふ)れる ❶ go mad; lose one's senses; Ⓢ Ⓘ lose one's marbles. ❷ be torn by conflicting emotions; be swayed. Ⓒ 〜が減(へ)る be mentally fatigued; suffer from nervous strain; feel worn down. Ⓒ 〜が細(ほそ)い be timid; be faint-hearted; be cautious. 〜が紛(まぎ)れる be diverted (from one's worries); be (pleasantly) distracted. 〜が回(まわ)る ❶ be attentive; be thoughtful; be considerate. ❷ suspect *sb* without reason; expect the worst; be prejudiced. 〜が短(みじか)い have a quick temper; be short-tempered. 〜が向(む)く be inclined to do *sth*; feel like doing *sth*; be in the mood (to do *sth*). Ⓒ 〜が結(むす)ぼれる become depressed; fall into a depression; become cast down. 〜が滅入(めい)る lose courage; be dispirited; be downhearted. ◎ 〜が戻る lose interest (in doing sth); change one's mind; ◎ ① be turned off. 〜が揉める be anxious; be nervous; ① wring one's hands. 〜が休まる feel relieved; feel at ease. 〜が和らぐ relent toward sb. ⓥ ③ 〜に行く have an orgasm. 〜が緩む slacken one's attention; ① drop one's guard; let up. 〜が良い ❶ feel good; be in good spirits. ❷ be good-natured; have a friendly disposition. 〜が弱い be faint-hearted; be weak-kneed; be timid. 〜が弱る lose spirit; run out of energy; ⓒ become enervated; ⓔ lose one's zest for life. 〜が若い be young at heart.

A. 〜で食う ❶ get a hold on oneself; control oneself. ❷ endure sth; put up with sth. ❸ persevere in sth; be patient.

N ◎ 〜に合う suit one's taste; take one's fancy; like sb/sth. ◎ 〜に当たる be offended; feel hurt. ◎ 〜に当てる offend sb; hurt sb's feelings. 〜に入る ❶ suit one's taste; take one's fancy; like sb/sth. ❷ humor sb; ingratiate oneself with sb; ① curry favor with sb. 〜に掛かる ① weigh on one's mind; feel uneasy about sth; be anxious about sth; be bothered by sth. 〜に掛ける ❶ have sth on one's mind; fret over sth; worry about sth. ❷ be haunted by sth. に適う suit one's taste. 〜に障る ❶ have sth on one's mind; fret over sth; worry about sth. ❷ be displeased about sth; be irritated by sth; be irked by sth; ◎ ① be rubbed the wrong way. ⓐ 〜に逆う go against sb's feelings; hurt sb's feelings. 〜に障る be offended; feel hurt. 〜に済む ❶ feel refreshed. ❷ be satisfied; be appeased. 〜にする be bothered by sth; make an issue of sth; ◎ let sth get to one. 〜に染む suit one's taste; take one's fancy; like sb/sth. ⓐ 〜に違う be displeased; feel hurt; be put out of humor. 〜に留まる be concerned about sth; take notice of sth; draw one's attention. 〜に留める keep sth in mind; bear sth in mind. 〜になる ❶ care about; be concerned about; worry about. ❷ be in the mood (to do sth); feel like doing. ❸ feel as if; feel that. ⓐ 〜に向く suit one's taste; please one's fancy. 〜に持つ ① weigh on one's mind. 〜に病む worry deeply about sth; be worried sick; fret incessantly over sth.

ヲ 〜を痛める fret over sth; worry about sth. 〜を入れる ❶ care about sth; make an issue of. ❷ be impatient; be eager to do sth. ❸ apply oneself to sth; do sth in earnest;

ⓘ put one's heart into *sth*. 〜を失う ❶ lose interest; be discouraged; ⓒ ⓘ be turned off. ❷ lose consciousness; faint; pass out; ⓒ black out. ⓞ 〜を打つ ❶ become depressed; fall into a depression. ❷ be shocked; be frightened; be startled. 〜を移す ❶ change one's mind. ❷ direct one's attention towards. 〜を奪われる be absorbed in *sth*; be engrossed in *sth*. ⓐ 〜を得る recover one's spirit; take heart; ⓢ buck up. ⓐ 〜を負う be eager; ⓘ be on one's mettle (for success). ⓞ 〜を置く ❶ respect *sb*'s feelings. ❷ feel relieved; be at ease. 〜を落ち着ける calm down; settle down; ⓒ regain one's composure. 〜を落とす be discouraged; be disappointed; lose heart. 〜を変える change one's mind. 〜を兼ねる ❶ feel hesitant; have scruples about (doing *sth*); hold back; shy away from. ❷ have regard for *sb*'s feelings; show constraint toward *sb*. 〜を利かす have the sense to (do *sth*); be considerate; ⓢ ⓘ use one's loaf. 〜を食う ❶ get a hold on oneself; control oneself. ❷ endure *sth*; put up with *sth*. ❸ persevere in *sth*; be patient. 〜を腐らす be dejected; feel depressed; feel frustrated; lose courage. 〜を挫く be discouraged; lose heart. 〜を砕く fret over *sth*; worry over *sth*; ⓒ ⓘ rack one's brains. ⓐ 〜を下す behave oneself; act as one should. ⓐ 〜を屈す be daunted; give in; cave in. 〜を配る pay attention; be attentive; ⓘ be on one's guard. 〜を狂わせる drive *sb* mad. 〜を込める do *sth* with devotion. ⓒ 〜を懲らす ❶ have had enough of; ⓒ be fed up with *sb*. ❷ take pains over; make strenuous efforts. ❸ be worried by *sth*; ⓒ ⓘ rack one's brains. 〜を静める ease one's mind; calm down; ⓒ get a hold on oneself. 〜を殺ぐ discourage *sb*; dampen *sb*'s enthusiasm. 〜をそそる arouse one's interest; be aroused by *sth*; ⓢ ⓘ push *sb*'s buttons. ⓒ 〜を背く offend *sb*'s feelings. 〜を逸らす ❶ be distracted; lose concentration. ❷ divert *sb*'s attention; distract *sb*. 〜を揃える pull together. 〜を損ずる ❶ hurt *sb*'s feelings. ❷ be disheartened. ⓐ 〜を嗜む be determined to do; firmly resolve to do; be fully resigned (to one's fate). ⓐ 〜を出す be full of vigor. ⓐ 〜を扶ける put *sb* on his/her mettle. 〜を通ず have the same mind; be in agreement. 〜を遣う ❶ care about *sb*; worry about *sb*; take care of *sb*; look after *sb*. ❷ pay attention to *sth*; be mindful of *sth*. ⓐ 〜を尽かす put one's heart and

79

soul into *sth*; devote all one's energy to *sth*. ⓐ 〜を尽くす ❶ exert oneself; apply oneself to *sth*. ❷ be mentally fatigued. 〜を付ける ❶ pay attention to *sth*; be mindful of *sth*. ❷ get active; be enlivened. ❸ bring *sb* round. ❹ liven *sth* up; give *sth* a boost. 〜を詰める strain one's nerves. ⓐ 〜を通す have the sense to (do *sth*). 〜を留める pay particular attention to. 〜を取られる be diverted with *sth*; forget oneself in *sth*; lose oneself in *sth*. 〜を取り直す collect oneself; ⓒ pull oneself together. ⓒ 〜を取る humor *sb*; flatter *sb*; try to please *sb*; ⓒ curry favor with *sb*. 〜を直す recover one's mental strength; ⓐ bounce back. 〜を抜く ❶ relax the tension; become unconcerned about *sth*; ⓒ let up. ❷ startle *sb*; frighten *sb*. ⓐ 〜を上す ❶ have a rush of blood to the head; feel dizzy. ❷ get excited; be worked up (over *sth*). 〜を呑まれる be overwhelmed; be taken aback. 〜を吐く ❶ make a good showing; do a good job; outdo oneself. ❷ brim with confidence; be in high spirits. 〜を励ます rouse oneself to action. 〜を晴らす cheer oneself up; take one's mind off *sth*; divert oneself (pleasantly). 〜を張り詰める be on edge; be nervous; ⓒ be on tenterhooks. 〜を張る ❶ pay attention to; be watchful; be on the lookout. ❷ exert oneself; make an effort. 〜を引き締める pluck up courage; brace oneself; ⓒ pull oneself together. 〜を引き立てる ❶ pluck up courage; brace oneself; ⓒ pull oneself together. ❷ encourage *sb*; cheer *sb* up; ⓢ buck *sb* up. 〜を引く rouse *sb*'s excitement; seek *sb's* attention. ⓐ 〜を触る ❶ be offended; take offense. ❷ turn one's attention to *sth* else; be diverted by *sth*. 〜を紛らす divert one's attention; take one's mind off *sth*. 〜を回す be suspicious; read too much into (a situation); ⓒ read between the lines. ⓒ 〜を迎える humor *sb*. 〜を持たす ❶ encourage *sb*; embolden *sb*; ❷ raise *sb's* hopes; ⓒ lead *sb* on. 〜を揉む be anxious about *sth*; fret over *sth*; worry about *sth*; ⓒ fidget about *sth*. 〜を養う nurse one's spirit; feel refreshed. 〜を休める take a rest; ⓢ kick back. 〜を病む worry deeply about *sth*; be worried sick; fret incessantly over *sth*. ⓐ 〜を遣る ❶ be in the mood (to do *sth*); feel like doing. ⓥ ⓢ ❷ have an orgasm. 〜を許す ❶ relax one's attention; ⓒ drop one's guard; ⓒ let one's guard down. ❷ let *sb* into one's heart; open up to *sb*. 〜を緩める relax one's attention; ⓓ drop one's guard; ⓔ unbend one's mind.

機 ⓔ an opportunity; a chance

[A] ⓔ 〜が熟す the time ripens. [N] ⓔ 〜に応ずる act in accordance with circumstances; take the proper steps to meet the situation. ⓔ 〜に乗じる seize an opportunity. ⓔ 〜に投ずる take advantage of a situation; capitalize on an opportunity. ⓔ 〜に乗る take advantage of a situation; capitalize on a opportunity. ⓔ ⓔ 〜に触れる be fortunate; be lucky; ⓒ ⓓ hit good luck. [を] ⓔ 〜を逸する let a chance slip by; miss an opportunity. ⓔ 〜を失う lose an opportunity; let a chance slip by. ⓒ 〜を待つ wait until the time is ripe; wait for an opportunity; ⓔ bide one's time. ⓔ 〜を見る seize an opportunity; look for an opportunity.

奇 ⓔ strangeness; oddity

[を] ⓔ 〜を争う compete with each other in novelty; try to outdo each other in eccentricity. ⓔ 〜を好む be eccentric. ⓔ 〜を衒う affect eccentricity.

気合い a yell; a shout; spirit

[A] 〜が入る be spirited.

[N] ⓐ 〜に当たる worry about. ⓐ 〜に構う ❶ be offended. ❷ fall ill. [を] 〜を入れる ❶ show courage; display spirit. ❷ inflict corporal punishment; punish sb. ❸ reprimand sb; ⓒ tell sb off; ⓓ haul sb over the coals. 〜を掛ける spur sb on; encourage sb; yell at sb.

気受け popularity; reception

[A] 〜が良い be popular; be well recieved; ⓓ be in sb's good books. 〜が悪い be unpopular; be badly recieved; ⓓ be in sb's bad books.

気炎 high spirits; big talk

[A] 〜が上がる be in high spirits. [を] 〜を上げる ❶ argue heatedly in favor/against sth; debate sth hotly. ❷ brag about sth; boast about sth; ⓓ talk big; ⓓ blow one's own horn. 〜を吐く ❶ argue heatedly in favor/against sth; debate sth hotly. ❷ brag about sth; boast about sth; ⓓ talk big; ⓓ blow one's own horn.

記憶 memory; recollection

[A] 〜が良い have a good memory. 〜が悪い have a poor memory. [N] 〜に留める register sth in one's memory. [を] 〜を失う lose one's memory. 〜を辿る retrace one's memory. を取り戻

す regain one's memory. 〜を呼び起こす call *sth* to mind. 〜を呼び戻す recall *sth*; call *sth* to mind.

気後れ "belated spirit"

[A] 〜がする lose one's nerve; back down; ⓘ get cold feet.

機会 an opportunity; a chance

[を] 〜を与える give *sb* a chance. 〜を免する miss an opportunity; let a chance slip by. 〜を窺う look for an occasion (to do *sth*). 〜を得る find an opportunity; get a chance. 〜を捕える seize an opportunity; ⓒ grab one's chances. 〜を狙う look for an opportunity. 〜を逃す miss an opportunity; let a chance slip by. 〜を見逃す overlook an opportunity; fail to spot an opportunity. 〜を待つ wait for an opportunity. 〜を持つ have an opportunity.

危害 an injury; harm; danger

[を] 〜を受ける sustain an injury. 〜を加える inflict an injury on *sb*. 〜を免れる escape unhurt; ⓒ ⓘ save one's skin.

危機 a crisis; a critical moment

[A] 〜が去る a crisis passes. 〜が迫る a crisis approaches; danger is imminent. [N] 〜に襲われる be caught in a crisis; ⓒ ⓘ be up the creek. 〜に陥る be plunged into a crisis; ⓘ be in deep waters. 〜に陥れる bring to a crisis; bring a crisis to a head. 〜に備える prepare for a crises; provide against emergencies. 〜に達する reach a crisis; come to a head. 〜に臨む face a crisis. [を] 〜を切り抜ける get through a crisis; see one's way out of a crisis; ⓘ weather the storm. ⓔ 〜を脱する pass through a crisis. ⓒ 〜を孕む be fraught with danger.

忌諱 offense; humbrage

[N] 〜に触れる give offence to *sb*; incur *sb's* displeasure; cause *sb* to take humbrage.

聞き耳 attentive ears

[を] 〜を立てる strain one's ears; ⓘ be all ears. ⓒ 〜を潰す turn a deaf ear.

危険 danger; peril; a hazard

[A] 〜が迫る be in danger. 〜が伴う be fraught with danger. [N] 〜に陥る fall into danger; get in harm's way; ⓘ be in deep waters. 〜に曝す expose oneself/*sb* to danger; put oneself/*sb* in harm's way. 〜に臨む face danger.

キケン　　　　　　　　　　　　　　　　　　　　　　　　　　キセキ

を ～を冒す brave danger; run a risk; take a chance. ～を避ける avoid danger; keep out of harm's way. ～を救う save sb from danger. ～を免れる escape from danger; keep out of harm's way. ～を招く court danger.

機嫌 humor; a mood

A ～が良い be in good humor; be in a good mood. ～が直る regain one's good humor; recover one's temper. ～が悪い be displeased; be out of humor; be in a bad temper.
を ～を取る flatter sb; humor sb; ⓘ curry favor with sb; ⓘ find sb's soft side. ～を損ねる offend sb. ～を直す regain one's good humor; recover one's temper.

技巧 art; craftsmanship; artifice

を ～を懲らす employ one's skill. ～を用いる use art. ⓒ ～を弄する resort to artifice; use a trick.

旗幟 ⓔ a flag; a banner

を ⓒ ～を鮮明する make one's position clear; take a clear stand.

記事 a (news) story; an article

を ～を送る send in a story; submit an article. ～を書く write an article. ～を差し止める ban an article. ～を取る get a story; get copy. ～を載せる carry a story.

傷 an injury; a wound; a scar

A ～がつく get hurt; be injured.
を ～を受ける receive a wound; ⓒ sustain an injury. ～を負う be wounded; ⓒ sustain an injury. ～をつける wound sb; inflict a wound. Ⓐ ～を求む look for sb's weak points; ⓒ find sb's Achilles heel.

瑕 a scratch; a crack; a flaw

A ～がつく be damaged; be scratched; be marred; be spoiled.
を ～をつける damage sth; mar sth.

気勢 spirit; ardor; enthusiasm

A ～が上がる be in high spirits; be elated.
を ～を上げる raise sb's spirit; drum up opposition. ～を示す display nerve; show spirit. ～を添える inspire sb; give sb moral support. ～を殺ぐ dampen sb's spirit. ～を増す be inspired; gain strength.

犠牲 self-sacrifice; sacrifice

を ～を払う make a sacrifice; pay dearly for sth.

奇蹟 a miracle; a wonder

を ～を現わす achieve a miracle. ～

を行う perform a miracle; work wonders.

鬼籍 Ⓔ the register of Hades

Ⓝ Ⓒ ～に入る pass away; be numbered among the dead; Ⓘ pass over to the majority.

機先 beforehand

Ⓦ ～を制する be the first to movel take the initiative; get a headstart on *sb*; Ⓘ beat *sb* to it; Ⓘ get the drop on *sb*.

偽善 hypocrisy

Ⓦ ～を行なう play the hypocrite.

基礎 the foundation; the basis

Ⓝ ～に有る lie at the base of *sth*; be at the root (of a problem). Ⓦ ～を固める strengthen the basis; consolidate the foundation. ～を築く ❶ Ⓒ lay a foundation (for a house). ❷ Ⓐ lay the basis for *sth*; pave the way for *sth*. ～を作る ❶ Ⓒ lay a foundation (for a house). ❷ Ⓐ lay the basis for *sth*; pave the way for *sth*.

規則 rules; a regulations; law

Ⓝ ～に訴える appeal to law. ～に拘泥する adhere to regulations. ～に反する go against regulations. ～に

よる be according to regulations. Ⓐ ～で縛られる be bound by regulations. ～で縛る tie *sb* down by rules. Ⓦ ～を定める lay down the rules; establish regulations; set the rules. ～を外れる deviate from the rules. ～を守る observe regulations. ～を設ける establish regulations; lay down rules. ～を破る flout the rules; violate regulations; break the law.

驥足 Ⓔ genius; great talent

Ⓦ ～を伸ぶ give full reign to one's talents; show one's full ability.

期待 expectation; anticipation

Ⓝ ～に添う meet one's/*sb's* expectations. Ⓦ ～を抱く harbor expectations. ～を裏切る betray one's/*sb's* expectations. ～を掛ける rely upon *sb*; put confidence in *sb/sth*; give credence to *sb/sth*; Ⓒ repose trust in *sb/sth*.

吉兆 Ⓔ an auspicious omen

Ⓦ Ⓒ ～を示す be auspicious; be of good omen; augur well.

狐 a fox; a vixen

Ⓐ ～が落ちる come to one's senses; extricate oneself from a spell. ～につ

ままれる be baffled; be flabbergasted; ⑤ ⓘ be blown away.
[を] ～を落とす bring sb to their senses; release sb from a spell.

気褄 a mood; humor
[を] ～を合わす ❶ please sb; humor sb. ❷ flatter sb; ingratiate oneself with sb; ⓘ curry favor with sb.

轡 a bit
[を] ～を並べる ride abreast; ride side by side. ～を嵌める offer a bribe; bribe sb; ⓘ grease sb's palm; ⓘ shut sb up.

規定 stipulations; provisions
[N] ～に従う be in conformity with regulations; observe the rules; comply with stipulations; ⓘ fall into line. ～に反する go against regulations; be in contravention of the rules.
[を] ～を設ける make provisions for; lay down the rules. ～を作る make provisions for; lay down the rules. ～を破る violate stipulations; infringe the rules.

機転 quick-wittedness; tact
[A] ～が利く be quick-witted; be sharp; ⓘ have one's wits about one.
[を] ～を利かせる use one's head;

ⓘ use one's loaf; be sensible; be discreet; use tact.

軌道 an orbit; a track; a line
[N] ～に乗る ❶ go into orbit; get on track. ❷ get started; launch (a project); ⓒ get going.

危難 E danger; peril; distress
[N] ～に遭う be in danger; face danger; be confronted with danger. ～に曝す expose oneself/sb to danger; put oneself/sb in harm's way; endanger oneself/sb.
[N] ～を免れる escape danger; get out of harms way.

疑念 doubt; suspicion; distrust
[を] ～を抱く have doubts; harbor suspicions; entertain misgivings. ～を起こさせる raise doubts; arouse suspicion. ～を解く dispel doubts; clear oneself/sb of suspicion. ～を晴らす clear oneself/sb of suspicion; dispel doubts. ～を持つ have doubts; harbor suspicions; entertain misgivings.

気乗り "mounted spirit"
[AJ] ～がする take interest in sth; be excited by sth; be inclined to do sth; ⓘ warm up to (an idea).

牙 a tusk; a fang

[を] ～を返す step back; turn back; retrace one's steps. ⓐ ～を噛む ❶ grind one's teeth; gnaw one's teeth. ❷ be vexed. ⓒ be cross. ～を研ぐ ❶ sharpen one's fangs. ❷ prepare for battle; ⓘ gird up one's loins; ⓘ clear the decks. ❸ have an eye on sb/sth; look envious at sb/sth; cast covetous eyes on sth. ❹ watch vigilantly for (a chance); scheme against sb. ⓒ ～を鳴らす ❶ show one's fangs; bare one's teeth. ❷ grind one's teeth; gnaw one's teeth. ❸ snarl at sb; be blunt with sb. ～を抜く defang (an animal). ～を剥く snarl at sb; be blunt with sb. ～を廻らす step back; turn back; retrace one's steps.

機微 Ⓔ niceties; inner workings

[N] ～に触る touch on the niceties of sth. ～に通じる have a keen insight into the inner workings of sth; understand the niceties of sth. [を] ～を穿つ reveal the niceties of sth; penetrate the inner workings of sth. ～を開く uncover the inner workings of sth.

驥尾 Ⓔ the tail of a fine horse

[N] ⓒ ～に付す ❶ follow suit; follow sb's lead; follow sb's (splendid) example; emulate (one's master). ❷ serve sb; be in a subordinate position; ⓘ play second fiddle to sb.

踵 Ⓔ the heel ▶ 踵 ▶ 踵

[を] ⓒ ～を返す go back; retrace one's steps. ⓒ ～を接する follow sb heel after heel; ⓘ breathe down sb's neck. ⓒ ～を巡らす go back; retrace one's steps.

詭弁 sophistry; sophism

[を] ⓒ ～を弄する use sophistry; ⓒ ⓘ chop logic (with sb).

希望 hope; a wish; aspiration

[N] ～に生きる live on hope. ～に応じる meet sb's wishes. ～に反する go against one's wishes. ～に満ちる be full of hope. ～に目覚める find renewed hope.
[を] ～を失う lose hope. ～を叶える fulfill one's hopes. ～を挫く stifle one's hopes; crush one's hopes. ～を捨てる give up hope; abandon one's hopes. ～を達する realize one's wishes. ～を繋ぐ hinge one's hopes (on sth); ⓒ pin one's hopes (on sth). ～を取り戻す restore hope in sth; reassure sb. ～を述べる express one's hopes. ～を吹き込む infuse sb with hope. ～を持つ have hope; cherish an aspiration.

き ぼね
気骨 "mind and bones"
[A] 〜が折れる be a great burden on one's mind and body; be wearisome; cause one great distress.

き まえ
気前 generosity; liberality
[A] 〜が良い be generous; ⓘ have an open hand.
[を] 〜を見せる display one's generosity; act generously.

き
決まり settlement; arrangement
[A] 〜がつく be settled; be arranged; be brought to a conclusion; come to an arrangement. 〜が悪い be embarrassed by sth; feel awkward about sth; be ashamed.
[を] 〜を付ける settle sth; bring sth to a conclusion; set things straight.

き みゃく
気脈 ⓔ a connection; coherence
[を] ⓒ 〜を通じる collude with sb; conspire with sb; share a secret; have a tacit understanding; be in secret communication with sb.

ぎ む
義務 duty; an obligation
[A] 〜が有る have a duty; be obliged; ⓒ be bound in duty.
[を] 〜を感じる have a sense of duty; feel an obligation. 〜を尽くす do one's duty; ⓒ discharge one's duty; ⓒ honor one's obligations. 〜を怠る neglect one's duties; shirk one's responsibilities. 〜を果たす do one's duty; ⓒ discharge one's duty; ⓒ honor one's obligations.

き め
木目 (skin) texture; grain
[A] 〜が荒い be course; have a rough (skin) texture. 〜が細かい ❶ be fine-grained; have a smoothe (skin) texture. ❷ be carefully done; be well-considered; be thought-through.

きも
肝 the liver; courage; pluck
[A] ⓒ 〜が煎れる feel vexed; be annoyed; be irritated. 〜が大きい be daring; be brave; ⓒ have pluck. 〜が据る ❶ have nerves of steel; be brave; have a lot of pluck. ❷ regain one's presence of mind; ⓒ recover one's composure; ⓘ pull oneself together; ⓘ gather one's wits. 〜が小さい be cowardly; be fainthearted; ⓢ be chicken. 〜が潰れる be terrified; ⓘ be scared out of one's wits; ⓢ be scared stiff. ⓒ 〜が抜ける be terrified; ⓘ be scared out of one's wits; ⓢ be scared stiff. 〜が冷える be struck with terror; ⓘ be scared to death. ⓘ break into a cold sweat. 〜が太い have courage; be bold; be brave; ⓒ have guts; ⓒ have pluck. ⓒ 〜が焼ける feel vexed; be annoyed; be irritated.

Ⓝ ～に堪える be shocked; be upset. ～に染みる be deeply impressed; be deeply moved. ～に染む be deeply impressed; be deeply moved. ～に銘ずる be deeply impressed; be brought home to one; ⓔ have sth impressed on one's mind; ⓘ take sth to heart.
Ⓦ ～を煎る ❶ endure great hardships; be upset; be nettled. ❷ become eager; become enthusiastic. ❸ take care of sb; help sb out; give assistance to sb. ～を落とす lose heart; be discouraged; be disheartened. ～を砕く ❶ be on edge; be nervous; ⓘ be on tenterhooks. ❷ ponder on; ⓔ exercise one's ingenuity; work out a plan. ～を消す be terrified; ⓘ be scared out of one's wits; ⓢ be scared stiff. ～を焦がす fret over sth; worry about sth. ～を据える resolve to do sth; make up one's mind. ～を出す show fight; pluck up courage; brace oneself. ～を潰す be terrified; ⓘ be scared out of one's wits; ⓢ be scared stiff. ～を飛ばす be terrified; ⓘ be scared out of one's wits; ⓢ be scared stiff. ～を取られる be terrified; ⓘ be scared out of one's wits; ⓢ be scared stiff. ～を投げ出す show fight; pluck up courage; brace oneself. Ⓐ ～を嘗める ❶ make sacrifices for future success. ❷ have a bitter experience; suffer hardships. ～を抜かす be terrified; ⓘ be scared out of one's wits; ⓢ be scared stiff. ～を拉ぐ be terrified; ⓘ be scared out of one's wits; ⓢ be scared stiff. ～を冷やす be struck with terror; ⓘ be scared to death. Ⓐ ～を焼く fret over sth; worry about sth.

きもごころ
肝心 the liver and the heart

Ⓐ ⓐ ～が騒ぐ feel a presentiment; have a sense of foreboding; feel uneasy; ⓔ experience a flutter of heart.
Ⓦ ～を失せる faint for fear. ～を砕く ❶ take pains over sth; make strenuous efforts. ❷ be worried by sth; ⓒ ⓘ rack one's brains. ❸ be terrified; ⓘ be scared out of one's wits; ⓢ be scared stiff. Ⓐ ～を惑わす be confused by; be deluded by sb/sth.

きも ち
気持ち feeling; mood; sensation

Ⓐ ～が良い feel good; feel comfortable. ～が悪い feel sick; feel uncomfortable; ⓘ give one the creeps.
Ⓝ ～になる feel good; feel at ease.
Ⓦ ～を抑える suppress one's feelings. ～を落ち着かせる compose oneself. ～を害される be hurt; be offended. ～を隠す hide one's feelings. ～を汲む consider sb's feel-

ings; take sb's feelings into consideration. ～を込(こ)める put more feelings into sth. ～を撮(と)り直(なお)す pull oneself together.

疑問(ぎもん) doubt; a question; a query

を ～を抱(いだ)く be wary of sb/sth; have doubts; be skeptical. ～を挟(はさ)む be wary of sb/sth; have doubts; be skeptical.

脚光(きゃっこう) the footlights; floats

N ～を浴(あ)びる be in the limelight; be in the spotlight; be performed; be put on stage; be staged.

急(きゅう) urgency; an emergency

N ～に応(おう)じる meet an urgent need. ～に赴(おもむ)く respond to an emergency; meet a crisis. ～に備(そな)える provide against an emergency. ～に止(と)まる stop short.
を ～を救(すく)う help sb in distress; help sb out of danger. ～を告(つ)げる ❶ give a distress signal; raise the alarm. ❷ become critical; grow threatening; be urgent. ～を要(よう)する demand immediate attention; be pressing.

灸(きゅう) moxibustion; moxa cautery

を ～を据(す)える burn moxa on sb's skin; cauterize the skin with moxa; give sb a moxy treatment.

笈(きゅう) a wicker suitcase

を Ⓐ ～を負(お)う go away from home to study; study abroad.

久闊(きゅうかつ) (one's) long silence

を Ⓒ ～を叙(じょ)する appologize for one's long silence.

旧歓(きゅうかん) former happyness

を ～を暖(あたた)める restore one former happyness; ① go back to the good old days.

旧観(きゅうかん) the former appearance

を Ⓒ ～を取(と)り戻(もど)す return to its former appearance.

牛耳(ぎゅうじ) the ears of an ox

を Ⓓ Ⓔ ～を取(と)る take the lead; head a group.

急所(きゅうしょ) a vital spot; the vitals

を ～を蹴(け)る kick sb in the groin. ～を逸(そ)れる miss the vital parts. ～を掴(つか)む grasp the crux (of a matter); get it right; ① be on the mark; Ⓒ ① get the point. ～を突(つ)く ❶ hit sb in the vitals; ① go for the jugular. ❷ hit sb where it hurts; ① touch sb on the raw. ❸ guess right; ① be on the mark; ① hit the nail on the head. ～を握(にぎ)る have a hold over sb. ～を外(はず)れる fail to understand the crux (of a matter); get it wrong; ⓘ be off the mark; ⓘ miss the point. ⓒ ～を遣る hit *sb* in the vitals; ⓘ go for the jugular.

きゅうじょう
旧情 回 former friendship
を ⓒ ～を温める renew one's former friendship; ⓒ restore a jaded friendship.

きゅうち
窮地 回 a predicament
N ⓒ ～に在る be in a sad plight; be in a quandary. ⓒ ～に追い込む drive *sb* into a corner; corner *sb*. ⓒ ～に陥る be driven into a corner; ⓒ ⓘ get into a scrap; ⓒ ⓘ be up the creek.
を ⓒ ～へ追い込む drive *sb* into a corner; corner *sb*.
を ⓒ ～を訴える complain of one's sad plight; ⓒ lament one's predicament. ⓒ ～を察する empathize with *sb's* predicament. ⓒ ～を救う help *sb* out of a predicament. ～を打開する resolve a predicament. ⓒ ～を脱する get out of a predicament; ⓘ weather the storm.

きゅうとう
旧套 回 a conventionalism
を ⓒ ～を脱する be free from conventionalism; be unconventional. ⓒ ～を守る be conventional; ⓘ fall in the old grooves.

きゅうり
旧離 回 disinheritance; disowning
を ⓒ ～を切る ❶ be disinherited; be disowned; ⓘ be cut off with a shilling. ⓘ ❷ be exiled; be cast out; be excommunicated.

きょ
居 回 a dwelling; a house
を ～を移す move house; change residence. ⓒ ～を構える make (a place) one's home; settle somewhere. ⓒ take up residence. ⓒ ～を卜する make (a place) one's home (having consulted a fortune teller); settle somewhere; ⓒ take up residence.

きょ
虚 回 emptiness; hollowness
N ⓒ ～に乗じる take advantage of an unguarded moment; catch *sb* off guard.
を ～を突かれる be caught off guard. ～を衝く catch *sb* off guard; take (the enemy) unawares.

きょ
炬 回 a bonfire; a torch
N ⓒ ～に付す put *sth* on the fire; throw *sth* onto the fire; torch *sth*; relinquish *sth* to the flames.

きょ
拳 回 a plan; a project; a scheme
N ⓒ ～に出る act upon a plan; put a plan into action.

きょう
興 interest; fun; amusement

[A] ～がある be interesting; ⓒ be fun. ～が醒める interest fades; the mood is dampened. ～が乗る become interested; be excited.

[N] ～に入る be absorbed in *sth*; ⓒ get in the mood (for *sth*). ～に乗ずる be driven by curiosity. ～に乗る be driven by curiosity.

[を] ⓐ ～を栄す arouse *sb's* interest; ⓢ ⓘ push *sb's* buttons. ～を醒ます spoil the fun; dampen the mood. ～を添える add to the merriment. ～をそそる arouse *sb's* interest; ⓢ ⓘ push *sb's* buttons. ⓒ ～を尽きる enjoy oneself; ⓒ have fun.

きょう
凶 misfortune; bad luck

[N] ～に乗る abuse *sb's* misfortune; exploit *sb's* weak position.

きょうおく
胸臆 one's own mind

[を] ～を行なう do as one pleases; do as one sees fit; carry through one's ideas; realize one's ideas.

きょうかん
共感 sympathy; empathy

[を] ～を得る gain *sb's* sympathy. ～を覚える feel sympathy for *sb*. ～を呼ぶ excite *sb's* sympathy.

きょうきん
胸襟 [E] the heart; the soul

[を] ⓒ ～を開く open oneself up to *sb*; take *sb* into one's confidence; ⓘ pour out one's heart to *sb*; ⓒ unbosom oneself.

ぎょうぎ
行儀 manners; deportment

[A] ～が良い be well-behaved; have good manners; be well-mannered. ～が悪い be ill-behaved; have bad manners be bad-mannered.

[を] ～を見習う learn good manners.

きょうくん
教訓 a (moral) lesson

[を] ～を与える give *sb* a lesson. ～を得る learn a lesson from (an experience). ～を織り込む attach a moral to (a story). ～を引き出す draw a lesson from (an experience).

きょうげん
狂言 a drama; a play

[を] ～を書く ❶ ⓒ write a play. ❷ hatch a plot; set out to deceive *sb*; spread a rumor; ⓘ frame *sb*; ⓘ set *sb* up. ～を懸ける hatch a plot; set out to deceive *sb*; spread a rumor; ⓘ frame *sb*; ⓘ set *sb* up. ～を残す have doubts; harbor suspicions; entertain misgivings.

きょうしゅう
郷愁 homesickness; nostalgia

[N] ～に駆られる feel homesick; ⓒ be stricken by homesickness. ～に耽る be given to nostalgia; pine for home.

キョウショウ / キョシュウ

を ～を感じる feel homesick; long for home.

きょうだん
教壇 a platform

N ～に立つ take the platform to teach; be a teacher.

を ～を追われる be removed from one's teaching post.

きょうちゅう
胸中 one's bosom; one's heart

N ～に浮かぶ enter one's mind; spring to mind; occur to one. ～に秘める keep sth to oneself.

を ～を明かす open oneself up to sb; take sb into one's confidence; ⓐ pour out one's heart to sb; ⓒ unbosom oneself. ～を察する sympathize with sb; empathize with sb; feel for sb.

きょうふ
恐怖 fear; terror; angst

A ～で死ぬ die from fear.

N ～に襲われる be seized with fear; be struck with terror. ～に戦く tremble with fear; give a shudder; be terrified.

を ～を感じる be afraid of sb/sth; be frightened at sth; be scared.

きょうみ
興味 interest; zest; curiosity

を ～を失う lose interest in sth. ～を起こさせる arouse interest in sth. ～を覚える take an interest in sth. ～

を添える add zest to sth. ～を殺ぐ spoil sb's pleasure; ⓒ spoil the fun. ～を持つ take an interest in sth. ～を養う foster sb's interest in sth.

ぎょうめい
驍名 Ⓔ bravery; heroic fame

を ⓔ ～を馳せる win fame; become a public hero; be known for one's bravery.

きょく
局 a bureau; a department

N ～に当たる take charge; deal with a situation; ⓐ step in.

を ⓒ ～を結ぶ bring sth to a conclusion.

きょくめん
局面 a situation; a phase

A ～が一変する a situation changes; ⓐ the tables are turned; ⓒ be a new ball game.

を ～を改善する improve the situation. ～を打開する bring a deadlock to an end; ⓐ break the ice.

きょせい
虚勢 a bluff; a bold front

を ～を張る make a bluff; ⓐ put on a bold front. ～を挫く ⓒ call sb's bluff.

きょしゅう
去就 one's course of action

N ～に迷う be at a loss (about what to do); ⓐ be at one's wits' end; ⓐ be all at sea.

を ~を誤る take the wrong course of action. ~を決する decide on one's course of action.

挙措 ⓔ carriage; deportment
を ⓒ ~を失う lose one's composure; act rudely; act without decorum; be a boor.

魚腹 a fish stomach
を ⓒ ~に葬せらる be drowned; ⓘ feed the fishes; ⓘ become food for the fishes. ⓒ ~に葬らる be drowned; ⓘ feed the fishes; ⓘ become food for the fishes.

距離 a distance; an interval
Ⓐ ~がある be distant; be different from. ~が開く get a lead on *sb*; lag behind *sb*. ~が勝つ get a lead on *sb*; lag behind *sb*.
を ~を置く leave an interval. ~を保つ keep a distance. ~を詰める catch up on; reduce *sb's* lead. ~を走る run (a certain) distance.

虚礼 ⓔ empty formalities
Ⓝ ⓒ ~に陥る slip into empty formalities; lapse into empty formalities.
を ⓒ ~を廃する do away with empty formalities; dispense with empty formalities.

義理 duty; debt; gratitude
Ⓐ ~が有る be bound by duty. ~が立つ be vindicated; ⓘ save one's face.
Ⓝ ~に欠ける fail in one's duties; ⓒ swerve from the path of duty. ~に絡まれる be bound by duty. ~に迫る be dictated by one's sense of duty. ~に詰まる stand to reason.
を ~を欠く fail in one's duties. ~を立てる do one's duty (by *sb*); be loyal (to *sb*). ~を詰める appeal to *sb's* sense of duty. ~を張る stick to one's duties.

規律 order; discipline; rules
Ⓝ ~に反する violate the rules; go against the rules.
を ~を正す restore discipline; put *sth* in order. ~を守る observe discipline; act according to the rules; ⓘ toe the line. ~を乱す loosen discipline; upset the order. ~を破る break the rules.

記録 a record; a document
Ⓝ ~に載る be recorded; be on record. ~に残す put *sth* on record.
を ~を更新する better one's record; establish a new record. ~を作る make a record. ~を取る keep a record of *sth*; put *sth* on record. ~を破る break a record.

議論 an argument; a discussion

[A] ～で遣り込める corner *sb* in an argument.
[N] ～に勝つ win an argument. ～に負ける lose an argument.
[図] ～を仕掛ける challenge *sb* to an argument. ～を覆す demolish an argument. ～を戦わす take issue with *sb*; ⓒ engage in a battle of words; ⓘ cross swords with *sb*. ～を始める start an argument; get into an argument (with *sb*). ～を申し進める pursue an argument. ～を持ち出す put forward an argument.

疑惑 doubt; suspicion; mistrust

[図] ～を抱く be wary of *sb*/*sth*; have misgivings about *sb*/*sth*. ～を解く clear one's doubts. ～を招く invite suspicion; arouse suspicion.

襟 a collar; a neckband ▶襟

[図] ～を開く ❶ loosen one's colar. ❷ open oneself up to *sb*; take *sb* into one's confidence; ⓘ pour out one's heart to *sb*; ⓒ unbosom oneself.

金看板 a gold-lettered signboard

[図] ～を掛ける ❶ assume an air of importance; make *sth* look more important than it is. ❷ be true to one's name; ⓘ sail under one's true colors.

均衡 equilibrium; balance

[図] ～を失う lose the balance. ～を回復する restore the balance. ～を保つ maintain the equilibrium; keep the balance. ～を取る put *sth* in balance; get the right balance. ～を求める find a balance. ～を破る upset the balance; ⓘ rock the boat.

琴線 the strings of a *koto*

[N] ～に触れる be touched by *sth*; ⓘ tug at one's heartstrings; ⓘ strike a (sympathetic) chord.

巾着 [A] a purse; a money pouch

[図] ～を切る pinch *sb*'s wallet. ⓒ ～を叩く empty one's purse.

緊張 tension; strain

[図] ～を欠く lack seriousness. ～を高める heighten tensions; raise the pressure. ～を解す wind down; ⓒ ⓘ take it easy. ～を緩める ease the tensions; ⓘ break the ice.

金的 the bull's eye

[図] ～を射止める ❶ hit the bull's eye; hit the mark. ❷ have great success; ⓒ ⓘ bring home the bacon.

金星 a win; a victory

[図] ～を挙げる make a win; claim victory; beat the chamion.

ク

苦 pain; hardships; privation

[N] ⓐ ～に掛ける worry about *sth*; fret over *sth*. ～にする ⓘ take *sth* to heart; be anxious about. ～になる ⓘ weigh on one's mind; cause one anxiety. ～に病む ⓘ take *sth* to heart; be anxious about.

愚 folly; stupidity; silliness

[N] ⓐ ～に返る go senile; grow feeble minded; ⓔ fall into one's dotage; ⓢ go gaga. ⓐ ～にする fool *sb*; make a fool of *sb*.
[を] ～を学ぶ follow a foolish example. ⓐ ～を守る play the fool; feign ignorance.

杭 a post; a pile; a stake

[を] ～を立てる put up a post. ～を引き抜く pull out a post. ～を守る be conservative; be unwilling to change; ⓘ be in a rut.

食い物 foodstuffs; provisions

[N] ～にする prey on *sb*; exploit *sb*; live on *sb*; sacrifice *sb*; thrive on (*sb*'s misfortune). ～になる be victimized; fall victim to *sb*.

空 space; emptiness ♦ 空♦ 空

[N] ～に消える vanish into thin air. ～に帰する come to nothing; end in failure; ⓘ go up in smoke.
[を] ～を打つ beat the air; hit empty air. ～を切る cut the air. ～を掴む clutch at thin air; claw the air.

苦役 ⓔ hard toil; drudgery

[N] ⓔ ～に服する serve a sentence; do penance; ⓒ ⓘ do time; ⓢ ⓘ do one's bird.

釘 a nail; a spike

[A] ～が利く be effective. ～が応える be effective; have effect; have the desired result.
[A] ～で打ち付ける nail *sth* down.
[N] ⓐ ～になる be frozen stiff; freeze with cold.
[を] ～を打つ drive in a nail. ～を刺す tell *sb* off beforehand; remind *sb* of *sth*; warn *sb* of *sth*; ⓘ haul *sb* over the coals. ～を抜く pull out a nail; draw out a nail.

苦言 bitter counsel; a bitter pill

[を] ～を浴びる accept *sb's* candid counsel; ⓘ swallow the bitter pill. ～を呈する offer bitter advice; give *sb* candid counsel.

草 grass; weeds; herbs

[を] ～を刈る mow the grass. ～を食

う feed on grass. 〜を取る weed (the garden). Ⓐ 〜を結ぶ ❶ return a favor; repay sb for received favors. ❷ stay at an inn; pass a night on one's journey; sleep rough. ❸ leave roadmarks; point the way.

楔 a wedge; a chock

Ⓣ 〜となる be the tie that binds.
Ⓦ 〜を打ち込む ❶ⓒ drive in a wedge. ❷ drive a wedge between (one's opponents); wedge (two parties) apart. ❸ drive a wedge into the enemy camp; scatter the enemy's troops. ❹ drive one's point home; call sb's attention to sth. 〜を打つ drive in a wedge. 〜を刺す remind sb of sth; call sb's attention to sth; make sure of sth.

籤 a written oracle

Ⓐ 〜が強い be lucky; have luck (in winning lotteries). 〜が弱い be unlucky; have no luck (in winning lotteries).
Ⓐⱽ 〜で決める draw lots; decide by drawing lots.
Ⓝ 〜に当たる win a prize (in a lottery); draw a winning ticket. 〜に外れる fail to win a prize; draw a losing ticket.
Ⓦ 〜を探る draw a written oracle; consult a written oracle. 〜を引く draw a written oracle.

苦汁 Ⓔ a bitter broth

Ⓔ ⓒ 〜を嘗める suffer a bitter experience; have a hard time.

薬 medicine; a drug; a pill

Ⓐ 〜が利く ❶ the medicine works. ❷ have the desired effect on sb; ⓒ come home; ⓒ strike a chord; ⓒ ring a bell.
Ⓝ 〜になる ❶ be medicinal; be good for one's health; be healthy. ❷ be good for one; do one good; be beneficial.
Ⓦ 〜を掛ける glaze (a vase); enamel (a plate). 〜を使う take medicine; be on medication. 〜を付ける apply an ointment. 〜を塗る glaze (a vase); enamel (a plate). 〜を飲む take medicine; swallow a pill.

癖 a habit; a way; a kink; a friz

Ⓐ 〜が有る ❶ have a habit; be in the habit (of doing sth). ❷ have kinks; have frizzy hair. 〜が付く fall into a habit; get into a habit; ⓒ contract a habit.
Ⓝ 〜になる become a habit; be a bad example.
Ⓦ 〜を付ける form a habit. 〜を直す ❶ get out of a habit; ⓒ break oneself of a habit; ⓒⓒ kick the

habit. ❷ iron out a friz; straighten (one's hair).

糞 Ⅳ Ⓢ excrement; feces; shit

[を] Ⓥ Ⓢ 〜をする evacuate the bowels; Ⓔ relieve oneself; Ⓘ go to the powder room; Ⓥ Ⓢ take a shit. Ⓥ Ⓢ 〜を垂れる ❶ be unjust to sb; do sb wrong; be ungrateful; forget one's social obligations. ❷ act dishonestly; be dishonest.

管 a pipe; a tube

[を] 〜 を巻く blather about sb/sth; Ⓒ blurt sth out.

口 the mouth; the lips

[A] 〜が合う understand each other; get on well; agree with each other. 〜が上がる ❶ become eloquent; become a good talker. ❷ lose one's means of living; lose one's livelihood. 〜が開く ❶ have a vacancy; a position is open. ❷ make a beginning. ❸ find a clue; have a key to sth. 〜が旨い be glib-tongued; be fair-spoken; Ⓒ Ⓘ have the gift of the gab. 〜が煩い be much talked about; be notorious. 〜が多い ❶ be talkative; Ⓔ be loquacious; Ⓒ be a chatterbox; Ⓘ talk people's head off. ❷ have many mouths to feed; have a large family to support. 〜が奢る be used to exquisite food; have an expensive taste. 〜が重い be incommunicative; be taciturn; be slow of speech. 〜が堅い be discreet; be tight-lipped; be able to keep a secret. 〜が掛かる be offered a position; be called in; be given a job. 〜が軽い be indiscreet; Ⓐ have a loose tongue. 〜が利く ❶ have a fluent tongue; be eloquent; Ⓒ Ⓘ have the gift of the gab. ❷ be influential; have authority. 〜が利ける be able to speak. 〜が臭い have bad breath. 〜が肥える be a gourmet. 〜が過ぎる go too far in what one says; say too much. 〜が滑る Ⓘ make a slip of the tongue; Ⓘ let sth fall/slip; Ⓒ blurt sth out. 〜が早い Ⓐ have a loose tongue; be loose-lipped. 〜が干上がる lose one's means of living; lose one's livelihood; run out of food; fall on hard times. 〜が殖える have new mouths to feed. 〜が減る ❶ have fewer mouths to feed. ❷ have no reply; be lost for words; Ⓘ throw in the towel. 〜が解れる start to talk; become talkative. 〜が曲がる be extremely bitter (in taste). Ⓐ 〜が脆い Ⓒ have a loose tongue; be loose-lipped. 〜が悪い be foul-mouthed; Ⓐ have a venomous tongue.

[N] 〜に合う suit one's taste; find sth to one's taste. Ⓐ 〜に入る ❶ be lionized; ⓒ ① become the talk of the town. ❷ be edible. ～に掛かる be the topic of conversation; be talked about. ～に掛ける say *sth*; express *sth*; put *sth* into words. ⓐ ～に藉く give a pretext; make an excuse. ～にする ❶ put (food) into one's mouth. ❷ speak of *sb/sth*; mention *sb/sth*; be on one's lips. ～に出す put *sth* into words; give voice to *sth*; ① let *sth* fall. ～に絶つ ❶ abstain from (a certain) food. ❷ remain silent; be reticent. ～に上せる talk about *sth*. ～に上る be the topic of conversation; be talked about. ～に乗せる deceive *sb*; ① take *sb* in; ⓒ ① lead *sb* by the nose. ～に乗る ❶ be the topic of conversation; be talked about. ❷ be deceived; ① be taken in. ～に入る be able to eat; be edible. ～に運ぶ bring (the bowl) to one's lips. ～に任せる say what comes into one's mind; talk without thinking.

🗾 ⓐ ～を開く ❶ open one's mouth. ❷ be staggered; be amazed. ～を開ける ❶ open one's mouth. ❷ say what is on one's mind; make a confession; own up to *sth*. ～を合わす ❶ arrange not to contradict each other; make each other's stories match. ❷ chime in with *sb*; ① pay lipservice to *sb*. ～を入れる interrupt *sb*; ① put in a word; ① put a word in edgeways; ① cut in; ⓢ ① butt in. ～を掩う laugh up one's sleeve. ⓒ ～を置く shut one's mouth. ～を掛ける ❶ make pre-arrangements. ❷ get in touch; call *sb* in; hire *sb*. ～を固める impose silence on *sb*; forbid *sb* to say anything; muzzle *sb*. ～を藉る make a pretext; give an excuse. ～を箝す ❶ hold one's tongue; keep silent; ⓒ ① button one's lips. ❷ silence *sb*; shut *sb* up. ～を利く ❶ speak to *sb*; pass a remark. ❷ be influential; have authority. ❸ have a fluent tongue; be eloquent; ⓒ ① have the gift of the gab. ❹ mediate between (two parties); speak up for *sb*. ～を切る ❶ open the conversation; speak out; break the silence. ❷ broach a matter; ① break the ice. ❸ open (a bottle/a box). ～を極める be persuasive; go out of one's way to express (praise). ⓐ ～を消す ❶ remain silent; ① bite one's lip; ⓒ ① button one's lips. ❷ withdraw one's testimony. ～を捜す look for work; ⓢ seek employment. ～を吸う give *sb* a kiss; kiss *sb*. ～を過ぎる make a living; ⓔ earn one's daily bread; support oneself. ～を過ごす ❶ make a living; ⓔ earn one's daily bread; support oneself. ❷ say too much; go too far. ～を滑らす

ⓞ make a slip of the tongue; ⓘ let sth fall/slip; ⓒ blurt sth out. 〜を狭める purse one's lips. 〜を添える ❶ take a sip. ❷ speak on sb's behalf; second sb. 〜を揃える ❶ speak with one voice; sing in chorus. ❷ make each other's stories match. 〜を出す ❶ interrupt sb; ⓘ put one's oar in; ⓘ put a word in edgeways; ⓘ cut in; ⓢⓘ butt in. ❷ interfere in (sb's affairs); meddle with; interfere with; ⓒⓘ poke one's nose into (the affairs of others). ⓒ 〜を叩く be garrulous; babble. 〜を立てる ❶ make an assertion; point sth out. ❷ make a living; earn one's daily bread; support oneself. ⓒ 〜を垂れる speak subserviently; speak obsequiously. 〜を噤む hold one's tongue; keep silent. ⓒⓘ button one's lips. 〜を付ける taste sth; eat sth. 〜を慎む be careful in speech; ⓘ weigh one's words; ⓘ guard one's words, ⓘ curb one's tongue. 〜を窄める purse one's lips. 〜を尖らす ❶ pout one's lips. ❷ be upset; sulk over sth. 〜を閉ざす remain silent; ⓘ bite one's lip; ⓒⓘ button one's lips. 〜を直す take the nasty taste out of one's mouth; take off the aftertaste. 〜を抜く tap; broach (a barrel). 〜を拭う ❶ wipe one's mouth. ❷ feign ignorance; pretend not to know. 〜を濡らす ❶ make one's living; eke out a living; ⓒ get by; ⓘ make ends meet; ⓘ keep the pot boiling. ❷ live on rations. 〜を糊する make a meager living. 〜を挟む ❶ interrupt sb; ⓘ put one's oar in; ⓘ cut in; ⓢⓘ butt in. ❷ interfere in (sb's affairs); meddle with; interfere with; ⓒⓘ poke one's nose into (the affairs of others). 〜を開く ❶ open one's mouth; begin to speak; start talking. ❷ open a bottle; uncork a bottle. 〜を封じる silence sb; shut sb up. 〜を塞ぐ silence sb; shut sb up. 〜を見つける find work; find employment; ⓒ get a job. Ⓐ 〜を毟る wheedle sth out of sb; milk sb for (information). 〜を歪める curl one's lips (in contempt). 〜を寄す become the mouthpiece of a spirit; be a medium. ⓒ 〜を割る break one's silence; speak out; confess to sth; own up to sth.

愚痴 idle complaints; lament

Ⓔ 〜を零す grumble over sth; lament (one's fate); be querulous; complain of things.

口占 Ⓑ infer sth from sb's words

Ⓐ ⓔ 〜で察する gather sth from sb's words; infer sth from what sb says; ⓘ read between the lines.

[を] 〜を合わせる make each other's stories match; arrange to tell the same story. 〜を引く fathom sb's thoughts; ⓘ feel sb's pulse; ⓘ pulse sb; ⓘ tap sb's mind.

口数 talk; loquaciousness

[を] 〜が多い be talkative; talk (too) much; ⓔ be loquacious. 〜が少ない be silent; be reticent; be sb of few words; ⓔ be incommunative.

口車 "mouth cart"

[N] 〜に乗る be taken in by sb; be cajoled into sth.

口先 a mouth; a snout; tongue

[A] 〜が旨い have a clever tongue; ⓒⓘ have the gift of the gab.

[A] 〜でごまかす talk one's way out of a situation; ⓔ rub along with honeyed words. 〜で騙す talk one's way out of a situation; ⓔ rub along with honeyed words.

[N] 〜に出掛かる ⓐ be on the tip of one's tongue.

嘴 a bill; a beak

[A] 〜が黄色い be immature; be inexperienced; ⓘ be green.

[を] 〜を入れる ❶ interrupt sb; ⓘ put one's oar in; ⓘ put a word in edgeways; ⓘ cut in; ⓢⓘ butt in. ❷ interfere in sb's affairs; meddle with; ⓒⓘ poke one's nose into the affairs of others. ⓐ 〜を鳴らす ❶ chatter about sth; babble over sth. ❷ repent one's actions. 〜を挟む ❶ interrupt sb; ⓘ put one's oar in; ⓘ put a word in edgeways; ⓘ cut in; ⓢⓘ butt in. ❷ interfere in sb's affairs; meddle with; ⓒⓘ poke one's nose into the affairs of others.

口火 a fuse; a spark plug

[と] 〜となる trigger sth; touch off.
[を] 〜を切る ❶ ignite a fuse. ❷ start on sth; begin sth; trigger off (an incident); touch sth off.

唇 the lips

[A] 〜が薄い be talkative; ⓔ be loquacious; ⓒ be a chatterbox; ⓘ talk people's head off.

[を] 〜を奪う kiss sb unexpectedly; ⓘ steal a kiss. ⓞ 〜を返す slander sb; speak ill of sb. 〜を噛み締める swallow one's frustration; but a brave face on things; ⓘ bite one's lip. 〜を噛む swallow one's frustration; suppress one's anger; ⓘ bite one's lip. 〜を尖らす ❶ pout one's lips. ❷ sulk over sth; be upset. ⓞ 〜を翻す slander sb; speak ill of sb.

口鉾 "mouth halbert"

Ⓝ 〜に掛かる be taken in by *sb*; be cajoled into *sth*; ⓒ be duped.

口脇 the corners of one's mouth

🅚 〜を下ぐ make a grimace; show one's displeasure; be annoyed. 〜を引き垂れる make a grimace; show one's displeasure; be annoyed.

靴 shoes; boots; sneakers

🅚 〜を取る take care of *sb/sth*; look after *sb/sth*. 〜を脱ぐ take off one's shoes/boots. 〜を履く put on shoes/boots. 〜を磨く polish one's shoes/boots.

句読 punctuation (marks)

🅚 〜を切る punctuate a sentence; divide a composition with punctuation marks.

苦杯 ⒺⒶ a bitter cup

🅚 ⓒ 〜を嘗める drink a bitter cup; suffer a defeat.

首 the neck; the head

Ⓐ 〜が危ない ❶ be in grave danger; ⓔ be in peril of one's life. ⓒ ❷ be on the point of being fired. 〜が落ちる be beheaded; be decapitated. 〜が繋がる keep one's position; hang on to one's job. 〜が飛ぶ ❶ be beheaded; be decapitated. ❷ lose one's job; be dismissed ⓒ be fired; ⓢ ⓘ get the sack. Ⓐ 〜が細る be in danger of one's life. 〜が回らない be deeply in debt; ⓘ be in dire straits.

Ⓝ 〜に齧り付く throw one's arms around *sb's* neck. 〜にする ❶ break off connections with *sb*; break with *sb*. ❷ dismiss *sb*; ⓒ fire *sb*; ⓢ ⓘ give *sb* the sack. 〜になる ❶ be beheaded; be decapitated. ❷ lose one's job; be dismissed ⓒ be fired; ⓢ ⓘ get the sack.

🅚 〜を集める confer with each other; ⓔ counsel together; ⓒ get together; ⓘ compare notes. 〜を項垂れる bow one's head (in defeat); hang one's head. 〜を折る ❶ ⓘ break one's/*sb's* neck. ❷ drop one's head; hang one's head. Ⓐ 〜を掻く ❶ behead *sb*; decapitate *sb*. ❷ scratch one's head (with bewilderment). Ⓐ 〜を懸く gibbet a (decapitated) head; display a (decapitated) head. 〜を賭ける ❶ risk one's life; ⓘ stick out one's neck. ❷ risk one's job; ⓘ put one's head on the block. 〜を傾げる incline one's head in doubt; look doubtful; be skeptical. Ⓐ 〜を刻む put *sth* in writing; set *sth* in stone. 〜を切り落とす cut off *sb's* head; behead *sb*; decapitate *sb*. 〜を切る ❶ behead *sb*; decapitate sb. ❷ dismiss sb; ⓒ fire sb; ⓢ ⓘ give sb the sack. 〜を縊る hang oneself; strangle oneself; commit suicide. 〜を曝す gibbet a head. 〜を竦める shrug one's shoulders; duck one's head (to avoid a blow). 〜を挿げ替える replace sb. 〜を揃える confer with each other; ⓒ counsel together; ⓒ get together; ⓘ compare notes. 〜を出す look out of (a window); ⓒ pop one's head out of (a doorway). 〜を垂れる droop one's head; let one's head hang; bow one's head. 〜を縮める duck one's head; shrug one's shoulders. 〜を継ぐ get away with murder; go unpunished; ⓒ do sth with impunity. 〜を突っ込む ❶ delve into sth; ⓒ plunge (headlong) into sth. ❷ interfere in (sb's affairs); get involved in sth; ⓒ ⓘ stick one's nose into (the affairs of others). ❸ be taken up with sth; be deeply involved with sth; go too far into sth. 〜を繋ぐ ❶ pardon sb. ❷ keep sb on (in his/her job). 〜を吊る hang oneself; strangle oneself; commit suicide. 〜を長くする stretch one's neck; crane one's neck. 〜を振る turn one's head (with disapproval); turn sth down; refuse to do sth. ⓢ 〜を延ばす stretch one's neck; crane one's neck. 〜を刎ねる behead sb; decapitate sb. 〜を捻る

❶ twist one's/sb's neck. ❷ think hard about sth; ⓒ ⓘ rack one's brains. 〜を振る shake one's head in denial; turn sth down; refuse to do sth. ⓢ 〜をやる ❶ behead sb; decapitate sb. ❷ dismiss sb; ⓒ fire sb; ⓢ ⓘ give sb the sack. 〜を回す go out of one's way (to do sth); bend over backwards (to accomodate sb).

踵 the heel ▶ 踵 ▶ 踵

を 〜を返す go back; retrace one's steps. 〜を接する follow sb heel after heel; ⓘ be hot on sb's heels; ⓘ breathe down sb's neck. 〜を巡らす go back; retrace one's steps.

工夫 a device; a means; a plan

N ⓐ 〜に落つ hit on (a plan); think sth out; call sth to mind.
を 〜を凝らす work out a plan; ⓒ tax one's ingenuity.

組み a class; a party; a group

A 〜で働く work in groups.
N 〜になる join forces; co-operate with sb; team up with sb. 〜に分ける divide into groups.
を 〜を選ぶ choose sides. 〜を作る create a group; make up a party.

雲 a cloud; the clouds

A 〜が切れる clouds are breaking.

クモ　　　　　　　　　　　　　　　　　　　クルマ

N ～に隠(かく)れる be hidden by the clouds; E be shrouded in clouds. ～に聳(そび)える reach into the skies; rise above the clouds; soar sky-high. A ～に臥(ふ)す live in the mountains.
を ～を上(あ)がる clouds gather; rain is coming; a storm gathers. ～を焦(こ)がす burn well; burn like tinder. ～を凌(し)ぐ rise above the clouds. ～を掴(つか)む be at a loss (about what to do); ① be in the dark. ～を衝(つ)く pierce the skies; be extremely tall. ～を遏(とど)む have a brilliant voice. ～を吹(ふ)き払(はら)う blow away the clouds. ～を踏(ふ)む ❶ walk in the mountains. ❷ live in the imperial palace; belong to the nobility.

鞍(くら) a saddle

N ～に慣(な)らす break a horse to the saddle. ～に跨(また)がる get into the saddle; saddle up.
を ～を置(お)く saddle a horse. ～を降(お)ろす unsaddle a horse ～を替(か)える ❶ change saddles; change horses. ❷ take another partner; take another lover. ❸ change jobs; change one's regular haunt.

蔵(くら) a storehouse; a treasury

を ～が建(た)つ become rich; become a millionaire.

位(くらい) grade; rank

A ～が上(あ)がる rise in rank. ～が下(さ)がる fall in rank. ～が付(つ)く gain in dignity.
N ～に付(つ)く ascend to the throne; accede to the throne.
を ～を落(お)とす lower sb in rank; demote sb. ～を返(かえ)す resign from one's post; leave office. ～を極(きわ)む rise to the highest rank; reach high office. ～を進(すす)める raise sb in rank; promote sb. ～を付(つ)ける invest sb with esteem; bestow dignity on sb. ～を取(と)られる be overwhelmed; be browbeaten. ～を取(と)る ❶ show dignity. ❷ give oneself airs; be pompous; E be ostentatious; ① put on airs; © be stuck-up. ～を譲(ゆず)る abdicate.

暮(く)らし a living; livelihood

A ～が立(た)つ be able to make one's living; eke out a living; © get by; ① make ends meet; ① keep the pot boiling.
N ～に困(こま)る be in financial trouble; E be in straitened circumstances; be in dire straits.
を ～をする live. ～を立(た)てる make a living; earn one's daily bread; support oneself.

ぐる a conspirator

N ⑤ ～になる conspire with sb; ⑤ ① be in cahoots with sb.

103

車 <small>くるま</small> a wheel; a car; a vehicle

N ⓐ ～に切る cut *sth* in round slices; cut clockwise. ～に乗る get into a car; take a cab; get a taxi. を ～を降りる get out of a car. ⓐ ～を懸く step down from office; ⓒ retire from public office; leave government service. ⓐ ～を摧く be abandoned; be frustrated; ⓘ be out on a limb. ～を捨てる get out of a car; ⓔ alight from a car. ～を飛ばす hurry somewhere in a car. ～を拾う get a taxi; get a cab. ～を呼ぶ call a taxi; call a cab.

苦労 <small>くろう</small> hardships; difficulty

を ～をかける give *sb* trouble; cause *sb* anxiety. ～を忘れる forget one's troubles.

鍬 <small>くわ</small> a hoe; a mattock; a grub hoe

A ⓐ ～が抜ける ❶ be perplexed; be puzzled; be baffled; be at a loss (about what to do); ⓒ ⓘ be in a fix. ❷ relax one's attention; ⓘ drop one's guard; be careless. ❸ be exhausted; become tired out; ⓢ be knackered. A ～で掘る hoe the soil. を ～を入れる break ground; cultivate land. ～を取る hoe (in the field); engage in farming. ⓐ ～を抜かす ❶ be perplexed; be puzzled; be baffled; be at a loss (about what to do); ⓒ ⓘ be in a fix. ❷ relax one's attention; ⓘ drop one's guard; be careless. ❸ be exhausted; become tired out; ⓢ be knackered.

群 <small>ぐん</small> a crowd; a flock; a swarm

を ～を為す flock together; form a crowd. ～を抜く outdo one's peers; outstrip *sb*; stand out; ⓒ rise above the common herd.

軍 <small>ぐん</small> an army; a military force

N ～に従う follow the army; go to the front. を ～を起こす raise an army; raise troops.

軍営 <small>ぐんえい</small> ⓘ a military camp

N ⓒ ～を布く set up camp.

君側 <small>くんそく</small> ⓘ the side of one's lord

N ⓐ ⓔ ～に侍する serve one's master; wait upon one's lord. を ⓐ ⓔ ～を清む protect one's lord from evildoers; clear the court of evil elements.

軍配 <small>ぐんばい</small> a *sumō* umpire's fan

を (人に)～を揚げる declare *sb* the winner; decide in favor of *sb*. ⓐ ～を振る give instructions; lead an army; conduct one's men.

グンモン　　　　　　　　　　　　　ケイカク

ぐんもん
軍門 a camp gate

[N] ⓔ ～に降る ❶ capitulate at the enemy's camp gate; admit defeat; acknowledge defeat; ⓘ throw in the towel. ❷ be routed; be beaten; ⓘ bite the dust.

くんれん
訓練 training; drilling

[A] ～が行き届く be well trained.
[を] ～を受ける be disciplined; be trained. ～を重ねる drill sb over and over again.

ケ

け
毛 hair; feathers; down

[A] ～が抜ける lose one's hair.
[を] ～を染める dye one's hair. ⓐ ～を立つ feel one's hairs stand on end. ～を縮らす frizzle one's hair. ～を抜く pull out a hair; pluck feathers.

けい
刑 punishment; a penalty

[N] ～に処する sentence sb. ～に服する serve a sentence; ⓒ ⓘ do time; ⓢ ⓘ do one's bird.
[を] ～を言い渡す pass sentence on sb; ⓔ pronounce a sentence on sb. ～を受ける be penalized; be punished. ～を加える inflict a penalty on sb. ～を勤める serve a sentence; ⓒ ⓘ do time; ⓢ ⓘ do one's bird. ～を逃れる escape punishment; ⓢ ⓘ beat the rap. ～を免れる escape punishment; ⓢ ⓘ beat the rap.

げい
芸 an art; an accomplishment

[A] ～が立つ be master of an art; be proficient in an art. ～が無い ❶ be unacomplished; lack talent; have no ability (in an art). ❷ lack taste; be unrefined. ❸ be good for nothing; have no (saving) virtues. ～が細かい be mindful of details.
[を] ～を教える teach (an animal) tricks. ～を覚える learn a trick. ～をさせる teach (an animal) tricks. ～を仕込む train sb in the arts. ～を磨く cultivate an art.

けいい
敬意 respect; regard; esteem

[を] ～を表わす show one's respect; pay homage to sb. ～を払う pay sb respect.

けいかい
警戒 caution; precaution

[を] ～を緩める relax one's attention; ⓘ drop one's guard. ～を要する require caution.

けいがい
謦咳 hawking; a cough

[N] ⓔ ～に接する meet (a superior) in person; talk to (one's senior) in person.

けいかく
計画 a plan; a project

を ～を起こす set a plan in action. ～を覆す upset a plan; ① rock the boat. ～を進める proceed with a plan; ① carry a plan forward. ～を立てる make a plan.

けいかく
圭角 an angle; a corner

N ① ～が取れる ❶ round off one's rough edges; become sociable; become affable. ❷ be sophisticated; be refined; be polished.

けいき
景気 things; business

を ～を上げる boost one's business; liven up; be enlivened. ～を付ける boost one's business; liven up; be enlivened. ～を直す revive the economy; mend one's market.

けいけん
経験 experience

A ～がある have experience; be experienced. ～が増す grow in experience.
N ～に富む have vast experience; be widely experienced.
を ～を生かす make use of one's experience; employ one's experience. ～を得る gain experience. ～を積む gather experience. ～を広げる widen one's experience.

けいこく
警告 a warning; a caution

N ～に従う heed a warning; take warning from.
を ～を受ける receive a warning; be warned. ～を発する issue a warning.

けいじ
掲示 a notice; a bulletin

を ～を出す put up a notice.

けいしき
形式 form; formality

N ～に流れる become formal.
を ～を廃する do away with formalities. ～を踏む go through the formalities.

けいちょう
傾聴 attentive listening

を ① ～に値する be worth listening to; be noteworthy; be worth one's attention. ① ～を怠る fail to listen carefully; ① drop one's guard.

けいべつ
軽蔑 contempt; disdain; scorn

を ～を表わす express one's contempt. ～を受ける be held in contempt. ～を示す show contempt.

けいほう
警報 an alarm; a warning signal

を ～を伝える give an alarm. ～を解く give an all clear. ～を鳴らす sound the alarm; beat an alarm.

げき
檄 a manifesto; a declaration

を ～を飛ばす ❶ draw up a manifesto; issue a declaration. ❷ appeal to sb; give a stimulus to sth.

逆鱗 [E] Imperial wrath

[N] ～に触れる incur the wrath of sb in power.

袈裟 a Buddhist priest's stole

[N] ～に掛く cut sb down slantwise from the shoulder.
[を] ～を斬る cut sb down slantwise from the shoulder.

けじめ a line; a distinction

[を] ⓐⓢ ～を食う be discriminated against; be looked down upon. ～を付ける ① draw a line; make a distinction. ～を守る honor a tradition; adhere to a custom; observe the difference between (good and bad); stick to the rules.

桁 a figure; a unit; a beam

[A] ～が違う be no match for one; ① be in a different league; ① be on different scales. ～が外れる ❶ be unexpected; be extraortinary (priced). ❷ be in a different class; stand on different levels; ① be in a different league.

下駄 geta; wooden clogs

[を] ～を預ける pass authority to sb else; leave sth to sb else; ① pass the ball to sb else; ① pass the buck. ～を履かせる inflate the figures; pad the results. ～を履く ❶ put on geta. ❷ take graft; accept a bribe; be bribed. ～を脱ぐ take off one's geta; remove one's geta.

けち stinginess; meanness

[を] ～を付ける find fault with sb/sth; carp at sb's faults.

けつ
穴 [V][E] the butt; the arse ▶ 穴

[A] ⓥⓢ ～が青い be immature; ⓔ be green; ⓔ be callow; ⓒ ① be wet behind the ears. ⓐⓥⓢ ～が痒い be slightly offended; feel somewhat vexed; ① go against the grain.
[を] ⓥⓢ ～を捲る come out fighting; take the offensive; ⓒ stick one's chin out. ⓥⓢ ～を見せる run away; take flight. ⓥⓢ ～を向ける be against sth; turn sth down. ⓥⓢ ～を割る ❶ expose oneself; ① make a clean breast of sth. ❷ betray oneself; reveal one's true character; ① give oneself away; ① show one's true colors. ❸ give up halfway; ① throw in the towel. ❹ go bankrupt; go out of business; ⓢ go bust.

決 a decision; a vote

[を] ～を採る take a decision; put sth to the vote; ⓔ go into division.

結果 a result; a consequence

血気 hot blood; youthful vigor
[N] 〜に逸る be impetuous; have youthful ardor; be full of vigor.

結婚 marriage; matrimony
[を] 〜を取り消す annul a marriage; dissolve a marriage. 〜を取り持つ be a matchmaker; arrange a marriage; act as a go-between. 〜を延ばす postpone a marriage; ⓒ put off a marriage. 〜を申し込む propose marriage; ask a girl's hand in marriage; ⓢ ⓘ pop the question.

決心 resolve; determination
[A] 〜が鈍る be weakened in one's resolution; lose resolve; ⓒ ⓘ get cold feet.
[を] 〜を動かす shake one's resolve. 〜を固める stiffen one's resolve. 〜を翻す break one's resolve; change one's mind; have second thoughts.

血相 complexion; countenance
[を] 〜を変える change color; turn pale (with fury); lose color; ⓘ turn black in the face (with anger).

[を] 〜を生む produce results. 〜を得る obtain results. 〜を収める secure results. 〜を及ぼす have an effect. 〜を齎す bring about a result.

決定 a decision; a settlement
[を] 〜を延ばす postpone a decision; defer a settlement; put off a decision. 〜を待つ await a conclusion.

欠点 a fault; a flaw; a mistake
[を] 〜を揚げる point out sb's flaws. 〜を補う cover up sb's faults. 〜を捜す find fault with sb; carp at sb's faults. 〜を直す correct a fault; mend a mistake.

決闘 a duel; a man to man fight
[を] 〜を挑まれる be challenged to a duel. 〜を申し入れる challenge sb to a duel.

血涙 旧 tears of blood
[N] ⓒ 〜に沈む weep one's eyes out; cry one's eyes out; drown in sorrow; ⓒ be dissolved in tears.
[を] ⓒ 〜を誘う induce tears; move sb to tears. ⓒ 〜を絞る shed bitter tears; weep profusely. ⓒ 〜を流す shed bitter tears; weep profusely.

血路 旧 an escape route
[N] ⓒ 〜を開く ❶ find an escape route; be able to escape. ❷ find a way out; resolve a situation; find a solution. ⓒ 〜を求める ❶ ⓒ look for a way out; try to escape. ❷ try and resolve a situation; look for a solu-

tion; ⓐ look for a way out.

結論 a conclusion

[N] 〜に来る come to a conclusion. 〜に達する reach a conclusion. 〜になる come to a conclusion. 〜に導く lead to a conclusion; bring about a conclusion.

[を] 〜を与える give a conclusion. 〜を急ぐ hasten to a conclusion. 〜を下す draw a conclusion. 〜を出す form a conclusion.

気配 a sign; indications

[を] 〜を感じる discern the signs of. 〜を示す show signs of.

煙 [図] smoke; fumes ▶ 煙

[A] ⓢ 〜が懸かる meet with disaster; come to grief; ⓔ be visited by a calamity.

[N] ⓢ 〜になる be wasted; ⓞ go up in smoke; ⓞ come to nothing. ⓢ 〜に巻く be evasive; be ambiguous; mystify sb.

煙 smoke; fumes ▶ 煙

[と] 〜と消える disappear; vanish into thin air.

[N] 〜になる ⓞ go up in smoke. 〜に巻かれる be suffocated. 〜に巻く ❶ envelop sth in smoke. ❷ be evasive; be ambiguous; mystify sb. 〜に

咽せる be suffocated by smoke; choke with smoke.

[を] 〜を出す emit smoke. ⓐ 〜を立てる make a living; earn one's daily bread; support oneself. 〜を吐く emit smoke; puff out smoke; cough up smoke; ⓔ pour forth smoke.

けり an end; a close

[A] 〜が付く be settled; be brought to a conclusion; come to a close.

[を] 〜を付ける settle sth; reach an agreement; bring sth to a close.

権 authority; power

[N] ⓞ 〜に借る hide behind sb's authority; abuse (one's father's) authority; ⓞ ride on sb's coat-tails. 〜に付く attach oneself to sb of authority. ⓞ 〜に募る give oneself airs under the protection of sb's authority.

[を] ⓞ 〜を冠る hide behind sb's authority; abuse (one's father's) authority; ⓞ ride on sb's coat-tails. 〜を取る seize power; hold power.

剣 a sword; a blade

[を] 〜を帯びる put on a sword; wear a sword. 〜を構える hold one's sword. ⓐⓔ 〜を弾ず lament over one's misfortunes; complain about one's lot; bewail one's predicament.

〜を研ぐ sharpen a sword; burnish a sword. 〜を抜く draw a sword. 〜を振るう brandish a sword. 〜を学ぶ study the art of fencing. 〜を磨く polish a sword; burnish a sword.

険 ⓘ steep; severe; grim; sharp

🅐 ⓔ 〜が有る have a sting; have a dangerous edge.

暄 ⓘ warmth

🅐 ⓒ ⓔ 〜を負う have one's little pleasures in life.

妍 ⓘ beauty; splendor

🅔 ⓒ 〜を競う vie in beauty; rival each other in splendor.

言 a word; a remark; speech

🅔 ⓐ 〜を絶つ be unspeakable. ⓐ 〜を食む ⓘ take back one's words; ⓘ eat one's words. ⓐ 〜を践む act on one's word; carry out what one has said. 〜を守る keep one's word; live up to one's words. 〜を用いる follow sb's advice.

権威 authority; influence

🅐 〜が有る have authority.
🅝 〜に従う submit to authority.
🅔 〜を与える give sb influence (over sth). 〜を落とす debase oneself. 〜を添える lend authority to (a claim). 〜を握る seize power. 〜を奮う wield power; exercise authority. 〜を持つ have authority.

検閲 censorship; inspection

🅔 〜を受ける be subject to censorship; be submitted for censorship; be inspected. 〜を行う impose censorship. 〜を通る pass censorship; pass muster. 〜を解く lift censorship. 〜を逃れる evade the censors.

喧嘩 a fight; a quarrel; a row

🅔 〜を売る spoil for a fight. 〜を収める settle a dispute; ⓘ bury the hatchet. 〜を買う take up a quarrel; ⓒ pick a fight with sb. 〜を仕掛ける start a fight; pick a fight with sb. 〜をする have a fight. 〜を始める have a quarrel; ⓘ come to blows. 〜を吹っかける pick a fight with sb. 〜を止める put down a fight.

玄関 the porch; the vestibule

🅔 ⓒ 〜を張る make an outward show; ⓘ keep up appearances.

嫌疑 suspicion; doubt; distrust

🅐 〜が掛かる be under suspicion; come under suspicion.
🅔 〜を受ける be under suspicion. 〜を掛ける cast suspicion on sb; suspect sb (of a crime). 〜を晴らす dis-

pel suspicion; clear oneself/sb of suspicion. 〜を招く invite suspicion; arouse suspicion.

元気 vigor; vitality; energy

[A] 〜が良い be in high spirits; be full of vigor; ⓒ ⓘ be on top of the world. 〜が衰える lose vigor; be enfeebled; ⓔ fall into low spirits. 〜が付く be encouraged; take heart; cheer up; ⓔ become heightened in spirits; ⓢ buck up. 〜が出る be encouraged; take heart; ⓔ become heightened in spirits; ⓢ buck up. 〜が無い be gloomy; feel dejected; be cast down; be in low spirits; ⓒ ⓘ have the blues.

[N] 〜になる ❶ recover from an illness; improve in health; get better. ❷ be refreshed; take heart; cheer up; ⓢ buck up.

[を] 〜を失う lose vigor; be enfeebled; ⓔ fall into low spirits. 〜を出す brace oneself; cheer oneself up; ⓢ ⓘ get up steam. 〜を付ける encourage sb; cheer sb up; ⓘ put sb on his/her mettle; ⓢ ⓘ buck sb up.

権限 authority; competence

[を] 〜を与える authorize sb; empower sb. 〜を越える exceed one's power; go beyond one's authority. 〜を持つ have power; have authori-ty.

言語 language; speech ▶言語

[N] 〜に絶する be beyond words; defy description; ⓔ beggar belief.

健康 health; wholesomeness

[A] 〜が勝れない be poorly; be unwell; ⓘ be out of sorts.

[N] 〜に適する be good for one's health; be wholesome. 〜に響く affect one's health. 〜に恵まれる be blessed with good health

[を] ⓔ 〜を害する injure one's health; damage one's health. 〜を損なう injure one's health; damage one's health. 〜を保つ preserve one's health.

言辞 [E] words; speech; language

[を] ⓔ 〜を弄する state a case; declare sth; say sth.

見当 an estimate; a guess

[A] 〜が付く be possible to guess; have a general idea. 〜が外れる guess wrong; ⓘ be off the mark.

[を] 〜を付ける ❶ take aim at sth; aim at sth; ❷ make an estimation; have a guess; ⓔ make a conjecture.

現場 the scene (of a crime)

[を] 〜を押さえられる be caught in the

act; ⓘ be caught red-handed.

厳秘(げんぴ) Ⓔ a closely guarded secret
Ⓝ ⓒ 〜に付する keep *sth* a strict secret; ⓘ be as silent as the grave.

源平(げんぺい) Ⓓ the Genji and the Heike
Ⓝ 〜に別(わ)ける create two rival parties; make two teams.

権利(けんり) a right; a claim; a title
ⓔ 〜を与(あた)える give *sb* rights. 〜を争(あらそ)う contest the rights. 〜を失(うしな)う lose one's rights. 〜を売(う)る sell the rights. 〜を犯(おか)す infringe on a right. 〜を買(か)う purchase a claim to *sth*; buy the rights. ⓒ 〜を踏(ふ)む trample upon *sb's* rights.

権力(けんりょく) power; influence
Ⓝ 〜に屈(くっ)する yield to power.
ⓔ 〜を与(あた)える give *sb* power; empower *sb*; ⓒ invest *sb* with power. 〜を得(え)る gain power; ⓒ be in the ascendant. 〜を掴(つか)む seize power. 〜を握(にぎ)る seize power; hold power. 〜を揮(ふる)う wield power; have a hold on *sb/sth*.

コ

子(こ) a child; children
Ⓐ 〜が出来(でき)ない be unable to have children; be sterile; ⓒ be barren.
ⓔ 〜を生(う)む give birth to a child. 〜を下ろす have an abortion; abort a pregnancy. 〜を孕(はら)ませる get a woman pregnant; ⓒ get a woman with child; ⓥ ⓢ knock a girl up. 〜を孕(はら)む concieve a child. 〜を儲(もう)ける father a child; get a child. 〜を持つ have children.

粉(こ) powder; flour; meal; dust
Ⓐ 〜が吹(ふ)く have a bloom; be (sugar) coated.
Ⓝ 〜にする ❶ grind *sth* to powder; pulverize *sth*. ❷ give one's all; do one's utmost; do what lies in one's power; ⓘ keep one's nose to the grindstone; ⓘ work one's fingers to the bone. 〜に碾(ひ)く grind *sth* to powder; pulverize *sth*.

碁(ご) go [boardgame]
ⓔ 〜を打(う)つ have a game of *go*.

期(ご) a time; an occasion
ⓔ ⓐ 〜を押(お)す call *sb's* attention to *sth*; make sure of *sth*; tell *sb* twice; ⓒ ⓘ rub it in. ⓐ 〜を突(つ)く call *sb's* attention to; make sure of *sth*; tell *sb* twice; ⓒ ⓘ rub it in.

恋(こい) love; tender passion
Ⓐ 〜がさめる fall out of love.

コイ

N ～に泣く pine for love. ～に悩む be lovesick; be lovelorn. ～に破れる be thwarted in love.

を ～を打ち明ける declare one's love. ～を囁く whisper words of love. ～を仕掛ける make love to sb; flirt with sb. ～を知る know what it is to be in love. ～をする love sb; fall in love with sb.

鯉口 the mouth of a sheath

を ～を切る partly unsheathe a sword; get ready to draw one's sword. ～を寛ぐ partly unsheathe a sword; get ready to draw one's sword.

功 E merit; services; success

を ～を争う claim credit for sth; ⓒ contend for distinction. ～を急ぐ be too eager for success. ～を入る have a long experience (in a specific field); work for many years on sth. Ⓐ ～を終える complete one's task; accomplish one's mission. ⓒ ～を奏する be successful; ⓘ bring home the bacon. ～を立てる distinguish oneself in duty; ⓒ render meritorious services. ～を積む exert oneself in one's service. ～を誇る boast of one's success; ⓘ blow one's own trumpet. ～を認める give sb credit for sth; recognize sb's qualities.

コウ

香 incense; fragrance; a scent

を ～を聞く smell incense. ～を焚く burn incense. ⓒ ～を闘わす play a game of incense smelling. ～を練る make incense.

公 the public; the state

N ⓒ ～に奉じる serve the public; ⓒ put oneself at the service of the state.

甲 a shell; armor; grade "A"

N Ⓐ ～に着る hide behind sb's authority; do sth under sb's shelter.
を ⓒ ～を付ける give sb grade "A". ⓒ ～を取る get grade "A".

稿 E a draft; a manuscript

を ⓒ ～を改める ❶ alter a draft; rewrite a manuscript. ❷ discuss an issue with a different group of people. ～を起こす start on a draft; begin on a novel. ⓒ ～を脱す finish writing; complete a novel.

紅 E crimson; red ▶ 紅(べに)

N ⓒ ～を注す go red in the face; blush; be ashamed. ⓒ ～を徴する go red in the face; blush; be ashamed.

孝 E filial piety

を ⓒ ～を尽くす be devoted to one's parents; be faithful to one's parents;

be filial.

却 [E] long years; long experience

[を] ⓒ ～を経(へ)る live to an old age; gain years of experience.

貢 [A] tribute

[を] ～を納(おさ)め占(し)める levy tribute on. ～を納(おさ)める pay tribute to.

業 [E] karma; one's actions

[A] ⓒ ⓔ ～が煎(い)れる lose patience; be vexed; have one's patience tried. ⓐ ⓔ ～が蹲(つくば)う be sinful; be full of sins; ⓔ be beyond redemption. ⓒ ⓔ ～が煮(に)える lose patience; be vexed. ⓔ ～が深(ふか)い be sinful; be full of sins; ⓔ be beyond redemption. ⓒ ～が滅(めっ)する be absolved of one's bad karma; pass away; die in peace. ⓒ ⓔ ～が湧(わ)く lose patience; be vexed; have one's patience tried. [N] ⓒ ～に沈(しず)む be past saving; ⓔ be beyond redemption. [を] ⓒ ～を曝(さら)す be disgraced. ⓒ ～を煮(に)やす be vexed; lose one's patience. ⓒ ～を晴(は)らす suffer the retributions of one's past misdeeds. ⓒ ～を沸(わ)かす lose patience; be vexed.

号 a number; a title; a pen name

[を] ～を追(お)う follow each other in number. ～を付(つ)ける use a pen name; use a pseudonym.

公安 public order; public peace

[を] ～を保(たも)つ maintain public order. ～を破(やぶ)る disturb the peace.

好意 goodwill; kindness

[N] ～に報(むく)いる return sb's favors. [を] ～を得(え)る receive sb's favors. ～を持(も)つ mean well; ⓒ be favorably disposed toward sb. ～を寄(よ)せる convey one's good wishes to sb.

公益 public interest

[を] ⓒ ～を害(がい)する harm public interest. ～を図(はか)る work for the public good.

口角沫 [E] "mouth froth"

[を] ⓒ ～を飛(と)ばす ❶ foam at the mouth; froth at the mouth. ❷ discuss sth passionately; debate sth with passion; engage in a heated debate.

好感 a good feeling

[を] ～を与(あた)える make a good impression on sb; give sb a good feeling. ～を抱(いだ)く be well disposed toward sb; like sb; ⓒ be favorably disposed to sb.

コウキ

こうかん
後患 E future troubles

㊅ ～を断つ remove the source of future trouble. ㊅ ～を宿す ㊅ sow the seeds of future trouble.

こうき
好機 a good opportunity

㊅ ～を逸する miss a golden opportunity; let slip a good chance. ～を捕える seize a good opportunity; ㊅ take the tide as it offers. ～を待つ wait for a good opportunity.

こうぎ
交誼 E friendship; amity; favor

㊅ ～を請う request sb's (continued) favor. ㊅ ～を結ぶ make friends with sb.

こうぎ
厚誼 E kindness

N ㊅ ～に報いる return a favor.
㊅ ～を謝す thank sb for a favor.

こうけい
肯綮 E the point; a vital point

N ㊅ ～に中る be relevant; ㊅ ㊀ be to the point; ㊀ be on the mark; ㊀ hit the nail on the head.

こうげき
攻撃 an attack; an assault

㊅ ～を受ける be attacked. ～を加える launch an attack. ～を撃退する repel an attack. ～を防ぐ defend oneself against an attack.

こうけつ
膏血 E sweat and blood

コウジツ

㊅ ㊅ (人民の)～を絞る exploit the people; squeeze the people; suck the life-blood out of a people.

こうげん
公言 big talk; a boast; a brag

㊅ ～を吐く boast about sth; brag about sth; ㊅ ㊀ talk big.

こうげん
巧言 E flattery; fair words

㊅ ㊅ ～を用いる use sweet words; flatter sb; say nice things to sb.

こうこ
江湖 E the public; the world

N ㊅ ～に訴える appeal to the public. ㊅ ～に勧める commend (a work of art) to the public.

こうさい
光彩 E luster; brilliancy

㊅ ～を失う lose luster; go into eclipse. ㊅ ～を添える add luster; enhance a reputation; crown an achievement. ～を放つ outshine others; eclipse others.

こうし
公私 public and private (affairs)

㊅ ～を混同する mix up public and private (affairs). ～を分ける keep public and private (affairs) separate.

こうじ
好餌 E a bait; a lure

と ～となる fall prey to (a scheme).
N ㊅ ～にぱくつく snap at the bait (of easy money).

こうじ
後事 ⓔ future affairs

㋾ ⓒ ～を托(たく)す entrust sb with future affairs.

こうじつ
口実 an excuse; a pretext

㋾ ～を作(つく)る trump up an excuse. ～を設(もう)ける trump up an excuse.

こうじょう
口上 a verbal message

㋐ ～で伝(つた)える convey a message verbally. ～で述(の)べる deliver a verbal message.
㋾ ～を述(の)べる deliver a verbal message.

ごうじょう
強情 stubbornness; obstinacy

㋾ ～を張(は)る be stubborn; be obstinate; ⓒ be pigheaded.

こうじょうしん
向上心 ambition; aspiration

㋾ ～を抱(いだ)く have ambitions; aspire to greatness. ～を養(やしな)う inspire aspirations in sb.

こうじん
後塵 ⓔ a trail of dust

㋾ ⓒ ～を拝(はい)する play a subordinate role; ⓘ take second billing to sb; ⓒⓘ play second fiddle to sb.

こうじん
後陣 a rear guard

㋾ ～を打(う)つ establish a rear guard; back sb up.

こうそう
構想 a conception; an idea

㋾ ～を立(た)てる devise a plan; work out an idea. ～を練(ね)る think hard about sth; ⓒⓘ rack one's brains.

こうちゃ
紅茶 black tea

㋾ ～を入(い)れる make tea. ～を沸(わ)かす brew tea.

こうちょう
高潮 high tide; the climax

Ⓝ ～に達(たっ)する reach the climax; attain the zenith.

こうとう
後図 ⓔ plans for the future

㋾ ⓒ ～を策(さく)する plan for the future; provide for future contingencies.

こうどう
行動 action; behavior; an act

Ⓝ ～に表(あら)わす show sth in one's conduct. ～に移(うつ)す put (a plan) into action. ～に入(はい)る go into action.
㋾ ～を起(お)こす set to work; make a move. ～を取(と)る take action.

こうなん
後難 ⓔ future trouble

㋾ ～を恐(おそ)れる fear future trouble. ～を避(さ)ける avoid future trouble. ～を残(のこ)す ⓒ sow the seeds of future trouble.

こうばい
勾配 a slope; a gradient; a fall

㋾ ⓒ ～が温(ぬる)い ❶ have a soft slope. ❷ be slow in one's movements. ⓒ ～

が鈍い ❶ have a soft slope. ❷ be slow in one's movements. ⓒ ～が早い be quick in one's movements; be agile; be nimble.

好評 Ⓔ favorable criticism
ⓐ ⓒ ～を博する be well received; ⓒ be lauded; ⓒ meet with public acclaim; ⓘ have good press.

幸福 happiness; well-being
Ⓝ ～に溢れる be full of happiness. ～に暮らす live a happy life; ⓢ sit pretty. ～に死ぬ pass away in peace; die happily.
ⓐ ～を祈る wish sb happiness. ～を受ける enjoy happiness. ～を失う forfeit happiness. ～を羨む envy sb's happiness. ～を得る secure happiness (in life). ～を傷つける injure sb's happiness; spoil sb's happiness. ～を掴む gain happiness.

口吻 Ⓔ one's way of speaking
ⓐ ⓒ ～を学ぶ imitate sb's way of speaking; parrot sb. ～を真似る imitate sb's way of speaking; parrot sb. ⓒ ～を洩らす ❶ betray one's feelings; show one's emotions; ⓒ give vent to one's feelings. ❷ hint at; intimate sth; imply sth.

紅粉 Ⓔ rouge and powder
ⓐ ⓒ ～を施す powder one's face.

首 Ⓔ the head ♦ 首
ⓐ ～を傾く incline one's head in doubt; look doubtful; be skeptical. ～を垂れる ❶ drop one's head. ❷ be discouraged; ⓘ lose heart. ～を廻らす ❶ look round; turn round; face about. ❷ look back upon the past; reflect on sth. ❸ ruminate on sth; ponder over sth; ⓒ ⓘ rack one's brains (over sth). ～を割る apply one's mind to sth; think hard about sth; ⓒ ⓘ rack one's brains.

公平 impartiality; equity
ⓐ ～を欠く be partial. ⓒ ～を期する attempt to be fair; seek to be impartial. ～を保つ maintain impartiality.

後報 Ⓔ further news
ⓐ ～を待つ await further details.

甲羅 a shell; a carapace
Ⓐ ～が生える live to an old age; be old and experienced; have long experience.
ⓐ ～を経る have long experience (in an office); work for many years. ～を干す sun oneself; ⓒ bask in the sun.

こうるい
紅涙 🄔 tears of blood

🄽 ⓔ ～に沈む weep one's eyes out; cry one's eyes out; drown in sorrow; ⓔ be dissolved in tears.

🄥 ⓔ ～を誘う induce tears; move *sb* to tears. ⓔ ～を絞る shed bitter tears; weep profusely. ⓔ ～を流す shed bitter tears; weep profusely.

こうろう
劫﨟 🄔 long years of service

🄥 ～を経る have long experience (in an office); work for many years.

こえ
声 a voice; a cry; notes; a song

🄐 ～が掛かる ❶ be called; be hailed. ❷ be encouraged; ⓔ be lauded; ⓒ be cheered on. ❸ be asked; be invited. ～が嗄れる grow hoarse. ～が詰る speak in a choked voice. ～が通る have a piercing voice.

🄥 ～を上げる raise one's voice; cry out; speak up. ～を合せる talk in unison; speak with one voice. ～を落とす lower one's voice. ～を掛ける ❶ call out; hail *sb*. ❷ encourage *sb*; cheer *sb* on. ～を嗄らす shout oneself hoarse. ⓔ ～を曇らす speak in a tearful voice; falter out; murmur wistfully. ～を殺す talk in a low voice; speak in a whisper. ～を絞る ❶ strain one's voice. ❷ speak in a whisper; ⓔ speak with bated breath. ～を揃える talk in unison; speak with one voice. ～を出す raise one's voice; speak up. ～を立てる cry out; raise one's voice. ～を尖らす speak harshly; sneer at *sb*. ～を呑む swallow one's words; be speechless. ～を励ます raise one's voice. ～を弾ませる shout for joy. ～を放つ shout out; ⓒ blare *sth* out. ～を張り上げる raise one's voice; yell at the top of one's voice. ⓔ ～を潜める lower one's voice; speak in a whisper; ⓔ speak with bated breath. ～を振り絞る cry at the top of one's voice; strain one's voice.

こおり
氷 ice

🄐 ～が張り詰める be frozen over/up with ice; be covered in frost. ～が張る freeze up.

🄽 ～に被われる be frozen over/up; be covered with ice. ～に座す expose oneself to grave danger; put oneself in harm's way; endanger oneself. ～に鏤む do *sth* in vain; do *sth* that is to no avail; waste one's time. ～に詰める pack (foodstuffs) in ice.

🄥 ～を歩む expose oneself to grave danger; put oneself in harm's way; endanger oneself. ～を落とす remove the ice; deice (a fridge). ～を掻く shave ice. ～を砕く crush ice. ～を踏む expose oneself to grave danger; put oneself in harm's way; endanger oneself.

戸外 outdoors; the open air

[N] 〜に出る go out of doors. 〜に飛び出す dash out of the door.

[を] 〜へ追い出す show sb the door; ⓐ give sb the door; ⓒ throw sb out; ⓢ kick sb out.

小刀 a (pocket)knife

[A] 〜が利く be intricately done; be detailed; be delicately done.

古稀 E seventy years of age

[N] 〜に達する reach seventy.

[を] 〜を過ぎる pass seventy; be on the wrong side of seventy.

呼吸 breathing; respiration

[A] 〜が絶える stop breathing; ⓔ reathe one's last. 〜が分る be familiar with sth; know how to do sth; ⓘ know the ropes; ⓒ get the knack of sth.

[を] 〜を合わす keep in tune with sb; keep in step with sb; keep time with sb. 〜を覚える become familiar with sth; learn how to do sth; ⓘ learn the ropes; ⓒ get the knack of sth. 〜を呑み込む become familiar with sth; learn how to do sth; ⓘ learn the ropes; ⓒ get the knack of sth. 〜を

計る plan sth (to coincide with sth); time sth (to be on time for sth).

虚空 E the sky; empty space

[A] 〜を掴む clutch at thin air; claw the air. 〜を見詰める stare into space.

[N] 〜に消える vanish into thin air; disappear from the face of the earth.

小首 a head; a neck

[を] 〜を傾げる incline one's head a little in doubt; look somewhat doubtful; be slightly skeptical. ⓐ 〜を投げる hang one's head; droop one's head; bow one's head (in submission). 〜を捻る turn one's head a little in doubt; look somewhat doubtful; be slightly skeptical.

黒白 E black and white

[を] 〜を争う argue the rights and wrongs (of an issue). 〜を付ける decide on the merits and demerits (of a case). 〜を分かつ tell right from wrong; discriminate between right and wrong. ⓒ 〜を弁う be able to tell right from wrong.

虚仮 E a fool; an idiot; a dunce

[N] ⓢ 〜にする ❶ make a fool of sb; ridicule sb; make fun of sb. ❷ slight *sb*; ignore *sb*; ⓒ pay no consideration to *sb*. ❸ look down on *sb*; dispise *sb*; ⓒ hold *sb* in contempt. ⓢ ～に踏む ❶ make a fool of *sb*; ridicule *sb*; make fun of *sb*. ❷ slight *sb*; ignore *sb*; ⓒ pay no consideration to *sb*. ❸ look down on *sb*; dispise *sb*; ⓒ hold *sb* in contempt. ⓢ ～に回す ❶ make a fool of *sb*; ridicule *sb*; make fun of *sb*. ❷ slight *sb*; ignore *sb*; ⓒ pay no consideration to *sb*. ❸ look down on *sb*; dispise *sb*; ⓒ hold *sb* in contempt.

虎穴 Ⓔ a tiger's den

Ⓝ ⓒ ～に入る ❶ enter a tiger's den. ❷ put oneself in danger; ⓘ put one's head in the lion's mouth.

沽券 esteem; credit; honor

Ⓐ ～が下がる fall in public estimation; be disgraced; ⓘ lose face.
Ⓝ ～に関わる affect one's esteem; ⓒ inpinge on one's reputation; be below one's dignity; bring discredit on (an organization).

糊口 Ⓔ bare livelihood

Ⓔ ～を凌ぐ eke out a living; ⓒ get by; ⓘ make ends meet; ⓒ ⓘ keep the pot boiling.

故国 Ⓔ one's homeland

Ⓝ ⓒ ～に帰る go back to one's homeland; return home.
Ⓔ ～を思う pine for home; yearn for one's homeland. ～を去る leave one's homeland; go into exile. ～を離れる leave one's homeland; go into exile.

小言 a scolding; a rebuke

Ⓔ ～を言う give *sb* a scolding; find fault with *sb*; rebuke *sb*.

心 the spirit; the heart ▶ 心

Ⓐ ～が洗われる feel purified; feel spiritually cleansed. ～が動く ❶ become interested in *sb*/*sth*; ⓒ take a fancy to *sb*/*sth*. ❷ be moved; be tempted. ❸ be swayed; be unsettled; ⓒ be torn by conflicting emotions. ～が躍る get carried away; get excited. ～が傾く be inclined to(ward) *sth*. ～が通う understand each other. ～が軽い be cheerful; be light-hearted. ～が変わる fall out of love; be fickle; be unfaithful. ～が利く be alert; keep an eye out. ～が腐る be corrupted; have a wicked heart. ～が挫ける be discouraged; lose heart. ～が籠る be considerate; be thoughtful; be tactful. ～が定まる make up one's mind. ～が騒ぐ feel uneasy; be ill at ease. ～が沈む be in low spirits; feel depressed. 〜が進(すす)む be in the mood for; be willing (to do sth). 〜が狭(せま)い be intolerant; be narrow-minded. ⓒ 〜が通(つう)ずる (be able to) convey one's feelings to sb else. Ⓐ 〜が付(つ)く ❶ notice sth. ❷ come round. 〜が咎(とが)める have a guilty conscience; feel guilty; be sorry. 〜が解(と)ける be cheered up; feel refreshed. 〜が届(とど)く ❶ be careful; be attentive (to details). ❷ be tactful; be considerate. ❸ communicate one's feelings; convey one's feelings. 〜が和(なご)む calm down; come to oneself; ⓔ find peace of mind. 〜が根腐(ねぐさ)る be corrupted; have a wicked heart. 〜が弾(はず)む be elated; feel excited; be proud. 〜が引(ひ)かれる be attracted by; be interested in; be concerned with. 〜が引(ひ)き締(し)まる be tense; brace oneself. 〜が広(ひろ)い be tolerant; be broad-minded. 〜が触(ふ)れ合(あ)う see things the same way; see eye to eye. 〜が乱(みだ)れる be distracted; be distraught; become upset; be confused. 〜が揉(も)める be anxious; be nervous. 〜が優(やさ)しい have a soft heart; be kind-hearted. 〜が疾(やま)しい have a guilty conscience. ⓒ 〜が悪(わる)い feel strange; feel weird; feel unwell.

N 〜に合(あ)う be agreeable; be pleasing. 〜に当(あ)たる occur to one; strike one; hit one; spring to mind. 〜に抱(いだ)く cherish (a thought); harbor (a feeling); entertain (an idea). 〜に入(い)る pierce the heart; ⓘ sting to the quick. 〜に浮(う)かぶ cross one's mind; come to mind. 〜に描(えが)く picture sth in one's mind; imagine sth vividly; come before one's eyes. 〜に思(おも)う think to oneself. 〜に懸(か)かる ❶ be troubled by; fret over sth; ⓘ weigh on one's mind. ❷ rely on sb's benevolence; appeal to sb's mercy. Ⓐ 〜に掛(か)く take sth into consideration; bear sth in mind; ⓘ take sth on board. 〜に及(およ)ぶ think of sth; hit upon an idea; come to one. 〜に適(かな)う meet one's taste; suit one's fancy. 〜に刻(きざ)む be deeply impressed by sth; Ⓐ be engraved on one's memory; ⓘ take sth to heart. 〜に焦(こ)がす secretly pine for sb/sth; be distracted; be torn by hidden emotions. Ⓐ 〜に障(さわ)る be annoying; be irritating. 〜に染(し)みる penetrate one's heart; ⓔ have sth impressed on one's mind. 〜に留(と)める bear sth in mind; keep sth in mind; Ⓐ make a mental note of sth. 〜に残(のこ)す leave (an impression) in sb's (one's) heart. 〜に残(のこ)る linger in one's mind; remain in one's heart. (考えが) 〜に閃(ひらめ)く suddenly think of sth; have a sudden idea; ⓘ hit upon sth. 〜に触(ふ)れる touch one's heart. 〜に任(まか)せる

ココロ

do as one pleases; have one's way. 图 (人に)〜を明かす reveal one's feeling to sb; open up to sb. 〜を暖める warm one's heart; be heartwarming. 〜を改める change one's habits; ① turn over a new leaf. 〜を合わせる put one's hearts and minds together; be in accord; be of one mind. ⑩ 〜を致す devote oneself to. 〜を痛める be worried by sth; fret over sth. 〜を入れ替える change one's habits; ① turn over a new leaf. 〜を入れる apply oneself to sth; do sth in earnest. 〜を動かす unsettle one; stir one up; move one. 〜を打たれる be touched by sb/sth; be moved by sb/sth; be impressed by sb/sth. 〜を打ち拉ぐ break sb's heart; crush sb's heart. 〜を打つ touch sb; move sb; impress sb. 〜を移す change one's mind; have a change of heart. 〜を奪う charm sb; ① steal sb's heart; ① put a spell on sb. 〜を奪われる be fascinated by; be spellbound by; be captivated by. ⑩ 〜を置く ❶ take sth into consideration; bear sth in mind; ① take sth on board. ❷ be attached to; hold fast to; cling to. ❸ be modest; be shy. ❹ be cautious; ① be on one's guard; be on the alert. ⓐ 〜を起こす pluck up courage; brace oneself. 〜を押し潰す break sb's heart; crush

sb's heart. 〜を躍らせる make one's heart leap; grow excited; be worked up (about sth). 〜を掻き乱す upset sb; shake sb's heart. 〜を掛ける ❶ pay attention to sb/sth; take note of sb/sth. ❷ give one's heart to sb; take a fancy to sb; set one's heart on sth. ❸ have faith in sb; pray for sb/sth. 〜を傾ける ❶ be absorbed in sth; be keen on sth; apply oneself to sth. ❷ take an interest in sb; take to sb; have sympathy for sb. 〜を固める prepare oneself for sth; get ready for sth; resolve to do sth; ① gird up one's loins. 〜を通わせる reach an understanding. 〜を交わす feel a deep sympathy for each other. 〜を決める make up one's mind. 〜を砕く ❶ worry about sth; ⓒ ① rack one's brains. ❷ pay attention to; make strenuous efforts; take pains over sth. 〜を配る ❶ be careful; be attentive. ❷ be watchful; be vigilant. (人の)〜を汲む sympathize with sb; empathize with sb. 〜を苦しめる agonize over sth; fret over sth. 〜を焦がす pine for sb; languish for sb. 〜を込める apply oneself to sth; give one's heart to sth; ⓔ devote one's mind to sth. 〜を凝らす think hard on sth; ⓒ apply one's mind to sth; ⓢ ① use one's loaf. 〜を定める make up one's mind; resolve to do sth. 〜

を察する read sb's mind. 〜を騒がす upset one; be disturbing; be disquieting. 〜を締め付ける break sb's heart; be heartrending. 〜を静める ease ones heart; compose oneself. 〜を据える be prepared; be resigned to (one's fate). 〜を注ぐ pour one's heart into sth; devote oneself to sb/sth. 〜をそそる arouse one's interest; be aroused by sth; ③ ① push sb's buttons. 〜を逸らす be distracted; be distraught. 〜を遣う be considerate; care about. 〜を掴む win sb's heart. 〜を尽くす ❶ devote oneself to sth. ❷ fret over sth; worry about sth; fidget about sth. 〜を付ける ❶ give sb a tip; take sb into consideration (financially). ❷ revive sb; bring sb round. 〜を留める bear sth in mind; keep sth in mind; ④ make a mental note of sth. 〜を捉える attract sb's attention; draw sb's attention. 〜を取られる be diverted with; forget oneself; lose oneself in sth. 〜を取り直す pluck up courage; brace oneself. 〜を慰める ease one's mind. 〜を悩ます fret over sth; be troubled by sth; worry about sth. 〜を煮やす lose patience; be vexed; have one's patience tried. ④ 〜を延ぶ ❶ feel relieved; feel reassured. ❷ pluck up courage; brace oneself. 〜を馳す think about;

long for; pine for. 〜を引き締める pluck up courage; brace oneself; ③ buck up; ① pull oneself together. 〜を引く ❶ sound sb out; feel sb out; ⓒ check sb's mood. ❷ attract one's/sb's attention; be appealing. (人に)〜を開く open one's heart to sb; unbosom oneself; ① pour out one's heart to sb. 〜を翻す be penitent; mend one's ways; ① turn over a new leaf. 〜を惑わせる delude sb; decieve sb. ④ 〜を回す ponder over sth; turn sth over in one's mind. 〜を見抜く see through sb. 〜を向ける direct one's attention toward sth. 〜を用いる take care; give attention to sth. 〜を安んずる ease one's mind; set one's heart at rest. ④ 〜を遣る ❶ cheer oneself up; divert oneself (pleasantly). ❷ do as one pleases; have one's own way. ❸ think about (home); long for sb; pine for sb/sth. 〜を和らげる appease sb; disarm sb; calm sb down. ④ 〜を行かす satisfy oneself; be satisfied with sth; be happy with sth. 〜を許す ❶ relax one's attention; ① drop one's guard. ❷ give one's heart to sb; trust sb blindly. ❸ let oneself go; abandon oneself to sth; indulge oneself. (人に)〜を寄せる take an interest in sb; warm to sb; take to sb; have sympathy for sb. (人の)〜を読む read sb's mind; read sb's thoughts.

こころざし
志 N will; resolve; spirit

を ~を得る attain one's aim; achieve one's goal; realize one's aspirations. ~を立てる set an aim in life; have a purpose in life; aspire after *sth*; resolve to do *sth*. ~を継ぐ carry out (one's father's) ambitions; follow in *sb's* footsteps. Ⓐ ~を尽くす be faithful; be trusting. ~を遂げる attain one's aim; achieve one's goal; realize one's aspirations. ~を果す attain one's aim; achieve one's goal; realize one's aspirations. ~を翻す change one's mind. ~を養う cultivate one's spirit; foster one's spirit.

こころだま
心魂 N the soul; the spirit

N Ⓐ ~に乗る be keen to do *sth*; show interest in *sth*; display enthusiasm for *sth*.
を Ⓐ ~を込める be careful; take care; be prudent; be cautious. Ⓐ ~を飛ばす be terrified; be scared out of one's wits; Ⓢ be scared stiff.

こし
腰 the waist; the loin; the hip

を ~が落ち着く take root; get settled. ~が重い be unwilling to work; be slow to act; Ⓘ drag one's heels. ~が折れる be frustrated; suffer a setback; be disheartened. Ⓐ ~が屈る ❶ have a stomach ache; one's stomach aches. ❷ go into convulsions; have a convulsive fit; be seized with cramps. ❸ be seized with labor pains; go into labor. ~が軽い ❶ be quick to act; be willing to work. ❷ be agile; be nimble. ~が砕ける lose one's stance; lose enthusiasm. ~が据る ❶ hold fast; be steadfast; be unswayed. ❷ hold on (to one's job); stand one's ground. ~が高い ❶ be arrogant; be haughty; be high-handed. ❷ [*sumō*] lack stability. ❸ have long legs; have a short trunk. ~が強い ❶ take a firm stand; be firm. ❷ be resilient; be flexible. ❸ be firm; be sticky; be chewy. [sports] ❹ have a powerful lift. ~が無い ❶ be timid; be a coward. ❷ have no stamina; lack tenacity; have no perseverance. ~が抜ける ❶ lose one's legs; Ⓛ be floored. ❷ lose heart; get scared; Ⓘ get cold feet. ~が冷える have a chill in one's kidneys. ~が低い ❶ be courteous; be humble; Ⓘ keep a low profile. ❷ [*sumō*] have stability. ❸ have short legs; have a long trunk. ~が弱い ❶ be weak-kneed; lack firmness; have no stamina. ❷ be timid; have no push; lack tenacity; have no perseverance. ❸ be limp; be thin (in

コシ

texture); be soggy.

[N] ⓐ 〜に下げる ❶ wear (a sword). ❷ take posession of *sth*; make *sth* one's own; confiscate *sth*. ❸ have one's will with *sb*; ⓒ have *sb* at one's beck and call; ⓒ wrap *sb* around one's little finger. 〜に付ける ❶ wear (a sword). ❷ take possession of *sth*; make *sth* one's own.

[を] 〜を上げる ❶ stand up; rise to one's feet. ❷ take action; come into action. 〜を入れる set about in earnest; commit oneself to *sth*; ⓒ put one's shoulders to the wheel; ⓢ go for it. 〜を浮かす get ready to stand up; be about to rise. 〜を打ち抜く flatter *sb*; humor *sb*; ⓒ curry favor with *sb*; ⓒ find *sb's* soft side. 〜を押す ❶ push (a cart). ❷ support *sb*; back *sb*; stand behind *sb*. ❸ put *sb* up; egg *sb* on. 〜を落ち着ける settle down; unwind. 〜を折る ❶ bend over; stoop at. ❷ yield to (pressure); be subordinate to *sb*. ❸ interrupt *sb*; spoil a story. ❹ ⓒ take the wind out of *sb's* sails. ❺ write a bad song; compose a poor poem. 〜を下ろす sit down; drop into a chair; plop oneself down. 〜を屈める ❶ stoop; bend over. ❷ greet *sb*; make a bow; bow to *sb*. 〜を掛ける sit oneself down; seat oneself. 〜を据える ❶ steady oneself; sit

コジリ

tight. ❷ settle down (to do *sth*); ⓒ buckle down (to do *sth*). 〜を突く be discouraged; lose heart. ❶ lose one's legs; lose one's footing; fall over. 〜を抜かす ❶ lose one's legs. ❷ ⓐ grow weak at the knees; lose heart; get scared; ⓒ get cold feet. ❸ lose oneself in *sth*; forget oneself; get carried away. 〜を抜く ❶ flatter *sb*; humor *sb*; ⓒ curry favor with *sb*; ⓒ find *sb's* soft side. ❷ lose one's legs; lose one's footing. ❸ ⓐ grow weak at the knees; lose heart; get scared; ⓒ get cold feet. 〜を伸ばす straighten up; stand up straight; stretch one's limbs. 〜を引く ❶ [*jūdō*] throw one's waist backwards (to throw one's opponent). ❷ limp along; walk with a limp. 〜を振る swing one's hips; sway one's hips. 〜を曲げる bend over; stoop at. 〜を持つ support *sb*; back *sb*; stand behind *sb*. ⓐ 〜を縒る fall over laughing; ⓒ kill oneself laughing 〜を割る [*sumō*] take a firm stance.

故事 [を] a historical fact

[を] 〜を引く allude to a historical event.

五指 "five fingers"

[N] 〜に余る be too numerous to count (on the fingers of one hand);

be in superior number. 〜に入る turn in one's finger (when counting); count on one's finger.

こしゃく
小癪 impudent; saucy; pert

[N] 〜に障る feel somewhat vexed; be slightly offended; Ⓘ go against the grain.

こじり
鐺 a chape; the tip of a sheath

[A] Ⓒ 〜が詰まる be in financial trouble; Ⓘ be in dire straits.

こせい
個性 personality; individuality

[を] 〜を失う lose one's dignity. 〜を抑える suppress one's ego. 〜を欠く lack individuality. 〜を伸ばす cultivate one's personality. 〜を発揮する display individuality. 〜を持つ have personality.

こせき
戸籍 census; registration

[を] 〜を洗う check sb's family register. 〜を調べる inquire into sb's family register; take the census.

ごぞう
五臓 Ⓑ the five viscera

[を] Ⓐ 〜を絞る suffer extreme hardships. Ⓐ 〜を煮やす be irate; burn with rage/resentment. Ⓐ 〜を揉む ❶ regret sth bitterly; feel chagrined (at sth); be grieved (at sth); feel sorry for sb. ❷ express one's true sentiments; speak from the heart. ❸ pour all one's energy into sth; Ⓘ give it one's all.

ごたい
五体 Ⓑ "the five limbs"

[を] Ⓒ Ⓔ 〜を投ぐ suffer extreme hardships; endure the unendurable.

ごたく
御託 Ⓑ whining; impertinence

[を] Ⓒ 〜を並べる ❶ dwell on a matter; labor a point; Ⓒ keep on about sth; Ⓘ harp on the same string. ❷ boast about sth; brag about sth; Ⓘ talk big; Ⓒ blow one's own horn (trumpet).

ごたまぜ
ごた混ぜ Ⓑ a jumble; a muddle

[N] Ⓒ 〜にする make a muddle of sth; juble sth up; mix sth up. Ⓒ 〜になる be mixed up; be in a mess; Ⓘ go to pie.

こち
故知 Ⓑ ancestral wisdom

[を] Ⓒ 〜に習う follow sb's example; Ⓘ follow in sb's footsteps; Ⓘ take one's cue from sb. Ⓒ 〜に学ぶ follow sb's example; Ⓘ follow in sb's footsteps; Ⓘ take one's cue from sb.

こつ
骨 bones; a trick; a knack ▶ 骨ほね

[A] 〜が難しい require tact; be difficult; be sensitive; be delicate. 〜が分かる become familiar with sth;

learn how to do *sth*; ⓘ learn the ropes; ⓒ get the knack of *sth*.

N ～にする cremate *sb's* remains. を ～を納める bury *sb's* ashes; entomb *sb's* remains. ～を教える learn *sb* how to do *sth*; ⓘ teach *sb* the ropes; ⓘ put *sb* up the ropes. ～を覚える become familiar with *sth*; learn how to do *sth*; ⓘ learn the ropes; ⓒ get the knack of *sth*. ～を呑み込む become familiar with *sth*; learn how to do *sth*; ⓘ learn the ropes; ⓒ get the knack of *sth*. ～を拾う gather *sb's* ashes; collect *sb's* remains.

滑稽 Ⓔ comic; humor

を ～を言う make a joke; ⓒ crack jokes; ⓒ be witty. Ⓔ ～を解する have a sense of humor.

骨髄 the marrow (of a bone)

N ⓐ ～に入る ⓘ sting to the quick; pierce the heart. ⓐ ～に徹する pierce the heart; ⓘ sting to the quick. を ⓐ ～を砕く have a hard time; suffer great hardships.

骨箱 a wooden urn

を ～を叩く talk loudly; wag one's tongue; be excessively garrulous.

小爪 the root of a nail

を ～を拾う pick on *sb*; ⓘ catch *sb* in his/her own words; ⓐ trips *sb* up.

後手 a rear guard

N ～に回る be outmanouvred; be forced into the defensive; lose the initiative; be forestalled.

事 a thing; a matter; an issue

N ～に当る see to *sth*; attend to *sth*; take care of *sth*. を ～を荒立てる make *sth* worse; worsen a situation; agravate a matter; ⓒ precipitate trouble. ～を起こす cause trouble; ⓘ stir *sth* up. ～を欠く be lacking; fall short; be pressed for *sth*. ～を構える worsen a situation; agravate a matter; ⓒ precipitate trouble. ～を好む be a trouble maker; be mischievious; ⓒ be bent on causing trouble. ～を運ぶ go ahead with (a plan); proceed with *sth*; put *sth* into action. ～を分ける reason (with *sb*); be sensible.

言 Ⓐ words; protest; a lie

N ～に出ず ❶ state *sth* plainly; speak out; vent one's spleen. ❷ be rumored; be the topic of conversation; be talked about. ～を食む break one's word; go back on one's word.

孤独 solitude; loneliness

A ～を愛する love one's own company; ⓒ be a loner. ～を味わう experience loneliness. ～を感じる feel solitude; feel lonely. ～を楽しむ enjoy one's own company; be reclusive; ⓒ be a loner.

言葉 words; speech; language

A ～が過ぎる say too much. ～が通じる be understood. ～が尖る speak stern words.

N ～に甘える take sb's word for it; accept sb's words. ～に余る be lost for words; be beyond description. ～に表わす put into words. ⓐ ～に付く comply with sb's wishes; do as sb says. ～に詰まる be at a loss for words. ～に触れる let sth fall; blurt sth out. ～に任せる comply with sb's words; do as sb says.

A ～を返す rebuke sb; talk back; ⓒ give sb backtalk. ～を交わす have a word with sb; talk with sb. ～を換える change one's words. ～を掛ける address sb; speak to sb. ～を飾る use fancy words; use fine language. ～を固める commit oneself; make a promise. ～を交わす ❶ exchange words with sb; have a word with sb; talk with sb. ❷ make a verbal agreement. ～を下げる ❶ speak in a humble way. ❷ be rude in one's speech; patronize sb; speak down to sb. ～を添える speak up for sb; put in a good word for sb. ～を違える break one's word; go back on one's word. ⓐ ～を番う commit oneself; make a promise. ～を継ぐ resume one's speech; ① pick up the thread. ～を尽くす exhaust one's words. ～を慎む watch one's words; be careful of what one says; ① weigh one's words. (人の)～を咎める censure sb's words; criticize sb; rebuke sb. ～を直す speak formally; use polite words. ～を濁す speak ambiguously; be vague. ～を練る choose one's words carefully; ① weigh one's words. ～を残す ❶ leave things unsaid. ❷ say sth for posterity. ～を呑む swallow one's words. ～を挟む interrupt sb; butt in. ⓐ ～を外す parry a remark. ～を放つ speak unreservedly; ① shoot off one's mouth. ⓐ ～を食う ❶ take back what one has said; ⓒ eat one's words. ❷ break one's word; go back on one's word. ～を引き出す entice sb to speak; draw sb out; pump out a secret.

言葉尻 the ending of a word

A ～を捕らえる ① catch sb in his/her own words; ⓐ trip sb up.

子供 a child; children

[A] ～が出来る conceive a child; be with child.
[を] ～を生む give birth; have a child. ～を下ろす have an abortion; abort a pregnancy.

粉 flour; meal; powder ▶ 粉

[N] ～にする grind *sth* to powder; pulverize *sth*. ～に碾く grind *sth* to powder; pulverize *sth*.
[を] ⓒ ～を掛ける seduce a girl; lure a girl; ⓒ ⓘ chat a girl up.

コネ connections; a pull

[A] ～が有る have connections; have influence; ⓘ have an in (with *sb*); ⓒ ⓘ have pull.
[を] ～を付ける establish relations with *sb*; set up (business) contacts.

小鼻 the nostrils

[A] ～が落ちる be emaciated; be close to dying.
[を] ～を蠢かす ❶ be elated; look triumphant. ❷ be haughty; ⓘ have airs and graces; ⓒ ⓘ have a swelled head; ⓒ be stuck-up. ～を膨らます ❶ flare one's nostrils. ❷ show one's displeasure; boil with rage.

小腹 [E] a (small) stomach

[A] ～が立つ be slightly annoyed; be slightly irritated. ～が減る feel slightly hungry.
[を] ～を立てる get slightly annoyed; get slightly irritated.

媚び flattery; cajolery

[を] Ⓐ ～を入る sound *sb's* feelings; ⓒ consult *sb's* pleasure. ～を売る sell one's favors. ⓒ ～を呈する use flattery; use blandishments.

御幣 a sacred Shintō staff

[を] ～を担ぐ be superstitious; believe in omens.

胡麻 sesame; a sesame seed

[を] ～を擦る ❶ grind sesame seeds. ❷ flatter *sb*; ⓘ curry favor with *sb*.

小股 short steps; the groin

[N] ～に歩く walk with short steps; take short steps; mince one's steps.
[を] ～を掬う [sumō] trip *sb* up; sweep *sb's* legs from under him. ～を取る ❶ [sumō] trip *sb* up; sweep *sb's* legs from under him. ❷ exploit *sb's* weak point.

小耳 a (small) ear

[N] ～に挟む overhear *sth*; come to one's knowledge; ⓘ hear *sth* on the grapevine.

米櫃 a rice chest; a rice bin

Ⓐ ～がたつく ❶ have little rice left in store. ❷ be in financial trouble; Ⓒ be in straitened circumstances; be in dire straits.

Ⓦ ～を潤す ❶ have much rice in store. ❷ make a profit; earn money; do well out of *sth*.

ごめん
御免 sb's pardon

Ⓦ ～を蒙る ask to be excused; ask permission; Ⓒ seek *sb*'s leave.

ころも
衣 clothes; garments; attire

Ⓦ Ⓐ Ⓗ ～を返す turn one's coat inside out (to ward off evil spirits) when meeting one's lover. ～を掛ける ❶ Ⓒ enhance *sth*; make *sth* more attractive. ❷ exaggerate *sth*; Ⓒ indulge in hyperbole; Ⓘ stretch the facts; Ⓢ Ⓘ pile it on; Ⓢ Ⓘ lay it on thick. ❸ glaze meat; frost a cake; coat fish. ～を付ける glaze meat; frost a cake; coat fish. ～を纏う wear a robe.

こわいろ
声色 tone of voice

Ⓦ ～を遣う imitate *sb*'s voice.

こん
根 a root; a radical; stamina ♦ 根

Ⓐ ～が尽きる lose patience with *sb*/*sth*.

Ⓦ ～を詰める apply oneself to (one's studies); concentrate on *sth*;

work hard on *sth*.

こんき
根気 perseverance; patience

Ⓐ ～が有る be patient; have perseverance; have stamina. ～が衰える lose patience; lose stamina. ～が尽きる reach the end of one's tether; run out of steam. ～が無い lack perseverance; have no staying power. ～が良い be persevering; Ⓒ be indefatigable.

Ⓦ ～を積める strain one's nerves; give all one's attention to *sth*. ～を要する require patience.

こんげん
根源 Ⓘ the origin; the root

Ⓝ Ⓒ ～に遡る trace *sth* to its origin. Ⓒ ～に触れる touch on the root of (a matter).

Ⓦ Ⓒ ～を究める trace *sth* to its origin; go to the root of *sth*. ～を絶つ root out the cause of trouble.

ごんご
言語 language; speech ♦ 言語

Ⓝ ～に絶する be beyond words; defy description; Ⓒ beggar belief.

こんじょう
根性 nature; disposition; spirit

Ⓐ ～が有る be tenacious; have guts. ～が汚い ❶ be perverted; be blackhearted. ❷ be treacherous; be cowardly; be unfair; be mean. ～が腐る be corrupted; be perverted; be depraved. 〜が小さい be mean; be ungenerous. 〜が突っ張る be stubborn; be obstinate; ⓒ be pigheaded. 〜が無い be weak; have no guts; 〜が根腐る be thoroughly corrupted; be totally perverted. 〜が捻くれる be perverse; have a warped nature. 〜が曲がる be unreasonable; be perverse; be cross-grained. 〜が悪い be ill-natured; be malicious. ［を］ 〜を入れ替える change one's habits; ⓞ turn over a new leaf. 〜を見せる show spirit. 〜を歪める irritate one; ⓘ rub one the wrong way; ⓒ get on one's nerves.

根底 ⓔ the root; the bottom

［を］ 〜を築く lay the basis for (an idea); pave the way for (a movement). ⓔ 〜を究める reach bedrock; get down to the root of (a matter). ⓔ 〜を為す form the basis (of a theory); be the foundation of (a belief).

困難 difficulties; trouble

［N］ 〜に遭う encounter difficulties; run into trouble. 〜に打ち勝つ overcome difficulties; ⓘ weather the storm. 〜に陥る fall into difficulties; get into trouble; ⓘ be in deep waters. 〜に堪える endure hardships; ⓘ weather the storm. 〜に臨む face difficulties.

［を］ 〜を感じる find sth difficult. 〜を切り抜ける overcome problems; surmount difficulties; get out of trouble; ⓘ weather the storm; ⓘ get out of the woods. 〜を除く relieve one's difficulties. 〜を招く invite difficulties; ask for trouble.

サ

差 a difference; a balance

［を］ 〜を付ける distinguish between two things; discriminate between two things; make a distinction. 〜を詰める narrow sb's lead.

座 a seat; a position; status

［A］ ⓞ 〜が醒める ❶ the mood is spoiled; spoil an occasion. ❷ interest wanes; lose interest. 〜が白ける the mood is spoiled; spoil an occasion. ⓞ 〜が長い outstay one's welcome; stay too long.

［N］ 〜に着く ❶ take a seat; assume a position. ❷ occupy a position; hold a post. 〜に連なる attend a meeting; join a party. 〜に直る sit down on one's own seat; sit down on one's seat; sit up straight.

［を］ 〜を構える take a seat. 〜を組む sit cross-legged. 〜を冷ます cast a chill over a room; spoil the mood; ⓘ be a wet blanket. 〜を占める

❶ take a seat; assume a position. ❷ occupy a position; hold a post. 〜を立つ leave one's seat; slip out of the room. 〜を取り持つ mediate between two parties; act as a go-between. 〜を守る maintain one's position; stay in power; hold a post; ⓒ ⓘ stay in the saddle. 〜を持つ carry on a conversation; entertain a company. 〜を外す leave one's seat; slip out of the room. 〜を譲る offer one's seat to sb.

才 talent; ability; aptitude

[A] 〜がある have talent.
[N] 〜に溺れる rely too much on one's talent; be too confident in one's talents.
[を] ⓞ 〜を頼む rely too much on one's talent; be too confident in one's talents. 〜を伸ばす develop one's talent. 〜を働かす exercise one's talents.

采 a baton of command

[を] 〜を振る be in command; act as leader; hold the leadership; ⓘ pull the strings.

財 money; riches; wealth

[を] 〜を惜しむ be parsimonious; ⓒ be tight-fisted. 〜を作る make a fortune. 〜を積む amass a fortune; grow rich. 〜を成す accumulate riches; grow rich. 〜を残す leave an estate. 〜を貪る covet riches.

骰子 a bone; a dice; a die

[を] 〜を振る throw dice; cast dice.

最期 one's last moment

[を] 〜を飾る ⓒ bring glory to one's last moments. 〜を遂げる die a pitiful death; meet with a tragic end; ⓔ come to an untimely end. 〜を見届ける be at sb's deathbed.

採算 commercial profit

[A] 〜が合う be a commercial success; be profitable; be worthwhile; pay (off). 〜が取れる be a commercial success; be profitable; be worthwhile; pay (off).

災難 a calamity; a misfortune

[N] 〜に遭う meet with misfortune.
[を] 〜を避ける avert a calamity. 〜を免れる escape disaster.

采配 a baton of command

[を] 〜を振る be in command; act as leader; hold the leadership; ⓘ pull the strings.

裁判 justice; a trial; a hearing

[N] 〜に掛ける go to court (over

sth); have a litigation against sb; ⓒ take sb to court. 〜に勝つ win a court case. ⓒ 〜に付ける put (a case) on trial; bring sb to justice. 〜になる be brought to trial; go to court. 〜に負ける lose a court case. 〔を〕 〜を仰ぐ submit (a case) to the court; bring a suit against sb; ⓒ sue sb. 〜を行なう hold court. 〜を受ける come up for trial; be on trial. 〜を行う pass judgment on sb; try sb. 〜を開く hold a court.

さいふ
財布 a purse; a wallet

〔を〕 〜を落とす drop one's purse. 〜を取り出す draw out one's purse. 〜を叩く empty one's purse. 〜を満たす fill one's purse.

さかい
境 a border; a frontier

〔N〕 〜に入る reach a high status; attain a superior position. 〔を〕 〜を荒らす harass the frontier. 〜を決める set up a borderline; define the boundary. 〜を接する border on (a place). 〜を為す represent a border. 〜を広げる extend the border(s). 〔A〕 〜を隔つ leave this world (behind); pass away; draw one's last breath; ⓒ ⓘ breathe one's last.

さかずき
盃 a (sake) cup

〔を〕 〜を上げる ❶ drink sake; have a drink. ❷ raise one's cup; toast to sth. 〜を合わせる touch (sake) cups. 〜を受ける accept a (sake) cup. 〜を返す offer a (sake) cup in return. 〜を重ねる drink one (sake) cup after another. 〜を傾ける have a drink. 〜を差す offer a (sake) cup. 〜をする drink a parting cup. 〜を伏せる reserve a (sake) cup. 〜を回す pass the (sake) cup around. 〜を貰う pledge one's loyalty (over a sake cup).

さかて
酒手 ⓢ drink money; a tip

〔を〕 〜を強請る demand a tip; ⓒ importune sb for drink money. ⓢ 〜を遣る give sb a tip.

さかやき
月額 ⓐ the shaven front-head

〔を〕 ⓐ 〜を伸ばす be unshaven. ⓐ 〜を剃る shave one's head.

さか
盛り the summit; prime; rut

〔A〕 〜が付く go to rut; get on heat. 〔N〕 〜に咲ける be in one's prime; ⓒ be in the bloom of one's life. 〔を〕 〜を過ぎる be past one's prime; ⓘ be in eclipse; ⓘ be on the wane.

さき
先 the head; the future ▶ 先

〔A〕 〜が有る be promising; have potential. 〜が見える ❶ be able to

see into the future; be clairvoyant; be far-sighted. ❷ be within reach; near completion; ① see light at the end of the tunnel.
N ～に行く go before sb else; go first. ～にする give priority to sth. ～に立つ ❶ be in the lead; ① be in the front van. ❷ be a priority; be placed above others. Ⓐ (人を)～に使う involve sb; use sb's name (in one's excuse). ～に出る come out first; top the list; be the first. ～になる get ahead of sb; get the lead.
を ～を争う strive to be first. ～を急ぐ rival sb for priority; try to be first. Ⓐ ～を追う clear the way (for a dignitary). Ⓐ ～を折る spoil sb's enthusiasm; ① be a wet blanket. Ⓐ ～を駆く take the lead; be in the forefront; ① set the tune. ～を担ぐ lead the way; Ⓐ pave the way (for sb). Ⓐ ～を切る ❶ cut the tip off. ❷ cut across sb; speak before one's turn. Ⓐ ～を潜る forestall sb; get a start on sb; preempt sb's actions; anticipate sb (in doing). ～を越す forestall sb; get a start on sb; pre-empt sb's actions; anticipate sb (in doing sth). Ⓐ ～を払う ❶ pay in advance; Ⓒ pay up front. ❷ pay on delivery. ❸ clear the way (for a dignitary). Ⓐ ～を回す forestall sb; get a start on sb; pre-empt sb's actions;

anticipate sb (in doing). ～を見る look ahead. ～を譲る give sb the lead; Ⓒ yield precedence to sb. ～を読む look into the future; plan ahead.

先棒 Ⓒ a front palanquin bearer
を Ⓒ ～を担ぐ ❶ be a palanquin's fron bearer; carry the front bar of a palanquin. ❷ be in the vanguard; take the lead; spearhead (a campaign); be a ringleader; ① be in the front van (of a movement). Ⓒ ～を振る be in the vanguard; take the lead; spearhead (a campaign); ① be in the front van.

策 a step; a measure; a means
A ～が尽きる be at the end of one's resources; ① be driven to the wall; ① be at one's wits' end; Ⓒ ① be in a fix. ～が無い be unresourceful.
N ～に窮する be at the end of one's resources; ① be driven to the wall; ① be at one's wits' end; Ⓒ ① be in a fix. ～に富む be resourceful; be a shrewd tactician.
を ～を与える instill wisdom in sb; furnish sb with knowledge; ① teach sb the ropes. ～を誤る take the wrong step; go astray. Ⓒ ～を講ずる devise a means; consider the (necessary) means. ～を立てる formu-

late a plan. ～を施(ほどこ)す adopt measures; take steps. ～を廻(めぐ)らす devise a scheme; draw up a plan. ⓒ ～を弄(ろう)する use artifice; ⓔ resort to wiles; play tricks on *sb*.

朔(さく) 回 New Year's Day [lunar]

囮 ⓞ ～を奉(う)く submit to a new emperor; accept the rule of a new emperor.

畝(さく) 回 a ridge; a rib; a row

囮 ⓞⓔ ～を切(き)る till the soil.

探(さぐ)り a spy; a probe; a stylet

囮 ～を入(い)れる sound *sb* out; probe a wound; plunge a probe into *sth*.

酒(さけ) *sake*; wine; liquor

N ⓐ ～に痛(いた)む destroy oneself with drinking; ⓢ get dead drunk; ⓢ get smashed. ～に耽(ふけ)る indulge in sake; give oneself up to drinking. ⓒ ～に回(まわ)される be enslaved to drinking; lose oneself in liquor.

囮 ～を傾(かたむ)ける drink from a sake cup. ～を嗜(たしな)む be fond of the bottle. ～を出(だ)す serve sake; put out sake. ⓐ ～を使(つか)う do *sth* under the influence of liquor; do *sth* with Dutch courage. ～を注(つ)ぐ pour out sake. ～を慎(つつし)む refrain from drinking; abstain from alcohol. ～を飲(の)む drink sake; take wine.

匙(さじ) a spoon

A ⓐ ～が回(まわ)る be good at mixing medicine.

囮 ～を投(な)げる give *sth* up as hopeless; ⓘ throw in the towel.

瑣事(さじ) 回 a trifle; trivialities

N ～にこだわる bother about trifles; ⓘ split hairs.

指図(さしず) directions; instructions

N ～に従(したが)う obey *sb's* directions.

囮 ～を仰(あお)ぐ ask for instructions. ～を受(う)ける receive instructions. ～を待(ま)つ await instructions. ～を守(まも)る obey *sb's* directions.

札片(さつびら) 回 bank notes; paper money

囮 ⓢ ～を切(き)る waste one's money; squander one's money.

里子(さとご) a farmed out child

N ～に出(だ)す farm out a child; send out a child to nurse with *sb*.

里心(さとごころ) homesickness; nostalgia

A ～が付(つ)く get homesick; pine for one's hometown; grow nostalgic.

悟(さと)り enlightenment; insight

A ～が良(い)い be quick to understand

sth; be quick-witted. 〜が早(はや)い be quick to understand *sth*; be quick-witted. 〜が悪(わる)い be slow to understand *sth*; be quick-witted.

🅆 〜を開く ❶ be enlightened; be spiritually awakened. ❷ resign oneself to one's fate; submit to fate.

鯖(さば) a mackerel

🅆 〜を読(よ)む cheat in counting; give *sb* the wrong number; misrepresent one's age.

様(さま) looks; condition; shape ▶ 様(ざま)

Ⓝ 〜になる be in good shape; look well; be complete.

様(ざま) a state; a plight ▶ 様(さま)

🅆 Ⓐ 〜を見(み)ろ serves you right!

鞘(さや) a sheath; a scabbard; a case

🄰 〜が有(あ)る be cunning be sly; ⒸⒹ have *sth* up one's sleeve; ⒸⒹ be up to *sth*.

🅆 〜を取(と)る take a commission; take a percentage. 〜を払(はら)う draw a sword; unsheathe a sword. ⒸⒹ 〜を寄(よ)せる narrow the spread.

左右(さゆう) left and right

Ⓝ Ⓒ 〜に托(たく)する dodge an issue; Ⓔ equivocate on an issue; Ⓘ beat about the bush; ⒸⒹ pussyfoot on an issue. Ⓒ 〜に侍(は)る wait on *sb*; attend on *sb*. 〜に揺(ゆ)れる roll from side to side. 〜に分(わ)ける part left and right. 🅆 〜を顧(かえり)みる look around. 〜を見(み)る look left and right; look around.

産(さん) 🅇 childbirth; a fortune

🅆 ⒸⒺ 〜を傾(かたむ)ける ❶ waste a fortune; exhaust one's fortune; Ⓔ dissipate one's possessions. ❷ invest one's family fortune; use private funds. Ⓔ (お)〜をする give birth to a child; have a baby. Ⓔ 〜を成(な)す amass a fortune; grow rich. ⒸⒺ 〜を破(やぶ)る lose one's fortune; go bankrupt; Ⓢ go bust.

算(さん) 🅇 Chinese divining blocks

🅆 Ⓐ 〜を置(お)く see into the future; divine the future; prophesy the future. Ⓐ 〜を散(ち)らす upset the ranks; throw the ranks into confusion; cause mayhem. Ⓐ 〜を乱(みだ)す cause mayhem; upset the ranks; throw the ranks into confusion.

賛(さん) 🅇 praise; eulogy; a legend

🄰 Ⓐ 〜が付(つ)く be criticized; be reviewed.

🅆 Ⓐ 〜を打(う)つ criticize (a work of art); review (a book). Ⓐ 〜をする write a legend (on a picture). Ⓐ 〜を付(つ)ける criticize (a work of art);

review (a book).

ざんがい
残骸 Ⓝ the remains of a corpse

を Ⓒ 〜を晒(さら)す be wrecked; be in ruins.

さんじ
賛辞 Ⓝ a eulogy; a compliment

を Ⓒ 〜を呈(てい)する pay tribute to *sb*; speak highly of *sb*.

さんした
三下 Ⓝ an underling; small fry

Ⓝ Ⓒ 〜に見(み)る ❶ slight *sb*; ignore *sb*; Ⓒ pay no consideration to *sb*. ❷ look down on *sb*; dispise *sb*; Ⓒ hold *sb* in contempt.

さんせい
賛成 approval; agreement

を 〜を得(え)る gain *sb's* approval. 〜を示(しめ)す express one's approval. 〜を求(もと)める seek *sb's* approval.

シ

し
死 death; decease; demise

Ⓝ (人を)〜に至(いた)らしめる cause *sb's* death. Ⓒ 〜に着(つ)く meet death; meet one's end; Ⓘ bite the dust. 〜に臨(のぞ)む face death; Ⓒ look death in the face.

を Ⓐ Ⓒ 〜を致(いた)す pass away; Ⓒ Ⓘ breathe one's last. Ⓒ (人の)〜を悼(いた)む mourn *sb's* death; lament over *sb's* death. 〜を祈(いの)る wish *sb* dead.

〜を恐(おそ)れる fear death. 〜を期(き)する expect to die; be ready to die. 〜を極(きわ)む be resolved to die. 〜を決(けっ)する be resolved to die. Ⓘ 〜を賜(たま)る be allowed to commit suicide. 〜を遂(と)げる meet one's end. 〜を賭(と)す risk one's life; hazard one's life; Ⓒ put one's life at stake. 〜を早(はや)める hasten *sb's* death. 〜を免(まぬが)れる escape death. 〜を招(まね)く court death.

し
歯 Ⓝ teeth; old age; frailty

を Ⓐ Ⓒ 〜を没(ぼっ)す reach the end of one's life; Ⓒ Ⓘ breathe one's last.

し   とげ
刺 Ⓝ a name card ▶ 刺

を Ⓒ 〜を通(つう)じる present one's card; send in one's name card.

じ
字 a character; a letter

を 〜を書(か)く write a character. 〜を崩(くず)す reduce a square Chinese character to the running style; write cursively. 〜を加(くわ)える add a character. 〜を削(けず)る erase a character.

じ
地 ground; texture; reality ▶ 地

Ⓐ Ⓒ 〜が積(つ)む be dense in texture. 〜が出(で)る one's true nature comes through; Ⓘ show the cloven hoof.

Ⓐ 〜で行(い)く put *sth* into practice; experience *sth* in reality; come true.

シアン　　　　　　　　　　　　　　　　シオドキ

国 ～を均(なら)す roll the ground; level the ground. ◎ ～を弾(ひ)く play accompaniment.

辞(じ) 国 a word; an expression
国 ⓔ ～を低(ひく)くする use humble words; speak in a humble way.

次(じ) 国 order; degree; sequence
国 ～を追(お)う follow a sequence; go in order; do *sth* in sequence.

思案(しあん) thought; consideration
N ～に余(あま)る be at a loss (about what to do); ⓘ be at one's wits' end; ⓘ be all at sea. ～に落(お)ちる be satisfied; be convinced; ⓔ ⓘ get the point. ～に暮(く)れる be lost in meditation; ponder over *sth*. ～に沈(しず)む think *sth* over; ponder over *sth*; be lost in thought. ～に尽(つ)きる be at the end of one's resources; ⓔ be at one's wits' end; ⓘ be all at sea. ～に耽(ふけ)る be sunk in meditation; be lost in thought. ◎ ～に塞(ふさ)がる think *sth* over; ponder over *sth*.
国 ～を重(かさ)ねる think on *sth* long and hard; ponder on *sth* repeatedly. ～を凝(こ)らす bury oneself in meditation. ～を廻(めぐ)らす think hard about *sth*; ⓔ cast *sth* about in one's mind; ⓒ ⓘ rack one's brains over *sth*.

辞意(じい) one's intention to resign
国 ～を翻(ひるがえ)す reconsider one's resignation. ～を洩(も)らす hint at one's resignation; ⓔ intimate one's intention to resign.

支援(しえん) support; aid; backing
国 ～を与(あた)える give *sb* support; support *sb*; ⓔ back *sb* up. ～を求(もと)める ask for support; ⓔ seek *sb's* support; look for support.

私怨(しえん) 国 a personal grudge
国 ～を抱(いだ)く hold a grudge against *sb*; ⓔ harbor a private malice; ⓒ have it in for *sb*; ⓘ have a chip on one's shoulder. ～を晴(は)らす satisfy one's grudge.

紫煙(しえん) 国 tobacco smoke
国 ～を燻(くゆ)らす send up a puff of smoke; pull away at one's cigarette; have a leisurely smoke.

塩(しお) salt; seasoning with salt
A ⓐ ～が浸(し)む go through a lot of hardships; suffer all sorts of privations.
N ～に漬(つ)ける preserve *sth* in salt; salt *sth* down.
国 ⓐ ～を踏(ふ)む experience lot of hardships; have a hard time.

138

しお
潮 the tide; a current

A ～が上げる the tide comes in. ～が引く the tide goes out. ～が満ちる the tide is at the full.
N ～に乗る take the tide.
を ⓐ ～を踏む go through a lot of hardships; suffer all sorts of privations. ～を待つ ❶ await a favorable tide. ❷ wait until the time is ripe; wait for a chance; ⓒ bide one's time.

しおどき
潮時 time and tide

を ～を外す ❶ miss a favorable tide. ❷ miss an opportunity; let a chance slip by. ～を待つ ❶ await a favorable tide. ❷ wait until the time is ripe; wait for a chance; ⓒ bide one's time. ～を見る ❶ wait for a favorable tide. ❷ watch for an opportunity; look for an opportunity; ⓒ bide one's time.

しか
鹿 a deer; a hind; a stag; a doe

を ～を争う contend for mastery; ⓒ vie for supremacy; compete for a prize; pursue political power. ～を逐う contend for mastery; ⓒ vie for supremacy; compete for a prize; pursue political power.

しが
歯牙 the teeth

N (事を)～に掛ける be bothered by sth; make an issue of sth; ⓒ let sth get to one.

しかく
資格 qualifications; capability

A ～が有る be qualified; have the qualifications (for a post).
を ～を与える qualify sb (for a post). ～を失う be disqualified; lose one's qualifications. ～を奪う disqualify sb (for a post). ～を得る qualify (for a post); ① become eligible (for a post). ～を取る obtain qualifications; get a license.

しかた
仕方 a method; a means; a way

A ～が無い it can't be helped. ～無しに…する be forced to do sth; ⓒ be obliged to do sth.

じがね
地金 ground metal; bullion

を ～を現わす betray oneself; reveal one's true character; ① show one's true colors. ～を出す betray oneself; reveal one's true character; ① show one's true colors.

じかん
時間 an hour; time

A ～が有る have time; be free; be vacant; have time on one's hands. ～が掛かる take time; be time-consuming. ～が迫る be under time pressure; time is closing in. ～が立つ time passes by.
N ～に遅れる be behind time; be

late. 〜に追われる be pressed for time; run out of time. 〜に縛られる be pressed for time; run out of time. ⓐ 〜を得る gain time; win time. 〜を稼ぐ play for time; buy time. 〜を繰り合わせる arrange hours. ⓒ 〜を食う be time-consuming; take time. ⓒ 〜を消す while away time. 〜を過ごす pass the time; spend time (on sth). 〜を進める bring time forward. 〜を費す spend time; waste (precious) time. 〜を潰す fill the time; ⓒ kill time. 〜を取る take time. ⓒ 〜を塞ぐ fill in the hour. 〜を守る be on time; be punctual; ⓢ ⓘ be on the button. 〜を持て余す have enough time; ⓘ have time on one's hands.

時機 ⓔ an opportunity; a chance

Ⓝ ⓒ 〜に投ずる take advantage of a situation; ⓒ capitalize on an opportunity.

Ⓐ 〜を捕える take one's chances; grab the chance; ⓒ seize an opportunity. ⓒ 〜を逸する let a chance slip by; miss an opportunity.

時儀 ⓔ seasonal compliments

Ⓐ 〜を交わす exchange seasonal compliments. ⓒ 〜を述べる give the compliments of the season.

児戯 ⓔ child's play; puerile

Ⓝ ⓒ 〜に等しい be puerile; be childish; be mere child's play. ⓒ 〜に類する be puerile; be childish; be mere child's play.

敷居 a threshold; a doorsill

Ⓐ 〜が高い feel awkward to visit sb; have leaden feet.

Ⓐ 〜を跨ぐ cross a threshold; enter/leave a house.

色彩 a color; a hue; a tint

Ⓝ 〜に富む be colorful; be rich in color.

Ⓐ 〜を与える give color to sth. 〜を帯びる take on color.

色情 desire; sexual appetite

Ⓐ 〜が起こる be seized with desire.

Ⓐ 〜をそそる arouse one's desire; excite one's sexual appetite.

事業 an enterprise; a project

Ⓐ 〜を営む run a business. 〜を起こす start an enterprise. 〜を引き受ける undertake a business. 〜を目論む have a project in view.

資金 funds; capital

Ⓐ 〜が切れる run out of funds.

Ⓐ 〜を集める raise funds. 〜を出す provide funds; put up funds.

ジケン　　　　　　　　　　　　　　　　シジョウ

死刑 capital punishment
　[N] ～に処する put sb to death.
　[を] ～を下す condemn sb to death; pass a death sentence on sb. ～を免れる escape capital punishment.

刺激 a stimulus; an impetus
　[を] ～を与える give impetus to sth; give a stimulus to sb. ～を受ける receive a stimulus; be stimulated.

試験 an examination; a test
　[N] ～に受かる pass an exam. ～に落ちる fail an examination; ⓒ flunk a test.
　[を] ～を受ける take a test; sit for an examination. ～を行う organize an examination; hold a test.

事件 an event; an incident
　[を] ～を起こす cause an incident; start trouble; stir up trouble; ⓒ raise Cain. ～を引き受ける take up a matter. ～を揉み消す hush up a scandal; cover up an affair; ⓒ sweep sth under the carpet.

嗜好 [E] a taste; a fancy; a liking
　[N] ⓒ ～に適う suit one's taste. ⓒ ～に投じる catch the (public) taste; capture sb's fancy.

時好 [E] the fashion of the moment

　[N] ⓒ ～に合う suit the latest fashion; be in vogue; be fashionable. ⓒ ～に投じる capture the fashion of the moment.
　[を] ⓒ ～を追う follow the fashion of the moment; pursue the latest fad.

仕事 work; labor; a job
　[N] ～に在り付く find work; ⓒ ⓘ land a job. ～に追われる be pressed with business. ～に掛かる set to work; get down to business. ～に疲れる be tired with work; be workworn.
　[を] ～を宛がう assign work to sb. ～を終える finish work; ⓒ round off a job. ～を捜す look for work; hunt for a job. ～を始める start work; get on with the job. ～を任せる entrust sb with work. ～を見付ける find work; ⓒ ⓘ land a job. ～を求める seek employment. ～を休む absent oneself from work; take time off from work. ～を辞める quit work; ⓒ ⓘ throw up one's job.

凝り a muscle-stiffness
　[A] ～が来る become interested in sth; ⓒ warm up to sth. ～が付く become interested in sth; ⓔ be engrossed in sth; ⓒ warm up to sth. ～が出来る suffer from a stiff muscle; ⓔ have an induration.
　[を] ～を残す leave an unpleasant

feeling.

指示 instructions; directions
N ～に従う comply with sb's directions; follow sb's instructions.
を ～を与える give instructions. ～を受ける receive directions.

市場 a market; a mart
N ～に出す put (a product) on the market. ～に出る come on the market; © hit the market.
を ～を操る manipulate the market. ～を荒らす spoil the market; upset the market. ～を築く build up a market. ～を狂わせる upset the market; spoil the market. ～を見付ける find a market.

私情 personal feeling
N ～に駆られる be swayed by personal feelings.
を ～を差し挟む take personal feelings into consideration. ～を捨てる set aside one's personal feelings. ～を挟む bring one's personal feelings into play.

私心 self-interest; selfishness
を ～を捨てる discard selfish feelings. ～を差し挟む act out of self-interest; ⓘ have an axe to grind; ⓘ have a hidden agenda.

自信 self-confidence
A ～が有る have self-confidence; be confident; © be cocky. ～が付く acquire confidence in oneself.
を ～を失う lose confidence; become insecure; ⓢ lose one's cool. ～を得る gain confidence; become sure of oneself; © get cocky. ～を欠く lack confidence; be insecure. ～を覆す undermine sb's self-confidence. ～を付ける acquire confidence in oneself. ～を持たせる give sb self-confidence. ～を持つ have self-confidence; be confident; © be cocky.

自説 one's own view
を ～を改める revise one's views. ～を捨てる give up one's own view. ～を曲げる change one's position.

視線 one's gaze; a glance
を ～を集める attract the public gaze. ～を浴びる attract sb's attention. ～を避ける avoid sb's gaze. ～を逸らす avert one's eyes; look away. ～を向ける turn one's gaze upon sb/sth.

慈善 charity; benevolence
を ～を行う do good; perform an act of charity. ～を施す render aid (to the poor); do good.

子孫 offspring; descendants

与 (...の)〜と称する claim descent from sb.

N 〜に伝える hand sth down to posterity; pass sth on to one's offspring.

を 〜を残す ❶ leave offspring. ❷ live on; survive.

自尊心 self-esteem; pride

を 〜を失う lose one's self-esteem. 〜を押える swallow one's pride. 〜を傷つける hurt sb's pride. 〜を保つ maintain one's self-esteem.

舌 the tongue; a clapper ▶ 舌

A 〜が肥える develop a taste for sth; be a gourmet. 〜が滑る ⓘ make a slip of the tongue; ⓘ let sth fall/slip; ⓒ blurt sth out. 〜が長い be talkative; ⓔ be loquacious; ⓒ be a chatterbox; ⓘ talk people's head off. ⓒ 〜が伸びる exaggerate sth; overstate sth; ⓘ stretch the facts; ⓢⓘ pile it on. 〜が回る have a glib tongue; be a good talker; ⓒⓘ have the gift of the gab. 〜が縺れる speak inarticulately; speak in a thick tone; talk with a lisp; have a slur in one's speech.

を 〜を打つ click one's tongue (with displeasure). ⓒ 〜を返す come back on what one has said; ⓘ change

one's tune. 〜を噛む bite one's tongue. ⓢ 〜を食う bite off one's tongue and die. 〜を滑らす blurt sth out; come out with sth inadvertently; let (a secret) slip out of one's mouth. 〜を出す ❶ make a fool of sb (behind their back); talk behind sb's back; ⓒ poke fun at sb (behind their back); ⓒⓘ thumb one's nose at sb. ❷ be embarrassed; be ashamed. 〜を鳴らす ❶ click one's tongue with (dis)pleasure. ❷ marvel at sth; be struck with wonder. ⓐ 〜を吐く be appalled by sth; be disgusted with sth; ⓒ be fed up with sth. ⓐ 〜を引く hold one's tongue; fall silent; ⓢ shut up. ⓐ 〜を翻す be struck dumb; be astonished; be flabbergasted; ⓢⓘ be blown away. ⓐ 〜を振る be terrified; ⓘ be scared out of one's wits. 〜を振う ❶ speak fluently; make an eloquent speech. ❷ be talkative; ⓔ be loquacious; ⓒ be a chatterbox; ⓘ talk people's head off. ❸ be terrified; ⓘ be scared out of one's wits. 〜を巻く ❶ be silenced; fall silent. ❷ be dumfounded; marvel at sth; ⓢⓘ be blown away. 〜を見る examine sb's tongue.

時代 an era; a (time) period

A 〜が付く become antiquated; atain a patina; acquire the appear-

ance of age.
N ～に先んじる be ahead of one's age; be a head of the times.
を ～を帯びる become antiquated; atain a patina; acquire the appearance of age. ⓢ ～を食う become antiquated; atain a patina; acquire the appearance of age. ～を下る come down in time. ～を遡る go back in time.

下心 an ulterior motive
N ～が有る have an ulterior motive; have a secret reason for *sth*; ⓘ have an axe to grind.

舌鼓 tongue-clicking
を ～を打つ ❶ smack one's lips. (食べ物に) ❷ enjoy one's food; eat with relish; ⓒ dig in.

下手 [nautical] wearing
N ～に出る condescend to *sb*; ⓔ asume a subordinate position. ～に着く serve *sb*; be in a subordinate position; ⓘ play second fiddle to *sb*.
を ～を持つ [*shōgi*] have the weaker side of the board.

事端 ◉ the origin of an event
を ⓔ ～を構える find a pretext for a deed. ⓞⓔ ～を繁くする give rise to complications; stir up troubles.

下紐 ◉ an undergarment belt
を ～を解く ❶ loosen the belt of one's undergarment. ❷ open oneself up to *sb*; take *sb* into one's confidence; ⓘ pour out one's heart to *sb*; ⓔ unbosom oneself. (男に) ❸ give oneself to a man; sleep with a man; ⓒ ⓘ go all the way. ⓒ (男に)～を許す give oneself to a man; sleep with a man; ⓒ ⓘ go all the way.

下目 an downward glance
N ～に見る look down on *sb*; dispise *sb*; ⓔ hold *sb* in contempt.

質 a pawn; a pledge ▶質 ▶質
A ～が流れる forfeit a pawn.
N ～に入れる give *sth* in pledge; give *sth* as collateral; pawn *sth*; ⓒ give *sth* in hock. ～に置く ❶ offer *sb* as a hostage; leave *sb* as a hostage. ❷ give *sth* as collateral; give *sth* in pledge; pawn *sth*; ⓒ give *sth* in hock. ～に取る ❶ accept *sth* in pledge; take *sth* in pawn. ❷ take a hostage; hold *sb* hostage.
を ⓐ ～を受ける pay off one's pledge. ～を置く give *sth* as collateral; give *sth* in pledge; pawn *sth*; ⓒ give *sth* in hock. ～を埋める give *sth* as collateral; give *sth* in pledge; pawn *sth*; ⓒ give *sth* in hock. ～を流す forfeit a pawn.

死地 ⓔ the jaws of death

を ～に追い込む drive sb into a corner; corner sb. ～に陥る be driven into a corner; ⓒ ⓘ get into a scrap; ⓒ ⓘ be up the creek. ⓔ ～に赴く face certain destruction; ⓘ throw oneself into the jaws of death; ⓘ burn one's boats/bridges (behind one).
を ～を求める face death; ⓔ look death in the face; court destruction.

質 quality; nature ▶ 質 ▶ 質

A ～が良い be of good quality. ～が悪い be of bad quality.
を ～を落とす reduce the quality of sth; ⓒ debase the quality of sth. ～を下げる debase the quality of sth.

実 the truth; the fruit ▶ 実

を ～を明かす reveal the truth; expose the truth. ～を挙げる bring sth to fruition; realize a goal; live up to one's principles. ～を言う speak the truth. ⓒ ～を立てる keep faith with sb. ⓒ ～を尽くす be truthful; act sincerely toward sb; show fidelity toward sb. ⓒ ～を告げる tell sb how things stand; undeceive sb. ⓒ ～を吐く confess the truth; ⓒ own up to the truth.

失言 a slip of the tongue

を ～をする ⓘ make a slip of the tongue; ⓘ let sth fall/slip; ⓒ blurt sth out. ～を取り消す take back what one has said; ⓒ eat one's words. ～を詰る reproach sb (for their indiscretions); scold sb; ⓘ tell sb off. ～を詫びる apologize for one's indiscretions.

失策 a blunder; a mistake

を ～を演じる commit a blunder; make a mistake; ⓒ ⓘ drop the ball.

尻尾 a tail; the end; the tip

A ⓐ ～が裂ける be bewitched by sb/sth; be under sb's spell. ～が出る betray oneself; reveal one's true character; ⓘ reveal one's true colors; ⓘ show the cloven hoof.
N ～に着く queue up; join a queue.
を ⓐ ～を嗅がれる be caught out; be exposed; be found out. ～を切る take a percentage; ⓒ take a rake-off. ～を出す betray oneself; reveal one's true character; ⓘ reveal one's true colors; ⓘ show the cloven hoof. ～を掴む ❶ obtain evidence; uncover a scandal. ❷ find fault with sb; catch sb out. ～を振る ❶ wag its tail. ❷ ingratiate oneself with sb; ⓘ curry favor with sb. ～を巻く acknowledge one's inferiority; beat a retreat; ⓢ ⓘ hightail it. ～を見せ

る betray oneself; reveal one's true character; ⓒ reveal one's true colors; ⓓ show the cloven hoof.

質問 a question; a query

[N] 〜に応ずる respond to a question. 〜に答える answer a question; reply to a question.
[を] 〜を受ける be questioned; answer a question; ⓒ take a question. 〜を受け流す turn a question aside; ⓔ parry a question. 〜を打ち切る bring an interview to a close; put an end to the questioning. 〜を逸らす turn a question aside; ⓔ parry a question. 〜を放つ fire questions at sb; ⓔ hurl questions at sb. 〜を向ける address a question to sb; put a question to sb.

指導 guidance; leadership

[を] 〜を与える give sb guidance. 〜を誤る lead sb amiss. (人の)〜を受ける receive guidance. (人の)〜を求める turn to sb for guidance.

品 a thing; quality; coquetry ▶ 品

[A] ⓒ 〜が落ちる be inferior in quality; be cheap; ⓓ be below par. 〜が劣る be inferior in quality; be cheap. 〜が切れる run out of stock. ⓒ 〜がだぶつく there is glut in the market; be overabundant. 〜が違う be different in quality. 〜が良い be of high quality.
[を] 〜を落とす reduce the quality of sth; ⓔ debase the quality of sth. 〜を作る behave coquettishly; play the coquette; give oneself airs; ⓓ put on airs; ⓒ be stuck-up. 〜を付ける ❶ find a pretext; ⓔ assign a reason for sth; make an excuse. ❷ behave coquettishly; give oneself airs; play the coquette; ⓓ put on airs; ⓒ be stuck-up. Ⓐ 〜を踏む gather experience; make headway. Ⓐ 〜を遣る behave coquettishly; play the coquette; ⓓ put on airs.

死に際 the hour of death

[A] 〜が悪い leave a bad name behind; die in infamy.

死に恥 a shameful death

[を] ⓒ 〜を曝す die a shameful death; die an ignominious death.

死に場所 one's place of death

[を] 〜を捜す seel a chance to die decently; seek a place to kill oneself.

死に花 posthumous fame

[を] 〜を咲かせる ❶ die in (a blaze of) glory; come to a glorious end. ❷ win posthumous fame; gain

篠 a small species of bamboo

[を] ～を束ねる rain heavily; pour with rain; fall down in sheets; ⓘ rain cats and dogs. ～を突く pelt with rain; come down in torrents. ～を乱す have a blustery shower.

鎬 ⑬ ridges on a sword blade

[を] ⓔ ～を削る fight desperately; ⓒ engage in a fierce contest; fight to the death.

芝居 a play; a drama; a fake

[を] ～を演じる perform a play; enact a scene. ～を打つ ❶ stage a play; play a piece. ❷ play a trick on *sb*; ⓢ put *sb* on; ⓘ put up a false show. ～を見る see a play.

自腹 ⑬ "one's own stomach"

[を] ⓢ ～を切る pay out of one's own pocket; ⓐ untie one's purse strings; ⓘ foot the bill.

支払い payment; disbursement

[を] ～を受ける receive payment. ～を断る refuse payment. ～を迫る press *sb* for payment. ～を停止する suspend payment; stop a check. ～を延ばす postpone payment.

地盤 the ground; the base

[を] ～を得る gain a foothold. ～を固める solidify the foundation. (市場に)～を築き上げる get a footing (in a market). ～を築く lay the foundation; establish a constituency. ～を造る prepare the ground. ～を作る establish a foothold. ～を取り戻す recover one's footing; regain one's foothold. (地方に)～を持つ have a foothold in (a district). ～を養う nurse one's constituency.

慈悲 mercy; charity; pity

[を] ～を掛ける do an act of charity; show mercy (to *sb*). ～を請う beg for mercy; plea for mercy. ⓐ ～を垂れる have mercy on *sb*.

痺れ a cramp; numbness

[を] ～を切らす ❶ have a cramp. ❷ lose one's patience; grow impatient; ⓒ get tired of waiting.

渋 persimmon tanin

[A] ～が来る be complained about. ～が出る complaints are made; grudges are vented; be complained about.

[を] ⓢ ～を食う be scolded; be told off; be given a dressing-down. ～を抜く sweeten *sth*; take away the astringency. ～を引く tan (paper).

私腹 one's own stomach
[を] ～を肥やす enrich oneself by way of graft; ⓘ line one's pocket; ⓘ feather one's own nest.

脂粉 ⓔ cosmetics; make-up
[を] ～を施す powder one's face; paint one's face.

時分 time; hour; season
[を] ～を窺う watch for a (good) moment; look for an opportunity; ⓔ bide one's time.

辞柄 ⓔ a pretext; an excuse
[を] ⓔ ～を設ける find an excuse; give a pretext; make excuses.

資本 a capital; a fund
[を] ⓞ ～を下ろす lay out capital (in a venture); put in capital. ～を出す provide capital; finance (an enterprise). ～を投じる invest capital (in). ～を寝かせる let capital lie idle.

始末 circumstances; settlement
[A] ～が良い ❶ be easy to settle; be under control. ❷ be easy to deal with; be pliant; be docile. ❸ be prudent; be frugal; be thrifty; be economical. ～が悪い ❶ be difficult to settle; be out of control; be hard to manage. ❷ be unruly; be hard to deal with; be intractable; be incorrigible. ❸ be unthrifty; be uneconomical.
[N] ～に負えない ❶ be difficult to settle; be out of control; be hard to manage. ❷ be unruly; be hard to deal with; ⓔ be intractable; be incorrigible. ～に困る be hard to deal with.
[を] ～を付ける settle one's accounts; do away with sth.

死命 ⓔ life and death; fate
[を] ⓔ (人の)～を制する have a hold upon sb; have sb in one's power.

締め括り control; conclusion
[を] ～を付ける round (a matter) off; settle (an affair); put an end to sth; bring sth to a close. ⓞ ～を遣る control (a department); supervise (an activity).

耳目 ⓔ the ears and eyes
[N] ～に触れる come to one's knowledge; learn sth by chance; find sth out; ⓒ ⓞ get wind of sth.
[を] ～を驚かす create a sensation; be much talked about; ⓐ shake the world; ⓘ make a stir. ⓞ ～を属す prick up one's eyes and ears; strain one's eyes and ears. ～を欹てる

prick up one's eyes and ears; strain one's eyes and ears. 〜を引く attract public interest; draw the attention of the world. 〜を避ける avoid public notice; shun publicity; ⓘ keep a low profile.

斜 a slant; a diagonal; an oblique

[N] 〜に構える ❶ [kendō] hold one's sword upward at an anle away from one's opponent. ❷ stand ready for (an atack); be on guard; ⓘ square up to *sth*; ⓘ square off (for a fight). ❸ intersect *sth* at an angle; run oblique (to *sth*). ❹ fail to face *sth* head-on; ⓘ laugh *sth* off.

視野 one's field of vision

[N] 〜に入る come into view; come in sight.
[を] 〜を去る go out of sight. 〜を広げる broaden one's outlook; widen one's mental/intellectual horizon.

邪気 malarial air; malice

[を] 〜を払う purge noxious vapors.

癪 spasms; convulsions

[A] ⓐ 〜が上る have a spasm; suffer a fit; have convulsions.
[N] 〜に障る be offended; feel vexed; take offense.
[を] ⓐ 〜を言う say offensive things; hurt *sb's* feelings; upset *sb*.

尺 a *shaku* (0.9 ft.); a measure

[を] ⓒ 〜を打つ measure the length of *sth*; take *sb's* measurements. 〜を取る measure the length of *sth*; take *sb's* measurements.

酌 serving *sake* at a table

[A] 〜が強い be generous in the serving of *sake*; serve copious amounts of *sake*.
[を] 〜をする pour sake into *sb's* cup; help *sb* to sake; serve sake. ⓒ 〜を取る pour sake into *sb's* cup; help *sb* to sake; serve sake.

錫 ▣ a priest's staff

[を] ⓐ ⓔ 〜を飛ばす travel on foot; go on a pilgrimage; ⓒ hit the road.

杓子 a ladle; a scoop; a dipper

[を] 〜を取る manage a household; run a household. 〜を渡す hand the management of the household (to one's daughter-in-law).

弱点 a weak point; a defect

[N] (人の)〜に触れる touch *sb* on a sore spot; ⓒ hit *sb's* Achilles heel; ⓘ touch *sb* on the raw. ⓒ (人の)〜に乗ずる take advantage of *sb's* weak point.

⦅を⦆ ～を暴く expose a defect. ～を突く strike (the enemy) at a weak point; ⓒ hit where it hurts; ⓔ hit sb's Achilles heel. ～を握られる ⓘ give a handle (to the enemy). ～を見抜く see sb's weak points; ⓔ find sb's Achilles heel; ⓘ get the length of sb's foot. ～を持つ have a weak point; have a flaw; ⓔ have an Achilles heel.

邪慳 cruelty; hardheartedness

⦅N⦆ ～にする be hard on sb; be cruel to sb; treat sb with cruelty.

奢侈 ⓔ luxury; extravagance

⦅N⦆ ～に流れる fall into luxurious habits. ～に耽る indulge in luxury.
⦅を⦆ ～を戒める admonish against luxurious living.

車軸 a wheel axle; an axle

⦅を⦆ ～を下す rain heavily; pour with rain; fall down in sheets; ⓘ rain cats and dogs. ～を流す rain heavily; pour with rain; fall down in sheets; ⓘ rain cats and dogs. ～を降らす rain heavily; pour with rain; fall down in sheets; ⓘ rain cats and dogs.

邪道 the wrong way; an evil way

⦅N⦆ ～に陥る fall into evil ways. ～に

入る be led astray; ⓐ stray from the right path. (人を)～に導く lead sb astray; ⓔ set sb on the road to perdition.
⦅を⦆ ～を取る ⓐ take the wrong road (in life); chose the wrong.

邪念 an evil thought; malice

⦅A⦆ ～が有る have wicked thoughts.
⦅N⦆ ～に耽る indulge in wicked thoughts.
⦅を⦆ ～を払う free oneself of evil thoughts.

娑婆 the outside world

⦅を⦆ ～へ出る be released from captivity; get out of prison; be set free.

娑婆気 ⓔ worldly desires

⦅A⦆ ⓒ ～が有る entertain worldly desires; have vulgar ambitions.
⦅を⦆ ⓒ ～を捨てる discard one's worldly desires; ⓘ rise above the world. ⓒ ～を出す be unable to shed one's worldly desires.

邪魔 a hindrance; cumbersome

⦅A⦆ ～が入る be hindered; be thwarted; be frustrated.
⦅N⦆ ～になる be in sb's way; be a hindrance; stand in the way.
⦅を⦆ ～を入れる frustrate sb's plans; thwart sb's aims; ⓘ put a spoke in

sb's wheels. 〜をする disturb sb; interrupt sb; thwart sb's plans.

砂利 gravel; pebbles

[を] 〜を敷く gravel a road; ballast a railroad. Ⓐ 〜を掴む be called before a magistrate; be cross-examined by a magistrate.

朱 ◨ cinnabar; vermilion ▸ 朱

[N] Ⓔ 〜に交わる associate with the wrong people; keep bad company. [を] Ⓔ 〜を入れる red-pencil sth; correct sth. 〜を差す paint sth red; paint one's lips. Ⓐ Ⓔ 〜を雪ぐ go purple with rage; be flushed with rage.

主 one's master; one's lord

[を] Ⓐ 〜を取る enter sb's service.

綬 ◨ a ribbon (of office)

[を] Ⓒ Ⓔ 〜を釈く step down from office; Ⓔ retire from public office; leave government service. Ⓒ Ⓔ 〜を結ぶ take up public office.

寿 ◨ a long life; longevity

[を] Ⓔ 〜を上る pray for sb's health; wish that sb may live a long life.

衆 great numbers; the masses

[N] 〜に抜きん出る surpass the masses; Ⓘ cut a prominent figure. [を] 〜を頼む rely on one's superior number. 〜を率いる lead the masses.

銃 a rifle; a gun; firearm; arms

[を] 〜を担ぎ変える change arms. 〜を構える hold a rifle at the ready. 〜を組む stack arms. 〜を捧げる present arms. 〜を解く unstack arms. 〜を担う shoulder a rifle. 〜を向ける point a gun at sb.

重 weight

[を] 〜を越す ❶ exaggerate sth; Ⓔ indulge in hyperbole; Ⓘ stretch the facts; Ⓢ Ⓘ pile it on; Ⓢ Ⓘ lay it on thick. ❷ exacerbate sth; make sth worse; Ⓔ enhance sth; make sth more attractive.

雌雄 male and female

[を] 〜を争う fight for supremacy; try conclusions with sb. 〜を決する fight it out with sb; come to a showdown with sb.

自由 liberty; freedom

[N] (人を)〜にする ❶ set sb free; liberate sb. ❷ have one's will with sb; Ⓘ wrap sb round one's little finger. ❸ deceive sb; Ⓘ take sb in; Ⓒ Ⓘ lead sb by the nose. 〜になる ❶ be set

free; be liberated. (人の) ❷ be at sb's disposal; be at sb's mercy; be at sb's will.
〖を〗 ～を与える set sb free; give sb liberty. ～を失う lose one's freedom; ⓒ be robbed of one's liberty. ～を得る gain one's liberty. ～を尊ぶ value liberty; ⓒ hold freedom dear; prize freedom.

銃火 rifle fire; musket fire
〖を〗 ～を冒す brave enemy fire. ～を浴びる come under fire. ～を交える exchange fire; fight a battle; ⓒ engage an enemy.

習慣 a custom; usage; habit
〖A〗 ～が有る have a habit/custom. ～が付く pick up a habit; take to a habit; ⓒ acquire a custom.
〖N〗 ～に従う stick to one's habit.
〖を〗 ～を捨てる abandon a usage; do away with custom; break off a habit; discard a custom. ～を付ける form a habit; ⓒ cultivate a custom. ～を取り入れる adopt a custom; take over a habit. ～を直す mend a habit; change a custom. ～を発する abolish a custom; ⓒ abrogate a custom. ～を守る observe an old custom; ⓒ stick to old habits.

銃口 the muzzle of a rifle

〖を〗 ～を向ける level a gun at sb; point a rifle at sb; hold a gun on sb.

十字 a cross
〖を〗 ～を切る cross oneself; cross one's heart. ⓒ ～を引く cross out (a word).

十字架 a crucifix; a cross
〖N〗 ～に懸ける crucify sb.
〖を〗 ～を背負う bear one's cross; carry a cross.

終止符 a period; a full stop
〖を〗 ～を打つ put an end to sth; bring sth to an end; ⓒ write finis to sth; ⓒ ⓘ call it a day.

十字路 a crossroads
〖N〗 ～に立つ stand at a crossroads; be at a crossroads.

醜態 shameful behaviour
〖を〗 ～を演じる act disgracefully; behave in a shameful way; ⓘ cut a sorry figure; ⓒ ⓘ come a cropper. ～を曝す act disgracefully; behave in a shameful way; ⓘ cut a sorry figure; ⓒ ⓘ come a cropper.

秋波 an amourous glance
〖を〗 ～を送る wink at sb; ⓘ give sb the eye; ⓘ make eyes at sb.

ジュギョウ　　　　　　　　　　　　　　　　　　ジュッチュウ

愁眉 knitted eyebrows
〔を〕 ⓒ ～を開く feel relieved; be reassured; be put at ease.

主義 a principle; a cause
〔N〕 ～にこだわる stick to one's principles; ⓞ stick to one's guns. ～に殉じる die for one's principles; sacrifice oneself for a cause.
〔を〕 ～を捨てる give up a cause; abandon one's principles. ～を曲げる compromise one's principles. ～を守る defend a cause; live up to one's principles; ⓞ stick to one's guns.

授業 teaching; class; a session
〔N〕 ～に出る attend lessons; go to school.
〔を〕 ～を受ける take lessons; be taught; receive instruction. ⓒ ～をサボる dodge a lesson; play truant. ～を休む miss a lesson; stay away from a lesson.

宿怨 a deep-seated grudge
〔を〕 ～を晴らす get one's revenge on sb; ⓞ settle old scores (with sb); ⓞ square accounts with sb.

趣向 a plan; an idea
〔A〕 ～が浮ぶ think of sth; hit upon an idea; come up with an idea; come to one.

〔を〕 ～を変える bring variety to sth; vary one's approach. ～を凝らす work out a plan; devise a scheme.

数珠 a rosary; a string of beads
〔を〕 ～を切る ❶ renounce the Buddhist faith; be converted from Buddhism. ❷ abandon one's ideals; resign oneself to one's fate; give sth up; let go of an idea.

手段 a means; a measure; a way
〔A〕 ～が尽きる be at the end of one's resources; ⓞ be at the end of one's tether; ⓞ be at one's wits' end.
〔を〕 ～を誤る ⓐ take a wrong step; use the wrong methods; go astray. ～を選ばず try all possible means; stop at nothing; ⓞ do sth by hook or by crook. ～を講じる devise a means; work out a way. ～を尽くす leave no means untried; try every means; ⓞ leave no stone unturned. ～を取る take measures; resort to (certain) means.

手中 in one's hand
〔N〕 ～に在る be in sb's control; be at sb's mercy; be in sb's posession. ～に納める take posession of sth; sieze control over sth; get a hold on sth; get hold of sth. ～に落ちる fall into one's/sb's hands; come under

one's/*sb's* control. 〜に帰する fall into one's/*sb's* hands; come under one's/*sb's* control. 〜に握る take posession of *sth*; sieze control over *sth*; get a hold on *sth*; get hold of *sth*.

術計 (じゅっけい) N a ploy; a ruse; a scheme

A ⓒ 〜が尽きる pass away; reach the end of one's life; ⓔ ⓘ breathe one's last.

N ⓒ 〜に陥る become the victim of a plot; ⓐ fall into a trap.

術中 (じゅっちゅう) N a ploy; a strategem

N 〜に陥る become the victim of a plot; play into *sb's* hands; become; be entrapped; ⓐ fall into a trap. 〜に嵌まる become the victim of a plot; play into *sb's* hands; become; be entrapped; ⓐ fall into a trap.

手套 (しゅとう) N gloves

を ⓒ 〜を脱ぐ reveal one's true strenth; ⓘ play one's trump card.

首尾 (しゅび) N alpha and omega

A 〜が良い ❶ have a favourable outcome; be successful; be a success. ❷ enjoy *sb's* favor; be in *sb's* favor. 〜が悪い ❶ have an unfavourable outcome; be unsuccessful; be a failure. ❷ be out of favor with *sb*.

朱筆 (しゅひつ) N a brush with red ink

を ⓒ 〜を入れる red-pencil *sth*; correct *sth*. ⓔ 〜を加える red-pencil *sth*; correct *sth*.

趣味 (しゅみ) a taste; an interest; a hobby

A 〜が有る be interested in *sth*; have a taste for *sth*. 〜が良い be tasteful; have a good taste. 〜が悪い be tasteless; have a poor taste.

N 〜に合う suit one's taste; be to one's taste. 〜に適う meet one's taste; be to one's taste.

を 〜を持つ have an interest; have a hobby.

寿命 (じゅみょう) one's span of life

を 〜を縮める shorten one's span of life. 〜を延ばす lengthen one's span of life.

修羅 (しゅら) a scene of bloodshed

を 〜を燃やす ❶ burn with envy; be consumed with jealousy. ❷ go wild with rage; be beside oneself with rage; be consumed with wroth; ⓒ go beserk.

順 (じゅん) order; a turn

A 〜が来る be next in line; one's turn comes round. 〜が狂う be out

ジュンジョ

of order.
N ～に送る pass sth on. ～に並ぶ stand in order. ～に並べる put sth in order. ～に回す pass sth around. ～に遣る take one's turn.
を ～を追う go in order; do sth in sequence. ～を変える change the order. ～を繰り上げる move up in order. ～を狂わす put sth out of order. ～を待つ await one's turn.

春秋 E spring and autumn
N ⓒ ～に富む be still very young; be in the prime of one's life; have still many years before one.

順序 order; sequence
A ～が違う be out of order; be inappropriate.
N ～に従う go in order; do sth in sequence.
を ～を誤る follow the wrong order. ～を狂わす upset the order; disturb the order; put sth out of order. ～を立てる put sth in order. ～を整える adjust the order. ～を踏む follow procedures; ⓒ go through due formalities. ～を乱す disturb the order; put sth out of order.

春情 E sexual passion; lust
を ⓒ ～をそそる arouse one's sexual passions; be tempting; be suggestive;

ジョウ

① turn sb on; ⓒ be sexy. ⓔ ～を催す be sexually aroused; ① be turned on ⑧ feel horny.

順番 order; turn; rotation
N ～に働く work in shifts; take turns.
を ～を狂わす upset the order; put sth out of order. ～を待つ await one's turn. ～を守る keep one's turn; observe the order.

諸 E the beginning; the start
N ⓒ ～に就く get under way; be started; be on foot.

賞 a prize; a reward
を ～を与える bestow a reward on sb; award a prize to sb; give sb a reward. ～を争う compete for a prize (with sb). ～を受ける receive a prize. ～を懸ける offer a prize (for sth); (人の首に) put a price on (sb's head). ～を攫う carry off an award. ～を取る win an award.

性 nature; disposition
A ～が合う ❶ have the same temperament. ❷ have the same social standing. ⓒ ～が付く be steady; be resolved; be firm. ～が抜ける become feeble-minded; lose vigor.
N ～に合う agree with one; come nat-

ural to one; ⓒ be congenial to one.

掌 しょう 🅴 the palm of the hand ▶ 掌 てのひら

🅆 ～を返 かえ す ❶ be easy (to do); be simple (to understand). ❷ be fickle; be inconstant; be changeable. ～を指 さ す be clear; be apparent.

情 じょう feelings; passion; pity

🅐 ～が有 あ る have a kind heart. ～が薄 うす い be unfeeling; be heartless; be hardhearted; be coldhearted. ～が移 うつ る become attached to *sb*; begin to love *sb*. ～が強 こわ い ❶ be headstrong; be obstinate; ⓒ ⓘ be stiff-necked. ❷ be amorous; be sensual; be lustful; be lascivious. ～が無 な い be unfeeling; be heartless; be hardhearted; be coldhearted. ～が激 はげ しい be passionate; be *sb* of strong passions. ⓐ ～が張 は る refuse to give in; be obstinate; be stubborn. ～が深 ふか い ❶ be warmhearted; be kindhearted. ❷ have a passionate disposition; ⓒ be a great lover. ～が弱 よわ い be *sb* of weak emotions.

🅽 ～に厚 あつ い be compasionate; be sentimental; ⓒ have a tender heart; ⓒ have a soft spot. ⓐ ～に入 い れる apply oneself to; do *sth* in earnest. ～に絆 ほだ される be moved by one's pity for *sb*; be swayed by emotions; ⓒ be tied to *sb* by affection. ～に脆 もろ い have a tender heart; be sentimental; ⓒ have a soft spot.

🅆 ⓒ ～を明 あ かす confide in *sb*; tell things as they are. ～を売 う る prostitute oneself; ⓒ sell one's favors. ⓒ (人 ひと の)～を起 お こす affect *sb's* emotions; touch *sb's* heart. ～を覚える be swayed by emotions; feel (a surge of) passion. ～を交わす have sexual intercourse; sleep with each other. ～を込 こ める sympathize with *sb*; empathize with *sb*; feel for *sb*. ～を立 た てる be faithful to *sb*. ⓒ ～を矯 た める repress one's desires; restrain one's passions. (人 ひと と)～を通 つう じる ❶ have an affair (with *sb*); ⓢ carry on with *sb*. ❷ make secret overtures (to the enemy). ～を張る refuse to give in; be obstinate; be stubborn. ～を燃 も やす burn with love (for *sb*); lust after *sb*. (人 ひと の)～を催 もよお す affect *sb's* emotions; touch *sb's* heart. ～を寄 よ せる make overtures to *sb*.

錠 じょう a padlock; a snaplock

🅐 ～が下りる ❶ (the door) locks. ❷ be settled; be brought to an end. ～が掛 か かる (the door) locks.

🅆 ～を開 あ ける remove a lock; unlock (a door). ～を下ろ おろ す ❶ fasten a lock; lock (a door). ❷ grow stubborn; become set in one's ways. ～を掛ける fasten a lock; lock (a door). ⓒ 〜を狂わす hamper a lock; meddle with a lock. 〜を挟じ開ける prize open a lock; force a lock. 〜を付ける put a lock on (a door). 〜を捩じ切る prize open a lock; force a lock. 〜を外す remove a lock; unlock (a door).

しょうがい
障害 an obstacle; a barrier

と 〜と成る become an obstacle.
N 〜に遭う run into difficulties; ⓒⓘ hit a snag. 〜に打ち勝つ overcome an obstacle. 〜に成る be an obstacle. 〜にぶつかる encounter an obstacle; ⓒⓘ hit a snag.
を 〜を築く build a barrier; erect a barrier. 〜を飛び越える [sports] clear a hurdle. 〜を乗り越える overcome an obstacle; surmount difficulties.

しょうがい
生涯 a life(time); livelihood

を 〜を失う ❶ lose one's life; pass away. ❷ lose one's means of living; lose one's livelihood; run out of food; fall on hard times. ❸ be put to death; ⓒ mount the scaffold. 〜を終える end one's life; pass away. 〜を送る spend a life; live a life.

じょうかく
城郭 F a castle; a fortress

を 〜を構える maintain a castle. ⓒ 〜を設ける ❶ build a castle; errect a fortress; fortify oneself. ❷ keep people at bay; withdraw into oneself; be intensely private.

しょうき
正気 consciousness; sanity

N 〜に返る recover one's sanity; come to oneself; come to one's senses.
を 〜を失う ❶ lose consciousness; pass out; ⓒ black out. ❷ lose one's senses; go mad; ⓈⓘⓄ lose one's marbles; Ⓢ go crazy.

じょうき
常軌 F the proper course

を ⓒ 〜を逸する be eccentric; break conventions; go off the beaten track.

しょうげき
衝撃 a shock; an impact

を 〜を与える give sb/sth a shock. 〜を受ける receive a shock.

じょうこう
情交 friendship; liaison

を 〜を迫る force attentions upon sb. 〜を結ぶ keep company with sb; become intimate with sb; have a relationship with sb.

しょうじ
生死 F life and death

を ⓒ 〜を出づ ❶ be delivered from worldly attachments. ❷ be enlightened; be spiritually awakened. ⓒ 〜を離る ❶ be delivered from worldly attachments. ❷ be enlightened; be spiritually awakened.

じょうじつ
情実 personal considerations

图 ～を排(はい)する set aside personal considerations.

しょうそく
消息 news; word; a letter

图 ～を聞(き)く hear of sb; get news of sb. ～を伝(つた)える bear news of sb.

しょうたい
正体 the true shape

图 ～を現(あら)わす reveal one's true character; ⓘ show one's true colors; ⓘ show the cloven hoof. ～を失(うしな)う ❶ lose consciousness; pass out; ⓒ black out. ❷ lose one's senses; lose one's wits; go mad; ⓒ lose it; ⓢ ⓘ lose one's marbles; ⓢ go crazy. ～を隠(かく)す ❶ wear a mask; disguise oneself. ❷ hide one's true character; ⓐ put on a mask. ～を無(な)くす ❶ lose consciousness; pass out; ⓒ black out. ❷ lose one's senses; lose one's wits; go mad; ⓒ lose it; ⓢ ⓘ lose one's marbles; ⓢ go crazy.

しょうだく
承諾 consent; acceptance

图 ～を与(あた)える give one's consent. ～を得(え)る obtain sb's consent.

じょうだん
冗談 a joke; jest

Ⓐ ～が分(わ)かる understand a joke; see a joke; ⓒ ⓘ get it. Ⓝ ～に言(い)い紛(まぎ)らす turn sth into a joke; laught sth off; ⓘ make sport of sth. ～にする take sth as a joke; laugh sth off; ⓘ make sport of sth. 图 ～を言(い)う tell a joke; make a joke; ⓒ ⓘ crack a joke.

じょうどう
常道 ⒺⒺ the beaten track

图 ⓒ ⓢ ～を辿(たど)る follow the beaten track. ～を踏(ふ)み外(はず)す stray from the beaten track; get out of compass.

しょうね
性根 nature; disposition

Ⓐ ～が腐(くさ)る be corrupted; be depraved. ～が付(つ)く ❶ come to one's senses; come to oneself; be oneself again. ❷ be penitent; mend one's ways; ⓘ return to the straight and narrow; ⓘ turn over a new leaf. ～が曲(ま)がる have a warped mind; be corrupted; be depraved. Ⓝ ⓒ ～に返(かえ)る come to oneself; come to one's senses. 图 ～を入(い)れ換(か)える mend one's ways; ⓘ turn over a new leaf. ⓒ ～を失(うしな)う ❶ lose consciousness; pass out; ⓒ black out. ❷ lose one's senses; go mad; ⓢ go crazy; ⓢ ⓘ lose one's marbles. ⓒ ～を奪(うば)う drive sb mad; ⓒ rob sb of his/her senses; corrupt sb's mind. ～を定(さだ)める make up one's mind; decide to do sth; resolve to do sth. 〜を叩き直す straighten sb out; set sb right. ⓐ 〜を付ける ❶ pluck up courage; brace oneself; become emboldened. ❷ bring sb round to his/her senses.

しょうぶ
勝負 victory or defeat

[A] 〜が付く the game is up. [N] 〜に勝つ win a game. 〜にならない be no match for sb. 〜に負ける lose a game; ⓒ be beaten. [を] 〜を争う compete with sb. 〜を付ける fight to the finish; fight it out.

じょうまえ
錠前 a lock

[を] 〜を開ける remove a lock; unlock (a door). 〜を下ろす fasten a lock; lock (a door). 〜を掛ける fasten a lock; lock (a door). 〜を狂わす hamper a lock; meddle with a lock. 〜を抉じ開ける prize open a lock; force a lock. 〜を付ける put a lock on sth. 〜を捩じ切る prize open a lock; force a lock. 〜を外す remove a lock; unlock (a door).

しょうめん
正面 the front; head-on

[を] 〜を切る ❶ face sb head-on; take a stand; ⓘ stand one's ground. ❷ meet the occasion; ⓘ face the music; ⓘ bite the bullet.

しょうらい
将来 the future (prospects)

[N] 〜に備える prepare for the future. [を] 〜を戒める warn for the future. 〜を考える have the future in mind; think of the future. ⓒ 〜をトする predict the future; see into the future; tell sb's fortune.

しょうり
勝利 victory; triumph

[を] 〜を得る gain a victory. 〜を収める gain victory; ⓘ gain the upper hand. 〜を占める gain a victory; be victorious. 〜を誇る boast of victory; revel in one's success; ⓒ glory in victory; ⓒ ⓘ blow one's own horn (trumpet).

じょうれい
条例 a usage; a custom

[N] 〜に従う follow precedent; do sth in the conventional way. 〜に背く be contrary to custom; ⓘ go against the grain.

しよく
私欲 selfish desires

[N] 〜に走る pursue one's selfish desires. [を] 〜を離れる rise above one's selfish desires. 〜を満たす gratify one's selfish desires.

しょく
職 work; a post; a calling

[N] 〜に就く take employment; get a

job. ～に留(とど)まる remain in office; stay in a job.
【を】 ～を与える employ sb; give sb employment; hire sb. ～を失(うしな)う be dismissed; lose one's job; ⓒ be fired; ⓢⓛ get the sack. ～を得(え)る obtain a position; secure employment; get a job. ⓒ ～を覚(おぼ)える learn a trade. ～を代(か)える change one's job; switch jobs. ～を探(さが)す seek employment; look for a job. ⓒ ～を仕込(しこ)む teach sb a trade. ⓒ ～を辞(じ)する resign one's office; tender one's resignation; leave one's job. ～を解(と)かれる be dismissed from one's post. ～を投(な)げ打(う)つ resign from office; leave one's post. ～を奉(ほう)ずる hold office. ～を辞(や)める resign one's office; leave one's job. ⓒ ～を汚(よご)す abuse one's position.

食(しょく) a meal; food; appetite
【A】 ～が進(すす)む have a good appetite.

食指(しょくし) ⓔ the index finger
【A】 ⓒ ～が動(うご)く ❶ intend to do *sth*; be about to do *sth*. ❷ have a desire to do *sth*; have an itch to do *sth*; have a mind to do *sth*.

触手(しょくしゅ) a tentacle; a feeler
【を】 ～を伸(の)ばす ❶ extend a tentacle; ⓛ put out a feeler. ❷ try to obtain *sth*; reach for *sth*; aspire to *sth*; ⓒ entertain an ambition for *sth*.

食欲(しょくよく) appetite
【を】 ～を失(うしな)う lose one's appetite. ～をそそる excite one's appetite. ～を殺(そ)ぐ dull one's appetite.

助言(じょげん) advice; counsel
【を】 ～を得(え)る get counsel from *sb*. ～を求(もと)める seek *sb's* counsel; ask for *sb's* advice.

女色(じょしょく) ⓔ feminine charms
【N】 ⓒ ～に耽(ふけ)る indulge in lewdness; ⓒ be given up to amours. ⓒ ～に迷(まよ)う be infatuated with a woman; ⓒ be enamored of a woman.
【を】 ⓒ ～を好(この)む be lascivious; be licentious. ⓒⓒ ～を近付(ちかづ)ける keep company with woman.

所帯(しょたい) a home; a household
【を】 ～を構(かま)える set up house; get married; start a life together. ～を畳(たた)む give up one's home; give up married life; get divorced. ～を張(は)る set up house; get married; start a life together. ～を持(も)つ set up house; get married; start a life together.

処置(しょち) a measure; disposition

N ～に窮する be at a loss; ⓘ be at one's wits' end; ⓘ be all at sea. ～に困る be at a loss; ⓘ be at one's wits' end; ⓘ be all at sea.
图 ～を誤る take the wrong measures; make an error. ～を得る reach a solution; solve (a matter). ～を取る take measures; deal with sth; ⓒ use one's discretion.

初日 the premiere/opening night
A ～が出る [sumō] have one's firsth win; have a victory at last.

助力 help; aid; assistance
图 ～を仰ぐ ask for help; seek aid; ⓒ turn to sb for assistance. ～を得る receive assistance; get help. ～を求める seek sb's assistance; ask for sb's help.

白 white; blank
图 ～を切る pretend not to know; feign ignorance; ⓘ play the innocent. ～を付ける prove one's/sb's innocence; vindicate oneself/sb.

尻 the rear; the buttocks; the hips
A ～が青い be immature; be inexperienced; ⓘ be green. ～が有る have long-term consequences. ⓒ ～が暖まる stay on; linger behind (at a place). ⓒ ～が重い be lazy; ⓒ be indolent; be slow; ⓘ drag one's heels. ⓒ ～が軽い ❶ be quick; be nimble. ❷ act light-heartedly; ⓒ be flighty. ⓥ ⓢ ❸ be promiscuous; have loose morals; ⓔ be wanton; ⓒ sleep around; ⓒ ⓘ put oneself about. ～が切れる stop sth midway; leave sth unfinished. ⓢ ～が腐る outstay one's welcome; stay too long. ～が来る ❶ be complained about; ⓔ have a complaint lodged against one. ❷ get involved in the affairs of others; be embroiled in a quarrel. ⓐ ⓒ ～が肥える shirk one's duties; be lazy; be impudent. ⓐ ⓒ ～がこそばゆい be ill at ease; have a guilty conscience; feel awkward. ⓒ ～が据わる ⓐ be glued to a spot; ⓒ stay put; ⓘ stick it out. ⓐ ～が出る be complained about; ⓔ have a complaint lodged against one. ⓒ ～が長い outstay one's welcome; stay too long. ⓒ ～が抜ける be slothful; be forgetful; ⓒ be sloppy. ⓐ ～が剥げる be exposed; be found out. ～が早い ❶ be quick to boil. ⓥ ⓢ ❷ be promiscuous; have loose morals; ⓔ be wanton; ⓒ sleep around; ⓒ ⓘ put oneself about. ⓐ ⓢ ～が破れる be exposed; be found out. ⓐ ⓒ ～が揉める have troubles; be troubled (by sth); have a dispute. ⓐ ⓢ ～が割れる be exposed; be found out.

シリ / ジリ

Ⓝ Ⓐ Ⓒ ～に聞かす listen without interest; pay little attention; pass over *sth*. Ⓒ (妻の)～に敷かれる be dominated by one's wife; Ⓘ be tied to one's wife's apron strings; Ⓒ Ⓘ be henpecked. Ⓐ ～に立つ ❶ follow *sb* closely; Ⓘ breathe down *sb's* neck. ❷ accompany *sb* through life. Ⓒ ～に付く ❶ Ⓘ be hot on *sb's* heels; Ⓘ breathe down *sb's* neck. Ⓒ ❷ imitate *sb*; copycat *sb*. Ⓥ Ⓢ ～に挟む ignore *sb*; make light of *sth*; Ⓘ close one's eyes to *sth*.

図 Ⓒ ～を上げる ❶ get up; stand up; rise up. ❷ speak with a rising intonation. Ⓒ ～を暖める ❶ warm one's buttocks. ❷ remain in the same position (for a long time); hold a post (for many years). Ⓒ (女の)～を追い回す dangle after a girl; chase a girl. Ⓒ (人の)～を押す ❶ give *sb* assistance. ❷ encourage *sb*; egg *sb* on; Ⓒ Ⓘ fire *sb* up. ❸ abet *sb* in a crime. Ⓒ ～を落ち着ける make oneself at home; linger behind (at a place). Ⓒ ～を掛ける ❶ sit oneself down; take a seat. ❷ cause *sb* trouble; leave a problem for *sb* else (to settle). ～を絡げる ❶ tuck one's *kimono* (into one's *obi*). ❷ run off; Ⓘ take to one's heels; Ⓘ make a run for it; Ⓒ Ⓘ cut and run. Ⓐ ～を切る stop mid-sentence; check oneself; break off

short. Ⓐ Ⓢ ～を食う ❶ set matters right; wind *sth* up; deal with the aftermath (of an affair). ❷ be left to deal with a problem; Ⓘ be left with the broken pieces. ❸ be involved in (a quarrel); Ⓒ get a by-blow. Ⓐ Ⓢ ～を括る do *sth* with great care; stay concentrated (to the end). Ⓒ ～を下げる ❶ sit down. ❷ speak with a falling intonation. Ⓐ Ⓒ ～を捌く set matters right; wind *sth* up; deal with the aftermath (of an affair). Ⓒ ～を据える ❶ squat on one's haunches. ❷ settle down; resolve to do *sth*; Ⓒ buckle down. Ⓒ (人の)～を叩く encourage *sb*; egg *sb* on; Ⓒ Ⓘ fire *sb* up. Ⓐ Ⓒ ～を溜める make oneself at home. Ⓐ Ⓒ ～を突く press *sb* to settle an affair; demand that *sb* clear their debts. Ⓥ Ⓢ (人の)～を拭う bear *sb's* burden; bear the consequences of *sb's* error; pay off *sb's* debt; Ⓐ clean up *sb's* mess. Ⓒ Ⓢ (人の)～を剥ぐ bring *sth* to light; expose *sb*. ～を端折る ❶ tuck one's *kimono* (into one's *obi*). ❷ cut short (one's stay); abridge (a story). ❸ run off; Ⓘ take to one's heels; Ⓘ make a run for it; Ⓒ Ⓘ cut and run. Ⓒ ～を引く remain unsettled; remain unresolved. Ⓒ ～を振る swing one's hips; wag one's behind. Ⓒ ～を捲る assume a defiant attitude. Ⓒ ～を向

ける turn one's back on *sb*; ⓘ give *sb* the cold shoulder. Ⓐ ～を結ぶ finish *sth* off; put an end to *sth*; bring a matter to a (satisfactory) close. ⓒ ～を持ち込む complain about *sb*; Ⓔ lodge a complaint; seek a settlement. ⓒ ～を持つ ❶ give *sb* assistance. ❷ encourage *sb*; egg *sb* on; ⓒⓘ fire *sb* up. ❸ abet *sb* in a crime. ⓒ ～を遣る seek reparation; demand a settlement; sue *sb*. ⓒ ～を寄越す be complained about; be sued. ⒶⓈ (人の)～を割る bring *sth* to light; expose *sb*.

私利 Ⓔ self-interest
を ～を計る look to one's own interests; ⓒⓘ look after number one; ⓘ feather one's own nest.

自利 Ⓔ one's own interest
を ⓒ ～を図る be self-seeking; Ⓔ consult one's own interests; ⓘ look after number one.

事理 Ⓔ reason; facts; propriety
を Ⓔ ～を弁える be sensible; have good sense; listen to reason.

尻馬 a byrider on a horse
Ⓝ ～に乗る go along with *sb*'s ideas; ⓘ climb onto the bandwagon; ⓘ ride on *sb*'s coattails.

尻口 Ⓔ the rear door of an oxcart
Ⓐ ⒶⒺ ～で物言う give an evasive reply; dodge an issue; Ⓔ equivocate on an issue ⓘ beat about the bush; ⓒⓘ pussyfoot on (an issue).

尻毛 Ⓔ hairs on the buttocks
を ⓒ ～を抜く take advantage of an unguarded moment; ⓘ catch *sb* off guard.

尻目 a sidelong glance
Ⓝ (人を)～に懸ける ❶ give *sb* a sidelong glance; look sideways at *sb*; look at *sb* out of the corner of one's eyes. ❷ take no notice of *sb*; have no eye for *sb*; think nothing of *sb*; ignore *sb*; Ⓔ set *sb* at naught.

尻餅 Ⓔ a birthday rice cake
Ⓐ ⓒ ～を搗く fall on one's backside; fall over backwards; land on one's rear; ⓒ make a pratfall.

時流 Ⓔ the current of the times
Ⓝ Ⓔ ～に阿る ⓘ curry favor with (the public). Ⓔ ～に逆らう be out of tune with the times; go against the stream. Ⓔ ～に従う go along with the current; follow the fashion of the day; ⓘ climb onto the bandwagon. Ⓔ ～に投じる catch the public fancy. Ⓔ ～に乗る go with the times;

be trendy.
⟨を⟩ ⓒ ～を追う pursue the fashion of the day; follow the latest fad.

白黒 white and black
⟨N⟩ ～に成る be mixed up; be in a mess; be in disorder; be in chaos.
⟨を⟩ ～を決める decide on what is just; distinguish between right and wrong.

皺 wrinkles; creases; furrows
⟨A⟩ が寄る ❶ become wrinkled. ❷ (顔に) have a wrinkled face, be marked with old age; become old.
⟨N⟩ ～にする make a crease. ～に成り become wrikled; crease.
⟨を⟩ (アイロンで)～を伸ばす iron out creases. (顔に)～を付ける line sb's face; mark sb with old age. ～を寄せる ❶ gather sth in. ❷ (顔に) wrinkle (up) one's face; make a grimace.

信 faith; fidelity; trust; truth
⟨を⟩ ⓐⓒ ～を致す have a deep faith; deeply believe. ～を失う lose sb's confidence; lose credit. ～を得る gain sb's confidence; get credit; enjoy sb's trust. ～を置く rely upon sb; put confidence in sb/sth; give credence to sb/sth; ⓒ repose trust in sb/sth. ～を問う test sb's belief in one. ⓐ ～を取る ❶ take sth to be true; accept sth as true. ❷ gain sb's trust; win sb's confidence; uphold sb's trust. ⓐ ～を為す ❶ take sth to be true; trust in sth; put one's faith in sb/sth; place reliance on sb/sth. ❷ deepen one's faith; strengthen one's belief.

心 heart; mind, soul; core ♦ 心
⟨A⟩ ～が腐る ❶ ⓒ have a rotten core. ❷ ⓐ be rotten at the core; be corrupted; have a warped nature. ～が疲れる suffer from nervous stress; be mentally fatigued; be sapped of vitality.
⟨を⟩ ～を入れる line a coat; pad a sash. ～を切る snuff a candle; trim a wick. ～に触る grate on one's nerves; wear one down. ～を出す turn up the wick; screw up a lamp. ⓒ ～を止める top a tree; make a pollard. ～を取る core (an apple).

真 ᴱ truth; genuineness ♦ 真
⟨N⟩ ⓒ ～に迫る be realistic; be lifelike; be true to nature.
⟨を⟩ ⓒ ～を穿つ be relevant; ⓘ be to the point; ⓘ be on the mark; ⓘ hit the nail on the head. ～を打つ be the last to enter; be the star performer; ⓘ top the bill. ～を切る be the last to enter; be the star per-

former; ⓒ top the bill. ⓔ 〜を保(たも)つ stay lifelike; remain true to nature.

神(しん) god; spirit; divinity ▶ 神(かみ)

Ⓝ 〜に入(い)る reach a superior level of attainment (in an art); have divine skills.

寝(しん) a bed; a bedstead; a birth

Ⓝ 〜に着(つ)く go to bed; turn in for the night; ⓔ retire to rest; ⓒ ⓓ hit the hay.

紳(しん) Ⓑ a wide sash (of office)

Ⓝ ⓒⓔ 〜に書(しょ)す keep sth in mind; ⓔ commit sth to memory; make a mental note of sth.

陣(じん) a camp; quarters

ⓦ 〜を固(かた)める close the ranks. 〜を構(かま)える pitch a camp; take up a position; encamp (for battle). 〜を敷(し)く pitch a camp; take up a position; encamp (for battle). 〜を撤去(てっきょ)する break camp. 〜を取(と)る pitch a camp; take up a position; occupy a place; seize a position. 〜を張(は)る pitch a camp; take up a position; encamp (for battle).

塵界(じんかい) Ⓔ the dusty world

ⓦ ⓒ 〜を脱(だっ)する ❶ get away from the hustle and bustle of the world. ❷ go into seclusion; become a hermit; renounce the world; ⓔ retire from the world. ❸ become a Buddhist priest; take the tonsure; ⓔ retire into religion.

心気(しんき) mood; feeling; spirit

Ⓐ 〜が涌(わ)く be anxious about sth; be worried about sth; be troubled by sth; fret over sth.
ⓦ 〜を凝(こ)らす think hard on sth; apply one's mind to sth; ⓒ ⓓ rack one's brains. 〜を砕(くだ)く fret over sth; fidget over sth; ⓒ ⓓ rack one's brains. 〜を取(と)る cheer oneself up; take one's mind off sth; divert oneself (pleasantly). 〜を燃(も)やす be anxious about sth; be worried about sth; fret over sth. 〜を病(や)む worry deeply about sth; be worried sick; fret incessantly over sth.

仁義(じんぎ) humanity and justice

ⓦ 〜を切(き)る greet a fellow yakuza. 〜を通(とお)す do what is right; ⓓ stick to the straight and narrow. 〜を守(まも)る do what is right; ⓓ stick to the straight and narrow.

神経(しんけい) a nerve; nerves

Ⓐ 〜が高(たか)ぶる become nervous; become excited; be on edge. 〜が鋭(するど)い be sensitive; ⓒ be touchy; ⓓ have

a thin skin. 〜が鈍い be insensitive; be callous; ⓘ have a thick skin. 〜が太い have a lot of nerve; ⓘ have nerves of steel. 〜が細い have sensitive nerves; have a nervous temperament.
Ⓝ 〜に堪える be a strain on one's nerves. 〜に触る grate on one's nerves; wear one down.
ⓦ 〜を苛立たせる set one's nerves on edge; get on one's nerves; jar sb's nerves. ⓒ 〜を起こす get excited; become nervous. 〜を静める soothe one's nerves. 〜を摩り減らす grate on one's nerves; wear one down. 〜を使う tax one's nerves; be stressed by sb/sth. 〜を疲らせる exhaust one's nerves. 〜を尖らす set one's nerves on edge. ⓒ 〜を悩ます worry about sth; fret over sth. 〜を抜く ⓘ extract a nerve.

心血 Ⓔ the heart's blood
ⓦ ⓔ 〜を注ぐ do sth with all one's heart; do sth with heart and soul; devote all one's energies to sth.

人後 Ⓔ second in rank
Ⓝ ⓔ 〜に落ちる come second; fall behind; ⓘ bite the dust; ⓘ take a back seat.

信仰 (religious) faith; belief

Ⓝ 〜に殉じる be a martyr for one's faith. 〜に入る find faith.
ⓦ 〜を固める strengthen one's faith. 〜を実践する practice one's faith. 〜を捨てる forsake one's faith; renounce one's beliefs. 〜を深める deepen one's faith. 〜を持つ have faith; believe in God.

親交 friendship; intimacy
ⓦ 〜を得る win sb's friendship. 〜を図る promote friendly relations. 〜を断つ break off one's friendship with sb; ⓔ sever connections with sb. 〜を結ぶ cultivate a friendship with sb; make friends with sb.

人口 population; common talk
Ⓝ 〜に入る be talked about; ⓒ ⓘ become the talk of the town; ⓒ ⓘ go the rounds. 〜に落つ be talked about; ⓒ ⓘ become the talk of the town; ⓒ ⓘ go the rounds. 〜に乗る be talked about; ⓒ ⓘ become the talk of the town; ⓒ ⓘ go the rounds.

心骨 Ⓔ spirit and body
Ⓝ ⓔ 〜を刻す be deeply hurt; be profoundly affected; ⓒ feel gutted.

心魂 Ⓔ heart and soul
Ⓝ ⓔ 〜に徹する feel sth deeply;

ⓞ come home to one; ⓞ strike home; ⓞ cut to the quick.

しんさん
辛酸 国 hardships; privations

Ⓐ ⓞⓔ ～が浸む experience hardships; ⓔ suffer life's vicissitudes.
图 ～を嘗める go through many hardships; ⓔ suffer life's vicissitudes.

しんしょく
侵食 sleeping and eating

图 ～を共にする live under the same roof; share the same house. ～を忘れる lose oneself in *sth*; forget oneself; get carried away.

じんしん
人心 国 people's hearts

图 ⓒ ～を収める win the hears of the people. ⓒ ～を静める appease the people. ⓒ ～を惑わす mislead the public.

じんすけ
甚助 国 jealousy

Ⓝ ⓞⓒ ～を起こす be envious of *sb's* love; be jealous of (one's wife).

しんぞう
心臓 the heart

Ⓐ ～が強い have nerve; be brazen; ⓒ have guts. ～が弱い be timid; ⓔ be bashful; ⓒ be a whimp.

しんだい
身代 one's property

图 ～を継ぐ inherit *sb's* property; come into a fortune. ～を潰す lose one's property; ⓔ dissipate one's fortune; go bankrupt; ⓢ go bust. ～を減らす damage one's fortune.

しんだん
診断 a diagnosis; diagnostication

图 ～を誤る make a wrong diagnosis. ～を受ける have one's case diagnosed. ～を下す give a diagnosis.

じんち
陣地 a position; an encampment

图 ～を維持する keep the field. ～を失う lose the field. ～を敷く take up a position. ～を占領する carry a position. ～を撤退する withdraw from a position. ～を守る hold a position.

しんとう
心頭 国 the mind; the heart

Ⓝ ⓒ ～に落とす think *sth* over; ponder over *sth*; be lost in thought. ⓒ (怒り)～に発す fly into a rage; ⓒ ⓞ fly off the handle.

じんとう
陣頭 the head of an army

Ⓝ ～に立つ be at the head of an army; lead the vanguard; ⓞ be in the front van.

じんどう
人道 国 humanity

Ⓝ ⓒ ～に背く be inhumane; go against humanity; be cruel. ⓒ ～に悖る go against humanity; be inhumane; be cruel.

シンプク　ス

しんにゅう
之繞 囗 the radical for movement

[を] ⓒ ～を掛ける exaggerate *sth*;
① stretch the facts; ⓢ ① pile it on;
ⓢ ① lay it on thick.

しんねん
信念 convictions; beliefs; faith

[A] ～が堅い have strong convictions;
have a deep belief in *sth*; hold
strong opinions. ～がぐらつく have
one's beliefs shaken; waver in one's
faith. ～が強い have strong convictions; have a deep belief in *sth*;
hold strong opinions.
[を] ～を固める harden in one's convictions; strenthen one's belief. ～を
曲げない be unbending in one's convictions; have unswerving faith.

しんぱい
心配 anxiety; worry

[を] ～を掛ける cause *sb* to worry. ⓒ
～を去る relieve *sb's* anxiety.

しんぷく
心腹 囗 the bosom; the heart

[A] ⓒ ～が立つ fly into a rage; lose
one's temper; ⓒ ① fly off the handle; ⓢ ① blow a fuse.
[N] ⓒ ～に落つ ❶ make sense of *sth*;
grasp the meaning; ① catch the
idea. ❷ be convinced; be won over;
be persuaded; ① come round to *sb's*
point of view.
[を] ⓒ ～を輸写す open oneself up to
sb; take *sb* into one's confidence;

① pour out one's heart to *sb*;
ⓒ unbosom oneself.

しんぽ
進歩 progress; improvement

[を] ～を妨げる hinder progress. ～を
遂げる make progress. ～を見せる
show progress.

しんめい
身命 囗 one's life

[N] ⓒ ～を捧げる sacrifice one's life;
devote one's life (to a cause). ⓒ ～
を賭する risk one's life; ⓒ put one's
life at stake. ⓒ ～を投げ打つ throw
away one's life; give up one's life.

じんもん
陣門 囗 a camp gate

[N] ⓒ ～に降る ❶ capitulate at the
enemy's camp gate; admit defeat;
acknowledge defeat; ① throw in the
towel. ❷ be routed; be beaten;
① bite the dust.

じんよう
陣容 battle array; a lineup

[を] ～を立て直す ❶ close ranks.
❷ reshuffle (a cabinet) ～を整える
marshal an army; array the forma-
tion of troops; get ready for battle;
① clear the decks.

じんりん
人倫 囗 humanity; morality

[N] ⓒ ～に背く go against humanity;
transgress morality; be inhumane.

信頼 trust; reliance; faith

[N] ～に値する deserve sb's trust; ⓔ be worthy of sb's trust. ～に答える be reliable; be trustworthy; live up to sb's expectation; ⓔ prove oneself worthy of sb's trust. ～に背く betray sb's trust; ⓒ let sb down. [を] ～を失う lose sb's trust. ～を裏切る betray sb's trust. ～を得る win sb's trust; gain sb's confidence. (人に)～を置く put one's trust (in sb); rely on sb.

針路 a course; a flight path

[を] ～を誤る take the wrong course. ～を定める set one's course. ～を取る take (a certain) course.

ス

巣 a nest; a beehive; a web

[N] ～に帰る ❶ return to the nest. ⓒ ❷ return home; come home. ～に着く settle in the nest.
[を] ～を替える ❶ move house; change residence. ❷ change one's haunt; begin to frequent a different establishment. ～を懸ける spin a web; weave a web. ～を構える buld a nest; nest (in a hedge). ～を構う ❶ buld a nest; nest (in a hedge). ❷ infiltrate an area; set up shop. ❸ take root (in people's minds); ⓘ catch on. ～を組む buld a nest; nest (in a hedge). ～を造る buld a nest; nest (in a hedge). ～を離れる ❶ leave the nest. ⓒ ❷ leave home; ⓘ learn to stand on one's own (two) feet.

酢 vinegar

[A] ～が過ぎる be excessive; go too far; ⓒ ⓘ be over the top.
[N] ～に漬ける pickle sth in vinegar.
[を] ～を買う agitate sb; stir up trouble; ⓘ breed bad blood. ～を乞う agitate sb; stir up trouble; ⓘ breed bad blood. ～を刺す agitate sb; stir up trouble; cause resentment; ⓘ breed bad blood.

図 a drawing; a picture; a map

[A] ⓐ ～が外れる go wrong; guess wrong; ⓒ get it wrong.
[N] ～に当たる go according to plan; prove a success; work out well. ～に乗る ❶ go according to plan; prove a success; work out well. ❷ get carried away; be elated; get excited. ❸ be haughty; be puffed up; ⓘ have airs and graces; ⓒ be stuck-up.
[を] ⓐ ～を失う be stupefied; be dumfounded; be struck dumb; ⓢ ⓘ be blown away. ⓐ ～を抜かす ❶ miss an opportunity; let a chance slip by. ❷ relax the tension; ⓘ break

the ice. ④ ～を外(はず)す let a chance slip by; miss an opportunity. ～を引く draw (up) a plan.

頭(ず) Ⓔ the head; the brain ▶ 頭(あたま) ▶ 頭(かしら)

Ⓐ ⑤ ～が高(たか)い be arrogant; be haughty; have an overbearing attitude; be proud.
Ⓝ ～に乗(の)る ❶ go according to plan; prove a success; work out well. ❷ get carried away; be elated; get excited. ❸ be haughty; be puffed up; show off; ⓘ have airs and graces; ⓒ be stuck-up.
Ⓦ ～を切(き)る [*kabuki*] assume a posture; make a defiant gesture; strike an attitude. ～を遣(つか)う [*bunraku*] turn the head of a doll towards the audience.

粋(すい) the best; refined; delicate

Ⓦ ～を利(き)かす be discreet; be considerate; be tactful; take *sb's* feelings into account.

水(すい) water; a river; the sea ▶ 水(みず)

Ⓐ ～が墓(ぼ)れる pour with rain.
Ⓦ ⑤ ～を咬(か)める water down *sake*; add water to *sake*.

衰運(すいうん) Ⓔ waning fortune

Ⓝ ⑥ ～に向(む)かい go into decline; ⓘ be on the wane; ⓒ ⓘ go downhill.

Ⓦ ⑤ ～を辿(たど)る go into decline; ⓘ be on the wane; ⓒ ⓘ go downhill. ～を挽回(ばんかい)する retrieve one's fortunes.

水火(すいか) Ⓔ water and fire

Ⓦ ⑥ ～を踏(ふ)む ❶ take great risks; ⓘ be skating on thin ice. ❷ be cornered; be in trouble; ⓘ be with one's back against the wall; ⓘ be brought to bay.

水草(すいそう) Ⓔ a water plant

Ⓦ ⑤ ～を追(お)う lead a nomadic life; ⓒ have no fixed abode; be a drifter.

水泡(すいほう) a water bubble; foam

Ⓝ ～に帰(き)す come to nothing; end in failure; fall through; ⓘ go up in smoke. ～に属(ぞく)す come to nothing; end in failure; fall through; ⓘ go up in smoke.

姿(すがた) a figure; a form; an aspect

Ⓦ ～を現(あら)わす show oneself; come into sight; make one's appearance. ～を隠(かく)す hide oneself; cover one's traces. ～を消(け)す drop from view; fade away; ⓘ keep a low profile. ～を窶(やつ)す disguise oneself (as *sb*).

隙(すき) an opening; a gap; a space

Ⓝ ～に乗(じょう)じる take advantage of an unguarded moment; catch *sb* off guard. 　〜を伺う seek an opening; watch for an unguarded moment; try to catch *sb* off guard. 〜を狙う watch for an opportunity; ⓒ bide one's time. 〜を見せる lay oneself open to attack; ⓘ drop one's guard. 〜を見付ける find an opportunity (to attack).

数奇 a cultivated taste
を 〜を好む enjoy a cultivated life; pursue an aesthetic life. 〜を凝らす be sophisticated; be well designed; display a cultivated taste.

ずき 🄺 a police detective
を ⓒ 〜が回る ❶ be detected; be found out. ❷ be on the lookout for *sb*; be on *sb's* track.

救い rescue; relief; salvation
🄰 〜が無い be past saving; ⓒ be beyond redemption. 🄽 ⓒ 〜に与る ❶ find relief; be saved. ❷ find salvation; ⓒ partake of salvation. 〜に行く go to *sb's* rescue; help *sb* in distress. を 〜を見い出す find salvation; be converted. 〜を求める ❶ ask for help; seek relief. ❷ seek salvation.

救い舟 a lifeboat
を 〜を出す ❶ launch a lifeboat. ❶ go to *sb's* rescue; help *sb* in distress.

凄み ghastliness; dreadfulness
を 〜を利かす intimidate *sb*; threaten *sb*; ⓒ bully *sb*.

凄文句 🄺 threatening words
を ⓒ 〜を並べる use threatening language; intimidate *sb*; ⓒ bully *sb*.

筋 a muscle; a fiber; logic
🄰 ⓒ 〜が切れる make progress; get better. 〜が立つ be reasonable; be logical; stand to reason; be right. 〜が違う be unreasonable; do not stand to reason; be in the wrong. 〜が通る be reasonable; stand to reason; be right. 〜が良い have talent; have an aptitude; have a head for (figures). 〜が悪い ❶ have a bad nature; have a bad temperament. ❷ have little talent; lack artistic skill. を ⓒ 〜を言う be argumentative; object to *sth*; find fault with *sb*; ⓘ split hairs. 〜を書く form a plan; have *sth* in mind. ⓐ 〜を出す lose one's temper; ⓒ ⓘ fly off the handle; ⓢ ⓘ blow a fuse. 〜を通す ❶ be steadfast; stick to one's principles; ⓘ stick to one's guns. ❷ follow the

correct procedures; go through the proper channels.

筋骨 (すじぼね) sinews and bones

[を] 〜を抜く (ぬく) be severely scolded; be told off in no uncertain terms; be given a thorough dressing-down.

素性 (すじょう) birth; lineage; origin

[A] 〜が怪しい (あやしい) have no clear family background; have a shady lineage; have doubtful antecedents. 〜が良い (いい) be of good birth; come from a good family. 〜が卑しい (いやしい) be lowborn; ⓔ be of humble birth.

[を] 〜を暴く (あばく) disclose *sb's* identity; ⓒ ① blow *sb's* cover. 〜を隠す (かくす) conceal one's identity; hide one's history. 〜を調べる (しらべる) inquire into *sb's* background; ⓒ check *sb* out; ① give *sb* the once over.

煤 (すす) soot

[を] 〜を払う (はらう) sweep away soot; clean the house.

鈴 (すず) a bell

[を] 〜を鳴らす (ならす) ring a bell.

裾 (すそ) the skirt; the cuffs; the base

[を] ⓞ 〜を掻く (かく) ❶ trip *sb* up; sweep *sb's* legs from under him/her. ❷ outwit *sb*; cheat on *sb*. 〜を絡げる (からげる) tuck in a skirt. ⓞ 〜をする clean the hoofs of a horse. ⓞ 〜を揃える (そろえる) tidy one's hair. ⓞ 〜を遣う (つかう) clean the hoofs of a horse. 〜を曳く (ひく) trail the skirt (of a wedding dress). 〜を捲る (まくる) roll up the cuffs (of one's trousers). 〜を持つ (もつ) hold up the train (of a wedding dress).

素手 (すで) a bare/empty hand

[を] 〜を引く (ひく) be left empty-handed; come to nothing; get nowhere; be in vain; ① go up in smoke. 〜を振る (ふる) do nothing; remain motionless.

砂 (すな) sand; grit

[N] 〜にする spoil *sth*; ruin *sth*.

[を] 〜を噛ます (かます) [*sumō*] throw one's opponent; topple one's opponent. 〜を掴む (つかむ) ❶ [*sumō*] be defeated; lose a fight; ① bite the dust. ❷ make useless efforts; ① catch at shadows.

脛 (すね) the leg; the shin ▶ 脛 (はぎ)

[A] ⓞ 〜が流れる (ながれる) lose out against *sb*; lose ground; give way; give in.

[N] 〜に疵持つ (きずもつ) ❶ have a criminal past; have bad credentials. ❷ have a guilty conscience; ⓔ feel the pangs of conscience.

[を] ⓞ 〜を掛ける (かける) stay at (a place); make a stay (at a place). 〜を齧る (かじる) live on *sb's* expenses; be dependent on sb; ⓒ sponge on sb. ⓓ ～を払う trip sb up; sweep sb's legs from under him/her. ⓔ ～を拾う refrain from going somewhere.

図星 ⑤ the bull's-eye; the mark

を ⓐ ～を指される have one's plans seen through; be exposed. ⓑ ～を指す guess right; ⓘ be on the mark; ⓘ hit the nail on the head. ～を突く ❶ hit sb in the vitals; ⓘ go for the jugular. ❷ guess right; ⓘ be on the mark; ⓘ hit the nail on the head.

住居 a dwelling; an abode

を ～を定める take up one's abode; make (a place) one's home. ～を尋ねる ask for sb's address.

墨 India (China, Japan) ink

A ⓐ ～が入る ❶ recieve a tatoo to mark one out as a criminal. ❷ be sentenced; be brought to justice.
を ⓐ ～を打つ ink a line. ～をする rub down ink. ～を付ける dip (a brush) in ink. ⓑ ～を引く ink a line.

隅 a corner; a nook

を ～に置けない be shrewd; be insiduous; not to be triffled with; not to be taken lightly.

素矢 ⑤ an off-the-mark arrow

N ⓔ ～を食う ❶ come to nothing; be in vain; ⓒ be to no avail; ⓘ go up in smoke. ❷ be disappointed (in one's hopes); be frustrated; prove a disappointment; be thwarted. ⓔ ～を引く ❶ come to nothing; be in vain; ⓒ be to no avail; ⓘ go up in smoke. ❷ be disappointed (in one's hopes); be frustrated; prove a disappointment; be thwarted.

寸 a sun (3.03 cm)

A ～が約む be (too) short. ～が詰む be (too) short.

寸陰 ⑤ a moment; an instant

N ⓔ ～を惜しむ waste no time; lose not a moment.

寸暇 ⑤ a spare moment

N ⓔ ～を盗む use every spare moment; waste no time; lose not a moment.

寸鉄 ⑤ a small weapon

N ⓔ (身に)～を帯びず carry no weapons; be unarmed.

寸法 measurements; a plan

N ～に入れる take sth into consideration; ⓘ take sth on board. ～を取る take a measurement.
を ～を付ける map out a plan; lay

out a schedule; make arrangements; prepare a plan.

セ

背 the back; the spine ▶ 背

[A] ～が高い be tall; be of great stature. ～が低い be short; be of small stature.
[N] ～に負う carry *sth* on one's back; shoulder (a load). ～にする ❶ carry *sth*; shoulder (a load); ❷ leave *sb/sth* behind. ❸ turn one's back toward *sth*; put one's back against *sth*.
[を] ～を伸ばす straighten one's back. ～を曲げる bend one's back. ～を見せる turn one's back toward *sth*; turn one's back on *sb*. ～を向ける ❶ turn one's back toward *sth*; turn one's back on *sb*. ❷ reject *sb/sth*; ⓒ give *sb* the cold shoulder; ⓓ turn one's back on *sb/sth*. ⓐ ～を縒る writhe in agony; be in agony.

瀬 a rapid; a shoal; a shallow

[N] ～に乗り上げる run ashore; be grounded; ⓔ take the ground.
[を] ～を下る descend a rapid. ～を乗り切る pass a rapid. ～を踏む ❶ test the depth of a shallow. ❷ check out a situation; probe *sth*; try *sth* out. ❸ sound *sb* out; ⓕ send up a trial

balloon; ⓖ put out one's feelers. ～を渡る ford a rapid.

精 spirit; vigor; vitality

[N] ⓗ ～に入る pay attention to detail. ～に入れる ❶ do *sth* with heart and soul; ⓘ put one's heart into *sth*. ❷ take pains over *sth*; fret over *sth*; ⓒ ⓘ rack one's brains.
[を] ⓗ ～を入れる do *sth* with heart and soul; ⓘ put one's heart into *sth*; throw oneself into *sth* heart and soul. ⓗ ～を落とす lose courage; be discouraged; be dejected; be disappointed; be frustrated. ⓗ ～を切る breathe hard; gasp for breath. ～を出す exert oneself; apply oneself (to one's work). ⓗ ～を尽かす be discouraged; be dejected; lose courage; be disappointed; be frustrated. ～を付ける invigorate *sb*; tone *sb* up; cheer *sb* on. ⓗ ～を励ます be devoted to *sth*; be enthusiastic about *sth*; do *sth* with zeal.

背 stature; height; tallness ▶ 背

[A] ～が高い be tall; be of great stature. ～が立つ be able to stand with one's head above water. ～が伸びる grow in stature; grow taller. ～が低い be short; be of small stature.
[を] ～を測る measure *sb's* height.

生 ᴇ life; living

ⓔ 〜を営む lead a life; ⓔ spend one's days. ⓔ 〜を享ける come into the world; be born. ⓐ ⓔ 〜を偸む outlive one's span of life; live to no purpose; live a useless life. 〜を貪る outlive one's span of life; live to no purpose; live a useless life.

姓 a surname; a family name

ⓐ 〜を冒す use the name of sb else; misappropriate sb's name. 〜を変える change one's name.

贅 ᴇ luxury; extravagance

ⓐ 〜を言う boast about sth; brag about sth; ⓘ blow one's own horn; ⓘ talk big. 〜を尽くす indulge in luxury; behave extravagantly; be exorbitant. ⓐ 〜を張る show off; be vain. ⓐ 〜を遣る ❶ show off; be vain. ❷ boast about sth; brag about sth; ⓘ talk big.

税 a tax; a duty

〜を納める pay a tax. 〜を課する levy a tax; impose a tax. 〜を取り立てる collect taxes; draw a tax.

誠意 sincerity; good faith

〜を疑う question sb's sincerity. 〜を欠く lack sincerity. 〜を示す show one's good faith.

生気 vitality; vigor; life; verve

ɴ 〜に満ちる brim with vitality. 〜を与える give animation to sth; put life into sth. 〜を奪う sap the vitality of sb/sth.

制限 a restriction; a limit

〜を受ける be subject to restriction. 〜を越える exceed restriction levels. ⓔ 〜を付する place restrictions on sth.

成功 success; a coup; a hit

〜を焦る be (too) eager for success; hunger for success. 〜を祈る pray for success; wish sb success. 〜を祝う celebrate one's success; congratulate sb on his/her success. 〜を収める achieve success; be successful; ⓒ make a hit 〜を期する expect success; be sure of success; anticipate success.

正鵠 ᴇ the bull's eye; the point

〜を射る ❶ hit the target; hit the mark; strike home. ❷ be relevant; ⓘ be on the mark; ⓘ hit the nail on the head; ⓘ be to the point. 〜を得る ❶ hit the target; hit the mark; strike home. ❷ be relevant; ⓘ be on the mark; ⓘ hit the nail on the head; ⓘ be to the point. ⓔ 〜を失する be irrelevant; ⓘ be off the mark;

⓪ miss the point.

精彩 (せいさい) E brilliance; luster

[を] ⓒ ～を欠く be lackluster; be tame; lack in vitaliy; be dull. ⓒ ～を放つ be brilliant; ba startling; be charismatic; be conspicuous.

生色 (せいしょく) E an animated look

[を] ⓒ ～を失う look very pale; have an exeedingly pale countenance; look as white as a sheet.

贅沢 (ぜいたく) luxury; extravagance

[N] ～に暮らす live in luxury; lead a life of luxury. ～に育つ be brought up in luxury.
[を] ～を言う ask for too much; expect too much. ～をする indulge in luxury; ⓪ have one's bread buttered on both sides. ～を尽す make sth exquisite; explore the boundaries of luxury. ～を慎む abstain from luxuries. ～を始める take to extravagance.

掣肘 (せいちゅう) E restraint; restriction

[を] ⓒ ～を受ける be retrained; be restricted. ⓒ ～を加える put sb under restraint.

正道 (せいどう) E the right path

[N] ～に就く be on the right track. ～に立ち返らせる lead sb back to the right way. ～に外れる be astray from the right path. ～に導く guide sb to the right path. ～に戻る get back on the right path; mend one's ways; ⓪ return to the straight and narrow.
[を] ～を逸れる deviate from the right path. ～を外す stray from the right path. ～を踏む keep to the right path; pursue an honest career; ⓪ stick to the straight and narrow; ⓒ do the right thing.

生命 (せいめい) life; existence; the soul

[を] ～を預ける put one's life in sb's hands; ⓒ entrust one's life to sb. ～を失う lose one's life. ～を奪う take sb's life. ～を賭ける risk one's life. ⓒ ～を捧げる devote one's life (to a cause). ～を救う save sb's life. ⓒ ～を托す place one's life in sb's hands; ⓒ entrust one's life to sb ⓒ ～を賭する risk one's life. ～を尊ぶ value life; ⓒ hold life dear. ～を投げ打つ throw one's life away. ～を狙う seek sb's life; ⓒ have a design on sb's life.

生面 (せいめん) a new area/field

[を] ～を開く open up a new field; explore new possibilities.

誓約 (せいやく) a vow; an oath; a pledge

[を] ～を果(は)たす fulfill one's vow; live up to one's word. ～を守(まも)る keep one's vow; be true to one's word. ～を破(やぶ)る break one's word; ⓒ violate one's pledge.

勢力 (せいりょく) influence; power; weight

[A] ～がある have influence; exercise power; wield power. ～が増(ま)す gain in influence; win gravity. [を] ～を得(え)る acquire influence. ～を挫(くじ)く undermine sb's influence. ～を張(は)る establish one's influence. ～を挽回(ばんかい)する regain power. ～を揮(ふる)う wield power; ⓒ hold sway. ～を増(ま)す increase one's influence.

席 (せき) a seat; a gallery

[N] ～に着(つ)く take one's seat; seat oneself. ～に戻(もど)る return to one's seat. [を] ～を改(あらた)める ❶ change seats. ❷ change venue; ⓒ adjourn to another room. ❸ find another occasion (to do sth). ～を移(うつ)す change venues; ⓒ adjourn to another room. ～を替(か)える change one's seat; change seats. ⓒ ～を汚(けが)す attend a meeting; participate in a meeting; join a party. ～を蹴(け)る leave (a meeting) in a row; ⓒ storm out of the room. ～を進(すす)める come closer to; draw near to; be drawn into. ～を取(と)る take sb's seat. ～を外(はず)す leave one's seat; make a seat free; leave the room. ～を離(はな)れる leave one's seat; quit one's seat. ～を譲(ゆず)る ❶ offer one's seat to sb. ❷ hand over one's position to sb; make place for sb else.

籍 (せき) domicile; membership

[を] ～を入(い)れる become a member (of a club); be enrolled (at a university); ⓒ affiliate oneself with (an organization). ～を置(お)く become a member (of a club); be enrolled (at a university); ⓒ affiliate oneself with (an organization).

堰 (せき) a dam; a weir

[を] ～を切(き)る ❶ burst a dam; break a dam. ❷ ⓐ open the flood gates; let (one's tears) flow unrestrained.

責任 (せきにん) responsibility; duty

[A] ～が有(あ)る bear responsibility; be responsible. [を] ～を失(うしな)う lose responsibility. ～を移(うつ)す turn over a duty to sb else; shift the responsibility (for one's actions) to sb else; ⓒ ⓘ pass the buck to sb else. ～を負(お)う bear the responsibility for (one's actions); be responsible. ～を押(お)し付(つ)ける shift the responsibility (for one's actions) to *sb* else; ⓒ ① pass the buck to *sb* else. 〜を感じる feel responsible; have a sense of responsibility. 〜を避ける avoid responsibility; ⓒ shirk one's duty. 〜を棄てる desert one's duty; abandon one's responsibilities. 〜を問う call *sb* to account; make *sb* answerable; call *sb* to task for *sth*. 〜を解く relieve *sb* from his/her duty. 〜を取る assume responsibility; take responsibility. 〜を果たす fulfill one's duty; carry out one's responsibility; do one's duty. 〜を放棄する relinquish one's responsibilities; ⓔ abdicate responsibility. 〜を持つ be responsible; hold responsibility. 〜を分け合う share the responsibility.

世間 the world; the public

Ⓐ 〜が狭い ❶ have a small circle of acquaintances. ❷ feel inferior; be shy; ⓒ ① be a shrinking daisy. Ⓐ 〜が立つ do one's worldly duties. Ⓐ 〜が詰まる be unable to manage (financially); ⓒ hit hard times. Ⓐ 〜が張る make a great outlay (to impress people); ⓔ be ostentatious. 〜が広い have a wide circle of acquaintances. Ⓝ 〜に知れる become public; come to light; ① spread abroad; ① take wind. 〜に出る go out into the world; enter the real world. ⓒ 〜に成る return to secular life; renounce the cloth. 〜に広まる gain publicity; become widely known; gain repute. Ⓐ 〜に凭れる follow the world; do as others do; ⓒ go with the flow.
囮 〜へ出る go out into the world; enter the real world.
匿 〜を恐れる be afraid of people's opinions; fear what people will say. Ⓐ 〜を兼ねる take account of the public eye; ① keep up appearances. 〜を騒がす be much talked about; create a sensation; ① make a stir. Ⓐ 〜を済ます fool the world; ① lead the public by the nose. Ⓐ 〜を包む hide *sth* from the outside world; keep *sth* secret. 〜を憚る be wary of people's opinions; heed public opinion. Ⓐ 〜を張る play the *bon vivant*; show off; ⓔ be ostentatious. Ⓐ 〜を塞げる lose contact with the world; be shut off from the outside world. 〜を見る see the world; gain in worldly experience. Ⓐ 〜を辞める ❶ go into seclusion; become a hermit; ⓒ retire from the world; renounce the world. ❷ become a Buddhist priest; take the tonsure; ⓔ retire into religion. 〜を渡る go through the world.

世間体 appearances

[A] ～が良い be respectable; appear decent. ～が悪い be disreputable.
[を] ～を構う take account of the public eye; heed public opinion. ～を繕う save appearances; ⓘ keep up appearances.

せこ a pile of saucers

[を] ～を入れる ❶ wait on all the guests; attend to the needs of all guasts. ❷ do *sth* with heart and soul; ⓘ put one's heart into *sth*. ❸ take pains over *sth*; pay meticulous attention to detail.

世故 worldly affairs

[N] ～に長ける know what makes the world go round; be worldly-wise; ⓒ be street-wise.

瀬越し fording a shallows

[を] ～を掛ける drive *sb* into a corner; put *sb* in a difficult position.

世帯 a household; a home

[N] ～に迫る be in financial trouble; ⓒ be in straitened circumstances; be in dire straits.
[を] ～を破る be divorced; break up; ⓒ split up.

節 a season; constancy ▶節

[を] ⓒ ～を売る prostitute oneself; ⓒ sell one's honor. ～を折る yield to *sb*; give in to *sb*. ～を屈する yield to *sb*; give in to *sb*. ⓒ ～を捨てる abandon one's principles; ⓘ desert one's colors. ～を遂ぐ achieve one's aim; win through. ～を曲げる betray one's principles; ⓢ sell out. ～を全うする be faithful; remain constant; stick to one's principles; stand firm; ⓘ hold to one's colors; ⓘ stick to one's guns. ～を守る be faithful; remain constant; stick to one's principles; stand firm; ⓘ hold to one's colors; ⓘ stick to one's guns. ⓒ ～を破る stain one's virtue; be unchaste.

拙 E poor; unskillful; clumsy

[を] Ⓐ Ⓒ ～を蔵す hide one's flaws. Ⓐ Ⓒ ～を守る be content with one's mediocrity; accept one's flaws.

舌 the tongue ▶舌

[N] ～に掛ける win *sb* over; get round *sb*; seduce *sb*.

背中 the back; one's back

[A] ～が禿げる be cunning; be sly; be crafty; be wily; be street-wise.
[を] ～を向ける ❶ turn one's back toward *sth*; turn one's back on *sb*. ❷ reject *sb*/*sth*; ⓘ give *sb* the cold shoulder; ⓘ turn one's back on

sb/*sth*.

銭(ぜに) money; coin; cash

[N] ～になる be profitable; bring in money; make money.

[を] ◎ ～を売る exchange (small) cash for gold/silver buiIion. ◎ ～を買う exchange gond/silver buiIion for (small) change. ◎ ～をつく count out one's money; pay in cash. ◎ ～を読む count money.

是非(ぜひ) right and wrong

[を] ～を犯(おか)す go against reason; be unreasonable; do not stand to reason; be in the wrong. ～を極(きわ)める distinguish right from wrong. ～を問(と)う call *sth* into question. ～を弁(べん)じる distinguish between right and wrong. ～を論(ろん)じる discuss the pros and cons (of an issue).

台詞(せりふ) one's lines; one's words

[を] ～を言(い)う speak one's lines; read the lines. ◎ ～を付(つ)ける ❶ appear on the stage; perform on stage. ❷ explain a situation; throw light on a matter; explain oneself. ～をとちる bungle up one's lines; ⓒ fluff one's lines. ～を忘(わす)れる forget one's lines; freeze up.

世話(せわ) care; assistance; help

sb/*sth*. [A] ～が焼(や)ける give *sb* trouble; require care; be a nuisance to *sb*. [N] ◎ ～に砕(くだ)ける ❶ [*kabuki*] slip into the common vernacular. ❷ speak in a plain and friendly manner; speak in the language of the man of the street. ～になる be under *sb*'s care; receive assistance.

[を] ～をかく take care of *sb*/*sth*; look after *sb*/*sth*; see to *sb*/*sth*. ～をする look after *sb*. ～を掛(か)ける trouble *sb*. ⓐ ～を拾(ひろ)う carry the burden. ～を焼(や)かす give *sb* trouble; require care. ～を焼(や)く ❶ take care of *sb*/sth; look after *sb*/sth; see to *sb*/*sth*. ❷ exert oneself on *sb*'s behalf; do one's best for *sb*. ⓐ ～を病(や)む take utmost care; look after *sb* at one's own cost.

先(せん) the future; priority ▶先(さき)

[を] ～を越(こ)す anticipate *sb*/*sth*; take the initiative; get a start on *sb*; be the first to act. ～を取(と)る get a lead on *sb*; preempt *sb*'s actions; get ahead of *sb*.

選(せん) selection; choice

[N] ～に入(い)る be selected; be chosen. ～に漏(も)れる be rejected; be left out of the selection.

線(せん) a line; a wire; a route; a track

[A] ～が太い ❶ be strongly built; be sturdy; be robust; have a strong physique. ❷ be headstrong; ⓒ be indomitable; be dauntless. ❸ be generous; be magnanimous; have a big heart. ～が細い ❶ be thin; be frail; have a weak physique. ❷ be timid; be fainthearted; ⓒ be timorous; ⓒ be chicken.
[を] ～を引く ❶ draw a line. ❷ make a distinction between two things; ⓘ draw the line.

膳 a (small) table; a tray

[N] ～に出す serve a meal; put a meal on the table. ～に就く sit down to table. ～に向かう sit down to table.
[を] ～を片付ける clear the table; remove the tablecloth. ～を据える ❶ put a tray in front of *sb*; lay the table; set a table. ❷ woo a man; force one's attentions on a man. Ⓐ ～を引く clear the table; remove the tablecloth.

善 good; goodness; virtue

[を] ～を成す do good; practice virtue.

前後 before and behind; order

[N] ～に暮れる be bewildered; be at a loss; ⓘ be at one's wits' end; ⓘ be all at sea. ～に迷う be bewildered; be at a loss; ⓘ be at one's wits' end; ⓘ be all at sea.
[を] ～を失う ❶ forget oneself; be at a loss; be distraught; be flabergasted; be nonplussed. ❷ be fast asleep; sleep like a log. ❸ drink oneself into a stupor; get blind drunk. ～を顧みる reflect on the consequences (of one's actions). ～を失する ❶ forget oneself; be at a loss; be distraught; be flabergasted; be nonplussed. ❷ be fast asleep; sleep like a log. ❸ drink oneself into a stupor; get blind drunk. ～を忘ずる ❶ forget oneself; be at a loss; be distraught; be flabergasted; be nonplussed. ❷ be fast asleep; sleep like a log. ❸ drink oneself into a stupor; get blind drunk. ～を見回す look around one. ～を忘れる ❶ forget oneself; be at a loss; be distraught; be flabergasted; be nonplussed. ❷ be fast asleep; sleep like a log. ❸ drink oneself into a stupor; get blind drunk.

善根 Ⓔ a good deed; charity

[を] ⓒ ～を積む lead a good life; accumulate good deeds. ⓒ ～を施す do good; practice charity.

全盛 the height of prosperity

[を] ～を極める attain the highest

stage of prosperity. ～を誇る be in all its glory.

せんそう
戦争 war; a battle; warfare
[A] ～が起こる war breaks out. [N] ～に訴える resort to arms. ～に勝つ win a battle; win the day. ～に出る go to war; go into battle. ～に備える prepare for war; ⓒ clear the decks. ～に負ける be defeated in battle; lose a battle. [को] ～を逃れる escape from war; ⓔ be spared from (the ravages) of war. ～を始める open hostilities.

せんて
先手 the first move
[को] ～を打つ ❶ [shōgi] make the first move. ❷ forestall sb; get a start on sb; anticipate sb (in doing). ～を取る ❶ [shōgi] make the first move. ❷ get a lead on sb; get ahead of sb.

ぜんてつ
前轍 ⒺⒶ the rut of the car in front
[को] ⓒ ～を踏む repeat sb's mistake; share sb's fate; ⓔ follow in the wake of sth; ⓘ fall into the same rut.

せんど
先途 ⒺⒶ one's destination
[को] ⓒ ～を磨く accomplish one's purpose; attain one's object; reach on'e goal; achieve one's aim.

せんとう
先頭 the forefront; the lead
[N] ～に立つ lead the vanguard; take the lead; spearhead (a campaign); ⓘ be in the front van. [को] ～を切る take the lead; ⓘ be in the front van (of a campaign). ～を走る lead the race; be in the lead.

ぜんび
善美 ⒺⒶ the good and beautiful
[को] ～を極める make sth exquisite; explore the boundaries of luxury. ～を尽す make sth gorgeous; furnish sth lavishly.

ぜんぴ
前非 ⒺⒶ one's past folly
[को] ⓒ ～を悔いる repent of one's past sins. ⓒ ～を悟る see the error of one's own ways.

せんべん
先鞭 ⒺⒶ the initiative; the lead
[को] ～を付ける ❶ get a headstart on sb; ⓘ blaze one's trail. ❷ take the initiative; take the lead. ❸ preempt sb's action; forestall sb; outwit sb.

ぜんぼう
全貌 ⒺⒶ the whole picture/story
[को] ～を現わす come into full view; ⓔ emerge into view. ～を示す give sb the full details; ⓒ put sb in the picture. ～を掴む grasp the full story; ⓒ get the whole picture. ⓒ ～を尽す give an exhaustive account; describe sth in all its details.

せんみょう
宣命 🅱 an Imperial decree

🅰 ⓒ 〜を含める tell sb to accept the inevitable; ⓒ persuade sb to reconcile themselves to their fate.

ぜんりょく
全力 all one's power

🅰 〜を上げる muster all one's strength; exert all one's power; ⓒ go all out. 〜を注ぐ pour all one's energy into sth. 〜を尽す do one's utmost; do everything in one's power; give one's all.

せんれい
先例 a precedent; an example

🅣 〜とする take sth as a precedent. 〜となる become a precedent (for). 🅝 〜に背く contravene precedent; depart from precedent. 〜による be according to precedent; comply with precedent. 🅰 〜を作る set a precedent. 〜を破る violate a precedent.

せんれい
洗礼 baptism

🅰 〜を受ける be baptized. 〜を施す baptize sb.

ソ

ぞう
臓 the intestines; the bowels

🅰 〜を揉む ❶ be anxious about sth; fret over sth; worry about sth;

ⓒ fidget about sth. ❷ regret sth bitterly; feel chagrined (at sth); be grieved (at sth); feel sorry for sb.

そうが
爪牙 🅱 nails and fangs; clutches

🅝 ⓒ 〜に掛かる fall victim to (sb's evil intent); fall into sb's clutches. 🅰 ⓒ 〜を脱する free oneself from sb's hold; get out of sb's clutches. ⓒ 〜を研ぐ ❶ sharpen its clutches. ❷ keep a vigilant eye on sb/sth; have an eye on sb/sth.

そうけん
双肩 🅱 one's shoulders

🅝 ⓒ 〜に懸かる bear sth with both shoulders; rest fully on one's shoulders. ⓒ 〜に担う carry a heavy burden; be charged with all the responsibilities for sth.

そうごう
相好 facal features; looks

🅰 〜を崩す break into a smile; beam with joy; be all smiles.

そうぞう
想像 imagination; fancy

🅐 〜がつく be imaginable; be understandable; have a notion; one can guess; ⓒ get the idea. 🅝 〜に描く make a mental picture of sth; picture sth to oneself; see sth in one's imagination. 〜に絶する defy all imagination. 〜に基づく be a figment of one's imagination.

[を] ～を廻らす be imaginative; use one's imagination; ponder over sth.

相談 counsel; a talk; an offer

[N] ～が纏まる come to an agreement; reach a settlement; come to terms.
[N] ～に預かる be asked for one's advise; consulted by sb. ～に行く go to seek sb's advice; go to consult sb. ～に入れる take sb into council. ～に応じる ❶ give counsel to sb; advise sb. ❷ give sb assistance; assist sb; Ⓒ give sb a helping hand. ❸ accept sb's offer; respond to sb's proposal. ～に加える take sb into council. ～に乗る ❶ give counsel to sb; advise sb. ❷ give sb assistance; assist sb; Ⓒ give sb a helping hand. ❸ accept sb's offer; respond to sb's proposal.
[を] ～を受ける be asked for one's advise; consulted by sb. ～を決める come to an agreement; reach a settlement; come to terms. ～を持ち出す put forward a proposal; make an offer.

相場 the market (price)

[A] ⑦ ～が上がる prices rise; go up in price; quotations advance. ～が良い the prospects are good; the situation is favorable; Ⓒ things look good. ～が決まる be taken for granted; be a widely held view; stand to reason; speak for itself. ⑦ ～が下がる prices fall; go down in price; quotations decline. ⑦ ～が立つ be quoted; gotations are given. ～が悪い the prospects are gloomy; the situation is unfavorable; Ⓒ things look bad.
[Av] ～で儲ける lose money in speculation.
[を] ⑦ ～を操る manipulate the market; rig the market. ⑦ ～を狂わす affect the price; upset the market. ⑦ ～を付ける offer a price; quote an article.

臓腑 the intestines; the bowels

[を] ～を抉る break one's/sb's heart; be heartrending. ～を揉む ❶ be anxious about sth; fret over sth; worry about sth; Ⓒ fidget about sth. ❷ regret sth bitterly; feel chagrined (at sth); be grieved (at sth); feel sorry for sb.

俗 Ⓔ customs; manners

[N] ～に言う use a vulgar turn of phrase; use everyday language. ～に落ちる be liked by the masses; be well recieved by the commoner; be the darling of the public.
[を] ⓓ Ⓔ ～を追う pursue worldly things. Ⓔ ～を脱する rise above the world.

ソコ　　　　　　　　　　　　　　　　　　ソデ

ぞくじん
俗塵 国 the world; earthly affairs
を ～を洗(あら)う disengage one's mind from worldly cares. ～を避ける live secluded from the world; keep aloof from everyday life.

そくばく
束縛 a restraint; a restriction
を ～を受(う)ける be placed under restraint. ～を加(くわ)える impose restraints upon *sb*; put restrictions on *sb*. ⓒ ～を脱(だっ)する free oneself from restraint; ⓔ throw off a yoke.

そこ
底 the bottom; the bed
Ａ ～が浅(あさ)い ❶ ⓑ be shallow; have little depth. ❷ ⓐ be shallow; ⓐ have no depth; be superficial. ～が知(し)れない be unfathomable; be a mystery. ～が深(ふか)い ❶ ⓑ be deep; have depth. ❷ be profound; ⓐ have depth; ⓒ be deep. ～が見(み)える be seen through. ～が割(わ)れる be exposed; be seen through; ⓒ be shown up (for what one is).
Ｎ ～に着(つ)く find bottom; touch bottom; reach the bottom.
を ⓐ ～を入(い)れる ❶ have a starter; have an appetizer. ❷ make sure of *sth*; tell *sb* twice; bring *sth* home to *sb*; ⓒ ⓘ rub it in. ❸ reach the rock-bottom price; ⓒ bottom out. ⓐ ～を押(お)す remind *sb* (of *sth*); call *sb*'s attention to *sth*; make sure of *sth*;

tell *sb* emphatically of *sth*. ～を極(きわ)める master the essence of *sth*. ⓐ ～を叩(たた)く ❶ empty (a vessel) totally. ❷ reach the rock-bottom price. ～を突(つ)く ❶ touch bottom; reach the bottom. ❷ exhaust (one's savings); run out of (petrol). ⓗ ～を付ける fail in dying fabric. ～を抜(ぬ)く knock out the bottom (of a box). ⓐ ～を叩(はた)く empty (a vessel) totally. ⓐ ～を払(はら)う empty (a vessel) totally. ⓖ ～を割(わ)る ❶ open one's heart to *sb*; unbosom oneself; speak one's mind; ⓘ pour out one's heart to *sb*. ❷ (prices) fall through the bottom. ⓖ ～を破(やぶ)る expose (a secret); reveal the truth.

そしょう
訴訟 a lawsuit; an action
Ｎ ～に勝(か)つ win a lawsuit. ～に負(ま)ける lose a lawsuit.
を ～を起(お)こす raise a suit; go to court. ～を取(と)り下(さ)げる drop a suit.

そじょう
俎上 国 a chopping block
Ｎ ～に載(の)せる ❶ put (meat) on the chopping block. ❷ put *sth* under review; take *sth* up for discussion.

そで
袖 a sleeve; an arm; a wing
Ｎ ～にあしらう assume a cold attitude; treat *sb* stiffly; ⓘ give *sb* the cold shoulder; ⓘ hold *sb* at arm's lenght. ⓐ ⓢ ～に食(く)らう hide *sth* in

185

one's sleeve; ⓒ pinch *sth*; ⓓ nick *sth*. 〜にくらぶ pinch *sth* on impulse; steal *sth* on a whim. ⓐ 〜に時雨る cry in one's sleeve; shed tears. 〜に縋る ❶ hang on to *sb's* sleeve; cling to *sb's* sleeve. ❷ entreat *sb* for mercy; appeal to *sb's* compassion. ⓐ 〜に墨付く have proof that one is the object of *sb's* love; recieve a token of *sb's* love. 〜にする ❶ jilt one's lover; walk out on *sb*. ❷ rebuff *sb*; ⓘ leave *sb* in the lurch; ⓘ give *sb* the cold shoulder. 〜に付く ❶ hang on to *sb's* sleeve; cling to *sb's* sleeve. ❷ entreat *sb* for mercy; appeal to *sb's* compassion. 〜に為す ❶ jilt one's lover; walk out on *sb*. ❷ rebuff *sb*; ⓘ leave *sb* in the lurch; ⓘ give *sb* the cold shoulder. 〜になる assume a cold attitude; treat *sb* stiffly; ⓘ give *sb* the cold shoulder; ⓘ hold *sb* at arm's lenght. 〇 〜を折り返す fold back one's sleeves. ⓗ 〜を返す turn one's sleeve inside out (in the hope of dreaming of one's lover). ⓐ 〜を片敷く have a rest; have a (cat)nap; have a snooze. 〜を構える hold *sb* by the sleeve; buttonhole *sb*. 〜を絞る cry in one's sleeve; be moved to tears. 〜を詰める shorten the sleeves of a long-sleeved kimonos (due to one's coming of age). ⓘ 〜を

連ねる ❶ line up; stand in line. ❸ do *sth* in a body; act as a group. ❸ sleep with *sb*; share the same bed; make love. 〜を通す put on a garment (for the first time). 〜を留める stop wearing long-sleeved kimonos (due to one's coming of age). 〜を捕える hold *sb* by the sleeve; ⓒ ⓘ buttonhole *sb*. 〜を濡らす cry in one's sleeve; shed tears. 〜を払う brush (an obstacle) aside. 〜を控える hold *sb* by the sleeve; buttonhole *sb*. 〜を引く ❶ pull *sb* by the sleeve; pluck *sb's* sleeve. ❷ woo a woman; try to win a girl. ❸ warn *sb*; call *sth* to *sb's* attention. ⓒ 〜を拡ぐ beg for alms. 〜を塞ぐ sow up the plackets in one's kimono sleeved (due to one's coming of age). 〜を干す stop grieving. 〜を捲る ⓘ roll up one's sleeves. 〜を分かつ part from *sb*; part company with *sb*; break off relations with *sb*.

外 the outside; outdoors

Ⓐᵥ 〜で遊ぶ play outdoors; play in the open.

Ⓝ 〜にいる be outside; be out. 〜に立つ stand outside (the door). 〜になる be futile; come to nothing; be wasted; ⓘ go up in smoke. 〜に漏る come to light; leak out; ⓘ spread abroad; ⓘ take wind.

ソラ

外(そと) ～へ出(で)る go outside; go out of doors. ～へ向(む)ける turn outward.
外(そと)を ～を見(み)る look outside; look out of (the window).

外堀(そとぼり) the outer moat (of a castle)
を ～を埋(う)める remove an obstacle to one's immediate goal; attain one's goal in a roundabout way.

傍(そば) a side; vicinity; proximity
N ～にいる be at sb's side. ～に置(お)く keep sth/sb near at hand. ～に座(すわ)る sit down next to sb. ～に寄(よ)る draw near to sb.
を ～を通(とお)る pass sb by. ～を離(はな)れる leave sb's side.

側杖(そばづえ) ⓐ a by-blow
を ⓢ ～を食(く)う ❶ get a by-blow from a fight between others. ❷ get involved in the affairs of others; be embroiled in a quarrel. ❸ meet with misfortune; be the hapless victim of circumstance.

側目(そばめ) a sidelong glance
N (人(ひと)を)～に懸(か)く ❶ give sb a sidelong glance; look sideways at sb; look at sb out of the corner of one's eyes. ❷ take no notice of sb; have no eye for sb; think nothing of sb; ignore sb; ⓒ set sb at naught.

ソロバン

空(そら) the sky; the air ▶ 空(から) ▶ 空(くう)
A ～で覚(おぼ)える learn sth by heart; know sth by heart. ～で読(よ)む recite sth from memory; read sth by rote.
N ～に舞(ま)い上(あ)がる pierce the skies; soar into the sky.
を (旅(たび)の)～を仰(あお)ぐ be in a strange land; be away from home. ⓐ ～を歩(あゆ)む be on edge; be nervous; ⓑ be on tenterhooks. ⓒ ～を使(つか)う ❶ pretend not to know; feign ignorance. ❷ lie about st; tell a lie. ～を吐(つ)く ❶ pretend not to know; feign ignorance. ❷ lie about st; tell a lie. ～を飛(と)ぶ fly in the air. ～を眺(なが)める look at the sky. ～を見上(みあ)げる look up at the sky. ～を渡(わた)る cross the skies; sail across the sky.

空鼾(そらいびき) feigned snoring
を ～を掻(か)く pretend to be asleep; feign sleep (by snoring).

空耳(そらみみ) feigned deafness
を ～を使(つか)う pretend to be deaf; feign deafness; pretend not to hear. ～を潰(つぶ)す pretend to be deaf; feign deafness; pretend not to hear. ～を走(はし)らす ❶ pretend to be deaf; feign deafness; pretend not to hear. ❷ pretend to be listening. ❸ imagine one has heard sth.

空目 feigned blindness

[を] ～を使う ❶ pretend to be blind; feign blindness. ❷ pretend not to see. ❸ look upwards; cast one's eyes upwards. ❹ look blankly; have a hollow look; ❺ wear a vacant look.

反り a warp; a curve; an arch

[A] (人と)～が合う be like-minded; get along with *sb*; ⓘ see eye to eye; ⓒ ⓘ hit it off. ～が有る be curved. ⓢ ～が来る become warped.

[を] (人と)～を合わせる try to get along with *sb*. Ⓐ ～を打つ ❶ be ready to draw one's sword; have one's sword at the ready. ❷ have a recurved shape; be bent backwards. Ⓐ ～を返す turn one's sword (so that the curve faces downward); be ready to draw one's sword; have one's sword at the ready.

算盤 a Japanese abacus

[A] ～が合う be a commercial success; be profitable; be worthwhile; pay (off). ～が取れる be a commercial success; be profitable; be worthwhile; pay (off).

[を] ～を入れる (re)calculate sth; make adjustments. ～を置く ❶ calculate the loss and gain on an abacus. ❷ act on selfish motives; ⓒ be guided by self-interest; have ulterior motives. ～を弾く ❶ calculate the loss and gain on an abacus. ❷ act on selfish motives; ⓒ be guided by self-interest; have ulterior motives.

損 a loss; damage; a drawback

[A] ～が行く suffer a loss; sustain financial losses; suffer damage. Ⓐ ～が立つ result in a loss.

[N] ～になる result in a loss.

[を] ～を埋める recoup a loss; make good a loss. ～を掛ける cause a loss; inflict a loss upon *sb*. ～を被る sustain a loss; suffer damage. ～をする suffer a loss. ～を償う recoup a loss; make good a loss.

尊敬 respect; esteem; regard

[を] ～を受ける be esteemed; get respect. ～を得る earn *sb's* respect; gain *sb's* esteem. ～を払う pay one's respect to *sb*; show respect.

存在 existence; being

[を] ～を疑う doubt the existence of. ～を認める recognize *sb's* existence.

田 a rice field; a paddy field

[を] ～を植える plant rice seedlings. ～を打つ plow a rice field; till a rice field. ～を耕す plow a rice field; till a rice field. ～を作る crop a rice field; cultivate a rice field; grow rice; till a rice field.

体 the body; an object ▶ 体

[A] ～が無い ❶ lack perseverance; have no staying power. ❷ be useless; be a good-for-nothing; be a bumbler. ❸ [sumō] have no staying power; lack endurance; be on the verge of defeat.

[を] ～を預ける [sumō] throw one's full weight against one's opponent. ～を躱す dodge (a blow); get out of the way. ～を成す take form; get into shape; be organized. ⓒ ～を引く draw back; withdraw (one's body).

題 a subject; a title; a problem

[を] ～を出す ❶ [writing] set the subject for a composition. ❷ lay down specific conditions; set conditions; ⓘ lay down the rules. ～を付ける give a title to a book; attach a headline to an article.

大 largeness; greatness; size

[を] ～を為す attain greatness; rise to fame; realize a great feat; become eminent; ⓒ make it big.

大概 moderation; generally

[N] ～にする do *sth* in moderation; refrain from taking things too far; keep within bounds.

大魚 [E] a large fish; a big catch

[を] ⓒ ～を逸する miss a great opportunity; make a big mistake.

退屈 boredom; tedium; enui

[を] ～を凌ぐ drive away the enui; fill in the hours; ⓒ ⓘ kill time. ～を紛らす drive away the enui; fill in the hours; ⓒ ⓘ kill time.

太鼓 a drum; a tomtom

[を] ～を打つ ❶ beat a drum. ❷ keep in tune with *sb*; go along with *sb*; play along with *sb*. ❸ cater to *sb's* wishes; try to please *sb*. ❹ mediate between two parties; act as a go-between. ～を叩く ❶ pound on drums. ❷ flatter *sb*; ⓘ chime in with *sb*; ⓘ curry favor with *sb*. ～を鳴らす beat a drum. (人の)～を持つ flatter *sb*; ⓘ chime in with *sb*; ⓘ curry favor with *sb*.

太鼓判 [E] a large seal

[を] ⓒ ～を押す give one's seal of approval; sponsor *sb/sth*; give *sb* a clean bill of health.

台座 a pedestal

[A] ⓒ ～が来る ❶ be complained

about; ⓒ have a complaint lodged against one. ❷ get involved in the affairs of others; be embroiled in a quarrel.
🈺 ～を据える resolve to do *sth*; settle down; ⓒ buckle down. ⓐ ～を放す cut off *sb's* head; behead *sb*; ⓒ decapitate *sb*.

大事 a serious matter; prudence
🈯 ～に至る get out of control; become serious; take on serious proportions. ～にする ❶ take good care of *sth*; give *sth* much care. ❷ think much of *sth*; set great value on *sth*; cherish *sth*. ～になる get out of control; become serious; take on serious proportions.
🈺 ～を取る be prudent; take no chances; play it safe. ～を為す achieve a great success; accomplish *sth* great. ～を引き起こす bring about a disaster; give rise to a crises; lead to trouble.

体重 body weight
🈯 ～が減る lose weight. ～が増す gain weight; put on weight.
🈺 ～を計る weigh oneself. ～を減らす reduce one's weight.

大地 the ground; the earth
🈺 ～を見抜く see through a plot;

penetrate a mystery; discern the truth; read *sb's* thoughts.

大抵 moderation; general
🈯 ～にする do *sth* in moderation; refrain from taking things too far; keep within bounds.

態度 an attitude; a manner
🈺 ～を改める revise one's attitude. ～を変える change one's attitude. ～を決める determine one's attitude. ～を持する retain one's attitude. ～を取る take a stand.

台無し ruin; chaos; a mess
🈯 ⓢ ～にする ❶ ruin *sth*; wreck (one's career); mar *sth*. ❷ make a muddle of *sth*; juble *sth* up; mix *sth* up. ⓢ ～になる ❶ come to nothing; ⓘ end in tears; ⓘ go to pie. ❷ be mixed up; be in a mess.

太平 peace; quiet; tranquility
🈺 ～を並べる say what one likes; ⓒ indulge in idle talk; ⓒ title-tattle. ～を抜かす talk nonsense; ⓘ talk through one's hat; ⓒ ⓘ talk rubbish. ～を打ち挙げる say whatever one likes; ⓒ indulge in utter idle talk.

太平楽 🅵 a fool's paradise
🈺 ⓢ ～を言う say what one likes;

ⓔ indulge in idle talk; ⓒ title-tatle. ⑤ 〜を並(なら)べる say what one likes; ⓔ indulge in idle talk; ⓒ title-tatle.

大砲(たいほう) a canon; an artillery gun

圏 〜を据(す)える mount a gun. 〜を造(つく)る build a gun. 〜を放(はな)つ fire a gun. 〜を向(む)ける train a gun.

大枚(たいまい) 図 a large sum of money

圏 ⑤ 〜を叩(はた)く pay a large sum of money; ① pay through one's nose.

体面(たいめん) appearances; face; honor

圏 〜を重(おも)んじる respect sb's honor; ⓔ ① keep sb in countenance. 〜を汚(けが)す be disgraced; ① lose face. 〜を保(たも)つ ① save one's face; ① keep up appearances. 〜を繕(つくろ)う ① keep up appearances.

ダイヤ a diagram; a schedule

圏 〜を変(か)える revise the time-table. 〜を狂(くる)わす upset the schedule; disrupt the time-table.

タオル a towel

圏 〜を投(な)げる admit defeat; give in; yield to sb; ① throw in the towel.

高(たか) a quantity; an amount; a sum

A 〜が知(し)れる be not worth considering; be of little account.

圏 〜を括(くく)る ❶ make light of sth; think little of sth. ❷ feel where things are going; be confident about the outcome. ❸ underestimate sth; minimize (the danger).

箍(たが) a (metal/bamboo) hoop

A 〜が外(はず)れる feel relieved; feel relaxed. 〜が緩(ゆる)む ❶ the hoop comes off. ❷ feel relieved; feel relaxed. ❸ lose one's vigor; lose one's edge; ① go out of gear.
圏 〜を掛(か)け代(か)える put on new hoops; rehoop a barrel. 〜を掛(か)ける put on a hoop; bind a barrel. 〜を外(はず)す ❶ take the hoops off; unhoop a barrel. ❷ free oneself from restrictions; ⓔ throw off the yoke; ⓔ cast off the fetters. ❸ have fun; make merry; ① paint the town red; ⓒ ① let one's hair down.

高腰(たかごし) a haughty posture

圏 〜を掛(か)く be haughty; be proud; ⓔ have an overbearing attitude; ① have airs and graces; ⓒ ① have a swelled head; ⓒ be stuck-up.

多岐(たき) 図 manyfold; multifarous

N ⓔ 〜に渡(わた)る ❶ include many; be manyfold; take up various topics. ❷ wander from the (main) subject; get sidetracked; be diverted.

惰気 E idleness; sluggishness

を Ⓔ 〜を生じる be bored; be tired; be wearied. Ⓒ 〜を催す be boring; Ⓔ cause enui.

卓 a table; a desk

を 〜を囲む sit around the table; gather around the table. 〜を立つ leave the table.

丈 height; length; measure

A 〜が知れる ❶ be fathomable; be comprehensible. ❷ be trifling; be not worth considering; be of little account. 〜が高い be tall; be of great stature. 〜が伸びる grow tall. 〜が低い be short; be of small stature. 〜が短い be (too) short.

を (思いの)〜を述べる open oneself up to sb; take sb into one's confidence; Ⓘ pour out one's heart to sb; Ⓒ unbosom oneself.

胼胝 a callus; a corn

A 〜が入る ❶ one's (leg) goes to sleep; lose the feeling in a limb. ❷ get borded of sth; lose interest in sth; be bored to distraction; Ⓒ get sick and tired of sth.

N 〜になる become callous.

出汁 broth; a pretext; a tool

N 〜に使う use sb; involve sb in (one's excuses); Ⓘ make a cat's paw of sb; Ⓘ make a scapegoat of sb.

駄洒落 a dull joke; a poor pun

を 〜を言う make a bad joke; Ⓒ crach a cheap joke.

助け assistance; help; aid

と 〜となる be a help to sb; be of assistance; contribute to sth.

N 〜に行く go to sb's aid; help sb out. 〜に来る come to sb's aid. 〜になる be of assistance; be helpful; be a help.

を (人の)〜を借りる get sb's help; recieve sb's assistance. 〜を求める ask help; ask for sb's help; seek (sb's) assistance. 〜を呼ぶ call for help; cry out for assistance.

助け舟 a lifeboat

を 〜を出す ❶ launch a lifeboat. ❷ go to sb's rescue; help sb in distress.

駄々 E sulking; petulance

を Ⓒ 〜を言う sulk over sth; be petulant; Ⓘ make a scene. Ⓒ 〜を捏ねる sulk over sth; be petulant; Ⓘ make a scene; Ⓒ Ⓘ have the sulks.

戦い war; a battle; a struggle

N 〜に倦み疲れる be tired of fighting; ⓒ be battle weary. 〜に赴(おもむ)く go to war; go to the front; head for the battlefield. 〜に勝つ gain victory; win a game; win a battle; ⓘ win the day. 〜に備える prepare for battle; make oneself ready for combat; ⓘ clear the decks. 〜に出(で)る go to the front; go off to war; ⓔ take the field. 〜に負(ま)ける be defeated; lose a game; ⓘ lose the day. [を] 〜を挑(いど)む offer battle; challenge sb to a game; ⓘ throw down the gauntlet to sb. 〜繰(く)り広(ひろ)げる widen the battle. ⓔ 〜を宣(せん)する declare war (against a country). 〜を交(まじ)える join battle (with sb); ⓔ do battle; engage the enemy. 〜を求める seek battle; challenge sb to battle.

踏鞴(たたら) a foot bellows

[を] 〜を踏(ふ)む ❶ work to foot bellows. ❷ ⓘ make a misstep; lose one's balance; ⓒ totter.

質(たち) a temperament ▶質 ▶質

[A] 〜が良(い)い have a good nature; be good-natured; ⓔ be of a good disposition. 〜が悪(わる)い have a bad nature; be bad-natured; ⓒ be wicked.

立場(たちば) a standpoint; a position

[N] (人の)〜に在(あ)る be in sb's position; ⓘ be in sb's shoes. (人の)〜に 成(な)る put oneself in sb's place; ⓘ put oneself in sb's shoes.

[を] 〜を失(うしな)う lose one's footing. 〜を奪(うば)う cut the ground from under sb's feet. 〜を得(え)る gain one's footing. 〜を換(か)える change one's ground; take a different standpoint. 〜を尊(とうと)ぶ respect sb's position. 〜を取(と)る take a (certain) position; take a stand. 〜を守(まも)る hold one's ground.

手綱(たづな) a bridle; the reins

[を] 〜を取(と)る hold the reins; be in control; ⓢ ⓘ call the shots. ⓒ 〜を控(ひか)える draw in the reins; rein in (a horse); call sb to order. 〜を引(ひ)き締(し)める tighten the reins; rein in (a horse); call sb to order; ⓘ keep a tight rein. 〜を引(ひ)く pull the reins; draw in the reins. 〜を緩(ゆる)める slacken the reins; give sb free rein; ⓘ allow a free rein. 〜を渡(わた)す pass the reins to sb else; make place for sb else; transfer control.

盾(たて) a shield; a buckler

[N] 〜に突(つ)く seek to protect oneself; get back-up; act under sb's protection; act on sb's authority. 〜に取(と)る ❶ use sth/sb as a shield; ⓘ hide oneself behind sth. ❷ use sth as an excuse; ⓐ hide behind sth; ⓐ shield oneself behind sth.

棚 (たな) a shelf; a rack; a trellis
　N ～に上げる ❶ (物を) put sth on a shelf. ❷ (事を) be blind to one's own faults; ⓘ fail to see the beam in one's own eye.
　を ～をつる put up a shelf.

掌 (たなごころ) the palm of the hand ▶ 掌 (てのひら)
　N ～に握る be in one's hands; be under one's control; ⓢ ⓘ call the shots. ～にする ❶ make sth one's own. take possession of sth. ❷ do as one pleases; have one's own way.
　を ～を返す ❶ be easy (to do); be simple (to understand). ❷ be fickle; be inconstant; be changeable. Ⓐ ～を指す be clear; be apparent.

種 (たね) a seed; a stone; a kernel
　A ～が割れる be exposed; be revealed; ⓘ come to light.
　を ～を明かす reveal a secret; explain a trick. ～を蒔く ⓘ sow seeds; Ⓐ sow seeds (of discontent). ～を宿す become pregnant; have sb's child; ⓒ be with child. Ⓐ ～を割る expose sb; reveal a secret.

頼み (たのみ) a favor; a request
　A ～が有る have a favor to ask.

　N ～に応じる do sb a favor; answer sb's request; ⓒ oblige sb. ～に来る turn to sb for a favor; make a request to sb. ～にする rely on sth; trust in sth; count on sth. ～になる be sb one can rely on; be trustworhty; be reliable.
　を ～を掛ける rely upon sb; put confidence in sb/sth; give credence to sb/sth; ⓒ repose trust in sb/sth. ～を聞く answer sb's request; do sb a favor; oblige sb.

駄法螺 (だぼら) a brag; a boast; big talk
　を ～を吹く ❶ boast about sth; brag about sth; ⓘ talk big; ⓘ blow one's own horn (trumpet). ❷ exaggerate sth; ⓒ indulge in hyperbole; ⓘ stretch the facts; ⓢⓘ pile it on; ⓢⓘ lay it on thick.

他聞 (たぶん) ⓔ publicity
　を ⓒ ～を憚る be afraid of what others may say; shun publicity.

玉 (たま) a ball; a globe; a bulb; a gem
　A ～が上がる be exposed; be revealed; ⓘ come to light. ～が切れる the lamp reaches the end of its life; the bulb blows.
　と (露を)～と欺く (dewdrops that) look as if they were gems.
　N ～に掛ける trap sb; ensnare sb;

ⓒ take *sb* in; ⓢ dupe *sb*. 〜にする roll *sth* into a ball; make *sth* into a ball. 〜に使う use *sb*; use *sb* as a decoy; make a cat's paw of *sb*.
を 〜を抱く have great ambitions; have huge aspirationsn. ⓐ 〜を種う take a beautiful woman as one's wife; marry a beauty. 〜を受ける catch a ball. 〜を打つ hit a ball; strike a ball. 〜を選ぶ wait for a good opportunity; ⓔ bide one's time. 〜を転がす ❶ roll a ball. ❷ have a clear voice; be transparent in tone. 〜を転がす have a powerfull voice; have a billowing voice. 〜を突く hit a ball; play billiards. ⑦ 〜を繋ぐ deposit a margin on the stocks. 〜を投げる throw a ball. 〜を吐く ❶ use flowery language; be eloquent. ❷ compose an exquisite poem. ⓔ ⓐ 〜を転ぼす be melifluous; have a flowing style; be fluent. 〜を磨く polish a gem.

弾 a bullet; shot; a shell

A 〜で打ち抜く send a bullet through (a wall).
N 〜に当る be hit by a bullet.
を 〜を打ち込む put a bullet in (sb's stomach). 〜を打つ fire a shot; shoot at *sb*. 〜を打ち尽す empty one's magazine; fire away all one's shot. 〜を込める load a gun; charge a gun. 〜を抜く unload a gun; extract a bullet.

だま ⑩ pay out the string of a kite

を ⓐ 〜を食う be deceived; ⓘ be taken in; ⓒ be conned; ⓒ be duped. ⓐ 〜を暮れる deceive *sb*; ⓘ take *sb* in; ⓒⓘ lead *sb* by the nose; ⓢ dupe *sb*. ⓐ 〜を出す open oneself up to *sb*; take *sb* into one's confidence; ⓘ pour out one's heart to *sb*; ⓔ unbosom oneself. ⓐ 〜を遣る deceive *sb*; ⓘ take *sb* in; ⓒⓘ lead *sb* by the nose; ⓢ dupe *sb*.

卵 an egg; spawn; spat

を 〜を抱く sit on an egg; incubate an egg. 〜を孵す hatch an egg. 〜を渡る expose oneself/*sb* to danger; put oneself/*sb* in harm's way; endanger oneself/*sb*.

魂 the soul; the spirit

A 〜が抜ける ❶ the spirit leaves the body. ❷ lose one's spirit; lose vigor. ❸ faint; pass out; lose consciousnesess.
を 〜が据わる recover one's presence of mind; come to oneself.
を ⓐ 〜を揚ぐ be terrified; ⓘ be scared out of one's wits; ⓢ be scared stiff. 〜を入れる breathe (new) life into *sth*. 〜を入れ替える have a

change of heart; mend one's ways; ⓘ turn over a new leaf. 〜を打ち込む throw oneself into *sth* heart and soul; ⓘ put one's heart into *sth*. 〜を奪う charm *sb*; ⓘ steal *sb's* heart; ⓘ put a spell on *sb*. 〜を消す ❶ be deeply hurt; be profoundly affected; ⓒ feel gutted. ❷ be at a total loss; be utterly bewildered; be stunned; be perplexed in the extreme. 〜を込める do *sth* with all one's heart; do *sth* with heart and soul; devote all one's energies to *sth*. 〜を飛ばす be in raptures; be in a state of extacy; ⓘ be in seventh heaven. 〜を抜く charm *sb*; ⓘ steal *sb's* heart; ⓘ put a spell on *sb*. 〜を冷やす be struck with terror; ⓘ be scared to death. ⓘ break into a cold sweat. 〜を吹き込む breathe (new) life into *sth*.

玉無し 🅒 a total loss

Ⓝ ⓒ 〜にする ❶ ruin *sth*; wreck (one's career); mar *sth*. ❷ make a muddle of *sth*; juble *sth* up; mix *sth* up. ⓒ 〜になる ❶ come to nothing; ⓘ end in tears; ⓘ go to pie. ❷ be mixed up; be in a mess.

玉の緒 🅒 a string of beads

🅐 ⓔ 〜が切れる leave this world (behind); pass away; draw one's last breath; ⓔ breathe one's last. ⓔ 〜

絶える leave this world (behind); pass away; draw one's last breath; ⓔ breathe one's last.

🅚 ⓔ 〜絶つ kill oneself; commit suicide; ⓔ cut the thread of life.

玉の輿 🅒 a nobleman's palanquin

Ⓝ 〜に乗る marry into wealth; get married to a man with money; ⓒ ⓘ marry money.

駄味噌 🅒 bad *miso*

🅚 ⓒ 〜を上げる praise oneself; flatter oneself; ⓔ sing one's own praises; ⓘ blow one's own horn (trumpet).

惰眠 🅒 indolence; idle slumber

Ⓝ ⓔ 〜を覚ます rouse *sb* from his/her slumber; stir *sb* into action. ⓔ 〜を貪る idle one's time away; live in idleness.

駄目 no good; useless; futile

Ⓝ 〜にする spoil *sth*; ruin *sth*. 〜になる be spoiled; be ruined; go wrong; go bad.

🅚 〜を押す make doubly sure; tell *sb* twice; ⓒ ⓘ rub it in. 〜を出す ❶ [theater] demand changes to the script; set conditions for a performance. ❷ point out shortcomings in *sb's* work. ❸ lay down specific conditions (in reply to a request); ⓒ lay down the rules. ⓓ ～を踏む do *sth* in vain; do *sth* that is to no avail; waste one's time.

例 a precedent; an example ▶ 例

A ～が無い ❶ be unprecedented; be unheard-of. ❷ have no experience of *sth*; have not heard of *sth*.

袂 a sleeve; a sleeve pocket

N ～に入れる put *sth* in one's (*kimono*) sleeve; pocket *sth*. ～に縋る ❶ hang on to *sb's* sleeve; cling to *sb's* sleeve. ❷ appeal to *sb*; ⓔ beseech *sb* (to grant a favor). ～に取り付く ❶ hang on to *sb's* sleeve; cling to *sb's* sleeve. ❷ appeal to *sb*; ⓔ beseech *sb* (to grant a favor). ヲ ～を絞る shed a flood of tears; ⓔ weep bitterly. ⓓ ～を連ねる do *sth* in a body; act as a group. ～を払う brush *sb* aside; rebuff *sb*; ⓒ leave *sb* in the lurch; ⓒ give *sb* the cold shoulder. ～を分かつ break off relations with *sb*; part company with *sb*.

戯け ③ (tom)foolery; foolishness

ヲ ⓢ ～を言う talk nonsense; ⓒ talk through one's hat; ⓒⓒ talk rubbish. ⓢ ～を尽す act foolish; fool around; ⓒ play the clown.

戯言 nonsense; silly talk; rubbish

ヲ ～を言う talk nonsense; ⓒ talk through one's hat; ⓒⓒ talk rubbish.

胆 the liver; spirit; guts; pluck

A ～が据る ❶ have nerves of steel; be brave; have a lot of pluck. ❷ regain one's presence of mind; ⓔ recover one's composure; ⓒ pull oneself together; ⓒ gather one's wits. ヲ ⓒ ～を奪う strike terror into *sb's* heart; ⓒ scare the living daylights out of *sb*. ⓒ ～を練る muster courage; gather one's nerves; ⓒ gird up one's loins.

短 ③ shortness; brevity; a fault

ヲ ⓒ ～を補う make up for one's defects. ⓒ ～を捨てる do away with what is bad.

痰 sputum; phlegm; spittle

ヲ (人に)～を掛ける spit on *sb*. ～を吐く cough up phlegm; spit out.

端 ③ origin; beginning

ヲ ⓒ (事に)～を発する originate in *sth*; have its origin in *sth*; arise from *sth*; stem from *sth*. ～を開く make a new start; create new opportunities.

暖 Ⓔ warmth; heat

Ⓐ ⓒ ～を取る warm oneself (at a stove); warm oneself up. ⓒ ～を貪る huddle around (the stove); hug (the fire).

啖呵 harsh words; caustic words

를 ～を切る ❶ speak harshly; speak caustic words. ❷ insult sb; abuse sb; call sb names; ⓒ fling dirt at sb.

端緒 Ⓔ the beginning; a start

と ～と成る lead to (a success); become the first step (to a success); pave the way to success.

を ～を失う lose the clue; lose the plot. ～を得る find a clue; have a key (to a mystery). ～を捜す look for a clue; search for a key (to a problem). ～を摑む find a clue; have a key to. (事に)～を発する originate in sth; have its origin in sth; arise from sth. ～を開く make a beginning; pave the way.

丹精 Ⓔ "one's true heart"

を ⓐ ～を致す do one's utmost. ～を尽くす exert oneself. ～を込める do sth with all one's heart; do sth with heart and soul; devote all one's energies to sth. ～を凝らす spare no pains; make every effort.

嘆声 Ⓔ a sigh of grief/wonder

を ⓒ ～を発する gasp with wonder; sigh with despair. ～を漏らす gasp with wonder; sigh with despair.

旦夕 Ⓔ morning and evening

N ⓒ ～に迫る ❶ be in imminent danger; be in great perril; ⓘ hang on a silk thread. ❷ face death; be on the brink of death; ⓒ be at death's door.

段取り a program; a plan

を ～を決める make arrangements; work out a plan. ～を付ける pave the way for (a project); bring sth about; push sth through.

旦那 a master; a patron

Ⓐ ～が有る ❶ have a patron; enjoy sb's protection. ❷ be married; have a husband.

を ～を取る ❶ find a patron; obtain sb's protection. ❷ become sb's mistress; become sb's concubine.

チ

血 blood

Ⓐ ～が上がる ❶ feel dizzy; be giddy. ❷ lose one's temper; fly into a rage; ⓒ ⓘ fly off the handle; ⓢ ⓘ blow a fuse. ～が起こる ❶ feel dizzy; be giddy. ❷ lose one's temper; fly into a rage; ⓒ ① fly off the handle; ⓢ ① blow a fuse. 〜が通う be made of flesh and blood; be kind-hearted; be humane. 〜が騒ぐ tingle with excitement; become worked up; get excited. 〜が繋がる be related by blood; be a blood relative. 〜が出る blood oozes out; lose blood. 〜が付く be tainted with blood. 〜が止まる stop bleeding; the bleeding stops. 〜が上る ❶ feel dizzy; be giddy. ❷ lose one's temper; fly into a rage; ⓒ ① fly off the handle; ⓢ ① blow a fuse. 〜が引く ❶ turn pale (with fright); go white (in the face). ❷ shudder with fear; shiver with horror. 〜が沸く be exiting; be stirring. N 〜に飢える thirst for blood; be bloodthirsty. 〜に狂う go mad at the sight of blood. 〜に染まる be tainted with blood. ⓘ 〜に啼く utter a sorrowful cry; sing sorrowfully. 〜に塗れる be smeared with blood. 〜に迷う lose control; behave irrationally; forget oneself; ① lose one's head. ⓐ 〜に酔う go mad (with the sight of blood); get worked up. を 〜を上げる have a rush of blood to the head; feel dizzy; feel giddy. 〜を受ける descend from; inherit one's parents' traits. 〜を通わす

liven up (an occasion). 〜を清める purify the blood. ⓐ 〜を啜る vow solemnly; make a solemn oath. 〜を出す draw blood. 〜を止める staunch blood; arrest the bleeding. 〜を流す shed blood; let blood; bleed (for one's country). 〜を吐く cough up blood. 〜を引く carry the same blood; descend from; inherit one's parents' traits. 〜を見る cause casualties; lead to bloodshed. 〜を沸かす cause the blood to tingle; ⓔ inflame the blood; be thrilling; be stirring. 〜を分ける be related by blood; be blood relatives. 〜を汚す spoil the blood.

地 the earth; soil; a place ▶ 地

N 〜に墜ちる ❶ fall to the ground; hit the gorund. ❷ be born (into this world). ❸ lose vigor; lose power; be in decline; be on the wane. 〜に墜つ ❶ fall to the ground; hit the gorund. ❷ be born (into this world). ❸ lose vigor; lose power; be in decline; be on the wane. 〜に塗れる suffer a crushing defeat; be defeated; lose a contest; ① bite the dust. を 〜を固める strengthen one's foothold; secure a foothold. ⓐ 〜を払う disappear from the face of the earth; ① vanish into thin air. 〜を掘る dig the ground.

智 intellect; intelligence

を ~を磨く improve one's mind; sharpen one's mind; polish one's intellect. ⓒ ~を巡らす devise a stratagem; work out a plan.

治安 public peace; public order

を ~を保つ maintain public order. ~を破る disturb the peace.

地位 a position; a rank; a post

A ~が上がる climb in rank; rise in social standing. ~が高い have a high rank; be of high social standing. ~が違う differ in social standing. ~が低い have a low rank; be of low social standing.

N ~に就く take a position.

を ~を争う contest a position. ~を維持する maintain a position. ~を得る acquire a position. ~を向上する improve one's position. ~を占める occupy a position; hold a post. ~を捨てる abandon one's position; give up a position. ~を高める elevate one's position; raise one's status. ~を求める seek a position; apply for a post. ~を譲る yield one's position to; make room for sb; step down for sb. ~を乱用する abuse one's position. ~を弁える be aware of one's position.

知恵 wisdom; intelligence

A ~がある be wise; be intelligent; be full of ideas. ~が尽きる be at the end of one's tether; ⓘ be at one's wits' end; ⓘ be all at sea. ~が付く grow wise; ⓒ get smart. ~が増す gain in wisdom; grow wiser. ~が回る be resourceful; be inventive.

を ~を貸す give sb advice; offer counsel to. ~を借りる ask for sb's advice. ~を絞る think hard about sth; ⓒⓘ rack one's brains. ~を出す show wisdom. ~を付ける give sb a hint; plant an idea in sb's head; incite sb to sth. ~を磨く cultivate wisdom; sharpen one's intellect; polish one's intellect.

地下 underground; in the grave

N ~に埋める bury sth in the earth. ~に潜る go into hiding; ⓘ go to earth; ⓘ go to ground. ~に眠る sleep in the grave; rest in peace. ~に潜る go underground; go into hiding.

誓い a vow; an oath; a pledge

を ~を交す exchange vows. ~を立てる make a vow. ~を守る honor one's vow; stand by one's oath; be true to one's word. ~を破る break one's word; ⓒ violate one's pledge.

ちから
力 strength; force; power

[A] ～がある be strong; have strength. ～が尽きる be spent; ⓒⓐ be wrung out; ⓢ be knackered. ～が付く ❶ gain strength; gather strength. ❷ gain in proficiency; gather knowledge; make progress (in one's studies). ～が抜ける be enervated; lose strength.
[と] ～と頼む rely on *sb*.
[N] ～に余る be beyond one's powers; lie outside one's ability. ～に及ぶ be within one's power; lie within one's ability. ～に屈する yield to (brute) force. ～にする ❶ be reinvigorated; be strengthened by. ❷ rely on *sb*; get (moral) support from *sb*. ～になる be a help; be a source of strength.
[を] ～を合わせる work together; join forces. ～を入れる ～を入れる ❶ labor hard; work hard; do one's utmost; exert oneself; give one's all. ❷ be dedicated to *sth*; show great interest in *sth*. ❸ give *sth* one's active support to *sb*/*sth*; support *sb*; back (a project). ～を失う lose strength. ～を得る gain strength from *sth*; be encouraged by *sth*. ～を落とす be weakened; lose courage; be discouraged. ～を貸す give assistance to *sb*; stand by *sb*. ～を借りる ask for *sb's* help; enlist *sb's* help. ～

を比べる measure one's strength with *sb*. ～を込める put one's back into *sth*. ⓐ ～を立つ put one's back into *sth*. ～を尽くす exert oneself; make efforts. ～を付ける ❶ encourage oneself/*sb*; cheer oneself/*sb* up; put *sb* on his/her mettle; brace oneself. ❷ gain in proficiency; gather knowledge; make progress (in one's studies). ～を取り戻す regain one's strength. ～を働かす exercize one's faculties; ⓘ flex one's muscles. ～を揮う exert force; be influential. ～を養う cultivate a faculty; ⓘ polish one's skills.

ちからこぶ
力瘤 muscles; biceps

[を] ～を入れる ❶ labor hard; work hard; do one's utmost; exert oneself; give one's all. ❷ be dedicated to *sth*; show great interest in *sth*. ❸ give *sth* one's active support to *sb*/*sth*; support *sb*; back (a project). ～を出す ❶ ⓘ flex one's muscles. ❷ display one's strenth; demonstrate one's power; ⓘ flex one's muscles. ～を作る ❶ ⓘ flex one's muscles. ❷ display one's strenth; demonstrate one's power; ⓘ flex one's muscles.

ちぎり
契り a pledge; a vow

[を] ⓐ ～を籠む make a solemn vow. ～を結ぶ ❶ make a pledge; vow to

do *sth*. ❷ make the vows of marriage; get married; ⓒ ① tie the knot.

知識 knowledge; learning

[A] ～が進む advance in knowledge. ～が増す grow in knowledge.
[を] ～を与える impart knowledge to *sb*. ～を得る obtain knowledge. ～を蓄える accumulate knowledge; gather knowledge. ～を積む accumulate knowledge; gather knowledge. ～をひけらかす show off one's knowledge; parade one's knowledge. ～を広める broaden one's knowledge. ～を深める deepen one's understanding. ～を増す increase one's knowledge. ～を磨く improve one's knowledge.

恥辱 disgrace; shame; a stigma

[を] ～を与える humiliate *sb*; put *sb* to shame; ① take *sb* down a peg. ～を受ける be humiliated; be insulted; ① be taken down a peg. ⓒ ～を来たす bring shame upon *sb*. ～を被る suffer disgrace. ～を忍ぶ suffer an insult; ① eat humble pie. ～を濯ぐ wipe away a stigma; clear one's name. ～を招く disgrace oneself; bring shame upon one's head.

馳走 a treat; a feast; hospitality

[N] (ご)～になる be treated with hospitality; recieve *sb's* hospitality; be entertained by *sb*.
[を] (ご)～を受ける be treated with hospitality; recieve *sb's* hospitality; be entertained. (ご)～を出す set a rich table; make a feast.

乳 milk; the breast; a breast

[を] ～を絞る milk (a cow). ～を飲ませる suckle a baby; breastfeed a baby. ～を飲む take the breast; suck milk. ～を離す wean a child.

帙 [N] a book case; encased books

[を] ⓞ ⓒ ～を繙く open and read a book; peruse a book; delve into a book; read a book.

地歩 a foothold; a stand

[を] ～を失う lose ground; lose one's foothold. ～を得る gain a foothold; establish a foothold. ～を固める strengthen one's foothold; secure a foothold. ～を築く establish a foothold ～を占める gain a footing; secure a niche; take one's stand. ～を保つ maintain one's foothold; keep one's footing. ～を取り戻す regain one's foothold; recover lost ground.

血道 [N] a blood vessel

[を] ⓞ ⓢ ～を上げる be mad about a

woman; be infatuated with a woman; ⓒ ① run after a woman.

茶 green tea; nonsense

<u>N</u> ～に受かされる be kept awake by too much tea. ～に受ける take *sth* as a bit of a joke; ⓒ take *sth* with a grain of salt. ～にする ❶ make fun of *sb*; slight *sb*; insult *sb*. ❷ have a short rest; ⓒ have a nap; ⓒ have a breather. ❸ use and abandon *sb*; use *sb*; ① make a cat's paw out of *sb*. ❹ make *sth* simple and sober; do *sth* in good taste. ～に為す ❶ make fun of *sb*; slight *sb*; insult *sb*. ❷ have a short rest; ⓒ have a nap; ⓒ have a breather. ❸ use and abandon *sb*; use *sb*; ① make a cat's paw out of *sb*. ❹ make *sth* simple and sober; do *sth* in good taste. ～になる ❶ be tea-time. ❷ come to nothing; end in failure; fall through; ① go up in smoke. ❸ be not worth mentioning; be too ridiculous for words. (お)～に呼ぶ invite *sb* to a tea party.

<u>を</u> Ⓐ ～を言う ❶ talk nonsense; ① talk through one's hat; ⓒ ① talk rubbish. ❷ make fun of *sb*; tease *sb*; ridicule *sb*; ① pull *sb*'s leg; ⓒ ① poke fut at *sb*. ～を入れ替える make fresh tea. ～を入れる make (a pot of) tea. ～を煎じる make tea; brew tea. ～を出す serve tea. ～を点てる ❶ make tea (the formal way); hold a tea ceremony. ⓒ ❷ hold a Buddhist mass. ～を注ぐ pour out tea. ～を摘む pick tea. (お)～を濁す ❶ do *sth* in a halfhearted way; muddle on. ❷ give an evasive reply; ① beat about the bush; ⓒ ① pussyfoot on (an issue). ～を飲む drink tea. ～を挽く grind tea. (お)～を引く have no engagement; be without engagement. ～を焙じる roast tea. ～を沸かす ❶ make tea; brew tea. ❷ be greatly tickled at *sth*; ① split one's sides with laughter.

茶々 an interruption

<u>を</u> ～を入れる ❶ interrupt *sb*; ① put in a word; ① put a word in edgeways; ① cut in; ⓢ ① butt in. ❷ talk mischief; make destructive criticism. ❸ discourage *sb*; put a damper on (*sb*'s enthusiasm); ① pour cold water on (*sb*'s enthusiasm).

茶代 E a tip; a gratuity

<u>を</u> ～を受け取る receive a tip. ～を置く leave a tip (on the plate). ～を弾む tip *sb* generously; give *sb* a big tip. ～を遣る give *sb* a tip.

茶柱 an erectly floating tea stalk

<u>A</u> ～が立つ be auspicious; be lucky; ⓒ Ⓐ hit good luck.

宙 space; the air; midair

[A] ⓐ 〜で言う ⓘ say *sth* off the top of one's head. ⓑ 〜で読む recite *sth* from memory; read *sth* by rote.
[N] ⓐ 〜に行く be unresolved; ⓘ be up in the air; ⓘ be in limbo. 〜に浮く ❶ float in midair. ❷ be unfinished; be unresolved; ⓒ be in limbo. 〜に舞う drift in midair; flutter in the air. ⓐ 〜に迷う be unfinished; be unresolved; be in limbo.
[を] 〜を掛ける ⓘ have wings on one's heels. 〜を飛ぶ ❶ fly in the air. ❷ ⓘ have wings on one's heels.

注意 attention; notice; heed

[A] 〜が行き届く be very careful; take great care.
[を] 〜を与える give *sb* advice. 〜を促す call *sb's* attention to *sth*. 〜を怠る be careless; be negligent. 〜を逸らす divert one's attention. 〜を捕える capture *sb's* attention. 〜を払う pay attention to *sth*. 〜を引く draw *sb's* attention. 〜を向ける turn one's attention to *sth*.

忠告 advice; counsel

[N] 〜に従う follow *sb's* advice. 〜に背く go against *sb's* advice.
[を] 〜を与える give *sb* (a piece of) advice. ⓒ counsel *sb*. 〜を容れる accept *sb's* advice. 〜を聞く ask *sb's* advice; listen to *sb's* advice. 〜を守る act upon *sb's* advice; heed *sb's* advice. ⓒ stick to *sb's* advice. 〜を求める seek *sb's* advice.

注文 an order; a request

[N] 〜に応じる accept an order.
[を] 〜を集める collect orders. 〜を受ける accept an order. 〜を促す invite orders. 〜を付ける make conditions; make special requests. ⓐ 〜を取り極める close an order. 〜を取り消す cancel an order. 〜を取る take orders; secure an order. 〜を流す fail to secure an order.

中庸 ⓑ the middle path

[を] ⓒ 〜を得る be moderate; be middle-of the road. ⓒ 〜を取る take an average. ⓘ take the golden mean. ⓒ 〜を外れる lose one's moderation; be unreasonable. ⓒ 〜を守る be moderate; keep within bounds; ⓘ take the golden mean.

中立 neutrality; independence

[を] 〜を侵す violate (a country's) neutrality. 〜を守る maintain neutrality.

聴覚 hearing; auditory sense

[A] 〜が鋭い have good hearing; have a sharp ear.

N ～に訴える appeal to the ear. を ～を失う lose one's hearing. ～を働かす use one's ears.

調査 ちょうさ an investigation; an inquiry

を ～を打ち切る discontinue an investigation. ～を行う conduct an investigation. ～を進める pursue an investigation; ⓒ look into *sth*. ～を始める start an investigation.

調子 ちょうし a tune; a pitch; a manner

A ～が合う be in tune. ～が良い feel good; be in good condition. ～が高い be in a high key; have a high pitch. ～が出る warm up (to work); ⓒ get into one's stride. ～が外れる be out of tune. ～が低い be in a low key; have a low pitch. ～が悪い feel unwell; be out of order; be not well tuned; be awry; ⓘ be out of sorts.

N ～に乗る ❶ get into one's stride; get on the ball; get into the swing of things. ❷ get carried away; be elated; ⓒ ⓘ let oneself loose. ❸ be haughty; be puffed up; show off; ⓘ have airs and graces; ⓒ be stuck-up.

を ～を上げる raise the pitch. ～を合わせる keep in tune (with *sb*); keep in step (with *sb*); play along with *sb*. ～を落とす slow down; be in recession. ～を変える modulate one's tone; ⓒ change one's tune. ～を崩す lose condition. ～を下げる lower the pitch. ～を示す show a trend; display a tendency. ～を揃える be in tune; be in harmony. ～を高める raise one's pitch. ～を付ける intone (a poem). ～を整える work on one's shape; tone up one's condition; fine tune (a machine). ～を取り戻す regain one's form. ～を取る ❶ beat time; mark time. ❷ maintain a steady trend; keep things in balance. ～を飲み込む learn how to do *sth*; ⓒ get the knack of *sth*. ～を外す strike a false note; be out of tune. ～を乱す put *sth* out of tune.

嘲笑 ちょうしょう ridicule; derision; scorn

を ～を招く invite ridicule. ～を浴びせる cast ridicule upon *sb*.

提灯 ちょうちん a (paper) lantern

を ～を持つ ❶ carry a lantern. ❷ flatter *sb*; ⓘ curry favor with *sb*.

長蛇 ちょうだ 日 a long queue

を ⓒ ～を逸する miss a great opportunity; fail to win a coveted prize; let an enemy escape.

徴兵 ちょうへい conscription

N ～に出る serve in the army. ～に取られる be enlisted; ⓘ join up.

ちょうわ
調和 harmony

圏 ～を欠く lack harmony. ～を損なう disturb the harmony.

ちょっかい 图 one's fingers

А ⑤ ～が回る be skilled with one's hands; be good with one's hands; ⓒ ① be a dab hand at *sth*.

圏 ⑤ ～を掛ける ❶ interfere in (*sb's* affairs); meddle with; interfere with; ⓒ ① poke one's nose into (the affairs of others). ❷ make a move; ⓒ make advances to *sb*; ⓒ ① make a pitch for a girl; ⓒ ① chat a girl up. ⑤ ～を出す ❶ interfere in (*sb's* affairs); meddle with; interfere with; ⓒ ① poke one's nose into (the affairs of others). ❷ make a move; ⓒ make advances to *sb*; ⓒ ① make a pitch for a girl; ⓒ ① chat a girl up.

ちり
塵 dust; dirt; the madding crowd

N ⓐ ～に立つ a rumor spreads. ⓐ ～に継ぐ inherit *sb's* legacy; take over *sb's* unfinished work. ⓑ ～に同ず ❶ submerge oneself in the world; go up in the crowd; keep company with the vulgar; hide one's virtues. ❷ hide one's talents; ① hide one's light under a bushel. ⓐ ～に交わる submerge oneself in the (workaday) world; go up in the madding crowd; ① keep one's head down; ① keep a low profile. ～に塗れる be defeated; lose in a contest.

圏 ⓐ ～を出つ ❶ escape from the madding crowd; get away from the hustle and bustle of the world. ❷ go into seclusion; become a hermit; ⓒ retire from the world; renounce the world. ❸ become a Buddhist priest; take the tonsure; ⓒ retire into religion. ～を切る [*sumō*] rub the salt off one's hands (by way of purification). ⓐ ～を据える mar one's good name; put a blot on one's reputation. ⓐ ～を絶つ ❶ go into seclusion; ⓒ retire from the world; renounce the world. ❷ be peerless; outstrip one's peers. ⓐ ～を逃れる escape from the madding crowd; get away from the hustle and bustle of the world. ～を払う dust *sth* off. ⓐ ～を捻る squirm (in one's seat); fidget with embarrassment. ⓐ ～を攪てる upset a settled matter; ① stir up dust; ① raise a dust. ⓐ ～を結ぶ ❶ send a small gift out of courtesy; give *sb* a small token of one's goodwill. ❷ [*sumō*] rub the salt off one's hands (by way of purification).

ちりょう
治療 medical treatment

圏 ～を受ける receive medical treatment. ～を施す subject *sb* to medical treatment.

ちんせき
枕席 国 a bed; a birth

N ⓔ ～に侍る ❶ wait on a man as his concubine; be *sb's* mistress; attend on *sb* at night. ❷ sleep with a man; go to bed with a man; share a bed with a man.

N ⓔ ～を薦む ❶ wait on a man as his concubine; be *sb's* mistress; attend on *sb* at night. ❷ sleep with a man; go to bed with a man; share a bed with a man.

ちんもく
沈黙 silence; reticence; quiet

を ～を守る remain silent; ⓒ bite one's lip; ⓒ ⓘ button one's lips. ～を破る break one's silence; break the silence; speak out.

ツ

つ
唾 spit; spittle; saliva

を ⓐ ⓒ ～を返す rebuke *sb*; talk back; ⓒ give *sb* backtalk. ～を呑む hold one's breath; catch one's breath; be intensely anxious. ⓐ ～を引く ❶ hold one's breath; catch one's breath; be intensely anxious. ❷ drool with envy; lust for *sth*.

つうげき
痛撃 国 a severe attack

を ⓒ ～を加える deal a crushing blow to *sb*; crack down on *sb*; hit *sb* hard.

つうげん
痛言 国 scathing remarks

を ⓒ ～を加える scold *sb*; ⓘ tell *sb* off; ⓘ give *sb* a dressing-down; ⓘ haul *sb* over the coals.

つうぼう
痛棒 国 [Zen] a disciplining stick

を ⓒ ～を加える ❶ deal a crushing blow to *sb*; strike a blow at *sb*; crack down on *sb*. ❷ scold *sb*; ⓘ tell *sb* off; ⓘ give *sb* a dressing-down; ⓘ haul *sb* over the coals. ～を食わす ❶ deal a crushing blow to *sb*; crack down on *sb*. ❷ scold *sb*; ⓘ tell *sb* off; ⓘ give *sb* a dressing-down; ⓘ haul *sb* over the coals.

つうよう
痛痒 国 pain and itching

を ⓔ ～を感じない be indifferent to *sth*; be unaffected by *sth*; do not care about *sth*.

つえ
杖 a (walking) stick

N ～に突く use a walking stick; rely on a walking stick.

を ～を突く lean on a stick; use a walking stick. ～を留める interrupt one's journey; stay at an inn; pass a night on one's journey. ～を曳く ❶ go for a walk; have a stroll; take a walk. ❷ visit a place; pay *sb* a visit.

つか
柄 a hilt, a haft; a handle

を ⓐ ～を取る be at home in (a subject); get used to *sth*; ⓒ be well versed in (a subject). ⓐ 〜を握る be at home in (a subject); get used to *sth*; ⓒ be well versed in (a subject).

使い出 ⑤ durability
[A] ⓐ 〜が有る last a long while; be durable; wear well; ⓒ ⓓ go far.

支え an obstruction
[A] (胸の)〜が降りる ❶ give a sigh of relief; be able to breathe again. ❷ feel relieved; be reassured; feel relaxed; be put at ease. ⓓ feel a weight taken off one's chest.

疲れ fatigue; exhaustion
[A] 〜が出る begin to suffer from fatigue; look run down. 〜が取れる recover from one's fatigue; feel refreshed. 〜が抜ける recover from one's fatigue; feel refreshed.
[을] 〜を癒す relieve one's fatigue; freshen up. 〜を覚える feel tired; be done in; ⓢ be knackered. 〜を取る relieve one's fatigue; freshen up. 〜を抜く relieve one's fatigue; freshen up. 〜を休める rest oneself; take a rest.

月 the moon; a month; a moon
[A] 〜が欠ける the moon wanes. 〜が重なる the months pass; take sevral months. 〜が満ちる ❶ the moon waxes. ❷ reach the last month of pregnancy; expect a baby within a month; the baby is due.
[N] 〜に磨く reveal its true beauty in the moonlight; be thrown into full relief by the moonlight.
[을] 〜を跨ぐ last for more than a month; take untill the next month.

付き an impression; appearance
[A] 〜が良い ❶ look well on *sb*; fit *sb* well; suit *sb*; sit well on *sb*; give *sb*/*sth* a good appearance. ❷ leave a good impression; have a favourable impression; be sociable. ❸ light up easily; be quick to kindle. ❹ print well; take well to paper. 〜が悪い ❶ look bad on *sb*; fit *sb* badly; sit poorly on *sb*; give *sb*/*sth* a bad appearance. ❷ leave a bad impression; have a bad impression; be unsociable. ❸ light up with difficulty; be slow to kindle. ❹ print with difficulty.

付け a bill; a charge; a check
[A] 〜で売る sell *sth* on credit; charge *sth* to *sb*'s account; ⓒ extend credit to *sb*. 〜で買う buy *sth* on credit; have *sth* charged to one's account; ⓓ buy sht on the cuf.
[A] 〜が利く have credit (with *sb*);

have a charge account (at a store). ~が溜まる the bills pile up; run into debts; ⓘ be in the red.

[N] ~にする ❶ make a fool of *sb*; ridicule *sb*; make fun of *sb*. ❷ use *sb*; involve *sb* in (one's excuses); ⓒ make a cat's paw of *sb*; ⓘ make a scapegoat of *sb*.

辻占 a paper slip with an omen

[を] ~が良い be auspicious; be of good omen; augur well. ~が悪い be inauspicious; be of bad omen; augur ill.

辻褄 coherence; logic

[A] ~が合う be coherent; be logical; be plausible; make sense; ⓒⓘ hang together; ⓒⓘ add up.

土 earth; soil; mud; the ground

[A] ~が付く [*sumō*] be defeated; lose a fight; ⓘ bite the dust. ~が離れぬ ❶ be countrified; be a country bumpkin. ❷ be unsophisticated; be unrefined; be a boor.
[と] ~と成る be buried; ⓔ be laid to rest.
[N] ~に埋める bury in the ground. ~に帰る pass away; return to dust. ~に親しむ live close to the soil; feel kinship with the earth. ⓐ ~に成る be buried; ⓔ be laid to rest.

[を] ~を懸ける heap up earth; cover *sth* with earth. ~を嘗める ❶ suffer extreme poverty; be destitute; ⓘ be in dire straits; ⓒⓘ hit on hard times. ❷ eke out a living; ⓒ get by; ⓘ make ends meet; ⓒⓘ keep the pot boiling. ~を掘る dig in the ground. ~を踏む set foot on (foreign) soil.

綱 a rope; a cord; a string

[を] ~を打つ make rope. ~を繰り出す pay out a rope; let out a rope. ~を手繰る haul in a rope. ~を張る ❶ stretch a rope; rope off (an area). ❷ [*sumō*] become a grand champion. ~を放す let go the rope. ~を引く pull a rope; haul in a rope.

角 a horn, an antler ▶ 角

[A] ~が生う ❶ sprout horns. ❷ get mad; lose one's temper; be vexed by *sth*; ⓢⓘ blow a fuse. ❸ exhibit jealousy; become jealous; be envious. ~が折れる ❶ lose its horns. ❷ become obedient; become tractable. ❸ be nonplussed; be embarrassed; ⓒ be stumped. ~が生える ❶ sprout horns. ❷ get mad; lose one's temper; be vexed by *sth*; ⓢⓘ blow a fuse. ❸ exhibit jealousy; become jealous; be envious.
[A] ~で突く gore *sth* with its horns; horn *sth*.

ツボ　　　　　　　　　　　　　　　　　　　　　　　　　　ツムジ

[を] 〜を落とす dehorn (an animal). 〜を折る give in to *sb's* demand; drop one's stubborn attitude. 〜を出す display jealous anger; Ⓢ ① get one's back up. (人と)〜を突き合わせる be at odds with *sb*; ① be at daggers drawn with *sb*; ① be at loggerheads with *sb*. 〜を付ける attach horns to *sth*. 〜を生やす be jealous of *sb*; envy *sb*; Ⓔ have a fit of jealousy; ① wear horns. Ⓒ 〜を引っ込ます draw in its feelers. 〜を振り上げる lift up its horns.

鍔 a handguard; the guard

[を] Ⓒ 〜を割る fight desperately; have fierce competition.

粒 a grain; a drop

[A] 〜が揃う ❶ be the same size; have the same size. ❷ meet the same standards; have the same quality; be of even quality. ❸ be of even ability; be well matched.

潰し crushing; smashing

[A] 〜が効く ❶ be good for some other work; be widely skilled; Ⓔ have marketable skills. Ⓒ ❷ sell *sth* for the price of the material; have scrap value.

[N] 〜にする demolish *sth*; melt *sth* down; pulp (books).

壺 a pot; a jar; a vessel

[N] 〜に嵌まる ❶ go according to plan; prove a success; work out well. ❷ grasp the crux (of a matter); get it right; ① be on the mark; Ⓒ ① get the point.

[を] 〜を押える grasp the crux (of a matter); get it right; ① be on the mark; Ⓒ ① get the point; understand *sb/sth*; Ⓒ know what is what. 〜を被く ❶ be unsuccessful; Ⓒ make a mess of things; Ⓒ bungle *sth*; Ⓒ be a loser. ❷ suffer a loss; sustain financial losses; suffer damage; ① lose out. 〜を被る ❶ be unsuccessful; Ⓒ make a mess of things; Ⓒ bungle *sth*; Ⓒ be a loser. ❷ suffer a loss; sustain financial losses; suffer damage; ① lose out. 〜を外す be irrelevant; ① be off the mark; ① be beside the point.

褄 Ⓘ the hem of a *kimono*'s

[を] Ⓐ Ⓔ 〜を重ねる make love; have sexual intercourse; have sex. 〜を取る ❶ hold up a *kimono* by the (left) hem. Ⓒ ❷ become a *geisha*.

罪 a crime; an offense; a sin

[A] 〜が無い be harmless; be innocent; be innocuous. 〜が深い be sinful; be full of sin.

[N] 〜に陥れる incriminate *sb* in a

crime. 〜に問う accuse sb of a crime; bring a charge against sb; charge sb with an offense. 〜に服する admit an offense; submit to a sentence; plead guilty.
⑧ 〜を贖う atone for one's sins; do penance. 〜を暴く disclose a crime; ⓔ bring a misdemeanor to light. 〜を負う take (the guilt for) an offense; hold oneself accountable for an offense. 〜を犯す commit a crime; commit a sin; ⓔ perpetrate a misdemeanor. 〜を行なう do wrong. 〜を隠す hide an offense; ⓔ cloak a sin. 〜を重ねる commit one crime after another. 〜を庇う cover up a sin. 〜を着せる put the guilt on sb; pin the blame on sb; ⓘ lay the blame at sb's door. 〜を着る take the blame for an offense; ⓔ ⓘ take the fall. 〜を定める sentence sb for an offense. 〜を正す inquire into an offense. 〜を作る act criminally; do sth outrageous. 〜を鳴らす accuse sb of an offense. 〜を免れる evade punishment. 〜を認める plead guilty to an offense. 〜を許す condone an offense.

旋毛 a whorl of hair
⑧ 〜を曲げる become mean; be cantankerous; ⓒ get cross (at sth).

爪 a nail; a claw; a talon
Ⓐ 〜が長い ❶ have long fingernails. ❷ be envious; be greedy; covet sth; ⓘ bite off more than one can chew. 〜が伸びる ❶ one's fingernails grow long. ❷ covet sth; look enviously at sb/sth; watch sb with envy; crave for sth.
⑧ 〜を隠す ❶ draw in one's claws. ❷ hide one's talents. 〜を切る cut one's nails; trim one's nails. ⓢ 〜を食う ❶ bite one's finger nails. ❷ feel uneasy; be nervous; be uncertain; be anxious; be ill at ease. 〜を銜える ❶ bite on one's nails. ❷ covet sth; look enviously at sb/sth; watch sb with envy. ❸ remain an onlooker; stand by idly; ⓘ sit on the fence. 〜を染める paint one's nails. 〜を研ぐ ❶ sharpen its claws. ❷ prepare oneself for a fight; resolve to do sth; ⓘ gird up one's loins. 〜を延ばす ❶ let one's nails grow long. ❷ lust after sth. Ⓐ 〜を弾く ❶ snap one's nails. ❷ show one's disapproval; vent one's frustration. ❸ reject sb/sth; shun sb; ⓘ give sb the cold shoulder; ⓘ turn one's back on sb/sth. ⓡ 〜を放す [prostitution] favor a customer.

艶 gloss; luster; glaze
Ⓐ 〜が消える lose its luster. 〜が出る a gloss appears.

ツラ　　　　　　　　　　　　　　　　　　　　テ

㊁ ～を消す take off the gloss; subdue the luster. ～を出す make *sth* glossy; give luster to *sth*; polish *sth* up. (話に)～を付ける give color to a story; make a story colorful. ～を取る take away the luster.

露 dew; dewdrops; tears

Ⓐ ～が降りる dew falls.
㋤ ～と消える end one's days; fade away; sink into oblivion.
Ⓝ ～に濡れる be moist with dew. ⓒ ～に結ぶ be frosted with dew. (目に)～を宿す be reduced to tears; ⓔ melt into tears.
㊁ ⓐ ～を打つ tip *sb*; give a tip; give a gratuity. ～を帯びる be covered with dew. ～を払う brush off the dew.

面 ㋛ a face; the surface ▶ 面 ▶ 麺

Ⓐ ⓢ ～が良い be cheeky; be impudent. ⓢ ～が大きい be proud; be haughty; be arrogant. ⓢ ～が憎い hate the sight of *sb*; detest *sb*.
㊁ ⓢ ～を売る make oneself known; gain influence. ⓐⓢ ～を食わす hit *sb* in the face; strike *sb* in the face. ⓢ ～を下げる act with good grace; be unashamed; be unabashed. ⓢ ～を顰める make a grimace; scowl. ⓢ ～を出す make an appearance; show one's face; visit *sb*; call on *sb*. ⓐⓢ

～を拭う pocket one's pride; swallow one's pride. ⓐⓢ ～を張る ❶ hit *sb* in the face; give *sb* a slap in the face. ❷ make grimaces; scowl; make a wry face; ⓒ wrinkle one's face. ❸ become famous; become widely known; be popular. ⓢ ～を膨らす show one's displeasure. ⓢ ～を踏む injure *sb*'s dignity; cause *sb* to lose face; ⓔ blight *sb*'s honor. ⓐⓢ ～を見返す ❶ look back at *sb*; glare back at *sb*. ❷ put a former enemy to shame; ⓘ get one's own back.

手 the hand; the arm

Ⓐ ～が上がる ❶ show greater skill; get better at *sth*; improve one's hand(writing). ❷ (be able to) drink more. ❸ be at a loss (about what to do); ⓘ be at one's wits' end; ⓘ be all at sea. ～が空く have time (for *sb*); be free; be vacant; ⓘ have time on one's hands. ～が有る ❶ have means at one's disposal; have options open to one. ❷ have assistance; be in no short supply of hands. ❸ be skilled with one's hands; ⓔ be dexterous. ～が要る require assistance; need help; ⓘ need a hand. ～が掛かる require a great deal of trouble; be troublesome; ⓒ be a handful. ～が利

く be skilled; be good with one's hands; ⓒ ① be a dab hand at *sth*. 〜が切れる break off (relations) with *sb*; fall out with *sb*. 〜が込む be elaborate; be intricate. 〜が冴える be skilled; be good with one's hands; ⓒ ① be a dab hand at *sth*. 〜が下がる lose one's skill; get out of practice. 〜が空く have time (for *sth*); be free; be vacant; ① have time on one's hands. 〜が足りない be short of hands. 〜が尽きる be at a loss (about what to do); ① be at one's wits' end; ① play one's last card; ① be all at sea. 〜が付かない be unable to settle down; be restless. 〜が付く ❶ set about (doing *sth*); start out on *sth*. ❷ become intimate with (a servant); enter into a sexual relation with (a maid). 〜が付けられない ❶ be out of control; be unmanageable. ❷ be incorrigible; be beyond help. 〜が詰まる be busy; be occupied; ① have one's hands full. 〜が出ない ❶ be beyond one's means; be too expensive. ❷ be too difficult for one; lie outside one's ability. 〜が届く ❶ be thorough; offer good service; ① go the whole hog. ❷ lie within one's ability; be within one's sphere of influence. ❸ be within reach of (a goal); get close to (an objective); be getting on for (a certain age). 〜が無い ❶ have a shortage of man power; ① be short of hands; ① be short-handed. ❷ have no recourse; have no (other) options; be without means. ❸ be comonplace; be mediocre; ① have no saving graces; ① be run of the mill. ❹ be boorish; be curt; be brusque; be rude. 〜が長い be a kleptomaniac; be light-fingered; ⓔ be given to pilfering. 〜が鳴る hear the clapping of hands. 〜が入る ❶ correct *sth*; process *sth*; refine *sth*; ❷ take charge; take control; ① take *sth* in hand; ⓐ step in. 〜が離せない be extremely busy with *sth*; require constant attention. 〜が離れる ❶ become independent; be no longer connected with; ① cut the cord. ❷ require no (further) work; ① be on the rails. 〜が省ける save one trouble. 〜が早い ❶ be quick; be nimble. ❷ be a lady's man; ⓢ be a quick mover. ❸ be quick to fight; be quick-tempered. 〜が塞がる ① have one's hands full; be fully occupied. 〜が回る ❶ attend to everything; leave nothing undone; be attentive to *sb*. ❷ be on *sb's* track. 〜が見える be exposed; see through *sb*; ① see in *sb's* cards. 〜が焼ける be troublesome; be a bother. 〜が良い ❶ write in a good hand. ❷ be good at *sth*;

テ　　　　　　　　　　　　　　　テ

have nimble hands; ① be a dab hand at *sth*. ～が笑う lose control over one's hands; have shaky hands. ～が悪い ❶ write in a bad hand. ❷ be a poor hand at *sth*; ① have two left hands.
N ～に余る be beyond one's control; lie outside one's powers; be too much for *sb* (to handle). ～に合わない ❶ lie uneasily in one's hands; be a dad tool; be unwieldy. ❷ be beyond one's control; lie outside one's powers; be too much for one/*sb* (to handle). ～に入る ❶ do *sth* with complete control; be skilled at *sth*; be proficient at *sth*; ① be at home in *sth*; ① be a dab hand at *sth*. ❷ gain possession of *sth*; ① fall into one's hands. ～に入れる ❶ get hold of *sth*; get one's hands on *sth*; come by. ❷ be in one's hands; be under one's control; ③ ① call the shots. ～に負えない be beyond one's control; lie outside one's powers; be too much for one/*sb* (to handle). ～に落ちる come under *sb's* control; ① fall into *sb's* hands. ～に掛かる ❶ be looked after; be taken care of; be dealt with. ❷ ① fall into *sb's* hands; ① die by *sb's* hand; ① bite the dust. ～に掛ける ❶ take care of *sth*/*sb*; look after *sb*. ❷ kill *sb* with one's own hands. ～に帰す come under

one's/*sb's* control; ① fall into one's/*sb's* hands. ～にする take *sth* into one's hands; come into the possession of *sth*; make *sth* one's own. ◎ ～に立つ be worthy of *sb's* attention; have effect on *sb*. ～に足る be worthy of *sb's* attention; have effect on *sb*. ～に付かない be unable to settle down; be restless. ～に唾する ❶ ① spit in one's hands. ❷ get ready; ① roll up one's sleeves. ～に取る take *sth* into one's hands. (人の)～に成る be by *sb's* hand; be the work of *sb*. ～に握る be in one's hands; be under one's control; ③ ① call the shots. ～に乗る ❶ fall into a trap; be taken in; ① play into (the enemy's) hands. ❷ be at *one's*/*sb's* beck and call; be at *one's*/*sb's* disposal; be at *one's*/*sb's* mercy; be at *one's*/*sb's* will. ～に入る gain possession of *sth*; ① fall into one's hands. ～に渡す hand *sth* to *sb*; place *sth* in *sb's* hands. ～に渡る pass into *sb's* possession; fall into *sb's* hands.
を ～を頒つ devide work (among laborers); mete out work; split up (for a search). ～を空ける make time for *sb*; make oneself available; ① free one's hands. ～を上げる ❶ raise one's hands; throw up one's hands. ❷ improve one's skill; get better at *sth*; improve one's

hand(writing). ❸ (be able to) drink more. ❹ throw one's fists around; attack *sb*; be violent; ⓒ throw a punch. ❺ give up; give in; yield to; ⓘ throw in the towel. 〜を洗う wash one's hands. 〜を合わす ❶ fold one's hands (in prayer). ❷ have a game with *sb*; have a bout with *sb*. 〜を入れる ❶ put one's hand into *sth*; reach into *sth*. ❷ touch *sth* up; smarten (a place) up. ❸ meddle with *sth*; ⓘ cook the books. ❹ sound *sb* out; ⓘ send up a trial balloon. ❺ devise a means to *sth*; find a means to *sth*. ❻ make a raid on; conduct a raid (into). 〜を失う be deprived of a means. 〜を打つ ❶ clap one's hands. ❷ adopt a measure; take action; make a move. ❸ come to an understanding; strike a bargain; close a deal; ⓘ shake hands on *sth*. ❹ [*shōgi*] make a smart move. 〜を負う be wounded; be hurt. ⓐ 〜を置く ❶ be at a loss (about what to do); ⓘ be at one's wits' end; ⓘ be all at sea. ❷ be reserved; hold back. ❸ stand back; acknowledge *sb's* superiority; yield to *sb*. (人の)〜を押える seize *sb* by the hand. ⓐ 〜を歛む ❶ restrain one's hands. ❷ salute *sb*; give a salute. 〜を下ろす ❶ take the initiative; ⓘ swing into action. ❷ unfurl a flag. 〜を返す ❶ be easy (to do); be simple. ❷ be volatile; be changeable; be fickle. 〜を変える change one's approach; resort to other means. ⓐ 〜を搔く signal with one's hands. ⓓ 〜を書く have a taste for calligraphy; be fond of writing. 〜を掛ける ❶ take charge; get a hold on *sth*; ⓘ take *sth* in hand; ⓐ step in. ❷ lay one's hands on *sth*; take *sth*; ⓒ pinch *sth*; ⓢ nick *sth*. ❸ put *sb* to trouble over *sth*; trouble *sb* with *sth*; cause trouble. ❹ attack *sb*; ⓔ assail *sb*. 〜を翳す shield one's eyes with one's hand. 〜を貸す assist *sb*; give *sb* help; help *sb*; ⓘ lend *sb* a helping hand. 〜を借りる receive help; ask for help; call in *sb's* aid. 〜を切る ❶ cut one's hand. ❷ (人と) break off (relations) with *sb*; ⓘ drop *sb*. ⓢ 〜を食う be deceived; ⓘ be taken in; ⓒⓘ be led by the nose. ⓐ 〜を砕く exert oneself; ⓔ give *sth* one's all. 〜を下す ❶ do *sth* in person. ❷ set out to do *sth*; undertake *sth*. 〜を配る make arrangements; take (the necessary) steps. 〜を組む ❶ fold one's arms; link arms with *sb*. ❷ cooperate with each other; work together; join forces; ⓘ join hands. 〜を加える ❶ correct *sth*; process *sth*; refine *sth*. ❷ falsify *sth*; tamper with *sth*.

テ

~を拱ねく ❶ fold one's hands in prayer. ❷ fold one's arms. ❸ stand by idly; remain an onlooker; ⓘ sit on the fence. ~を込める give full play to one's skill; exercise one's utmost skill. ⓐ ~を下げる ❶ beg sb's pardon; express one's regret. ❷ humble oneself (towards sb); ⓘ play up to sb; ⓘ fawn on sb. ~を差し出す hold out one's hands; offer one's hand. ~を縛られる have one's hands tied. ~を知らせる declare one's hand; show where one stands. ~を締める ❶ squeeze sb's hand; give sb's hand a squeeze. ❷ close a deal; strike a bargain. ❸ tighten (the rules); draw in the reins; ⓘ keep a tight rein. ~を擦る rub one's hands; wring one's hands. ~を添える ⓘ lend sb a helping hand. ~を染める ❶ set out to do sth; make a start; ⓐ get one's hands dirty. ❷ be involved in; ⓘ have a hand in (a plot); ⓢⓘ be in cahoots. ~を揃える gather to do sth; work together. ~を出し過ぎる do more than one can handle; ⓘ have too many irons in the fire; ⓘ bite off more than one can chew. ~を出す ❶ throw one's fists around; attack sb; be violent; ⓒ throw a punch. ❷ meddle with sth; dabble in (stocks); get involved in sth; ⓔ turn one's hand to sth. ❸ take sth; ⓒ pinch sth; ⓢ nick sth. ❹ make advances to sb; make a move; get involved with a woman. ~を携える take sb's hand; hold sb's hand. ~を叩く ❶ clap one's hands. ❷ strike a deal. ~を使う ❶ use one's hands. ❷ resort to (every possible) means. ~を束ねる ❶ fold one's arms. ❷ stand by idly; remain an onlooker; ⓘ sit on the fence. ~を突く put both hands on the floor (when greeting). ~を尽くす do one's utmost; do all one can; ⓘ leave no stone unturned. ⓐ ~を造る put one's hands together (in worship). ~を付ける ❶ lay one's hand on sth; touch sth. ❷ set out to do sth; take sth on; ⓘ take sth in hand. ❸ become intimate with (a maid); enter into a sexual relation with sb (below one's standing). ❹ embezzle money; pocket (other people's) money. ~を繋ぐ fold one's hands; join hands. ~を通す put on a garment (for the first time). ~を取る ❶ take sb by the hand; grab sb's hand. ❷ introduce sb into an art; teach sb kindly. ❸ be flurried; be baffled; be at a loss (about what to do); ⓘ be at one's wits' end; ⓘ be all at sea. ❹ be deceived; ⓘ be taken in; ⓒⓘ be led by the nose. ❺ [sumō] use a technique; resort to a trick. ~

を鳴らす clap one's hands (to call sb). 〜を握りしめる clench one's hands. 〜を握る ❶ clench one's fists; wring one's hands. ❷ shake *sb's* hand; grasp *sb's* hand. ❸ form an alliance; cooperate with *sb* on *sth*. ❹ make peace with *sb*; ⓒ be reconciled; ⓒ make up (with *sb*). ❺ be nervous; be on edge; ⓒ be kept on tenterhooks. 〜を抜く skimp one's work; ⓒ cut corners; ⓢ ⓒ skate on the job. 〜を濡らさず ❶ do *sth* without effort; win a contest hands down. ❷ make no effort; do *sth* without toil. 〜を濡らす make an effort; exert oneself; do one's best. ⓒ 〜を舐む ❶ ⓒ spit in one's hands. ❷ get ready; ⓒ roll up one's sleeves. 〜を延ばす ❶ stretch one's arms; reach out for *sth*. ❷ try one's hand at (*sth* new); venture into (a new area); ⓒ turn one's hand to *sth*. 〜を放す let off *sth*; loose one's hold on *sth*. 〜を離れる ❶ be out of one's hands; be off one's hands. ❷ become independent; stand on one's own feet; ⓒ cut the cord. 〜を省く skimp one's work; ⓒ cut corners; ⓢ ⓒ skate on the job. 〜を引く ❶ lead *sb* by the hand. ❷ draw one's hands away. ❸ withdraw oneself from *sth*; retreat from a controversy; ⓒ wash one's hands of *sth*; opt out ⓒ back

out/down. 〜を広げる ❶ spread one's arms. ❷ be finished; be done for. ❸ extend one's activities; expand a business. ❹ go on a spending spree; ⓒ live it up. 〜を拭く dry one's hands. 〜を振る wave one's hand. 〜を触れる touch *sth*. (人の) 〜を経る pass through *sb's* hands. 〜を真似る imitate *sb's* hand(writing). 〜を回す ❶ make full arrangements; take measures; work out a plan. ❷ resort to spying; employ an agent; ⓒ send out tracers. 〜を結ぶ join forces with *sb*; cooperate with *sb*; form an alliance with *sb*. 〜を揉む ❶ rub one's hands together; wring one's hands. ❷ fret over *sth*. 〜を焼く ❶ burn one's hands. ❷ be at a loss (about what to do); ⓒ be put out by *sb*; ⓒ have one's hands full (with a child). ❸ have a bitter experience; be unsuccessful (in dealing with *sth*); ⓒ burn one's fingers. 〜を休める have a rest; take a break; stop doing *sth*. 〜を許す forgive *sb*; deal leniently with *sb*; ⓒ be magnanimous. 〜を緩める loose one's grip on *sth*; relax one's hold; make allowances; slacken in vigilance. 〜を汚す ❶ dirty one's hands. ❷ set out to do *sth*; make a start; ⓒ get one's hands dirty; ⓢ get cracking. 〜を分つ ❶ divide work; mete out work.

❷ break off relations; ⓒ sever one's connections with *sb*. ❸ divorce *sb*; get divorced; get separated; ⓔ secure a divorce; ⓒ split up. 〜を別（わ）ける break off relations; ⓒ sever one's connections with *sb*. 〜を煩（わずら）わす trouble *sb* with *sth*; bother *sb*; rely on *sb*'s help; be a burden to *sb*.

手足（てあし） arms and legs
图 〜を伸（の）ばす stretch one's arms and legs; relax; unwind.

泥（でい） 回 mud; mire; paint ▶ 泥（どろ）
图 ⓒⓔ 〜を切（き）る have no recourse; have no (other) options; be without means; ⓘ clutch at thin air.

体裁（ていさい） appearance; style
A 〜が良（い）い look nice; have a pleasant appearance; make a good figure. 〜が悪（わる）い look bad; be unsightly; ⓘ cut a sorry figure.
图 〜を言（い）う ma〜を飾（かざ）る make outward show; save appearances; ⓘ keep up appearances. 〜を取（と）り繕（つくろ）う make outward show; save appearances; ⓘ keep up appearances.

貞女（ていじょ） 回 a constant woman
图 〜を立（た）てる be a constand wife; be faithful to one's husband.

貞操（ていそう） chastity; constance; virtue
图 〜を売（う）る sell one's chastity; prostitute oneself. 〜を捧（ささ）げる surrender one's chastity. 〜を守（まも）る remain faithful; ⓔ defend one's virtue; be chaste. 〜を弄（もてあそ）ぶ trifle with (a girl's) chastity. 〜を破（やぶ）る lose one's chastity. 〜を汚（よご）す defile (a girl's) chastity; deflower a girl.

手掛（てが）かり a handhold; a clue
A 〜が有（あ）る have a clue. 〜が無（な）い have no clue.
图 〜と成（な）る give one a clue; ⓘ put *sb* on the scent.
图 〜を失（うしな）う lose the clue; ⓘ lose the scent. 〜を得（え）る find a clue; find traces (of a criminal); ⓘ get on the scent of *sb*. 〜を辿（たど）る follow the lead. 〜を掴（つか）む find a clue; find traces (of a criminal); ⓘ get on the scent of *sb*. 〜を作（つく）る establish relations with *sb*; set up (business) contacts.

手柄（てがら） a feat; an acomplishment
图 〜を揚（あ）げる perform a feat; accomplish *sth*; ⓘ win one's spurs. 〜を立（た）てる perform a feat; accomplish *sth*; ⓘ win one's spurs.

敵（てき） an enemy; a foe; a rival
N 〜に襲（おそ）われる be attacked by the

enemy. ～に勝つ conquer the enemy. ～に付く go over to the enemy; desert to the enemy. ～に投じる go over to the enemy; desert to the enemy. ～に成る become enemies; turn against each other. ～に臨む face the enemy; confront the enemy. ～に回す antagonize sb; make an enemy of sb.

と ～とする antagonize sb; make an enemy of sb; have sb for an enemy. ～と戦う fight with the enemy. ～と渡り合う engage an enemy; close with the enemy.

を ～を愛する love the enemy. ～を受ける be under attack from the enemy; be attacked by the enemy. ～を押える check the enemy; keep the enemy in check; pin down the enemy. ～を襲う make a raid on the enemy; attack the enemy. ～を作る make enemies; antagonize people.

手際 dexterity; workmanship

A ～が良い ❶ be skilled with one's hands; be good with one's hands; ⓒ ① be a dab hand at sth. ❷ be well done; be of superior workmanship. ～が悪い ❶ be a poor hand at sth; ① have two left hands. ❷ be badly done; be of inferior workmanship.

を ～を見せる ❶ display one's skill; demonstrate one's dexterity; show one's talent. ❷ display one's skill (in handling an affair); show tact (in dealing with people).

て

手ぐすね pine resin glue

を ～を引く watch eagerly for a chance; be on the lookout for an opportunity.

手癖 "the habit of one's hands"

A ～が悪い be a cleptomaniac; ① have light fingers; ① be light-fingered; ⓒ ① have sticky fingers.

手管 wiles; female charm

を (女の)～に掛かる be taken in by a woman; be led astray by a woman; fall into a woman's trap. (女の)～に乗る be taken in by a woman; be led astray; play into a woman's hands.
を ～を尽す use all one's female charm; exhaust one's wiles. ～を弄する use one's wiles; play the coquette; use one's female charm.

手口 a trick; a way of doing sth

を ～を真似る imitate sb; mimic sb; copycat sb.

梃子 a lever; a handspike

を ～を入れる ❶ boost the market; bolster prices. ❷ back sb up; support sb; prop sb up; shore sth up.

テダテ　　テマ

手心(てごころ) ◨ consideration; allowance
◪ ⓔ ～を加(くわ)える make allowances (for *sb*); use one's discretion; ⓒ go easy on *sb*; ⓢ ⓘ pull one's punches.

手先(てさき) the fingers; a tool; a pawn
Ⓐ ～が痺(しび)れる get numb fingers.
Ⓐ ～で稼(かせ)ぐ live by one's finger's end.
Ⓝ ～に使(つか)う involve *sb* in (one's excuses); use *sb* as a tool; ⓘ make a cat's paw of *sb*. ～に成(な)る be an agent in *sth*; act as an instrument.

手塩(てしお) ◨ table salt
Ⓝ ～に掛(か)ける raise (a child) with tender loving care.

手数(てすう) trouble; pains; concern
Ⓐ ～が掛(か)かる require a great deal of trouble; be troublesome; ⓒ be a handful. ～が省(はぶ)ける be spared the trouble; save one/*sb* the trouble.
◪ ～を掛(か)ける put *sb* to (a lot of) trouble over *sth*; trouble *sb* with *sth*; cause trouble. ～を省(はぶ)く save one/*sb* trouble; spare one/*sb* the trouble.

手立(てだ)て a device; a trick
Ⓐ ～が無(な)い have no recourse; have no (other) options; be without means; ⓒ run out of tricks.
◪ ～に乗(の)る become the victim of a plot; play into *sb's* hands; become; be entrapped; ⓐ fall into a trap; ⓘ step into a snare; ⓘ be taken in; ⓒ be duped; ⓒ be conned.

手玉(てだま) a hand ball; a small ball
Ⓝ ～に取(と)る trifle with a person; ⓘ take *sb* in; ⓒ ⓘ lead *sb* by the nose; ⓒ ⓘ twist *sb* round one's little finger.

轍(てつ) ◨ a wheel track; a rut
◪ ⓔ ～を踏(ふ)む repeat *sb's* mistake; share *sb's* fate; ⓔ follow in the wake of *sth*; ⓘ fall into the same rut.

鉄(てつ) iron; steel
◪ ～を被(かぶ)せる iron (a garment).

手付(てつ)け a deposit; a guarantee
◪ ～を置(お)く leave a deposit. ～を打(う)つ make a deposit.

鉄槌(てっつい) ◨ an iron hammer
◪ ⓔ ～を下(くだ)す deal a crushing blow (to *sb/sth*); crack down on *sb/sth*.
ⓔ ～を加(くわ)える deal a crushing blow (to *sb/sth*); crack down on *sb/sth*.

鉄砲(てっぽう) a gun; a rifle; a firearm
◪ ～を撃(う)つ ❶ fire a gun. ❷ tell a lie. ⓒ ⓘ talk through one's hat. ❸ exaggerate; ⓔ indulge in hyperbole;

① stretch the facts; ⑤ ① pile it on; ⑤ ① lay it on thick. ～を放つ ❶ fire a gun. ❷ tell a lie; ⓒ ① talk through one's hat. ❸ exaggerate; ⓔ indulge in hyperbole; ① stretch the facts; ⑤ ① pile it on; ⑤ ① lay it on thick. ～を向ける level a gun at *sb*/sth; aim a gun at *sb*.

掌 the palm of the hand ▶ 掌

[N] ～に隠す palm (a card/coin).
[を] ～を返す be inconstant; be changeable; be fickle.

手筈 a plan; a schedule

[を] ～を決める make a plan; draw up a plan; fix a schedule. ～を狂わせる thwart a plan; cause a plan to miscarry; upset a schedule. ～を整える get a plan ready; prepare a schedule; make arrangements.

出端 ⑬ the outset; the start

[を] ⓔ (人の)～を折る snub *sb*; spoil *sb's* headstart; dampen *sb's* initial enthusiasm. ⓔ (人の)～を挫く snub *sb*; spoil *sb's* headstart; dampen *sb's* initial enthusiasm.

手間 time; trouble; labor

[A] ～が掛かる ❶ take (much) time; be time-consuming. ❷ cost labor; take (much) trouble; be labor-intensive.
[を] ～を取る ❶ take (much) time; be time-consuming. ❷ cost labor; take (much) trouble; be labor-intensive.

手前味噌 ⑬ self-made *miso*

[を] ⓒ ～を上げる praise oneself; flatter oneself; ⓔ sing one's own praises; ① blow one's own horn (trumpet). ⓒ ～を並べる praise oneself; flatter oneself; ⓔ sing one's own praises; ① blow one's own horn (trumpet).

手味噌 ⑬ self-made *miso*

[を] ⓒ ～を上げる praise oneself; flatter oneself; ⓔ sing one's own praises; ① blow one's own horn (trumpet). ⓒ ～を並べる praise oneself; flatter oneself; ⓔ sing one's own praises; ① blow one's own horn (trumpet).

天 the heavens; the sky

[N] ～に謝す heaven be thanked!; thank heaven! ～に誓う swear by heaven. ⓒ ⓔ ～に沖する soar into the sky; shoot up skyward. ～に衝く soar into the sky; shoot up skyward. ～に唾する fall into one's own trap. ⓒ ～に

則る submit to the will of heaven; follow the way of heaven. 〜に任せる put one's faith in heaven; trust to providence; rely on fate. 〜に召される pass away; leave this world (behind); ⓔ be called by God.
を 〜を仰ぐ look up to heaven; raise one's gaze skyward. 〜を恐れる fear the gods. (火が)〜を焦がす (flames) scorch the heavens. ⓐⓔ 〜を摩する touch the heavens.

点 a spot; a point; a mark

A 〜が甘い be (too) liberal in marking; be (too) lenient in marking. 〜が辛い be strict in marking; be severe in marking. 〜が良い have good marks. 〜が悪い have bad marks.
を 〜を与える award marks. 〜を得る gain a point. 〜を打つ ❶ mark sth with a dot; punctuate a sentence. ❷ criticize sb; point out sb's shortcomings. 〜を稼ぐ gain (good) marks; get a good score. ⓒ 〜を記す keep the score. 〜を付ける give marks; mark sb's work. 〜を取る get a rating; score a point.

天下 the whole country

を 〜を治める pacify the whole country; rule over the whole country. 〜を取る conquer the whole country; take the reigns of government; gain absolute control.

天寿 one's natural life-span

を 〜を全うする die of old age; live out one's natural life-span.

天井 the ceiling; the roof

A 〜が支える ❶ reach the top (price); reach the ceiling; ⓒⓘ hit the roof. ❷ have no room for progress; reach the top capacity. 〜が抜ける ❶ be able to do sth in public; ⓒⓘ be out of the closet. ❷ be elated; ⓘ tread on air; ⓘ be in seventh heaven.
を 〜を打つ reach the top (price); reach the ceiling; ⓒⓘ hit the roof. 〜を抜ける ❶ do sth in public; ⓒⓘ come out of the closet. ❷ make merry; make a racket; ⓒⓘ let one's hair down. ⓒ 〜を見せる ❶ pin sb down on his/her back. ❷ torment sb; give sb distress; treat sb harshly. ❸ scold sb; ⓘ tell sb off; ⓘ give sb a dressing-down; ⓘ haul sb over the coals.

点数 marks; points; rates

を 〜を稼ぐ humor sb; ⓔ ingratiate oneself with sb; ⓘ curry favor with sb; ⓒⓘ earn Brownie points with sb. 〜を付ける give sb marks; rate sth.

てんびん
天秤 a pair of scales

N ～に掛(か)ける weigh the pros and cons (of a matter).

ト

と
戸 a door; a sliding door

を ～を開(あ)ける open a door. Ⓐ ～を下(お)ろす ❶ close a door; bolt the door. ❷ go out of business; go bankrupt; ③ go bust. Ⓐ ～を鎖(さ)す ❶ close a door; bolt the door. ❷ go out of business; go bankrupt; ③ go bust. ～をしめ直(なお)す reclose a door. ～を閉(し)める close a door. ～を叩(たた)く knock on a door.

と
堵 E a fence; an enclosure

Ⓐ Ⓐ Ⓔ ～に安(やす)んず ❶ live in peace; enjoy the safety of peace. ❷ be relieved; be at ease; feel at ease.

を Ⓐ Ⓔ ～を安(やす)くす ❶ live in peace; enjoy the safety of peace. ❷ be relieved; be at ease; feel at ease.

ど
度 a degree; an extent

Ⓐ ～が過(す)ぎる be excessive; go too far; © ⓘ be over the top. Ⓐ ～が抜(ぬ)ける ❶ have bad timing. ❷ relieve the tension; ⓘ break the ice.

N Ⓐ ～に当(あ)たる be moderate; be in the right degree.

を ～を失(うしな)う be rattled; lose one's presence of mind; be flustered; be flurried; ⓘ lose one's head. ～を越(こ)す go too far in *sth*; take *sth* too far; ⓘ carry *sth* too far. ～を過(す)ごす go too far in *sth*; ⓘ take *sth* too far; ⓘ carry things too far.

とう
当 E right; justice; fairness

を ～を得(え)る be right; be in order; be proper; ⓘ be to the point. Ⓔ ～を失(しっ)する be wrong; be improper; Ⓔ be ill conceived; ⓘ be off the mark; ⓘ be beside the point.

とう
薹 E a flower stalk; a peduncle

Ⓐ Ⓒ ～が立(た)つ ❶ go to seed; run to seed. ❷ go hard; become fibrous. ❸ pass one's prime; Ⓔ lose the bloom of youth; Ⓐ get old and rusty; ⓘ be over the hill.

どう
胴 the trunk; the body

Ⓐ Ⓐ ～が据(す)わる be resolute; pluck up courage; brace oneself; gather one's strength. ～が潰(つぶ)れる ❶ be hungry; get hungry. Ⓗ ❷ [gambling] ⓘ break the bank. ～が長(なが)い have a long trunk. ～が細(ほそ)い be slender; be thin in the flanks. ～が短(みじか)い have a short trunk; have a short waist.

N Ⓒ ～に上(あ)げる toss *sb* into the air. Ⓐ ～に突(つ)く toss *sb* into the air.

を ～を据(す)う brace oneself; gather

one's nerves; ⓘ gird up one's loins. Ⓐ ～を据(す)える pluck up courage; become emboldened.

堂 a hall; a temple; a shrine

Ⓝ ～に入(い)る become an expert; master a craft; be at home in (a certain field of expertise).

堂奥 Ⓔ the inner sanctum

Ⓝ Ⓒ ～に入(い)る master the secrets of (an ancient craft); be initiated in the mysteries of (an art).

頭角 Ⓔ the top of the head

Ⓦ ～を現(あら)わす distinguish oneself; stand out (among one's peers); ⓘ cut a dashing figure.

等閑 Ⓔ irresponsibility; neglect

Ⓦ Ⓒ ～を付(ふ)する ❶ do sth in a half-hearted way; act irresponsible; ⓘ make light of sth. ❷ neglect sth; pay no heed to sth; overlook sth.

峠 a (mountain) pass; a crisis

Ⓦ ～を越(こ)す ❶ cross over a ridge; traverse a (mountain) pass. ❷ pass the critical point; ⓘ turn the corner; Ⓒ ⓘ be over the hump.

東西 east and west

Ⓦ ～を失(うしな)う be bewildered; be at a loss; ⓘ be at one's wits' end; ⓘ be all at sea. ～を知(し)らず be at a total loss; be utterly bewildered; be stunned; be perplexed in the extreme. ～を分(わか)らず be at a total loss; be utterly bewildered; be stunned; be perplexed in the extreme. ～を弁(わきま)えず be at a total loss; be utterly bewildered; be stunned; be perplexed in the extreme.

同情 sympathy; compassion

Ⓝ ～に値(あたい)する deserve sb's sympathy; Ⓒ be worhty of sb's compassion. ～に訴(うった)える appeal to sb's sympathy. Ⓦ ～を浴(あ)びせる lavish sympathy on sb. ～を表(あら)わす express one's sympathy; display compassion. ～を失(うしな)う lose sb's sympathy. ～を得(え)る have sb's sympathy; win sb's sympathy. ～を誘(さそ)う arouse sb's sympathy. ～を強(し)いる press sb for his/her sympathy. ～を示(しめ)す show sympathy; display compassion. ～を棄(す)てる stop feeling sorry for sb. ～を引(ひ)く attract sb's sympathy. ～を求(もと)める seek sb's sympathy; Ⓒ enlist sb's compassion. ～を寄(よ)せる feel for sb; Ⓒ extend one's sympathy to sb.

答弁 Ⓔ a reply; an answer

Ⓝ Ⓒ ～に窮(きゅう)する be at a loss for an answer; be speechless.

[を] ⓒ 〜を差し控える reserve one's answer. ⓒ 〜を求める call *sb* to account; require an explanation.

道理 righteousness; reason

[A] 〜が分かる see reason; listen to reason; be sensible; be reasonable; be down-to-earth.
[N] 〜に合う be logical; stand to reason; be reasonable; make sense. 〜に適う be reasonable; be logical; stand to reason; makie sense.
[を] ⓐ 〜を言う ❶ explain oneself; make an excuse; defend oneself. ❷ be given to too much reasoning; be argumentative; ⓘ split hairs; ⓒ ⓘ chop logic (with *sb*). 〜を詰める try to win out in an argument; argue *sb* down.

遠回し a roundabout way

[N] 〜に言う ❶ hint at *sth*; elude to *sth*; say *sth* in a roundabout way; insinuate *sth*. ❷ give an evasive reply; dodge an issue; ⓒ equivocate on an issue; ⓘ beat about the bush; ⓒ ⓘ pussyfoot on (an issue).

咎 a fault; an offense; blame

[を] 〜を受ける take the blame for an offense; ⓒ ⓘ take the fall. 〜を着せる put the guilt on *sb*; pin the blame on *sb*; ⓘ lay the blame at *sb's* door.

〜を蒙る be blamed; be accused of an offense; be scnsured.

時 time; an occasion; a chance

[A] 〜がある have time. 〜が掛かる take time. 〜が立つ time passes; time goes by; time elapses.
[N] ⓐ 〜に遇う have luck; have one's day. 〜に当たる be at the right time. 〜に従う go with the times; go with the flow. ⓐ 〜につく bend to the powers that be. 〜に臨む meet the occasion; ⓘ face the music; ⓘ bite the bullet. 〜に因る go with the times. ⓐ 〜に寄る bend to the powers that be.
[を] 〜を与える give *sb* time; allow *sb* time (to do *sth*). 〜を争う fight for time; try to buy time. 〜を窺う watch for an opportunity; ⓒ bide one's time. 〜を失う ❶ miss an opportunity; lose a chance; be untimely. ❷ be out of touch with the times; go into eclipse; go down in the world. 〜を打つ chime the hour; strike the hour. 〜を移す waste (precious) time; while away one's time; waste one's time. 〜を得る ride the wave of opportunity; ⓒ have one's day. 〜を置く (do *sth*) at regular intervals; (do *sth*) periodically. 〜を惜しむ spare time; be sparing of one's time. 〜を貸す give *sb* time. 〜

を稼ぐ play for time; buy time. 〜を切る (do sth) at regular intervals; (do sth) periodically. 〜を裂く find the time. 〜を過ごす pass time; spend one's time. 〜を費やす spend time; waste time. 〜を撞く toll the time; chime the hour; strike the hour. ⓐ 〜を作る announce the dawn; crow (at dawn). 〜を告げる announce the hour; toll the time. 〜を潰す idle one's time away; waste one's time; ⓒ kill time. 〜を待つ wait until the time is ripe; wait for an opportunity; ⓑ bide one's tim. 〜を巡らす waste (precious) time; while away one's time; waste one's time. 〜を忘れる forget the time; lose the time.

鬨 Ⓓ a battle cry; a war cry

Ⓔ (の声)〜を擧げる raise a war cry; shout in triumph. 〜を合わす respond to the enemy's battle cry. 〜をつくる raise a war cry; shout in triumph.

度胆 Ⓠ "the very liver"

Ⓐ ⓒ 〜を抜かす ❶ be dumfounded; be taken aback. ❷ be terrified; ⓘ be scared out of one's wits.

度胸 courage; pluck; grit

Ⓐ 〜が据る have great courage; have nerves of steel.

〜を定める muster courage; gather one's nerves; ⓘ gird up one's loins. 〜を据える pluck up courage; gather one's strength.

徳 moral goodness; virtue

Ⓔ 〜とする be grateful to sb for their benevolent influence; feel morally indebted to sb.
Ⓝ ⓐⓔ 〜に隠る benefit from sb; enjoy (sb's) benevolent influence; be placed under an obligation.
Ⓐ 〜を行なう do good; practice virtue. 〜を傷つける injure one's/sb's reputation; hurt one's/sb's character. 〜を備える have virtue; be virtuous. 〜を付ける ❶ make a profit; gain by sth; ⓒ do well out of sth. ❷ cause sb to gain from sth; ⓒ do well by sb. ⓐⓔ 〜を見る benefit from sb; enjoy (sb's) benevolent influence. 〜養う instill virtue in sb; breed sb with good character.

得 profit; gain; an advantage

Ⓝ 〜になる be profitable; bring profit; be to one's/sb's advantage.
Ⓐ 〜をする make a profit; benefit from sth; ⓒ do well out of sth.

毒 poison; venom; malice; spite

Ⓐ 〜が回る the poison takes effect; be poisoned.

トゲ

刺 a thorn; a splinter; ◆刺

[を] ⓒ 〜を含む have a sting.

床 a bed; a sickbed; a kip ◆床

[N] 〜に就く ❶ go to bed; retire to bed; turn in. ❷ take to a sickbed; be taken ill; be ill in bed; be laid up (with illness). 〜に入る go to bed; get into bed.

[を] 〜を上げる ❶ put away the bedding. ❷ get better; leave one's sickbed; ⓒ be up and about. 〜を敷く prepare a bed; lay out the bedding; make a bed. 〜を取る prepare a bed; lay out the bedding; make a bed. ⓒ 〜を延べる prepare a bed; lay out the bedding; make a bed. 〜を離れる ❶ get out of bed. ❷ leave one's sickbed; get better; ⓒ be up and about. 〜を払う ❶ put away the bedding. ❷ get better; leave one's sickbed; ⓒ be up and about.

所 a place; a spot; a scene

[N] ⓐ 〜に置く ❶ stand back; give way to sb; yield ground to sb. ❷ be reserved; hold back. ⓐ 〜に付く fall into place; find a niche; find one's feet; feel at home.

[を] 〜を得る ❶ be in (one's) place; be in one's element. ❷ fall into place; ⓒ attain a position; find a niche. ⓒ 〜を教える tell sb one's

トシ

[N] 〜に中る be poisoned; get poisoned. 〜に成る be venomous; be noxious; be harmful.

[を] 〜を仰ぐ take poison; poison oneself. ⓐ 〜を言う say malicious things; ⓒ speak venomous words; ⓐ spit venom. 〜を下ろす purge a toxin. 〜を飼う administer poison to sb; poison sb. 〜を書く write malicious things; ⓘ write with a poisonous pen. 〜を消す counteract the effects of poison; neutralize poison. 〜を吹き込む put a bad idea into sb's head; give sb bad ideas; incite sb to do wrong. 〜を盛る administer poison to sb; poison sb.

得意 prosperity; pride; a client

[A] 〜が多い have many customers; have a large clinetelle.

[と] 〜とする be one's strong point; be one's forte.

[N] 〜になる be proud (of oneself); swell with pride; be elated.

[を] 〜を争う compete for customers. 〜を失う lose customers; lose a client. 〜を得る gain customers; win a client. 〜を作る build a clientele.

塒 a coil

[を] 〜を巻く ❶ coil oneself up. ❷ hang around; loaf about; loiter around.

address; give *sb* one's address. 〜を
変える change one's position;
change place.

鶏冠(とさか) a cockscomb; a topknot

[を] 〜に来る ❶ have a rush of blood
to the head. ❷ get mad; lose one's
temper; be vexed by *sth*; ⑤ ① blow a
fuse. ❸ ① go to one's head; ① lose
one's head; ⑤ ① lose one's marbles;
⑤ freak out. ❹ become nervous; get
flustered; fret over *sth*.

年(とし) a year; years; age ◆ 年(ねん)

[A] 〜が明ける the year opens; the
year begins. 〜が改まる ❶ the new
year comes round. ❷ the era name
changes; enter a new era. 〜が行く
❶ grow old; reach old age. ❷ a year
passes by; the year draws to a close.
〜が替わる ❶ the new year comes
round. ❷ the era name changes;
enter a new era. 〜が足(た)る ❶ put on
years; grow older; gain in years.
❷ grow old; reach old age. 〜が長け
る put on years; grow older. 〜が立
つ years pass. 〜が寄る grow old;
reach old age.
[を] 〜を惜しむ fear old age; regret
the passing of the years. 〜を隠す
conceal one's age. (人の)〜を聞く
ask *sb* his/her age. ⑤ 〜を食う put
on years; grow older. 〜を越す

❶ send off the old year and greet
the new. ❷ keep *sth* over the win-
ter. 〜を取る ❶ put on years; grow
older; gain in years. ❷ welcome the
new year. ⑥ 〜を拾う take a new
lease of life. 〜を跨ぐ extend from
one year to the next; bridge the
new year. 〜を迎える welcome the
new year.

どじ [名] a blunder; a boner

[を] ⓒ 〜を組む commit a blunder;
① put one's foot in it; ⓒ ① pull a
boner; ⓒ ① make a bloomer. ⑤ 〜を
食らわす cause *sb* to commit a blunder; ① play a trick on *sb*; ⓒ ① take
sb in. ⓒ ⓒ 〜を捏ねる fly into a
drunken rage. ⓒ 〜を為出かす com-
mit a blunder; ① put one's foot in it;
ⓒ ① pull a boner. ⓒ 〜を働く commit a blunder; ① put one's foot in it;
ⓒ ① pull a boner. ⓒ 〜を踏む commit a blunder; ① put one's foot in it;
ⓒ ① pull a boner.

どす a dagger; grim; gruesome

[を] 〜を利かせる intimidate *sb*;
threathen *sb*; ⓒ bully *sb*. 〜を呑む
conceal a dagger; wear a dagger in
one's bosom.

渡世(とせい) [名] a means of living

[A] ⑤ 〜が成る be able to make one's

living; eke out a living; © get by; ① make ends meet; ① keep the pot boiling.

[N] ⑤ (何_{なに}かを)～にする make sth one's means of living; make a living by sth; live on sth; live by sth.

[を] ⑤ ～を送_{おく}る make one's living; eke out a living; © get by; ① make ends meet; ① keep the pot boiling.

土壇場_{どたんば} [E] an execution ground

[Av] © ～で逃_にげる make a narrow escape; make a last-minute exit.

[N] © ～に追_おい込む corner sb; drive sb to bay. © ～に成_なる be cornered; be driven to bay; ① have one's back against the wall.

土地_{とち} soil; land; a lot; a locality

[を] ～を買_かう buy a lot. ～を借_かりる lease land. ～を切_きり開_{ひら}く clear the land. ～を肥_こやす enrich the soil. ～を耕_{たがや}す till the soil.

毒気_{どっき} [E] poisonous air; spite

[N] ⑤ ～に当_あてられる be put out by sb's venomous words; be taken aback by sb's harsh words.

[を] ⑤ ～を取られる ❶ be surprised; be dumbfounded; © ① be put out; ① be taken aback. ❷ be terrified; ① be scared out of one's wits; ⑤ be scared stiff. ⑤ ～を抜_ぬかれる ❶ be surprised; be dumbfounded; © ① be put out; ① be taken aback. ❷ be terrified; ① be scared out of one's wits; ⑤ be scared stiff.

徒党_{ととう} a faction; a league; a cabal

[を] ～を組_くむ ❶ form a faction; band together; make a group. ❷ conspire together; form a conspiracy. ～を結_{むす}ぶ ❶ form a faction; band together; make a group. ❷ conspire together; form a conspiracy.

止め_{とど} [E] a finishing blow

[を] © ～を刺_さす ❶ kill sb by a stab in the neck. ❷ deal sb a decisive blow; clinch an argument; ① put the lid on sth.

迸り_{とばっち} [E] a by-blow

[を] ⑤ ～を食_くう ❶ get a by-blow from a fight between others. ❷ get involved in the affairs of others; be embroiled in a quarrel. ❸ meet with misfortune through no fault of oneself; be the hapless victim of circumstance.

帳_{とばり} [E] a curtain; hangings

[A] ⑤ ～が降_おりる darkness falls; night falls.

[N] © ～に包_{つつ}まれる be shrouded in mystery.

とほう
途方 an aim; reason; logic

[N] ～に暮れる be bewildered; ⓪ be at one's wits' end; ① be all at sea.

とみ
富 riches; a fortune; wealth

[A] ⓪ ～が落ちる win a prize (in a lottery).
[を] ～を作る create wealth; make a fortune. ～を積む amass a fortune; accumulate wealth; build up a fortune. ～を成す accumulate riches; create wealth; grow rich. ～を残す leave an estate (to *sb*). ～を誇る grow arrogant through one's wealth; be purse-proud.

とむらい
弔い a funeral; a burrial; a mass

[N] ～に行く attend a funeral service; attend a mass for the dead.
[を] ～を出す hold a funeral service; conduct a mass for the dead.

とむね
と胸 ⓪ "the very chest"

[を] ⓪ ～を突く be startled; be stunned; be shocked; be dumfounded; be flabbergasted; ① be taken aback; ⓪ ① be put out.

ともづな
艫綱 the stern mooring rope

[を] ～を解く ❶ untie the stern mooring rope; ① cast off (the moorings); ⓪ ① slip the paiter. ❷ leave port; ① set sail; ① put out to sea.

どや
どや ③ a dos house; a flophouse

[N] ⓪ ③ ～に着く ❶ return home; come home. ❷ stay at an inn; sleep away from home; pass a night on one's journey.

とら
虎 a tiger; a tigress

[N] ～になる get roaring drunk; get riotously drunk; be high on drink.
[を] ⓪ ③ ～を遣う take liquor; drink wine.

どら
どら ③ fast living; disspation

[を] ③ ～を打つ ❶ indulge oneself; ⓔ lead a life of dissipation; ① lead a fast life; ① sow one's wild oats. ❷ squander money; ⓔ dissipate one's fortune; ruin oneself. ⓪ ③ ～を渇く ❶ indulge oneself; ⓔ lead a life of dissipation; ① lead a fast life; ① sow one's wild oats. ❷ squander money; ⓔ dissipate one's fortune; ruin oneself. ⓪ ③ ～を遣る ❶ indulge oneself; ⓔ lead a life of dissipation; ① lead a fast life; ① sow one's wild oats. ❷ squander money; ⓔ dissipate one's fortune; ruin oneself.

どら
銅鑼 a gong

[を] ～を打つ ❶ strike a gong. ③ ❷ indulge oneself; ⓔ lead a life of dissipation; ① lead a fast life; ① sow one's wild oats. ③ ❸ squander money; ⓒ dissipate one's fortune; ruin oneself.

取り 回 the star performer

を ⓐ 〜を勤める be the last to enter; be the star performer; ⓘ top the bill.

鳥居 a Shintō shrine archway

を 〜を潜る ❶ pass through a torii. ❷ visit a Shintō shrine; worship at a Shintō shrine. ⓒ 〜を越す ❶ be old and experienced; have long experience. ❷ be worldly-wise; ⓑ be street-wise; ⓘ be a sly old fox.

鳥影 the shadow of a bird

A ⓒ 〜が射す expect visitors; feel sb coming; anticipate sb's arrival.

鳥肌 goose bumps; gooseflesh

A 〜が立つ give sb goose bumps; get goose pimples.

泥 mud; dirt; mire ▶ 泥

を 〜を齧る ❶ suffer extreme poverty; be destitute; ⓘ be in dire straits; ⓒⓘ hit on hard times. ❷ lead the life of a convict; spend one's years behind bars. 〜を被る assume sb else's responsibility; take the blame; ⓒⓘ take the fall. 〜を切る have no recourse; have no (other) options;

be without means; ⓘ clutch at thin air. 〜を擦る deride sb; ridicule sb; ⓒ stain sb's good name; ⓘ sling mud at sb; ⓒⓘ take sb down a peg. 〜を塗る deride sb; ⓘ sling mud at sb; stain sb's good name; ⓘ take sb down a peg. ⓢ 〜を吐く confess the truth; admit one's guilt; ⓒ own up (to a crime). ⓐ 〜を踏む have an unsteady gait; be unsteady on one's feet.

徒労 回 fruitless labor

N ⓒ 〜に終る come to nothing; be in vain; ⓔ be to no avail; ⓘ go up in smoke. ⓒ 〜に帰する come to nothing; be in vain; ⓔ be to no avail; ⓘ go up in smoke.

頓挫 回 a setback; a hitch; a balk

を ⓒ 〜を来たす suffer a setback; be checked; be brought to a halt.

遁辞 回 an excuse; a pretext

を ⓒ 〜を設ける give an evasive reply; dodge an issue; ⓒ equivocate on an issue ⓘ beat about the bush. ⓒ 〜を弄する give an evasive reply; dodge an issue; ⓒ equivocate on an issue ⓘ beat about the bush.

蜻蛉 a dragonfly

を ⓗ 〜を切る [kabuki] make a somersault in the air.

ナ

**な
名** a name; a title; esteem ▶ **名**

[A] ～が有る have a good name; be well known; ⓒ ① be *sb*. ～が売れる be widely known; be popular; be esteemed. ⓐ ～が朽ちる disgrace one's good name; lose one's reputation. ～が廃れる lose one's reputation; lose ground. ～が立つ win acclaim; ⓒ ① become the talk of the town. ～が通る be well known; be renowned. ⓐ ～が流れる win fame; become widely known. ～が泣く reflect badly on one's name; fall short of one's reputation. ⓒ ～が触れる be well known; be famous; be celebrated.

[N] ～に負う ❶ (do *sth*) in one's own name; (do *sth*) in the name of (honor). ❷ be true to one's name. ❸ be famous; have a great reputation. ～に係わる compromise one's reputation; reflect on one's good name. ～に聞く hear of *sth*; listen to *sth*; ① give rumor the ear. ～に背く belie one's name; be untrue to one's name; do not live up to one's name. ⓐ ～に立つ be well known; be famous; be celebrated. ⓐ ～に流る win fame; become widely known; rise in the world. ⓒ ～に恥ず have pride in one's name; wear one's name with pride. ⓐ ～に旧る have an illustrious name. ⓒ ～に触れる be famous; be celebrated.

[所] ～へ立つ become widely known; win acclaim; ① become the talk of the town.

[を] ～を明かす disclose one's/*sb's* name. ～を揚げる ❶ win fame; gain reputation; become celebrated. ❷ advertise oneself; make oneself well known; distinguish oneself. ～を挙げる mention *sb's* name; name *sb*. ～を現わす reveal one's/*sb's* name. ～を言う say one's name; mention *sb's* name. ～を偽る assume a false name; give a wrong name. ⓐ ～を埋む fade into obscurity; bury one's name. ～を売る achieve fame; acquire a reputation. ⓐ ～を得る become famous; gain reputation; win popularity. ～を惜しむ hold one's name high; honor one's name; be jealous of one's reputation. ～を落とす damage one's (good) name; lose one's reputation. ⓐ ～を折る injure one's/*sb's* reputation; mar one's/*sb's* reputation. ～を変える change one's name. ～を書く write down one's name. ⓐ ～を掛く ❶ enter one's name; allow one's name to be added (to a list). ❷ gain fame; grow in reputation. ❸ call *sb's* name. ～を貸す lend one's name (to a cause). ～を騙

る assume *sb's* name; impersonate *sb*. 〜を借りる ❶ do *sth* in *sb's* name; use *sb's* name. ❷ do *sth* under a pretext. Ⓐ 〜を腐す wreck one's/*sb's* name; ruin one's/*sb's* reputation. Ⓒ 〜を降す damage *sb's* (good) name; bring *sb* down. 〜を汚す damage one's/*sb's* name; disgrace one's/*sb's* name. 〜を指す mention *sb* by name; point out *sb's* name. 〜を沈む damage *sb's* (good) name; bring *sb* down. 〜を示す name oneself; publish one's name. 〜を濯ぐ clear one's/*sb's* name; restore one's/*sb's* reputation. 〜を雪ぐ clear one's/*sb's* name; restore one's/*sb's* reputation. 〜を出す put forth one's name; give one's name. Ⓐ 〜を正す tell right from wrong; define one's moral obligations. 〜を立てる ❶ win fame; gain a reputation; become celebrated. ❷ start a rumor; set afloat a rumor. 〜を保つ defend one's/*sb's* honor. Ⓐ 〜を散らす achieve fame; acquire a good reputation; Ⓒ Ⓘ be the talk of the town. ❷ cause a scandal; Ⓒ Ⓘ become the talk of the town; be talked about. 〜を付ける give *sb* a name; christen a child. 〜を連ねる enter one's name (on a list); have oneself enlisted. Ⓐ 〜を釣る seek fame; make oneself well known; distinguish oneself. Ⓐ 〜を遂げる attain a (certain) reputation; distinguish oneself. 〜を留む leave one's name behind; become immortal; Ⓔ leave one's mark. 〜を轟かす gain a bad name; become notorious; gain notoriety. Ⓑ 〜を唱える state one's name (to the enemy). 〜を取る win fame; become famous. 〜を流す cause a scandal; be talked about; Ⓒ Ⓘ be the talk of the town. 〜を成す acquire a name for oneself; win fame; become well known. Ⓓ 〜を偸む gain an unjustified reputation. 〜を残す leave one's name behind; become immortal; Ⓒ leave one's mark. Ⓓ 〜を恥ず have pride in one's name; wear one's name with pride. 〜を辱む bring shame on one's/*sb's* name; Ⓒ Ⓘ drag *sb's* name through the mud. 〜を辱める insult *sb's* reputation; disgrace oneself; Ⓔ bring disgrace upon one's/*sb's* name. 〜を馳せる win fame; become widely known. 〜を広む widen one's reputation; win fame. Ⓐ 〜を揮う do one credit; reflect well on one's name. Ⓐ 〜を許す recognize *sb's* reputation. 〜を汚す soil one's name; mar one's reputation. 〜を呼ぶ call *sb* by name.

菜 vegetables; greens

🦋 〜をつくる grow vegetables. 〜を漬ける pickle vegetables.

内証 secrecy; discretion

[Av] 〜で話す say *sth* in secret; talk confidentially; confide in *sb*.

[N] 〜にする make *sth* a secret; keep *sth* secret; ⓒ ⓘ hush *sth* up.

[を] 〜を締める make *sth* a secret; keep *sth* secret; ⓒ ⓘ hush *sth* up.

内証事 a private matter

[を] 〜を打ち明ける take *sb* into one's confidence; ⓘ pour out one's heart to *sb*; ⓔ unbosom oneself.

内証話 a private talk

[を] 〜をする talk in private; have a private talk; have a confidential talk; have a tête-à-tête.

等閑 negligence

[N] 〜にする neglect (one's duties); disregard *sth*; pay no heed to *sth*.

中 the inside; the interior

[Av] 〜で待つ wait inside (a place).
[N] (危険の)〜に居る be in danger; be in the midst of danger. 〜に埋める bury *sth* in (the sand/soil). 〜に数える number *sb* among (the great). 〜に佇む stand amid (a crowd). 〜に立つ ❶ stand inside (a place). ❷ mediate between (two parties); come between (two parties). 〜に入る ❶ go into a place; enter (a building); go inside. ❷ mediate between (two parties); come between (two parties).

[を] 〜へ入れる put *sth* into (a box). 〜へ立つ mediate between (two parties); come between (two parties). 〜へ入る ❶ go into a place; enter (a building); go inside. ❷ mediate between (two parties); come between (two parties).

[を] 〜を取る ❶ take the middle course; ⓒ go middle. ❷ mediate between (two parties); come between (two parties). 〜を直す reconcile (two parties); make peace. 〜を行く take the middle course; go middle.

仲 relations; relationship

[Av] 〜が良い be good friends; be on good terms; get on well. ⓒ 〜が旨い be good friends; be on good terms; get on well. 〜が悪い be enemies; be on bad terms; ⓘ be at daggers drawn; ⓒ ⓘ be on the out with *sb*.

[N] 〜に立つ mediate between (two parties); come between (two parties). 〜になる fall in love with each other; come to love each other. 〜に入る mediate between (two parties); come between (two parties). 〜に挟まる be caught between (the conflicting interests of) two parties.

⓳ ～へ立つ mediate between (two parties); come between (two parties). ～へ入る mediate between (two parties); come between (two parties).
を ～を裂く divide (two parties); drive a wedge between (two parties); estrange two people. ～を塞ぐ divide (two parties); drive a wedge between (two parties); estrange two people. ～を取り持つ act as a go-between; be a matchmaker. ～を取る mediate between (two parties); come between (two parties). ～を直す reconcile (two parties); make peace.

流れ a flow; a stream; a school
N ～に逆らう go against the flow; swim against the current. ～に従う go with the flow; swim with the current.
を ～を下る go downstream. ～を汲む ❶ drink from a stream. ❷ follow in a tradition; belong to a school (of thought); belong to the same bloodline. Ⓐ ～を立てる be a prostitute; remain a prostitute. ～を上る go upstream. ～を乱す wade through a stream; cross a stream.

泣き crying; weeping; lament
A ⓒ (芸に)～が入る become highly accomplished at an art; master a skill.
を ～を入れる plead for mercy; beg for mercy; ⓔ implore sb. ～を見る be in trouble; ⓘ come to grief; ⓒ get oneself into a fix.

泣き顔 a tearful face
を ～を隠す hide one's tears. ～を見せる show one's tears.

泣き言 a whimper; a sulk
を ～を言う whine about sth; sulk over sth; complain about sth.

無き手 the last resort
を ～を出す ❶ leave no means untried; try every means; ⓘ leave no stone unturned; ⓒ play one's last card. ❷ do the impossible; challenge the gods.

無き者 the dead; a goner
N ～にする ❶ kill sb; take sb's life; send sb to oblivion. ❷ take no notice of sb; have no eye for sb; think nothing of sb; ignore sb.

慰め comfort; consolation
を ～を得る take comfort in sth; draw comfort from sth. ～を求める seek for solace; take comfort in sth; find solace in (prayer).

情け sympathy; pity; charity

[を] ～を売る ❶ sell one's favors; prostitute oneself; ⓘ go on the streets. ❷ be kind to sb; show sb sympathy. ～を掛ける be kind to sb; show kindness; treat sb with sympathy; take pity on sb. ～を交わす love one another; treat each other with affection. ～を乞う ask sb for mercy; beg for mercy; plead for mercy. ～を知る ❶ know pity; have pity. ❷ penetrate the depths of love; know what it is to love; ⓔ understand the tender feelings. ～を尽す do good; practice charity.

馴染み intimacy; familiarity

[N] ～になる become intimate with sb; grow fond of each other; grow attached; make friends with sb.
[を] ⓒ ～を掛く take a liking to a prostitute; visit the same prostitute; frequent a prostitute. ～を重ねる become increasingly intimate; grow fond of sb.

謎 an enigma; a conundrum

[を] ～を掛ける ❶ set sb a riddle; give sb a puzzle; put a riddle to sb. ❷ hint at sth; elude to sth; say sth in a roundabout way; insinuate sth. ～を解く ❶ solve a riddle; work out a puzzle; untangle a mystery. ❷ read between the lines; ⓔ ⓘ get the picture ⓔ ⓘ catch sb's drift. ❸ penetrate deep mysteries; explain the inexplicable.

鉈 a hatchet; an axe

[を] ～を振るう ❶ wield a hatchet; swing an axe. ❷ take drastic measures; introduce sweeping reforms; make a huge cut in the budget; axe (extra expenditures).

納得 assent; consent

[A] ～が行く ❶ make sense of sth; grasp the meaning; ⓘ catch the idea. ❷ be convinced; be won over; be persuaded; ⓘ come round to sb's point of view.

名乗り 囲 name announcing

[を] ～を上げる ❶ give one's name; introduce oneself. ❷ stand for election; ⓔ let one's name go forward; run as a candidate; run for election. ❸ enter a competition; join a contest; compete in an event. ⓗ ❹ state one's name and pedigree (to the enemy); reveal one's identity.

鍋釜 pots and pans

[A] ⓐ ～が賑わう live in luxury; live the good life; be well off. ⓐ ～が割れる have a domestic quarrel.

生身 a living body

[を] 〜を削る be in agony; suffer extreme hardships; ⓒ ⓘ go through living hell.

波 a wave; a billow; a sea

[A] 〜が高い the waves are high; have high seas; ⓒ be choppy. 〜が立つ be wavy; have high seas; ⓒ be choppy.

[N] 〜に攫われる be carried away by the waves; be swept away by the waves. 〜に漂う drift on the waves. 〜に呑まれる be swallowed up by the waves. 〜に乗る ❶ ride a wave; surf on a wave. ❷ ride on the waves (of opportunity); ride the crest (of a movement).

[を] 〜を打つ be wavy; have high seas; ⓒ be choppy. 〜を被る ship water; be washed by the waves. 〜を切る plow the waves; cleave the waves; cut through the waves.

涙 tears; crying; sympathy

[A] 〜が込み上げる tears come to one's eyes; the eyes fill with tears.

[N] 〜に暗れる cry one's eyes out. 〜に暮れる live in misery; live a life of misery. 〜に沈む weep one's eyes out; cry one's eyes out; drown in sorrow; ⓒ be dissolved in tears. ⓐ 〜に迷う be distraught with grief; be lost in grief. 〜に咽ぶ be choked with tears.

[を] 〜を浮かべる tears stand in one's eyes. 〜を打ち払う dash one's tears away. 〜を押える fight back one's tears; repress one's tears. 〜を零す shed tears. 〜を誘う move sb to tears; be a tear-jerker. 〜を流す shed tears. 〜を拭う wipe one's tears away; wipe one's eyes. 〜を呑む ❶ swallow one's tears; gulp down one's tears. ❷ pocket an insult; brook an insult; ⓘ keep a stiff upper lip. 〜を払う dash one's tears away. 〜を拭く dry one's tears. 〜を振るう ❶ dash one's tears away. ❷ stop feeling sorry for oneself/sb. 〜を催す melt into tears; be moved to tears.

鳴り a sound; ring; ringing

[を] 〜を静める ❶ be silent; fall silent; be hushed; be still. ❷ be still; be inactive; ⓘ lie low. 〜を潜める ❶ fall silent; be hushed; be still. ❷ be still; be inactive; ⓘ lie low.

成り行き the course of events

[A] ⓘ 〜で買う buy at the market.

[N] 〜に任せる let events take their course; ⓘ let things ride.

[を] 〜を待つ wait how things will turn out. 〜を見る watch the course of events; see how things will turn out.

ナワメ

縄 a rope; a cord; bonds

N ～に掛かる be bound with a rope; be put in bonds; be arrested. を ～を入る measure the acreage (of a plot of land); take the measurements of a plot. ～を打つ ❶ bind sb with a rope; arrest sb; seize sb. ❷ measure the acreage (of a plot of land); take the measurements of a plot. ❸ stretch a rope; rope off (a place); draw a cordon. ～を掛ける ❶ bind sb/sth with a rope; tie sb up; put sb in bonds. ❷ arrest sb; put sb under arrest. ～を解く ❶ unbind sb/sth; untie sb/sth; untie sb's bonds. ❷ release sb; set sb free; ⓒ let sb go. ～を綯う twist a rope; strand a rope. ～を張る rope off (a place); draw a cordon; demarcate an area; mark one's territory. ～を引く pull a rope. ⓗ ～を結ぶ knot a rope (to convey a message).

縄張り roping off; territory

を ～を荒らす intrude into sb's domain; trespass on sb's territory. ～を争う contest a sphere of influence; quarrel over (one's) territory. ～をする rope off (a place); draw a cordon; demarcate an area. ～を広げる extend one's territory; widen one's beat. ～を守る defend one's territory; protect an area.

縄目 Ⓔ bonds; fetters; chains

N Ⓔ ～に遭う ❶ be bound with a rope; be put in bonds. Ⓒ ❷ be arrested; be put under arrest. を Ⓔ ～を切る untie one's bonds. Ⓔ ～を擦り抜ける free oneself from one's bonds; slip one's bonds. Ⓔ ～を解く ❶ unbind sb/sth; untie sb/sth; untie sb's bonds. ❷ release sb; set sb free; Ⓒ let sb go. Ⓔ ～を免れる escape arrest.

難 trouble; difficulty; hardship

N ～に遭う meet with disaster. ～に当たる face (up to) difficulty; tackle a difficult situation. を ～を言う point out sb's flaws. Ⓐ ～を構える take issue with sb; Ⓒ engage in a battle of words; ⓘ cross swords with sb. ～を避ける take refuge in (a place). ～を付ける find fault with sb; criticize sb; point out sb's shortcomings; carp at sb's faults. ～を免れる escape danger; escape censure.

難局 a difficult situation

N ～に当たる deal with a difficult situation; Ⓒⓘ take the bull by the horns; Ⓒⓘ face the music. ～に立つ be in a difficult situation; Ⓒⓘ be in a fix; Ⓢⓘ be up the creek を ～を切り抜ける find one's way

ニ

out of a difficult situation; ① tide over a crises; ① weather the storm. ～を乗り越える get through a difficult situation; ① tide over a crises; ① weather the storm.

難癖 a fault; a blemish
[を] ～を付ける find fault with *sb*; criticize *sb*; point out *sb's* shortcomings; carp at *sb's* faults.

二

荷 a load; a cargo; a burden
[A] ～が重い ❶ be a heavy load; be a taxing burden. ❷ be a great responsibility. ～が下りる be relieved from one's duty; be acquitted of one's responsibilities. ～が勝つ be too heavy a load for one; be unequal to the task.
[N] ～になる be a burden to one.
[を] ～を送る send freight; consign goods. ～を下ろす ❶ unload (a ship); unpack (a horse). ❷ fulfill one's duty; relieve oneself of one's responsibilities. ～を括る fasten a load; strap up a load. ⓒ ～を付ける load (a cart); pack (a horse). ～を積む load (a cart); pack (a horse); take on cargo. ～を解く unpack a box. ～を担う carry a load on one's shoulders. ～を刎ねる throw cargo over-

ニモツ

board; jettison (part of) the cargo. ～を引き取る receive goods; take delivery of goods.

匂 a smell; a scent; an odor
[を] ～を嗅ぐ smell *sth*. ～を付ける perfume *sth*. ～を取る take the smell off *sth*. ～を抜く remove an odor. ～を放つ give out a scent.

肉 flesh; meat; the flesh
[A] ～が落ちる lose weight. ～が付く put on weight.
[N] ～に飢える thirst for the flesh.
[を] ～を切る carve meat. ～を付ける fatten up; flesh out.

肉欲 lust; passion; carnal desire
[と] ～と戦う fight one's desires; combat sensuality.
[N] ～に耽る indulge in sensual pleasures; give oneself up to lust.
[を] ～を避ける abstain from sensuality; keep one's passions at bay. ⓔ ～を制する suppress one's carnal desires; restrain one's passions; be continent. ～を満たす gratify one's lusts; ⓥ ⓢ get laid.

逃げ flight; escape
[を] ～を打つ ❶ attempt to escape; try to get away; plan one's escape. ❷ excuse oneself; dodge (a ques-

tion); ⓒ back out (of a promise). 〜を張る ❶ attempt to escape; try to get away; plan one's escape. ❷ excuse oneself; dodge (a question); ⓒ back out (of a promise).

逃げ場 a refuge; a shelter
を 〜を失う have one's escape cut off; be cut off from escape; be trapped. 〜を作る find a pretext; set up one's escape.

錦 Japanese brocade
を 〜を飾る return home in glory; ⓒ have a glorious homecoming; ⓒ ① bring home the bacon. 〜を衣る return home in glory; ⓒ have a glorious homecoming; ⓒ ① bring home the bacon.

にち Ⓐ wheedling; extortion
を ⓐ 〜を入れる wheedle *sb* into *sth* by false arguments; talk *sb* into *sth*; ⓒ importune *sb* by illicit means.

日限 a date; a term
Ⓐ 〜が切れる the term expires. 〜が来る fall due.
を 〜を定める fix a term; set a date. 〜を早める advance the date.

荷物 a load; a burden; luggage
を 〜を預ける have one's baggage checked. 〜を下ろす unload (a cart). 〜を抱え込む bear a responsibility; carry a (heavy) burden. 〜を運ぶ carry a load. 〜を纏める pack up.

睨み a sharp look; authority
Ⓐ 〜が利く command respect; be authoritative; have influence; ① carry weight.
を 〜を利かせる wield authority; ① have *sb* under one's thumb.

任 a duty; a responsibility
Ⓝ 〜に当たる take charge of a duty; ⓒ undertake a responsibility; ⓒ take on a job. 〜に在る be in office; hold a post. 〜に赴く leave for one's post. 〜に帰る return to one's post. 〜に堪える be equal to the task; be up to the job. 〜に就く take up one's duties; take office. 〜に適す be fit for a post.
を 〜を辞す resign from one's post; ⓒ tender one's resignation; step down from office; leave office. 〜を果たす fulfill one's duties.

認可 approval; permission
を 〜を得る obtain authorization; be authorized.

人気 popularity; public interest
Ⓐ 〜がある be popular; be in favor;

be in vogue. 〜が落ちる fall in popularity; lose favor; go out of fashion; ⓘ fall from grace. 〜が増す win popularity; gain in popularity. 「を」 〜を失う lose popularity; go out of fashion. 〜を得る gain favor; become fashionable. 〜を落とす lose popularity; become unpopular. 〜を高める increase one's popularity; heighten one's popularity. 〜を取る become popular; win favor; ⓒ catch on. 〜を呼ぶ be much talked about; create a sensation; ⓘ make a stir.

人数 the number of persons

「を」 〜を限る limit the number of people. 〜を数える count heads; ⓒ ⓐ tell noses. 〜を揃える assemble the required number of people. 〜を増やす increase the number of persons. 〜を減らす reduce the number of persons.

人相 looks; appearance

「を」 〜を教える describe sb's looks. 〜を変える disguise oneself. 〜を見る read sb's face.

又

縫い揚げ a tuck (of a garment)

「を」 〜を下ろす let out a tuck. 〜をする tuck (a garment).

縫い目 a seam; a stitch

「A」 〜が綻びる a seam opens. 〜が解ける a seam starts.
「を」 〜を解く undo a seam.

盗み stealing; theft; larceny

「N」 〜に入る break into a house; burglarize an estate.
「を」 〜を働く steal sth; ⓒ commit larceny.

濡れ衣 a false charge

「を」 〜を着せる accuse sb unjustly; bring a false charge against sb. 〜を着る be falsely charged; be wrongly accused (of a crime).

ネ

根 a root; the source; nature 根

「A」 〜が付く ❶ ⓒ take root. ❷ catch on; ⓐ take root. 〜が遂げぬ fail to reach the ultimate goal; remain unacomplished. 〜が無い be unfounded; be ungrounded; be groundless. 〜が生える ❶ ⓒ take root. ❷ ⓐ take root; settle down.
「N」 〜に入る ❶ ⓒ take root. ❷ catch on; ⓐ take root. ❸ understand sth fully; be fully aware of sth; ⓘ sink in. 〜に持つ ❶ bare sb ill will; harbor a grudge against sb; have an underlying motive; ⓘ have an axe to

grind. ❷ entertain (an idea); harbor (a grudge); hold *sth*; hide *sth*. ❸ be engrained in *sth*; be in *sb's* nature. 🔄 〜へ入る ❶ⓒ take root. ❷ catch on; ⓐ take root. ❸ understand *sth* fully; be fully aware of *sth*; ⓓ sink in. 🔄 ⓐ 〜を押す pay attention to *sth*; elaborate on *sth*. 〜を下ろす take root; settle down. ⓐ 〜を切る ❶ cure *sb* radically; ⓑ effect a radical cure. ❷ root out a longstanding abuse; eradicate an old evil. 〜を差す ❶ⓒ take root. ❷ arise from *sth*; originate in *sth*; ⓐ take root in *sth*. 〜を締む pluck up courage; brace oneself; ⓑ buck up; ⓓ pull oneself together. 〜を絶つ root out (a problem); eradicate the roots (of evil). 〜を摘む ❶ nip a root. ❷ grasp *sb's* purpose; understand *sb's* motives. 〜を抜く root up; pluck up by the roots. 〜を生やす ❶ⓒ take root. ❷ⓐ take root; settle down. 〜を張る ❶ⓒ take root. ❷ catch on; ⓐ take root. ⓐ 〜を引く sow the seeds (of discord). ⓒ 〜を回す dig round the roots (of a tree).

音 🔄 a sound; a tone; a tune

🅰 ⓒ 〜が良い sound sweet. ⓒ 〜が悪い sound harsh.

🄽 ⓒ 〜に聞く listen to rumors; lend

rumor the ear; ⓓ hear *sth* on the grapevine. ⓐⓒ 〜に立つ raise one's voice; call out. ⓒ 〜に泣く burst out crying; wail. 🔄 ⓒ 〜を上げる ❶ complain about *sth*; make complaints; ⓒ ⓓ sing small. ❷ give in; admit one's defeat; ⓒ ⓓ cry uncle. ⓐ 〜を入れる stop singing. ⓐⓒ 〜を立つ raise one's voice; call out. ⓒ 〜を泣く burst out crying; wail.

値 a price; a cost; a value

🅰 〜が上がる rise in price; go up in price. 〜が決まる fix a price; set a price. 〜が下がる fall in price; go down in price. 〜が出る fetch a good price; improve in price. ⓐ 〜が成る ❶ fix a price. ❷ come to an understanding; arrive at an agreement; come to terms. 〜が張る be expensive; be dear.

🔄 〜を上げる raise the price. 〜を押える peg the price. 〜を聞く ask the price; inquire after the price. 〜を決める fix a price; set a price. 〜を下げる lower the price. 〜を競り上げる bid up the price. 〜を付ける ❶ put a price on *sth*; set a price on *sth*; price (an article). ❷ name a price; make an offer; estimate a price. 〜を踏む ❶ put a price on *sth*; set a price on *sth*; price (an article).

❷ name a price; make an offer; estimate a price.

寝息 a sleeper's breathing
[を] ～を窺う listen whether *sb* is asleep; see if *sb* is sleeping.

寝入り端 one's first sleep
[を] ～を起こされる be woken when one has just fallen asleep.

値打ち value; worth; merit
[A] ～が上がる ❶ rise in value; gain value. ❷ go up in public estimation; gain prestige. ～が有る have value; be worthy (of *sth*). ～が落ちる ❶ fall in value; lose value. ❷ go down in public estimation; lose prestige. ～が下がる lose value; drop in value; go down in public estimation. ～が出る become of value. ～が増す ❶ gain in value; increase in value. ❷ go up in public estimation; gain prestige; be widely recognized.
[を] ～を付ける put a value on *sth*. ～を増す increase the value of *sth*; make *sth* more valuable. ～を認める appreciate the value of *sth*; recognize the merit of *sth*.

寝返り tossing about in bed
[を] ～を打つ ❶ toss about in bed; turn over in one's sleep. ❷ betray an ally; play *sb* false; double-cross *sb*; go over to the enemy; defect to the other side; ① be a turncoat.

寝首 the neck of one who sleeps
[を] ～を掻く ❶ cut *sb's* throat in their sleep. ❷ betray *sb* when they expect it least; ① play foul on *sb*; ⓒ ① play a dirty trick on *sb*.

塒 a roost; a lie
[N] ～に帰る fly home to roost. ～に着く ❶ go to roost. ⓢ ❷ turn in for the night; sleep rough.
[を] ⓢ ～を定める find a place to sleep for the night; sleep rough.

猫 a cat
[を] ～を飼う keep a cat. ～を被る conceal one's real personality; feign ignorance; play the hypocrite; simulate modesty.

螺子 a screw; a spring
[A] ～が緩む ❶ a screw loosens. ❷ loosen up; relax; unwind.
[Av] ～で締める screw *sth* down. ～で停める screw *sth* up; fix *sth* with a screw; fasten *sth* with a screw.
[を] ～を締める drive home a screw. ～を抜く remove a screw. ～を巻く ❶ wind up (a watch). ❷ rouse *sb* to action; spur *sb* into action; call *sb* to

order. ～を回す turn a screw. ～を戻す unscrew a screw. ～を緩める loosen a screw.

妬 ⓔ envy; jealousy

を ⓔ ～に籠む bare *sb* ill will; harbor a grudge against *sb*; have an ulterior motive; ⓘ have an axe to grind. ⓔ ～に持つ bare *sb* ill will; harbor a grudge against *sb*; ⓘ have an axe to grind.

寝刃 a blunt sword

を ～を合わす ❶ sharpen a sword. ❷ carry out a wicked design; conspire against *sb*; lay a plot against *sb*; ⓢ ⓘ be in cahoots.

熱 heat; temperature; fever

Ⓐ ～が上がる one's temperature rises; increase one's fever. ～がある have a temperature; be feverish; run a fever. ～が籠る be filled with enthusiasm. ～が下がる one's temperature falls; ⓔ one's fever subsided. ～が冷める lose one's enthusiasm. ～が高い have a high fever; have a temperature. ～が出る run a temperature; become feverish. ～が入る get carried away by *sth*; put one's mind to *sth*; ⓘ warm up to *sth*. ～が引く one's temperature falls; ⓔ one's fever subsided.

Ⓝ ～に浮かされる ❶ be delirious with fever; fall into delirium. ❷ be obsessed with *sth*.

を ～を上げる ❶ push up the temperature; raise the heat. ❷ be enthusiastic about *sb*/*sth*; enthuse over *sb*/*sth*; be enthralled by *sth*; ⓘ be mad about *sb*; have a crush on *sb*. ～を加える apply heat to *sth*. ～を冷ます ❶ cool down; chill down. ❷ dampen one's enthusiasm; ⓘ be a wet blanket. ～を計る take one's temperature. Ⓐ ～を吐く ❶ argue heatedly in favor/against *sth*; debate *sth* hotly. ❷ brag about *sth*; boast about *sth*; ⓘ talk big; ⓘ blow one's own horn.

根葉 roots and leaves; rancor

Ⓝ ～に成る lead to discontent; be the seed of resentment. ～に持つ bear a grudge (against *sb*); be bitter about *sth*; feel resentment at *sth*; ⓔ nurse a rancor (against *sb*); ⓘ have a chip on one's shoulders.

根腹 "the root of one's stomach"

Ⓐ ～が立つ be truly mad; be genuinely upset.

根回し "digging round the roots"

を ～をする ❶ dig round the roots (before replanting a tree). ❷ lay the basis; win people over (for one's future plans); ⓘ pull strings.

寝耳 the ear of *sb* who sleeps

N ～に入る ❶ hear *sth* while one is asleep. ❷ gain possession of *sth* without expecting it; ⓘ drop into one's lap.

眠気 sleepiness; drowsiness

A ～がさす become sleepy; feel drowsy; be overcome with drowsiness.
N ～に襲われる be overcome with drowsiness.
を ～を覚ます keep oneself awake; shake off sleepiness; get over a sleepy spell. ～を払う shake off sleepiness; get over a sleepy spell. ～を催す become sleepy; feel drowsy.

眠り a sleep; a slumber; a nap

A ～が浅い have a poor sleep; sleep lightly; be a light sleeper. ～が深い have a sound sleep; sleep deeply; be a good sleeper.
N ～に落ちる fall asleep; drop off to sleep. ～につく go to sleep; go to bed; ⓔ retire to bed.
を ～を覚ます arouse *sb* from sleep. ～を催させる make *sb* feel drowsy; induce sleep.

狙い an aim; an end; an object

A ～が当たる ❶ hit the target. ❷ provoke a response; ⓘ touch a (raw) nerve; ⓘ sink in; ⓘ strike home. ～が良い ❶ ⓒ aim right. ❷ have a good objective; have the right ambitions. ～が高い ❶ ⓒ aim high. ❷ ⓐ aim high; ⓘ set one's sights high; have high ambitions. ～が外れる ❶ miss the target. ❷ fail to obtain the intended effect; ⓘ be off the mark. ～が悪い ❶ ⓒ aim wrongly. ❷ have the wrong objective; have the wrong ambitions.
を ～を誤る ❶ ⓒ aim wrongly. ❷ have the wrong objective; have the wrong ambitions. ～を定める ❶ take aim; fix one's aim; aim at (a target). ❷ focus on *sth*; ⓘ set one's sights on *sb*/*sth*; ⓘ have one's eye on *sb*/*sth*. ～を付ける ❶ take aim; fix one's aim; aim at (a target). ❷ focus on *sth*; ⓘ set one's sights on *sb*/*sth*; ⓘ have one's eye on *sb*/*sth*.

念 E a sense; an idea; a wish

A ⓔ ～が入る be attentive to detail; be prudent; be careful. ⓒ ～が届く ❶ have one's wish come true; see one's dream fulfilled. ❷ be tactful; be considerate; be attentive. ⓔ ～が残る be unable to give *sth* up. ⓒ ～が晴れる clear one's mind.

ネンコウ

[と] ⓒⒺ 〜とする be of concern.
[N] Ⓒ 〜に掛ける be troubled by *sth*; fret over *sth*; Ⓘ weigh on one's mind.
[を] Ⓒ 〜を入れる ❶ pay attention to detail; take care with *sth*; do *sth* with care. ❷ put *sb* to trouble; give trouble to *sb*; make trouble. Ⓒ 〜を押す remind *sb* (of *sth*); call *sb's* attention to *sth*; tell *sb* emphatically of *sth*. Ⓒ 〜を凝らす meditate on *sth*; ponder over *sth*. ⓒⒺ 〜を突く make sure of *sth*; call *sb's* attention to *sth*; remind *sb* of *sth*. Ⓒ 〜を残す pass away with regrets. Ⓒ 〜を晴らす clear one's mind.

年 a year; a grade; a term ▶ 年

[A] 〜が明ける ❶ end one's term of service; end one's apprenticeship. ❷ end one's role; Ⓔ bring one's mission to an end. ❸ go out of use; lose its effectiveness.
[N] Ⓒ 〜に行く be apprenticed to *sb*; apprentice oneself to *sb*.
[を] Ⓒ 〜を入れる go through a long period of training; put in a great deal of time; apply oneself to *sth* over many years. Ⓒ 〜を沈める be apprenticed to *sb*; apprentice oneself to *sb*.

年功 Ⓔ long years of service

[を] Ⓒ 〜を積む have long experience (in an office); apply oneself to *sth* over many years; work for many years; serve long.

ノド

能 ability; faculties; talent

[A] 〜が無い ❶ have no talents; be dull-witted. ❷ be uninteresting; be without merrit; be boring.
[を] 〜を隠す hide one's talents; Ⓘ hide one's light under a bushel. 〜を尽す give full scope to one's abilities; exert one's faculties to the utmost.

脳味噌 the brains; the grey cells

[を] 〜を絞る think hard about *sth*; Ⓔ apply one's mind to *sth*; ⓒⒾ rack one's brains.

軒 the eaves

[を] 〜を争う stand close together. 〜を借りる take shelter under the eaves (of *sb's* house). 〜を軋す stand side by side; stand in a row. 〜を連ねる stand side by side; stand in a row. 〜を並べる stand side by side; stand in a row.

熨斗 a strip of dried sea-ear

[を] Ⓒ 〜を添える give *sb* a present; send *sb* a present; present *sth* to *sb*;

make sb a present. 〜を付ける give sb a present; send sb a present; present sth to sb; make sb a present.

望み a wish; aspirations; hope

[A] 〜が有る there is hope.
[N] 〜に叶う meet one's hopes; answer one's prayers.
[を] 〜を抱く have an ambition; harbor a wish; ⓒ cherish a desire. 〜を失う lose hope; despair of achieving one's ambition. (人に)〜を掛ける expect much of sb; set one's hopes on sb. 〜を叶える fulfill sb's wishes. 〜を捨てる abandon one's dreams; give up hope. 〜を属す set one's hopes on sb; pin one's hopes on sb. (人に)〜を託す pin one's hopes on sb. 〜を繋ぐ cling to one's (last) hopes. 〜を遂げる realize one's dream; attain one's object; effect one's purpose. ⓒ 〜を懐く entertain hopes (of success); aspire to sth.

喉 the throat; a voice

[A] 〜が良い have a good voice (for singing). 〜が痛い have a sore throat. 〜が渇く ❶ be thirsty. ❷ be envious; be greedy; covet sth. 〜が詰まる be choked; choke on sth. 〜が鳴る ❶ smack one's lips; ⓢ ⓘ lick one's chops. ❷ covet sth; lust for sth; crave for sth. 〜が引っ付く be extremely thirsty; crave for water.
[N] 〜に支える have sth stuck in one's throat; get sth stuck in one's throat. 〜に引っ掛かる have sth stuck in one's throat; get sth stuck in one's throat.
[を] 〜を潤す quench one's thirst. 〜を押える hold one's/sb's throat; seize sb by the throat. 〜を嗄らす shout oneself hoarse. 〜を聞かす sing to others. 〜を締める grip sb's throat; strangle sb. 〜を絞る shout at the top of one's voice. 〜を突く stab oneself/sb in the throat. 〜を鳴らす ❶ purr. ❷ covet sth; lust for sth; crave for sth. ⓒ 〜を干す feel hungry; go hungry; starve from hunger.

野放し pasturing; *laissez-faire*

[N] 〜にする ❶ pasture (cattle); let (a dog) run loose. ❷ let sb do as they like; refrain from interfering; ⓘ let sth run its own course.

呑み込み understanding

[A] 〜が良い be quick to understand sth; be quick-witted. 〜が付く ❶ make sense of sth; grasp the meaning; ⓘ catch the idea. ❷ be convinced; be won over; be persuaded; ⓘ come round to sb's point

247

of view. ～が早い be quick to understand *sth*; be quick-witted. ～が悪い be slow to understand *sth*; be quick-witted.

乗り a ride; riding

[A] ～が来る ❶ be enlivened; live up; gain vigor; gain momentum. ❷ warm up to *sth*; ③ get into one's stride. ～が付く ❶ be enlivened; live up; gain vigor; gain momentum. ❷ warm up to *sth*; ③ get into one's stride.

矩 the law; teachings; standards

[N] ⓐ ～に蹈える transgress the law; be unlawful; be immoral.

暖簾 a shop curtain; reputation

[N] ～に関わる affect the name of a shop; reflect on the reputation of an enterprise.
[を] ～を売る sell out one's business. ～を下ろす ❶ close down (a shop); go out of business; ⓒ retire from business. ❷ close shop; put up the shutters; ⓒ wind up business. ⓐ ～を掛ける go out of business; go bankrupt; ⓢ go bust. ～を傷つける harm the name of a shop; damage the reputation of an establishment. ～を潜る frequent an establishment; visit a shop. ～を汚す harm the reputation of a shop. ～を分ける start

up in the same business; open up a branch store.

狼煙 a signal fire; a beacon

[を] ～を揚げる ❶ light a signal fire; send up a flare. ❷ launch (a campaign); start (a revolt); trigger (an incident); unleash (a revolution).

八

歯 a tooth; grinders; a cog

[A] ～が痛む have a toothache. ～が浮く be grating; be nauseating; be disgusting; ③ set one's teeth on edge. ⓐ ～が利く ❶ be effective; be of use. ❷ have influence; ③ carry weight. ～が立つ ❶ be edible. ❷ be within one's reach; be able to handle *sth*. ❸ be a match for *sb*; be able to resist *sb*.
[N] ⓐ ～に合う ❶ be edible. ❷ meet one's taste; be suitable.
[を] ⓐ ～を噛む grind one's teeth; gnash one's teeth. ⓐ ～を切る clench one's teeth; grit one's teeth. ～を食い縛る clench one's teeth; grit one's teeth. ⓐ ⓒ ～を切る clench one's teeth; grit one's teeth. ⓑ ～を染める blacken one's teeth. ⓒ ～を出す ❶ show one's teeth; bare one's teeth. ❷ get angry; be irate. ～を立てる sink one's teeth into *sth*.

ハ

~を抜く pull out a tooth; extract a tooth. ~を穿る pick one's teeth. ~を磨く brush one's teeth; polish one's teeth. ~を見せる show one's teeth; grin. ~を剥く ❶ show one's teeth; bare one's teeth. ❷ get angry; be irate; ⓒ ⓘ blow a fuse.

葉 leaves; foliage; needles

A ~が落ちる the leaves fall; lose its leaves. ~が出る the leaves come out; come into leaf.
を ~を枯らす ❶ lose the closs on its leaves; wither. ❷ lose its former splendor; become lack-lustre. ❸ go down in the world; ⓒ be down on one's luck; ⓢ ⓘ go to the dogs.

覇 ᴱ supremacy; leadership

を ~を争う contend for mastery; ⓒ vie for supremacy. ⓒ ~を唱える hold sway; assume the leadership; reign supreme.

刃 a blade; an edge ▶ 刃 (やいば)

を ⓒ ~を付ける sharpen a sword; give an edge to a blade; sharpen a knife; set a razor. ⓒ ~を拾う polish a sword; finish a sword blade.

羽 feathers ▶ 羽 (はね)

A ⓐ ~が利く have influence; ⓘ carry weight (with *sb*).

を ⓐ ~を伸す exert one's influence.

場 a place; a spot; a site

A ~が開く the market opens. ~が立つ a session is held.
を ~を取る occupy space. ~を外す quit a place; ⓒ ⓘ slip away. ~を離れる leave a place; quit a place; ⓒ ⓘ slip away.

場合 an occasion; a juncture

N ~に因る rely on circumstances; depend on the occasion.

場当たり grandstand play

を ~を言う tune one's talk to the company; ⓘ pay lipservice. ~を取る ⓘ win the gallery. ⓒ ~を遣る play to the gallery.

灰 ash; ashes; remains

と ~と成る ❶ be reduced to ashes; be burnt down. ❷ be cremated; be committed to the flames.
N ~にする ❶ reduce *sth* to ashes; burn *sth* down. ❷ cremate *sb's* remains; commit *sb* to the flames. ~に成る ❶ be reduced to ashes; be burnt down. ❷ be cremated; be committed to the flames.

肺肝 ᴱ lungs and liver

を ⓐ ⓒ ~を明かす unbosom oneself;

249

ⓔ admit sb into one's confidence ⓘ pour out one's heart to sb. ⓐⓔ 〜を出だす unbosom oneself; ⓔ admit sb into one's confidence ⓘ pour out one's heart to sb. ⓐⓔ 〜を穿つ see through sb's heart; penetrate sb's mind. ⓐⓔ 〜を砕く think hard about sth; ⓒⓘ rack one's brains. ⓐⓔ 〜を苦しむ think hard about sth; ⓔ tax one's ingenuity; ⓒⓘ rack one's brains. ⓐⓔ 〜を出す unbosom oneself; ⓘ pour out one's heart to sb. ⓐⓔ 〜を尽くす think hard about sth; ⓒⓘ rack one's brains. ⓐⓔ 〜を披く unbosom oneself; ⓔ admit sb into one's confidence ⓘ pour out one's heart to sb.

肺腑 one's inmost heart

を 〜を抉る break one's heart; be heartrending; ⓘ sting one to the quick. 〜を突く hit sb where it hurts; ⓘ touch sb on the raw.

敗北 defeat; a reverse; a rout

を 〜を喫する meet with defeat; taste defeat. 〜を招く court defeat. 〜を認める admit defeat; acknowledge one's defeat.

墓 a grave; a tomb; a sepulcher

N 〜に葬る consign (sb) to the grave. 〜に参る visit sb's grave. を 〜を暴く dig open a grave. 〜を建てる raise a tomb; erect a tombstone. 〜を掘る dig a grave.

捗 progress; advance

A 〜が行く make good progress.

馬鹿 a fool; a simpleton

N 〜にする ❶ make a fool of sb; make fun of sb; slight sb; insult sb. ❷ look down on sb; dispise sb; ⓔ hold sb in contempt. 〜になる ❶ become benumbed; grow dull; go blunt; go flat. ❷ lose one's sense of reason; become irrational; ⓒ go beserk. ❸ restrain oneself; play the fool; ⓘ keep a low profile. を 〜を言う talk nonsense; ⓘ talk through one's hat; ⓒⓘ talk rubbish. 〜を尽す be as stupid as one can be; make countless blunders; blunder on; commit one folly after another. 〜を見る make a fool of oneself; feel like a loser; be disappointed. 〜を遣る make a mistake; commit a stupidity; make a blunder.

場数 experience

を 〜を踏む gain experience; add to one's experience.

秤 a pair of scales

N 〜に掛ける ❶ weigh sth; measure

the weight of *sth*. ❷ compare A with B; weigh the pros and cons (of a matter).

はかりごと
謀 a plan; a scheme

[を] ～を廻らす work out a plan; devise a scheme; ① set a snare.

はぎ　　　　　　 すね
脛 the leg; the shin ▶ 脛

[N] ⓐ ～に上ぐ ❶ turn up one's skirt above the knees. ❷ (心を) open oneself up to *sb*; take *sb* into one's confidence; ① pour out one's heart to *sb*; ⓔ unbosom oneself.

ばきゃく
馬脚 a horse's legs

[を] ～を現わす betray oneself; reveal one's true character; ① show the cloven hoof.

はく
箔 (metal) foil; gold/silver leaf

[A] ～が落ちる ❶ the gilt comes off. ❷ lower one's dignity; lose prestige; lose one's reputation; reflect badly on one. ～が付く gather prestige; gain in reputation. ～が剥げる ❶ the gilt comes off. ❷ lower one's dignity; lose prestige; lose one's reputation; reflect badly on one.

[を] ～を置く gild (an object); cover *sth* with gold/silver leaf. ～を付ける make one/*sth* look more important; add to *sth*'s value; add to one's reputation; reflect well on one. ～を塗る gild (an object); cover *sth* with gold/silver leaf).

ばぐ
馬具 horse gear; harness

[を] ～を付ける harness a horse. ～を外す unharness a horse.

はくし
白紙 blank paper; white paper

[N] ～に返す start anew; begin afresh; ① start with a clean slate. ～に戻す return to the drawing board; start all over again.

はくしゃ
拍車 a spur

[を] (馬)に～を入れる spur on (one's horse). ～を掛ける ❶ spur on (one's horse). ❷ spur *sth* on; give impetus to (a project). ～を加える ❶ spur on (one's horse). ❷ spur *sth* on; give impetus to (a project).

ばくち
博打 gambling; speculation

[を] ～を打つ gamble; play for money; take a gamble. ～を止める give up gambling.

はくひょう
薄氷 thin ice

[を] ～を踏む court danger; ① tread on thin ice; ① play with fire.

はこ
運び a program; a plan

[を] ～を付ける pave the way for (a

project); bring *sth* about; carry *sth* forward; push through (a measure).

鋏 (a pair of) scissors
Ⓐ ～を入れる cut *sth* up; cut *sb's* hair; give *sb* a haircut; edit a film; prune a tree; trim a shrub.

箸 chopsticks
Ⓐ ～が進む eat a lot; eat one's fill. Ⓔ ～を合わす ❶ keep in tune (with *sb*); keep in step (with *sb*); play along with *sb*. ❷ make one's story sound plausible; arrange to tell the same story; say *sth* to suit the occasion; Ⓒ chime in with *sb*. ❸ fulfill one's promise; live up to one's promise. ❹ keep an appointment; Ⓒ meet one's engagement. ～を打つ place the chopsticks on the dining table; lay the table. ～を置く put one's chopsticks down. Ⓒ ～を下ろす start eating; begin to eat. Ⓐ ～を試みる ❶ taste *sth*; sample food; try the taste of *sth*. Ⓒ Ⓢ ❷ sleep with a woman; Ⓒ have intercourse with a woman; Ⓢ lay a woman. ～を使う use chopsticks. ～を付ける start eating; begin to eat. ～を取る ❶ hold chopsticks; take up one's chopsticks. ❷ start eating; begin to eat. ～を休める ❶ put one's chopsticks down. ❷ finish eating.

橋 a bridge
Ⓔ ～を架ける ❶ build a bridge; span (a river with) a bridge; bridge (a river). ❷ establish (friendly) relations; Ⓐ build bridges. ～を潜る pass under a bridge. ～を渡る ❶ build a bridge; span (a river with) a bridge; bridge (a river). ❷ establish (friendly) relations; Ⓐ build bridges. ～を渡る ❶ Ⓒ cross a bridge. ❷ take a risk; Ⓒ make a leap of faith; Ⓐ cross the bridge.

恥 shame; ignominy; disgrace
Ⓔ ～を掻く be put to shame; be embarrassed; be humiliated; Ⓒ be taken down a peg. ～を隠す hide one's shame; escape disgrace; Ⓒ save one's face. Ⓐ ～を雪ぐ exorcize one's feelings of shame. ～を堪える bear the shame; endure the ignominy. ～を曝す disgrace oneself; bring shame upon oneself. ～を忍ぶ swallow one's pride; suppress one's feelings of shame. ～を知る have a sense of shame/honor; be sensible to shame. ～を雪ぐ vindicate one's honor; clear one's name. Ⓐ ～を捨つ be unashamed. ～を雪ぐ vindicate one's honor; clear one's name. ～を包む hide one's shame; escape disgrace; Ⓒ save one's face. ～を取る be put to shame; be embarrassed;

be humiliated; ⓑ be taken down a peg. ⓐ ～を見す put sb to shame; humiliate sb; ⓑ take sb down a peg. ～を見る be put to shame; be embarrassed; be humiliated; ⓑ be taken down a peg. ～を忘れる forget one's shame; be unashamed.

梯子 a ladder; stairs

〚を〛 ～を外される be abandoned; be left to fend for oneself; ⓑ be left in the lurch.

場所 experience

〚を〛 ～を踏む gain experience; add to one's experience.

筈 the notch of an arrow/bow

〚A〛 ～が違う be unexpected; be unforeseen; fall short of one's expectations.

〚を〛 ～を合わす ❶ keep in tune (with sb); keep in step (with sb); play along with sb. ❷ make one's story sound plausible; arrange to tell the same story; ⓑ chime in with sb. ❸ fulfill one's promise; live up to one's promise. ❹ keep an appointment; ⓒ meet one's engagement.

弾み rebound; momentum

〚A〛 ～が付く gain momentum; gather pace; get under way.

〚と〛 ～となる be an impetus; act as an incentive; spur sb on.

〚を〛 ～を打つ spring back; bounce back; release the momentum; jump back. ⓒ ～を食う suffer unforeseen consequences; undergo a backlash.

旗 a flag; a banner; a standard

〚を〛 ～を掲げる ❶ raise a flag; hoist a flag. ❷ rise in arms; raise an army. ❸ set out (to do sth); set up in business. ～を押し立てる unfurl a flag. ～を下ろす take down a flag; strike a flag; lower the flag. ～を掲げる hoist a flag; put up a flag. ～を出す hang out a flag. ～を立てる hoist a flag; put up a flag. ～を振る ❶ wave a flag. ❷ lead a group. ⓓ ～を開く unfurl a flag; put up a flag. ～を広げる unfurl a flag. ⓒ ～を巻く ❶ furl a flag. ❷ withdraw from the battlefield; ⓒ back out (of a situation). ❸ close down (a shop).

肌 the skin; the grain

〚A〛 ～が合う be like-minded; get along well; ⓒ be congenial to one; ⓑ see eye to eye; ⓒ ⓑ hit it off. ～が荒い have a rough skin. ～が綺麗 have a smooth skin.

〚A〛 ～で感じる have first-hand experience; know sth from (bitter) experience.

253

ハダカ

裸
Ⓝ ～に合う suit one; be right for one. (女の)～に触れる know a woman; sleep with a woman; Ⓒ have carnal knowledge of a woman; Ⓢ lay a woman.
Ⓖ ～を合わせる ❶ be close to *sb*; Ⓢ Ⓘ be in cahoots with *sb*. ❷ have sexual intercourse; sleep with each other. ～を入れる slip one's arm(s) back into the sleeves of one's *kimono*. ～を汚す stain one's/*sb's* virtue; rape a woman. ～を脱ぐ ❶ strip oneself to the waist; bare one's shoulders. ❷ exert oneself; do one's utmost. ～を触れる sleep together; lay with a man/woman; have sexual intercourse. (男に)～を許す ❶ give oneself to a man; sleep with a man; Ⓒ Ⓘ go all the way. ❷ let *sb* into one's heart; give one's heart to *sb*; open up to *sb*. ～を汚す stain one's/*sb's* virtue; be unchaste; rape a woman.

旗色 flag color; the situation
Ⓐ ～が良い the prospects are good; the situation is favorable; Ⓒ things look good. ～が悪い the prospects are gloomy; the situation is unfavorable; Ⓒ things look bad.
Ⓖ ～を見る remain an onlooker; Ⓘ see how the wind blows; Ⓘ sit on the fences.

ハナ

裸 a naked body; a nude
Ⓝ ～にする undress *sb*; strip *sb* naked; strip (a tree) of leaves. ～になる ❶ strip oneself naked; get undressed; take off one's clothes. ❷ lose all one's money; become penniless; Ⓒ go broke; Ⓢ go bust.

畑 a field; a farm; a plantation
Ⓐ ～が違う lie outside one's field of expertise.

裸足 bare feet
Ⓝ ～に成る ❶ take of one's shoes. ❷ do *sth* in earnest; set about *sth* in earnerst; get serious about *sth*.
Ⓐ (玄人も)～で逃げる be no match for one; Ⓘ be in a different league; Ⓘ be on different scales.

働き work; workings; operation
Ⓐ ～が有る be a steady worker; be a good provider.

鉢 a (rice)bowl; a (flower)pot
Ⓐ ～が割る lose one's virginity; be deflowered.
Ⓖ ～を托く beg for alms.

蜂 a (honey)bee; a wasp
Ⓖ ～を払う ❶ drive a wasp away. ❷ shake one's head. ❸ deny *sth*; refuse *sth*; turn down (an offer).

罰 ⓑ divine punishment ▶ 罰

[A] ⓒ ～が当たる be punished by the gods; ⓔ feel the wrath of Heaven; ⓔ incur divine punishment.

ばつ ⓑ an occasion; a situation

[A] ⓢ ～が悪い be embarrassed; feel awkward; be ashamed; be abashed; be ill at ease.

[を] ⓒ ⓢ ～を合わせる make one's story sound plausible; arrange to tell the same story; say *sth* to suit the occasion; ⓒ chime in with *sb*.

罰 punishment; penalty ▶ 罰

[を] ～を受ける be punished. ～を加える inflict punishment on *sb*; impose a penalty on *sb*; mete out punishment.

発破 a blast

[を] ～を掛ける ❶ blast *sth* with explosives. ❷ urge *sb* to do *sth*; spur *sb* on (to do *sth*); egg *sb* on.

派手 gaudiness; flashiness

[を] ～を売る make a big show; ⓔ be ostentatious; ⓒ cut a splash.

花 a flower; a blossom; youth

[A] ～が咲く ❶ ⓒ be in bloom; be in blossom. ❷ be prosperous; do well. ❸ grow lively; liven up.

[と] ～と散る be killed in action; fall in battle; die on the battlefield.

[N] ～に酔う be intoxicated with the beauty of flowers.

[を] ～を活ける arrange flowers; put flowers in (a vase). ⓢ ～を折る ❶ dress oneself up; adorn oneself; smarten oneself up; ⓒ go in one's Sunday best. ❷ have good looks; have a graceful figure. ～を飾る decorate *sth* with flowers; dress *sth* up. ～を切る cut flowers. ～を咲かせる ❶ make something prosperous; make *sth* flourish; invigorate *sth*. ❷ win fame; be successful; ⓒ bring home the bacon. ～を添える add luster to *sth*. ～を散らす ❶ conduct the Buddhist rite of scattering flowers. ❷ fight at close quarters; exchange blows; ⓒ come to blows. ❸ take issue with *sb*; ⓔ engage in a battle of words; have a heated argument; ⓒ cross swords with *sb*. ❹ marr the beauty of *sth*; spoil *sth*. ～を作る grow flowers. ～を摘む pick flowers; gather flowers. ～を引く play cards. ～を持たせる let *sb* have the credit for (a success); give *sb* credit; ⓔ bestow favors on *sb*. ～を遣る ❶ dress oneself up; adorn oneself; smarten oneself up; ⓒ go in one's Sunday best. ❷ live in luxury; lead a life of luxury; ⓒ live the life of Riley. ❸ be popular; be (widely) praized; be lionized.

はな
鼻 a nose; a muzzle; a trunk

[A] ⓐ ～が明く be disappointed; be frustrated. ～が利く ❶ have a good nose; have a good scent. ❷ be good at making money; ⓘ have a nose for *sth*. ～が高い be proud; be vain; be haughty; ⓔ have a high opinion of oneself; ⓢ be stuck up. ～が閊える be exeedingly cramped. ～が詰まる have a stopped up nose. ～が強い be headstrong; be obstinate; ⓒ ⓘ be stiff-necked. ⓐ ～が拉げる be discouraged; be squashed; be crushed; give way. ～が凹む be talked down; be cornered; ⓘ be brought to bay. ～が曲がる smell offensive.

[Av] ～であしらう treat *sb* with contempt; snub *sb*; ⓘ thumb one's nose at *sb*. ～で笑う laugh sardonically at *sb*; ⓒ snicker at *sb*.

[N] ～に当てる boast about *sth*; be proud of *sth*; take pride in *sth*. (言葉が)～に掛ける speak through the nose; have a nasal voice. (何かを)～に掛ける boast about *sth*; be proud of *sth*; take pride in *sth*. ～に付く ❶ smell offensive; be disgusting. ❷ get sick and tired of *sth*; ⓒ be fed up with *sth*. (何かを)～にぶら下げる boast about *sth*; take pride in *sth*.

[No] (言葉が)～へ掛かる speak through the nose; have a nasal voice. (何かを)～へ掛ける boast about *sth*; be proud of *sth*; take pride in *sth*.

[wo] (人の)～を明かす ❶ forestall *sb*; get a start on *sb*; preempt *sb's* actions; anticipate *sb* in doing *sth*. ❷ outwit *sb*; surprise *sb*. ～を蠢かす be elated; be puffed up with pride. ～を打つ ❶ snort one's nose. ❷ smell offensive; ⓒ assail the nostrils. ～を折る humble *sb's* pride; ⓘ put *sb's* nose out of joint; ⓘ take *sb* down a peg. ⓐ ～を欠く suffer a loss; incur a setback. ～を挫く snub *sb*; ⓒ humble *sb's* pride; ⓘ take *sb* down a peg. ～を揃える line up (horses). (人の)～を出し抜く ❶ forestall *sb*; get a start on *sb*; preempt *sb's* actions; anticipate *sb* in doing *sth*. ❷ outwit *sb*; surprise *sb*. ～を突き合わせる be face to face. ～を衝く ❶ smell offensive; ⓒ assail the nostrils. ❷ be face to face. ❸ have a clash of personalities; have a conflict; fall out with *sb*. ❹ be disinherited; be cut off. ～を撮まれる be disliked; put people off. ～を撮む hold one's nose. ～を鳴らす ❶ sniff one's nose. ❷ coo at *sb*; sulk over *sth*; behave like a spoilt child. ❸ look down on *sb*; treat *sb* with contempt; snort at *sb*. ～を並べる line

up (horses). Ⓐ ～を舐（ねぶ）る loaf around; idle away one's time. ～を弾（はじ）く ❶ assail the nostrils; smell offensive. ❷ humble *sb's* pride; ⓘ put *sb's* nose out of joint. ～を拉（ひし）ぐ snub *sb*; ⓒ humble *sb's* pride; ⓘ take *sb* down a peg. ⓓ ～を放（ひ）る sneeze. ～を圧（へ）し折（お）る make *sb* bite the dust; ⓒ ⓘ put *sb's* nose out of joint. ～を穿（ほじ）る pick one's nose.

洟（はな） nasal muscus; snivel; drivel

[を] ～をかむ blow one's nose. ～を啜（すす）る snif one's nose. ～を垂（た）らす run at the nose; have a runny nose. ～を拭（ふ）く wipe one's nose.

鼻脂（はなあぶら） nose fat

[を] ～を引く ❶ smoothen (a surface) with nose fat. ❷ make things run smoothely; ⓒ ⓘ grease the wheels. ❸ put a finish on *sth*; give *sth* a finishing touch.

鼻息（はないき） nasal breath

[A] ～が荒（あら）い ❶ breathe hard through the nose. ❷ be arrogant; be haughty; be proud; have an overbearing attitude.
[を] ⓒ ～を仰（あお）ぐ sound out *sb's* feelings; ⓒ consult *sb's* pleasure. ～を窺（うかが）う sound out *sb's* feelings; ⓒ consult *sb's* pleasure.

鼻歌（はなうた） humming

[を] ～を歌（うた）う hum a tune.

鼻薬（はなぐすり） "nose medicine"; a bribe

[を] ～を嗅（か）がせる offer *sb* a bribe; bribe *sb*; ⓒ ⓘ grease *sb's* palm. ～を効（き）かせる offer *sb* a bribe; bribe *sb*; ⓒ ⓘ grease *sb's* palm.

鼻毛（はなげ） nasal hair

[A] ～が長（なが）い be infatuated with a woman; be keen on a girl; ⓒ be besotted with a woman.
[を] Ⓐ ～を数（かぞ）える make fun of *sb* who is infatuated with one; ⓘ wrap *sb* round one's little finger; ⓒ poke fun at one's suitor. ～を抜（ぬ）く ❶ pull out one's nasal hair. ❷ outwit *sb*; deceive *sb*; ⓒ ⓘ lead *sb* by the nose. ～を延（の）ばす be infatuated with a woman; be keen on a girl; ⓒ be mad about a woman; ⓑ be besotted with a woman. ⓒ ～を読（よ）む make fun of *sb* who is infatuated with one; ⓘ wrap *sb* round one's little finger; ⓒ poke fun at one's suitor.

鼻先（はなさき） the tip of one's nose

[A] ～で笑（わら）う laugh sardonically at *sb*; ⓒ snicker at *sb*.

話（はなし） a talk; a chat; a rumor

[A] ～が合（あ）う understand each other;

get on well; agree with each other. ～が有る have *sth* to say; have *sth* on one's mind. ～が遅い be a slow speaker; be slow of speech. ⓪ ～が落ちる talk wildly; talk indecently; talk lewdly. ～が染む have a lively conversation. ～が違う be a different matter; be a different story. ～が付く ❶ reach an agreement; come to an understanding. ❷ strike a bargain; close a deal; ① shake hands on *sth*. ～が出来る be able to talk; understand each other. ～が弾む have a lively conversation. ～が早い ❶ ube a quick speaker; be quick of speech. ❷ see eye to eye; ⓒ ① be on the same wavelength. ～が纏まる come to an agreement; reach a settlement; ⓒ wrap *sth* up. ～が分かる ❶ understand *sb*; empathize with *sb*. ❷ be sensible; know what is what. Ⓝ ～に乗る give *sb* counsel; counsel *sb*. ～にならない be not worth mentioning; be trivial; be not worth one's while; be too ridiculous for words. ～に触れる touch upon a subject; broach a subject. ⓩ ～を変える change the subject (of conversation). ～をし掛ける speak to *sb*; accost *sb*. ～を決める come to an agreement; reach a settlement; ⓒ ① wrap *sth* up. ～を切り出す broach a subject; raise an issue. ～をする have a conversation; have a chat. ～を逸らす turn the conversation to a different subject; steer the conversation in a different direction. ～を付ける settle a matter; make arrangements with *sb*; negotiate with *sb*. ～を続ける continue to talk; keep up the conversation. ～を始める start a conversation; begin a story. ～を端折る make a long story short; cut the matter short; ⓒ ① get to the point; ① cut to the chase. ～を纏める come to an agreement with *sb*; reach a settlement; ⓢ wrap *sth* up. ～を結ぶ conclude a conversation. ～を持ち掛ける approach *sb* with a matter; make *sb* a proposal. ～を持ち込む propose a matter; make *sb* a proposal. ～を持ち出す bring up a subject; put forward a matter; broach a subject.

はなすじ
鼻筋 the bridge of the nose

Ⓐ ～が通る have a straight nose.

はなばしら
鼻柱 the bridge of a nose; pride

Ⓐ ～が強い be headstrong; be obstinate; ⓒ ① be stiff-necked. ⓩ ～を折る snub *sb*; ⓔ humble *sb*'s pride; ① take *sb* down a peg. ～を挫く snub *sb*; ⓔ humble *sb*'s pride; ① take *sb* down a peg. ～を圧し折る

make sb bite the dust; ⓒⓘ put sb's nose out of joint.

鼻笛 humming

[を] 〜を吹く ❶ hum a tune. ❷ be in a good mood; be pleased with oneself; chuckle over sth.

花実 flowers and seeds

[Ａ] 〜が咲く achieve success; come to a good end; ⓒⓘ make good.

刎ね splashes (of mud); a close

[Ａ] ⓐ 〜が付く be settled; be brought to an end.
[を] (着物に)〜を上げる get spatters of mud on one's clothes. (着物に)〜を掛ける get spatters of mud on one's clothes. ⓐ 〜を付ける settle sth; bring sth to an end. ⓑ 〜を取る ❶ take a percentage; take a rake-off. ❷ be a great success; be a big hit; ⓘ pull off a great coup.

羽 a feather; a wing ▶ 羽

[Ａ] 〜が抜ける shed feathers. 〜が生える fledge.
[を] ⓐ 〜を交す act like two turtle doves; have a loving marriage. 〜を畳む fold the wings. ⓑ 〜を垂る ❶ go down on one's knees; grovel in the dirt. ❷ surrender oneself; capitulate (to the enemy); submit to one's rival; ⓘ hoist a white flag. ⓐ 〜を並べる ❶ act like two turtle doves; be a loving man and wife. ⓐ ❷ give collective counsel to (one's lord). 〜を伸ばす have a good time; ⓐ spread one's wings; ⓢⓘ kick up one's heels. 〜を広げる spread the wings.

幅 width; breadth; influence

[Ａ] 〜が利く have influence with sb; be influential.
[Ｎ] 〜にする ❶ get one's own way; see sth through. ❷ take pride in sth; be proud of sth. ⓐ 〜に成る gain prestige; win fame; be widely recognized.
[を] 〜を利かす make one's influence felt; lord it over sb; assert one's power. ⓐ 〜をする be vain; show off; ⓒ be ostentatious; be haughty. 〜を取る ❶ occupy a wide space. ❷ make one's influence felt; assert one's power. ❸ leave sufficient room; make allowances; allow for sth. ⓑ 〜を成す ❶ make one's influence felt; lord it over sb; assert one's power. ❷ make oneself at home; put oneself at ease. ⓑ 〜を遣る make one's influence felt; lord it over sb; assert one's power.

羽振り influence; authority

[Ｎ] 〜が利く command respect; be

authoritative; have influence; ⓘ carry weight. ～が良い command respect; be authoritative; have influence; ⓘ carry weight.

㋾ ～が利かす make one's influence felt; ⓘ lord it over *sb*.

羽目 a panel; a situation; a pass

Ⓝ ～に陥る be in a quandary; be in a sad plight; ⓒ ⓘ be in a fix; ⓢ ⓘ be up the creek. ～に落ちる be in a quandary; be in a sad plight; ⓒ ⓘ be in a fix; ⓢ ⓘ be up the creek. ～に掛かる get carried away by *sth*; get into *sth*; ⓘ do *sth* on the spur of the moment. ～に付く ⓐ ❶ welcome a new inmate by pressing him agenst the wainscot. ❷ be in a quandary; be in a sad plight; ⓒ ⓘ be in a fix; ⓢ ⓘ be up the creek. ～になる be in a quandary; be in a sad plight; ⓒ ⓘ be in a fix.

㋾ ～を外す make merry; make a racket; ⓒ ⓘ let one's hair down.

馬銜 a bit; a mouthpiece

㋾ ～を銜える ❶ take the bit; fret at the bit. ❷ be impatient; be anxious; be in a hurry; be eager; ⓘ chafe at the bit. ～を外す make merry; make a racket; ⓒ ⓘ let one's hair down. ～を放つ make merry; make a racket; ⓒ ⓘ let one's hair down.

刃物 cutlery; an edged tool

㋾ ～を渡る court danger; ⓘ tread on thin ice; ⓘ play with fire.

波紋 a water ring; a ripple

Ⓐ ～が広がる ❶ create a ripple (on a pond); ripple out. ❷ have repercussions; the rumor spreads; ⓘ make a stir.

㋾ ～を描く ❶ create a water ring; ripple out. ❷ have repercussions; ⓘ make a stir. ～を投じる have major repercussions; ⓘ make a stir. ～を投げ掛ける cause a sensation; ⓘ make a stir.

早耳 "a quick ear"; "quick ears"

㋾ ～を走らせる come to a hasty conclusion; ⓘ jump to conclusions.

腹 the stomach; the abdomen

Ⓐ ⓐ ～が合う be like-minded; get along well; ⓒ have the same disposition; ⓔ be congenial to one; ⓘ see eye to eye; ⓒ ⓘ hit it off. ～が有る harbor a secret; have a hidden agenda; have an ulterior motive; ⓘ have an axe to grind. ⓐ ～が癒える ❶ settle old scores; ⓘ get one's own back; revenge oneself on *sb*; wreak one's wrath. ❷ cool one's anger; calm down; ⓐ cool down; work off one's grudge. ❸ vent one's spleen; give vent to one's feelings. 〜が痛む ❶ have a stomachache; have the gripes. ❷ be a financial burden; bear the financial burden. ⓐ 〜が居る cool one's anger; calm down; ⓐ cool down; work off one's grudge. 〜が大きい be magnanimous; be big-hearted 〜が収まる calm down; ⓐ cool down. 〜が汚い ❶ be perverted; be blackhearted. ❷ be treacherous; be cowardly; be unfair; be mean. 〜が寂しい have little money; ⓒ be hard up; ⓘ be in dire straits. 〜が決まる have one's mind made up; be resolved; be determined. 〜が腐る be corrupted; be despicable. 〜が下る have loose bowels; suffer from diarrhea. 〜が黒い be treacherous; be perverted; be blackhearted. 〜が空く have an empty stomach; be hungry. 〜が据る have the stomach to do sth; ⓒ have guts; have pluck; be bold. 〜が立つ get angry; lose one's temper; ⓢ ⓘ blow a fuse. 〜が出来る ❶ be full; have eaten one's fill. ❷ have one's mind made up; be resolved; be determined. 〜が出る have a potbelly; ⓢ ⓘ have a spare tire. ⓒ 〜が無い ❶ be ungenerous; be mean. ❷ lack courage; be timid; be cowardly. 〜が煮え繰り返る be infuriated; be irate; be furious; ⓒ be beside oneself with rage. 〜が煮え become irritated; be upset over sth; be cross with sb. 〜が張る be fully fed; feel bloated. 〜が膨れる ❶ be full; have eaten one's fill. ⓓ ⓢ ❷ become pregnant; have sb's child; ⓔ be with child. ❸ hold a grudge against sb; ⓔ harbor a private malice; ⓘ have an axe to grind; ⓘ have a chip on one's shoulder. ❹ be frustrated; feel thwarted. 〜が太い ❶ be brazen; be cheeky. ❷ be magnanimous; be generous; be big-hearted. 〜が減る have an empty stomach; be hungry. 〜が見え透く be seen through; be exposed.

[Av] 〜で行く ❶ do sth in earnest; set about sth in earnerst; get serious about sth. ❷ be bold; be resolute; ⓘ face the music; ⓘ take the bull by the horns.

[N] ⓐ 〜に合う ❶ understand sb; get on well with sb; agree with sb; ⓘ see eye to eye with sb; ⓒ ⓘ hit it off. ❷ suit one's taste; agree with one. 〜に味わう savor sth; take sth in; let sth sink in. ⓒ 〜に入る grasp the meaning of sth; learn how to do sth; master the art of sth. 〜に収める keep sth in mind; bear sth in mind; make a mental note of sth. 〜に落ちる be convinced; be persuaded; come round to sb's point of view; give one's consent. 〜に据え兼

ねる be intolerable; be unbearable; ⓒ be insufferable. ～に持つ ❶ bare sb ill will; harbor a grudge against sb; have an underlying motive; ① have an axe to grind. ❷ entertain (an idea); harbor (a grudge); hold sth; hide sth.
[腹] Ⓐ ～へ落ちる be convinced; be persuaded; come round to sb's point of view; give one's consent.
[腹] ⓒ ～を合わす collaborate with sb; conspire with sb; ⓢ ① be in cahoots with sb. ～を痛める ❶ go into labor; give birth. ❷ suffer financial losses. ❸ pay out of one's own pocket; Ⓐ untie one's purse strings; ① foot the bill. ～を癒す ❶ settle old scores; ① get one's own back; revenge oneself on sb; wreak one's wrath. ❷ cool one's anger; calm down; Ⓐ cool down; work off one's grudge. ❸ vent one's spleen; give vent to one's feelings. ～を入れる calm oneself down; compose oneself; work off one's grudge. Ⓐ ～を入れる apply oneself to sth; do sth wholeheartedly. ～を括る wring one's heart; ① turn one's stomach upside down; ⓒ feel gutted. ～を抱える hold one's sides (with laughter). ～を貸す become a surrogate mother; carry the child of another couple. ～を固める make up one's mind; resolve to do sth; ① gird up one's loins. ～を決める make up one's mind; resolve to do sth; ① gird up one's loins. ～を切る ❶ disembowel oneself; commit suicide. ❷ resign from office; leave office; step down from office. ❸ take responsibility; ⓒ ① face the music; ⓒ ① bite the bullet. ❹ ① laugh one's head off; ⓒ ① kill oneself laughing. ❺ pay out of one's own pocket; Ⓐ untie one's purse strings; ① foot the bill. ❻ [rowing] make a faulty stroke; ① catch a crab. ～を括る brace oneself; resolve to do sth; ① gird up one's loins. ～を下す evacuate the bowels; have diarrhea. ⓒ ～を拵える have a meal to fortify oneself; satisfy one's appetite; eat one's fill. ～を肥やす enrich oneself; ① line one's pocket; ① feather one's nest. ～を壊す have stomach trouble; upset one's stomach. ～を探る ❶ sound sb out; feel sb out; ⓒ check sb's mood. ❷ examine sb's stomach; subject sb's stomach to a medical examination. ～を摩る rub one's stomach. Ⓐ ～を締める brace oneself; resolve to do sth; ① gird up one's loins. ～を据える ❶ make up one's mind; prepare oneself for sth; ① gird up one's loins. ❷ calm oneself; collect one's senses. ❸ cool

one's anger; vent one's spleen; give vent to one's feelings. ～を空かす work up an appetite. ～を立てる get angry; take offense at *sth*; get worked up over *sth*; lose one's temper; ⓢ ① blow a fuse. ～を解く evacuate the bowels; have diarrhea. ～を見せる display one's generosity; act magnanimously. ～を見抜く see through *sb*; read *sb's* mind. ～を見る see into *sb's* heart; read *sb's* mind. Ⓐ ～を召す disembowel oneself; commit suicide. ～を病む ❶ have a stomachache; have the gripes. ❷ have a stomach disorder; have an intestinal ailment. ❸ be seized with labor pains; go into labor. ～を捩じる ① hold one's sides with laughter; ① laugh one's head off; ⓒ ① kill oneself laughing. ～を読む fathom *sb's* thoughts; read *sb's* mind. ～を縒る ① split one's sides with laughter; ① hold one's sides with laughter. ～を割る speak one's mind; be outspoken; be candid; be frank.

ばら 图 loose

图 ⓢ ～で売る sell *sth* loose; sell *sth* in bulk. ⓢ ～で買う buy *sth* loose; boy *sth* in bulk.

はらわた
腸 the intestines; the bowels

Ⓐ ～が腐る become depraved; be perverted; be corrupted. ～が千切れる wring one's heart; be heartbroken; ⓒ feel gutted. ～が煮え返る be infuriated; be irate; be furious. ～が見え透く be exposed.

Ⓝ ～に沁みる ❶ have a pleasant sensation (when drinking alcohol). ❷ sink deeply into one's mind; be deeply impressed.

囲 ～を括る wring one's heart; ① turn one's stomach upside down; ⓒ feel gutted. ～を搔き毟る wring one's heart; ① turn one's stomach upside down; ⓔ rend one's heart; break one's heart. ⓢ ～を切る roll over laughing; ① laugh one's head off; ⓒ ① kill oneself laughing. ～を探る sound *sb* out; feel *sb* out; ⓒ check *sb's* mood. ～を絞る wring one's heart; ⓔ rend one's heart; ① turn one's stomach upside down; break one's heart. ～を断つ ❶ wring one's heart; ⓔ rend one's heart; ① turn one's stomach upside down; break one's heart. ❷ roll over laughing; ① laugh one's head off; ⓒ ① kill oneself laughing. ～を抜く remove the guts; gut (a fish).

はり
針 a needle; a pin; a pointer

囲 ～を吐く speak harshly; sneer at *sb*; use barbed words. ⓢ ～を含む have a sting.

馬力 horse power
- [A] ～が有る have stamina.
- [を] ～を掛ける exert oneself; ⓪ work one's fingers to the bone.

春 spring; springtime
- [N] ～に会う be prosperous; be fortunate; ⓒ do well.
- [を] ～を売る sell one's chastity; prostitute oneself. ～を鬻ぐ sell one's chastity; prostitute oneself.

ばれ [日] a failure
- [A] ⑤ ～が来る be a failure; come to grief; break down.
- [N] ⑤ ～に成る be spoiled; be ruined; go wrong; go bad.

馬齢 [日] one's age
- [を] ⓪ ～を重ねる gather years in idleness; grow old without any accomplishments. ⒶⒺ ～を加う gather years in idleness; grow old without any accomplishments.

判 a (hand) stamp; a seal
- [を] ～を押す seal (a bond); affix a seal. ⓪ ～を貸す stand surety for sb; go bail for sb.

範 [日] an example; a model
- [を] ～を示す set an example. ～を垂れる set an example. ⓪ ～を採る follow sb's example. ⓪ ～を似做う copy sb's example.

番 watch; guard; one's turn
- [A] ⓪ ～が明ける be off watch.
- [N] ～に当たる be on duty. ～に立つ be on guard; stand guard.
- [を] ～を狂わせる disturb the order. ～をする watch over (a house); stand guard; look after sth. ～を待つ wait for one's turn.

範囲 an extent; a scope; a sphere
- [を] ～を限る set limits; limit (the scope of) sth; fix the limits of sth. ～を越える exceed a limit; transcend the boundaries.

反感 animosity; antipathy
- [を] ～を抱く hold a grudge against sb; harbor ill feelings toward sb. ～を買う arouse sb's antipathy; incur sb's ill feeling. ～を示す show one's antipathy. ～をそそる provoke antipathy.

反旗 [日] a banner of revolt
- [を] ⓪ ～を翻す rise in revolt; take up arms (against sb); ⓒ raise the standard of revolt.

反響 an echo; reverberation
- [を] ～を起こす cause repercussions;

be much talked about; ⓒ make a stir. 〜を呼び起こす evoke a response; ⓒ make a stir.

はんけつ
判決 a judicial decision

[N] 〜に服する accept a judicial decision. [を] 〜を言い渡す deliver judgment; ⓒ pronounce sentence on *sb*. 〜を下す decide (on a case); pass judgment (on a case). 〜を取り消す reverse a decision. 〜を待つ await a descision. 〜を読み上げる read out the decision.

はんざ
反座 "half a seat"

[N] 〜に分く share a seat with *sb*.

はんじょう
半畳 half a *tatami*

[を] ⓐ 〜を入れる jeer at *sb*; hoot at *sb*; heckle *sb*; ⓒⓘ give *sb* the bird. ⓐ 〜を打つ jeer at *sb*; hoot at *sb*; heckle *sb*; ⓒⓘ give *sb* the bird.

はんだん
判断 judgment; decision

[を] 〜を誤る err in one's judgment; judge wrongly. 〜を下す take a decision; make a judgment.

バトン a baton

[を] 〜を渡す ❶ hand over the baton. ❷ transfer the reins of power; make place for one's successor.

ばんなん
万難 [E] innumerable difficulties

[を] ⓔ 〜を排する do *sth* at all costs; overcome all kinds of difficulties.

はんらん
反乱 a rebellion; a revolt

[を] 〜を起こす rise in revolt; rebel against. 〜を静める put down a revolt; pacify a rebellion.

ヒ

ひ
日 the sun; a day; a date

[A] 〜が上がる the sun rises; the sun goes up. 〜が浅い be not long since; be only recent. 〜が当たる ❶ be in the sun; bask in the sun. ❷ be favored by circumstances; ⓘ have one's day in the sun. 〜が良い ❶ be an auspicious day; be a good day (far a certain occasion. ❷ have a lucky day; have a good day. 〜が移る the sun moves (from east to west). 〜が落ちる the sun goes down; the sun sets. 〜が傾く the sun is getting low; the sun declines. 〜が陰る the sun goes behind the clouds; the sun is eclipsed. 〜が暮れる it grows dark; night falls; the day declines. ⓒ 〜が込む take time; be time-consuming. 〜が差す the sunlight stings. 〜が沈む the sun sets; the sun goes down. 〜が高い the sun is high; the day is (still) high; be still

early days. ～が詰(つ)まる the days grow shorter. ～が出(で)る the sun rises; the sun goes up. ～が長(なが)い the days are long. ～が昇(のぼ)る the sun rises. ～が入(はい)る the sun sets; the sun goes down. ～が短(みじか)い the days are short. ～が悪(わる)い ❶ be an inauspicious day; be a bad day (far a certain occasion. ❷ have an unlucky day; have a bad day.
Ⓝ ～に当(あ)てる bask in the sun; sun oneself; expose *sth* to the sun. ～に干(ほ)す dry *sth* in the sun. ～に焼ける get sunburned.
Ⓚ ～を改(あらた)める change the day; do *sth* another time. Ⓐ ～を入(い)れる let in the sunlight. ～を選(えら)ぶ choose a date; name the day. ～を追(お)う the days pass by. ～を重(かさ)ねる gather time. ～を数(かぞ)える count the days. ～を限(かぎ)る give a time limit; set a deadline. Ⓐ ～を切(き)る give a time limit; set a deadline. ～を暮(く)らす pass one's days; spend one's time. Ⓐ ～を消(け)す pass one's days; spend one's time. ～を定(さだ)める fix a date; set a date. ～を延(の)ばす put *sth* off; postpone *sth*. Ⓐ ～を旧(ふ)る gather years; grow old. ～を経(へ)る pass the days; go through the days. ～を見(み)る cast a horoscope for the day. ～を避(よ)ける avoid the sun; keep off the sun; shield oneself from the sun.

火(ひ) a fire; a flame; a blaze
Ⓐ ～が移(うつ)る the fire spreads; catch on fire. ～が高(たか)ぶる ❶ get carried away; get (too) excited; ⓘ lose one's head. ❷ be sexually aroused; ⓘ be turned on ⓢ feel horny. ～が付(つ)く ❶ catch fire. ❷ a (crisis) breaks out; erupt into (a crisis); (war) breaks out. ～が出(で)る see stars; see red. Ⓐ ～が降(ふ)る be badly off; ⓘ be in dire straits. ～が燃(も)える a fire is burning.
Ⓝ ～に当(あ)たる warm oneself at a fire. ～に入(い)る ❶ court danger; ⓘ tread on thin ice; ⓘ play with fire. ❷ ruin oneself; destroy oneself; ⓢⓘ go to the dogs. ～に掛(か)ける put *sth* over a fire. ～に焼(や)べる put *sth* into the fire; throw (logs) on the fire.
Ⓚ ～を扇(あお)ぐ fan a fire. Ⓐ ～を挙(あ)ぐ ❶ make a fire; light a fire. ❷ make a living. Ⓐ ～を活(い)ける bank up a fire; damp down a fire. ～を打(う)つ strike a spark; make fire. ～を起(お)こす build a fire. ～を落(お)とす rake out a fire. Ⓗ ～を易(か)う purify a ritual fire. ～を搔(か)き立(た)てる stir a fire. ～を掛(か)ける ❶ set fire to *sth*; set *sth* alight. ❷ open fire (on the enemy); take (the enemy) under fire. Ⓐ ～を被(かぶ)る be overcome with grief; grief over *sth*; Ⓐ cover oneself in ashes. ～を切(き)る strike a spark; make fire. ～を消(け)

す ❶ put out a fire; extinguish a fire. ❷ turn off the light; switch off the light. ❸ put a damper on (sb's enthusiasm); ④ pour cold water on (sb's enthusiasm). ～を失す cause a fire by accident. ④ ～を摩る ❶ make fire by friction. ❷ burn with resentment; boil with dissension. ～を焚き付ける kindle a fire; make a fire. ～を出す have a fire started. ～を立てる signal by way of making a fire. ～を散らす ❶ throw off sparks; emit sparks. ❷ fight desperately; ⓒ engage in a fierce contest; fight to the death. ❸ argue heatedly in favor/against sth; debate sth hotly; ⓒ engage in a heated debate; ④ sparks fly. ～を使う use fire. ～を注ぐ replenish a fire. ～を付ける ❶ set fire to sth; set sth alight. ❷ turn on the light; switch on the light. ❸ trigger an event; start a conflict. ⓒ instigate a row. ～を通す heat sth up; warm sth up. ～を灯す light a lamp. ～を吐く spit fire; emit fire; erupt into flames. ❷ argue heatedly in favor/against sth; debate sth hotly; ⓒ engage in a heated debate; ④ sparks fly. ～を放つ set fire to sth. ～を噴く ❶ blow life into a fire. ❷ erupt into flames; emit fire; breathe fire. ❸ snore loudly. ④ ～を振る ❶ stir a fire; rake up a fire. ❷ start a quarrel with sb; pick a fight with sb. ～を弄ぶ play with fire. ～を燃やす make a fire; light a fire; start a fire.

ひ
非 a fault; an injustice; a wrong

[A] ～が入る be criticized; ⓒ be the subject of criticism; be blamed; be reproached; ④ come under fire. [を] ～を暴く discover one's faults. ⓒ ～を打つ ❶ point out sb's error; find fault with sb. ❷ criticize sb; censure sb; blame sb. ～を飾る hide one's faults. ～を悟る realize one's error. ～を遂ぐ push sth through (though one should know better). ～を鳴らす reproach sb; denounce (a traitor). ～を認める admit one's error; acknowledge one's faults.

び
美 beauty; grace; charm

[を] ～を添える add beauty to sth; give added grace to sth. ～を尽す be dazzlingly beautiful.

びう
眉宇 Ⓔ the brow

[を] ⓒ ～を輝かす beam (with joy).

ひがら
日柄 the kind of day

[A] ～が良い ❶ be an auspicious day; be a good day (far a certain occasion. ❷ have a lucky day; have a good day. ～が悪い ❶ be an inauspi-

cious day; be a bad day (far a certain occasion). ❷ have an unlucky day; have a bad day.
[を] ～を選ぶ choose an auspicous day; set the right date.

光り a ray; a beam; a gleam
[を] (人の)～を奪う outshine others; eclipse others. ～を韜む ❶ hide one's talents; ⓘ hide one's light under a bushel. ❷ keep company with the vulgar; hide one's virtues. ～を放つ ❶ emit light; give out light; send out rays of light. ❷ display one's talents; demonstrate one's genius; show one's virtues. ～を和らぐ ❶ hide one's talents; ⓘ hide one's light under a bushel. ❷ ⓘ keep one's head down; ⓘ keep a low profile. ❸ hide one's virtues; keep company with the vulgar.

美観 a nice view; a fine spectacle
[を] ～を傷つける mar the beauty of sth; spoil the view. ～を添える add to the beauty of sth; lend beauty to sth. ⓒ ～を呈する present a fine spectacle.

引き合い reference; an inquiry
[N] ～に出す refer to (an instance); quote a precedent; mention a case. ～に付く become involved; be netangled (in a plot); be implicated (in a crime); get embroiled (in a quarrel). ～に付ける involve sb in a situation; entangle sb (in a plot); implicate sb (in a crime).
[を] ⓘ ～を受ける recieve an inquiry; recieve a letter of inquiry. ⓘ ～を出す send out an inquiry; write a letter of inquiry.

引き金 a trigger
[と] ～と成る begin sth; trigger off (an incident); touch sth off.
[N] ～に成る begin sth; trigger off (an incident); touch sth off.
[を] ～を引く pull the trigger; squeeze the trigger.

引出し a drawer
[A] ～が違う have a false idea of sth; ⓒ ⓘ hold the wrong end of the stick.
[を] ～を開ける open a drawer. ～を閉める close a drawer. ～を抜く remove a drawer.

引け a loss; a defeat; a close
[A] ⓐ ～が立つ sustain a (financial) loss; suffer a (financial) setback.
[N] ～に成る ❶ come to an end; be over; break up. ❷ be indebted to sb; be obliged to sb; owe sb a favor. ❸ be disgraced; ⓒ bring disgrace upon oneself; ⓘ lose face

を ⑩ ～を打つ sound the closing bell of the licensed quarters. ⑦ ～を立てる ❶ pay a commission; pay a charge. ❷ pay for damages; indemnify sb for a financial setback. ～を付ける ❶ outstrip sb; eclipse sb. ❷ make sb feel inferior; humble sb; ⓘ take sb down a peg. ～を取る ❶ be outstripped; be outdone; be eclipsed. ❷ be beaten; suffer a defeat; ⓘ bite the dust.

髭 a beard; a mustache

A ～が多い ❶ give oneself airs; be pompous; ⓒ be ostentatious; ⓘ put on airs; ⓢⓘ be stuck-up. ❷ say bad things about sb; abuse sb; speak ill of sb; bad-mouth sb; ⓢ slur sb.

を ～を扱く stroke one's beard. ～を剃る shave oneself; have a shave. ～を蓄える grow a beard/mustache; have a beard/mustache. ⓘ ～を取る shave off one's beard/mustache. ～を撫でる ❶ stroke one's beard/mustache. ❷ be in a good mood; be pleased with oneself; chuckle over sth. ～を生やす grow a beard/mustache; have a beard/mustache. ～を捻る twirl one's mustache.

引け目 inferiority; a weakness

を ～を感じる feel inferior; feel small (in sb's presence). ～を見せる show signs of weakness; display one's sense of inferiority.

鼻孔 the nostril

を ～を膨らませる flare one's nostrils.

膝 the knee; one's lap

A ～が流れる lose out against sb; lose ground; give way; give in. ～が抜ける one's knees give way. ～が笑う be unsteady on one's legs.

を ～を抱く ❶ be lonely; ⓒ be forlorn. ❷ entreat sb (for mercy); implore sb. ⓐ ～を容れる ❶ set foot in (a place). ❷ join the party; join the conversation; ⓒ join in. ～を打つ ❶ agree with sb. ❷ be impressed by sth. ❸ call sth to mind. ～を折る ❶ sit on one's knees; bend one's knees. ❷ bow to sb; yield to sb; submit to sb. ～を屈める ❶ bend one's knees. ❷ bow to sb; yield to sb; submit to sb. ～を崩す ❶ relax one's knees; sit at ease. ❷ yield to sb; give in (to a demand). ～を組む ❶ cross one's legs; sit cross-legged. ❷ sit (down) with sb; sit face to face with sb. ～を進める ❶ come closer to sb/sth; draw near to sb/sth; be drawn into sth. ❷ be drawn in; grow interested in sb/sth; warm up to sb/sth. ～を抱く ❶ be lonely; ⓒ be forlorn. ❷ entreat *sb* (for mercy); implore *sb*. 〜を叩く ❶ agree with *sb*. ❷ be impressed by *sth*. ❸ call *sth* to mind. 〜を正す sit upright. 〜を立てる draw up one's knees. 〜を突き合わせる have a serious talk. 〜を突く go down on one's knees. ⓐ 〜を直す relax one's knees; sit at ease. 〜を曲げる bend one's knees. 〜を交える ❶ sit (down) with *sb*; sit face to face with *sb*. ❷ have an informal chat; have a heart-to-heart; ⓢ have a chinwag.

肘 an elbow; an arm

[Av] 〜で押し退ける elbow *sb* aside. 〜で押し分ける elbow one's way through (the crowd).
[N] 〜にする ❶ elbow *sb*; give *sb* the elbow. ❷ rebuff *sb*; ⓘ brush *sb* aside; snub *sb*.
[を] 〜を当てる restrain *sb*; hold *sb* down. 〜を押し退ける elbow *sb* aside. 〜を折る grow wiser with experience; gain in years and wisdom. 〜を齧む make a solemn oath; vow to be victorious. ⓐ 〜を極める ignore *sb*; make light of *sth*. ⓢ 〜を食う be rebuffed; be rejected; get snubbed. 〜を突く elbow *sb*; poke one's elbow (into *sb's* side); rest one's elbow. 〜を張る ❶ square one's elbow; spread out one's elbows.

❷ refuse to give in; ⓒⓘ dig in one's heels; hold on. ❸ be proud; be overbearing; be haughty; ⓘ be stuck up. 〜を引く pull *sb's* arm. ⓐ 〜を曲げる ❶ make one's arms into a pillow; rest on one's arms. ❷ enjoy a life of honest poverty.

肘鉄砲 ⓔ a rebuff; a snub

[を] ⓢ 〜を食う be rejected; get snubbed; ⓒ suffer a rebuff; ⓢ be kicked ⓘ get the mitten.

非常識 absurdity; irrationality

[を] 〜を極まる be absurd; be preposterous; be rediculous.

非常線 a cordon; fire lines

[を] 〜を張る post a cordon.

顰み frowning; a frown

[N] 〜に倣う follow *sb's* example; imitate *sb* slavishly; ⓒ ape *sb*.

襞 a pleat; a fold; a crease

[を] 〜を取る ❶ crease (a trouser leg); make a pleat. ❷ tuck (a garment) in; gather (a sleeve) in.

額 the forehead; the brow

[Av] 〜で見る look upwards (without raising one's head); cast one's eyes upwards.

[N] 〜に汗する do *sth* with all one's might; try as hard as one can.
[を] ⓐ 〜を鳩む confer with each other; ⓑ counsel together; ⓒ get together; ⓓ compare notes. 〜を集める confer with each other; ⓒ get together; ⓓ compare notes. 〜を合わせる sit close together; be close to each other. ⓐ 〜を垂る have one's forehead shaven.

媚態 [E] coquetry
[を] 〜を示す play the coquet. 〜を作る behave coquettishly.

左 (the) left
[を] 〜へ曲がる turn to the left. 〜へ寄る lean to the left.
[を] 〜を見る look to the left.

左 [E] a carpenter's left hand
[A] ⓐ 〜が上がる ❶ get better at *sth*; acquire more skill. ❷ (be able to) drink more than before; increase one's intake of alcohol.

左褄 [E] the left hem of a *kimono*
[を] 〜を取る ❶ hold up a *kimono* by the left hem. ⓒ ❷ become a *geisha*.

跛 [E] lameness; a cripple
[N] ⓐ 〜に成る become lame; become crippled.

[を] ⓐ 〜を引く have a limp.

必要 necessity; requirement
[A] (...する)〜が有る be necessary to do *sth*; be required to do *sth*. 〜が迫る be pressing; be urgent.
[N] 〜に応じる respond to a need; meet a requirement. 〜に迫られる be driven by necessity.

批点 a point of criticism
[を] 〜を打つ ❶ mark *sth* with a dot; punctuate a sentence. ❷ criticize *sb*; point out *sb*'s shortcomings.

人 a human being
[A] 〜が良い have a good nature; be pleasant; have gentle manners. 〜が掛かる be pursued by people. 〜が変わる have a change of personality; become a different person. 〜が立つ gather round; throng together. 〜が無い be few in number; have a shortage of hands; be short of men. 〜が悪い ❶ have a wicked nature; be unpleasant; have bad manners; ⓒ be a difficult customer (to deal with). ❷ look shabby; look dishevelled; be bad-looking.
[と] 〜と成る ❶ grow up; become an adult; reach adulthood. ❷ come to oneself; ⓒ recover one's sanity; come to one's senses.

[を] ～を得る find a suitable person (for a position). ⑤ ～を食う ❶ practice cannibalism. ❷ look down upon *sb*; ⓒ hold *sb* in low esteem; think little of *sb*. ❸ make a fool of *sb*; ⓒ poke fun at *sb*; ⑤ ⓘ take the mickey (out of *sb*); ⑤ ⓘ take the piss (out of *sb*). ～を立てる ❶ send a messenger; dispatch an intermediary. ❷ give *sb* credit; ⓘ put *sb* on a pedestal; ⓘ put *sb* in the limelight. (中に)❸ mediate between two parties; act as a go-between. ～をつくる build a good character; make a fine person out of *sb*. ～(の目)を抜く play a trick on *sb*'s eyes; deceive *sb*; ⓘ pull the wool over *sb*'s eyes. ～を呑む look down upon *sb*; ⓒ hold *sb* in low esteem; think little of *sb*. ～を呪う put a curse on *sb*; curse *sb*. ～を分かず draw no distinction between people; treat people equally.

人影 the shadow of a person

[A] ～が射す catch a glimpse of *sb*. ～が見えない not a soul is to be seen; be deserted; be empty.

人柄 personality; character

[A] ～が良い have a good nature; be pleasant; have gentle manners. ～が悪い ❶ be unpleasant; have bad manners; ⓘ be a difficult customer (to deal with). ❷ look shabby; look dishevelled; be bad-looking.

[を] ～を作る give oneself airs; be pompous; ⓒ be ostentatious; ⓘ put on airs; ⑤ ⓘ be stuck-up.

人聞き one's reputation

[A] ～が良い be respectable; ⓒ be reputable; be be decent. ～が良く無い be bad for one's reputation; do not sound respectable. ～が悪い be scandalous; ⓒ be disreputable; be shameful.

美徳 virtues; good deeds

[を] ～を積む accumulate virtues. ～を養う cultivate virtuous habits.

人心地 one's conscience

[A] ～がつく feel relieved; be reassured; be put at ease; ⓘ feel a weight taken off one's chest.

人騒がせ a false alarm

[を] ～をする raise a false alarm; cause a scare; ⓘ cry wolf.

人質 a hostage

[と] ～と成る be taken hostage; be held (as a) hostage.
[N] ～に取る take *sb* hostage; hold *sb* hostage.

人集り a crowd of people
[A] 〜がする people throng together; people gather round; stampede.

人助け a kind deed
[N] 〜に成る be of help to sb.
[を] 〜をする help sb; give sb assistance; give sb a helping hand.

人伝 hearsay; word of mouth
[N] 〜に聞く ❶ hear of sb by word of mouth; hear from sb. ❷ ⓒ get wind of sth; ⓘ hear sth through the grapevine.

人手 sb's hand; a worker; help
[A] 〜が要る need help; ⓘ need a (helping) hand; require assistance. 〜が足りない have a shortage of man power; be short of hands; be short-handed.
[N] 〜に掛かる die by sb's hands; be murdered. 〜に渡る pass into sb's hands; change hands.
[を] 〜を借りる get sb's assistance; ask sb for assistance. 〜を加える be man-made; be artificial; ⓒ be by the hand of man.

人中 human company; society
[へ] 〜へ出る appear in public; be in company; keep the company of others; go into society; be outgoing.

一呑み one gulp; an easy prey
[N] 〜に飲む gulp sth down; drink sth at a draft; ⓒ knock back a drink.
[と] 〜と侮る consider sb an easy prey; think little of one's enemy.

人橋 a go-between
[N] 〜を架ける ❶ make a proposal by way of a go-between. ❷ send out messengers one after another.

人柱 [A] a human sacrifice
[と] ⓒ 〜と成る sacrifice one's life; give one's life (to a cause).

人払い clearance of people
[を] 〜をする ❶ clear a place of people; make people leave the room. ❷ make way for sb; give way to sb; clear the way (for a dignitary). 〜を願う ask sb to talk in private; seek a private interview.

人前 the people; the public
[N] 〜に出る appear in public; be seen in public.
[A] 〜で叱る give sb a public scolding; scold sb in public.
[を] 〜を繕う keep up appearances; keep on a brave face; hold one's head high. 〜を憚る be diffident to others; be wary of the public.

ひとみ
瞳 the pupil

[を] ～を凝らす strain one's eyes; ⓒ rivet one's eyes on *sb/sth*; look hard at *sb/sth*. ～を据える fix one's eyes on *sb/sth*; gaze at *sb/sth*.

ひとめ
人目 the public eye

[A] ～が煩い be a liability; be a threat to one's good name. ～が多い be (too) crowded (to do *sth* unnoticed). ～が無い ❶ be deserted; be without people; be empty (of people). ❷ do *sth* unnoticed; be on one's own; be alone; be unseen. [N] ～に余る be overconspicuous; be excessive. ～に現る be noticed; stand out; be conspicuous; attract (people's) attention. ～に晒す bring *sth* to light. ～に立つ be conspicuous; stand out. ～に付く be conspicuous; attract attention; draw people's attention. ～に留まらない escape public notice; do not catch the eye; slip from sight. [を] ～を奪う steal *sb's* attention; captivate the public. ～を飾る keep up appearances; keep on a brave face; hold one's head high. ～を兼ねる shy away from the public gaze; ⓒ shrink from people's gaze; shun publicity. ～を避ける avoid public notice; shun public notice. ～を忍ぶ avoid public notice; do *sth* in secret. Ⓐ ～をす ❶ shy away from the public gaze; ⓒ shrink from people's gaze; shun publicity. ❷ be afraid of strangers; fear strangers. Ⓐ ～を包む shun the company of others; avoid others. ～を盗む do *sth* in secret; ⓒ steal one's way (into a place). ～を憚る fear to be seen by others; ⓒ be shady. ～を引く attract attention.

ひとやま
人山 a great crowd

[A] ～が出来る ❶ form a pile of corpses. ❷ form a great growd; throng together; stampede. [を] ～を築く ❶ pile up corpses in a great heap. ❷ form a great growd; throng together; stampede.

ひとり
独り single; alone; solitude

[A] ～で暮らす ❶ live by oneself; live on one's own. ❷ be unmarried; be single; remain a batchelor/spinster. ～で笑う laugh to oneself; smile to oneself; chuckle over *sth*. [を] ～を慎む adhere to what is right (even when one is alone); act according to one's conscience. ～を楽しむ enjoy one's own company; enjoy solitude; ⓒ be a loner.

ひとりごと
独り言 words to oneself

[を] ～を言う talk to oneself; think aloud; soliloquize.

非難 criticism; blame; reproach
[を] 〜を浴びる be the focus of criticism; come in for criticism. 〜を招く incur *sb's* criticism; lay oneself open to censure.

皮肉 skin and flesh; irony
[A] ⓪ 〜が離れる be painful; be distressing; be heart-breaking. ⓪ 〜が貼れる be proficient; be skilled; be an expert.
[を] 〜を言う say ironic things; make cutting remarks; talk cynical. 〜を絞る wring one's heart; feel crushed; ⓒ feel gutted.

火花 a spark; sparks
[A] 〜が散る sparks fly; spark; be sparkling.
[を] 〜を散らす ❶ throw off sparks; emit sparks. ❷ fight desperately; engage in a fierce competition; fight to the death. ❸ argue heatedly in favor/against *sth*; debate *sth* hotly; ⓒ engage in a heated debate; ⓘ sparks fly.

罅 a crack; a fissure
[A] 〜が入る ❶ be cracked; form a fissure. ❷ impair one's health; upset one's health. ❸ mar one's record; damage one's prospects. ❹ upset a friendship; cause a rift (between two people). 〜が来る be hindered; be thwarted; be frustrated. 〜が割れる be cracked; form a fissure.
[を] 〜を入れる upset the balance; interfere with *sth*; throw up obstacles; ⓘ rock the boat.

皹 cracked skin; chaps
[A] 〜が切れる have cracked skin; be chapped; chap.

罅たけ a crack; a fissure
[A] 〜が入る ❶ be cracked; form a fissure. ❷ impair one's health; upset one's health.

火蓋 the apron of a gun
[を] 〜を切る ❶ open fire; fire the first gun; take (the enemy) under fire. ❷ launch (a campaign).

美貌 [E] good looks; beauty
[N] 〜に迷う be captivated by *sb's* beauty; be enchanted by *sb*; ⓒ be smitten with *sb's* charms.

暇 time; spare time; leisure ▶ 暇
[A] ⓐ 〜が明く have time off; be free; be vacant; ⓘ have time on one's hands. 〜が有る have time; be vacant. ⓐ 〜が入る have *sth* to do; be engaged. ⓪ 〜がかかる take up time; be time-consuming. 〜が出る

❶ be dismissed; ⓒ be relieved of one's post; ⓒ be fired; ⓢⓘ get the sack. ❷ get time off; have time off. ❸ be divorced.

N ～に飽かす make full use of one's free time; spare no time. ～になる be free; be vacant; ⓘ have time on one's hands.

を Ⓐ ～を明ける ❶ take time off; make oneself free; make time (to do *sth*). ❷ divorce from (one's wife); get separated. Ⓐ ～を入れる while away one's time; ⓒ kill time. Ⓐ ～を欠く while away one's time; waste one's time; ⓒ kill time. ～を拵える make time (to do *sth*). ～を割る find time (to do *sth*). ～を出す ❶ dismiss *sb*; discharge *sb*; ⓒ fire *sb*; ⓢⓘ give *sb* the sack; ⓒⓘ send *sb* packing. ❷ give *sb* time off. ❸ get divorced (from one's wife); get separated. ～を潰す while away one's time; pass (the) time; ⓒ kill time. ～を取る ❶ resign from one's post; ⓒ tender one's resignation. ❷ take time off; have a vacation. ❸ get divorced (from one's husband); get separated. ❹ take (a lot of) time; be delayed (on the way). ～を盗む ❶ steal time (to do *sth*); make time (to do *sth*). ❷ while away one's time; waste one's time; ⓒⓘ kill time. ～を弄ぶ do not know

what to do with oneself; be bored. ～を貰う ask for leave; get time off; leave *sb's* service. ～を遣る ❶ dismiss *sb*; discharge *sb*; ⓒ fire *sb*; ⓢⓘ give *sb* the sack; ⓒⓘ send *sb* packing. ❷ give *sb* time off. ❸ get divorced (from one's wife); get separated.

火水 fire and water

N ～に入る ❶ be in danger; face danger; be confronted with danger. ❷ fight for one's life; do one's utmost; give one's all. ～に成る become turbulent; grow frenzied.

を ～を飛ばす fight desperately; ⓒ engage in a fierce contest; fight to the death.

秘密 a secret; a mystery

を ～を明かす confide a secret to *sb*; share a secret with *sb*. ～を暴く reveal a secret; disclose a secret; uncover a mystery. ～を侵す spill a secret; intrude on *sb's* privacy; ⓘ spill the beans. ～を教える initiate *sb* into the mysteries of (an art). ～を探る pry into a secret; probe a secret. ～を解く unravel a mystery. ～を守る keep a secret; observe secrecy; ⓘ keep *sth* under one's hat. ～を漏らす leak out a secret; betray a secret.

ひめい
悲鳴 a shriek; a scream
[を] ～を上げる utter a shriek; raise a howl; cry out (in anguish).

びめい
美名 Ⓔ a good name
[N] ⓒ (慈善の)～に隠れる hide (do sth disreputable) under the good name (of charity).

ひも
紐 a string; a cord; a braid
[Av] ～で括る tie sth up.
[を] ⓒ ～を絞る fasten a string. ～を付ける find a clue; resolve an issue; find a way out (of a predicament); have a key (to a problem). ～を解く untie a string. ～を結ぶ tie a string. ～を緩める loosen a string.

びもく
眉目 Ⓔ a face; features; looks
[を] ⓒ ～を開く feel relieved; be reassured; be put at ease.

ひゃく
百 a hundred; one hundred
[Aj] ⓑ ～が抜ける ❶ be one coin short in (a string of) one hundred. ❷ fail to tally; do not add up. ❸ be an imbecile; be a dunce; ⓒ be a half-wit; ⓢ be a bonehead.
[Aj] ⓑ ～に足らぬ ❶ be one coin short in (a string of) one hundred. ❷ fail to tally; do not add up. ❸ be an imbecile; be a dunce; ⓒ be a half-wit; ⓢ be a bonehead.

ひゃっけい
百計 Ⓔ all means
[Aj] ⓒ ～が尽きる be at the end of one's resources; ⓘ be at the end of one's tether; ⓘ come to the end of one's rope.
[を] ⓒ ～を廻らす leave no means untried; try every means; ⓘ leave no stone unturned.

ひやみず
冷や水 cold water
[を] ～を飲む ❶ drink cold water. ❷ be a stuborn old man; be headstrong in one's old age.

ひやめし
冷や飯 cold rice
[N] ～にする ❶ let the rice go cold. ❷ assume a cold attitude towards sb; treat sb stiffly; ⓘ give sb the cold shoulder. Ⓐ ❶ fire an actor; remove sb from the cast. ～に成る ❶ the food goes cold; go cold. Ⓐ ❷ lose one's role in a play; be removed from the cast.
[を] ～を食う ❶ eat cold rice. ❷ live on sb's expenses; be dependent on sb; ⓒ sponge on sb. ❸ be treated coldly; ⓘ be left in the lurch; ⓘ be given the cold shoulder.

ひょう
評 criticism; comment
[N] Ⓐ ～に合わぬ ❶ remain unappreciated; go unnoticed. ❷ be unfit for one; be no match for one; ⓘ be in a

different league; ⓛ be on different scales.
[A]〜が付く ❶ come to an evaluation; reach a verdict. ❷ be criticized; be commented upon.

病気 sickness; illness
[A]〜が治る recover from one's disease; get over one's illness; get well. 〜が振り返す relapse into illness; suffer a relapse.
[Av]〜で倒れる come down with an illness; ⓒ succumb to a disease.
[と]〜と闘う combat a disease.
[N]〜に打ち勝つ survive an illness. 〜に掛かる fall ill; take a disease; lose one's health. 〜に効く be effective in curing a disease; be wholesome. 〜に堪える bear one's illness. 〜に成る fall ill; contract a disease; lose one's health. 〜に負ける give way to one's disease.
[を]〜を移す transmit a disease. 〜を拗らす complicate a disease; develop a complication. 〜を背負う carry a disease; be ill. 〜を治す cure a disease. 〜を防ぐ prevent a disease. 〜を見舞う ask after sb's health; inquire after sb's health. 〜を装う feign illness.

病苦 [E] the pain of ill health
[N] ⓒ 〜に打ち勝つ surmount the pains of ill health; get the better of one's illness. ⓒ 〜に悩む suffer the pains of ill health; be tormented by one's illness.

病根 [E] the cause of a disease
[を] ⓒ 〜を断つ root out an illness; strike at the root of an illness.

拍子 rhythm; measure; time
[N] 〜に掛かる ❶ keep good time with (the music). ❷ get (too) excited; be elated; ⓛ get carried away.
[を] 〜を合わす keep good time with (the music). 〜を取る keep time; beat time. 〜を踏む keep time; beat time.

病床 [E] a sickbed
[N] ⓒ 〜に就く take to a sickbed; go to bed ill; be taken ill; be ill in bed; be laid up (with illness). ⓒ 〜に侍る be by sb's bedside; sit watch by sb's bedside. ⓒ 〜に伏す lie in one's sickbed; keep one's bed; ⓒ be laid up with illness; be bedridden.

病勢 [E] the state of a disease
[A] ⓒ 〜が改まる grow worse; take a turn for the worse. ⓒ 〜が衰える grow less serious; get better. ⓒ 〜が募る grow worse; take a turn for the worse.

ひょうばん
評判 reputation; fame; credit

[A] 〜が良い be popular; have a good reputation; ⓔ be well spoken of. 〜が高い have a great reputation; be a sensation; be extremely popular. 〜が立つ a rumor spreads. 〜が出る become known; create a name for oneself; gain in popularity. 〜が悪い be unpopular; have a bad reputation; ⓔ be ill spoken of.

[N] 〜になる ❶ win fame; gain reputation; become celebrated. ❷ be talked about; ⓒⓘ be the talk of the town; ⓒⓘ make the rounds.

[を] 〜を落とす lose one's (good) reputation; fall into discredit. 〜を立てる start a rumor; ⓘ make a stir. 〜を取り返す regain one's character; restore one's reputation. 〜を取る win reputation; become popular; win credit.

びょうま
病魔 ⓕ the demon of ill health

[N] ⓔ 〜に侵される fall ill; be seized with an illness. ⓒ 〜に襲われる fall ill; be seized with an illness.

ひょうり
表裏 ⓕ inside and outside

[A] ⓒ 〜が有る play a double game; be a double-dealer; wear two hats.

[を] ⓒ 〜を使う ❶ try to have it both ways; play a double game; try to have the best of both worlds. ❷ out-wit *sb*; deceive *sb*; ⓘ take *sb* in; ⓒⓘ lead *sb* by the nose.

ひより
日和 weather; fair weather

[A] 〜が上がる the weather improves; brighten up; clear up.

[を] 〜を見る wait and see; ⓘ see how the wind blows; ⓘ sit on the fence; ⓒⓘ watch which way the cat jumps.

ひれ
鰭 a fin

[を] 〜が有る command respect; be influential; have influence; ⓘ carry weight. 〜が落ちる lose influence; lose one's dignity. 〜が付く ❶ grow broad; become broad in the waist. ❷ look dignified; gain in stature; have presence; have authority.

[を] 〜が付ける ❶ exaggerate *sth*; ⓔ indulge in hyperbole; ⓘ stretch the facts; ⓢⓘ pile it on; ⓢⓘ lay it on thick. ❷ gather prestige; gain in reputation; gain authority; increase one's stature; ⓘ gather weight.

ひん
品 grace; refinement ▶ 品

[A] 〜が有る be refined; have grace. 〜が無い be unrefined; lack grace; be vulgar.

[を] 〜をする behave coquettishly; play the coquette; give oneself airs; ⓘ put on airs; ⓢⓘ be stuck-up.

ひん
貧 poverty; destitution

[を] 〜に迫られる be impoverished; be reduced to poverty; be driven to destitution; ⓘ be in dire straits.

ひん
顰 frowning; a frown

[N] 〜に倣う follow sb's example; imitate sb slavishly; ⓒ ape sb.

ピン the first; the beginning

[を] 〜を撥ねる pocket some of the money; take a percentage; ⓒ take a rake-off; ⓒ take a cut.

ひんい
品位 dignity; grace; nobility

[を] 〜を落とす lose one's dignity; degrade oneself. 〜を高める give sb dignity; ennoble sb. 〜を保つ maintain one's dignity; keep up one's state; ⓢ keep one's cool.

ひんこん
貧困 poverty; destitution

[N] 〜に喘ぐ suffer extreme poverty; ⓘ be in dire straits. 〜に陥る be impoverished; be reduced to poverty; become destitute.

[を] ⓒ 〜を脱する rise from poverty; ⓔ emerge from poverty.

ひんしゅく
顰蹙 ⒼE frowning

[を] ⓒ 〜を買う be frowned on; disgust sb; ⓔ incur sb's displeasure.

びんた ⒼE a slap on the cheek

[を] ⓢ 〜を食う be slapped in the face. ⓢ 〜を張る slap sb in the face; give sb a slap in the face.

ピント a focus

[A] 〜が合う be in focus. 〜が外れる ❶ be out of focus. ❷ be be irrelevant; ⓘ be beside the point; ⓘ be off the mark; ⓘ miss the point.

[を] 〜が合わせる bring sth into focus; focus (one's camera) on sth.

びんわん
敏腕 ⒼE ability; capability

[を] ⓒ 〜を揮う show one's ability; ⓔ give full play to one's talents.

フ

ふ
腑 the viscera; the bowels

[A] ⓐ 〜が抜ける ❶ lose one's senses; lose one's wits; ⓢ ⓘ lose one's marbles. ❷ lose courage; have no stomach for sth. ❸ fall into one's dotage; go senile; get weak with age; ⓢ go gaga.

[N] ⓐ 〜に入る ❶ make sense of sth; grasp the meaning; catch the idea. ❷ be convinced; be won over; be persuaded. 〜に落ちる ❶ make sense of sth; grasp the meaning; catch the idea. ❷ be convinced; be won over; be persuaded.

符 ᴱ a tally; a charm; an amulet

[A] ⓐⒺ ～が悪い be unfortunate; be unlucky; be inauspicious.
[を] Ⓔ ～を合わす ❶ make sth tally; compare the tallies. ❷ tally with each other; coincide with each other; correspond with each other.
Ⓔ ～を合する ❶ make sth tally; compare the tallies. ❷ tally with each other; coincide with each other; correspond with each other.
ⓐⒺ ～を割く make a tally; give out tallies.

斑 a spot; a speck; a stripe

[A] ～が切れる ❶ be marked off; be distinguished; be set apart. ❷ be frank; be clear; be straightforward. ❸ be settled; be arranged; be brought to a conclusion; come to an arrangement.

譜 sheet music

[を] ～を付ける set (words) to music.

分 a percentage; a rate ▶ 分

[A] ～が有る stand a chance; have a chance (of success). ～が良い ❶ the percentage is good. ❷ have the edge; be favorable. ～が悪い ❶ the percentage is bad. ❷ have no edge; be unfavorable.

歩 an advantage; profitable ▶ 歩

[N] ⓐ ～に合う be profitable; pay for itself. ⓐ ～に掛かる be profitable; pay for itself. ⓐ ～に回る ❶ be very profitable. ❷ draw profit from sth; exploit sth.

武 ᴱ military/martial affairs

[を] Ⓔ ～を争う struggle for military supremacy. Ⓔ ～を講ずる practice military tactics. Ⓔ ～を尊ぶ pursue a policy of militarism. Ⓔ ～を練る train oneself in the arts of war. Ⓔ ～を学ぶ study martial arts.

不安 uneasiness; anxiety

[N] ～に思う be uncertain about sth; feel uneasy about sth; be anxious about sth. ～になる lose one's peace of mind; grow restless; Ⓘ get cold feet.
[を] ～を抱く be anxious; have misgivings; Ⓔ entertain apprehensions. ～を感じる feel uneasy; be uncertain; be anxious; be ill at ease.

ふい ᴱ wastage; annulment

[を] ⓢ ～にする ❶ discard sth as useles; throw sth away; do away with sth. ❷ waste sth; Ⓔ bring sth to naught; Ⓒ mess sth up; Ⓢ blow sth. ⓢ ～に成る be futile; come to nothing; be wasted; Ⓘ go up in smoke.

不意 sudden; unexpected
[を] 〜を打つ take sb by surprise; catch sb unawares. ⓐⓢ 〜を食う be taken by surprise; be caught unawares. 〜を突く take sb by surprise; catch sb unawares.

不意討ち a surprise attack
[を] 〜を食わす take advantage of an unguarded moment; make a surprise attack; take sb by surprise; catch sb off guard.

吹聴 an announcement
[Aj] 〜が回る a rumor spreads.

風 an air; a look; a trend ▶ 風（かぜ）
[Aj] (...の)〜が有る have an air of... (about it); reek of sth. 〜が悪い look bad; be unattractive; ⓔ be unseemly; look clumsy; ⓢ be uncool.
[を] ⓔ 〜を守る stick to one's habits; adhere to a custom; keep to the (good) old ways.

封 seal; closing
[を] 〜を開ける open a letter. 〜を切る break open a seal; cut (a letter) open. 〜をする seal a letter; put (a letter) in an envelope.

風位 the direction of the wind
[Aj] 〜が転ずる the wind shifts.

[を] 〜を示す show the wind-direction. 〜を測る determine the wind-direction.

風雲急 threatening clouds
[を] ⓔ 〜を告げる the situation is threatening; grow tense; become critical.

風月 beauties of nature
[を] 〜を楽しむ enjoy nature; ⓔ take delight in nature. ⓔ 〜を友とする enjoy the company of nature; ⓔ converse with nature.

封鎖 a blockade; blocking
[を] 〜を潜る run a blockade. 〜を解く lift a blockade; raise a blockade. 〜を破る break a blockade.

風采 one's appearance
[Aj] 〜が上がらない make a poor impression; be unattractive; lack dignity; ⓘ cut a sorry figure.

風説 a rumor; hearsay
[を] ⓔ 〜を生む give rise to rumors. ⓔ 〜を立てる set a rumor afloat.

風船 a balloon
[を] 〜を上げる let up a balloon; send up a balloon. 〜を飛ばす let up a balloon; send up a balloon. 〜を膨ら

ます inflate a balloon. 〜を割る burst a balloon.

風致 ㊥ elegance; scenic beauty
㊥ ⓒ 〜を害する spoil the view; disfigure the landscape. ⓒ 〜を増す add charms to a view.

風潮 the tide; the current
Ⓝ 〜に逆らう be out of tune with the times; go against the tide. 〜に従う go with the tide. 〜に乗る ride the tide.

風波 wind and waves; a storm
Ⓝ 〜に揉まれる ❶ be caught in a storm; ⓒ be buffeted by the wind and waves. ❷ experience adversity; have a hard time. Ⓐ 〜が起こる ❶ the wind and waves rise. ❷ trouble arises. 〜が絶えない ❶ the winds do not let off. ❷ tbe beset by constant troubles. 〜が立つ ❶ the wind and waves rise. ❷ trouble arises. ㊥ 〜を凌ぐ ❶ brave the wind and waves; face the storm. ❷ meet the occasion; ⓒ face the music; ⓒ bite the bullet. 〜を冒して...する ❶ do sth in the face of wind and waves. ❷ do sth in the face of fierce opposition.

不運 misfortune; bad luck
Ⓝ 〜に遭う fall on evil days; meet with a reverse.
㊥ 〜を忍ぶ bear misfortune.

不覚 ㊥ imprudence; negligence
㊥ ⓒ 〜を取る suffer a setback; be beaten; ⓒ come to grief.

武器 a weapon; arms
㊥ 〜を納める lay down arms. 〜を取る take up arms; rise in arms.

復讐 revenge; vengeance
㊥ 〜を企てる seek revenge on sb. 〜を誓う swear revenge on sb. 〜を計る plan to revenge sb.

腹心 one's confidant(e)
㊥ 〜を布く open oneself up to sb; completely; take sb into one's total confidence; ⓒ pour out one's heart to sb without reserve. 〜を開く open oneself up to sb; take sb into one's confidence; ⓒ pour out one's heart to sb; ⓒ unbosom oneself.

袋 a bag; a sack; a pouch
Ⓝ ⓒ 〜に入る lag behind during the planting of rice seedlings.
㊥ 〜を空ける empty a bag. 〜を担ぐ ❶ carry a bag (on one's shoulder); shoulder a sack. ⓒ ❷ lag behind; fol-

low sb closely; ⓑ be hot on sb's heels. ⓐ ❸ fail to guess the scent of (any of) the burnt pieces of incense in a game of incense smelling. ⓐ ～を貪る have an eye on sb's wallet; pry on sb's purse; covet sb's money.

武功 ⓔ military exploits

を ⓒ ～を立てる distinguish oneself in war; ⓒ render distinguished military service.

節 a joint; a knuckle; a knot ▶ 節

A ～が痛む one's joints ache; feel pain in one's joints; ⓒ have sore joints. ⓐ ～が立つ cause offense; arouse bitterness; aggravate sb; have a rough going.

を ～を合わせる play the same air. ～を付ける ❶ set a verse to music. ❷ find fault with sb; pick a quarrel.

侮辱 insult; indignity

を ～を受ける suffer an insult; be insulted. ～を加える insult sb; level an insult at sb. ～を忍ぶ bear an affront; brook an insult; ⓘ keep a stiff upper lip.

不審 doubt; suspicion

N ～に思う consider sth to be suspicious; have doubts about sth; ⓒ think sth odd.

を ⓒ ～を上ぐ raise suspicions; ⓒ cast doubts on sth. ～を抱く have a suspicion; entertain doubts about sth. ～を打つ raise doubts; ⓒ cast suspicions on sb; question (sb's credentials); have doubts; harbor suspicions; entertain misgivings. ～を立てる raise doubts; ⓒ cast suspicions on sb; question (sb's credentials); entertain misgivings. ～を解く dispel sb's doubts.

不信 distrust; bad faith

を ～を抱く have a suspicion; be suspicious of sb. ～を買う incur suspicion; be called into question. ～を来す cause distrust. ～を招く incur sb's mistrust.

不正 injustice; iniquity

を ～を正す redress injustice. ～を働く do a dishonest thing; do sb an injustice; do wrong.

不足 shortage; want

を ～を言う vent one's discontent; express dissatisfaction. ～を補う make good a deficiency; meet a shortage. ～を告げる run short of sth; prove deficient.

蓋 a lid; a cover; a flap; a cap

を ～を開ける ❶ open a play; begin

a performance. ❷ begin (work); start things up. ❸ make *sth* public; bring *sth* into the open. 〜を取る take the lid of (a barrel); uncover *sth*.

札 a card; a label; a tag; a charm

[A] Ⓒ 〜が落ちる have one's tender accepted. 〜が付く get a (bad) reputation; Ⓒ gain notoriety.
[を] 〜を頂く receive a charm (from a shrine). 〜を入れる make a bid; offer one's bid; tender for (a project). 〜を切る cut the cards; shuffle the cards. 〜を配る deal the cards. 〜を捨てる throw up one's cards. 〜を立てる put up a notice board. 〜を付ける paste a card; label *sth*; put a tag on *sth*. 〜を取る pick a card; take a card. 〜を張る paste a card; label *sth*; put a tag on *sth*. 〜を見せる show one's cards. 〜を捲る turn over a card; turn down a card.

舞台 the stage

[N] 〜に立つ appear on the stage; go on the stage; Ⓒ come before the footlights. 〜に載せる stage a play; put a play on stage.
[を] 〜を退く leave the stage; end one's acting career; Ⓒ retire from the stage. 〜を踏む go on the stage; make one's debut; Ⓒ come before the footlights.

二股 [E] a fork; a branch

[N] Ⓒ 〜になる fork off in two; fork into two branches; divide into two.
[を] Ⓒ 〜を掛ける try to achieve one's goal by two alternative ways; try to have the best of both worlds; play a double game; Ⓘ have two strings to one's bow; Ⓒ Ⓘ hedge one's bets.

二道 a crossroads

[を] 〜を掛ける ❶ try to achieve one's goal by two alternative ways; play a double game; Ⓘ have two strings to one's bow; Ⓒ Ⓘ hedge one's bets. Ⓒ ❷ have two lovers at the same time; Ⓘ have the best of both worlds.

縁 an edge; a verge; a side ▶ 縁

[N] 〜に立つ stand on the edge; be on the verge of *sth*.
[を] 〜を付ける frame (an area); delimit (an area). 〜を通る hug the side (of the road); stick to the roadside. 〜を取る hem (an area); border (an area). 〜を縫う border (cloth); hemstitch (cloth).

淵 an abyss; a pit; the depths

[N] 〜に落ち込む sink into the limbo of oblivion. 〜に沈む sink into the depth (of misery); fall into a slough (of despond).

285

打ち壊し ③ demolition

[を] ⓢ ～を言う talk mischief; make destructive criticism; ⓘ be a wet blanket. ⓢ ～を遣る make a mess of things; ⓘ throw a spanner in the works; ⓒ bungle *sth*; ⓒ botch *sth*.

不忠 ⓪ disloyal; unfaithful

[を] ⓒ ～を働く be disloyal (to one's master/country).

符牒 a sign; a token; a mark

[Av] ～で言う speak in sipher; speak a secret language.
[を] ～を付ける ❶ mark *sth* (out); put a label on *sth*. ❷ put a price-tag on *sth*; price an article.

物価 prices (of commodities)

[を] ～を上げる raise prices. ～を下げる lower prices; reduce prices. ～を調節する regulate prices.

物議 ⓪ public censure; unrest

[を] ⓢ ～を醸す give rise to a public discussion; cause dissent; arouse criticism; raise a scandal.

仏事 a Buddhist mass

[を] ～を営む hold a Buddhist mass.

筆 a (writing) brush; a pen

[A] ～が荒れる write in a poor style; be clumsily written; be cluttered; be a messy composition. ～が滑る a slip of the pen; touch the paper by accident (when writing). ～が立つ be facile with one's pen; write in a good style; be a good writer. ～が回る be facile with one's pen; be a good writer.
[Av] ⓢ ～で食う live by one's pen.
[N] ～に任せる let one's pen wander.
[を] ～を入れる make corrections; touch up (a document); add touches to (calligraphy). ～を擱く lay down one's pen; complete a draft; stop writing. ～を起こす start writing; begin to write; pick up the pen; ⓒ put pen to paper. ～を落とす pick up the pen; put pen to paper. ～を折る give up writing; end one's literary career. ～を下ろす ❶ use a new brush. ❷ pick up the pen; ⓒ put pen to paper; start on a (new) work. ⓥ ⓢ ❸ lose one's virginity; become a man. ⓐ ～を呵す force oneself to write; make an effort to write. ～を加える fill in; make corrections; add some touches. ⓐ ～を下す pick up the pen; put pen to paper. ～を棄てる stop writing; give up a writing carreer. ～を染める ❶ wet one's brush (with ink); dip one's brush in ink. ❷ (小説に) start on a (new) novel. ❸ try one's hand at writing;

take up a writing career. ～を絶つ give up writing; end one's literary career. ～を試す try one's pen. ～を尽す exert oneself in one's writing; write to the best of one's ability; work hard on a draft. ～を執る pick up the pen; ⓔ put pen to paper. ～を投げる stop writing in mid-sentence. ～を拭う ❶ clean one's brush; wipe one's brush. ❷ lay down one's pen; stop writing. ～を運ぶ write a draft; ⓔ move one's pen across the paper. ～を走らせる write off; scribble away. ⓐ ～を馳す write off; scribble away. ～を揮う wield a brush; write calligraphy; paint a picture. ～を舞わす write off; scribble away. ⓒ ⓔ ～を弄ぶ write in jest; doodle.

ふところ
懐 the bosom; a purse

Ⓐ ～が暖かい have a well-filled purse; ⓘ be well-heeled. ～が痛む be a financial burden; pay out of one's own pocket. ～が寂しい have little money; ⓒ be hard up; ⓘ be in dire straits. ～が寒い have little money; ⓘ have a cold purse; ⓘ feel the draught. ～が広い be generous; be hospitable. ～が深い ❶ be generous; be magnanimous; have a big heart; be understanding; be broadminded. ❷ have great ability; have abundant mental faculties. ❸ [sumō]

have long arms; have a long reach; be able to keep sb at arm's lenght. ～を膨らます line one's pocket; ⓔ enrich oneself by way of graft; ⓘ feather one's own nest. Ⓝ ～に入れる put sth in one's pocket; pocket sth; make sth one's own. ～にする pocket sth; make sth one's own. 를 ～を暖める enrich oneself by way of graft; ⓘ line one's pocket; ⓘ feather one's own nest. ～を痛める bear a financial burden; pay out of one's own pocket. ～を肥やす enrich oneself by way of graft; ⓘ line one's pocket; ⓘ feather one's own nest. ～を見透かす see through sb's designs.

ふところぐあい
袋具合 one's financial situation

Ⓝ ～が良い have plenty of money; be well off; ⓒ have a heavy purse. ～が悪い be short of money; be badly off; ⓒ have a light purse.

ふところつごう
袋都合 one's financial situation

Ⓝ ～が良い have plenty of money; be well off; ⓒ have a heavy purse. ～が悪い be short of money; be badly off; ⓒ have a light purse.

ふとん
布団 a futon

를 ～を上げる roll up one's futon. ～

〜を被る pull one's futon over one's head. 〜を敷く spread one's futon; make a bed. 〜を畳む fold up one's futon; clear away one's futon.

舟/船 a boat; a ship; vessel

Ⓐ ⓒ 〜が座る ❶ land a boat; a boat is pulled ashore. ❷ run aground; be stranded; go on the rocks. ❸ outstay one's welcome; stay too long. ❹ stay put; stay on (in power); remain in office.

Aᵥ 〜で行く go by boat; take a boat. 〜で運ぶ carry sth by boat.

Ⓝ 〜に強い be a good sailor. 〜に乗る get on board a ship. 〜に酔う get seasick. 〜に弱い be a poor sailor.

を 〜を通わせる sail between two ports; perate a ship. 〜を漕ぐ ❶ row a boat. ❷ nod off; fall asleep (on the job). 〜を出す put to sea; set sail; put out. 〜を造る build a ship. 〜を止める bring a ship to. 〜を回す bring up a ship; sail a ship. 〜を乗り捨てる abandon ship. 〜を雇う charter a ship; hire a boat.

不評 ill repute; a bad reputation

を 〜を買う ❶ become the target of criticizm; be criticized. ❷ lose one's popularity; become unpopular. 〜を招く lose one's popularity; become unpopular.

不憫 pity; compassion

Ⓝ 〜に思う feel pity; take pity on sb; ⓒ be moved to pity.

を 〜を掛ける treat sb with compassion; take pity on sb.

不平 discontent; dissatisfaction

を 〜を言う speak one's mind; grumble over sth; complain of sth; ⓒ voice one's discontent. 〜を抱く be discontented; hold a grudge against sb; ⓘ have an axe to grind; ⓒ nurse a grievance. 〜を訴える complain about sth; ⓒ lodge a complaint. 〜を押える restrain oneself; ⓒ repress one's dissatisfaction. 〜を鳴らす complain about sth; ⓒ air one's grievances. 〜を並べる grumble over; ⓒ whine over sth. 〜を洩らす vent one's discontent; ⓒ air one's grievances. 〜をやめる stop complaining; leave off complaining; ⓒ let it go.

不便 inconvenience

を 〜を掛ける inconvenience sb; cause inconvenience. 〜を感じる be inconvenienced. 〜を忍ぶ put up with an inconvenience; endure discomfort. 〜を生ずる be a source of discomfort; cause inconvenience. 〜を除く remove inconveniences.

不問 ⒠ disregard; connivance

[N] ⒠ ～に付する ignore sth; leave sth unquestioned; disregard sth; ⓘ pass sth over; ⓢ shut one's eyes to sth; ⓒ ⓘ wink at (sb's mistake).

部門 a class; a group

[N] ～に入れる bring sth under the division of sth; place sth in a (certain) category; categorize sth. ～に入る fall under the head of sth; fall into a category; belong to a category. ～に分ける classify (into orders); divide into sections.

無聊 ⒠ ennui; tedium

[を] ⒠ ～を慰める while away one's time; fill the time; ⓒ kill time.

篩 a sieve; a filter; a strainer

[N] ～に掛ける ❶ sieve sth; put sth through a sieve; filter sth out. ❷ screen (applicants); vet (candidates); make a selection.

触れ an official notice

[を] ～を出す issue an official notice. ～を回す send round an official notice.

ブレーキ a brake

[を] ～を掛ける ❶ put on the brake; apply one's brake; ⓒ step on the brakes. ❷ halt (a project); call a halt to the progress. ❸ obstruct sth in progress; ⓒ ⓘ throw a spanner in the works.

風呂 a (hot) bath; a public bath

[N] ～に行く go to a bathhouse. ～に入れる give sb a bath. ～に浸かる soak in a bathtub; sink into a hot bath. ～に入る take a bath.
[を] ～を落とす empty a bathtub; let the water out of the bath. ～を焚く heat a bath; prepare a bath. ～を立てる prepare a bath. ～を使う take a bath; use a bath. ～を沸かす heat the bath.

文 composition; writing

[を] ～を売る make a living by the pen; write to make a living; support oneself by writing. ～を書く write prose. ⒠ ～を飾る embellish a composition. ⓐ ⒠ ～を属す make a composition; write an article. ～を作る make a composition; write a composition. ～を綴る compose an essay; frame a sentence. ～を練る improve on one's writing; polish one's writing style. ～を奮う write high prose; compose literature.

分 a part; one's place ♦ 分

[を] ～を尽くす do one's duty; ⓒ do

one's bit. ～を守る keep to one's sphere in life; ⓘ keep within one's own province; ⓘ cut one's coat according to one's cloth. ～を弁える know one's place; ⓘ keep within one's own province.

紛議 dissension; controversy

を ～を醸す cause dissension.

紛擾 confusion; disorder

を ⓒ ～を起こす stir up trouble; cause a disturbance; ⓒ give rise to confusion; ⓢ ⓘ raise a dust.

文壇 the literary world

N ～に乗り出す enter upon a literary career; take up writing.

文通 correspondence

を ～を禁じられる be held incommunicado. ～を絶つ break off correspondence with sb. ～を続ける maintain correspondence with sb. ～を始める enter into correspondence with sb.

褌 a loincloth

を ⓒ ～を締める brace oneself; get ready to do sth; ⓘ gird up one's loins; ⓘ put one's best foot forward; ⓢ ⓘ get up steam.

分秒 a moment; a second

を ⓒ ～を争う fight for time; try to buy time; have no time to lose; run a race against time.

文名 literary fame

を ～を馳せる win literary fame.

へ

兵 a soldier; troops; warfare

を ～を挙げる take up arms; rise in arms; raise an army. ～を送る send troops. ～を構える (prepare to) do battle with sb. ～を交える cross swords with sb. ～を募る raise an army; collect an army. ～を解く disband an army. ～を率いる lead an army. ～を伏せる lay an ambush. ～を向ける direct an army against sb. ～を催す raise an army; rally an army.

塀 a wall; a fence

A ～で囲む fence in (an area); put a fence around (a place).
を ～を立てる build a wall. ～を乗り越える climb over a wall. ～を巡らす surround (a house) with a wall; wall in (an area).

平気 calmness; serenity

を ～を装う affect composure; be self-composed; ⓘ keep one's head.

へイ

へいこう
平衡 equilibrium; balance
　〜を失う lose one's balance. 〜を保つ keep one's balance.

へいこうせん
平行線 parallel railway lines
　〜を辿る fail to see each other's points of view; talk at cross purposes.

へいせい
平静 serenity; tranquility; calm
　〜を失う lose one's composure; become upset; be perturbed. 〜を保つ keep calm; maintain one's composure; ⓒ keep one's head cool.

へいぜい
平生 normally; ordinarily
　〜を失う upset routine; upset the regular pace (of life).

へいゆ
平癒 recovery from illness
　ⓒ 〜を祈る pray for sb's recovery.

へいわ
平和 peace; harmony
　ⓒ 〜を講ずる make peace with sb. 〜を乱す disturb the harmony. 〜を破る break the peace.

へそ
臍 the navel, the belly button
　Ⓐ ⓐ 〜がくねる be too ridiculous for words; be preposterous; be outrageous; ⓘ be beyond the pale. 〜が曲がる be corrupt; be perverse; be depraved; have a warped nature. 〜が縒れる be laughable; be ludicrous; be rediculous.
　Ⓐ ⓐ 〜で笑う be too ridiculous for words; be preposterous; be outrageous; ⓘ be beyond the pale.
　ⓐ 〜を動かす give sb fits of laughter; convulse sb with laughter. ⓐ 〜を固める be determined; make up one's mind. ⓐ 〜を噛む have regrets; be sorry for. 〜を曲げる become perverse; get awkward; sulk over sth; ⓒ get cross. 〜を振る be amused; take delight in sth; find pleasure in sth.

べそ Ⓑ "a blubbering face"
　ⓢ 〜をかく be ready to cry; be close to tears. ⓢ 〜を作る be ready to cry; be close to tears.

へど
反吐 Ⓑ vomit; puke
　Ⓐ ⓢ 〜が出る ❶ throw up; fetch up; be sick. ❷ feel unwell; feel sick; feel nauseous. ❸ be disgusted (with sb/sth); be appaled (with sb/sth); find sb/sth disagreeable.
　ⓢ 〜を吐く throw up; fetch up; be sick; puke; ⓒ ⓘ shoot the cat.

ペン

ペテン Ⓑ trickery; deception
　Ⓝ ⓢ 〜に掛かる be deceived; be cheated; ⓘ be taken in (by sb); ⓒ ⓘ be led by the nose. ⓢ 〜に掛け

る outwit sb; deceive sb; defraud sb; ⓘ take sb in.

紅 rouge; lipstick; nail polish ▶ 紅

图 ～を注す ❶ put on lipstick; put on rouge. ❷ paint one's nails; apply nail polish. ～を付ける ❶ put on lipstick; put on rouge. ❷ paint one's nails; apply nail polish.

篦 a spatula

图 ⓐ ～を使う be ambiguous; be evasive; ⓘ beat about the bush.

変 change; disturbance

A ～が変わる take a turn for the worse; deteriorate. ～が来る face death; ⓒ be at death's door.

弁 speech; eloquence; a dialect

A ～が立つ have a fluent tongue; be fluent in speech; ⓒ ⓘ have the gift of the gab. ～が拙い be a poor speaker. ～が良い be a good speaker; be eloquent.
图 ～を練る cultivate eloquence; improve one's oratory skills. ～を振るう speak without hesitation; speak forcefully; speak with vigor. ⓒ ～を弄する ❶ use one's eloquence; ⓒ resort to sophistry. ❷ quibble over sth; put forward a far-fetched argument; ⓘ split hairs.

便 convenience; facility

A ～が有る have facilities. ～が乏しい be poor in facilities; have scant facilities. ～が無い have no facilities. ～が良い be convenient. ～が悪い be inconvenient.
图 ～を与える provide for sb's convenience; provide accomodation; afford facilities. (…の)～を図る provide facilities for sb/sth; accomodate sb/sth.

ペン a (writing) pen; a ballpoint

图 ～を折る stop writing; end one's writing career; give up a writing career. ～を執る pick up the pen; ⓒ put pen to paper. ～を辞める stop writing; end one's writing career; give up a writing carreer.

偏見 prejudice; a biased view

N ⓐ ～に染まる be tainted with prejudice.
图 ～を抱く be prejudiced; hold a biased view. ～を捨てる discard one's bias; get over one's prejudices. ～を持つ be prejudiced; hold a biased view.

辺幅 outward appearance

图 ⓐ ⓒ ～を飾る be particular about one's appearance; ⓘ keep up appearances.

へんりん
片鱗 a glimpse; a part
を ～を示す get a glimpse of *sb's* erudition/talent.

ホ

ほ
歩 a step; a pace ▶ 歩
を ⓐ ～を失う be at a loss (about what to do); lose one's direction. ⓑ ～を移す step ahead. ～を進める ❶ advance; go ahead. ❷ make progress; push (a project forward); give impetus to *sth*. ～を運ぶ ❶ proceed; go ahead. ❷ head for a place; set out for a place; ⓒ direct one's steps towards a place. ～を廻らす turn back; retrace one's steps.

ほ
帆 a sail; a canvas
N ～に上ぐ ❶ raise the high; hoist *sth* up. ❷ raise one's voice; speak up; cry out.
を ～を揚げる hoist a sail. ～を下ろす lower a sail. ～を掛ける ❶ set a sail. ❷ run off; ⓒ make a run for it; ⓒ ⓓ cut and run. ～を絞る brail a sail. ～を畳む furl a sail; shorten sail. ～を詰める take in sail. ～を張る unfurl a sail. ～を増す make sail.

ほ
穂 an ear; a head; a spike
A ～が出る ears form (on the barley); come into ears; ⓒ ear up.

N ⓐ ～に出る come out into the open; become noticed; be revealed. ～になる ears form (on the barley); come into ears; ⓒ ear up.
を ～を出す ears form (on the barley); come into ears; ⓒ ear up. (話の)～を継ぐ take up the thread (of a story); take up (one's story); resume (one's story).

ほ
秀 excellence
N ⓐ ～に出づ become noticed; become apparent; come out into the open; be revealed.

ポイント a point
を ～を失う lose a point. ～を稼ぐ ❶ win a point; gain a point. ❷ get a good score; obtain good results. ❸ rise in *sb's* estimation; improve one's standing. ❹ ingratiate oneself with *sb*; ⓘ curry favor with *sb*. ～を取る ❶ win a point; gain a point. ❷ rise in *sb's* estimation; improve one's standing.

ぼう
棒 a rod; a stick; a club
N ～に振る make a mess of *sth*; waste *sth*; bring ruin on *sth*.
を ⓐ ～を折る be a failure; give up halfway; ⓘ bite the dust. ～を引く draw a line; cross *sth* out; strike *sth* off. ～を揮う conduct music.

ほうか
砲火 gunfire; artillery fire

△ ～を開ける open fire; fire the first gun; take (the enemy) under fire; ⓒ open hostilities. ～を浴びる be under fire. ～を蒙る be subjected to fire; be brought under fire. ～を交える exchange fire; fight a battle; ⓒ engage an enemy.

ほうがく
方角 a direction; a bearing

A ～が立たない ❶ be lost; be unable to find one's bearings. ❷ be lost for a solution; be unable to find a way out (of a situation). ～が付く ❶ find one's way out (of a place); find one's orientation; get one's bearings. ❷ reach a solution; find a way out (of a situation). ～が悪い be badly orientated; face in the wrong direction.

N ～に迷う lose one's bearings; lose direction; lose one's way.

△ ～を失う ❶ lose one's bearings; lose direction; lose one's way. ❷ be at a loss; ⓘ be at one's wits' end; ⓘ be all at sea. ～を間違える lose one's sense of direction; lose one's bearings. ❶ ⓐ lose direction; one's sense of purpose; ⓒ ⓘ lose it. ～を見定める take one's bearings; find one's orientation. ～を見る ❶ find one's way out (of a place); find one's bearings. ❷ reach a solution; find a way out (of a situation). ascertain the direction (of a building); see if the direction is lucky.

ぼうぎゃく
暴虐 an outrage; an atrocity

△ ⓒ ～を行う commit atrocities.

ぼうけい
謀計 a plot; a scheme

N ⓒ ～に陥る become the victim of a plot; ⓐ fall into a trap.

△ ⓒ ～を巡らす conspire against *sb*; devise a stratagem.

ぼうげん
妄言 a reckless remark

△ ⓒ ～を吐く make a reckless remark; utter *sth* thoughtless; talk without thinking.

ぼうげん
暴言 violent language

△ ～を吐く use violent language; utter wild words; ⓘ lash out at *sb*.

ぼうこう
暴行 violence; an outrage

△ ～を加える assault *sb*; molest *sb*; employ violence against *sb*. ～を働く resort to violence; ⓒ have recourse to violence.

ぼうさき
棒先 a front palanquin bearer

△ ～を切る take a percentage; take a commission; take a rake-off take graft; ⓘ line one's pocket; ⓘ feather one's own nest. ～を撥ねる take a percentage; take a commission; take a rake-off/take graft; ⓘ line one's pocket; ⓘ feather one's own nest.

帽子 a hat; a cap; headgear

[を] ～を押える hold one's hat/cap. ～を被る put on a hat/cap. ～を取る take off one's hat/cap. ～を脱ぐ take off one's hat/cap. ～を振るう wave one's hat/cap.

法事 a Buddhist mass

[を] ～を営む hold a Buddhist mass.

房事 [E] sexual intercourse

[N] ⓔ ～に耽る indulge in sexual pleasure.
[を] ⓔ ～を慎む abstain from sexual intercourse.

方針 a course; a line; an aim

[を] ～を誤る take a wrong course. ～を立てる frame a plan; map out one's course; decide one's policy. ～を採る adopt a course; aim for *sth*; take a (certain) line.

坊主 [z] a Buddhist priest

[N] ⓒ ～に刈る have one's hair closely cropped; trim (one's hair) closely. ⓒ ～になる ❶ become Buddhist a priest. ❷ have one's head shaved.

法廷 a law court; a court of law

[A] ～で争う go to law; take *sth* to court; ⓔ bring a suit against *sb*.
[N] ～に立つ stand at the bar. ～に引き出す take *sb* up to court; sue *sb*; ⓒ drag *sb* into court. ～に持ち出す bring a matter before the court; take *sth* to court.
[する] ～へ出る appear in court; go into court.
[を] ～を開く hold a court.

暴動 a riot; a disturbance

[を] ～を起こす raise a riot; create a disturbance. ～を静める suppress a riot; put down a riot.

方法 a method; a means; a way

[を] ～を誤る do *sth* the wrong way; use the wrong method; ⓔ resort to the wrong means. ～を変える change one's methods; resort do different means. ～を講じる take steps (to achieve *sth*); take measures; employ certain means. ～を見い出す find a way; obtain a method.

法網 [E] the meshes of the law

[を] ⓒ ～を潜る slip through the meshes (of the law.

砲門 the muzzle of a gun

[を] ～を開く open fire; fire the first

gun; take (the enemy) under fire; ⓒ open hostilities.

暴利 excessive profits
图 〜を貪る make undue profits.

暴力 violence; brute force
N 〜に訴える resort to violence; ⓒ have recourse to violence.
图 〜を加える assault sb; molest sb; ⓒ employ violence against sb. 〜を振るう use violence on sb.

吠え面 a tearful face
图 ⓢ 〜を掻く laugh sourly; ⓘ laugh on the wrong end of one's face.

頬 the cheek
A 〜が痩ける have hollow cheeks; have sunken cheeks. 〜が弛む smile; look glad.
图 〜を赤らめる go red in the face; blush. 〜を染める go red in the face; blush. 〜を叩く talk too much; ⓒ rattle on; ⓘ wag one's tongue; ⓒ ⓘ talk sb's ears off; ⓘ have a long tongue. 〜を抓る ⓘ pinch oneself. 〜を尖らす put on a sulky face. 〜を膨らます ❶ puff out one's cheeks; swell one's cheeks. ❷ sulk over sth; be petulant; ⓘ make a scene; ⓒ ⓘ have the sulks.

頬桁 cheekbones
A 〜が過ぎる talk too freely; divulge a secret; ⓘ give sth away; ⓒ ⓘ shoot off one's mouth.
图 〜を叩く talk too much; ⓒ rattle on; ⓘ wag one's tongue; ⓒ ⓘ talk sb's ears off; ⓘ have a long tongue.

頬杖 "cheek props"
图 〜を突く rest one's chin in one's hands; lean on one's hands.

墓穴 a grave
图 〜を掘る ❶ dig a grave. ⓒ ❷ go to ruin; ⓘ dig one's own grave; ⓢ ⓘ go to the dogs.

保険 insurance
图 〜を掛ける take out insurance.

鉾 a halberd; arms; weapons
图 〜を収める lay down arms; stop fighting. ⓐ 〜を倒にする turn on one's ally; betray an ally; go over to the enemy; ⓘ become a turncoat. 〜を取る take up arms; rise in arms. 〜を交える open hostilities; fight each other. 〜を向ける attack sb (in an argument); ⓒ lay into someone; ⓘ turn one's guns on sb.

反故 scraps of paper
N 〜にする ❶ throw sth away; do

保護 protection; shelter
を ～を与える give protection to sb. ～を受ける be protected by sb. ～を求める seek protection.

鉾先 the point of a spear
A ～が鈍る take the edge of one's/sb's argument; lose its sting.
を ～を争う fight at close quarters; be in a life-and-death struggle. ～を交える fight each other; grapple with an opponent; ⓒ cross swords with sb. ～を向ける ❶ point one's spear at sb; attack sb with one's spear. ❷ attack sb (in an argument); ⓒ lay into someone.

埃 dust
を ～が溜まる become dusty; gather dust; collect dust.
～を静める let sth rest; lay the dust. ～を立てる ❶ raise dust; stir up dust; kick up dust. ❷ cause a disturbance; ⓑ raise a dust; ⓒ stir up dust. ～を払う brush away the dust; wipe off the dust.

誇り pride; a boast
と ～とする take pride in sth; be proud of sth.
を ～を傷つける hurt sb's pride. ～を持つ have pride; be proud.

星 a star; a spot; a culprit
A ⓢ ～が割れる find out who the culprit is.
を ⓢ ～を挙げる ❶ arrest a culprit; seize a criminal. ❷ [sumō] win a match. ⓒ ～を戴く ❶ work till late into the night; work late shifts. ❷ labor hard; work hard; ⓒ work from dawn till dusk. ～を射る ❶ win a point; gain a point. ❷ get a good score; obtain good results. ⓒ ～を失う be beaten; suffer a defeat; ⓑ be worsted; ⓒ bite the dust. ⓒ ～を落す [sumō] lose a match. ～を被く ❶ work till late into the night; work late shifts. ❷ labor hard; work hard; ⓒ work from dawn till dusk. ⓒ ～を稼ぐ ❶ win a point; gain a point. ❷ get a good score; obtain good results. ❸ rise in sb's estimation; improve one's standing. ❹ ingratiate oneself with sb; ⓒ curry favor with sb. ⓐⓢ ～を食わす guess right; get it right; ⓒ be on the mark; ⓒⓒ get the point; ⓒ hit the nail on the head. ⓐⓒ ～を指す ❶ guess right; ⓒ be on the mark; ⓒⓒ hit the mark.

❷ see through (a plot); penetrate (*sb's* heart). ◎ 〜を付ける take aim at; have an eye on; mark *sb* out. ◎ 〜を潰す [*sumō*] lose a match. ⓗ ◎ 〜を唱える proclaim the year's star sign. ◎ 〜を拾う [*sumō*] rescue a victory; win in spite of the odds. ◎ 〜を見る tell *sb's* fortune.

臍 Ⓔ the navel; a tenon; a pivot

Ⓐ Ⓔ 〜を固める ❶ make up one's mind; resolve to do *sth*. ❷ believe firmly in *sth*; have unstinting faith in *sb*/*sth*. ◎ 〜を噛む repent *sth*; have regrets; regret *sth*. ◎ 〜を決める make up one's mind; be prepared for *sth*; be determined; be resolved (to do *sth*); gird up one's loins. 〜を食う regret *sth*; repent *sth*; have regrets. ◎ ◎ 〜を付ける have dinner; have *sth* to eat.

菩提 Buddhahood; enlightenment

Ⓐ ◎ 〜を弔う pray for the repose of *sb's* soul; hold a memorial service; hold a mass for *sb*.

釦 a button

Ⓐ 〜を押す ◎ push a button. 〜を掛ける fasten one's buttons; button up (a coat). 〜を付ける put on a button; sew a button on (a coat). 〜を毟り取る tear off a button.

歩調 a pace; a step

Ⓐ 〜が合う ❶ keep the same pace. ❷ be like-minded; get along well; ◎ see eye to eye; ◎ ◎ hit it off. Ⓐ 〜を合わす ❶ fall into step; keep pace with *sb*. ❷ work together; act in concert. 〜を定める set the pace. 〜を揃える ❶ fall into step; keep pace with *sb*. ❷ work together; act in concert. 〜を整える set the pace. 〜を取る keep step; keep pace with *sb*. 〜を早める quicken one's pace. 〜を乱す break step; walk out of step. 〜を緩める slacken one's pace.

没 rejection

Ⓝ 〜にする reject an article; turn down (a manuscript); consign (an article) to the wastepaper basket.

程 a limit; an extent; one's place

Ⓐ 〜が有る have one's limits. Ⓐ 〜が良い ❶ be refined; be stylish; be smart. ❷ have a clever tongue; ◎ ◎ have the gift of the gab. Ⓐ 〜を越す break bounds; go too far. 〜を知る know one's place; know one's limitations. 〜を守る observe moderation; keep within bounds; stay within good limits.

仏 Buddha; the departed soul

Ⓝ 〜になる ❶ become enlightened;

become a Buddha. ❷ pass away; draw one's last breath; ⓒ ① breathe one's last ❸ reach extacy; be in seventh heaven.

骨 bones; a skeleton ▶ 骨

[A] 〜が有る have fortitude; have strong convictions. 〜が折れる be laborious; be a hard job; find *sth* hard to do. 〜が太い ❶ have thick bones; be well built. ❷ be firm; be reliable; be sturdy; ⓒ be steadfast.
[N] 〜に刻む engrave *sth* on one's memory. 〜に沁みる sink deep into one's mind; feel *sth* deeply. 〜に徹する ❶ go straight to the heart; ① cut to the quick. ❷ master a skill fully; make (a skill) one's own. Ⓐ 〜に徹る go straight to the heart; feel *sth* deeply; ① cut to the quick. 〜になる pass away; draw one's last breath; ⓒ ① breathe one's last.
[を] 〜を埋める ❶ bury *sb's* remains; inter *sb*. ❷ make (a place) one's final home; settle permanently (in a place). ❸ devote one's life to (a cause); dedicate oneself to (a cause). 〜を惜しむ ❶ spare oneself (the trouble); be sparing of oneself. ❷ be idle; be lazy; neglect one's duty. 〜を折る ❶ break a bone; suffer a fracture. ❷ take pains to do *sth*; make serious efforts; exert oneself. ❸ have a hard time of it; go through a lot of trouble. 〜を粉にする work extremely hard; ① work one's fingers to the bone. 〜を刺す be frozen to the bones; have one's bones ache with cold. 〜を曝す be reduced to a skeleton. 〜を違える dislocate a limb. 〜を接ぐ set a broken bone; set a fracture. 〜を抜く ❶ bone a fish. ❷ emasculate *sth*; take the backbone out of *sth*; ① water *sth* down. ❸ emasculate *sb*; take the soul out of *sb*. Ⓐ 〜を盗む ❶ cause *sb* a lot of work; be a burden to *sb*. ❷ be idle; be lazy; neglect one's duty. 〜を拾う ❶ gather a deceased's ashes. ❷ look after a deceased's affairs; take the place (of a fallen comrade). 〜を休める take a rest; ⓒ have a breather.

骨身 flesh and bones

[N] 〜に応える be chilled to the bone. 〜に沁みる sink deep into one's mind; feel *sth* deeply. 〜に徹する feel *sth* deeply; ① come home to one; ① cut to the quick.
[を] 〜を惜しむ ❶ spare oneself (the trouble); be sparing of oneself. ❷ be idle; be lazy; neglect one's duty. 〜を削る ❶ work hard; do one's best; ① work one's fingers to the bone. ❷ suffer great hardships.

ボン / マ

歩武(ほぶ) 🇪 marching steps
🇳 ⓢ 〜を進(すす)める advance on (one's enemy); make a drive on (a stronghold). 〜を揃(そろ)える ❶ fall into step; keep pace with *sb*. ❷ work together; act in concert.

法螺(ほら) a boast; a brag; big talk
🇪 〜を吹(ふ)く boast about *sth*; brag about *sth*; ① tell a tall tale; ② talk big; ⓒ ① talk through one's hat; ① blow one's own horn (trumpet).

洞ヶ峠(ほらがとうげ) Hora pass
🇳 〜を決(き)め込(こ)む remain a passive onlooker; wait and see; ① sit on the fence; wait for the cat to jump.

襤褸(ぼろ) a rag; a shred; a fault
🇦 〜が出(で)る have one's faults exposed; be found out; ① show the cloven hoof; ⓒ ① show oneself up.
🇪 〜を隠(かく)す hide one's faults; cover up one's mistakes. 〜を出(だ)す expose one's faults; betray one's ignorance; ⓒ ① show oneself up. 〜を見(み)せる expose one's faults; betray one's ignorance; ⓒ ① show oneself up.

盆(ぼん) the Bon (Lantern) festival
🇳 〜を傾(かたむ)ける pour down with rain; rain hard; come down in torrents; ⓒ ① rain cats and dogs. 〜を覆(くつがえ)す

pour down with rain; rain hard; come down in torrents; ⓒ ① rain cats and dogs. 〜を敷(し)く ❶ run a gambling house. ❷ own one's own house. ❸ start one's own shop; set up shop. 〜をひく ❶ run a gambling house. ❷ own one's own house. ❸ start one's own shop; set up shop.

本気(ほんき) seriousness; earnestness
🇦 〜で言(い)う mean *sth*; speak in earnest; say *sth* in all seriousness.
🇳 〜にする take *sb* serious; believe what *sb* says. 〜になる become serious; get serious; ⓒ ① get real.

本腰(ほんごし) "a proper hip stance"
🇪 〜を入(い)れる do *sth* in earnest; make a serious effort; ① get down to business; ⓒ ① swing into full gear.

本音(ほんね) one's real intentions
🇪 〜を吐(は)く confess one's real intention; ⓒ owe up; ① show one's true colors; ① drop one's mask. 〜を吹(ふ)く confess one's real intention; ⓒ owe up; ① show one's true colors; ① drop one's mask.

マ

間(ま) space; room; an interval ▶ 間(あいだ)
🇦 〜が有(あ)る have the time (to do

sth); have time (for sth). 〜が合わな
い there is no time (to do sth); be
out of time. 〜が良い be fortunate;
be auspicious; be lucky. 〜が欠ける
be short of time; be too late. 〜が抜
ける ❶ be out of tune; be off-key;
be off-bear. ❷ look stupid; be out of
place; be absent-minded. 〜が延び
る be slovenly; be dull; be careless;
be untidy. 〜が持てない run out of
topics for conversation. 〜が悪い
❶ feel awkward; be embarrassed; be
ashamed. ❷ be unfortunate; be
unlucky; be inauspicious. ❸ be
untimely; be inconvenient.
[N] 〜に合う ❶ be on time; be in
time; meet a deadline. ❷ be of use;
ⓑ be opportune; ⓒ come in handy.
❸ be enough; be sufficient; meet
requirements.
[を] 〜を開ける leave a space; space
out. 〜を合わす ❶ keep good time
with (the music). ❷ act appropriate-
ly; do sth timely; ⓒ patch sth up for
the time being. 〜を窺う watch for
a good moment; ⓑ bide one's time.
〜を措く leave a space; leave an
interval; put a pause (between). 〜
を欠く be of no use; be incompe-
tent; be to no avail. 〜を貸す let a
room; rent a room. 〜を借りる take
a room; hire a room. 〜を配る leave
(enough) space; arrange things spaciously. 〜を詰める fill a gap; close
a gap. 〜を取る leave (enough)
space; arrange things spaciously. 〜
を塞ぐ fill a space. 〜を見る watch
for a good moment; ⓒ bide one's
time. 〜を持たす fill in the time;
use one's spare time (well). ⓐ 〜を
渡す do sth timely; act appropriate-
ly; act in time; meet the occasion.

魔 a demon; a devil

[A] 〜が刺す be tempted by a devil;
be possessed by an evil spirit; fall
victim to temptation. 〜が悪い have
no luck; be unlucky; be unfortunate.
[を] 〜を祓う exorcise an evil spirit.
〜を避ける avert evil influences;
keep evil spirits away.

真 truth; reality; seriousness ▶ 真しん

[N] 〜に受ける take sth as the truth;
accept sth as true; believe sth to be
true; accept sth as true. ⓐ 〜に成る
get serious; straighten one's face;
put on a serious look.

前 the front; forward

[A] 〜が有る ❶ have a criminal
record; be an ex-convict. ❷ have a
criminal past; have a shady past;
have bad credentials.
[と] 〜と変わらない be the same as
before; remain unchanged.

Ⓝ ～に座る sit in front; sit in the front seat.
㋣ ～へ出る step forward. ～へ呼び出される be called in front (of the class).
㋾ ～を隠す cover one's private parts. ～を通る pass in front of *sb*. ～を見る look in front of one. ～を向ける face the front.

巻き添え involvement

Ⓝ ～にする involve *sb* in a situation; entangle *sb* (in a plot); implicate *sb* (in a crime).
㋾ ⓐ ～を食う be entangled (in a plot); be implicated (in a crime); get embroiled (in a quarrel).

幕 a curtain; a hanging screen

Ⓐ ～が上がる ❶ the curtain rises; the play begins. ❷ *sth* starts; *sth* begins. ～が開く ❶ the curtain rises; the play begins. ❷ *sth* starts; *sth* begins. ～が下りる the curtain falls; the play comes to an end. ～が切れる an episode comes to an end. ～が支える be short of funds; be poorly funded. ～が通る ❶ make *sb* understand; get one's ideas across. ❷ become widely know; win fame.
Ⓝ ⓐ ～にする bring *sth* to an end; ⓘ bring down the curtain. ～になる come to an end.
㋾ ～を上げる raise the curtain; begin a play. ～を打つ ❶ close the curtain; bring *sth* to an end; ⓘ bring down the curtain. ⓑ ❷ an ally pitches a camp; set up camp. ～を下ろす drop the curtain; bring *sth* to an end. ～を切り上げる leave a place; ⓒ ⓘ pack up. ～を切り落とす begin *sth* in style; make a splendid start. ⓐ ～を切る ❶ raise the curtain; begin a play. ❷ start on *sth*; set about doing *sth*. ❸ drop the curtain; end a play. ❹ bring *sth* to an end; end *sth*; ⓘ bring down the curtain. ❺ patch things up for the moment; make temporary improvements. ❻ leave one's seat; leave a place. ⓐ ～を通す ❶ carry the stage; command a house. ❷ make oneself understood; get one's ideas across. ～を閉じる ❶ close the curtain; drop the curtain. ❷ bring *sth* to an end; end *sth*; ⓘ bring down the curtain on *sth*. ～を張る ❶ hang up a curtain. ⓑ ❷ pitch a camp; set up camp. ～を引く ❶ close the curtain; drop the curtain. ❷ bring *sth* to an end; end *sth*; ⓘ bring down the curtain. ⓑ ❸ an enemy pitches a camp; set up camp.

枕 a pillow; a headrest

Ⓐ ～が上がらない remain bed-ridden; fail to improve in health. ⓐ ～が浮く cry in one's pillow; shed tears in bed; cry oneself to sleep. 🅴 ⓐ ～と枕く go to sleep; curl up. 🅺 ～を重ねる sleep together regularly; share the same bed regularly; have regular intercourse. ～を傾ける go to bed; go to sleep; curl up. ～を交わす ❶ sleep together; share the same bed. ❷ have intercourse; have sex; ⓒ ⓘ do it. ⓐ ～を砕く fret over *sth*; be troubled by *sth*; worry about *sth*. ～を捜す steel *sth* from under *sb's* pillow; rob *sb* in their sleep; commit bedroom theft. ⓐ ～を定む ❶ decide in which direction to sleep. ❷ choose a place to sleep. ❸ [prostitution] choose a sleeping partner. ～をする use a pillow; use a headrest. ⓒ ～を欹てる raise one's head from one's pillow; rear one's head by propping up one's pillow. ～を高くする ❶ sleep in peace; sleep sound. ❷ have peace of mind; be free from care; feel at ease. ❸ feel reassured; feel relieved; be assured. ⓐ ～を付ける sleep together; share the same bed. ～を並べる ❶ sleep together; share the same bed. ❷ fall in great numbers; commit mass suicide. ～を濡らす cry in one's pillow; shed tears in bed. ～を振る ❶ [*rakugo*] make introductory remarks.

❷ begin a play; ⓘ raise the curtain. ❸ begin *sth* in style; make a splendid start. ～を結ぶ stay at an inn; sleep away from home; pass a night on one's journey; sleep rough. ⓐ ～を割る be troubled by *sth*; worry about *sth*; fret over *sth*.

負け defeat; a lost contest
🅰 ～が込む lose many contests; suffer defeat upon defeat.
🅽 ～になる lose a contest; be defeated; suffer a defeat; ⓒ ⓘ be licked; ⓒ ⓘ be whipped.

負けん気 🅱 fighting spirit; pluck
🅺 ⓢ ～を出す show fight; be indomitable; refuse to yield.

誠 truth; sincerity
🅺 ～を込めて…する do *sth* in good faith; (speak) from the heart. ～を尽す be truthful; be faithful.

呪い a spell; a charm
🅺 ～を掛ける put a spell on *sb*. ～を消す break a spell. ～をする put a spell on *sb*.

真面目 seriousness; gravity
🅽 ～になる ❶ become serious; turn grave; fall quiet. ❷ become dispirited; be cretfallen.

交わり acquaintance; society

[を] ～を絶つ part company; cut off relations; have a falling out. ～を深める become friendly; deepen one's acquaintance. ～を結ぶ become attached (to one another); form a fellowship.

股 the crotch; the fork

[N] ～に掛ける travel the world; be a globetrotter.
[を] (人の)～を潜る creep between sb's legs. be humiliated; ⓘ bite the dust; ⓒⓘ eat dirt; ⓒⓘ eat crow ～を広げる set one's legs apart; spread one's legs.

待ち伏せ an ambush

[を] ⓢ ～を食う fall into an ambush; be waylaid. ～をやめる break an ambush.

待ち惚け ⓔ waiting in vain

[を] ⓒ ～を食う wait in vain for sb; ⓒⓘ be stood up.

松 a pine (tree)

[A] ⓒ ～が取れる the first week of the New Year has passed.

真っ黒 deep-balck; pitch-black

[N] ～に焦げる be scorched black. ～になる ❶ become deeply tanned; ❷ⓘ be as brown as a berry. ❷ forget oneself; be absorbed in sth; ⓒ be engrossed in sth.

睫 eyelashes; lashes

[を] ～を濡らす be on the alert; watch out; ⓘ be on one's guard. ⓐ ～を読まれる ❶ be taken in by sb; be cheated on. ❷ be looked down on; be slighted; be made light of; ⓒ be held in contempt.

末席 ⓔ a back seat

[N] ⓒ ～に座る sit at the bottom end of the table; take a back seat.
[を] ⓒ ～を汚す have the honor of attending (a wedding).

マット a mat; a doormat; a rug

[N] ⓢ ～に沈む [boxing] be knocked out; be floored.

祭 a festival; a fete; a feast day

[A] ～が閧える the heat goes out of a quarrel; dampen down.

的 a mark; a target; an object

[A] ⓢ ～が立つ be punished by the gods; incur divine punishment; be served right.
[N] ～に当たる ❶ hit the target; hit the mark; strike home. ❷ grasp the crux (of a matter); get it right; ⓘ hit

the mark; ⓒ ① get the point.
图 ～を射る ❶ hit the target; hit the mark; strike home. ❷ be relevant; ① be on the mark; ① hit the nail on the head; ① be to the point. ～を越す overshoot the mark. ～を絞る focus on *sth*; set one's sights on *sth*; aim at (a target). ～を外す ❶ fail to hit the mark; miss the mark; miss in one's aim. ❷ be irrelevant; ① be off the mark; ① be beside the point.

俎板 a cutting board
N ～に載せる ❶ put (food) on the chopping block. ❷ put *sth* under review; take *sth* up for discussion.

眦 ⑥ the corner of the eye
图 ⓒ ～を決す glare (furiously) at *sb/sth*; stare one's eyes out; ① look daggers at *sb*.

瞼 an eyelid; the lid of an eye
A ～が重い feel sleepy; be tired; one's eyelids are heavy. N ～に浮かぶ come before one's eyes; come to mind; occur to one; ⓒ rise in one's thoughts. ～に残る linger before one's eyes; ① be engraved on one's memory. 图 ～を閉じる close one's eyes; shut one's eyes. ～を引っくり返す roll back one's/sb's eyelid(s).

魔法 magic; sorcery; witchcraft
图 ～を掛ける cast a spell on *sb*; put *sb* under a spell. ～を使う use magic; practice witchcraft.

幻 a phantom; an apparition
N ～に見る see *sth* in a vision. 图 ～を追う pursue phantoms.

眉 an eyebrow; one's brow
N ～に迫る draw close; come into view; enter one's field of vision. 图 ～を上げる ❶ raise one's eyebrows. ❷ look angered. Ⓐ ～を集める knit one's brows; ⓒ bend one's brows. Ⓐ ～を落とす ❶ shave off one's eyebrows. ❷ get married; become *sb's* wife; ⓒ ① tie the knot. ～を描く correct one's eyebrows; pencil one's eyebrows. ～を曇らす look troubled. ～を顰める contract one's eyebrows; knit one's brows; ⓒ bend one's brows. ～を皺める contract one's eyebrows; knit one's brows; ⓒ bend one's brows. ～を引く correct one's eyebrows; pencil one's eyebrows. ～を顰める frown on *sth*; knit one's brows; ⓒ bend one's brows. ～を開く feel relieved; feel assured. Ⓐ ～を広ぐ feel relieved; feel assured. ～を寄せる frown on *sth*; knit one's brows; ⓒ bend one's brows. Ⓐ ～を読む read *sb's* thoughts.

三

眉根 an eyebrow

[A] ～を寄せる frown on *sth*; knit one's brows; © bend one's brows.

満 fullness; ripeness

[を] © ～を侍す ❶ draw a bow fully. ❷ wait until the time is ripe; watch for an opportunity; © bide one's time. ～を搾る ❶ draw a bow fully. ❷ wait until the time is ripe; watch for an opportunity; © bide one's time. ～を引く ❶ draw a bow fully. © ❷ drink to one's heart's content; have one's fill; ⓘ lift one's elbow.

万一 a contingency

[N] ～に備える provide against contingencies.
[を] ～を頼む trust to chance.

三

身 the body; the flesh; oneself

[A] ～が入る become interested in *sth*; be absorbed in *sth*; © be engrossed in *sth*; © warm up to *sth*. ～が重くなる become pregnant; have *sb*'s child; © be with child. ～が固まる ❶ get on in life; settle down. ❷ get a job; find one's vocation. ❸ get married; © ⓘ tie the knot. ～が軽い ❶ be nimble; be agile. ❷ travel light; be lightly dressed. ©

～が極まる settle down; get a job; get married. ～が定まる settle down; get a job; get married. ～が竦む shrink with fear; draw back from *sth*; © recoil from *sth*. ～が立つ ❶ save one's honor; maintain one's dignity; ⓘ save one's face; ⓘ stand proud. ❷ make a living; get by; support oneself; © earn one's daily bread. ⓐ ～が詰まる be cornered; be in trouble; ⓘ be in dire straits; ⓘ be brought to bay. ～が入る become interested in *sth*; be absorbed in *sth*; © be engrossed in *sth*; © warm up to *sth*. ⓐ ～が燃える burn with (anger). ⓘ be on fire; © be consumed (with passion). ～が持てぬ ❶ lose one's maners; go astray; © stray from virtue; ⓢ ⓘ go to the dogs. ❷ ruin oneself; dissipate one's fortune; ⓢ ⓘ go bust.

[N] ～に合う be suitable; © be becoming; suit one. ～に当たる ❶ take charge; take control; ⓘ take *sth* in hand; ⓐ step in. ❷ sympathize deeply with; feel deeply for *sb*; © empathize with *sb*. ～に余る ❶ be too much for one; be more than one can deal with. ❷ be more than one deserves; be too great an honor. ～に入る feel *sth* deeply; ⓘ come home to one; ⓘ cut to the quick. ⓐ ～に入れる put oneself into *sth*; take an interest in *sth*; devote oneself to *sth*. 〜に受ける feel *sth* as if it happened to oneself; affect one personally. 〜に負う ❶ⓒ shoulder (a burden). bear responsibility; ⓐ carry the burden. ❷ take responsibility; take the blame; ⓓ be a fall guy. ❸ tax one's abilities to the full degree; match one's capacities. 〜に落ちる fall upon oneself (to do); be left to one (to do). 〜に代える value *sth* as much as one's own life; do *sth* in the face of death. ⓐ 〜に掛かる affect one; befall one. 〜に沁みる ❶ be chilled to the bone. ❷ sink deep into one's mind; ⓒ come home to one. 〜に過ぎる ❶ be too much for one; be more than one can deal with. ❷ be more than one deserves; be too great an honor. 〜に付く ❶ be nourishing; be good for one. ❷ make *sth* one's own; master (a craft). ❸ be eager to do; take an interest in *sth*; devote oneself to *sth*; ❹ be equipped with *sth*; fit one's body. 〜に付ける ❶ put on (a piece of clothing/jewelry); bear a weapon; carry *sth* on one's body. ❷ acquire *sth*; be equipped with *sth*. ❸ learn (a skill); master (a skill). 〜に詰まされる sympathize deeply with; feel deeply for; ⓒ empathize with *sb*. 〜に成す make oneself acquainted with *sb*/*sth*' familiarize oneself with *sth*; make oneself at home in (a topic). 〜になる ❶ be nourishing; do one good. (人の) ❷ put oneself in *sb's* place. ❸ join *sb*; become *sb's* ally. 〜に纏う put *sth* on; be wrapped in (a garment). 図 〜を誤る go astray; ⓒ stray from virtue; ⓓ go to the bad. 〜を合わす become one; ⓔ act in unison. 〜を入れる put oneself into *sth*; take an interest in; devote oneself to *sth*. ⓐ 〜を失う ❶ lose one's life; pass away. ❷ commit suicide; kill oneself. ❸ lay down one's life; throw away one's life. ⓐ 〜を打つ indulge in *sth*; give oneself up to *sth*; abandon oneself to *sth*. 〜を売る prostitute oneself; sell oneself (into slavery). 〜を起こす ❶ rise up; set to work. ⓢ get cracking. ❷ rise in the world; establish oneself; make one's way up. ⓐ 〜を修む get a grip on oneself; straighten oneself out. 〜を落とす ❶ drop oneself; let oneself fall. ❷ degrade oneself; descend to do *sth*; stoop to do *sth*. ❸ come down in the world; be down and out. 〜を踊らす ❶ jump in the air; leap (for joy). ❷ plunge into action. ⓐ 〜を変える be reborn. 〜を屈める stoop down; bend over. 〜を隠す ❶ hide oneself; go into hiding; ⓒ lie low.

❷ live a scluded life; live in seclusion. ❸ hide one's background; cover up one's past. 〜を固(かた)める ❶ settle down; get a steady job; get married. ❷ dress up (warm); ⓒ bundle up. ❸ stand ready; take a stance; stand on guard. 〜を躱(かわ)す avoid danger; dodge an attack; shirk one's duty; avoid responsibility; ⓘ dodge the column. 〜を浄(きよ)める purify oneself. 〜を切(き)られる be chilled to the bone; be extremely cold. 〜を切(き)る ❶ feel the cold. ❷ experience great hardships. ❸ pay sth out of one's own pocket. 〜を砕(くだ)く ❶ work oneself to the bone; do one's utmost. ❷ put one's body in the service of Buddha. ❸ become a Buddhist monk; take the tonsure. 〜を汚(けが)す defile oneself; lose one's chastity. 〜を削(けず)る suffer great hardships; be in anguish. 〜を焦(こ)がす burn with (unrequited) love; ⓒ be consumed with love. 〜を粉(こ)にする work extremely hard; ⓘ work one's fingers to the bone. Ⓐ 〜を懲(こ)らす do penance; mortify one's flesh. 〜を曝(さら)す expose oneself; lay oneself open to (an attack). 〜を沈(しず)める ❶ drown oneself; throw oneself into the water. ❷ sell one's body; prostitute oneself. ❸ be down and out; go to ruin; go down in the world. 〜を侍(じ)する lead a hard life; eke out a living. 〜を忍(しの)ぶ go into hiding; hide oneself; ⓘ go to ground. 〜を絞(しぼ)る give it one's all; ⓔ exert oneself to the utmost; go all out. 〜を仕舞(しま)う destroy oneself; ruin oneself. 〜を過(す)ぐ make a life for oneself; earn a livelihood; make a living. 〜を捨(す)てる ❶ lay down one's life; throw away one's life; sacrifice one's life; dedicate one's life (to a cause). ❷ go into seclusion; become a hermit; ⓒ retire from the world; renounce the world. ❸ become a Buddhist priest; take the tonsure; ⓒ retire into religion. ❹ leave one's body; ⓒ throw off one's mortal coil. 〜をする make a gesture; gesticulate. 〜を立(た)てる rise in the world; establish oneself (as an artist); set oneself up (in a trade). Ⓐ 〜を辿(たど)る reflect on one's life; relive one's past life. 〜を尽(つ)くす ❶ do one's utmost; do sth with one's whole heart. ❷ risk one's life; ⓘ put one's life on the line. 〜を慎(つつし)む behave prudently. Ⓐ 〜を抓(つ)む sympathize deeply with; feel deeply for sb. Ⓐ 〜を詰(つ)める live frugally; lead a frugal life. 〜を挺(てい)する risk one's life; offer one's life; throw oneself (into the breach). 〜を投(とう)じる ❶ throw oneself (into a river). ❷ plunge (headlong) into sth; go into (politics); ⓘ burn one's boats/bridges (behind one). 〜

を投げる ❶ throw oneself (off a building); hurl oneself (into the water); ❷ throw oneself into *sth* heart and soul; put one's heart and soul into *sth*. 〜を成す ❶ dress oneself; get oneself ready; fit oneself out. ❷ put oneself into *sth*; take an interest in; devote oneself to *sth*. 〜を盗む ❶ be idle be lazy; skimp one's work; ⓢ ⓘ skate on the job. ❷ enter/leave a place by stealth; steal into/out (of a place); ⓒ sneak in/out (of a place). ⓐ 〜を逃れる avoid danger; dodge an attack; shirk one's duty; avoid responsibility; ⓘ dodge the column. (窓から)〜を乗り出す lean out of (the window). ⓐ 〜を果たす ❶ risk one's life; ⓘ put one's life on the line; ⓘ throw oneself into the jaws of death. ❷ come to an untimely end; sacrifice one's life. ❸ ruin oneself; go bankrupt; ⓢ ⓘ go the the dogs. ⓐ 〜を填む do *sth* with devotion; throw oneself into *sth* wholeheartedly; pour all one's love into *sth*. 〜を退く ❶ draw one's body back; retreat; ⓘ step back. ❷ resign from one's post; leave an occupation; step down; ⓒ back out. 〜を潜める hide oneself. 〜を冷やす be struck with terror; ⓘ be scared to death. ⓘ break into a cold sweat. 〜を開く step back (in line).

〜を滅ぼす ruin oneself; destroy oneself; ⓢ ⓘ go to the dogs. (男に)〜を任す give oneself to a man; sleep with a man. 〜を任せる ❶ throw oneself on the mercy of *sb*. ❷ give oneself up to (an addiction/vice). ❸ give oneself to (a man); sleep with a man. ❹ resign oneself to (one's fate). 〜を毟る pick the flesh (from the bones). 〜を結ぶ ❶ bear fruit. ❷ be successful; carry fruit; produce results. ❸ concieve a child. 〜を持ち崩す destroy oneself; go to the bad; ⓢ ⓘ go to the dogs. 〜を持ち下げる come down in the world; go to the bad; ⓢ ⓘ go to the dogs. ⓐ 〜を持つ ❶ be independent; stand on one's own feet; ⓒ ⓘ cut the cord. ❷ get married; get settled; settle down. ❸ be well behaved; have good manners. ❹ conduct oneself (in a certain way); act (as if one were...); hold oneself. 〜を揉む writhe in agony; fret greatly over *sth*; worry about *sth*; fidget about *sth*. 〜を燃やす ❶ burn with unrequited love; ⓒ be consumed with love. ❷ burn with rage; ⓘ be on fire. ⓐ 〜を焼く ❶ suffer great agonies; be convulsed with anguish. ❷ burn with (unrequited) love; ⓒ be consumed with love. 〜を窶す ❶ disguise oneself; dress oneself (as *sb*/*sth*). ❷ devote oneself to sth; be absorbed in sth; pine for (sb's love). 〜を寄^よせる live with sb; stay with sb. 〜を分^わつ ❶ devide sth in two; split sth up. ❷ open up the body; enter a body.

実^み a fruit; a nut; a berry ▶ 実^{じつ}

Ⓐ 〜がなる bear fruit.
を 〜を結^{むす}ばせる carry sth to fruition. 〜を結^{むす}ぶ bear fruit; pay off.

見え^み show; display; ostentation

を 〜を切る ❶ [kabuki] asume a mie pose. ❷ assume a posture; make a defiant gesture; strike an attitude. 〜を拵^{こしら}える ❶ make outward show; save appearances; ⓘ keep up appearances. ❷ try to hide a short-coming; gloss over sth; put a gloss on sth. 〜をする ❶ make a (certain) face; look (strange/normal). ❷ tidy oneself up. ❸ make outward show; save appearances; ⓘ keep up appearances. ❹ make a good impression; look smart; be suave. 〜を作^{つく}る ❶ make outward show; save appearances; ⓘ keep up appearances. ❷ try to hide a shortcoming; gloss over sth; put a gloss on sth. 〜を張^はる show off; be vain; ⓔ be ostentatious.

見え坊^{みえぼう} Ⓝ a vain person; a swell

Ⓐ ⓒ 〜を言^いう talk pompously; show off; ⓘ have airs and graces; ⓢ ⓘ be stuck-up.

磨き^{みが} a polish; burnishing

を 〜をかける ❶ give sth a polish; polish sth up. ❷ improve one's skills; work on one's technique.

右^{みぎ} (the) right; the above

Ⓝ (人^{ひと}の)〜に出^でる Ⓐ ❶ occupy a higher rank; be superior in rank. ❷ surpass sb; be superior to sb.
を 〜へ曲^まがる turn to the right. 〜へ寄^よる lean to the right.
を 〜を見る look to the right.

見切り^{みき} forsaking; abandonment

Ⓐ 〜で買^かう buy sth at a reduced price.
を 〜を付^つける give sth up; be through with sb/sth; be done with sb/sth.

神輿^{みこし} a portable shrine

を 〜を擧^あげる ❶ lift up a portable shrine. ❷ rise from one's seat; get up. ❸ set to work; take action; ⓒ get on with sth. 〜を下^おろす ❶ put down a portable shrine. ❷ sit down; take a seat. 〜を担^{かつ}ぐ ❶ carry a portable shrine. ❷ cajole sb into sth; talk sb into sth. 〜を据^すえる ❶ settle oneself down; plant oneself (on a chair). ❷ outstay one's welcome. 〜を揉む push and shve a portable shrine.

見込み expectations; prospects

[A] 〜が当たる ❶ guess right; ⓒ ⓘ be spot on. ❷ meet one's expectations; come true. 〜が有る be promising; have bright prospects. 〜が薄い have a slim chance (of success). 〜が立たない be incalculable; be unfathomable. 〜が乏しい have a slim chance (of success). 〜が無い have no prospects (of succeeding); do not stand a chance; be hopeless. 〜が外れる ❶ guess wrong; ⓒ ⓘ be off the mark. ❷ fail to meet one's expectations.
[を] 〜を付ける ❶ make an estimate; make a prediction. ❷ make sure of sth; ⓒ ⓘ check sth out.

見殺し see sb die (and not help)

[N] 〜にする ❶ let sb die without giving help; see sb die without attempting to save him/her. ❷ abandon sb; leave sb in the lurch; sell sb down the river.

操 chastity; faithfulness

[を] 〜を立てる ❶ be faithful; remain constant; stick to one's principles; stand firm; ⓘ hold to one's colors; ⓘ stick to one's guns. ❷ remain faithful to sb; be chaste; ⓒ defend one's virtue. 〜を破る ❶ betray one's principles; ⓒ ⓘ sell out. ❷ be unfaithful; lose one's chastity; ⓒ be inconstant; ⓒ ⓘ sleep around.

水 water; a flood ▸ 水

[A] 〜が開く be in the lead. 〜が染む become a local; blend in with the locality; be a native. ⓒ 〜が回る become widely known.
[Aᵥ] 〜で割る water sth down; ⓘ put water in the wine/whiskey.
[N] 〜に逆らう be out of tune with the times; go against the stream. Ⓐ 〜にする ❶ put sth to waste; waste sth; spoil sth; throw sth away. ❷ let sth pass; forgive and forget; ⓒ let bygones be bygones; ⓒ ⓘ let sth go. ❸ have an abortion; abort a pregnancy. 〜に流す let sth pass; forgive and forget; ⓒ let bygones be bygones; ⓒ let sth go. Ⓐ 〜になる come to nothing; ⓘ go up in smoke; be wasted. 〜に馴れる ❶ get accustomed to the drinking water. ❷ get used to one's new environment; settle in. 〜に浸す soak sth in water.
[を] 〜を開ける open up a lead (between oneself and the competition). 〜を入れる ❶ [sumō] give water to sumō wrestlers to refresh

themselves. ❷ take a rest; have a break; ⓒ have a breather. 〜を打つ water (the lawn). 〜を切る ❶ drain the water. ❷ plow the water. 〜を好む take to water; be water-loving. 〜を注す ❶ pour water into (a kettle). ❷ estrange people from each other; cause ill feelings between people; ⓘ breed bad blood. ❸ discourage sb; put a damper on (sb's enthusiasm); ⓘ be a wet blanket; ⓘ pour cold water on (sb's enthusiasm). 〜を出す turn on the water. 〜を止める turn off the water. 〜を抜く drain off (a tub). 〜を弾く repel water; be water-repellent. 〜を向ける ❶ offer water on the altar. ❷ distract sb's attention; proposition sb to do sth; win sb over; draw sth out of sb. 〜を割る add water; dilute sth with water.

店 a store; a shop; a stall

A 〜を上ぐ close shop; put up the sutters; ⓒⓘ wind up bussiness. 〜を開ける open the store. 〜を買う buy out a business. 〜を閉める ❶ close down (a shop); go out of business; ⓒ retire from business. ❷ close shop; put up the shutters; ⓒ wind up business. 〜を出す open a store. 〜を畳む close down (a shop); go out of business; ⓒ retire from business. 〜を張る open up shop. ⓒ 〜を引く close shop; put up the shutters; ⓒ wind up business. 〜を広げる extend one's business; spread (one's things) all over the place. 〜を持たせる set sb up in business. 〜を譲る hand over one's business.

身銭 one's own money

A 〜を切る pay out of one's own pocket; ⓐ untie one's purse strings; ⓘ foot the bill.

味噌 miso [bean paste]

A ⓐ 〜が腐る ❶ the miso goes bad. ❷ have a bad voice (for singing). A 〜を明ける be boastful; take pride in oneself; ⓘ blow one's own horn; ⓘ talk big. ⓐ 〜を上げる be boastful; take pride in oneself; ⓘ blow one's own horn; ⓘ talk big. ⓒ 〜を擂る ❶ grind miso before it has been strained. ❷ become a Buddhist priest; ⓒ take the tonsure. 〜を付ける ❶ apply miso to sth. ❷ be a failure; ⓒ make a mess of things; ⓒ bungle sth.

道 a way; a road; the Way

A 〜が開く have renewed hope; the prospects brighten; ⓘ see light at the end of the tunnel. 〜がくねる the road twists and turns; the road meanders. 〜が付く find a route; find a way (out); reach a solution. 〜が捗る make good headway; the going is good; ⓔ be expeditious. 〜が開ける have renewed hope; ⓘ see light at the end of the tunnel. ⓐ 〜が行く make good headway; the going is good; ⓔ be expeditious. [N] 〜に非ず go about sth in the wrong way; take the wrong approach; be the wrong way (to do sth). ⓒ 〜に欠ける fail in one's duties; ⓔ swerve from the Way. 〜に適う comply with the Way; be reasonable; be rational. 〜に背く stray from the Way; err from the Way. 〜につく follow a road; take to the road; ⓢ ⓘ hit the road. 〜に出る come out into the road; lead onto a road. 〜に入る take a (certain) way. 〜に外れる stray from the Way; ⓘ leave the straight and narrow. 〜に迷う lose one's way; get lost. [去] 〜へ出る go out into the road. [を] 〜を開ける make way for sb; give way to sb; clear the way. 〜を誤る take the wrong turn; go astray. 〜を歩く walk (up/down/along) a road; follow a road. 〜を行く take a road; go one's way. 〜を急ぐ hurry along. 〜を失う lose one's way; be at a loss (about what to do). 〜を教える tell sb the way; direct sb to a place. (人に)〜を聞く ask sb the way; ask sb for directions. ⓐ 〜を切る ❶ obstruct the road; cut off a path. ❷ cut off all relations with sb; ⓔ sever one's connections with sb. 〜を遮る obstruct a path; block the road. ith sb. 〜を進む follow a (certain) road; pursue a path. 〜を尋ねる ask the way. 〜を立てる do one's duty; do what is right. 〜を辿る follow a road; retrace a path; follow in sb's path. 〜を付ける ❶ make a road; cut a path. ❷ lead the way; pave the way (for sb). 〜を通す drive a road through (a forest); cut a path. 〜を説く expound the Way; moralize a story. 〜をとる take a (certain) road. ⓐ 〜を払う make way for sb; give way to; clear the way. 〜を開く open up a road; break trail. 〜を拾う find one's way; pick one's way. 〜を塞ぐ stand in sb's way; block sb's passage; bar the way. (人の)〜を踏み外す stray from the Way; ⓘ leave the straight and narrow. 〜を守る uphold the Way; maintain one's integrity. 〜を間違える take the wrong way. 〜を求める look for a way; seek the Way; pursue the truth. 〜を譲る ❶ yield the right of way; step aside; make way for sb. ❷ let sb else take once place; make way for sb.

道草(みちくさ) grass along the road

[を] ～を食(く)う ❶ (let one's horse) eat the grass along the road. ❷ loiter on the way; be long about it; ⓒ dilly-dally on the way (home).

密計(みっけい) Ⓔ a secret plan

[を] ⓒ ～を巡(めぐ)らす weave a plot; devise a secret plan.

三つ指(みつゆび) three fingers

[を] ～を突(つ)く make a respectful bow while placing the three fingers of both hands on the floor.

皆(みな) everybody; everything; all

[N] ～にする ❶ use *sth* up; consume *sth*; exhaust one's supplies. ❷ waste *sth*; squander *sth*; ⓒ ⓘ burn *sth* up. ～になる ❶ be exhausted; be consumed; be depleted. ❷ be wasted; ⓘ go up in smoke; ⓘ come to nothing.

身分(みぶん) status; rank; identity

[A] ～が違(ちが)う have a different social standing; differ in social standing.
[を] ～を明(あ)かす reveal one's identity; disclose one's identity. ～を隠(かく)す hide one's identity.

耳(みみ) an ear; hearing; an edge

[A] ～が痛(いた)い ❶ have a pain in the ear. ❷ be unpleasant to the ears; be embarrassed to hear *sth*. ～が汚(よご)れる hear obscenities. ～が肥(こ)える have an ear for *sth*. ～が鋭(するど)い have a keen ear; be sharp-eared. ⓒ ～が近(ちか)い have good hearing; have a sharp ear. ～が遠(とお)い have poor hearing; have a bad ear. ～が鳴(な)る have a ringing in the ears; suffer from tinnitus. ～が早(はや)い have a quick ear; be quick of hearing. ～が良(よ)い have a good ear. ～が悪(わる)い have poor hearing; have a bad ear.

[N] ⓒ ～に当(あ)たる be upset by what one hears; ⓔ offend the ears. ～に入(い)る come to one's knowledge; learn *sth* (by chance); find *sth* out; ⓘ get wind of *sth*. ～に入(い)れる ❶ tell *sb*; bring *sth* to *sb's* attention. ❷ listen to *sb*; take notice of *sth*; ⓒ ⓘ lend *sb* an ear. Ⓐ ～に掛(か)かる ❶ listen attentively; prick up one's ears. ❷ linger in one's ears; strike one's ear. Ⓐ ～に応(こた)える be brought home to one; have effect on one. ～に逆(さか)らう sound harsh to the ear; jar upon one's ear; ⓔ offend the ear. ～に障(さわ)る sound harsh to the ear; jar upon one's ear; ⓔ offend the ear. ～にする happen to hear *sth*; find out about *sth*; ⓒ pick up a rumor; ⓘ get wind of *sth*. Ⓐ ～に立(た)つ ❶ listen attentively; prick up one's ears.

❷ linger in one's ears; strike one's ear. ～に付く ❶ strike one's ear; linger in one's ear. ❷ be tired of hearing; be wary of hearing *sth*. ～に留める ❶ keep *sth* in mind; linger in one's ears. ❷ take notice of *sth*; pay attention (to what *sb* says). ⓐ ～に成る have people's ears; give cause for rumor. ～に残す linger in one's ears. ～に入る come to one's knowledge; learn *sth* by chance; find *sth* out; ⓒ get wind of *sth*. ～に挟む ❶ put (a pencil/cigarette) behind one's ear. ❷ come to one's knowledge; learn *sth* by chance; find *sth* out; ⓒ get wind of *sth*. 🔲 ～を洗う ❶ clean one's ears. ❷ cleanse oneself of the impurities one has heard. ～を疑う doubt one's own ears; cannot believe one's ears. ～を打つ whisper *sth* into *sb's* ear; ⓒ put a word into *sb's* ear; ⓒ bend *sb's* ear. ～を覆う cover one's ears (with one's hands). ～を押える stop the ears; hold one's ears. (ページの) ～を折る turn down the edge of a page. (人に)～を貸す listen to *sb*; ⓒ lend *sb* an ear; ⓒ give one's ear to *sb*. ～を傾ける listen to *sb* attentively; pay attention to (what *sb* says); ⓒ bend one's ear to *sb*. ⓐ ～を借る whisper *sth* into *sb's* ear; ⓒ put a word into *sb's* ear; ⓒ have *sb's* ear; ⓒ bend *sb's* ear. ⓐ ～を聞く reach one's ear; come to one's knowledge. ⓐ ～を擦る make an insinuating remark; ⓒ give an indirect cut; ⓒ talk at *sb*. ～を肥やす develop an ear for (music). ～を濯ぐ cleanse oneself of the impurities one has heard. ～を澄ます listen intently; strain one's ears; ⓒ be all ears. ～をそ欹てる strain one's ears; prick up one's ears. ～を側める listen intently; strain one's ears; prick up one's ears. ～を揃える make a lump-sum payment; pay in full. ～を立てる listen intently; strain one's ears; prick up one's ears. ⓐ ～を潰す pretend not to listen. ～をつんざぐ be deafening; be ear-splitting. ⓐ ～を舐る ❶ whisper *sth* into *sb's* ear; ⓒ put a word into *sb's* ear. ❷ inform on *sb*; tell on *sb*; ⓒ let on about *sb*; ⓒ stab *sb* in the back. ❸ cast aspersions on *sb*; slander *sb*; speak ill of *sb*; ⓒ cast a slur on *sb's* name. ⓐ ～を引く share *sb's* good luck. ⓑ ～を吹く whisper *sth* into *sb's* ear; ⓒ put a word into *sb's* ear. ～を塞ぐ ⓒ listen with half an ear; ⓒ turn a deaf ear. ～を穿る pick one's ear(s). ⓐ ～を読む count one's money. ⓐ ～を聾する ❶ become deaf; lose one's hearing. ❷ be deafening; make a terrible clamour.

身持ち behaviour; conduct
　[A] ～が良い ❶ be well behaved; have good manners. ❷ be steady; ⓒ be continent. ～が悪い ❶ behave badly; have bad manners. ❷ be immoral; have loose morals; be a libertine.
　[N] ～になる become pregnant; have sb's child; ⓒ be with child.
　[を] ～を直す be penitent; mend one's ways; ⓘ turn over a new leaf.

脈 a vein; a pulse; deposits
　[A] ⓒ ～が上がる ❶ pass away; draw one's last breath; ⓒ ⓘ breathe one's last. ❷ lose hope; despair of *sth*. ～が有る ❶ have a pulse; have life in one yet. ❷ have room for hope. ⓒ ～が切れる ❶ pass away; draw one's last breath; ⓒ ⓘ breathe one's last. ❷ lose hope; despair of *sth*.
　[を] ～を打つ pulsate; throb. ～を数える count *sb's* pulse. ～を繋ぐ ❶ eke out a living; ⓒ get by; ⓘ make ends meet. ❷ have a glimmer of hope; hold out hope; be not lost yet. ～を取る take *sb's* pulse; feel *sb's* pulse. ⓐ ～を引く sound *sb* out; ⓘ feel *sb's* pulse. ～を見る ❶ take *sb's* pulse; feel *sb's* pulse. ❷ test the prospects of *sth*; try the viability of *sth*.

冥加 ⓒ divine protection
　[N] ⓒ ～に余る be blessed by divine protection; be too good for one. ⓒ ～に叶う be blessed by divine protection; be too good for one. ⓒ ～に尽きる ❶ be deserted by fortune; run out of good luck. ❷ be too good for one.

冥利 providence; divine favor
　[A] ⓒ ～が恐ろしい tough luck. ⓒ ～が尽きる ❶ be deserted by fortune; run out of good luck. ❷ be sinful; be wicked; be against the commands of Heaven. ⓒ ～が悪い be sinful; be wicked; be against the commands of Heaven.
　[N] ⓒ ～に尽きる ❶ be deserted by fortune; run out of good luck. ❷ be blessed by divine protection; be too good for one.

魅力 charm; appeal; lure
　[A] ～が有る have an appeal; be charming.
　[を] ～を失う lose one's appeal; lose its glamour; lose one's charm. ～を感じる be fascinated by *sb*/*sth*. ～を添える lend charm to; give *sth* additional charm.

ム

無 nothing; naught; nil
　[N] ～に帰す come to nothing; be

wasted; be a waste of time. ～にする waste *sth*; put *sth* to waste. ～になす waste *sth*; put *sth* to waste; ⓔ render *sth* futile; ⓔ bring *sth* to naught. ～になる come to nothing; be wasted; be a waste of time.

無為 ⓔ idleness; inactivity

[N] ⓒ ～に入る ❶ enter monastic life; go into a monastery. ❷ become a Buddhist monk; take the tonsure. ⓔ ～に暮らす live an idle life; idle one's time away.

昔 antiquity; ancient; old days

[を] ～を偲ぶ look back on one's past; think of one's younger days.

向き direction; inclination

[A] ～が有る be inclined towards *sth*; have an aptitude for *sth*; have a talent for *sth*. ～が変わる change direction; come round; swing round. ～が悪い ❶ feel awkward; be embarrassed; be abashed. ❷ be badly orientated; face in the wrong direction. [N] ～になる ❶ become serious; get serious; ⓒ ⓘ get real. ❷ have a quick temper; become irritable; ⓘ have a short fuse. [を] ～を変える change the direction (of *sth*); bring (a ship) about.

無下 direction; inclination

[N] ～にする ❶ reject *sth* out of hand; refuse *sth* flatly; turn *sb*/*sth* down. ❷ reject *sb*/*sth*; ⓘ give *sb* the cold shoulder; ⓘ turn one's back on *sb*/*sth*. ❸ render *sth* futile; bring *sth* to naught.

婿 a son-in-law

[N] ～に行く mary into the family of one's bride. ～に成る mary into the family of one's bride.
[を] ～を取る take a husband.

向こう the opposite side

[N] (人を)～に回す rival with *sb*; compete with *sb*.
[を] (人の)～を張る oppose *sb*; set oneself up against *sb*.

向こうっ面 the opponent

[N] ～に成る ❶ become opponents; be on opposite sides. ❷ go over to the enemy; ⓔ desert to the enemy. ❸ antagonize *sb*; make an enemy of *sb*; have *sb* for an enemy.
[を] ～へ回る go over to the enemy; ⓔ desert to the enemy.

虫 an insect; a bug; a worm

[A] ⓐ ～が合う be like-minded; get along well; ⓔ be congenial to one; ⓘ see eye to eye; ⓒ ⓘ hit it off. ⓐ ～

ムシ　　　　　　　　　　　　　　　　　　　　　　　　　　ムシ

がある feel confident; have confidence. ～が良い be selfish; take things for granted; do things one's own way. ⓐ ～が痛い have a stomach ache; one's stomach aches. ⓐ ～が入る ❶ be damaged; be spoiled; be marred. ❷ keep bad company; have a ne'er-do-well as a lover; have a good-for-nothing boyfriend. ～が起こる ❶ become fretful; get peevish. ❷ be (sexually) roused; be tempted. ～が納まる regain one's temper; settle down; ⓑ be mollified; ⓐ cool down. ⓒ ～が落ち着く regain one's temper; settle down; ⓑ be mollified; ⓐ cool down. ⓐ ～が降りる feel refreshed; feel relieved. ⓐ ～が齧る ❶ have a stomach ache; one's stomach aches. ❷ feel hungry; have an appetite. ❸ go into convulsions; have a convulsive fit; be seized with cramps. ❹ be seized with labor pains; go into labor. ⓐ ～が聞く agree fully; be in full agreement. ～が嫌う dislike sb; have an aversion to sb; feel uncomfortable with sb. ～が食う be eaten by worms. ～が込み上げる ❶ be aroused; feel a surge of passion; ⓢ be turned on. ❷ lose one's temper; fly into a rage; ⓢ lose one's cool. ～が刺す ❶ be damaged; be spoiled. ❷ keep bad company; have a ne'er-do-well as a lover; have a good-for-nothing boyfriend. ～が鎮まる calm down; ⓑ regain one's composure; ⓐ cool down. ～が知らず have a gut feeling; have a premonition; ⓑ have a sense of foreboding; ⓒ have a hunch. ～が好かない be disgusting; be disagreeable. ⓐ ～が据る be ready; be resigned (to one's fate); be resolved. ⓐ ～が堰く have a stomach ache; one's stomach aches. ～が集る ❶ get worms. ❷ become infested with worms; ⓒ become verminous. ～が付く ❶ be infested with insects; be insect-ridden. ❷ keep bad company; have a ne'er-do-well as a lover; have a good-for-nothing boyfriend. ～が出る ❶ fall ill. ❷ get worms. ⓐ ～が動じる be surprised; be startled. ⓐ ～が取り上ぐ lose one's temper; fly into a rage; ⓢ lose one's cool. ～が這う crawl with insects; teem with insects. ⓐ ～が早い ❶ be hasty; be rash. ❷ have a quick temper; be short-tempered. ⓒ ～が焼ける feel vexed; be annoyed; ⓑ be chagrined. ～が湧く get worms; become infested with worms; ⓒ become verminous. ⓐ ～が悪い be hypersensitive; ⓑ have delicate nerves; have a short temper.

Ⓝ ⓐ ～に当たる get angry; lose one's temper; take offense; ⓒ ⓓ fly off the handle; ⓔ ① blow a fuse. ⓐ ~に入る calm down; ⓔ regain one's composure; ⓐ cool down. ⓐ ~に障る ❶ feel unwell; have an upset stomach. ❷ feel vexed; be offended; ⓔ be chagrined; grate on one's nerves. 图 ⓒ ~を起こす ❶ have a stomach ache. ❷ go into convulsions; have a convulsive fit; be seized with cramps. ❸ be seized with labor pains; go into labor. ~を抑える ⓒ ❶ control one's temper; contain one's anger; suppress one's feelings. (腹の) ❷ have a snack. ~を下す drive out worms; expel worms. ⓒ ~を殺す control one's temper; contain one's anger; suppress one's feelings. ⓒ ~を堪える control one's temper; contain one's anger; suppress one's feelings. ⓐ ~を摩る control one's temper; contain one's anger; suppress one's feelings. ~を鎮める control one's temper; contain one's anger; suppress one's feelings. ⓒ ~を死なす control one's temper; contain one's anger; suppress one's feelings. ~を宥める control one's temper; contain one's anger; suppress one's feelings. ⓒ ~を持つ have a temper; be irritable. ~を病む ❶ have a stomach ache. ❷ go into convulsions; have a convulsive fit;

be seized with cramps. ⓒ ~を患う have a stomach ache; suffer from a stomach complaint.

むしず
虫酸 图 water brash

囚 ⓢ ~が来る ❶ have a fit of water brash. ❷ be disgusted (with *sb*/*sth*); be appalled (with *sb*/*sth*); find *sb*/*sth* offensive. ⓢ ~が出る ❶ have a fit of water brash. ❷ be disgusted (with *sb*/*sth*); be appalled (with *sb*/*sth*); find *sb*/*sth* offensive. ⓢ ~が走る ❶ have a fit of water brash. ❷ be disgusted (with *sb*/*sth*); be appalled (with *sb*/*sth*); find *sb*/*sth* offensive.

むじな
狢 a badger; a racoon dog

图 ~を使う deceive *sb*; ① take *sb* in; ⓒ ① lead *sb* by the nose; ⓒ ① throw dust in *sb's* eyes.

むしろ
筵 a straw mat; matting

图 ~を踏む share the same bed; sleep together; go to bed.

むしん
無心 innocence; detachment

图 ~を言う talk of trivial things; ⓔ indulge in idle talk; ① pay lipservice; ⓒ make small talk.

むだ
無駄 futility; idleness; useless

Ⓝ ~にする render *sth* futile; bring

sth to naught. 〜になる be futile; come to nothing; be wasted; ⓘ go up in smoke.
を 〜を省く avoid waste; be efficient.

無駄足 a wasted trip
を 〜を運ぶ make a wasted a trip; ⓘ go on a bootless errand. 〜を踏む make a wasted a trip; ⓘ go on a bootless errand.

無駄口 idle talk; wasted talk
を 〜を叩く indulge in idle talk.

無駄玉 a wasted bullet
N ⓐ 〜になる be to no avail; be useless; be futile; come to nothing.

無駄話 idle talk; tittle-tattle
を 〜をする say what one likes; ⓑ indulge in idle talk; ⓒ title-tatle.

無駄骨 wasted efforts
N ⓐ 〜に終わる prove fruitless.
を ⓐ 〜を折る make vain efforts; waste one's time; make useless efforts; ⓘ catch at shadows.

無駄飯 an idle life
を ⓐ 〜を食う lead an idle life; waste one's life.

鞭 a whip; a rod; a cane
A 〜で打つ lash *sb*; give *sb* a hiding.
を ⓐ 〜を揚ぐ whip (a horse); lash (a horse). 〜を加える give *sb* the rod; give *sb* a thrashing. 〜を取る take charge; take control; ⓘ take *sth* in hand; ⓐ step in. 〜を鳴らす crack a whip; swish a whip. 〜を振る wield a whip.

胸糞 "chest shit"
N ⓥ ⓐ 〜が悪い feel sick; be disgusted; be appalled; feel sick to the stomach; feel wrethced.

胸倉 the collar; the lapels
を ⓐ 〜を掴む sieze *sb's* collar; sieze *sb* by the collar. ⓐ 〜を取る sieze *sb's* collar; sieze *sb* by the collar.

胸尽し the collar; the lapels
を ⓐ 〜を掴む sieze *sb's* collar; sieze *sb* by the collar. ⓐ 〜を取る sieze *sb's* collar; sieze *sb* by the collar.

胸 the breast; the chest
A ⓐ 〜が合う be like-minded; get along well; ⓒ be congenial to one; ⓘ see eye to eye; ⓒⓘ hit it off. ⓐ 〜が開ける feel relieved; ⓘ feel a weight taken off one's chest. 〜が痛い have a chest ache; one's chest

aches. 〜が痛む ❶ have a chest ache; one's chest aches. ❷ be in agony; be in anguish; be worried about sb/sth. ❸ go against one's conscience; be troubled by one's conscience; ⓒ feel the pricks of conscience. 〜が収まる calm down; ⓑ regain one's composure; ⓐ cool down. 〜が躍る be excited; be lifted in spirit; ⓓ have butterflies in one's stomach. 〜が決まる make up one's mind; decide to do. 〜が苦しい have heartburn. ⓒ 〜が焦がる ❶ pine for sb; burn with passion for sb. ❷ be anxious; worry about sb/sth; be impatient. 〜が裂ける be heartbroken; be torn apart with grief. 〜が騒ぐ ❶ grow exited; get flustered. ❷ have a sense of foreboding; feel a presentiment; feel uneasy; ⓑ experience a flutter of heart. 〜が空く feel refreshed; feel relieved. ⓐ 〜が堰く be filled with sadness; feel wretched. ⓒ 〜が狭い be narrow-minded; be small-minded. ⓐ 〜が迫る be filled with emotions; ⓑ feel a stirring in one's breast; be excited by sth; become aroused by sth. 〜が支える lie heavy on one's stomach; feel a pressure on one's chest; ⓓ feel a weight on one's chest. 〜が潰れる ❶ be surprised; be startled; be taken aback; be flabbergasted. ❷ feel crushed; be heartbroken; ⓒ feel gutted. 〜が詰まる be filled with (gratitude); be overcome by (grief); ⓓ feel a weight on one's chest; ⓓ have a lump in one's throat; be choked up. 〜が轟く suffer heartthrobs; feel one's heart pounding. 〜が煮え返る burn with rage; be irate. ⓒ 〜が煮える burn with desire/rage; ⓔ be consumed with passion/hatred. 〜が弾む be excited; be lifted in spirit. 〜が張り裂ける be utterly heartbroken; be torn apart by grief. ⓐ 〜が張る be filled with (gratitude); be overcome by (grief); ⓓ feel a weight on one's chest; ⓓ have a lump in one's throat; be choked up. 〜が晴れる feel refreshed; feel relieved. ⓐ 〜が開く feel relieved; ⓓ feel a weight taken off one's chest. 〜が塞がる ⓓ feel a weight on one's chest; ⓓ have a lump in one's throat; be choked up. 〜が燃える burn with (desire/rage); ⓔ be consumed with (passion/hatred). 〜が焼ける have heartburn. 〜が弱い have a weak chest. 〜が悪い ❶ be sick to the stomach; ⓓ turn one's stomach upside down; be disgusted. ❷ be offended; feel vexed; take offense. ❸ have a bad nature; be bad-natured; ⓒ be wicked.

ムネ

N ～に当(あ)る be struck by; ⓐ come home to one; occur to one. ～に余(あま)る feel distressed. ～に抱(いだ)く hug (an idea) to one's heart; cherish a thought. (人を)～に抱(いだ)きしめる hug sb; ⓑ press sb to one's bosom. ～に浮(う)かぶ occur to one; ⓐ cross one's mind; ⓑ dawn on one; ⓒ strike one. ～に描(えが)く picture sth to oneself; picture sth in one's mind. ～に納(おさ)める keep sth to oneself; ⓐ hold sth in one's heart. ～に落ちる come to terms with sth; consent to sth; be satisfied with sth. ～に聞(き)く search one's heart; ponder sth deeply; ⓐ turn sth over in one's mind; ⓒ do some soul-searching. ～に刻(きざ)む ⓐ take sth to heart; bear sth in mind. ⓐ ～に釘打(くぎう)つ feel guilty; ⓑ weigh upon one's conscience; ⓒ feel the pricks of conscience. ～に応(こた)える go to one's heart; ⓐ tug at one's heartstrings; ⓐ come home to one; ⓒ cut to the quick. ～に閉(し)まる keep sth to oneself. ～に据(す)え兼(か)ねる be intolerable; be unbearable; ⓔ be insufferable. ～に迫(せま)る be filled with emotions; ⓒ feel a stirring in one's breast; be excited by sth; become aroused by sth. ～に抱(いだ)きしめる press sb to one's heart. ～に畳(たた)む keep sth to oneself; ⓐ hold sth in one's heart. ～に支(つか)える lie heavy on one's stomach; feel a pressure on one's chest; ⓐ feel a weight on one's chest. ⓒ ～に包(つつ)む ⓐ keep sth to oneself; hold sth in one's heart. ⓒ ～に詰(つ)まる be filled with (gratitude); be overcome by (grief); ⓐ feel a weight on one's chest; ⓐ have a lump in one's throat; be choked up. ～に響(ひび)く go to one's heart; ⓐ tug at one's heartstrings; ⓐ come home to one; ⓐ cut to the quick. ～に秘(ひ)める ⓐ keep sth to oneself; ⓐ hold sth in one's heart. ～に蘇(よみがえ)る come back to one; recurr to one.

S ～を明(あ)かす unbosom oneself; speak one's mind; ⓐ get sth off one's chest; ⓐ unburden one's heart. ～を痛(いた)む have a lung disease; be consumptive. ～を痛(いた)める ❶ have a chest ache. ❷ be worried about sth; fret over sth. ～を打ち明(あ)ける take sb into one's confidence; ⓐ pour out one's heart to sb; ⓔ unbosom oneself. ～を打つ be moved by sth; be impressed by sth; ⓐ tug at one's heartstrings; ⓐ strike a chord. ～を躍(おど)らせる be excited; be lifted in spirit. ～を貸(か)す ❶ express one's thoughts; give sb advice. ❷ [sumō] give sb a workout. ～を借(か)る ❶ ask sb's advice. ❷ [sumō] be given a workout. ～を焦(こ)がす ❶ pine for sb; burn with passion for sb. ❷ be anxious; worry about *sb/sth*; be impatient. 〜を定める prepare to do *sth*; ① make up one's mind; ② gird up one's loins. ④ 〜を摩る keep *sth* to oneself; suppress one's anger/feelings. 〜を締め付ける break one's/*sb's* heart; be heartrending. ④ 〜を据える prepare to do *sth*; ① make up one's mind; ② gird up one's loins. ④ 〜を堰く be nauseated by; feel sick; be vexed at *sth*. 〜を反らす ❶ throw one's chest out; straighten oneself up. ❷ take pride in *sth*; feel bolstered by *sth*. 〜を叩く ❶ beat one's chest. ❷ agree readily. 〜を突く ❶ be surprised; be taken aback; be flabbergasted. ❷ worry about *sb/sth*; feel anxious about *sb/sth*; ① go to the heart; ② cut one to the quick. ❸ be steep; ⑤ be precipitous. 〜を潰す ❶ upset one; be disturbing; be disquieting. ❷ be shocked; be amazed; be stunned; be astonished. 〜をときめかす suffer heartthrobs; be agitated; get excited (at the thought of *sth*); ⑥ go pit-a-tat. 〜を轟かす suffer heartthrobs; feel one's heart pounding (against one's chest); ⑥ go pit-a-tat. 〜を撫で下ろす ❶ give a sigh of relief; be able to breathe again. ❷ feel relieved; be reassured; be put at ease. 〜を弾ませる ⑥ one's heart leaps with antici-

pation. 〜を開ける expose one's chest; bare one's breasts. 〜を晴らす get rid of an unpleasant feeling; dispel a sense of gloom; ① take a load off one's mind. 〜を張る ❶ throw one's chest out; straighten oneself up. ❷ boast about *sth*; be proud of *sth*; pride oneself on *sth*; ① puff up one's chest. 〜を冷やす be terrified; tremble with fear; give a shudder. 〜を開く open one's heart; ⑥ unbosom oneself; ① get *sth* off one's chest; ① pour out one's heart to *sb*. 〜を膨らます ❶ heave one's chest. ❷ have high hopes; be full of *sth*; ⑥ be upbeat. 〜を病む suffer from a chest disease. 〜を割る speak frankly; be outspoken; be candid.

旨 effect; purport; command

匕 (...を)〜とする aim at doing *sth*; stand on doing *sth*.

匕 〜を受ける recieve orders; be ordered. 〜を含める issue orders; give *sb* directions. 〜を奉じる obey orders; follow *sb's* directions.

胸三寸 one's heart; one's mind

N 〜に納める hide one's feelings; suppress one's feelings.

謀叛 a rebellion; a revolt

匕 〜を起こす raise a rebellion; rise

in revolt. 〜を企てる plot a rebellion. 〜を静める suppress a rebellion.

無理 unreasonableness

⑲ 〜を言う be unreasonable; be cross-grained; say unreasonable things. 〜をする strain oneself; overtax oneself; go against nature. 〜を張る be unreasonable; be cross-grained.

メ

目 an eye; sight; eyesight

 〜が合う ❶ the eyes meet. ❷ be asleep. ⓪ 〜が明く ❶ be able to see (again). ❷ ⓐ one's eyes are opened; come to see; come to understand. ❸ [sumō] win a bout after a succession of defeats. 〜が粗い have a loose weave; be loosely woven. 〜が有る ❶ have a critical eye (for quality); be a connoisseur (of art). ❷ be heavy; weigh heavy. 〜が良い ❶ have good eyesight. ❷ have a critical eye (for quality); be a connoisseur. 〜が痛い have sore eyes. 〜が落ち込む have sunken eyes; have deepset eyes. 〜が霞む ❶ have a blurred vision; have one's eyes grow misty with tears; one's eyesight grows dim (with age). ❷ lose one's powers of judgment; become uncertain of oneself. ⓪ 〜が堅い be unable to sleep; ⓔ suffer from insomnia; be wide awake; be wide awake. 〜が利く ❶ have a critical eye for sth; have a keen eye. ❷ have an observant eye; have a watchful eye. 〜が曇る ❶ have a blurred vision; one's eyesight grows dim (with age). ❷ lose one's powers of judgment; become uncertain of oneself. 〜が眩む ❶ be blinded (by sunlight/greed); be dazzled. ❷ feel dizzy; get giddy. 〜が眩れる ❶ be blinded (by /sunlightgreed); be dazzled (by beauty). ❷ feel dizzy; get giddy; have a dizzy spell. ❸ have a blurred vision; have one's eyes grow misty with tears. 〜が肥える have a critical eye (for quality); be a connoisseur (of art). 〜が冴える be unable to sleep; ⓔ suffer from insomnia; be wide awake; become wide awake. 〜が覚める ❶ wake up; open one's eyes. ❷ be wide awake again; be aroused from one's slumber. ❸ come to one's senses; ⓔ be disillusioned; see reason. ❹ be startled; be dazzled; be amazed. 〜が鋭い be sharp-sighted; have eagle eyes. 〜が据る the eyes are set/fixed. 〜が高い have a critical eye for sth; have a keen eye. ⓐ 〜が

〜が　立つ be fortunate; be lucky; ⓒ ⓘ hit good luck. 〜が近い be shortsighted; be nearsighted; be myopic. 〜が付く take notice of *sb/sth*; pay attention to *sb/sth*; notice *sth*. 〜が散る be distracted; be diverted; be distraught. 〜が潰れる lose one's sight; go blind. 〜が詰む have a close weave; be closely woven. 〜が出る ❶ the die is cast. ❷ (良い〜) have luck on one's side; have a stroke of good luck; be lucky. ❸ be stunned (by the cost); be flabbergasted. 〜が届く keep an eye on *sb/sth*; pay careful attention; be attentive. ⓒ 〜が飛び出る ❶ be stunned (by the cost); be flabbergasted. ❷ be severely scolded; ⓘ be given a dressing-down. 〜が無い ❶ be blinded (by love); ⓒ be imprudent; ⓒ be mad about *sb/sth*. ❷ lack a critical eye; have no insight. 〜が早い be quick to see *sth*; be sharp-sighted. 〜が光る keep a close eye on *sb/sth*; keep a watch on *sb/sth*. 〜が回る ❶ feel dizzy; get giddy; be stunned. ❷ be extremely busy. 〜が行く ❶ notice *sth*; take to *sb*; catch one's fancy. ❷ feel dizzy; get giddy. 〜が良い have good sight. 〜が弱い have weak eyes; have poor eyes. 〜が悪い have bad sight; have poor eyesight.

Ⓝ (酷い)〜に遭う be in trouble; have a hard time. 〜に余る ❶ be too much to take in. ❷ be too much to bear; be intolerable. 〜に浮かぶ come before one's eyes; come to mind; occur to one; ⓒ rise in one's thoughts. ⓒ ⓒ 〜に映じる greet the eyes; be seen by one. 〜に懸かる ❶ come in sight; be noticed. ❷ (お〜に) see *sb*; meet with *sb*. 〜に懸ける ❶ notice *sth*; ⓘ catch one's eye. ❷ take care of *sb/sth*; look after *sb/sth*. ❸ (お〜に) display *sth*; put *sth* on show. ⓐ 〜に遮る block off one's sight. 〜に曝す expose *sth* to the eye. 〜に障る ❶ be hurtful to the eye. ❷ be offensive to the eye; be an eyesore; spoil the view. 〜に染みる ❶ smart the eyes; cause the eyes to water. ❷ be vivid (in color); be dazzling; be startling. ❸ grow tired of seeing *sth*; ⓒ get an eyeful of *sth*. 〜にする notice *sth*; take note of *sth*; happen to see *sth*. 〜に立つ stand out; draw one's attention. 〜に付く ❶ attract one's attention; be noticeable. ❷ haunt one; ⓘ stay with one. 〜に留まる ❶ attract attention; be noticed; catch one's eye. ❷ take to *sb*; catch one's fancy; ⓒ ⓘ give *sb* the (glad) eye. ⓐ 〜に留める notice *sth*; ⓘ catch one's eye. 〜になる keep an eye on *sb*/*sth*; watch out for *sb*/*sth*; look out for *sb*/*sth* 〜に残(のこ)る linger before one's eyes; ⓙ be engraved on one's memory. 〜に入(はい)る catch sight of *sb*/*sth*; come in sight; come into view. 〜に触(ふ)れる attract one's attention; come into view; ⓙ catch one's eye. 〜に見(み)える be obvious; be clear (for all to see); stand to reason. ⓢ 〜に見(み)る see *sth* clearly; have *sth* before one's eyes.

開(あ) Ⓐ 〜を明(あ)く come to one's senses; see reason; Ⓔ be disillusioned. 〜を開(あ)ける bring *sb* to his/her senses; Ⓔ disillusion *sb*; Ⓐ open *sb's* eyes. 〜を上(あ)げる look up; Ⓐ raise one's eyes; Ⓔ lift one's gaze. 〜を遊(あそ)ばす give one's eye free reign. 〜を合(あ)わす ❶ close one's eyes. ❷ meet each other's gaze; run across *sb*. 〜を痛(いた)める impair one's vision. 〜を射(い)る ❶ be blinding; be startling. ❷ catch sight of *sb*/*sth*; ⓙ catch the eye; ⓙ strike one. 〜を入(い)れる cast a favorable eye on *sb*; favor *sb*. 〜を疑(うたが)う doubt one's eyes; question what one sees. 〜を移(うつ)す shift one's gaze. 〜を奪(うば)う be fascinating; be an eye-catcher. 〜を奪(うば)われる be fascinated by *sth*; be spellbound by *sth*; be dazzled by *sth*. 〜を覆(おお)う ❶ cover one's eyes (with one's hands). ❷ ignore *sth*; turn a blind eye (to *sth*). ⓙ 〜を起(お)こす

❶ throw the dice; Ⓔ cast the die. ❷ be fortunate; be lucky; Ⓒ ⓙ hit good luck. 〜を押(おさ)える cover one's eyes. 〜を落(お)とす ❶ look down; cast a downward look. ❷ drop a stitch; let down a stitch. Ⓒ ❸ lose one's life; lay down one's life. 〜を驚(おどろ)かす be astonished; be startled; be flabbergasted. 〜を掛(か)ける ❶ take care of *sb*/*sth*; look after *sb*/*sth*. ❷ watch out for *sb*/*sth*. ❸ be partial to *sb*; biased toward *sb*. (人(ひと)の)〜を掠(かす)める do *sth* by stealth; Ⓢ do *sth* on the sly. 〜を切(き)る make a notch in *sth*; score (meat). Ⓒ 〜を極(きわ)む strain one's eyes; peer (into the distance). (人(ひと)の)〜を潜(くぐ)る elude *sb's* view. Ⓐ 〜を下(くだ)す take care of *sb*/*sth*; look after *sb*/*sth*; watch out for *sb*/*sth*. 〜を配(くば)る keep a watchful eye on *sb*/*sth*; remain vigilant; watch *sb*/*sth* carefully. (涙(なみだ)で)〜を曇(くも)らす blur the eyes (with tears). 〜を晦(くら)ます deceive *sb*; ⓙ throw dust in *sb's* eyes. 〜を呉(く)れる glance at *sb*/*sth*. Ⓐ Ⓢ 〜を食(く)わす wink at *sb*; exchange glances with *sb*. 〜を肥(こ)やす ❶ feast one's eyes on *sth*. ❷ develop an eye for *sth*; nourish the eye. 〜を凝(こ)らす ❶ gaze at *sb*/*sth*; stare a at *sb*/*sth*. ❷ strain one's eyes. 〜を遮(さえぎ)る bar *sth* from sight; obstruct one's/*sb's* view. 〜を覚(さ)ます ❶ wake up. ❷ be startled; be surprised. ❸ become conscious of *sth*; ⓐ have one's eyes opened; realize *sth*; awake to (the truth). ❹ come to one's senses; see reason; ⓒ be disillusioned. ⓒ ～を曝す draw one's eyes wide open; look straight ahead; look all over *sth*. (人の)～を忍ぶ elude *sb's* eyes. ～を据える fix one's eyes on *sb/sth*; gaze at *sb/sth*. ⓐ ～を擦る rub one's eyes; wipe one's eyes. ⓐ ～を澄ます gaze at *sb/sth*; stare at *sb/sth*; look hard at *sb/sth*. ～を注ぐ turn one's gaze toward *sb/sth*; keep one's eyes on *sb/sth*; pay attention to *sb/sth*. ⓐ ～を側める avert the eyes (in disgust); look away; look the other way. ～を背ける avert the eyes (in disgust); look away from; look the other way. ～を逸らす take one's eyes off *sb/sth*; turn the eyes away from *sb/sth*. ⓐ ～を立てる take notice of *sb/sth*; pay attention to *sb/sth*. ⓒ ～を使う use one's eyes; ⓐ keep one's eyes open. ～を付ける keep one's eyes on *sb/sth*; pay attention to; be interested in *sth*. ～を潰す put *sb's* eye out. ～を瞑る ❶ close one's eyes; go to sleep. ❷ pass away; draw one's last breath; ⓒ ⓘ breathe one's last. ❸ overlook *sth*; put up with *sth*; ⓘ turn a blind eye; ⓘ wink at *sth*. ～を通す run one's eyes over *sb/sth*;

look *sth* over; look through *sth*. ～を閉じる ❶ shut one's eyes; close one's eyes. ❷ pass away; draw one's last breath; ⓒ ⓘ breathe one's last. ⓐ ～を留める take notice of *sb/sth*; pay attention to *sb/sth*. ～を慰む soothe the eyes. ⓐ (人の)～を抜く play a trick on *sb's* eyes; ⓘ pull the wool over *sb's* eyes. ～を拭う wipe one's eyes. ～を盗む do *sth* in secret. ～を外す take one's eyes off *sb/sth*; turn the eyes away from *sb/sth*. ～を離す let *sb/sth* out of one's sight; ⓘ be off one's guard. ～を憚る shy away from the public gaze; ⓒ shrink from people's gaze; shun publicity. ～を光らす keep a watchful eye on *sb/sth*; be watchful; be vigilant. ～を引く ❶ draw one's/*sb's* attention; attract one's/*sb's* notice. ❷ wink at *sb*; ⓘ give *sb* the eye; ⓘ make eyes at *sb*. ～を開く ❶ open one's eyes. ❷ understand *sth*; become aware of *sth*; ⓘ dawn on one. ❸ be spiritually awakened; reach enlightenment; ⓘ see the light. ❹ become able to read; become literate. ～を塞ぐ ❶ shut one' eyes. ❷ pass away; draw one's last breath; ⓒ ⓘ breathe one's last. ❸ ⓘ turn a blind eye; ⓘ wink at *sth*. ～を伏せる lower one's eyes; ⓒ cast down one's eyes. ～を細める squint one's eyes; screw up one's eyes. 〜を回（まわ）す ❶ lose consciousness; pass out; ⓒ black out. ❷ be bewildered; be startled. ❸ be extremely busy. 〜を見合（みあ）わせる lock eyes with each other. 〜を見出（みだ）す gaze at *sb/sth*; glare a at *sb/sth* (with jealousy). ⓐ 〜を見（み）す ❶ wink at *sb*; ⓘ give *sb* the eye; ⓘ make eyes at *sb*. ❷ cause *sb* trouble; give *sb* a hard time. ❸ show one's feelings in one's eyes. 〜を見張（みは）る ❶ open one's eyes wide. ❷ be struck with wonder; be stunned; be awestruck; be flabbergasted; ⓢ ⓘ be blown away. 〜を見（み）る ❶ look *sb* in the eyes; look into *sb's* eyes. ❷ be in a (difficult) situation; ⓒ be in a fix. ❸ discriminate between two things; recognize *sb/sth*. ❹ be able to read; be literate. 〜を剥（む）く glare at *sb/sth*; stare one's eyes out; ⓘ look daggers at *sb*. 〜を向（む）ける turn one's eyes to *sb/sth*; become interested in *sb/sth*; turn one's attention to *sb/sth*. 〜を遣（や）る look at *sb/sth*; look toward *sb/sth*; ⓒ cast one's eyes on *sb/sth*. 〜を喜（よろこ）ばす please the eyes; be a feast for the eyes.

芽（め）a bud; a sprout; a spear

A 〜が出（で）る ❶ sprout up; burst into leaf. ❷ begin to prosper; start to thrive. ❸ come into luck; ⓒ get a lucky break. 〜が吹（ふ）く ❶ sprout up; burst into leaf. ❷ begin to prosper; start to thrive. ❸ come into luck; ⓒ get a lucky break. 图 〜を出（だ）す ❶ put out buds; burst into leaf. ❷ begin to prosper; start to thrive. 〜を摘（つ）む ❶ nip a bud. ❷ nip (a plot) in the bud; foil *sb's* evil designs. 〜を吹（ふ）く ❶ put out buds; burst into leaf. ❷ begin to prosper; start to thrive.

命（めい）E an order, life; fate ▶ 命（いのち）

N ⓒ 〜を革（あらた）む ❶ recieve a new mandate of Heaven. ❷ have a change of dynasty. ❸ cause a revolution; give rise to a revolution.

銘（めい）E an inscription; an epitaph

图 ⓒ 〜を打（う）つ ❶ stamp one's name (into a blade); impress a signature (onto a blade). ❷ name *sth*; style *sth*; brand *sth*. ⓒ 〜を刻（きざ）む carve an epitaph (into a stone); engrave an inscription (into stone).

名（めい）E distinction; greatness ▶ 名（な）

图 ⓒ 〜を謳（うた）う extol *sb's* name; praise *sb's* accomplishments.

命数（めいすう）E one's given span of life

A 〜が尽（つ）きる ❶ reach the end of one's days. ❷ run out of luck.

～を知る know one's time has come.

名声 fame; renown; celebrity

～が上げる rise in fame. ～が有る be celebrated; be popular. ～が落ちる lose one's reputation.
～を揚げる make one's name renowned; enhance one's reputation. ～を失う lose prestige; lose one's reputation. ～を落とす ruin one's reputation; ⓒ lower one's reputation. ～を傷つける damage one's name; injure one's reputation. ～を汚す mar one's name; ⓒ tarnish one's reputation; ⓒ cast a slur on one's reputation. ～を高める bring fame to one/*sb*; add to one's reputation; ⓒ enhance one's reputation. ⓒ ～を博する win fame; make a name for oneself; gain a reputation. ～を求める seek a name for oneself; desire fame.

瞑想 meditation

～に耽る be lost in meditation.

名分 one's moral duty

～を立てる justify oneself; explain one's conduct.

名望 repute; renown; fame

～を失う lose one's reputation;

ⓒ fall in public estimation. ～を得る gain reputation.

命脈 life; the thread of life

ⓒ ～が尽きる die out; come to an end.
ⓒ ～を保つ remain alive; maintain life; preserve life. ⓒ ～を繋ぐ stay alive; hang on to life; eke out a living; cling on to life.

迷夢 an illusion; a delusion

ⓒ ⓒ ～が覚める come to one's senses; come to oneself; ⓒ be disillusioned; see reason.
ⓒ ⓒ ～を覚ます bring *sb* to his/her senses; ⓒ disillusion *sb*.

名誉 honor; credit; glory

～に係わる affect one's honor.
～を与える award honor to *sb*; bestow honor on *sb*. ～を失う lose one's honor. ～を重んじる value honor. ～を回復する regain one's reputation; restore one's honor. ～を傷つける hurt *sb's* honor; injure *sb's* honor. ～を毀損する bring disgrace upon *sb*; stain *sb's* honor. ～を汚す bring disgrace upon *sb*; sully *sb's* reputation. ～を高める gain honor; do oneself proud. ～を保つ maintain one's honor; preserve one's good name. ～を担う take credit

for. ～を挽回(ばんかい)する retrieve one's honor; restore one's honor.

迷惑(めいわく) trouble; annoyance
[を] ～を掛(か)ける ❶ cause sb trouble; get sb into trouble. ❷ annoy sb; make oneself a nuisance.

目打(めう)ち worth; value; merit
[A] ～が有(あ)る have value; be worth (doing); be valuable; have merit. ～が無(な)い have no value; be not worth (doing); be worthless; be of no value; have no merit.
[を] ～を上(あ)がる increase in value; rise in (public) estimation. ～を落とす lower the value of sth; cause sb/sth to lose merit; depreciate sth. ～を下(さ)げる lose value; fall in value; drop in (public) estimation. ～を損(そん)ずる impair the value of sth; damage sb's worth. ～を付(つ)ける value sth; appraise sth; make an estimation. ～を増(ま)す increase in value; rise in (public) estimation.

メートル a meter
[を] ～を上(あ)げる be in high spirits; ⓒ be inebriated; ⓘ be in one's cups.

目顔(めがお) a look; an expression
[A] ～で知(し)らす give sb a significant look; wink at sb.

[を] ～を忍(しの)ぶ avoid public notice; shun public notice; do sth in secret.

目頭(めがしら) the inner corner of the eye
[を] ～を押(おさ)える fight back one's tears. ～を拭(ぬぐ)う wipe away one's tears.

目角(めかど) the corner of the eye
[N] ⓐ ～に取(と)る see sth clearly; recognize sth clearly; ⓒ take sth in.
[を] ⓐ ～を利(き)かす be sensible; be quick-witted. ⓐ ～を立(た)てる look fiercely at sb; ⓘ look daggers at sb.

眼鏡(めがね) a pair of spectacles
[A] ～が狂(くる)う misjudge a situation.
[N] ～に適(かな)う win sb's confidence; meet sb's approval; pass a test.
[を] ～を掛(か)ける ❶ put on one's glasses. ❷ have a biased view; be prejudiced; ⓘ see sth through colored spectacles. ～を外(はず)す take off one's glasses.

目釘(めくぎ) 団 a rivet of a sword hilt
[を] ～を湿(しめ)す ❶ moisten the rivet of a sword hilt. ⓐ ❷ prepare for battle; make oneself ready for combat; brace oneself; ⓘ gird up one's loins.

目串(めぐし) 団 a rough estimate
[A] ⓐ ～が付(つ)く ❶ be able to guess; have a general idea. ❷ be arrested;

be siezed; ⓒ ① the game is up. Ⓐ ～が抜ける be innocent; be free from blame; ⓔ be vindicated.

图 Ⓐ ～を立てる ❶ keep an aye on *sb/sth*; Ⓐ fasten one's eyes on *sb/sth*. ❷ make an educated guess. Ⓐ ～を付ける ❶ keep an aye on *sb/sth*; Ⓐ fasten one's eyes on *sb/sth*. ❷ have a guess; guess at *sth*; estimate; ⓢ ① take a shot.

目くじら the corner of the eye

图 ～を立てる ❶ raise one's eyebrows. ❷ call *sth* into question; look disapprovingly at *sb/sth*; make a fuss over *sth*; ① split hairs.

目先 at hand; immediate

A ～が利く be farsighted; have foresight; ⓔ be prescient.

N ～にちらつく see (recollect) *sth* vividly; be haunted by (an image).

图 ～を変える do something new. ～を暗ます play a trick on *sb's* eyes; fudge a matter; ① pull the wool over *sb's* eyes; ① throw dust in *sb's* eyes.

飯 cooked rice; a meal; food

N ⓒ ～に付く ❶ eat three times a day; eat regularly. ❷ make a living; ⓔ earn one's daily bread; support oneself. ❸ get a job; find employment; ⓒ land a job.

图 ⓒ ～を食う ❶ eat one's food; have a meal; have diner. ❷ make a living; ⓔ earn one's daily bread; support oneself. ～を炊く cook rice.

目尻 the corner of the eye

图 ～を下げる ❶ be all smiles; be pleased with *sth*. ❷ make eyes at *sb*; ⓔ cast amorous glances at *sb*; ① make sheep's eyes at *sb*.

メス a knife; a scalpel

图 (犯罪に)～を入れる take drastic measures (against crime); inquire deeply into (a corruption case).

目垂れ 旧 a sign of weakness

图 ⓒ ～を見る ❶ look for signs of weakness; sound *sb* out; test *sb*. ❷ take advantage of *sb*; use *sb*.

鍍金 plating; gilding; gilt

A ～が剥げる ❶ the gilt comes off. ❷ betray oneself; reveal one's true character; ① show one's true colors; ① show the cloven hoof.

图 Ⓐ ～をさす gild *sth*; plate *sth* (with gold/silver). ～を施す gild *sth*; plate *sth* (with gold/silver).

目褄 旧 public notice; publicity

图 Ⓐ ～を忍ぶ avoid public notice; do *sth* in secret; meet in secret.

目面 (めづら) the eyes and face

N ~を掴(つか)む be dispondant; be in deep grief; be cast down.

目処 (めど) an aim; a goal; a prospect

A ~が有(あ)る have hope of doing; lie within the realm of possibilities. ~が立(た)つ have renewed hope; the prospects brighten; ⓘ see light at the end of the tunnel. ~が付(つ)く have renewed hope; the prospects brighten; ⓘ see light at the end of the tunnel.

を ~を付(つ)ける have a guess; guess at *sth*; estimate; ⓢⓘ take a shot. ~を取(と)る ❶ have a guess; guess at *sth*; estimate; ⓢⓘ take a shot. ❷ set a target; aim for *sth*. ❸ forecast the future; make a prediction.

目端 (めはし) ready wits

A ~が利(き)く ❶ be quick witted; be tactful; have tact; be sensible. ❷ have a sharp eye; be shrewd; be catious; be perceptive.

目鼻 (めはな) the eyes and nose

A ~が付(つ)く reach completion; near completion; materialize; take shape; ⓒ get somewhere.

を ~を付(つ)ける give shape to *sth*; get *sth* into shape.

目星 (めぼし) an aim; an objective

を ~を付(つ)ける ❶ keep an eye on *sb/sth*; ⓐ fasten one's eyes on *sb/sth*. ❷ make an educated guess.

目安 (めやす) a standard; a yardstick

A ~が付(つ)く have a rough idea; get a general idea.

を ~を置(お)く set a standard. ~を立(た)てる set a standard; fix one's aim. ~を付(つ)ける ❶ set a standard; fix one's aim. ❷ submit a petition; lodge a complaint.

面 (めん) a mask; a (sur)face ▶ 面(おもて) ▶ 面(つら)

A ⓢ ~が有(あ)る know *sb* by face; be acquainted. ⓢ ~が通(とお)る ❶ be widely known; be notorious. ❷ command respect; be influential; ⓘ carry weight; ⓒⓘ get around. ~が割(わ)れる be unmasked; be identified; be exposed.

と ~と向(む)かう come face to face; meet face to face.

を ~を打(う)つ make a mask. ~を被(かぶ)る ❶ put on a mask. ❷ disguise oneself. ❸ hide one's face (in shame). ❹ feign innocence. ~を刻(きざ)む cut a facet (on a stone). ~を付(つ)ける put on a mask. ~を取(と)る ❶ take off one's mask; remove one's mask. ❷ take the corners off *sth*; plane off the corners of *sth*. ❸ [*kendō*] strike the mask of

メンボク

one's opponent; score a point. ⓐ 〜を脱ぐ take off one's mask; remove one's mask. 〜を外す take off one's mask; remove one's mask.

面倒 trouble; difficulty; care

を 〜を掛ける cause trouble to *sb*; trouble *sb*. 〜を見る take care of *sb*/*sth*; look after *sb*/*sth*.

面皮 ⓔ countenance

N ⓒ 〜が厚い be cheeky; be brazen be impudent; have (a lot of) nerve.

を ⓒ 〜を失う lose one's reputation; lose face; lose respect. ⓒ 〜を欠く lose one's reputation; fall into discredit. ⓒ 〜を剥ぐ ❶ unmask *sb*; expose *sb*; show *sb* for what they really are. ❷ put *sb* to shame; ⓒ ⓘ put *sb* in his/her right place.

面目 honor; face; dignity

A 〜が立つ save one's honor; maintain one's dignity; ⓘ save one's face; ⓘ stand proud. 〜が潰れる be disgraced; ⓒ bring disgrace upon oneself; ⓘ lose face. 〜が無い be ashamed of oneself.

N 〜に関わる concern one's honor; reflect on one's dignity; be a matter of honor. 〜に掛ける do *sth* for one's honor; be bound in honor.

を 〜を失う disgrace oneself;

ⓒ ⓘ lose countenance; ⓘ lose face. ⓐ 〜を凌ぐ bear the shame; suffer ignominy; ⓒ endure ignominy. 〜を保つ uphold one's honor; preserve one's honor; maintain one's dignity; ⓘ save one's face; ⓢ keep one's cool. 〜を立てる save *sb's* honor; ⓒ ⓘ keep *sb* in countenance. 〜を潰す injure *sb's* dignity; cause *sb* to lose face; ⓒ blight *sb's* honor. 〜を施す gain honor; get credit for *sth*; ⓘ do oneself proud.

モ

喪 mourning

A 〜が明ける go out of mourning; the period of mourning ends.

N 〜に服する go into mourning; the period of mourning begins.

を 〜を発する declare (a period) of mourning.

蒙 ⓔ ignorance

を ⓒ 〜を啓く enlighten (*sb's* mind); educate *sb*; open *sb's* eyes.

妄言 ⓔ reckless words

を ⓒ 〜を吐く utter reckless words.

申し分 one's say; a complaint

A 〜が無い be beyond reproach; be impeccable; be perfect.

モチ　　　　　　　　　　　　　　　　　　　モノ

毛氈(もうせん) a rug; a carpet

[を] Ⓐ ～を被(かぶ)る ❶ make an error; ⓒ commit a blunder; make a mess of sth; ⓒ bungle sth. ❷ be disowned; be disinherited; ⓒ be cut off (without a shilling). ❸ spend one's money on prostitutes; Ⓘ live a fast life; run out of money. ～を敷(し)く spread a rug; lay a carpet.

藻屑(もくず) seaweed

[と] ～となる be drowned; ⓒ be swallowed by the waves; Ⓘ find a watery grave; ⓒⒾ go to Davy Jones' locker.

目的(もくてき) a purpose; a goal; an aim

[N] ～に適(かな)う answer a purpose; serve a purpose; meet a goal.
[を] ～を抱(いだ)く have a purpose. ～を推(お)し進(すす)める advance a cause. ～を定(さだ)める set (oneself) a purpose. ～を達(たっ)する accomplish an aim; ⓒ attain one's object; ⓒ gain one's end. ～を遂(と)げる reach a goal; achieve one's aim; ⓒ do the trick. ～を持(も)つ have a purpose; have a goal.

餅(もち) a rice cake

[N] Ⓐ ～に搗(つ)く be at a loss (about what to do); be too much for one; be beyond one's control. Ⓐ ～に成(な)る ❶ form a group; stick together; cling together. ❷ curl up (in one's futon).

[を] ～を搗(つ)く ❶ pound steamed rice into cakes; make rice cakes. ⓒ ❷ make love; have sexual intercourse; have sex; ⓒ make whoopee.

持ち場(もちば) one's post; one's duty

[を] ～を捨(す)てる desert one's post. ～を守(まも)る keep one's post. ～を回(まわ)る make one's rounds.

畚(もっこ) Ⓐ a straw basket

[N] Ⓐ ～に乗(の)る be executed; be put to death; ⓒ receive the death sentence; ⓢⒾ kick the bucket.

物相飯(もっそうめし) Ⓑ prison rations

[を] ⓢ ～を食(く)う serve a sentence; ⓒⒾ do time; ⓢⒾ do one's bird.

勿体(もったい) pretensions; ostentation

[を] ～を付(つ)ける ❶ give oneself airs; be pompous; ⓒ be ostentatious; Ⓘ put on airs. ❷ give sth too much weight; attach undue importance to sth; overestimate sth.

元(もと) the origin; the beginning

[A] ～が掛(か)かる be expensive; cost much. ～が切(き)れる fall below the cost price; be unable to cover the cost. ～が取(と)れない be unable cover one's original outlay; fail to return the original investment.

モノ　　　　　　　　　　　　　　　　　　　　　　　モン

Ⓝ (...を)～にする make sth the basis of (one's opinion); take sth as a premise; base sth on sth.
Ⓔ ～を掛ける invest money in sth; put money in sth; Ⓒ sink money in sth. ～を調べる trace sth to its origin; investigate sth thoroughly; Ⓒ get to the bottom of sth. ～を糺す trace sth to its origin; investigate sth thoroughly; Ⓒ get to the bottom of sth. ～を取る cover one's original outlay; recoup one's investment; Ⓒ get one's money's worth.

もとどり
髻 Ⓐ a topknot
Ⓔ Ⓐ ～を切る ❶ become a Buddhist priest; take the tonsure; Ⓔ retire into religion. ❷ go into seclusion; become a hermit; Ⓔ retire from the world; renounce the world. ～を掴む seize sb by the topknot. Ⓐ ～を放つ wear one's topknot openly.

もの
物 a thing; an object; goods
Ⓐ ～が要る cost money; require funds; be expensive; be costly. ～が無い ❶ be insubstantial; be of no consequence; be insignificant. ❷ be lifeless; be dead; be without life; show no signs of life. ～が分かる know what makes the world go round; be worldly-wise.
Ⓝ Ⓐ ～に当たる get flustered; be confused; fidget over sth. ～に襲われる have a nightmare. Ⓐ ～に掛かる interfere with everything; meddle with everything; ⓘ have a finger in every pie. ～にする ❶ take possession of sth; make sth one's own. ❷ master a craft/skill/language. ❸ win sb's heart; make a conquest; Ⓒ ⓘ chat a girl up. ～になる ❶ turn sth into sth; amount to sth; be of consequence. ❷ come off; pass muster; be a success. ❸ become a full-grown human being; grow up; rise in the world; make sth of oneself. ～に似ず be in a different class; stand on different levels; be no match for sb; ⓘ be on different scales; ⓘ be in a different league.
Ⓔ ～を言う ❶ say sth; address sb. ❷ count for sth; be important; go a long way. ❸ speak for itself; be self-evident; ⓘ speak volumes. ❹ become close friends; get friendly with sb; Ⓔ get on intimate terms with sb. ❺ compain about sth; grumble (about sth). ～を言わす let sth speak for itself; utilize sth; make use of sth. ～を思う be bothered about sth; have sth on one's mind; fret over sth. ～を突く throw up; fetch up; be sick; puke; Ⓒ ⓘ shoot the cat. ～を見せる put sb in their place; show sb who's the boss.

335

物言い speech; a protest

[を] 〜を付ける protest against *sth*; object to *sth*; contest a verdict.

物心 consciousness; discretion

[A] 〜が付く reach the age of discretion; start noticing things.

喪服 a mourning dress

[を] 〜を着ける take to mourning; put on mourning; mourn *sb's* death.

紅葉 a Japanese maple

[を] (顔に) Ⓐ 〜を散らす blush shyly; have a flush in one's cheeks.

股立 apertures in a *hakama*

[を] 〜を取る pull (tuck) up one's *hakama*; prepare for a fight.

舫い綱 the mooring rope

[を] 〜を解く ❶ untie the mooring rope; ⓒ cast off (the moorings); ⓒ ⓘ slip the paiter. ❷ leave port; ⓘ set sail; ⓘ put out to sea.

諸肌 two bare shoulders

[A] 〜を脱ぐ ❶ strip oneself to the waist; bare both one's shoulders. ❷ exert oneself; do one's utmost.

門 a gate; an entrance ▶ 門

[N] 〜に入る ❶ pass through a gate; enter (a building). ❷ become *sb's* pupil; become a follower. 〜に立つ stand at the gate. 〜に学ぶ study under *sb*; ⓒ be under *sb's* tutelage. [を] 〜を開ける open the gate(s). Ⓐ 〜を出る ❶ leave home; go out into the world; enter the real world. ❷ become a Buddhist priest; enter a Buddhist monastery. Ⓐ 〜を打つ close the gate(s). 〜を潜る pass through a gate. 〜を閉める close the gate(s). 〜を叩く ❶ knock at the gate; call on *sb*. ❷ apply to become *sb's* pupil; ⓒ seek *sb's* tutelage. 〜を閉じる close the gate(s).

文句 Ⓔ a remark; a complaint

[を] ⓒ 〜を言う make a complaint; complain to *sb* (about *sth*); raise objections. ⓒ 〜を付ける criticize *sb*; make a complaint; object to *sth*; ⓒ grumble about *sth*.

門戸 Ⓔ the door

[を] ⓒ 〜を構える set up house; start housekeeping. ⓒ 〜を閉ざす ❶ shut the door (on *sb*); close the door (on *sb*). ❷ exclude *sb*; keep *sb* out. Ⓐ 〜を成す ❶ set up house; start housekeeping. ❷ found a school (of thought). ⓒ ⓒ 〜を張る ❶ live in a fine house; keep an establishment. ❷ put up a (good) front. ❸ found a school (of thought). ⓔ ～を開く ❶ open the door (to sb). ❷ give free access to sb; lift restrictions. ❸ open up relations (with a country).

ヤ

矢 an arrow; a bolt; a spoke

[A] ⓐ ～が入る be criticized; ⓔ be the subject of criticism; be blamed; be reproached; ⓐ come under fire. [を] ⓐ ～を刺す fix an arrow to the bowstring. ⓐ ～を番える fix an arrow to the bowstring. ⓐ ～を突く be quick; be expedient. ⓐ ～を矧ぐ ❶ feather an arrow; prepare an arrow. ❷ prepare for battle; make oneself ready for combat; ⓘ gird up one's loins; ⓘ clear the decks. ～を放つ ❶ discharge a volley; open fire; take sb under fire. (質問の) ❷ fire (questions) at sb. ～を向ける fix one's aim; aim for (a target); ⓘ set one's sights on sb/sth.

野 ❺ a plain; a field

[N] ⓐⓔ ～に居る be out of office; be in opposition. ⓔ ～に下る step down from office; ⓔ retire from public office; leave government service.

刃 a blade; a sword ▶ 刃

[N] ～に掛かる die by the sword. ～に 掛ける put sb to the sword; knife sb; strike sb down. ⓐⓔ ～に伏す throw oneself on one's sword; kill oneself by the sword.

八百長 ❺ a rigged affair; a fix

[A] ⓢ ～で負ける [sumō] lose a match on purpose; throw a match. [を] ⓢ ～を遣る [sumō] fix a match; ⓒ rig a fight.

矢面 ❺ the brunt of an attack

[N] ⓔ ～に立つ ❶ bear the brunt of an attack; ⓒ throw oneself into the breach. ❷ become the target of criticism; ⓐ bear the brunt of an attack; ⓘ step into the breach.

薬缶 a kettle; a tea kettle

[を] ～を掛ける put a kettle on (the fire). ⓐ ～を被る conceal one's real personality; feign ignorance; play the hypocrite; simulate modesty. ⓢ ～を脱ぐ be straightforward; come out strong; ⓘ call a spade a spade.

焼き ❺ baking; pottery; temper

[A] ～が回る ❶ [forging] be fired for too long. ⓢ ❷ become decrepit; grow senile. ⓢ ❸ become antiquated; go out of fashion. [を] ～を入れる ❶ [forging] forge a sword; temper a sword. ⓢ ❷ inflict corporal punishment; punish *sb*; harden *sb*. ⑤ ❸ torture *sb*; ⓒ put *sb* to torture; lynch *sb*. ⑤ ❹ reprimand *sb*; ⓘ haul *sb* over the coals; ⓘ teach *sb* a lesson. ⓒ ⑤ ～を掛ける drink away one's hangover.

焼餅 toasted rice cake

を ～を焼く be jealous (of one's wife); display signs of jealousy.

役 a post; a duty; a role

N ～に立つ be useful; be of help; serve a purpose.
を ～を演じる play a role. ～を退く resign a post; quit one's post; ⓒ retire from office. ～を勤める hold an office; perform a duty; play a role. ～を振る assign duties; allocate roles.

約束 a promise; an engagement

と ⓒ (前世からの)～と諦める come to terms with one's fate; resign oneself to one's karma.
N ～に縛られる be bound by a promise; be under a promise. ～に背く break one's promise; renege on one's promise.
を ～を交わす exchange promises; become engaged. ～をする make an appointment (with *sb*). ～を解く release *sb* from a promise. ～を取り消す withdraw one's promise; call off an engagement. ～を果たす ❶ fulfill one's promise; live up to one's promise. ❷ keep an appointment; ⓒ meet one's engagement. ～を守る ❶ keep one's promise; ⓔ honor one's promise; be true to one's word. ❷ keep an appointment; ⓒ meet one's engagement. ❸ observe the rules; abide by the rules; ⓒ stick to the rules. ～を破る break one's promise; renege on one's promise.

櫓 a (castle) turret; a scaffold

を ～を上げる ❶ build a (castle) turret; errect scaffolds; set up a scaffold. ❷ begin a (puppet) play; start a performance. ～を組む set up a scaffold; construct a scaffold.

自棄 ⑤ self-abandonment

N ⑤ ～になる become desperate; be driven to despair; grow reckless.
を ⑤ ～を起こす abandon oneself; become desperate; ⓒ give oneself up to despair; go mad with despair.

野次 ⑤ booing; jeering; hooting

を ⑤ ～を飛ばす hoot at *sb*; jeer at *sb*; ⓒ ⓘ give *sb* the bird.

鏃 an arrowhead; a flinthead

を ⓐ ～を争う fight a battle; do battle. Ⓐ ～を噛む engage an enemy; come to blows.

痩せ我慢 worn out patience
⓿ ～を張る put up with *sth* out of pride; endure *sth* stoically; Ⓒ Ⓘ grin and bear it.

厄介 a burden; trouble
Ⓝ ～になる be a burden to *sb*; be under *sb's* care; be dependent on *sb*; take up lodgings at *sb's* place.
⓿ ～を掛ける give *sb* trouble; bother *sb*; be a nuisance to *sb*.

躍起 exitement; franticness
Ⓝ ～になる become exited; grow eager (to do *sth*); become desperate; Ⓒ get worked up (over *sth*).

宿 a house; a lodging; a dwelling
⓿ ～を替える take up different lodgings; change one's lodgings. ～を貸す give *sb* a night's lodgings; put *sb* up for the night. ～を探す look for a hostel; look for a night's lodging. ～を取る take up one's lodgings; put up at an inn. ～を求める look for a hostel; Ⓒ seek shelter for the night.

柳 a willow tree
Ⓝ ～に受ける handle *sth* with resilience; tackle (a problem) in a flexible way; Ⓒ bend without yielding; be pliable. Ⓐ ～に出る comply without protest; be obedient; be docile; Ⓒ be tractable. Ⓐ ～に遭う handle *sth* with resilience; tackle *sth* in a flexible way; Ⓒ bend without yielding; be pliable.
⓿ Ⓐ ～を折る see *sb* off; give *sb* a send-off.

脂 resin; gum; nicotine; tar
⓿ ～を下げる give oneself airs; be self-complacent; Ⓒ be stuck-up.

藪蛇 a snake in the thicket
Ⓝ Ⓢ ～になる produce the opposite result; go against one; backfire.

山 a mountain; a mine; a gamble
Ⓐ ～が当たる guess right; get it right; Ⓘ be on the the mark. ～が外れる guess wrong; get it wrong; Ⓘ be beside the mark. Ⓐ ～が見える have renewed hope; the prospects brighten; Ⓘ see light at the end of the tunnel.
Ⓝ ～にする pile *sth* up; gather *sth* into a heap. ～に登る climb a mountain; Ⓒ ascend a mountain.
⓿ ～を当てる ❶ Ⓒ strike a vein (of gold). ❷ make a fortune; ❸ Ⓘ make it big time. Ⓐ ～を入れる sell one's

day's worth of goods; close shop; ⓒ wind up business. ～を下りる descend a mountain; come down a mountain. ⓓ ～を買う invest in mines. ～を掛ける ❶ speculate (in stocks); venture on *sth*; take a chance on *sth*. ❷ take chances on getting the right answer; guess at the right answer (in an exam). ～を越す ❶ cross the mountains. ❷ pass the critical point; ⓘ turn the corner; ⓒⓘ be over the hump. ❸ be beyond one's prime. Ⓐ ～を止める ❶ stop in the middle of one's work. ❷ close for the day; close shop; put up the shutters; ⓒ wind up business. ～を成す pile *sth* up; gather *sth* into a heap. ～を抜く have supernatural powers; have great strenght. ～を張る ❶ speculate (in stocks); venture on *sth*; take a chance on *sth*. ❷ take chances on getting the right answer; guess at the right answer (in an exam). ～を踏む commit a crime; ⓒ perpetrate a crime. ～を盛り上げる build up suspense (in a story). ⓒ ～を遣る speculate (in stocks); venture on *sth*; take a chance on *sth*.

病 Ⓔ an illness; a disease

Ⓝ ⓒ ～に犯される fall ill; be taken ill; contract a disease. ⓒ ～に掛かる fall ill; be taken ill; contract a disease. Ⓔ ～に沈む contract a grave disease; fall dangerously ill. Ⓐ ⓒ ～を癒す cure an illness. ⓒ ～を養う undergo medical treatment.

闇 darkness; the black market

Ⓐ ～で売る sell *sth* on the black market. ～で買う buy *sth* on the black market. Ⓝ ～に消える vanish into the night; Ⓔ be swallowed up by the dark. Ⓐ ～に暮れる ❶ go dark; Ⓒ descend into darkness. ❷ lose one's mind; go mad (with grief). ～に流す channel (goods) to the black market. ～に葬る cover *sth* up; ⓒ hush *sth* up. ～に惑う ❶ lose one's way in the darkness. ❷ be at a loss; ⓘ be at one's wits' end; ⓘ be all at sea. ❸ lose one's mind; go mad (with grief). ～に迷う ❶ lose one's way in the darkness. ❷ be at a loss; ⓘ be at one's wits' end; ⓘ be all at sea. ❸ lose one's mind; go mad (with grief). Ⓐ ⓒ ～を遣る trade in the black market; be a blackmarketeer; be an off-the-books dealer.

槍 a spear; a lance; a javelin

Ⓐ ～が入る be interrupted. ⓒ ～が出る be interrupted. Ⓐ ～が曲がる fall short of one's expectations; Ⓔ belie one's expectations.

[を] ～を入れる ❶ attack *sb* with a spear. ❷ jeer at *sb*; hoot at *sb*; heckle *sb*; ⓒ ① give *sb* the bird. ❸ interrupt *sb*; interfere in *sb's* affairs; meddle in *sb's* affairs; ⑤ butt in; ① put one's oar in. ⑥ ～を受ける ❶ be attacked with a spear. ❷ be jeered at; be heckled; ⓒ ① be given the bird. ⑤ ～を食う ❶ be attacked with a spear. ❷ be jeered at; be heckled; ⓒ ① be given the bird. ⑥ ～を出す ❶ thrust out one's spear. ❷ jut out; stick out; ⑥ protrude. ❸ criticize *sb*; make a complaint; raise objections; object to *sth*; ⓒ grumble about *sth*. ❹ [*nōraku*] sing before one's turn; be out of harmony.

やりだま
槍玉 E a victim; a sacrifice

N ⓒ ～に挙げる make an example of *sb*; victimize *sb*; ⓔ pillory *sb*; ⓒ make *sb* the but of criticizm; ① make a scapegoat of *sb*.

ユ

ゆ
湯 hot water; a hot spring

N ～に行く go to the bathhouse; visit a public bath. ～に漬かる have a dip in the bathtub; ⓒ have a good soak.
[を] ～を立てる ❶ heat water; boil water. ❷ get the bath ready; heat the bath. ～を使う take a bath. ～を使わせる give *sb* a bath. ⓐ ～を引く take a bath; wash oneself. ～を沸かす ❶ boil water. ❷ heat the bath; get the bath ready.

ゆう
雄 E supremacy; leadership

[を] ⓔ ～を争う compete for leadership; pursue power; contend for mastery; ⓔ vie for supremacy.

ゆう
勇 E bravery; courage; pluck

[を] ⓐⓔ ～を鼓す pluck up courage; ⓔ muster up courage; ① pull oneself together; ① gird up one's loins.

ゆう い
優位 E superiority; ascendancy

N ⓔ ～に立つ have an advantage over *sb*; ⓔ be in the ascendant; ⓒ ① have the drop on *sb*.
[を] ⓔ ～を与える give *sb* the lead. ⓔ ～を占める have an advantage over *sb*; ① have the upper hand over *sb*; ⓒ ① have the drop on *sb*.

ゆ えい
輸贏 E victory or defeat

[を] ⓐⓔ ～を争う contend for victory; ⓔ vie for supremacy.

ゆう き
勇気 courage; valor; bravery

A ～が有る have courage; be brave; be corageous; ⓒ have pluck; ⑤ have guts. ～が要る require courage; take nerve; ⑤ need guts. 图 ～を失う lose courage; lose heart. ～を挫く discourage *sb*; dishearten *sb*. ～を鼓す pluck up courage; ⓔ muster up courage; ⓞ pull oneself together; ⓘ gird up one's loins. ～を示す show courage; display courage. ～を殺ぐ discourage *sb*; dishearten *sb*. ～を出す pluck up courage; muster one's courage; get up one's nerve; ⓘ pull oneself together; ⓘ gird up one's loins. ～を付ける encourage *sb*; cheer *sb* on.

融通 accomodation; adaptability

A ～が利く ❶ have credit; have financial resources. ❷ be flexible; be versatile; be adaptable.

床 the floor ▶ 床

N ～に座る sit on the floor. 图 ～を掃く sweep the floor. ～を拭く wipe the floor; mop the floor. ～を踏み鳴らす stamp one's foot (with anger).

雪 snow; a snowfall

A ～が降る snow falls; it snows. N ～に埋もれる be buried in the snow; be snowed under. ～に閉ざされる be snowbound; be snowed up; be snowed in.

图 ⓞ ～を欺く be snow-white; be startlingly white. ～を戴く ❶ be covered with snow; be snow-crested. ❷ have (snow-)white hair. ⓞ ～を冒す brave the snow. ～をかく clear away snow. ⓐ ～を廻らす blow up the snow.

湯気 stream; vapor

A ⓞ ～が上がる get ahead in the world; succeed in life; rise in the world. ～が立つ ❶ give off steam. ❷ boil with rage.

ゆとり leeway; margin; latitude

A ～が有る be well provided for; be well stocked; be broad-minded. 图 ～を与える make room for *sth*; allow latitude; leave a margin. ～を持たせる leave sufficient room; ⓐ give play to the rope.

指 a finger; the thumb; a toe

N ～に嵌める put (a ring/a pick for playing *koto*, etc.) on a finger. 图 ～を折る turn in one's finger (when counting); count on one's fingers. ～を切る ❶ cut one's finger. ❷ make a vow; make a pledge. ⓞⓔ ～を屈する make a vow; pledge to do *sth*; make a pledge. ～を銜える ❶ put a finger in one's mouth. ❷ covet *sth*; look enviously at *sb*/*sth*; watch *sb* with envy. ❸ remain an onlooker; stand by idly; ⓒ sit on the fence. 〜を指す ❶ point to *sth*; point at *sth*; point *sth* out. ❷ talk behind *sb's* back; backbite. Ⓐ ❸ take part in *sth*; have a hand in *sth*. Ⓐ ❹ make an estimate; put *sth* down at a certain price. 〜を絞る extract blood from one's finger (to sign a document). 〜を染める try one's hand at *sth*; take *sth* up; have a try at *sth*; get a taste of *sth*. Ⓒ 〜を尽くす make a pledge; make a vow; pledge to do *sth*. 〜を鳴らす snap one's fingers. 〜を詰める ❶ crush one's finger; catch one's finger (in the door). ❷ [*yakuza*] cut of the tip of one's finger in atonement. ❸ make a pledge; make a vow; pledge to do *sth*. 〜を曲げる bend a finger; flex one's fingers.

弓 a bow; archery

Ⓐ 〜で射る shoot with bow and arrow. Ⓒ 〜を加う fix an arrow to the bowstring. Ⓐ 〜を鳴らす drive out (an evil spirit); put *sb* to flight. 〜を外す ❶ loosen the bowstring; remove the bowstring. ❷ lay down one's arms; disarm; stop fighting; ⓒ give up the struggle. 〜を引く ❶ draw a bow; shoot an arrow.

❷ drive out (an evil spirit); put *sb* to flight. ❸ rebel against (authority); rise against (an oppressor).

夢 a dream; a vision; an illusion

Ⓐ 〜が覚める ❶ be awakened; wake up; be roused from one's sleep. ❷ ⓒ be disillusioned; come to one's senses; see reason. Ⓔ (一生を)〜と過ごす dream one's life away. Ⓝ 〜に欺かれる entertain false hopes; ⓒ labor under an illusion. 〜に現れる appear in one's dream. 〜を買う buy a lot; buy a lottery ticket. 〜に通う appear in one's dream. 〜に見る dream about *sb*/*sth*; see *sth* in a dream; have a vision. Ⓔ ⓐ 〜を合わす interpret a dream. 〜を抱く ⓐ have a dream; have aspirations. 〜を描く aspire to *sth*; have aspirations. ⓐ have a dream. 〜を追う pursue a dream; live one's dream. ⓒ 〜を誘う bring out the best in *sb*. 〜を覚ます ❶ awake *sb*; rouse *sb* from sleep. ❷ disillusion *sb*; bring *sb* to his/her senses; make *sb* see reason. 〜を托する rely on *sb*/*sth*; place one's hope on *sb*/*sth*. 〜を違える counteract the spell of a bad dream (through incantation). 〜を解く interpret a dream. 〜を見る ❶ dream about *sth*; ⓒ have a dream. ❷ be lost

in daydreams; be a dreamer. 〜を結
ぶ get to sleep; have a dream.

夢路 "dream street"
㋕ 〜を辿る fall asleep; be fast
asleep; ⓒ nod off.

許し permission; pardon; leave
㋕ 〜を与える pardon sb; give sb
leave; grant permission. 〜を受ける
be pardoned; obtain leave; get permission. 〜を乞う ask for permission; request leave.

ヨ

世 the world; society; the public
Ⓝ Ⓐ 〜に合う ❶ win popularity;
meet the public taste. ❷ be prosperous; be fortunate; ⓒ do well. Ⓐ 〜に
出ず ❶ be born into the world; see
the light of day. ❷ start in life; go
out into the world. ❸ take up public
office; come into office. 〜に遅れる
fall behind the times. 〜に阿る
truckle to the times; buy popularity.
〜に従う go with the tide; go with
the flow. 〜に知らず ❶ be unique;
be unprecedented. ❷ be abnormal;
be other-worldly; be out of this
world. 〜に背く go against the tide.
〜に立つ succeed in life; go up in
the world; ⓘ make one's mark. 〜に
連れる change with the world; Ⓐ be
swept along with the tide. 〜に出る
❶ be born into the world; see the
light of day. ❷ start in life; go out
into the world. ❸ take up public
office. 〜に問う make sth public;
turn to the public; publicize sth. 〜
に泊まる live in this world; inhabit
this world. Ⓐ 〜に鳴る become
famous; win fame. 〜に似つ ❶ be
unique; be unprecedented. ❷ be
abnormal; be other-worldly; be out
of this world. 〜に憚る avoid public
notice; shun publicity. Ⓐ 〜に旧る
❶ grow old; become hackneyed.
❷ become rare; grow sparse. ❸ know
what it is to be married; have a
marital history.
㋕ 〜を挙げる come together; be
united. ⓒ 〜を出づ ❶ get away from
the hustle and bustle of the world.
❷ go into seclusion; ⓔ retire from
the world; become a hermit;
renounce the world. ❸ become a
Buddhist priest; take the tonsure;
ⓔ retire into religion. ⓒ 〜を厭う
become weary of life; get tired of
life. 〜を倦む become weary of life;
get tired of life. 〜を送る go
through life; make a living. 〜を驚か
す create a sensation; be much
talked about; Ⓐ shake the world;
ⓘ make a stir. Ⓐ 〜を籠む be young;

ⓒ be in the spring of life. ～を籠める the night is still long. ～を去る pass away; leave this world. ～を忍ぶ bury oneself in obscurity; live in seclusion. ～を知る ❶ know what makes the world go round; be worldly-wise. ⓐ ❷ subdue a country; rule a country. ～を捨てる ❶ become a hermit; go into seclusion; renounce the world; ⓒ retire from the world. ❷ become a Buddhist priest; take the tonsure; ⓒ retire into religion. ～を狭める make one's circle of acquaintances smaller. ⓐ ～を背く ❶ go into seclusion; renounce the world; become a hermit; ⓒ retire from the world. ❷ become a Buddhist priest; take the tonsure; ⓒ retire into religion. ⓐ ～を保つ rule over a country; govern a country; ⓒ manage the affairs of state. ⓐ ～を尽くす ❶ reach the end of one's life; end one's life; finish one's life. ❷ go through life; pass through life; spend one's life (doing sth). ～を取る sieze power; take the reigns of government; conquer the whole country; gain absolute control. ～を轟かす ❶ be widely known; make a name for oneself; become famous. ❷ arouse exitement; ⓘ create a stirr. ⓐ ～を遁れる ❶ go into seclusion; renounce the world; ⓒ retire from the world. ❷ become a Buddhist priest; take the tonsure; ⓒ retire into religion. ～を儚む be tired of life; get weary of the world. ～を離れる ❶ become a Buddhist priest; take the tonsure; ⓒ retire into religion. ❷ go into seclusion; renounce the world; ⓒ retire from the world. ～を憚る fear to be seen by others; live in obscurity; be reclusive. ⓐ ～を張る show off; be vain; ⓒ be ostentatious. ～を響かす create a sensation; be much talked about; ⓘ make a stir. ⓐ ～を済す save the world. ～を渡る ❶ go through life; earn one's living; make a living. ❷ pass on the family leadership. ❸ go into seclusion; become a hermit; renounce the world; ⓒ retire from the world.

夜 night; evening; dawn

Ⓐ ⓐ ～が詰まる the nights grow short.
图 ～を明かす keep an all-night vigil; stay up all night. ⓐ ～を籠む the night is young. ～を撤する sit up all night. ～を更かす stay up late; keep late hours.

酔い drunkenness; intoxication

Ⓐ ～が覚める become sober; get sober; sober up. ～が回る become

inebriated; get drunk; ⓔ be intoxicated; ⓕ be in one's cups.

よう
用 use; business; an errand

Ⓐ ～が足りる be useful; be of use; be of help; be competent; ⓔ meet the requirements.

Ⓝ ⓐ～に立つ be useful; be of use; serve a purpose; ⓒ come in handy.

Ⓦ ～を済ます get through with one's business; finish one's business; do one's errand. ⓓ ⓔ ～を節する save expenses; cut costs; be frugal. ～を足す ❶ conduct one's business; run errands. ❷ relieve oneself; go to the toilet; ⓔ answer the call of nature. ～を勤める serve *sb*; do *sb* a service; ⓔ be at *sb*'s service. ⓐ ⓔ ～を弁ずる conduct one's business; go on an errand. ⓒ ～を満たす cover the costs; meet the expenses.

よう
要 the main point; the essence

Ⓦ ⓐ ～を揚げる raise the main point; present the essence of one's message. ～を得る be brief; ⓕ be to the point. ⓒ ～を摘む give the main points; present the essence of one's message.

よう
陽 the positive; the male; *yang*

Ⓝ ～に開く come out into the open; take the initiative; initiate an attack.

よう
俑 (Chinese) burrial puppets

Ⓐ ⓐ ～を作る start on *sth* wrong; set a bad example; ⓔ set an evil precedent.

ようぎ
容儀 deportment; mien

Ⓦ ⓐ ⓔ ～を正す sit up straight. ⓐ ⓔ ～を乱す act rudely; act without decorum; be a boor.

ようきゅう
要求 a demand; a request

Ⓝ ～に応じる respond to a demand; comly with *sb*'s request; admit *sb*'s claim. ～に適う satisfy a demand; meet a request. ～に屈する succumb to *sb*'s demands.

Ⓦ ～を入れる accede to a demand. ～を叶える fulfill *sb*'s wish; grant *sb*'s request. ～を退ける turn down a demand; refuse a request; reject a claim. ～を撥ね付ける turn down a demand; refuse a request; reject a claim.

ようじ
用事 business; an errand

Ⓐ ～が有る have *sth* to do; be engaged.

Ⓦ ～を済ます finish one's business; complete an errand.

ようじ
楊枝 a toothpick

Ⓦ ⓐ ～を違える ❶ get a minor detail wrong; make a trivial mistake.

用心 care; heed; cation

図 ～を怠る be imprudent; ⓘ be off one's guard.

要領 the point; the gist

図 ～を得る be relevant; ⓘ be to the point; ⓘ be on the mark; ⓘ hit the nail on the head. ～を教える give sb an outline; tell sb the gist of sth; ⓘ teach sb the ropes.

欲 greed; avarice; desire

Ａ ～が突っ張る be greedy; ⓔ be avaricious; ⓘ bite off more than one can chew. ～が張る be greedy; ⓔ be avaricious; ⓘ bite off more than one can chew. ～が深い be greedy; be selfish; ⓔ be avaricious.

Ｎ ⓐ ～に耽る give oneself over to greed; indulge one's passions; be obsessed by sth; be a slave to love; ⓔ be ruled by avarice.

図 ～を言う say what one has on one's mind; speak unreservedly. ～を搔く ❶ be greedy; ⓔ be avaricious; ⓘ bite off more than one can chew. ❷ covet sth; lust for (a woman) desire sth; crave for sth. ⓐ ～を渇く be greedy; be avaricious; ⓘ bite off more than one can chew. ～を離れる be disinterested; be unselfish; be generous; ⓔ free oneself from greed.

横 the side; the flank; the width

と ⓐ ～と出る become cross at sb; be cross-grained; be perverse.

Ｎ ⓐ ～に行く ❶ be unreasonable; be cross-grained. ❷ [prostitution] sleep with another guest; tend to another guest. ～に置く lay sth on its side; put sth on its side. ～に切る intersect with a road; cross sb's path. ⓐ ～に暮らす live a carefree life. ～にする lay sth down. ⓐ ～に出る ❶ be unreasonable; be cross-grained. ❷ scare sb (into sth); threaten sb. ～になる ❶ lie oneself down; lie down. ⓒ ❷ be unreasonable. ⓐ ～に寝る ❶ lie on one's side; go to sleep; turn in for the night. ❷ fail to pay off one's debts; stay in arrears. ❸ embezzle money; misappropriate money. (首を)～に振る ❶ shake one's head. ❷ reject sth; turn down (an offer) ～に曲げる bend sideways; bend to one side. (船が)～に揺れる roll from side to side; roll to one side. ⓐ ～に渡る ❶ be unreasonable; be cross-grained. ❷ scare sb (into sth); threaten sb; bully sb.

へ ～へ切れる turn into a side road; turn the corner. ～へ退く move sideways; give way to sb.

図 ⓐ ～を言う ❶ be unreasonable; be cross-grained. ❷ scare sb into *sth*; intimidate *sb*; ⓒ bully *sb*. ⓓ ～を押す ram one's opinion through; force one's will on *sb*; go against all reason. ⓐ ～を切る [prostitution] sleep with another guest; attend to another guest. ～を向く ❶ look aside; look the other way. ❷ reject *sth*; turn down (an offer).

横紙 "sideway paper"
Ⓐ ～を破る be unreasonable; be perverse; be cross-grained.

横車 "a sideway cart"
Ⓔ ～を押す force one's will on *sb*; ram one's opinion through; go against all reason.

横手 the side
Ⓔ ～を打つ ❶ clasp one's hands; fold one's hands. ❷ be taken aback; be startled; be surprised.

横道 a side road; a byway
Ⓔ ～に入る deviate from virtue; be led astray; ⓘ leave the straight and narrow.
Ⓔ ～へ逸れる ❶ stray from the right way; be led astray; ⓘ leave the straight and narrow. ❷ wander from the (main) subject; get sidetracked; be diverted.

横目 a sidelong glance
Ⓝ (人を)～に見る ❶ give *sb* a sidelong glance; look sideways at *sb*; look at *sb* out of the corner of one's eyes. ❷ take no notice of *sb*; have no eye for *sb*; think nothing of *sb*; ignore *sb*; ⓒ set *sb* at naught.

横槍 an interruption
Ⓐ ～が入る be interrupted.
Ⓔ ～を入れる ❶ interfere in *sb's* affairs; pry in *sb's* affairs; ⓒⓘ poke one's nose into (the affairs of others). ❷ interrupt *sb*; ⓢ butt in; ⓘ put one's oar in.

誼み Ⓘ friendship; goodwill
Ⓔ ⓒ ～を重んじる be true in one's friendship; value friendship. ⓒ ～を通ずる enter into friendly relations with (the enemy); take *sb's* side. ～を結ぶ establish a friendship with *sb*; enter into friendly relations with *sb*.

余端 Ⓘ lingering life
Ⓔ ⓒ ～を保つ cling on to dear life; eke out a living; ⓘ be on one's last legs.

他所 another place
Ⓝ ～に聞く ❶ listen without interest; listen to *sb* without feeling

involved. ❷ pretend to be deaf; feign deafness; pretend not to hear. 〜にする do not care for *sth*; neglect *sth*; be indifferent to *sth*. 〜に成す do not care for *sth*; neglect *sth*; be indifferent to *sth*. 〜に成る ❶ lose interest; become indifferent. ❷ become estranged; become alienated (from *sb*). 〜に見る ❶ remain a passive onlooker; ⓘ sit on the fence. ❷ look away; pretend not to see *sth*.

予想 expectation; conjecture

Ⓐ 〜が明るい the prospects are bright; the outlook is good; be promising. 〜が付かない be unpredictable; ⓔ be beyond conjecture. 囲 〜を裏切る go against one's expectations; upset one's expectations. 〜を上回る be above expectations; exceed one's expectations. 〜を下回る be below expectations; fall short of one's expectations. 〜を許さない be unpredictable; ⓔ be beyond conjecture.

与太 Ⓑ idle talk; gossip; humbug

囲 ⓢ 〜を飛ばす ❶ talk nonsense; ⓔ indulge in idle talk; ⓘ talk through one's hat; ⓒⓘ talk rubbish.

涎 Ⓑ saliva; drivel; drool

Ⓐ ⓢ 〜が出る ❶ start to drool;

begin to drivel. ❷ be delicious; be ravishing; be tempting. 囲 ⓢ 〜を垂らす dribble over *sth*; lust for *sb/sth*; gloat on *sth*. ⓢ 〜を流す dribble over *sth*; lust for *sb/sth*; gloat on *sth*. ⓐ ⓢ 〜を舐る imitate *sb*; take *sb* off; ⓢ ⓘ take the mickey (out of *sb*).

余談 a diversion; a digression

N 〜に渡る wander away from the point; make a digression.

予断 Ⓑ a prediction; a prophecy

囲 ⓔ 〜を許さない be impossible to predict; be unpredictable.

四つ four

N 〜に組む ❶ [*sumō*]come to grapples; grapple with the opponent. ❷ tackle a job; ⓘ come to grips with a *sth*. 〜にする ❶ cut/devide *sth* into four parts; quarter (an apple). ⓐ ❷ punish adulterers by tying them together and cutting them in two. 〜に這う crawl on one's hands and knees; ⓘ go on all fours. 〜に渡る ❶ [*sumō*]come to grapples; grapple with the opponent. ❷ tackle a job; ⓘ come to grips with a *sth*.

余念 other thoughts

Ⓐ (…に)〜が無い have no time for

anything else; be absorbed in *sth*; ⓒ be engrossed in *sth*.

余白 a blank; a space; a margin
[へ] ～へ書く write in the margins.
[を] ～を埋める fill in a blank space. (...に)～を割く allow space for *sth*; accomodate space for *sth*. ⓒ ～を汚す have an article in print; have an article published.

輿望 ⓔ expectation; trust
[を] ⓒ ～を担う enjoy the trust of the people; ⓒ have the people's hopes thrust upon one's shoulders.

嫁 a (young) wife; a bride
[N] ～に行く marry a man (into the family); get married to a man; ⓒⓘ tie the knot. ～に遣る give one's daughter away in marriage; marry one's daughter off; ⓒ give *sb* the hand of one's daugher.
[を] ～を捜す look for a bride; search for a wife. ～を取る get married; take (a woman for one's) wife; ⓒⓘ tie the knot. ～を迎える get married; take a wife; ⓒⓘ tie the knot. ～を貰う have *sb* for a wife; marry a woman.

余裕 room; scope; time
[A] ～が有る have room to spare; leave ample scope; have time to spare; have money to spare.
[を] ～を付ける make allowances; allow for *sth*. ～を残す leave (sufficient) room. ～を持たせる leave sufficient room; ⓐ give play to the rope.

縒り a twist; a ply; a lay
[A] ～が戻る ❶ return to the original state; go back to the old days; become disentangled. ❷ be reconciled; make amends; make it up with *sb*. ❸ feel relieved; feel relaxed; be put at ease.
[を] ～を掛ける ❶ twist a rope; twine a rope. ❷ exert oneself; do one's best; concentrate on *sth*. ～を戻す ❶ disentangle (a knot). ❷ return *sth* to its original state. ❸ get reconciled; make amends.

夜 night; nighttime
[A] ～が更ける grow late; get late; the night wears on.
[N] ～になる become night; the night falls; it gets dark.

喜び joy; delight; rapture
[N] ～に湧く be delighted; be in raptures; ⓘ be over the moon.
[を] ～を得る derive pleasure from; draw joy from. ～を感じる take delight in; be happy about. ～を述べ

る offer one's congratulations; express one's joy.

齢 [E] age; years

[A] ⓒ ～を重ねる put on years; grow older; gain in years.

弱音 [E] feeble complaints

[A] ⓒ ～を吐く complain about *sth*; moan about *sth*; ⓒ ⓘ sing small.

ラ

来意 the purpose of one's visit

[を] ～を尋ねる ask for the reason of *sb's* call. ～を告げる state the reason of one's call; give the reason for one's visit.

楽 ease; comfort; relief

[N] ⓒ ～に居る stretch one's legs; make oneself at home.

[を] ～をする live in comfort; take life easy; have an easy life.

落着 a settlement

[を] ～を付ける reach a settlement; settle *sth*; come to a conclusion.

埒 [E] a fence; a boundary

[A] ⓒ ～が明く ❶ be settled; come to a settlement. ❷ make progress; make headway; come to an end.

[を] ⓐ ⓒ ～を明ける ❶ explain *sth*; justify *sth*; plead an excuse. ❷ settle a matter; bring *sth* to a settlement. ⓒ ⓒ ～を越える cross a boundary; ⓔ go beyond bounds; ⓘ be beyond the pale. ⓐ ⓒ ～を付ける ❶ explain *sth*; justify *sth*; plead an excuse. ❷ settle a matter; bring *sth* to a settlement.

喇叭 [E] a trumpet; a horn

[を] ⓒ ～を吹く ❶ blow a bugle. ❷ boast about *sth*; brag about *sth*; ⓘ tell a tall tale; ⓒ ⓘ talk through one's hat; ⓘ talk big; ⓘ blow one's own horn (trumpet).

乱 [E] a revolt; a rebellion; a riot

[A] ⓐ ～が入る be in turmoil; be in an uproar; be in a tumult.

[を] ⓐ ～を入れる make an uproar; make a tumult; ⓒ ⓘ raise the devil; ⓢ kick up a row. ～を起こす raise a rebellion; rise in revolt; ⓔ raise the standard of revolt. ～を治める suppress a rebellion; put down a revolt; crush a riot.

リ

利 benefit; profit; gains

[A] ⓢ ～が食う build up interest; run up interest.

N ~に走る be eager to make a profit. Ⓐ ~に耽る be engrossed in profit-making. ~に迷う be swayed by interests; be tempted by gain. Ⓦ ~を失う ❶ lose the advantage; be at a disadvantage; be handicapped. ❷ suffer a loss. ~を得る ❶ have an advantage (over sb). ❷ make a profit; profit from sth. ~をかく pay interest. Ⓢ ~を食う yield interest; get interest.

理 reason; a principle; logic

Ⓐ Ⓐ ~が済む be sensible; be fair-minded; be down-to-earth.
N ~に当たる be in the right; be right; be reasonable; Ⓘ be on the mark. Ⓐ ~に落ちる be given to too much reasoning; be argumentative. Ⓐ ~に折れる give in to reason. ~に適う be reasonable; stand to reason. ~に詰まる ❶ give in to reason; be won over. ❷ be given to too much reasoning; be argumentative; Ⓘ split hairs; Ⓒ Ⓘ chop logic (with sb). ~に反する go against reason; be unreasonable; be in the wrong. Ⓦ Ⓐ ~を言う ❶ explain oneself; make an excuse; defend oneself. ❷ be given to too much reasoning; be argumentative; Ⓘ split hairs; Ⓒ Ⓘ chop logic (with sb). Ⓐ ~を砕く reason with sb; tell sb what is what.

~を尽くす listen to reason; be reasonable; be down-to-earth. ~を曲げる pervert the truth; bend the truth. Ⓐ ~を持つ be reasonable; be in the right; Ⓘ be on the mark. Ⓐ ~を破る pervert the truth; bend the truth. ~を分ける see reason; know what is what.

裏 Ⓔ the reverse/other side ▶ 裏

N Ⓐ ~に入る ❶ [medical] strike inward. ❷ be depressed; be downhearted; be gloomy; feel down. Ⓐ ~に落ちる be downhearted; be depressed; be gloomy; feel down. Ⓐ ~に詰む be downhearted; be depressed; be gloomy; feel down.

利害 pros and cons; interests

Ⓦ ~を説く explain the pros and cons to sb; reason with sb; persuade sb; win sb over. ~を共にする have common interests.

力量 ability; capacity; capability

Ⓦ ~を示す display one's ability. ~を試す test sb's ability. ~を問う question sb's ability; call sb's ability into question.

理屈 Ⓔ reason; logic; theory

Ⓐ ~が良い ❶ be well off; have a heavy purse. ❷ be lucky; be fortu-

nate; have luck. ❸ be profitable; be advantageous; be economical. Ⓐ ◎ 〜が下る understand *sth*; comprehend *sth*; follow *sth*. ◎ 〜が立つ be reasonable; be logical; stand to reason; be right. ◎ 〜が付く resolve a situation; settle an affair. ◎ 〜が通る be sound; be reasonable; be sensible; stand to reason.
N ◎ 〜に合う be reasonable; be logical; stand to reason. ◎ 〜に適う be logical; make sense; be rational; be sensible; be down-to-earth.
を ◎ 〜を言う be argumentative; raise an argument; ① split hairs; ◎ ① chop logic (with *sb*). ◎ 〜を捏ねる argue for the sake of argument; ① put on an argument. ◎ 〜を付ける ❶ be argumentative; ① split hairs; ◎ ① chop logic (with *sb*). Ⓐ ❷ resolve a situation; settle an affair.

利子 interest

Ⓐ 〜がつく yield interest.
Ⓐv 〜で暮らす live on interest.
を 〜を生む yield interest. 〜を取る charge interest. 〜を払う pay interest.

理性 reason; reasoning power

を 〜を失う lose one's reason; go mad; ⓢ ① lose one's marbles. 〜を欠く be devoid of reason. 〜を保つ

maintain one's sanity; ① keep one's head. 〜を働かす use one's reason.

理想 an ideal

N 〜に適う measure up to one's ideal; conform to one's ideal.
を 〜を抱く cherish an ideal. 〜を追う pursue an ideal. 〜を立てる hold up an ideal.

律儀 honest; upright; straight

N 〜に構える act with integrity; behave in an honest way. 〜に働く do one's work faithfully; earn an honest living.

溜飲 🄴 water brash

Ⓐ ◎ 〜が起こる suffer from water brash. 〜が下がる ❶ be cured of water brash. ⓒ ❷ feel relieved; feel satisfaction over *sth*; be content with *sth*.
を ◎ 〜を下げる feel satisfaction (in doing *sth*); satisfy oneself (by doing *sth*); gloat over *sth*.

柳眉 🄴 beautiful eyebrows

N ◎ 〜を逆立てる raise one's eyebrows in anger; glare at *sb* (with indignation).

涼 the (evening) cool

を 〜を納る enjoy the cool. 〜を入

れる let in cool air. 〜を取る enjoy the cool. 〜を求める seek the evening cool.

料簡 目 an idea; a thought

Ⓐ ⓒ 〜が付く ❶ have an idea; think of *sth*; hit on an idea. ❷ realize one's error; become aware of one's mistake.
Ⓝ Ⓐ ⓒ 〜に付く act in accordance with *sb's* ideas; comply with *sb*.
Ⓦ ⓒ (悪い)〜を起こす conceive a bad idea; yield to temptation; ⓘ take *sth* into one's head. Ⓐ ⓒ 〜を加える take measures; take steps. Ⓐ ⓒ 〜を付ける be patient (with *sb*); put up with *sb*/*sth*; acquiesce in *sth*.

了見 a thought; a notion

Ⓝ 〜に及ばない have no clue; have no (other) options. (人の)〜に任せる leave *sth* to *sb's* discretion.
Ⓦ 〜を起こす conceive of an idea; think of *sth*. 〜を聞く ask *sb's* intention; questions *sb's* notions. 〜を加える think of a solution; devise a means; work out a way; work *sth* out. 〜を定める decide on *sth*; make up one's mind.

良心 conscience

Ⓐ 〜が咎める go against one's con- science; feel guilty; have a guilty conscience; ⓘ feel the pricks of con- science.
Ⓝ 〜に訴える appeal to *sb's* con- science; address *sb's* conscience. 〜に顧みる search one's soul; ⓒ consult one's conscience. 〜に従う follow one's conscience; listen to one's conscience; act according to one's conscience. 〜に背く go against one's conscience. 〜に問う listen to one's conscience; ⓒ heed conscience. 〜に恥じる feel guilty; have a guilty conscience; ⓒ weigh upon one's conscience; ⓘ feel the pricks of conscience. 〜に反する go against one's conscience.
Ⓦ 〜を傷つける wound one's con- science. 〜を慰める soothe one's conscience; ⓒ appease one's con- science. 〜を悩ます feel guilty; ⓒ weigh upon one's conscience; ⓘ feel the pricks of conscience.

両天秤 a pair of scales

Ⓦ 〜を掛ける try to achieve one's goal by two alternative ways; play a double game; ⓘ have two strings to one's bow; ⓒ ⓘ hedge one's bets.

両刀 two swords; both swords

Ⓦ 〜を遣う ❶ use two swords. ❷ be ambidextrous. ❸ be bisexual.

輪郭 (りんかく) contours; outlines; profile

[を] 〜を描く draw sb in outline; describe sth in outline. 〜を掴む grasp the general idea; get the picture; ⓒ ⓘ catch sb's drift. 〜を述べる give an outline (of a plan).

ル

累 (るい) trouble; implication

[A] 〜が及ぶ be negatively affected by circumstances; be troubled by circumstances; undergo a negative influence.
[を] 〜を及ぼす cause sb trouble; get sb into trouble; affect sth negatively; ⓒ have negative repercussions.

塁 (るい) a fort; a base; a rampart

[を] ⓐ 〜を摩する ❶ draw close to an enemy fort. ❷ be close rivals; be close contenders; run very closely. 〜を守る defend a fort. 〜を設ける build a fort; set up a parapet; erect a stronghold.

類 (るい) a species; a type; a sort

[A] 〜が無い ❶ be unique; unprecedented. ❷ be exquisite; be superior; be unparalelled.
[N] 〜に属する belong to a species.
ⓐ 〜に触れる check out sb's relations; hunt up one's connections.

[を] 〜を異にする be in a different category; be of a different order. ⓘ 〜を知らず be unable to value sth; get one's priorities wrong; ⓘ put the cart before the horse.

留守 (るす) being away; absence

[N] 〜にさせる ❶ make sb look after the house (while one is away). ❷ make sb take charge of a house's management. ❸ take sb as a wife; make sb one's wife. 〜にする be absent; be out. (お)〜になる neglect one's duties.
[を] 〜を預かる take charge of the house (while sb is absent); look after the house; ⓘ hold the fort. 〜を使う pretend to be out; feign absence.

レ

礼 (れい) a bow; etiquette; courtesy

[N] (お)〜に行く visit sb out of courtesy; call on sb to offer one's thanks.
[を] 〜を言う express one's thanks; make one's apologies; express one's gratitude; ⓒ tender an apology. 〜を欠く lack courtesy; be impolite. 〜を差し上げる offer a reward. ⓒ 〜を失する go against etiquette. 〜を知る be well-bred; be of good breeding. 〜をする ❶ make a bow; bow to sb;

salute *sb*; make a curtsy. ❷ offer a reward; remunerate *sb*; pay *sb* a fee. ～を尽くす show *sb* every courtesy; treat *sb* with honor. ～を述べる thank *sb*; express one's thanks. ～を貰う accept a reward; receive a reward; get a reward.

例 an example; a precedent
[N] ～に倣う follow suit; follow an example; take example by *sth*.
[を] ～を揚げる give an example; take an instance; refer to a precedent. ～を捜し出す ferret out an instance; find a precedent. ～を示す show an example; point out an instance. ～を作る establish a precedent; set a precedent. ～を引く cite an instance; draw an example; quote an instance. ～を設ける cite a case. ～を破る break the precedent.

霊 the spirit; someone's memory
[を] ～を鎮める appease the souls of the deceased. ～を慰める appease the souls of the deceased. ～を祭る perform religious services for the departed souls; worship the spirits; celebrate *sb's* memory.

霊感 inspiration; a brainstorm
[A] ～が働く be inspired; have a brain wave; get inspired. ～を与える give *sb* inspiration. ～を受ける be inspired; have a brain wave; get inspired. ～を見出す find inspiration; get inspiration. ～を求める seek inspiration; look for inspiration.

冷気 cold; chill; cold weather
[を] ～を感じる feel chilly. ～を催す the cold season has set in.

冷静 calmness; coolness
[N] ～に返る regain one's presence of mind; Ⓔ recover one's composure; Ⓘ pull oneself together. ～に構える affect composure; remain self-composed; Ⓘ keep one's head.

礼節 E courtesy; etiquette
[を] Ⓔ ～を失う lose one's sense of decorum; be perturbed. Ⓔ ～を保つ remain calm; maintain one's sense of decorum; be unruffled; Ⓘ keep one's head. Ⓔ ～を取り戻す regain one's self-possession. Ⓔ ～を磨く cultivate one's manners.

令名 E a good name; fame
[を] Ⓔ ～を博する win fame; become famous. Ⓔ ～を馳せる win fame; become famous. Ⓔ ～を汚す mar *sb's* name; Ⓔ tarnish *sb's* reputation.

レンラク / ロク

れいむ
霊夢 A an inspired dream

を ⓐ 〜を見る have an inspired dream.

れつ
列 a row; a line; a tire

N 〜に加わる step into line; join a queue. 〜に並ぶ stand in line; line up; form a queue.
を ⓒ 〜を切る cross a line; break through a line. 〜を作る form a line; line up; form a queue; queue up. 〜を詰める close up the ranks. 〜を解く break up the ranks. 〜を整える dress to ranks. 〜を離れる fall out of line; leave the ranks. 〜を乱す break the line; jump the queue; break rank.

れっとうかん
劣等感 an inferiority complex

を 〜を抱く feel inferior; have an inferiority complex. 〜を持つ feel inferior; have an inferiority complex.

れんぽ
蓮歩 E graceful steps

を ⓐⓒ 〜を運ぶ walk gracefully.

れんらく
連絡 contact; communications

を 〜を失う lose contact. 〜を絶つ break off communications; cut off contact. 〜を保つ maintain (radio) contact; keep in touch with sb. 〜を付ける establish contact; get in touch with sb; make contact. 〜を取る get in touch with sb; establish contact; make contact.

ロ

ろ
炉 a fireplace; a hearth; a forge

N 〜に掛ける hang (a kettle/pot) over the fire.
を 〜を囲む sit around the fireplace; gather around the hearth. ⓒ 〜を切る make a fireplace in the floor.

ろ
櫓 a scull; an oar

を ⓒ 〜を押す work a scull; pull an oar. ⓒ 〜を漕ぐ work a scull; pull an oar.

ろう
労 E trouble; labor; pains

N ⓒ 〜に報いる reward sb for his/her services.
を 〜を惜しむ stint one's efforts; be sparing of oneself. 〜を取る take the trouble to do sth; take pains to do sth. 〜を省く save sb trouble; spare sb the trouble. 〜を煩わす trouble sb to do sth.

ろう
牢 a prison; a jail; a gaol

N 〜に入る be imprisoned; be put in jail; be thrown into jail.
を 〜を出る be released from prison; come out of prison. 〜を破る escape from prison; break out of prison.

ロク　　　　　　　　　　　　　　　　　　　ワガモノ

老 old age; the aged; old men

[を] ～を労（いたわ）る be kind to old men. ～を敬（うやま）う honor age; respect the aged; revere old age.

狼藉（ろうぜき）[E] disorder; mayhem; havoc

[を] ⓔ ～を極（きわ）める commit all kinds of excesses. ⓔ ～を働（はたら）く run riot; work havoc; commit excesses.

櫓櫂（ろかい） sculls and oars

[A] ～が無（な）い ❶ have no recourse; have no options; be without means. be left to one's one devices; ⓔ be thrown upon one's own resources. ❶ have no one to turn to; be at a loss; ① be all at sea.

碌（ろく） gravel; corrosion

[A] ～で無（な）い ❶ be useless; fail to serve its purpose; be of no use. ❷ be a good-for-nothing; be a bumbler; be useless.

[N] ～に居（い）る ❶ be at ease; be at peace with oneself; feel relaxed. ❷ sit at ease; sit cross-legged. ❷ sit straight; sit upright; sit square.

禄（ろく）[E] a fief; a stipend; a ration

[A] ～が甘（あま）い ❶ [sumō] have a weak grip. ❷ be in a weak position; have a disadvantage.

[を] ～を受ける recieve a stipend. ⓐ

～を窃（ぬす）む hold a sinecure. ⓐ ～を食（は）む receive a stipend; become a vassal.

露店（ろてん） a street stall

[を] ～を出（だ）す open a street stall; set up a street stall; keep a street stall.

路頭（ろとう）[E] the roadside

[N] ⓔ ～に迷（まよ）う be adrift; be homeless; become a beggar; ⓔ be cast out by the world.

露命（ろめい）[E] a transient life

[を] ⓔ ～を繋（つな）ぐ eke out a living; ⓒ get by; ① make ends meet; ① keep body and soul together.

呂律（ろれつ） articulation

[A] ～が廻（まわ）らない be inarticulate; slur one's words.

ワ

輪（わ） a circle; a ring; a link

[A] ～が外（はず）れる the wheel comes off.

[N] ～になる sit in a circle; form a circle.

[を] ～を描（えが）く form a circle; describe a circle. ～を掛（か）ける ❶ exaggerate sth; overstate sth; ① stretch the facts; ⓢ ① pile it on. ❷ exacerbate sth; make sth worse; ⓔ enhance sth;

make *sth* more attractive. 〜を回す roll a hoop; drive a hoop.

和 peace; the sum; the total

を 〜を乞う sue for peace. ⓒ 〜を求める do the sum (of); add *sth* up.

賄賂 a bribe; bribery

を 〜を受け取る accept a bribe; be bribed. 〜を贈る offer *sb* a bribe; bribe *sb*; ⓒ ⓘ grease *sb's* palm. 〜を使う offer *sb* a bribe; bribe *sb*; ⓒ ⓘ grease *sb's* palm. 〜を貰う accept a bribe; be bribed.

我が意 one's own mind

を 〜を得る meet one's wishes; be satisfactory to one; be happy to hear *sth*.

我が身 oneself

を 〜を顧みる reflect on oneself; search one's soul; ⓒ consult one's conscience; ⓒ exercise introspection.

我が道 one's own way

を 〜を行く go one's own way; ⓘ plow one's own furrow.

我が物 one's own (property)

N 〜にする ❶ take possession of *sth*; make *sth* one's own. ❷ learn how to do *sth*; master a skill; learn a language/craft.

別れ parting; farewell

を 〜を告げる say good-bye; ⓒ bid *sb* farewell; ⓒ take one's leave. 〜を惜しむ dread parting; be sorry to part; ⓒ be loath to part.

脇 the side; another place

N 〜に置く lay *sth* aside; put *sth* beside one. 〜に抱える hold *sth* under one's arm. 〜に立つ stand beside *sb*; stand by *sb's* side. 〜になる take a backseat (to another problem). 〜に呼ぶ call *sb* to one's side. 〜に寄る step aside; go to one side; get out of the way.
する 〜へ退く step aside; go to one side; get out of the way. 〜へ反らす change the conversation; divert *sb's* attention from *sth*; ⓒ digress from the subject. 〜へ散らす take one's mind off *sth*; ⓘ wash one's hands of a matter. (人を)〜へ連れ出す take *sb* aside. 〜へ引き寄せる draw *sth* to one's side. 〜へ回る go somewhere else. 〜へ向く look aside; turn away.
を ⓐ 〜を掻く be eager to do *sth*; be proud to do *sth*; ⓘ be on one's mettle. ⓐ 〜を詰める grow up; come of age; attain manhood/womanhood. 〜を通る pass *sb* by. ⓐ 〜を塞ぐ

grow up; come of age; attain manhood/womanhood. ～を見る look away; take one's eyes off *sth*.

和議 ⓔ peace negotiations

㋳ ⓒ ～を請う sue for peace. ～を結ぶ make peace; conclude peace. ～を申し込む make overtures for peace; ⓘ hold out the olive branch.

脇道 a byway; a byroad

Ⓝ ～に反れる ❶ wander into a byroad; ⓒ stray into a sideroad. ❷ wander from the (main) subject; get sidetracked; be diverted.
㋳ ～へ反れる ❶ wander into a byroad; turn aside; ⓒ stray into a sideroad. ❷ wander from the (main) subject; get sidetracked; be diverted.

脇目 a sidelong glance

Ⓝ (人を)～に見る ❶ give *sb* a sidelong glance; look sideways at *sb*; look at *sb* out of the corner of one's eyes. ❷ take no notice of *sb*; have no eye for *sb*; think nothing of *sb*; ignore *sb*; ⓒ set *sb* at naught.

脇役 a supporting role

Ⓝ ～に回る ❶ take a subordinate part. ❷ take a subordinate role; ⓘ take a back seat to *sb*; ⓘ take second billing to *sb*.
㋳ ～を勤める ❶ play a subordinate part; support an actor. ❷ play a subordinate role; ⓘ take second billing to *sb*; ⓒ ⓘ play second fiddle to *sb*.
～を果たす ❶ play a subordinate part; support an actor. ❷ play a subordinate role; ⓘ take second billing to *sb*; ⓒ ⓘ play second fiddle to *sb*.

枠 a frame; a rim; a limit

Ⓝ ～に入れる frame (a picture). ～に嵌まる be conventional; be hackneyed; ⓘ be the same old fare. ⓒ ～に巻く reel thread.
㋳ ～を決める set restrictions; put a limit on *sth*. ～を越える exceed the framework; ⓘ be beyond the pale. ～を付ける frame (a picture). ～を嵌める impose restrictions; put restrictions on *sth*. ～を拡げる widen the scope. ～を設ける establish a framework; set a limit.

訳 a reason; a ground; a sense

Ⓐ ～が有る have a reason; be with reason. ～が立つ ❶ see reason; be sensible. ⓐ ❷ pay one's dues; clear off. ⓐ ❸ have intimate relations with *sb*; have an affair; ⓒ ⓘ carry on with *sb*. ～が違う be different; run counter to *sth*. ⓐ ～が付く ❶ give one's consent; understand *sth*. ❷ pay one's dues; clear off one's debts. ～

が無い ❶ be illogical; be unreasonable; be irresponsible. ❷ be meaningless; be nonsensical. 〜が分かる understand sb/sth; be sensible; ⓒ know what is what.
㊻ 〜を言う ❶ give one's reasons; explain oneself; ⓔ set forth one's reasons. ❷ make an excuse; give a pretext. 〜を聞く ask for a reason; ask for an explanation. 〜を尋ねる demand a reason. 〜を質す inquire into a reason for sth. ⓐ 〜を立てる ❶ reason with sb; tell sb what is what; resolve a problem. ❷ have intimate relations with sb; have an affair; ⓒ ⓘ carry on with sb. ❸ pay one's dues; clear off one's debts. ❹ conduct (one's amourous affairs) in a stylish manner. ⓐ 〜を付ける settle a matter; get through sth. 〜を通す persuade sb; convince sb; win sb over. 〜を説く explain oneself; ⓔ set forth one's reasons. 〜を話す give one's reasons; explain oneself; ⓔ set forth one's reasons.

業 an act; a technique ▶ 業
㊻ 〜を磨く polish one's technique; hone one's skills.

山葵 Japanese horseradish
Ⓐ 〜が利く ❶ the wasabi is strong in flavor. ❷ provoke a response; cut to the quick; ⓘ touch a (raw) nerve; ⓘ sink in; ⓘ strike home.

禍 a calamity; misfortune
と 〜となる lead to one's downfall; ⓔ be one's undoing.
㊻ 〜を招く invite a disaster; ask for trouble; ⓔ bring calamity upon oneself. 〜を避ける avoid a disaster; keep out of harm's way.

話題 a topic; a subject
Ⓝ 〜に困る be lost for a topic (of conversation). 〜に富む have a broad pallet of topics at one's disposal; be sb of wide interest. 〜に上る become the topic of a talk; come up in conversation.
㊻ 〜を選ぶ choose a topic (for conversation); ⓒ pick a subject. 〜を変える change the subject; shift the conversation; ⓘ take a new tack. 〜を賑わす be much talked about; ⓘ make a stir.

蟠り vexations; cares; grudges
Ⓐ 〜が有る have sth on one's mind; be vexed by sth. 〜が出来る cause ill feelings; ⓘ breed bad blood. 〜が解ける calm down; ⓔ regain one's composure; ⓐ cool down.
㊻ 〜を捨てる throw off reserve; forget one's ill feelings (toward sb).

渡り a ferry; a passage; transit

A 〜が付く **❶** come into contact with sb; enter into relations with sb. **❷** come to an understanding; ⓒ arrive at an understanding.
を 〜を付ける **❶** get in touch with sb; enter into relations with sb; start negotiations with sb; ⓒ effect a liaison with sb. **❷** reach an agreement; ⓒ arrive at an understanding.

罠 a snare; a trap; a gin

A 〜が掛かる be caught in a trap; fall into a trap.
N 〜に陥る be caught in a trap; be ensnared. 〜に落ちる fall into a trap; be trapped. 〜に誘き込む lure (an animal) into a trap. 〜に掛かる be trapped; be ensnared; be taken in; ⓒ be conned; ⓢ be duped. 〜に掛ける snare (an animal); ensnare sb (into doing sth). 〜に嵌まる be caught in a trap; be ensnared.
を 〜を掛ける lay a snare; set a trap; ⓒ ① set sb up.

詫び an apology; an excuse

を 〜を容れる accept an apology. 〜を入れる offer an apology.

藁 (rice) straw; a straw

A ⓐ 〜が出る have one's faults exposed; ⓒ ① show oneself up.
Av 〜で葺く thatch a house/roof.
を 〜を敷く cover the ground with straw; litter a stall down. ⓐ 〜を焚く **❶** entice sb; put sb up (to commit a crime); egg sb on. **❷** speak ill of sb; ⓒ disparage sb; abuse sb; ① run sb down. **❸** haggle over (a price); bargain for sth. ⓐ 〜を出す betray one's ignorance; ⓒ show oneself up. 〜を束ねる bind straw into a sheaf; tie up straw.

笑い a laugh; a smile; a sneer

N 〜に紛らす divert oneself with laughter; laugh sth away.
を 〜を浮かべる wear a smile. 〜を押える repress a laugh; stifle one's laughter; swallow a laugh. 〜を買う be laughed at; be ridiculed; ① make oneself a laughingstock. 〜を噛み殺す suppress a smile. 〜を含む wear a faint smile. 〜を招く invite ridicule; ⓒ incur derision. 〜を洩らす laugh in spite of oneself.

草鞋 straw sandals

を 〜を脱ぐ end one's journey; take up lodgings; stop over (at a place). 〜を履く **❶** set out on a journey. **❷** take a percentage; ⓒ take a rake-off; ⓒ take a cut. ❸ be on the run; ⓔ be at large.

割 a rate; a ratio; gain; profit

A ～が付く bear a premium; leave a surplus; remain in excess. ～が良い have a good yield; pay well. ⓐ ～が弱い have a poor return; be unprofitable. ～が悪い have a bad yield; be unprofitable.

N ～に合う be profitable; pay for itself; ⓒ pay off. ⓐ ～に当たる be profitable; pay for itself. ⓓ ～に返る be disadvantageous to one; be to one's disadvantage; ⓘ be a fall guy. ～に入る mediate between two parties; act as a mediator.

を ⓐ ～を言う ❶ explain oneself; make an excuse; defend oneself. ❷ be given to too much reasoning; be argumentative; ⓘ split hairs; ⓒ ⓘ chop logic (with *sb*). ～を入れる ❶ employ a mediator; resort to arbitration. ❷ inser (extra) material (to widen a *kimono* or *obi*). ❸ make (minor adjustments; readjust *sth*); touch *sth* up. ⓐ ～を打つ ❶ drive in a wedge; wedge two things apart. ❷ mix *sth* with water; water *sth* down. ⓢ ～を食う turn out to one's disadvantage; be disadvantageous to one. ⓓ ～をする allot (space) to *sb*; assign (money) to *sb*. ⓒ ～を付ける

❶ pay out a premium. ❷ act as a mediator; mediate between two parties. ❸ bring *sth* to a conclusion; settle *sth*; put an end to *sth*.

割符 a tally; a check

A ⓓ ～が合う ❶ the tallies meet. ❷ be like-minded; get along well; ⓔ be congenial to one; ⓘ see eye to eye; ⓒ ⓘ hit it off.

を ⓓ ～を合わす make *sth* tally; compare the tallies.

割前 a share; one's lot

を ⓓ ～を出す bare one's share; pay one's due; contribute one's quota. ⓔ ～を貰う get one's share; receive one's quota.

悪遊び a prank; evil pleasures

を ～を覚える get into mischief; take to evil pleasures; take up gambling.

悪口 abuse; slander

を ～を言う say bad things about *sb*; speak ill of *sb*; foul *sb*'s name.

悪巧み wiles; an evil design

を ～をする carry out a wicked design; conspire against *sb*; lay a plot against *sb*; ⓢ ⓘ be in cahoots.

Index

A

abacus 187
abandonment 310
abdomen 260
ability 131, 246, 280, 352
abode 172
absence 355
absurdity 270
abuse 4, 10, 363
abyss 285
acceptance 3, 158
accomodation 341
accomplishment 105
account 74
acomplishment 218
acquaintance 303
action 116
actor 11
adaptability 341
admonition 21
advance 250
advantage 226, 281
advice 73, 160, 203
affairs 178
affection 1
afterpains 12
aftertaste 11
age 24, 227, 263, 350
aged 41, 357
agreement 136
aid 40, 138, 160, 192
aim 10, 26, 229, 245, 331, 332, 333
air 187, 203
alarm 106
alive 33
all 313
allowance 219
alone 274
alpha 154
amazement 10
ambition 116
ambush 303
amiability 2
amity 115
amorous 29
amount 190
amourous 152
ample 42
amulet 280
amusement 91
anchor 17
anger 17
angle 106
animosity 264
announcement 281
annoyance 329
answer 224
anticipation 84
antipathy 264
antler 209
anxiety 167, 281
aperture 72
apology 16, 361
apparition 305
appeal 316
appearance 42, 70, 89, 208, 217, 240, 282, 292
appearances 62, 178, 190
appetite 159, 160
applause 62
appreciation 73
approval 74, 136, 240
aptitude 131
arch 187
ardor 62, 83
argument 94
arista 38
arm 33, 269
arms 7, 71, 217, 283, 296
army 104, 167
arrangement 87
arrival 25
arrogance 42
arrow 24, 173, 336
arrowhead 338
arse 107
art 23, 83, 105
article 70, 83
articulation 358
artifice 83
artillery 190
ascendancy 341
ash 4, 249
ashes 52, 249
aspect 170
aspiration 86, 116
aspirations 246
ass 13
assault 115
assent 236
assistance 40, 160, 180, 192
astonishment 23
atrocity 294
attack 115, 206, 281, 337
attention 203
attire 129
attitude 190
audacity 44
authority 16, 109, 110, 111, 240, 259
autumn 3, 154
avarice 346

365

aversion 28
awake 33
awareness 21
awn 38
axe 42, 47, 236
axle 150

B

back 10, 32, 55, 173, 179
backbiting 56
backing 32, 138
badger 319
bag 283
bait 39, 47, 115
balance 94, 131, 290
ball 194, 220
balloon 282
ballpoint 292
bamboo 146
banner 83, 253
banquet 40
baptism 182
barrier 66, 156
base 147, 354
basis 84
basket 334
bath 289
baton 264
battle 25, 168, 181, 192, 225
beacon 248
beads 153, 195
beak 100
beam 267
beard 268
bearing 293
beautiful 182
beauty 110, 267, 275
bed 184, 206, 227
bee 254

beehive 168
beforehand 84
beginning 26, 155, 197, 279, 334
behavior 116
behaviour 315
being 188
belief 166
beliefs 167
bell 65, 172
bellows 192
belt 47
benefit 351
benevolence 142
berry 309
best 169
bewilderment 14
biceps 201
bill 100, 208
billow 236
birth 171, 206
bit 64, 85, 259
black 163
blade 109, 248, 336
blame 274
blank 160, 349
blast 2, 254
blaze 266
blemish 238
blindness 187
blockade 282
blocking 282
blood 4, 19, 108, 115, 117, 198
bloodshed 154
blossom 254
bluff 92
blunder 57, 145, 228
board 22
boast 115, 194, 297, 299
boasting 42

boat 287
body 24, 68, 166, 188, 223, 305
bone 132
bones 14, 42, 126, 171, 298, 299
bonfire 90
bonito 62
booing 338
books 202
boots 101
border 133
boredom 189
bosom 92, 167, 286
bottom 184
bough 39
boundary 350
bow 342, 355
bowels 182, 184, 262, 280
brag 115, 194, 299
bragging 42
braid 276
brain 8, 169
brains 246
brainstorm 355
brake 288
brambles 28
branch 39, 285
bravery 20, 92, 341
breadth 259
breast 202, 320
breath 17
breathing 17, 119, 242
breeze 58
brevity 197
bribe 358
bribery 45, 358
bride 349
bridge 252
bridle 193

brilliance   collar

brilliance 175
brilliancy 115
brocade 239
broth 96, 191
brow 267, 270, 305
brush 41, 285
bubble 170
bubbles 14
bud 327
bug 317
build 68
bulb 194
bulk 56
bull 32
bullet 194
bulletin 106
bullion 139
burden 50, 238, 239, 338
bureau 92
burnishing 310
burrial 229
burrow 12
business 106, 345, 346
butt 107
buttocks 161
button 297
by-blow 186
byway 347, 359

C

cajolery 129
cajoling 45
calamity 132, 361
call 31
calling 159
callus 191
calm 15, 290
calmness 290, 356
camp 104, 168
candy 13

cane 320
canon 190
canvas 292
cap 294
capability 139, 280, 352
capacity 352
capital 140, 147
car 103
card 284
care 180, 346
cargo 238
carpet 333
carving 31
cash 179
casket 70
castle 157
cat 243
cation 346
cattle 32
cauldron 66
cause 30, 152
caution 105, 106
ceiling 222
celebrity 328
censorship 110
census 126
certificate 50
chains 238
chair 22
chance 50, 81, 82, 139, 225
change 291
chaos 190
chape 125
chaps 275
character 25, 137, 271
charge 16, 40, 64
charity 142, 147, 181, 235
charm 219, 267, 280, 303, 316

charms 1, 160
chastity 218, 310
chat 257
check 208, 363
cheek 295
cheekbones 296
chest 320
child 112, 128
childbirth 136
children 112, 128
chill 356
chin 5, 46
choice 180
chopping 185
chopsticks 251
chord 26
cinnabar 4, 150
circle 40, 358
circumstances 148
claim 112
class 102, 152
claw 211
clearance 11
climax 116
clogs 107
close 50
closing 281
clothes 39, 129
clouds 37, 102, 282
clue 26, 55, 218
clumsy 179
clutches 183
coals 43
coat 39
cockscomb 227
coffin 70
cog 248
coherence 87, 208
coil 226
cold 59, 356
collar 39, 94, 320

367

color   dagger

color 28, 140
comfort 235, 350
comic 127
command 132
commandment 52
comment 277
commission 36
committee 29
communications 356
compassion 14, 224, 288
competence 111
complaint 16, 22, 333, 336
complaints 99, 350
complex 356
complexion 54, 108
compliment 45, 136
compliments 140
composition 289
composure 45
conception 116
concern 74, 219
conclusion 44, 108, 148
conduct 315
confidant 283
confidence 142
conflagration 57
confusion 289
conjecture 348
connection 39, 87
connections 129
connivance 288
conquest 62
cons 352
conscience 272, 353
conscious 33
consciousness 21, 157, 335
conscription 205
consent 158, 236
consequence 107

consideration 74, 137, 219
considerations 157
consolation 235
conspiracy 30
conspirator 103
constancy 179
contact 356
contempt 106
content 39
contingency 305
contours 354
control 44, 148
controversy 289
conundrum 235
convenience 292
conventionalism 90
convictions 167
convulsions 149
cool 353
coolness 356
coquetry 146, 270
cord 209
cordon 270
core 164
corner 23, 63, 106, 173
coronet 71, 75
corpse 136
correspondence 289
corrosion 357
corruption 45
cosmetics 147
cost 242
counsel 73, 95, 160, 183, 203
countenance 54, 108, 332
counting 73
coup 175
courage 87, 225, 341
course 25, 168, 294

court 295
courtesy 355, 356
cover 284
cow 32
crack 83, 274, 275
craftsmanship 83
crag 29
cramp 147
crease 270
creases 163
credit 120, 278, 329
crime 4, 111, 210
cripple 270
crisis 82, 223
criticism 116, 274, 277
criticizm 22, 271
cross 152
crossroads 152, 285
crotch 303
crowd 104, 272, 274
crown 41, 71, 75
crucifix 152
cruelty 149
crushing 209
crux 74
cry 34
crying 234, 236
cuffs 172
culprit 297
cumbersome 150
curiosity 92
current 138
curtain 16, 229, 301
curve 187
custom 73, 75, 151, 159
customs 184
cutlery 260

D

dace 3
dagger 228

dam   drool

dam 25, 177
damage 52, 188
danger 82, 85
dark 55
darkness 340
date 239, 265
dawn 345
day 265
dead 235
deafness 187
death 42, 137, 146, 148, 157
debt 93
debts 41
deception 291
decision 107, 108
declaration 106
decoy 47
decree 182
deer 139
defeat 158, 249, 268, 303, 341
defect 149
deficit 3
degree 137, 222
deity 67
delay 44
delicate 169
delight 71, 350
delusion 329
demand 346
demise 137
demolition 285
demon 301
department 92
deportment 93, 346
deposit 220
derision 205
descendants 142
design 21, 26, 68
desire 140, 239, 346

desires 150, 159
desk 191
destination 181
destiny 37
destitution 279
detachment 319
detective 170
determination 108
device 102, 219
devil 47, 301
dew 211
dewdrops 211
dexterity 218
diagnosis 167
diagonal 148
diagram 190
dialect 291
difference 131
difficulties 131, 265
difficulty 104, 238, 332
dignity 21, 49, 75, 279, 332
digression 349
diligence 38
direction 293
directions 135, 141
dirt 3, 205, 230
discipline 93
discontent 288
discretion 233, 335
discussion 94
disdain 106
disease 278, 339
disgrace 45, 201, 252
disgust 28
disinheritance 90
dislike 28
disloyal 285
dismissal 47
disorder 289, 357
display 309

disposal 60
disposition 21, 130, 155, 158, 160
disregard 288
dissatisfaction 288
dissension 289
disspation 230
distance 93
distinction 107, 328
distinguished 20, 280, 283
distress 2, 85
distrust 85, 110, 284
disturbance 291, 295
diversion 23, 349
divination 38
divining 136
doctrine 37
document 93
dog 27
domicile 177
door 63, 222, 336
doormat 304
doubt 33, 85, 89, 94, 110, 283
down 105
draft 113
dragnet 13
dragonfly 231
drama 91, 146
drawback 188
drawer 268
drawing 169
dread 45
dreadfulness 171
dream 343, 356
dress 39
drilling 105
drive 19
drivel 256, 348
drool 348

369

drop 209
drowsiness 244
drudgery 95
drug 96
drum 189
drunkenness 345
duck 68
duel 108
dunce 119
dust 112, 116, 205, 296
duty 87, 93, 177, 240, 334, 337
dwelling 90, 172, 338

E

eagerness 38
ear 129, 313
earnestness 300
ears 148
earth 189, 199, 208
ease 350
east 223
eating 166
eaves 246
echo 264
edge 63, 285
effect 30, 38, 52, 323
egg 195
ego 363
elbow 25, 269
eloquence 291
embers 43
emergency 89
emotions 73
empathy 91
emptiness 68, 90
encampment 167
enclosure 222
enemy 8, 218
energy 110
engagement 25, 337

enigma 235
enlightenment 135, 297
enmity 20, 35, 36
ennui 288
enterprise 140
enthusiasm 83
entrance 335
enui 189
envy 243
epitaph 328
equilibrium 94, 290
equity 117
era 143
errand 345, 346
error 13, 57
escape 108, 239
essence 345
esteem 105, 120, 188, 231
estimate 111, 330
etiquette 355, 356
eulogy 136
evening 198, 345
event 140
events 237
everybody 313
everything 313
evidence 3
evil 3, 4, 72, 150
exageration 42
examination 140
example 182, 196, 263, 355
excellence 293
excrement 97
excuse 16, 115, 147, 231, 361
exhaustion 207
existence 176, 188
exitement 338
expectation 84, 348, 349

expectations 310
experience 106, 113, 250, 252
exploits 283
expression 137, 329
extent 222, 264, 298
exterior 36, 49
extortion 239
extra 42
extravagance 149, 174, 175
eye 61, 62, 71, 323
eyebrow 305
eyebrows 152, 353
eyelashes 304
eyelid 304
eyes 148, 331
eyesight 71, 323

F

face 53, 211
facility 292
faction 229
facts 163
faculties 246
failure 44, 263
fair 22, 48
fairness 223
faith 164, 166, 167, 168, 175
faithfulness 310
fake 146
fall 3
falsehood 32
fame 92, 146, 278, 290, 328, 356
familiarity 235
family 12, 23
fan 33, 42
fancy 141, 183
fang 86

farewell   futon

farewell 359
farm 254
fashion 141
fat 13
fate 37, 148
fatigue 207
fault 14, 57, 108, 224, 238, 267
favor 1, 50, 74, 115, 193
fear 44, 45, 92
feast 40, 201
feat 218
feather 258
feathers 105, 248
features 53, 183, 276
feces 97
feeler 160
feeling 71, 72, 88, 141, 165
feelings 48, 73, 155
feet 7, 254
feighning 44
female 151
fence 55, 222, 290, 350
ferry 361
festival 48, 299, 304
fete 48, 304
fetters 238
fever 243
few 23
fidelity 164
fief 357
field 24, 336
fight 110
figure 61, 170
filament 25
filter 288
filth 3
fin 48, 279
finger 24, 160, 342
fingers 205, 219, 313

fire 57, 170, 266, 276
firearm 151, 220
fireplace 357
first 279
fish 39
fissure 274, 275
fix 337
flag 83, 253
flame 266
flank 347
flashiness 254
flattery 44, 45, 48, 115, 129
flavor 6
flaw 83, 108
flesh 239, 274, 299, 305
flight 239
flock 104
flood 311
floor 341
flophouse 230
flour 112, 128
flow 234
flower 254
flowers 258
foam 14, 170
focus 280
foe 8, 218
fold 270
foliage 248
folly 95, 182
food 159, 330
foodstuffs 95
fool 13, 119, 250
foolishness 196
foot 5
foothold 7, 202
footing 7
footlights 89
force 33, 104, 295
forefront 182

forehead 270
forethought 41
fork 285, 303
form 61, 62, 106, 170
formalities 93
formality 106
forsaking 310
fort 354
fortress 157
fortune 37, 136, 170, 229
foundation 21, 84
fox 84
fragrance 113
frailty 137
frame 360
franticness 338
freedom 151
fresh 14
friendliness 2
friendship 90, 115, 157, 166, 348
fright 44, 45
front 11, 159, 301
frontier 133
frown 270
frowning 270, 279
fruit 57, 145, 309
fullness 305
fumes 109
fun 72, 91
fund 147
funds 140
funeral 229
fur 69
furnace 66
furrows 163
fuse 100
futile 196
futility 319
futon 287

371

future 10, 116, 133, 159, 180

G
gain 362
gains 351
gallantry 20
gallery 176
gambling 251
gap 12, 72, 170
garments 129
gate 63, 335
gaudiness 254
gaze 142
generation 24
generosity 71, 87
genius 84
genuineness 164
ghastliness 171
gibberish 36
gilding 331
gills 39
girdle 47
gist 346
glance 29, 37, 142, 144, 152, 163, 186, 348, 359
glaze 211
glimpse 292
globe 194
gloom 30, 31
glory 38, 329
gloss 211
gloves 154
glume 38
go-between 273
goal 331, 333
goblin 47
god 67
goddess 67
gong 65, 230

good 180, 182
goodness 180, 226
goods 334
goodwill 70, 74, 114, 348
gooseflesh 230
gossip 36, 348
government 70
grace 50, 267, 279
graceful 356
grade 103
gradient 116
graft 45
grain 87, 209, 253
grasp 63
grass 95
gratitude 73, 93
gratuity 203
grave 200, 249, 296
gravel 150, 357
gravity 20, 176, 303
greatness 188, 328
greed 346
greens 233
grief 14, 64, 198
grim 110, 228
grime 3
grinders 248
grit 172, 225
groin 129
ground 137, 147, 189
group 102, 288
grudge 35, 138, 153
grudges 361
gruesome 228
guard 116, 127, 264
guess 10, 111
guidance 146
gulp 273
gun 151, 190, 220, 295
gunfire 293

gust 2
gut 26
guts 197

H
habit 73, 96, 151
hair 67, 105, 210
hairdo 67
halberd 296
hall 223
hammer 220
hammering 2
hand 153, 155, 172, 193, 212, 220, 272
handguard 209
hands 32
hangings 16
happiness 117
happyness 89
hardheartedness 149
hardship 238
hardships 31, 95, 104, 166
harm 52, 82
harmony 205, 290
harshness 4
hat 294
hatchet 42, 47, 236
haughtiness 42
haughty 191
havoc 357
hazard 82
haze 58
head 8, 25, 57, 101, 117, 119, 133, 169
headdress 57
headgear 39, 294
headrest 302
health 111
hearing 132, 204, 313
hearsay 272, 282

heart 15, 18, 75, 88, 91, 92, 120, 164, 166, 167, 249, 323
hearth 357
heat 243
heavens 221
hedge 55
heed 346
heel 55, 86, 102
height 174, 191
helm 57
helmet 66
help 160, 180, 192, 272
herbs 95
hidden 15, 29
hide 69
hilt 207
hindrance 150
hip 124
history 40
hit 9, 175
hitch 231
hobby 47, 154
hoe 104
hole 12
hollowness 90
home 16, 33, 63, 160, 178
homeland 120
homesickness 91, 135
honest 353
honor 38, 53, 61, 120, 190, 329, 332
hook 55, 66
hoop 191
hooting 338
hope 86, 246
horn 209, 351
horror 45
horse 34
hostage 272

hour 139, 147
house 3, 16, 23, 90, 338
household 16, 23, 63, 160, 178
hue 28, 140
hull 68
human 271
humanity 165, 167, 168
humbug 348
humming 257, 258
humor 83, 85, 127
hunch 69
hundred 276
hunger 30
hurt 52
husk 68
hyperbole 42
hypocrisy 84

I
ice 32, 118, 251
idea 14, 116, 153, 245, 353
ideal 353
ideas 71
idiot 119
idleness 191, 319
ignominy 45, 252
ignorance 333
illness 277, 339
illusion 329, 343
imagination 183
imbalance 31
immediate 330
impact 157
impartiality 117
impertinence 126
impetus 140
implication 354
impression 30, 208
improvement 168

imprudence 283
impudent 125
incense 113
incident 140
inclination 20, 316, 317
inconvenience 288
indebtedness 41
independence 204
indications 109
indignity 283
individuality 126
indolence 196
indulgence 29
infer 99
inferiority 268
influence 16, 38, 110, 112, 176, 259
influnece 2
iniquity 284
initiative 182
injury 52, 82, 83
injustice 267, 284
ink 172
innocence 319
inquiry 31, 204, 267
inscription 328
insect 317
inside 33, 47, 233, 278
insight 62, 135
inspection 110
inspiration 72, 355
instant 173
instructions 135, 141
insult 283
insurance 296
intellect 199
intelligence 199, 200
intent 26
intention 20, 21, 300, 353
intentions 300

373

intercourse 294
interest 72, 74, 91, 92, 154, 352
interests 352
interference 73
interior 33, 233
interpretation 52
interruption 203, 348
interval 2, 93, 300
intestines 182, 184, 262
intimacy 166, 235
intoxication 38, 345
intuition 69
investigation 204
involvement 301
iron 220
irony 274
irrationality 270
irresponsibility 223
issue 127

J

jail 357
jar 210
jaw 5
jealousy 166, 243
jeering 338
jest 158
job 141
joint 283
joke 22, 158, 192
joy 39, 71, 350
judgment 264
jumble 126
juncture 249
justice 132, 165, 223

K

karma 30, 114
kernel 193
kettle 43, 64, 66, 337

key 55
kickback 36, 58
kindness 114, 115
king 41
kite 195
knee 269
knife 331
knowledge 37, 201
knuckle 283

L

label 284
labor 59, 61, 141, 220, 231, 357
ladder 252
ladle 149
lament 99, 234
lamp 3
lance 340
language 111, 127, 130
lantern 205
lap 269
larceny 241
largeness 188
lashes 304
latitude 342
laugh 23, 362
law 43, 84, 247
lawsuit 185
lead 182
leader 57
leadership 146, 248, 341
league 229
learning 201
leaves 248
leeward 57, 66
leeway 342
left 136
leg 4, 5, 172, 250
legs 7
leisure 26, 70, 275

length 191
leniency 71
lesson 44
letter 137
lever 219
liaison 157
liberality 87
liberty 151
license 29
lid 284
lie 32
life 23, 24, 27, 31, 148, 151, 154, 157, 168, 174, 175, 176, 328, 329, 348
lifeboat 171, 192
lifetime 24
light 3, 55
liking 141
limb 39
limit 175, 298
line 25, 26, 85, 107
lineage 171
lips 97, 100
lipstick 291
liquor 135
listening 106
live 62
livelihood 103, 120
livelyhood 156
liver 74, 87, 88, 197, 249
living 103, 174, 228
load 36, 238, 239
locality 228
lock 158
lodging 338
logic 171, 208, 229, 351, 352
loin 124
loincloth 289
loneliness 127

longevity 151
look 37, 329
looks 53, 135, 183, 240, 276
loose 262
lord 150
loss 188, 195, 268
lot 363
love 1, 28, 112
luck 31
luggage 239
lungs 249
lure 39, 47, 115
lust 28, 155, 239
luster 115, 175, 211
luxury 149, 174, 175
lye 4

M

mackerel 135
magic 305
make-up 147
male 46, 151, 345
malice 4, 149, 150, 226
man 46
manifesto 106
manner 59, 204
manners 91, 184
manuscript 113
manyfold 191
map 169
margin 342, 349
mark 11, 221, 304
market 22, 141, 183
marks 222
marriage 108
marrow 127
mask 68, 332
mass 229, 294
massage 15
masses 151

masseur 15
master 150, 198
mat 304, 319
matrimony 108
matter 127
mayhem 357
meal 159, 330
meaning 28
meanness 107
means 102, 139, 153, 277, 295
measure 134, 153, 160, 278
measurements 173
meat 239
meddling 73
medicine 96
meditation 328
meeting 51
melancholy 31
member 29
membership 177
memory 81
mercy 147
merit 62, 113, 242, 329
merriment 75
mess 190
message 116
metal 139
meter 329
method 139, 295
mettle 70
mind 15, 21, 23, 75, 164, 167, 323
mine 339
miracle 83
mire 230
mirth 75
mischief 22
misfortune 91, 132, 283, 361
miso 196, 221, 312

mist 58
mistake 13, 108, 145
mistrust 94
moat 186
model 60, 263
moderation 188, 190
mold 17, 60, 65
moment 173, 290
momentum 19, 252
monarch 41
money 132, 135, 179, 190, 312
month 207
mood 83, 85, 88, 165
moon 207
morale 18
morality 168
morning 198
motion 31
motive 143
mountain 339
mourning 333, 335
mouth 97, 100, 101
mouthpiece 259
movement 31
moxibustion 89
mud 208, 217, 230
muddle 126
multifarous 191
muscle 171
muscles 201
mustache 268
muzzle 255
mystery 276

N

nail 95, 127, 211
nails 183
name 231
nap 244
nape 34

375

nature 130, 155, 158, 241
naught 316
navel 290, 297
necessity 271
neck 34, 39, 101, 119
neckband 39
needle 263
needles 248
neglect 223
negligence 233, 283
negotiations 359
nerve 165
nerves 165
nest 168
net 13
neutrality 204
new 14
newborn 34
news 117, 157
niceties 86
night 345, 350
nighttime 350
nil 316
nobility 279
nobleman 39
noise 46
nonsense 197
nook 23, 173
normally 290
nose 255, 331
nostalgia 91, 135
nostril 269
nostrils 129
notes 118
nothing 316
notice 106, 203
notion 71, 353
notoriety 4
now 28
nude 254
number 58, 114

numbness 147
nut 309

O

oak 58
oar 52, 357
oath 176, 200
object 10, 188, 304
objection 18
objective 332
obligation 50, 87
obscurity 35
obstacle 156
obstinacy 60, 116
obstruction 207
occasion 30, 50, 112, 225, 249, 254
ocean 34
odd 46
oddity 81
odor 239
offense 82, 210, 224
offer 183
offing 43
offspring 142
ogre 47
oil 12
omega 154
omen 84, 208
oneself 47, 51, 358, 363
opening 170
opinion 19
opponent 2, 317
opportunity 81, 82, 114, 139
oppression 10
oracle 48, 96
orbit 85
order 23, 93, 114, 137, 154, 155, 181, 199, 204, 328

ordinarily 290
origin 40, 130, 171, 197, 334
ornament 57
ostentation 309, 334
outdoors 118, 186
outlines 354
outrage 294
outset 220
outside 36, 186, 278
ovation 62

P

pace 7, 292, 298
paddle 52
padlock 156
pain 95, 207
pains 219
paint 217
painting 38
palanquin 12, 19, 44, 61, 134, 196, 294
palaver 45
palm 193, 220
panel 259
pans 236
paper 67, 251, 296
paradise 190
pardon 129, 343
particulars 20
parting 38, 359
partner 2
party 40, 51, 102
pass 223, 259
passage 361
passion 112, 155, 239
past 56
pasturing 247
pathos 14
patience 130
patron 198
patronage 1

pattern 60, 68
pawn 144, 219
payment 147
peace 15, 114, 190, 199, 358
pebbles 150
pedestal 189
pelt 69
pen 285, 292
penalty 105, 254
people 273
percentage 280
peril 82, 85
period 143, 152
permission 240, 343
perseverance 130
personality 126, 271
perspiration 7
pert 125
petulance 192
phantom 305
phase 92
phlegm 197
picture 38, 169
piece 25
piety 113
pile 95
pill 96
pillow 302
pin 263
pine 303
pipe 97
pit 285
pitch 71, 204
pitch-black 303
pity 14, 147, 155, 235
place 227, 249
plain 336
plan 14, 90, 102, 105, 153, 173, 198, 220, 250, 251, 313

plank 22
plantation 254
plate 22
platform 92
plating 331
play 91, 140, 146
plaything 49
pleasure 71, 75
pleat 270
pledge 60, 144, 176, 200, 201
plight 135
plot 30, 294
ploy 153
pluck 87, 197, 225, 303, 341
ply 350
pocket 196
point 221, 293
poison 226
polish 310
pony 34
poor 179
popularity 31, 81, 240
population 166
porch 110
position 22, 131, 192, 199
post 22, 95, 199
postponement 12
pot 43, 66, 210
potato 28
pots 236
pottery 337
poverty 279
powder 112, 128
power 109, 112, 176, 182
praise 136
prank 22, 363
prayer 48, 71
prayers 28

precaution 105
precedent 182, 196, 355
predicament 90
prediction 349
prejudice 292
presence 75
present 28
pressure 10, 44
prestige 21
pretensions 334
pretext 115, 147, 191, 231
price 242
prices 285
pride 19, 142, 226, 258, 297
priest 294
principle 152, 351
principles 37
priority 180
prison 357
privation 95
privations 166
prize 155
probe 134
problem 188
profile 354
profit 132, 226, 351, 362
profits 295
program 198, 251
progress 168, 250
project 90, 105, 140
promise 337
proof 3
property 167
prophecy 349
propriety 163
pros 352
prospect 331
prospects 310
prosperity 181, 226
protection 296, 315

377

protest 18, 127
providence 316
provisions 85, 95
proximity 186
public 113, 115, 177, 273
publicity 194, 331
puerile 140
puke 291
pulse 315
pun 192
punctuation 101
punishment 105, 140, 254
pupil 273
purport 323
purpose 333
purse 94, 132
push 44

Q

qualifications 139
quality 146
quantity 190
quarrel 110
queer 46
query 89, 145
question 89, 145
queue 205
quiet 190, 206

R

rack 193
rag 299
rage 17
railing 55
rampart 354
rancor 33, 244
rank 103, 199, 313
rapid 173
rapture 350
rashness 62
rate 280, 362

rations 334
ray 267
reality 137
rear 11, 32, 161
reason 163, 224, 229, 351, 352, 360
rebellion 265, 323, 351
rebound 252
rebuff 270
rebuke 120
reception 81
reckoning 73
recollection 81
record 93
recovery 290
red 4, 113
reef 15
reel 70
reference 267
refined 169
refinement 279
reflection 55
reform 24
refuge 239
regard 105, 188
registration 126
regulation 43
regulations 84
reins 193
rejection 298
relation 39, 72
relations 234
relationship 72, 234
reliance 168
relief 31, 170, 350
remains 249
remark 110, 336
remarks 207
remonstrance 21
renewal 24
renown 328

reply 224
report 36, 46
reproach 274
reputation 53, 247, 272, 278, 287
repute 328
request 193, 204, 346
rescue 170
resentment 33, 35
reserve 41
resign 138
resignation 3
resolve 108, 123
resort 43
respect 105, 188
respiration 119
responsibility 177, 240
restraint 175, 184
restriction 175, 184
result 52, 107
resuscitation 62
reticence 206
revenge 283
reverberation 264
reverse 35, 36, 352
revolt 264, 265, 323, 351
reward 155
rhyme 29
rhyming 30
rhythm 278
ribbon 151
rice 277, 330
riches 132, 229
ride 247
ridge 134
ridicule 205
rifle 151, 152, 220
right 136, 179
righteousness 224
rigmarole 36
ring 40, 358

ringing　　　　　　　　　　　　　　　　　　　　shoes

ringing 237
riot 295, 351
ripeness 305
ripple 260
rival 218
river 69, 170
road 23, 25, 312
roadside 358
rock 29
rod 64, 293
role 337, 359
roll 25
romance 31
roof 28
room 349
roost 243
root 130, 131, 241
rope 209, 229, 237, 335
rosary 153
rotation 155
rouge 291
rout 249
route 180
row 110, 356
rubbish 197
rudder 57
rug 304, 333
ruin 190
rule 43
rules 84, 93
rumor 36, 257, 282
ruse 153
rut 181, 220

S

sack 283
sacrifice 83, 273, 340
saddle 2, 103
sadness 64
safety 15
sail 292
sake 24, 70, 135, 149
saliva 61, 69, 206, 348
salt 138, 219
salvation 170
sand 172
sandals 362
sanity 157
sash 47
saucers 178
saucy 125
scabbard 136
scaffold 338
scales 222, 250, 354
scalpel 331
scandal 31
scar 83
scene 227
scent 113, 239
schedule 190, 220
scheme 14, 90, 153, 250, 294
scissors 251
scope 264, 349
scorn 106, 205
scratch 83
scream 276
screw 243
scull 357
scum 14
scythe 66
sea 34, 170, 236
seal 29, 30, 189, 263, 281
seam 241
season 147, 179
seasoning 138
seat 131, 176
secrecy 233
secret 111, 276
secrets 43
seed 193
seeds 258
selection 180
self-abandonment 338
self-esteem 142
self-interest 142, 162
selfishness 142
sensation 71, 72, 88
sense 15, 72, 73, 245
sequence 137, 154
serenity 45, 290
seriousness 300, 301, 303
service 20
sesame 129
session 152
setback 231
settlement 11, 44, 60, 87, 108, 148, 350
severe 110
shade 29
shadow 30
shallow 173
shame 19, 201, 252
shameful 152
shape 60, 61, 62, 157
share 363
shares 65
sharp 110
sharpness 38
sheath 113, 136
shelf 193
shell 68, 113, 117, 194
shellfish 51
shelter 239, 296
shield 193
shin 172, 250
ship 287
shit 97
shoal 173
shock 14, 157
shoes 101

379

shop 311
shortage 284
shortness 197
shoulder 59, 61
shoulders 183, 335
shout 81
show 309
shred 299
shriek 276
shrine 223, 310
shrubs 28
sickbed 227, 278
sickle 66
sickness 277
side 285, 347, 359
sieve 288
sight 323
sign 55, 109, 285
signboard 74, 94
significance 28
silence 89, 206
silliness 95
simpleton 13, 250
sin 210
sincerity 175, 303
sinews 171
single 274
site 249
situation 92, 253, 254, 259
size 56, 188
skeleton 52, 298
sketch 38
skill 33
skin 69, 253, 274
skirt 36, 172
sky 119, 187, 221
slander 10, 363
slant 148
sleep 242, 244
sleepiness 244
sleeping 166

sleeve 185, 196
slope 116
sluggishness 191
sluice 25
slumber 196, 244
slur 48
smashing 209
smell 239
smile 24, 362
smiling 39
smoke 109, 138
snare 361
snivel 256
snore 28
snoring 187
snow 341
snowfall 341
snub 270
society 303, 343
soil 199, 208, 228
soldier 290
soles 7
solitude 127, 274
soot 171
sophistry 86
sorcery 305
sorrow 14, 31, 64
soul 91, 124, 164, 166, 176, 195
sound 46, 47, 237, 241
source 241
space 2, 119, 170, 203, 300, 349
sparks 274
spasms 149
spatula 291
spawn 195
spear 296, 340
species 354
specifics 19
speck 280

spectacle 267
spectacles 330
speculation 251
speech 110, 111, 127, 130, 291, 335
spell 303
spike 95
spine 173
spirit 18, 19, 62, 75, 81, 83, 120, 123, 124, 165, 166, 174, 195, 197, 303, 355
spit 206
spite 20, 226, 228
spittle 197, 206
splendor 65, 110
splinter 227
spoon 135
spot 227, 249, 280
spring 154, 243, 263
springtime 263
sprout 327
spur 251
sputum 197
spy 134
ßdurability 207
stage 284
stain 11
stairs 252
stake 95
stalk 223
stamina 130
stamp 29, 263
standard 332
standpoint 192
star 37, 297
start 26, 155, 197, 220
starvation 30
stature 174
status 131, 313
stealing 241

steel 220
steep 110
steer 32
step 7, 25, 134, 292, 298
steps 129
stick 207, 293
stiffness 141
stigma 48, 201
stimulus 140
stinginess 107
stipend 357
stipulations 85
stitch 241
stocks 65
stomach 47, 129, 147, 260
stone 21, 24, 193
store 311
storehouse 43, 103
story 83
strain 94
strangeness 16, 81
strategem 153
straw 362
stream 69, 234, 342
string 26, 209, 276
struggle 192
stubbornness 60, 116
stump 65
stupidity 95
style 217
subject 188, 361
success 9, 113, 175
successor 11
sudden 281
sugar 13
suitcase 89
sulk 235
sulking 192
sum 190, 358
summit 133
sumō 104

sun 265
superiority 341
supplication 28
support 31, 32, 138
supremacy 248, 341
surface 49, 211
surname 174
surplus 42
surprise 10, 23
surroundings 10
suspicion 33, 64, 85, 94, 110, 283
swarm 104
sweat 7, 115
sweet 13
sword 61, 109, 146, 243, 330, 336
swords 354
sycophancy 48
sympathy 91, 224, 235

T

table 180, 191
tablet 28
tact 85
tag 284
tail 41, 48, 145
taint 48
talent 84, 131
talk 100, 257
tallness 174
tally 25, 280, 363
target 304
taste 6, 141, 154, 170
tax 37, 174
tea 116, 202
teaching 152
teachings 44, 247
tears 75, 117, 211, 236
technique 360
tedium 189, 288

teeth 137, 139
temper 21, 70
temperament 192
temperature 243
temple 223
tenon 297
tension 94
tentacle 160
term 239, 245
territory 237
terror 45, 92
test 140
texture 87
theft 241
thing 334
thirst 62
thorn 227
thought 48, 71, 137, 353
thoughts 349
thread 25
threshold 140
throat 30, 246
throne 41
thumb 342
thunder 68
tide 116, 138
tiger 230
tile 28
time 139, 147, 220, 225, 275, 349
times 163
tint 140
tip 133, 145, 203
title 188, 231
tittle-tattle 319
toe 32, 342
together 24
toil 95
token 285
tomb 249
tome 70

tone 241
tongue 100, 142, 143, 145, 179
tool 191, 219
tooth 248
toothpick 346
topic 361
topknot 227, 334
torch 90
towel 190
toy 49
trace 11
track 85, 180, 220
tradition 73
train 41
training 105
tranquility 15, 190, 290
trap 13, 361
tray 180
treacherous 22
treasury 103
treat 201
treatment 206
trellis 193
trend 281
trial 132
tribute 114
trick 5, 43, 72, 126, 219
trickery 291
trifle 135
trigger 268
triumph 159
trivialities 135
troops 290
trouble 116, 131, 219, 238, 329, 332, 338, 354, 357
troubles 114
trump 43
trumpet 351
trunk 223, 255

trust 164, 168, 349
truth 145, 164, 301, 303
tube 97
tune 204, 241
turn 154
turret 338
tusk 86
twist 350
type 354

U

umbrella 56
uncommonness 16
underground 200
underling 136
understanding 63, 247
uneasiness 281
unexpected 17, 28, 281
unfaithful 285
unforeseen 17
united 24
unreasonableness 323
unrest 285
unskillful 179
untruth 32
upright 353
upstream 36
upturn 37
urgency 89
urn 127
usage 151, 159
useless 196, 319

V

vacancy 68
valor 20, 341
value 62, 242, 329
vapor 342
vegetables 233
vehicle 103
vein 2, 315

vengeance 283
venom 226
verge 285
vessel 287
vestibule 110
vexations 361
vice 4
vicinity 10, 186
victim 340
victory 62, 94, 158, 159, 341
view 19, 142, 267
vigor 19, 62, 108, 110, 174, 175
vinegar 169
violence 294, 295
virtue 180, 218, 226
virtues 38, 272
viscera 126, 280
vision 148, 343
visit 31, 350
vitality 110, 174, 175
vitals 89
vixen 84
voice 47, 118, 130, 246
volition 21
volume 56, 70
vomit 291
vortex 32
vote 107
vow 71, 176, 200, 201

W

waist 124
wall 66, 290
wallet 132
war 181, 192, 225
warehouse 43
warfare 181, 290
warmth 110, 197
warning 106

warp 187
wasp 254
wastage 281
water 170, 276, 277, 311
wave 236
way 25, 312
weakness 268, 331
wealth 132, 229
weapon 173, 283
weapons 71, 296
weather 4, 72, 279
web 168
wedge 96
weeds 95
weeping 234
weight 44, 49, 151, 176, 189
weir 177
welfare 15
west 223
wheedling 239
wheel 103
whimper 235
whining 126
whip 320
whirlpool 32
white 160, 163
width 259
wife 349
wiles 219, 363
will 15, 21, 123
willfulness 63
willpower 19
win 94
wind 2, 3, 58
windhole 57
windward 57
wine 135
wing 23, 258
wire 180
wisdom 126, 200
wish 71, 86, 245, 246
witchcraft 305
wits 331
woman 51
womenfolk 51
wonder 83
word 110, 137
words 30, 111, 127, 179
work 59, 61, 141, 159, 254
workings 254
world 177, 184, 343
worry 167
worth 62, 242, 329
wound 83
wrath 17, 33
wretched 31
wrinkles 163
wrist 33
writing 289
wrong 179

Y

yarn 25
yawn 4
year 227, 245
years 350
yell 81
yen 40

Z

zest 62, 92

TOYO PRess: Explore Dream Discover
Editorial supervision: Hiromi Miyagi-Lusthaus. Book and cover design: Chōkei Studios. Printing and binding: IngramSpark. The typefaces used are Osaka and Trebuchet MS.

www.ingramcontent.com/pod-product-compliance
Lightning Source LLC
Chambersburg PA
CBHW072100050526
44107CB00126B/1471/J